Read What People Are Saying About

"I thought I knew a lot about online games and virtual worlds, but this book not only showed me that for every nugget of knowledge I had there were five others, but also how they are all connected and interrelated into a giant tapestry."

Kevin O'Gorman
Sr. Designer, Cosmic Origins, LLC
Guest Lecturer, University of Texas at Dallas

"If you're thinking of creating your first massively multiuser game and you haven't read Bartle's Designing Virtual Worlds, *you're about to waste millions of dollars making the same mistakes that so many others have made. This book is the history, analysis, textbook, and reference companion for virtual worlds designers."*

F. Randall Farmer
Veteran designer and implementer of over a dozen text and graphical virtual worlds

"This book makes two important contributions. First, it lays a clear blueprint identifying the traps and pitfalls that a designer new to virtual worlds may encounter. Second it covers a range of topics from the history of MUDs to more complex issues such as ethical considerations in online games. This book is an essential component to assist designers in joining the fastest growing segment in the game industry from the man who was there to see the genre's birth."

Dustin Clingman
Professor of Game Development, Full Sail

"This book is so densely packed with information, you'll be reading it over and over again to get it all."

Bridgette Patrovsky
Co-author of *Developing Online Games: An Insider's Guide* (New Riders Publishing)

"If you want to know the reality behind virtual worlds, you'd be silly not to get this book. It is prime source material from the father of online games, himself."

Jessica Mulligan
Co-author of *Developing Online Games: An Insider's Guide* (New Riders Publishing)

Designing Virtual Worlds

Richard A. Bartle

New
Riders

1249 Eighth Street, Berkeley, California 94710
An Imprint of Peachpit,
A Division of Pearson Education

Designing Virtual Worlds

International Standard Book Number: 0-1310-1816-7

Library of Congress Catalog Card Number: 2003106801

Printed in the United States of America

Trademarks

Warning and Disclaimer

Publisher
Stephanie Wall

Production Manager
Gina Kanouse

Acquisitions/Development Editor
Chris Zahn

Project Editor
Michael Thurston

Copy Editor
Linda Seifert

Indexer
Julie Bess

Proofreader
Debbie Williams

Composition
Gloria Schurick

Manufacturing Coordinator
Dan Uhrig

Interior Designer
Kim Scott

Cover Designer
Aren Howell

Marketing
Scott Cowlin
Tammy Detrich
Hannah Onstad Latham

Publicity
Susan Nixon

To the players.

Table of Contents

Acknowledgments

This book would not have been written were it not for:

John Neidhart at Pearson Education, who was willing to indulge my desire to write about virtual world design despite the fact that he was actually looking for a book about AI.

Stephanie Wall and Chris Zahn at New Riders, who gave me an enthusiastic welcome when I appeared on their doorstep at short notice as a result of a Pearson reorganization. They gave me the time and freedom I needed to finish the job properly.

My wife, Gail Bartle. From June 2002 until April 2003, I turned down all consultant and design work I was offered so I could write this book. Without her quiet but unfailing support, you wouldn't be reading this now.

I'd also like to thank Damion Schubert and Matt Mihaly for the many insightful comments they made in their reviews (sometimes several to a page). This book would still have been written without them, it just wouldn't have been as worth reading.

About the Author

Richard Allan Bartle, Ph.D., co-wrote the first virtual world, MUD ("Multi-User Dungeon"), in 1978, thus being at the forefront of the online gaming industry from its very inception. A former university lecturer in Artificial Intelligence, he is an influential writer on all aspects of virtual world design and development. As an independent consultant, he has worked with almost every major online gaming company in the U.K. and the U.S. over the past 20 years.

Richard lives with his wife, Gail, and their two children, Jennifer and Madeleine, in a village just outside Colchester, England. He works in virtual worlds.

About the Technical Reviewers

These reviewers contributed their considerable hands-on expertise to the development process for *Designing Virtual Worlds*. As the book was being written, these dedicated professionals reviewed all the material for technical content, organization, and flow. Their feedback was critical to ensuring that *Designing Virtual Worlds* fits our readers' need for the highest-quality technical information.

Matt Mihaly is the founding partner, lead designer, and CEO of Achaea LLC. Founded in 1996 in San Francisco, Achaea designs and produces some of the world's most popular and successful commercial text MUDs, including *Achaea, Dreams of Divine Lands* (http://www. achaea.com), *Aetolia*, the *Midnight Age* (http://www.aetolia. com), and *Imperian* (http://www.imperian.com)—all of which run on Achaea's proprietary network engine, Rapture.

Matt graduated from Cornell University in 1994 with a degree in Political Science and is a licensed stockbroker. These experiences have informed his game design tendencies and he is an expert on business models, political systems, and community dynamics in virtual worlds. Along with the inevitable interest in games, he spends his free time pursuing Brazilian jujitsu and kickboxing, cooking, travelling, hiking, kayaking, skiing, and scuba diving.

 **Damion Schubert** has been working in online world design professionally for over seven years. He was originally the lead designer of *Meridian 59* (and several expansions), as well as the lead designer for the defunct *Ultima Online 2*. He has also served as a contractor for such projects as *The Sims Online* and Kalisto's *Highlander Online*. Currently Damion is serving as a senior designer at Wolfpack, which shipped *Shadowbane* in March 2003.

Tell Us What You Think

As the reader of this book, you are the most important critic and commentator. We value your opinion and want to know what we're doing right, what we could do better, what areas you'd like to see us publish in, and any other words of wisdom you're willing to pass our way.

When you contact us, please be sure to include this book's title, ISBN, and author, as well as your name and email address. We will carefully review your comments and share them with the author and editors who worked on the book.

Email: errata@newriders.com

Preface

The aim of this book is to make people *think* about virtual world design. Whether you agree with any of it is not an issue, as long as you advance your own thoughts on the subject.

Too much virtual world design is derivative. Designers take one or more existing systems as foundations on which to build, sparing little thought as to why these earlier worlds were constructed the way they were. This is troubling, not because it leads to artistic sterility—designers are always imaginative enough to make their creations special—but because the resulting virtual worlds might not *work* as well as they could. If designers don't know the reasoning behind earlier decisions, how can they be sure that the conditions that sustained those decisions still apply when they act on them?

Are designers even aware that there *are* decisions they can unmake?

Although a good deal of design is evolutionary, that does not mean designers can't be revolutionary too. Virtual worlds are all about freedom—for their inhabitants, yes, but also for their designers. Just because every virtual world you can think of classifies characters using some variation of a basic four-profession model, that doesn't mean *your* virtual world has to classify them that way; more to the point, it doesn't even mean that your virtual world has to classify characters at all.

Virtual worlds are unlike anything else. You can't approach them from a background in some other area—game design, literature, media studies, architecture, or whatever— and expect all the normal rules to apply. Unfortunately, it doesn't *look* that way from the outside. "How hard can it be?" is a question often asked by people entering the field from some related area that is considered to be Pretty Damned Tough.

Then they find out.

If they're lucky, they find out quickly. If they're unlucky, they only find out after 18 months and half their budget. Designing virtual worlds is *very* difficult, unless you know what you're doing; then, it's no harder than any other complex design activity.

The key is in recognizing the fact that what seems eminently logical to you from your usual perspective might turn out to be disastrous when viewed from another angle—and then realizing that the worlds you're drawing inspiration from almost certainly contain elements designed by people who *didn't* recognize that fact until it was too late.

To design a virtual world is perhaps the greatest act of creative imagination there can be. The possibilities are absolutely limitless—you can make and do anything in them. *Anything!* Today's virtual worlds are mere children's scribbles compared to the masterpieces to come.

We see these scribbles, but have no concept of how the masterpieces will appear; the virtual worlds of the future will not be like the virtual worlds of today, in ways we cannot yet know. Thus, much of what you read in this book is doomed, eventually, to be proven wrong. However, it might well point the way to discovering what is right. All it takes is for people to think about what they're designing; if reading this book helps in that respect, then it has done its job.

I don't care *what* you think, so long as you *think*.

Introduction

Every day, over a million people visit virtual worlds—a figure set to grow over the coming years. What is it that draws them to these imaginary places? What do they do after they've arrived? How can the people who create such worlds—their designers—ensure that players' needs are met? Can they do this while satisfying their *own* needs, too?

Who Should Read This Book?

This is a book for people who design virtual worlds.

Because of this, it's also a book for people who implement, operate, study, or play virtual worlds.

Because of *this*, it's also a book for people interested in entertainment, education, creativity, art, society, culture, philosophy, space, architecture, psychology, identity, language, economics, government, theology, drama, literature, or cognition.

Virtual worlds are of the future. If you want to create or understand that future, this is the book for you.

Overview

The material presented here is organized such that it begins with concrete facts and moves gradually toward abstract conjecture. As it does so, theories of virtual world play and creation are developed that ultimately demonstrate the validity of virtual world design as an object of study.

Chapter 1: Introduction to Virtual Worlds

What are virtual worlds? Beginning with an historical account of how they came to be where they are today, this chapter moves on to describe the various categories of virtual worlds that exist and what these categories mean for designers. Influences from other art forms are presented to explain some directions virtual world design has taken.

Chapter 2: How to Make Virtual Worlds

This is a relatively short chapter that outlines the development process commonly employed for virtual worlds and the effects this process has on what designers can do. It includes an examination of how virtual worlds are typically implemented and the constraints this implies.

Chapter 3: Players

This major chapter concerns the people who play virtual worlds. Only by fully understanding why people play can designers hope to accommodate these players' needs. It focuses on two important concepts, *immersion* and *identity*, and how they can be related using an enhanced "player types" model. It follows with a discussion about community in virtual worlds, and how it fits in with all this.

Chapter 4: World Design

Here, the practical decisions designers must make concerning the creation of virtual worlds are described, with reference to the theory developed in Chapter 3. The various options available at each stage are presented, with explanations as to why designers may or may not want to incorporate them into their creations.

Chapter 5: Life in the Virtual World

In this chapter, the spotlight falls on characters, rather than the players behind them. Various ways to represent character skill, experience, and advancement are discussed, along with different systems for allowing characters to form groups. Combat and crafting activities are described, as are the various "endgames" to which they can lead. The theory of Chapter 3 is mainly used in application here, but it does receive a final extension that makes clear exactly why players *do* play virtual worlds.

Chapter 6: It's Not a Game, It's a...

This is an academic chapter that shows the design of virtual worlds to be a serious topic of research. By studying what other fields find interesting in virtual worlds, the boundaries of the subject can be ascertained and its worth assessed. Also, insights from research by experts from other disciplines can be picked up by designers and applied directly. The aim of this chapter is credibility: Virtual worlds are not "just a game," they're something entirely new.

Chapter 7: Toward a Critical Aesthetic

This is another credibility exercise, although in this case it's to defend virtual world designers from their critics within the arena of virtual worlds rather than their critics not involved in virtual worlds. The purpose of this chapter is to justify this statement: Virtual world design is an art form. To do this, it develops a critical aesthetic—a way of extracting meaning from designers' work that frees them to innovate further.

Chapter 8: Coda: Ethical Considerations

This final chapter discusses the morals of virtual world design. It asks plenty of questions, but doesn't provide many answers; the idea is to alert designers to their responsibilities, rather than lecture them about how they should behave.

Chapter 1

Introduction to Virtual Worlds

What are virtual worlds? In this context, a *world* is an environment that its inhabitants regard as being self-contained. It doesn't have to mean an entire planet: It's used in the same sense as "the Roman world" or "the world of high finance."

So what about the *virtual* part? Not to get too philosophical about it:

➤ *Real*. That which is.

➤ *Imaginary*. That which isn't.

➤ *Virtual*. That which isn't, having the form or effect of that which is.

Virtual worlds are places where the imaginary meets the real.

Some Definitions

Virtual worlds are implemented by a computer (or network of computers) that simulates an environment. Some—but not all—the entities in this environment act under the direct control of individual people. Because several such people can affect the same environment simultaneously, the world is said to be *shared* or *multi-user*. The environment continues to exist and develop internally (at least to some degree) even when there are no people interacting with it; this means it is *persistent*.

Although virtual worlds now have many applications beyond that of being mere entertainment products, they began as computer games; furthermore—perhaps because of the large sums of money involved in their creation and the guaranteed huge monthly incomes they can generate—computer games remain at the cutting edge of virtual world development.

For these reasons, much of the vocabulary commonly used to describe virtual worlds is games-based. Thus, the human beings who interact with the simulated environment are known as *players* rather than *users*; the means by which the environment introduces goals for the players is called *gameplay*; the activity of interacting with the environment is referred to as *playing*.

Specialists may adopt a different vocabulary that is formal for their particular area of expertise, for example a cultural anthropologist might prefer to talk of "individuals" exhibiting "behaviors" in response to "pressures;" however, for any broader discussion of the subject the dominance of game-oriented terminology is impossible to resist, and it is therefore the one that shall be used here.

The exception is the very term "virtual world" itself. Over the years, a number of words, phrases, and contrived acronyms have been used to describe these projected milieux, none of which have been entirely successful. For reasons that will be explained shortly, virtual worlds were originally known as *MUDs* (Multi-User Dungeons).

Although this term is still in common currency to the extent that it has made it into several regular dictionaries, it is not universally accepted. In particular, many players of certain of its subcategories see it as implying some kind of combat-oriented world view, and prefer the term *MU** instead (MU for Multi-User and * for anything that could conceivably follow).

This would be analogous to calling dinosaurs *saurs on the grounds that "dinosaurs" vaguely implies[1] that they were all pea-brained carnivorous monsters, whereas in fact many were pea-brained herbivorous monsters—and hey, there are pterosaurs and plesiosaurs, too.

---

1. "Dino" comes via New Latin from the Greek *deinos*, meaning "fearful." *Saurus* merely means "lizard."

The first virtual worlds were text-based, in that their environments and the events occurring within them were described using words rather than images. Confusingly, although the term MUD applies to virtual worlds in general, the term MU* does not— it's used strictly for text-based worlds. The introduction of computer graphics into the mix therefore caused a second spate of naming, in order to make a distinction between *graphical MUDs* and *text MUDs*. At first the new games were called *persistent worlds*, but when the enormous numbers of simultaneous players they were attracting became their defining feature this changed to *MMORPGs* (Massively-Multiplayer Online Role-Playing Games). Said acronym dominates at present, but it is rarely used with enthusiasm (not least because it's unpronounceable) and it is therefore likely to be abandoned the instant some viable alternative emerges.

Although, properly, all these persistent, shared, computer-moderated environments can and should be referred to as MUDs, the term is sufficiently loaded that outside the cognoscenti it is unlikely to be universally interpreted this way. Enough people think that MUDs are a mere category of MU*s (rather than the reverse) for it to be confusing. Therefore, this book prefers the more descriptive and less emotive "virtual worlds" as an alternative.

It is important to note that virtual worlds are not the same as *virtual reality* (VR), which has a much more specific meaning. Virtual reality is primarily concerned with the mechanisms by which human beings can interact with computer simulations; it is not especially bothered by the nature of the simulations themselves. People who visit virtual worlds may some day benefit from research into visors, data gloves, and beyond, but the fundamental attraction for them is what awaits when they enter a virtual world, not the means by which they do so.

What They Are and Whence They Came

Although more abstract versions can, and do, exist, most virtual worlds adhere to certain conventions that distinguish them from related non-real spaces. The most important of these are

> ➤ The world has underlying, automated rules that enable players to effect changes to it (although not to the rules that grant them this ability). This is the world's *physics*.

➤ Players represent individuals "in" the world. They may wield partial or total influence over an army, crew or party, but there is only one game entity that represents them in the world and with which they strongly identify. This is their *character*. All interaction with the world and other players is channeled through characters.

➤ Interaction with the world takes place in *real time*. When you do something in the world, you can expect feedback almost immediately.

➤ The world is shared.

➤ The world is (at least to some degree) persistent.

A chat room would not be a virtual world because it has no physics; a strategic wargame doesn't map the player onto a single character through which that player acts; a play-by-email game doesn't run in real time; a single-player game is not shared; a first-person shooter isn't persistent.

For some examples, the case is not so clear-cut. Are tabletop role-playing games virtual worlds, for example? No, because they're not automated, but it's a close call. Would a two-player educational MUD be a virtual world? Probably. Would a 500-player game with a world so vast that the players could never find each other? Yes, but under protest.

In practice, it's fairly easy to determine what is or isn't a virtual world simply by looking at its heritage. If its design draws heavily from the design of an existing virtual world, it almost certainly is one; if it doesn't, it almost certainly isn't.

The First Age: 1978–1985

Virtual worlds are often called MUDs because *MUD* was the name of the first one to prosper. Although earlier games had been written that might today be described as virtual worlds, they were seeds that fell on stony ground. *MUD*, by contrast, grew to produce seeds of its own.

MUD was programmed in MACRO-10 assembler on a DecSystem-10 mainframe at Essex University, England, in the fall of 1978. Its author was a talented Computer Science undergraduate, Roy Trubshaw. Version I was a simple test program to establish the basic principles by which a shared world could be maintained. When it worked, Roy immediately started on version II, a text-based virtual world that would be instantly recognizable as such even today. It was also written in MACRO-10, a decision that led to its becoming increasingly unwieldy as more and more features were added. Because of this, in the fall of 1979 Roy made the decision to begin work on version III of the game. He split it in two: The game engine was written in BCPL (the fore-runner of C); the game world was written in a language of his own devising, MUDDL (Multi-User Dungeon Definition Language). The idea was that multiple worlds could be constructed in MUDDL but would run on the same, unmodified engine (which was effectively an interpreter).

Roy had a basic working program by Easter 1980, but it only amounted to a fraction of what he envisaged. This being the final year of his degree, he realized that he did not have time to complete the project. Someone else would have to do it.

From the beginning, Roy had been open to suggestions from his friends as to how *MUD* could be extended and improved. Most of these ideas came from fellow under-graduates Richard Bartle (that's me) and Nigel Roberts. Unlike Nigel, I was younger than Roy and did not have to leave the university for another year (in fact, I was to stay until 1989; first as a postgraduate and then as a lecturer). Luckily, I was also a first-class programmer and had a strong background in gaming. Roy therefore passed *MUD* on to me, and I subsequently wrote the remainder of the engine and nearly all the world to produce what became the paradigm for the entire genre. That's enough blowing my own trumpet, you'll be relieved to know.

Roy had two motivations to write *MUD*. First, he had enjoyed single-player adventure games (Crowther and Woods' *ADVENT*; Anderson, Blank, Daniels, and Lebling's *ZORK*; Laird's *HAUNT*) and liked the idea of creating a multiplayer game along those lines. Secondly, he had a strong academic interest in writing programming language parsers and interpreters. The two came together when he discovered a means of sharing write-enabled areas of memory on the DEC-10 mainframe and mused on its potential uses.

The "D" in *MUD* stands for "Dungeon." Contrary to what many people assume, this has nothing to do with the role-playing game *Dungeons & Dragons* and does not mean that the game world had a dungeon setting[2]. Instead, it is due to the fact that the version of *ZORK* Roy played was a Fortran port called *DUNGEN*[3]. Roy wanted something that was like a multi-user *DUNGE(o)N*, and the acronym MUD immediately presented itself.

---

2. This is just as well, as it didn't.

3. The DEC-10 used six-character, all uppercase filenames. This is why "Dungeon" is referred to as DUNGEN and "Adventure" as ADVENT by old-time hackers like me.

Essex University is a mere 45 minutes by road from the main (what was then the Post Office, but is now) British Telecom research facility, located at Martlesham Heath near Ipswich. This caused the university to be selected to pilot a new, experimental packet-switching service called *EPSS*. Among other things, EPSS allowed contact to and from the ARPA (Advanced Research Project Agency) net in the United States. Roy could therefore tell people in the U.S. about *MUD*, and some of them came to try it out[4]. The ARPA net eventually evolved to become what is known today as the Internet.

Nevertheless, *MUD* remained a mainly Essex University phenomenon in its formative years, existing primarily because of the largesse of the Computer Services team and their manager, Charles Bowman. In the teeth of complaints about wasted resources, members of the university's Computer Society were allowed to spend off-peak time doing anything non-academic they liked. Many of them chose to play *MUD*.

Some, however, were inspired to write their own games in MUDDL for use with the *MUD* engine. There were a number of these, of which the pre-eminent were *ROCK* (based on TV's *Fraggle Rock* Muppet show), *MIST* (original and anarchic), *BLUD* (original and bloody), and *UNI* (the Computer Science Department as a sword-and-sorcery virtual world).

Besides its EPSS connections, Essex University also had a number of modems for dial-up use. News of *MUD* reached the U.K.'s small community of BBS (bulletin board system) users, and they obtained permission to play the game by direct dial—just as long as they did so at times when any sane person would have been in bed for two hours. This they did, and demand grew so much that that they clubbed together and bought the university some extra modems so it could cope…!

Network uptake increased, and eventually all U.K. universities were connected to a system called *JANet* (Joint Academic Network). EPSS ceased to be experimental and became PSS, which enabled people with access to either company PSS accounts or substantial amounts of money to connect to the university's computer systems in yet greater numbers. In 1984–85, there were articles on *MUD* in practically all the specialist computer games magazines in the U.K. The floodgates opened.

---

4. A fact that has busted more than one twisted patent claim.

The *MUD* engine had its limits. It could hold a maximum of 36 players at once[5], and if more wanted to play then a second game would have to be cranked up to supersede the first. Furthermore, it only ran on a DEC-10, and although copies were sent to other institutions in the U.K., Sweden, and Norway, only two of these allowed outsiders access (Dundee Technical College and Oslo University).

While Roy was still working on version II of *MUD*, another student at Essex University, Stephen Murrell, had written from scratch his own virtual world using a different means of handling inter-player communication (that of assigning devices). His game, *PIGG*, was also written in MACRO-10 and eventually ran into the same maintainability problems as *MUD*. Nevertheless, the precedent was set. A number of external players of *MUD* became inspired, or frustrated enough by it, to set about writing their own games.

The Second Age: 1985–1989

The first such virtual worlds to appear were Neil Newell's *Shades*, Ben Laurie's *Gods*, and *AMP*[6]. They were followed shortly by Pip Cordrey, *et al*'s very active *MirrorWorld*. As these games were all derived from *MUD*, they became collectively referred to as "MUDs" or, occasionally, "MUGs" (Multi-User Games). The original *MUD* was dubbed *MUD1* (even though it was in its third version) to disambiguate it from the class of MUDs. This marked the beginning of the second age of virtual worlds.

The possibility of making money from these games arose, so *MUD1* went live both on the dominant U.S. online service of the time, CompuServe, and a U.K. look-alike, CompuNet. A programmer at CompuNet, Alan Lenton, was moved to write his own virtual world, *Federation II*, which has the distinction of being the first MUD to have a non-Fantasy setting (it was Science Fiction).

MUD1, *Federation II*, *Shades* (on the Prestel Micronet teletext system), and *Gods* (in a German translation) went on to achieve commercial success. Scores of other MUDs were created in the U.K., written mainly by players of the Big Four. It was a

---

5. The DEC-10 used a 36-bit world, and Roy assigned 1 bit per player for internal reference.

6. Unfortunately, I only ever met the husband-and-wife team behind *AMP* once, and have been unable to recall their names. I don't think I ever did know for what AMP is an acronym.

time of great experimentation in both game world and game engine design, with much original work coming from the *MirrorWorld* group on their IOWA (Input/Output World of Adventure) system[7].

Around this time, the decision was made to rewrite *MUD1* from scratch as *MUD2* (although it was actually version IV). The original architecture and its DEC-10 platform had proved too limiting, and MUDDL (which owed much to the database definition scheme employed by *ADVENT*) was not sufficiently powerful to handle advanced concepts. A new language, *MUDDLE* (Multi-User Dungeon Definition LanguagE), was developed from first principles specifically for writing MUDs. It turned out to be expressive enough to stand the test of time, and this was therefore the last occasion on which the game *MUD* was to be rewritten in its entirety.

Virtually all the key issues of virtual world design were identified in the first and second ages. By 1987, for example, all the protocols and in-game tools for dealing with player problems were in place and reasonably well codified, thanks to the pioneering efforts of people like Mark Longley (*MUD1*), Michael Lawrie (*MIST*), and Pip Cordrey (*MirrorWorld*). Sadly, however, this kind of knowledge was not passed on in its entirety.

Developers of descendent games usually knew what they *ought* to have, but not necessarily *why* they ought to have it, with the result that after several generations a number of important concepts had been forgotten.

Games that were launched 10 years later, therefore, had to rediscover some of the fundamentals the hard way.

Most of the MUDs that were written in the second age were programmed by enthusiasts at home[8]. At this time (but not for much longer), single-player text adventures were a very important part of the computer game market, so there were plenty of people who understood the principles. Because few academic institutions in the U.K. were as liberal with their computer resources as Essex University, those MUDs that were written at such places tended to achieve only local success.

---

7. This period of experimentation parallels that which took place in early conventional computer game design, although the two occurred quite separately.

8. For a reasonably comprehensive survey of these, see http://www.mud.co.uk/richard/imucg.htm.

The exception was *AberMUD*, so called because it was written at the University of Wales at Aberystwyth. Its programmer, Alan Cox, wrote it in B (another fore-runner of C) for a Honeywell L66 mainframe under GCOS3/TSS in 1987. A year later, it was ported to C. This was a turning point in virtual world history. The game wasn't particularly advanced either technologically or in terms of content (it was very combat-oriented), but it was great fun. More importantly, in C it was positioned to make a huge advance: It could run under Unix.

The Third Age: 1989–1995

AberMUD spread across university computer science departments like a virus. Identical copies (or *incarnations*) appeared on thousands of Unix machines. It went through four versions in rapid succession, spawning several imitators. The three most important of these were *TinyMUD*, *LPMUD*, and *DikuMUD*.

TinyMUD, by Jim Aspnes at Carnegie Mellon University, arrived in 1989. It had two main ancestors: *AberMUD*, and a VAX VMS game called *Monster* that had been released a year earlier. *Monster* (by Rich Skrenta at Northwestern University) was unusual in that it was written independently of the general *MUD1* hierarchy. Its main innovation was the facility to create elements of the virtual world from within the world itself. This was something that had been removed from *MUD1* in the switch from version II to version III.

TinyMUD was basically a stripped-down version of *Monster*. Although still a virtual world, it had practically no "game" aspect to it at all. Players could create new locations and objects (but not much functionality) almost with impunity. Whereas *MUD1* and *AberMUD* had boasted around 400–500 discrete locations, a popular 1990 incarnation of *TinyMUD* called *Islandia* racked up over 14,000 of them in the few months of its existence.

The lack of game in *TinyMUD* meant that players spent most of their time creating things and talking about their creations. Although not the first primarily "social" virtual world (Clive Lindus' cleverly conceived *Void*[9] beat it by a few months), it was the one from which virtually all subsequent such worlds sprang. *TinyMUD* was deliberately intended to be distanced from the prevailing hack-and-slay *AberMUD* style, and

---

9. Its name over the years has been variously *Void*, *The Void*, and *Vortex*, but they're all the same place. *Void* is adult in nature, and was directly inspired by the first such virtual world, *The Zone*.

the "D" in its name was said to stand for "Dimension" (or, occasionally, "Domain") rather than "Dungeon;" this is the ultimate cause of the MUD/MU* distinction that was to arise some years later.

LPMUD was named after its author, Lars Pensjö of the University of Gothenburg, Sweden. Having played both *AberMUD* and *TinyMUD*, he decided he wanted to write his own game with the adventure of the former and the user-extensibility of the latter. Whereas most early MUD designers were of the haughty opinion that players weren't as good at world creation as they, Lars believed the opposite: that players could build a better world than he could himself. To this end, he developed an in-game programming language called *LPC* that allowed players of sufficient experience to add not only objects, but also powerful functionality to the game as it ran.

This was a major advance, and introduced many people to the wonders of programming without frying their brains in the manner that conventional academic learn-to-program courses tend to do. LPC was sufficiently well designed that it is still very much in use today.

DikuMUD was created at the Department of Computer Science at the University of Copenhagen (Datalogisk Institutved Københavns Universitet), Denmark. Released in 1990, its authors were a group of student friends: Katja Nyboe, Tom Madsen, Hans Henrik Staerfeldt, Michael Seifert, and Sebastian Hammer. It was designed purely as a better *AberMUD*, and made no reference to either *TinyMUD* or *LPMUD*. Whereas these other two games had moved toward allowing on-the-fly changes to be made to the virtual world, *DikuMUD*'s designers went in the opposite direction and hard-coded everything they could.

However, they hard-coded it very well: *DikuMUD* ran "out of the box" and was organized very well internally. A reasonable C programmer could easily modify the original *DikuMUD* code and produce a new world of their own, or change the data files to create a differently-appearing one. Many did.

As a result, several major *codebases* (standalone MUD program suites) were created from the basic *DikuMUD* original, the main ones being *Circle*, *Silly*, and *Merc*. *Merc* spawned *ROM* (Rivers of MUD) and *Envy*, among others, and these in turn had their own spin-offs. All appeared—and continue to appear—in a dizzying number of sub-versions.

LPMUD did not inspire quite so many offshoots, because LPC was flexible enough to allow people to write their own games without writing their own game engines. Although most LPMUDs are combat-oriented, critically (and unlike DikuMUDs) they don't *have* to be[10].

The *TinyMUD* family tree is perhaps the most interesting of the three main *AberMUD*-inspired branches. *TinyMUD* itself was little more than a mere proof of concept. Incarnations of the game would appear on some long-forgotten university Unix machine, enjoy a few short months of brilliant existence, and then collapse under the weight of acrimony, apathy, and full disk packs that they caused. Those players who weren't put off virtual worlds for life would then migrate[11] to another nascent *TinyMUD* and the cycle would repeat, slash-and-burn style.

The problem was that players couldn't actually *do* much in *TinyMUDs* except invite one another to admire their latest piece of what might as well have been wallpaper. One player, Stephen White, decided in 1990 to extend the functionality of *TinyMUD* and wrote *TinyMUCK* (muck being a kind of mud). Using this as his template, he then produced *MOO* (MUD, Object Oriented). *MOO* introduced a fully functional *scripting language* (as such in-world programming languages[12] are called) and thus brought the LPC-like capabilities to social-oriented virtual worlds. *MOO* had two important off-spring: Pavel Curtis' *LambdaMOO* (which was to become a favorite of journalists, academics, and social misfits) and, via *CoolMUD*, *ColdMUD* (an attempt to create a software-engineering quality virtual world authoring system).

MOO's descendents have found a niche in the educational world, as they are easy to use and (like *LPMUDs*) can demonstrate the principles of programming to youngsters without scaring the wits out of them. They were not, however, the only important codebase family to come out of *TinyMUCK*.

Larry Foard released *TinyMUSH* later in 1990. The "MUSH" part originally didn't mean anything special, but was later retrofitted as "Multi-User Shared Hallucination." The *TinyMUSH* codebase introduced several advanced features, such as event triggering

---

10. For a comparison between LPMUDs and DikuMUDs, see Rawn Shah's and James Romine's, *Playing MUDs on the Internet*. New York, John Wiley, 1995.

11. Those that had Internet access would. It was by no means universal at the time, and not every player could find another home when his or her local *TinyMUD* was shut down.

12. So are some out-of-world programming languages, as we'll see later in this chapter.

and software automatons (known as *puppets*), which together facilitated role-playing. Consequently, most of the derivatives of *TinyMUSH* (known as *MUSHes*) are role-playing in nature: What you do defines what you are, rather than the reverse.

From a non-historical perspective, the significant property of MOOs, MUSHes, and other descendents of *TinyMUCK* (known as MUCKs) is that they don't have computer-controlled monsters for players to seek out and, within the context of the virtual world, kill. Players of these classes of virtual worlds are the ones most likely to use the term MU*, reserving MUD to mean those games that do have computer-controlled monsters for players to seek out and kill[13].

The third age of virtual worlds was thus a period of huge expansion. More people sampled virtual worlds than ever before. Indeed, a study of traffic on the NSFnet backbone in 1993 showed that just over 10% of the bits belonged to MUDs; in other words, before the advent of the World Wide Web (WWW) MUDs constituted some 10% of the Internet!

There were less positive consequences, however. Whereas in earlier times anyone who wanted to run a virtual world would have to write one from first principles, the sudden preponderance of codebases meant that this was no longer the case. If you wanted to run a virtual world, you simply downloaded an off-the-shelf one and *voila!*—one virtual world! Although in theory developers could change any aspect of what they had downloaded (particularly for LPMUDs and *TinyMUD* derivatives), in practice most people simply built on what they already had. This meant that two worlds using the same codebase would probably have the same basic geography and physics, with multiple extensions. Although some old-timers have complained that this leads to homogeneity and thereby stifles creativity, that's not the main bugbear. Rather, it's that if designers don't understand *why* the partial design they begin with does what it does (and doesn't do what it doesn't do), how can they be sure their changes are for the best? Come to that, how can they be sure the template they begin with isn't itself flawed in some way?

Were only undergraduates and amateur enthusiasts considered, the third age of virtual worlds is still very much upon us. Several thousand LPMUDs, DikuMUDs, MOOs, MUSHes, and MUCKs exist, some of them with impressive numbers of players. However, the torch of innovation was soon to be picked up by a different bearer—business.

---

13. In this context, MUDs are frequently dismissed somewhat haughtily as inferior game forms. Players of MUDs reciprocate by calling the MU* brigade *carebears*.

The Fourth Age: 1995–1997

MUDs might very well have been called SOGs had things turned out differently.

Around the same time that Roy Trubshaw began work on what was to become *MUD1*, Alan Klietz wrote *Sceptre of Goth* on the CDC Cyber run by MECC (the Minnesota Educational Computer Consortium). The game (also known as *Empire* and *The Phoenix*) was based on an earlier MECC game called *Milieu*. It was developed completely independently; its mechanics owed more to *Dungeons & Dragons* than did *MUD1*'s, particularly in its use of character classes.

Sensing the commercial possibilities, Klietz ported it to run on a PC and ran it as a dial-up game. It met with local success, so incarnations were set up in several major U.S. cities. Klietz's company (GamBits) then sold the software to another company. Unfortunately, this second company ran into severe legal problems and ran out of money. *Sceptre of Goth* passed to a creditor, and was never released again. Thus, through bad luck, the first commercial virtual world did not have the impact that it might have had, although it did make enough of a mark to influence the design of some later codebases, in particular *Mordor*.

In the U.K., offshoots of the *MUD1* family tree had done well, but were stymied by the system of high telephone charges that was then in place in that part of the world.

When it costs more to connect to a game than it does to play it, there will inevitably be problems. People were running up phone bills of £2,000 to £3,000 a quarter—this at a time when the average salary was under £9,000 for an entire year.

The situation was little better in the rest of Europe; *Gods* did well in Germany, but couldn't really be said to have cracked the market. *Shades*, released in a French translation for the Minitel teletext system, made nowhere near the £70,000 or more a year it had been clearing in the U.K.

The picture was different in the U.S., where local phone calls were basically free. CompuServe recruited over a million subscribers to its system, charging them at premium rates to access data. Games formed a big part of its profit: Whereas it takes only two minutes to check how your stocks are performing, you might spend two hours playing a game. However, CompuServe did not promote its games, fearing that to do so would discourage parents from signing up to the service lest it corrupt their children.

Rivals to CompuServe were not so coy. GEnie was launched in 1985 by the former head of games at CompuServe, Bill Louden. Naturally, it put games to the fore, as did another 1985 start-up called QuantumLink. Although QuantumLink carried a very influential precursor to graphical virtual worlds (Lucasfilm's *Habitat*, designed by F. Randall Farmer and Chip Morningstar) and was destined to become the mighty America Online (AOL), at the time it was GEnie that drew all the attention. Genie's games-first strategy worked well, in that by the early 1990s hard-core gamers accounted for nearly 70% of GEnie's revenue. However, GEnie suffered from lack of investment (most of its profits went back to parent company General Electric) and the fact that CompuServe's concerns about the side effects of promoting games were not entirely unfounded. At this time, people still needed "noble content" such as news or educational products as an excuse to sign up for a service, even if they were only intending to play games when they got there.

Much of GEnie's flowering at this time was due to the efforts of its Games Product Manager, Jessica Mulligan. Jessica had worked for QuantumLink, where she had recommended acquiring the *Advanced Dungeons & Dragons* license for an online game (which was eventually to become *NeverWinter Nights*).

When QuantumLink began to de-emphasize games, she moved to GEnie. There, she assembled an impressive stable of some of the finest games of the day. Because of her, GEnie was the launch point for many classic online games, including two very important virtual worlds: *Gemstone II* in 1988 and *Dragon's Gate* in 1990 (a year in which earlier U.K. favorite *Federation II* made it to GEnie).

Gemstone had been created by David Whatley and his company, Simutronics, in 1987; the II was added when it went live on GEnie. Simutronics' expertise grew from BBS technology, and *Gemstone II* was a descendent of neither *MUD1* nor *Sceptre of Goth*.

In 1989, Darrin Hyrup, the lead programmer on another Simutronics game (*Orb Wars*), left to join a company called Adventures Unlimited Software, Inc. (AUSI). AUSI was started in 1984 by entrepreneurial programmer Mark Jacobs to run a text-based virtual world named *Aradath* he had also written independently. Like *Sceptre of Goth*, *Aradath* ran on a home computer dial-up system, but unlike all other virtual worlds for the next decade it charged its users a flat fee to play. Although it was turned down by QuantumLink, its promise was enough to tempt Darrin to join Mark to write *Dragon's Gate*. This was a smart move.

At the end of the pre-WWW era in 1993, five U.S. services dominated the online market: CompuServe, Prodigy, AOL, Delphi, and GEnie. Smaller, games-specific services, such as MPG-Net and the ImagiNation Network, were also players in the games market (or tried to be). These services had a stranglehold on virtual world development: If you couldn't get your game on one of them, you were in for a hard time. At this point, third-age virtual worlds were still the biggest and most important.

The WWW changed it all. People were suddenly excited by the concept of "online." They flocked in droves to those services that offered Internet connection (which had previously been mainly the preserve of colleges). Some, such as AOL, embraced it. Others, particularly the ever-conservative CompuServe, tried to weather the storm and failed. A price war in 1993 among the major services had made Internet access affordable for all. Come 1995, hordes of inexpert computer users were knocking on the door, looking for interesting things. Some of them—rather a lot of them, in fact—wanted to play games.

Thus, the short but extraordinary fourth age of virtual worlds began. AOL went for the throat and signed up *Gemstone III*, *Dragon's Gate*, and *Federation II* (it already had *NeverWinter Nights*). In common with other services, its business model was based on time spent connected to its system, a legacy of how computer bureaux used to charge for mainframe timeslices in the days when not every company had its own hardware. Also like everyone else, if its customers were accessing content provided externally, AOL paid a royalty. Unlike most of its competitors, however, it paid a *fair* royalty[14]. Unlike all its competitors, it picked up a vast user base[15].

The consequence of this was that games like *Gemstone III* and *Dragon's Gate* were making their authors over a million dollars a month. Even the "failing" *NeverWinter Nights* (NWN) took around $5,000,000 in 1996, despite being limited to 500 simultaneous players. It was an amazing time to be in the industry—if your game was on AOL. If not, it was hugely frustrating.

Disaster struck when the business model suddenly changed.

---

14. CompuServe in particular was resented among developers for its arrogant "tell me why we only deserve 92% of the income that *our* customers generate" approach.

15. This was basically because they gave away the client software, I should add. I don't mean to imply that it was due to their paying a fair royalty to game designers!

Small companies that used to run local BBSs began setting themselves up as Internet Service Providers. Initially, they used the same, pay-per-hour tariffs as the big boys. Then, in response to customer pressure, they broke ranks and switched to flat rate charging. AOL followed suit in December 1996, so as not to lose customers to these upstarts.

Unfortunately, AOL's contracts with external information providers assumed a per-hour charge, which AOL had to honor. They tried to persuade game developers to accept a flat fee or a much reduced per-hour royalty, and some indeed went along with it. Others, however, held their ground. It was their opinion that the reason their games were successful was because they were good games; it had nothing to do with standing directly in the flow of AOL's newbie hose.

A compromise dual-pricing scheme was implemented similar to one introduced by GEnie some years earlier, whereby "premium" content (that is, games) was charged by the hour and everything else was flat rate. This was not a great success, though, and by mid-1997 the gravy train had stopped running.

Most of the virtual worlds that had been on the big services set themselves up as independent games on the (now easy-access) Internet. After all, if they were able to keep *all* the money that players paid, they could afford to shed 80% of their player base and still make a huge profit. Unfortunately, they had not anticipated three major obstacles that would humble them greatly:

1. Most of their players objected to paying for a game they had previously considered to be free. Only the hard core—around 5% to 10% of the total—ever made the move.

2. Attracting newbies is very, very difficult. As existing players gradually drift away, from where do their replacements come?

3. Over a thousand virtual worlds were already accessible via the Internet for free—the LPMUDs, DikuMUDs, MOOs, MUSHes, and MUCKs. Sure, they were "free, and worth every penny," but hey, free is free!

These for-pay virtual worlds (and others) do still exist, and do still make money, but it's nowhere near the amount they did in the halcyon days of 1995–1997. It would be nice to think that developers have learned from this the dangers of over-estimating the intrinsic value of their products; nice, but unlikely.

Off-the-shelf codebases are free to use and free to play, but they are not freeware. They come with strict licensing conditions that preclude their being used commercially. This means that there is still some innovation, as people who want to make money from virtual worlds must perforce write their own from scratch. The days when people would willingly pay more per hour to access a commercial virtual world than they would later pay per month[16] are long gone, however.

Yet all was not entirely lost. At its peak, *Gemstone III* on AOL was attracting 2,000–2,500 players simultaneously. In theory, if a product could attract players in sufficiently large numbers—say, 10 times this number in total—then it might be possible to levy an inexpensive monthly fee and still make a respectable profit.

In 1997, Origin Systems Inc. (OSI) launched *Ultima Online*.

The Fifth Age: 1997–Present

There had been graphical virtual worlds before.

The seminal *PLATO* (Programmed Logic for Automatic Teaching Operations) system went live at the University of Illinois way back in 1961, and many games were written to take advantage of both its network connectivity and graphics-capable plasma display units. Some of these laid down principles that would greatly influence the development of later computer games; some came close to being virtual worlds; some actually were virtual worlds.

Orthanc, by Paul Resch, Larry Kemp, and Eric Hagstrom, was an overhead view graphical game that, although not implementing a shared world, nevertheless allowed communication between individual players. It was written as early as 1973. Jim Schwaiger's 1977 game *Oubliette* (inspired by *Dungeons & Dragons* and Chuck Miller's earlier multiplayer game, *Mines of Moria*) had a first-person point of view and used line graphics to render the scene ahead. It had persistent characters, but was not a persistent world. Also, the interaction it allowed between characters was very limited; it was almost there, but not quite.

---

16. In 1990, GEnie was charging nearly $20 an hour for daytime access—more than double what the major games were charging for an entire month a decade later.

In late 1979, the first ever fully functional graphical virtual world was released: *Avatar*. Written by a group of students to out-do *Oubliette*, it was to become the most successful PLATO game ever—it accounted for 6% of all the hours spent on the system between September 1978 and May 1985[17]. Again using a Fantasy setting, it introduced the concept of *spawning* to repopulate areas automatically after players killed all the monsters.

Despite the fact that PLATO was very important in the development of computer games in general, its virtual worlds had little external impact. This was almost certainly because the twin strengths of the PLATO system—its fast network and superior graphics—would not generally become available to home users for another 15 years. If your screen can only display text and your modem only runs at 300 baud, online pictures aren't exactly a major priority. Insofar as the history of graphical virtual worlds is concerned, the second to fourth ages are pretty much dark ages.

Some of the second age virtual worlds *almost* went graphical. There were plans to produce Atari ST and Commodore Amiga clients for *Bloodstone*, a virtual world by Robert Muir that ran on Microlink, but they amounted to nothing. The coordinate-based *Mosaic* system (nothing to do with the browser of that name) pioneered by the *MirrorWorld* team was ideal material for conversion to graphics, but Pip Cordrey was vehemently anti-graphics and blocked the move. Others toyed with the idea, only to be put off by the expense involved.

A graphical virtual world that did influence others was *Island of Kesmai*, (*IOK*) written by Kelton Flinn and John Taylor in 1981. It grew from a six-player game called *Dungeons of Kesmai* that the pair had completed a year earlier, and was independent of the other work on virtual worlds going on at the time (the pair hadn't even heard of *ADVENT*, let alone *MUD1*!). *IOK* debuted on CompuServe in December, 1985.

The game did not have graphics as such. What it did have was a display that used individual letters and other ASCII characters to represent a bird's-eye view of the immediate vicinity. Because of the ersatz graphics, the degree of interaction allowed between players wasn't as high as in a purely text-oriented game (a state of affairs that continues to this day), but it was good enough to qualify *IOK* as a virtual world.

---

17. Source: http://www.thinkofit.com/plato/dwplato.htm.

The graphics capabilities of home computers gradually improved, and it was therefore only a matter of time before someone wrote a game that coupled an *IOK*-style tessellated world with a hardware-specific means of displaying it. Indeed, by the early 1990s the Kesmai Corporation had already done it for their multiplayer flight simulator game, *Air Warrior*, which had clients for the PC, Atari ST, Commodore Amiga, and Apple Macintosh. The basic principle was for the virtual world software itself (the *server*) to send data to software running on the home user's computer (the *client*), which it could use as the basis to construct an image[18].

Although Kesmai eventually produced a (disappointing) graphical version of *IOK* called *Legends of Kesmai*, they were well beaten to the punch by *NeverWinter Nights* (1991 on AOL), *Kingdom of Drakkar* (1992 on MPG-net), and *Shadows of Yserbius* (1992 on ImagiNation Network). These games basically took the same approach: a bird's-eye view of a 2D world built from squares, with flat sprites to represent players, objects, walls, and things to be fought. They maintained separate text areas for information, descriptions, and communications.

This is a very effective way to do it. The bandwidth and server load requirements are comparatively light, the design tools are cheap to develop, and you can create large, interesting worlds with a fair degree of interaction among the players. Such worlds can lack flexibility—you won't see many circular buildings in them—but they pay for it by their ease of creation. The scale is usually an issue, in that there's a conflict between the amount of space in the virtual world that characters appear to occupy (because of the fidelity of the graphics) and the amount they seemingly ought to occupy (because they represent people), but it's nothing too serious.

Note that although all tessellated worlds are essentially 2D, they don't have to be shown in the same, boring, map-like way that a newspaper typically displays a chessboard. Instead, they can be shown *isometrically*. By fixing the camera (that is, the player's viewpoint) at an angle other than directly overhead (say, at 60°), the impression of a 3D world can be given.

---

18. Many players seem naïvely to imagine that an entire image is transmitted each time one needs to be displayed, as with TV pictures. This is not, however, yet the case.

This is sometimes referred to as a 2½D world. It was inevitable that as soon as computer video cards were up to the job, new games would appear in the more realistic-looking 2½D rather than plain old 2D[19].

At this point, the story changes continents.

In Europe and North America, individuals wanting to use the Internet for fun would generally do so from home. This was not necessarily the case in other countries. In particular, the trend in South Korea was to use Internet cafés, where people could share their online experiences in a friendly, social atmosphere (with broadband connections). Large chains of such establishments soon spread across the country. This presented Korean game developers with a business model not available in the West: licensing game access to the Internet cafés, rather than to the players.

Two companies took advantage of this: Nexon launched *The Kingdom of the Winds* in 1996, with NCSoft's *Lineage* following in 1997. *Lineage* was designed by Jake Song, who had previously worked on *The Kingdom of the Winds* (TKOW) and was later voted South Korea's best game designer. Both *TKOW* and *Lineage* used a 2½D perspective, but the latter had vastly superior graphics and almost immediately became the virtual world with the most real-world players anywhere. It opened in Taiwan and was a huge hit there, too. Attempts to repeat this success in the U.S. market failed, however; for some reason, the game did not appeal to American tastes. It was therefore almost completely ignored in the West, until something happened that forced developers to pay attention: Revenue figures for *Lineage* in the first quarter of 2000 were posted at 6,500 million Won, that is over five million dollars. Virtual worlds were becoming a global phenomenon, and Korea was a leading marketplace.

In terms of advances in game design, though, the plot returns to the U.S. in 1997.

Although *The Kingdom of The Winds* predated it, the product that truly proved virtual worlds had come of age was OSI's *Ultima Online* (UO).

It is hard to understate the impact that this work had on the consciousness of developers and publishers. Prior to *Ultima Online*, virtual worlds had been regarded as all potential: It was clear from the devotion they inspired that they could probably make

---

19. Strictly speaking, any implementation of a 3D space that fakes height is 2½D. This means that games like *Doom*, which have a first-person perspective but can't implement bridges, can also be described as 2½D.

pots of money, but as no one had managed to do so outside of peculiar market conditions few companies were willing to invest in producing one. This was soon to change.

When *Ultima Online* garnered 50,000 subscribers within 3 months, people took notice. When it broke 100,000 within a year, jaws dropped. Never mind the substantial income from retail sales: 100,000 people were *each* paying $9.95 *per month* having already bought the game—and none of that money was going to retailers!

OSI was directly taking 12 million dollars a year from that one virtual world!

Ultima Online set the standard: 100,000 subscribers by the end of year one is the benchmark—anything less than that, and a graphical game-oriented virtual world can't honestly call itself a success.

So how did *Ultima Online* manage to pick up so many subscribers so quickly? Part of it was being the right product at the right time, of course, but the Ultima name—one of the best loved and respected by role-playing gamers—was probably the main reason people were so keen to try it. The virtual world it promised really caught the game-playing public's imagination.

Trying a game doesn't mean that people will continue to *play* it, though. With ordinary boxed games, the publishers don't particularly care whether anyone actually plays their products, so long as they *buy* them. *Ultima Online* had to be good enough that people *would* want to play—and would shell out nearly 10 bucks a month to do so.

That people did play is a tribute to the game's design team, led by Raph Koster. Raph had a background in virtual world design, having worked on 1992's *Worlds of Carnage* (the first DikuMUD to have an embedded scripting language) before moving on to found *LegendMUD* in 1994 with Kristen Koster (his wife), Rick Delashmit, and others. In 1995, Delashmit signed up as lead programmer for *Ultima Online* and recommended the Kosters to OSI.

LegendMUD was itself an innovative game, boasting a number of features to promote role-playing that had never been implemented before. For example, unlike other *DikuMUD* derivatives, *LegendMUD* was *classless* (players don't elect to be fighters, magic-users, healers, thieves, or whatever); this concept was to shape the design of *Ultima Online* powerfully. The wide-ranging playing experience of the designers meant that they could draw on ideas from many other codebases, too.

Perhaps most importantly, however, *Ultima Online* was conceived from the start to be a richer and deeper virtual world than a typical MUD, with an emphasis on community building, player-driven action, and the ability to accommodate different playing styles. These were tremendously important insights; they had a powerful impact on the graphical virtual worlds that appeared in the two to three years following *UO*'s release, and are now regarded as absolute prerequisites in the designs for new virtual worlds. Although later games could take aspects of *UO* on board, their designers were not always aware of the reasoning that had led the *UO* team to include or exclude some concept or other[20].

This led to balance issues (among others), and is one of the reasons why, in design terms, *UO* remained pre-eminent until the arrival of *Star Wars Galaxies* in 2003. It is no coincidence that the lead designer of *Star Wars Galaxies* (SWG) was also Raph Koster.

UO nevertheless did have its problems, the two principal ones being

> ➤ It was at times too innovative. Some of the ideas it field-tested did not work as planned and had to be altered. Examples: The means by which players were punished for attacking each other's characters wasn't effective; the detailed ecological model employed broke down when players rapidly killed everything that moved; the economy collapsed after a bug led to hyper-inflation.

> ➤ It was a victim of its own success. Although OSI was expecting tens of thousands of players, they weren't expecting hundreds of thousands of them. The sheer number of people involved meant that the pressure was on to correct any problems as soon after discovery as possible. This caused several management decisions to be made that, in retrospect, set precedents which perhaps ought not to have been set. Customer service doesn't scale well or rapidly.

All in all, *UO* was a game ahead of its time, but not so far ahead as to be regarded as a failure.

The same could not be said of Archetype Interactive's *Meridian 59*.

---

20. This is a theme I will return to again and again in this book. You already noticed, huh?

Launched a year ahead of *UO* (after the company had been bought by 3DO), it was the first graphical virtual world since the days of *Avatar* to employ a first-person point of view (that is, where the screen shows what the player's virtual character sees, rather than what someone sitting on a low cloud would see—if they could remove rooftops).

Because players could move around and view their surroundings from almost any angle, *Meridian 59* gave a far greater sense of being a 3D virtual world than did *UO* or *Lineage*. Indeed, this is the kind of viewpoint people typically mean when they're talking about a *3D* world or viewpoint in respect of any computer game[21].

Meridian 59 (M59) was designed by Mike Sellers and Damion Schubert, the latter having been recommended by Raph Koster (who had accepted a job at OSI by then so was unavailable). It was intended to become the first "3D MUD," and in this it succeeded.

However, it was not the huge success that it might have been (and that the designers of other in-development graphical virtual worlds feared it would become) mainly due to a lack of experience. The designers, the developers, and especially the publishers (3DO) made several mistakes that are classic to virtual worlds and therefore should have been easily avoided. To be fair, the designers did know their stuff, but they were working to a small budget and a short deadline.

Among the mistakes made were

> ➤ Allowing access permissions for certain features (for example, in-game shops) to be determined by the (soon-to-be-hacked) client software.

> ➤ Not fully testing the software. It was very stable, but one particular show-stopping bug rendered the in-game currency completely worthless overnight.

> ➤ Community-alienating changes of business plan. Originally costing each player $10 per month, they switched to $2.49 per day ("but never more than $30 a month") and lost a third of their players in the process[22].

> ➤ Self-defeating customer service work (due to a "no comment" policy).

---

21. Actually, it used a *DOOM*-like engine and was, technically speaking, therefore only 2½D.

22. Their player base had stopped growing by then, but this hastily shrank it.

Of course, these errors were also made by many of the virtual worlds that followed *Meridian 59* (indeed, they're still being made today). These other virtual worlds didn't all fail, however, so why did *M59*?

M59's problem was that it didn't garner enough players early on to weather its storms. There are several reasons for this, but they all come down to the fact that it was launched too soon. *M59* is remembered for being the first 3D virtual world; if it hadn't gone to market prematurely, then it wouldn't have been able to claim this title, but instead of being the pioneer it could well have become the paradigm.

What *M59* did wrong that actually hurt it was

- ➤ It had poor marketing. Few people outside the online gaming community knew it existed. The computer games press didn't care about it.

- ➤ Its graphics didn't compare well to those of other 3D games around at the time (particularly *Quake*'s). This is probably why the computer press didn't care about it.

- ➤ It had insufficient content. The world felt very small, and it lacked many features traditional to the Fantasy genre that potential players were surprised to find missing.

- ➤ There weren't enough people with Internet connections when it launched. Ironically, if they hadn't launched early to get the drop on *Ultima Online* then there almost certainly would have been.

In other words, it wasn't the design that killed it but the business decisions made. Design is hugely important, but it can't do everything.

Even so, *Meridian 59* did a lot of things right. In particular, it released expansion sets to keep players interested and (until it changed its pricing scheme) it made the total number of *players* important, rather than the total number of *hard-core players*. It also ran multiple incarnations of its virtual world on different servers, some of which it licensed to other countries (which although it had been done commercially back in the days of *Shades* had by then gone out of fashion).

Although the *M59* team was inexperienced to begin with, they soon learned. *M59* graduates are now among the most sought-after personnel in the industry. Mike Sellers (who left before *M59* shipped) went on to become lead designer of *The Sims Online*; Damion Schubert accepted the same position for *Ultima Online 2* before setting up as an independent creative consultant and eventually winding up working on the much-anticipated *Shadowbane*[23]; producer Rich Vogel took over from Starr Long at *Ultima Online* shortly before that game's launch, later beating all opposition to land the plum position of producer for *Star Wars Galaxies*.

The main reason for *M59*'s only modest success was that it came to market a touch too soon. In 1996, few people had a graphics card in their PCs and their modems were 14400 baud. *M59* therefore had to be written for this level of client hardware, or no one would have played it.

A year later, when *UO* launched, prospective players had upgraded and the OSI team was able to deliver a far more feature-rich product. *UO* had a somewhat bigger budget, too.

UO wounded *M59*, but not mortally. The fatal[24] blow was only to come in the spring of 1999, with the launch of 989 Studios, *EverQuest*.

If ever there was a case of being in the right place at the right time, *EverQuest* (*EQ*) is it. It was basically a DikuMUD with a graphical client bolted on—the similarities are so close that under legal threat its server programmers were forced to sign sworn statements to the effect that they didn't use any actual *DikuMUD* code in *EverQuest*[25].

Graphically, *EverQuest* took the same first-person 3D view as *Meridian 59*, but allowed the camera to roam instead of fixing it to the character's eyes. If players wanted a bird's-eye view or to see their own character from behind, they could do so. The graphics also occupied a good deal more of the screen, which greatly improved players' feelings of being immersed in the environment.

---

23. http://www.shadowbane.com

24. As with many of the characters in them, "fatal" is only a relative term for virtual worlds. *Meridian 59* was resurrected a few years later, and can now be found at http://meridian59.neardeathstudios.com.

25. There are copies at http://www.dikumud.com/diku/swornstatement.asp.

In terms of gameplay, *EverQuest* wasn't especially deep (although neither was it shallow). Had it been launched even a few months later, it would probably have had only moderate success; it was never exactly innovative, and there were other games in development which would have made it look inferior by comparison. However, it was launched at precisely the right moment. Its designers (Steve Clover, Brad McQuaid, and Bill Trost) had done a sound job.

It looked good, there were plenty of computer gamers actively seeking an online game to play, its *DikuMUD* heritage guaranteed a compelling experience, and *Ultima Online* was getting bad publicity because of its unpopular way of handling combat between players' characters and its generally poor newbie experience.

EverQuest had no great publicity campaign, which is probably just as well: News of this beautiful virtual world spread by word of mouth so rapidly that it was only through good fortune that enough Internet bandwidth became available in San Diego (where the servers were located) to cope with the demand[26]. *EQ* overtook *UO* in terms of subscriber numbers within six months and its usage figures were ordained to grow relentlessly, month after month, for years.

EQ's developers were just as inexperienced as *M59*'s, and they also made a number of novice errors. Indeed, their customer relations department was so systematically bad that at times it seemed people were playing in spite of their efforts, not because of them. So why did *EQ* put the final nail in *M59*'s coffin, rather than suffering a similar experience itself?

Essentially, the answer is that *EQ* reached a *critical mass* of players.

Whatever the reasons people had for starting to play the game, they continued to play because of the other people they had met there. *EQ* was constructed to encourage players to form small groups and play regularly with one another; if the team was short a member, players would persuade their real-world friends to make up the numbers. This bonding was something *M59* lacked, and in due course led to *EQ*'s all-conquering progress.

---

26. It is a not entirely unfounded rumor that around this time its competitor *Ultima Online* had more incoming Internet bandwidth than New York City. Before then, *Meridian 59* had regularly caused the Internet to slow down—in Silicon Valley—on patch days.

EQ's impact on subsequent graphical virtual world design was profound. It became the *de facto* paradigm for the genre. This had three main consequences:

➤ Players who "grew up" on *EverQuest* viewed its user interface, gameplay, and feature set as standard. New games that did not conform to this were viewed as flawed. This is not a new phenomenon. Players of *Shades* who tried out other games were often disparaging about what were actually superior (but non-*Shades*) ways of doing things. Similarly, after AOL purchased the ImagiNation network and dropped *NeverWinter Nights*, *Meridian 59* received a flood of refugees who then proceeded to demand every *NWN* feature that *M59* didn't already have, irrespective of how appropriate it was to the game.

➤ The sheer amount of money *EverQuest* generated caused developers considering writing a virtual world to want to jump on the bandwagon. Within two years of *EverQuest*'s launch, over a hundred graphical virtual worlds had been announced as being in development, of which the vast majority were *EverQuest* near-clones.

➤ *EverQuest* sucked in newbies who might otherwise have tried some other game, thereby depressing the market for the games that immediately followed it and forcing them to survive on their ability to attract the non-mainstream gamers.

One of the products to suffer was Turbine's *Asheron's Call*. Designed by Toby Ragaini (lead), Chris Foster, Eri Izawa, and Chris Pierson, it launched nine months after *EverQuest* (at least a year late, due to the inexperience of the production team[27]).

It broke new ground with a number of inventive ideas[28], primary among which was the *story arc*: Structures, objects, and new functionality would be added to (and in some cases, removed from) the virtual world on a regular basis (monthly) to unfold an overall narrative.

Asheron's Call (*AC*) also had some technical innovations that impacted virtual world design. One of the more irritating things about *EQ* was that it partitioned its world into *zones*. Rather than having a single, expensive computer to act as a server for the whole virtual world, each zone ran on its own computer as part of a cluster that comprised the server. Players moving from one zone to another would experience some delay

---

27. *Ultima Online* and *EverQuest* weren't exactly launched on time either, though....

28. Inventive for graphical worlds, that is; textual worlds, as usual, got there first.

while any initialization information concerning the new zone was transmitted to their PC. Once in the zone they were sharing its governing computer with only a fraction of the other players in the game, and therefore the response was good; however, moving between zones was a pain.

AC didn't have zones, which meant it presented itself as a single, seamless world—a far more player-friendly proposition. It still used a cluster of computers to manage the world, but didn't assign individual machines to specific zones. Instead, it used a technique called *dynamic load balancing* to determine which cluster member was in charge of which location set. If players congregated their characters in one area of the virtual world, the server responsible for it would offload part of that area (and the players associated with it) to another, less heavily loaded machine. Similar distributed server technology had been used by Nexon in 1999 (the year *AC* launched) to cram 12,263 users in a single incarnation of *The Kingdom of the Winds*, albeit with a tessellated 2½D world rather than a fully 3D one.

AC managed to build up a player base of around 80,000 by the end of its first year—20,000 short of the total needed for it to be considered an unqualified success. Had it launched before *EQ*, as originally planned, the story might have been rather different.

By the end of 2000, the state of play among the "big three" virtual worlds was as follows:

➤ *Ultima Online* (launched 1997) had 230,000+ subscribers from boxed unit sales of 380,000+ and expansion pack sales of 100,000+.

➤ *EverQuest* (launched early 1999) had 300,000+ subscribers from boxed unit sales of 600,000+ and expansion pack[29] sales of 300,000+.

➤ *Asheron's Call* (launched late 1999) had 90,000+ subscribers from 200,000+[30] boxed unit sales. It hadn't released any expansion packs.

What is most interesting here is not so much that *EQ* had a staggering 300,000 subscribers, but that it had lost another staggering 300,000 players who originally purchased the boxed unit. *UO's retention* rate, at 60% overall, was significantly better. Although continuing good word-of-mouth and large-scale advertising campaigns brought *EQ* yet more swathes of players in the coming years, its *churn* only got worse.

---

29. The first of these included the *EQ* client itself, but subsequent ones didn't.

30. Estimated.

The next significant release of a graphical virtual world was Funcom's *Anarchy Online* in June 2001. The first such world to be written by Europeans (a Norwegian/ Irish team), it was a departure in that it took a Science Fiction theme rather than the traditional[31] Fantasy. To provide some context, lead designer Gaute Godager buttressed it with a story arc. Unfortunately, the game suffered a disastrous launch, from which it took some time to recover. Consequently, it also failed to accumulate 100,000 players within 12 months. This was a shame, because its overall design was quite attractive.

By contrast, the launch of Mythic Entertainment's *Dark Age of Camelot* in October 2001 was a model of how to do things right. This is perhaps not surprising, given that Mythic was a direct descendent of AUSI, the company responsible for *Dragon's Gate*. The design team, under the guidance of Mark Jacobs, created a world that was both familiar (from the Camelot legends) and superficially compelling (because of its *realm versus realm* (RvR) approach to combat between players' characters[32]).

These factors made the game attractive to a large constituency, and well-targeted marketing let potential players know. *Dark Age of Camelot* (*DAoC*) racked up 200,000 subscribers by May 2002, easily supplanting *Asheron's Call* as the third most popular virtual world in the West.

All these games are PC-based. It was not surprising, therefore, that console companies with their enormous installed user bases and tightly regulated platforms would want to get in on the act. The SEGA Dreamcast was bold enough to take the first step (with *Phantasy Star Online*[33]), but the company did not really understand the concept of Internet games and the venture was not a success.

Sony, as owners of *EverQuest*, did understand it, however, and in May 2002 launched Square's *Final Fantasy XI* on the PlayStation 2. By the end of August, they had 120,000 users in Japan, each paying a monthly fee of ¥1,280 ($10.71 at the time). Although this qualified the game as a success, Sony's overheads were such that 200,000 users were needed to break even. Their target was 400,000 users, but they could only

---

31. Traditional for graphical virtual worlds—text-based ones had long since expanded into other genres.

32. This splits the player base into three factions that can fight each other in certain areas of no man's land. *Anarchy Online* did something similar but was less successful. The concept had already been around in text-based virtual worlds for many years, of course, but not on *Dark Age of Camelot's* scale.

33. http://www.sonicteam.com/pso/

envision reaching that number by releasing a PC client. This is not unreasonable: Consoles are secure development platforms, but not so secure that a developer would be foolish enough to trust a client not to be hacked. Therefore, there is no inherent technical reason why a virtual world targeted at console owners should not have a PC client too. It is likely that in the future, major virtual worlds will be expected to support a range of platforms; how this affects the design of the world itself depends on the nature of the lowest common denominator of those platforms[34].

And so we come to today[35].

The Sims Online (*TSO*), launched December 2002, has yet to break the 100,000 subscribers mark. Given the popularity of the *Sims* franchise, this has to be considered disappointing. My guess is that if the publishers hold their nerve, things will improve in the long term. At the moment, too many people are treating it as a game, then complaining that its only gameplay involves making pizzas for one another. *The Sims* is more a toy than a game, and the same is true of *The Sims Online*. Gamers are typically early adopters, but *The Sims Online*'s core players aren't. If they come in sufficient numbers to replace those gamers who leave, all will be well. Nevertheless, *TSO*'s slow start could have some knock-on effects for virtual worlds in general, depending on how the marketers who used it for product placement assess its less than spectacular beginnings.

The Sims Online had over 100,000 beta-testers and has sold over 100,000 boxes. Large numbers of beta-testers are currently quite fashionable: *Star Wars Galaxies* hit 150,000 in August 2002, and even soon-to-launch *EVE: The Second Genesis*[36]—hardly a guaranteed hit—is claiming 140,000. Whether this trend will continue in the light of the experience of *The Sims Online*, remains to be seen. Skeptics might be forgiven for wondering how many of these beta-testers are beta-testing several virtual worlds simultaneously, and therefore whether the perceived marketing benefit of a large beta-test is as strong as is normally assumed.

---

34. *EverQuest*'s PlayStation 2 debut, *EverQuest Online Adventure*, barely qualifies as being a virtual world.

35. March 2003 at the time of writing.

36. `http://www.eve-online.com/`

There is further evidence from the experience of *Asheron's Call 2*[37] (*AC2*). This virtual world also launched December 2002; it has beautiful graphics, but again seems to be struggling to attract newbies. Original *AC* players have been reluctant to switch over to it, and its attempts to pander to popular player opinion by diluting anything inconvenient (character "death," the economy) may have backfired—it reduces the challenge somewhat. As with *The Sims Online*, *AC2* had over 100,000 beta-testers but has yet to pick up that many subscribers[38].

Wolfpack's *Shadowbane* launches the day I write this. Long in development, it has been hyped relentlessly to some effect: There's little doubt exactly what kind of virtual world it is (violent) and no danger that people who don't consider this to be fun will even play it, let alone complain that it doesn't address their needs. Other virtual worlds have been prematurely hyped more (Glitchless's *Dawn*[39] and Artifact Entertainment's *Horizons*[40] spring to mind), but *Shadowbane* seems to have got its act together first. It therefore starts with a relatively small but highly dedicated core player base upon which to build. Time will tell whether it succeeds or not.

It's clear that the fifth age of virtual worlds will last for some years to come, but eventually its time will pass. Perhaps free 3D graphical engines will herald a new era of homegrown virtual worlds, or maybe advances in virtual reality interfaces or mobile telephony will have an impact. It could be any one of a number of things currently known and unknown that triggers the eventual paradigm shift.

What wonders will the sixth age of virtual worlds bring?

That, perhaps, may be for you to determine.

---

37. http://www.microsoft.com/games/zone/asheronscall/

38. It's hard to be absolutely certain, because Turbine doesn't release official subscriber numbers. Industry rumor is that it's short, however.

39. http://www.glitchless.com/dawn.html

40. http://www.istaria.com/

The Past Affects the Future

Very few graphical virtual worlds that are announced as being in development actually wind up being played. This situation may change as the barriers to entry fall, but probably not significantly so.

Estimates vary, but at least a hundred graphical virtual worlds—perhaps up to two hundred—were announced in the two years following *EverQuest*'s launch in 1999. Some were down to wishful thinking on the part of talented (or otherwise) amateurs; some failed in preproduction because funding was not available; some failed when the money they did raise ran out; some built up a community and reached live testing before they went belly-up.

Some, however, were set to become bestsellers yet were inexplicably cancelled. Three of these were to have repercussions for the industry as a whole.

Missed Opportunities

OSI, which wrote *Ultima Online*, was part of Electronics Arts (EA). Given the positive effect of the Ultima name on sales, other brands from the EA stable were considered contenders for implementation as virtual worlds. Thus began the *Privateer Online* project. Raph Koster was installed as lead designer, with Rich Vogel as producer. Work was well advanced when the project was suddenly, bizarrely cancelled. Raph, Rich, and others were immediately snapped up by Sony Online Entertainment (SOE) to work on the *Star Wars* license they had recently acquired. SOE was the new name of Verant, a company spun off from 989 Studios to develop *EverQuest*. In other words, EA presented some of its best virtual world experts to one of its two major competitors. It would shortly give most of its remaining experts to its other major competitor.

Ultima Online 2 was planned to be set in the same universe as *UO*, but to be fully 3D with an *EQ*-style moveable camera. Early screen shots showed it to be much superior in looks to *EQ*, and with Damion Schubert (of *Meridian 59* fame) as lead designer and Starr Long (Rich Vogel's predecessor at *UO*) as producer it was sure[41] to be a hit. Also involved was Jeremy Gaffney, who was a founder of Turbine and had worked on *Asheron's Call*.

---

41. Well, as sure as anyone ever can be in virtual world design.

Signs of strangeness appeared when the game was renamed as the unwieldy *Ultima Worlds Online: Origin*, but it wasn't until 2001—three years into the project—that it was insanely canned.

Starr Long, Jeremy Gaffney, and most of the other talent involved left almost immediately to set up with the designer of the Ultima series itself, Richard Garriott. Their new company, Destination Games, was shortly thereafter acquired by NCSoft, developers of *Lineage*, who saw an opportunity to use their Korean profits to break into the American market. Jake Song moved from Korea to Austin, Texas, to work with them. Electronic Arts had done it again. They were not the only company capable of such monumental gaffes, however.

Venerable games publisher Sierra had dipped its toes in the online marketplace before, having set up The Sierra Network in 1991; they sold it in 1994 for around $50,000,000 to AT&T, who renamed it ImagiNation Network[42]. Sierra had maintained an interest in a virtual world called *The Realm*, designed by Steve Nichols, which was eventually launched early 1997. *The Realm* was graphical, but had separate, static 2D pictures for each location that acted as a stage across which animations of the players' characters moved. It dated rapidly and failed to attract more than about 25,000 subscribers at its peak (late 1997). Nevertheless, it was proof of concept, and Sierra had an ace up its sleeve.

Some mainstream entertainment properties would make poor virtual worlds. The *Harry Potter* universe, for example, doesn't really allow for more than one Harry Potter in it. There are three franchises, however, that are especially well suited to being embodied as graphical virtual worlds[43] and which would produce a guaranteed hit: *Star Wars*, *Star Trek*, and *The Lord of the Rings*. Sierra had a *Lord of the Rings* license.

In 1998, Steve Nichols signed up as lead designer of *Middle Earth Online*, along with Janus Anderson (also of *The Realm*), Daniel James (from a top-notch commercial text-based virtual world called *Avalon*), and Jay Esparza (already with Sierra). The designers were keen to discuss all aspects of the development with prospective players,

---

42. AT&T sold it to AOL two years later for about $10,000,000. Way to go, AT&T.

43. Naturally, text-based versions of these have been around for many years, not necessarily with permission from the license owner.

and consequently generated a lot of buzz. They also generated a lot of friction with Sierra executives, who didn't like some of what was being mooted—especially with regards to plans for the permanent death of player characters.

The project continued, however, until during a company-wide reorganization of Sierra in 1999 the opportunity was taken to put it on ice. The design team was removed. Sierra also decided to abandon *The Realm* because it didn't look good against *Ultima Online* and it looked worse against *EverQuest*. The game was taken up by Codemasters; newly released Steve Nichols joined them.

The story does not quite end there, however. Sierra secretly hired a new design team to work on *Middle Earth Online*. This was perhaps not unrelated to the fact that the first of the *Lord of the Rings* movies was due to be released in 2001, which would generate massive, free publicity. Again, though, Sierra mystifyingly canned the project— although at least this time the developers, MM3D, sued.

Sierra had missed its chance. In December 2001, the movie *The Lord of the Rings: The Fellowship of the Ring* was released. It grossed $155,862,412 in its first two weeks[44].

That is how out-of-touch management decisions shape an industry.

Theory and Practice

It should be clear by now that virtual worlds have a long and varied history—much longer and more varied than many of the people who play and design them realize. But so what?

It's not entirely the case that only by understanding the past can people understand the future. Virtual worlds have been "invented" at least seven times (*MUD1*, *Sceptre of Goth*, *Avatar*, *Island of Kesmai*, *Aradath*, *Monster*, and *Gemstone* were all developed autonomously), and the designers of these games had no sense of any "past" in what they were doing. Originality is entirely possible without rehashing other people's ideas.

However, to ignore completely what has gone before would be extremely foolish. Time and time again, designers have made the same mistakes their predecessors made, either because they were simply not aware of the earlier work or they were too arrogant to believe it could possibly be relevant to their greatly superior product.

---

44. Source: http://www.boxofficemojo.com/data/lordoftherings/.

Conversely, some designers look *too* hard at what has gone before. To use some admired virtual world as a prototype is fine if you fully understand that world, but very limiting if you don't. A designer whose major experience of virtual worlds is *EverQuest* might, for example, think "what character classes should we have in our new game?" rather than "should we have character classes in our new game at all?" Some of the more basic assumptions go right back to *MUD1*, with few designers even realizing that they *are* assumptions, let alone that they can be questioned. That can't be right!

Nobody wants to repeat the mistakes of the past, but people don't always realize that what they're repeating *is* a mistake. That's because they're learning the wrong lessons. The past delivers facts—the practice. History delivers the *understanding* of those facts—the theory. It provides the causal links.

This is especially true for the design of virtual worlds. Each must be conceived as a complete entity. Each one can't really be modularized: Every component affects every other. Sometimes newspapers put together composite pictures made of the best features of famous faces—Bette Davis' eyes, Julia Roberts' mouth, Doris Day's nose, and so on. The result is usually more like Frankenstein's monster than "the world's most beautiful woman." So it is with virtual worlds: It doesn't matter how perfect the parts, it's by the whole that they are judged.

Thus, designers who know not only the choices available to them but also the wider effects of those choices are better able to create a virtual world that *works* than those designers who don't.

Whither Innovation?

The design of virtual worlds proceeds by a process of evolution rather than revolution. New virtual worlds usually draw heavily from one or more "parent" worlds, even to the extent that it's possible to map out an entire family tree for all the various codebases[45]. This being so, it is becoming increasingly important that designers of new virtual worlds become aware of innovations arising in other branches of the tree. Not only does this ensure that the best ideas spread, but there is less danger of standards problems arising from the same concept being implemented differently in different virtual worlds.

---

45. It's called "The MUD Tree," and lives at
    `http://camelot.cyburbia.net.au/~martin/cgi-bin/mud_tree.cgi`.

Because graphical virtual worlds take so long to develop, their designers in particular must keep an eye on what's happening elsewhere. These games (they do tend to be games) have their own strengths, of course: Their visual representation demands new levels of virtual world physics, and the huge number of players they have opens the door to all manner of interesting developments that would be impossible on a smaller scale. However, they are still several years behind text-based virtual worlds in nearly all other areas.

Furthermore, they'll probably stay behind for some time. When it comes to implementing new ideas, text-based worlds are more

> ➤ *Responsive*. Adding a new object doesn't mean adding a new texture map.

> ➤ *Enfranchising*. Many more people can write well than can draw well.

> ➤ *Adaptable*. Program changes can quickly be made anywhere in the system.

> ➤ *Experimental*. The test/edit cycle is much shorter, so changes can be made almost on impulse to be later refined, retained or rejected.

> ➤ *Open*. Players give new ideas more of a chance.

> ➤ *Pragmatic*. Players accept crashes and other failures more readily if they're not paying.

> ➤ *Tunable*. Minor changes don't mean major down-time.

> ➤ *Promising*. More is possible with text than with graphics.

> ➤ *Robust*. Balance is less of an issue with fewer players.

Besides, the consequences of a failed programmed-in-your-spare-time virtual world are far less agonizing than they would be for a $15,000,000 graphical extravaganza.

So how does a designer keep up to date?

Anyone with time on their hands[46] can check out a sample of the several thousand text-based virtual worlds that there are in existence[47] if they want to find out "the word

---

46. This rules out most designers, then....

47. For example:
- The Mud Connector (http://www.mudconnect.com).
- Mudlinks (http://www.cuddle-puddle.org/~mudlinks/lg.html)
- Muds Online (http://www.mudsonline.com/)
- MudRanger (http://www.mudranger.com/)

on the street." However, as I pointed out earlier, knowing what is available without knowing the theory behind it can be disastrous. It's therefore in the best interests of all virtual world designers to discuss ideas with one another. It isn't for sentimental reasons that luminaries such as Raph Koster, Damion Schubert, Brad McQuaid, and Jessica Mulligan not only subscribe to the MUD-DEV[48] mailing list, but are active posters to it. Neither is it surprising that the best informative and speculative articles about virtual world design are being written for—and made publicly available for free by—a company specializing in immersive text-based worlds, Skotos[49]. There's even a print magazine, *The Mud Companion*[50].

The future of virtual world design is therefore rosy, although obviously not as rosy as it would be if people richer than Skotos were to throw money at it.

The future is just that, however: the future. There's little point in discussing what *may* happen to virtual worlds unless you understand what *has* happened and what *is* happening.

The timeline I've presented here has outlined how things came to be the way they are in the virtual worlds of today[51], but it has given few hints as to what actually comprises a virtual world, let alone the wider effects of including or excluding particular components in a design.

It is to this topic that the major part of the remainder of this book is concerned.

The Basics

People often want to categorize the various virtual worlds, to make it easier to discuss their particular interests or find a world that is most suited to their needs. Prospective players, for example, will want to know what a world looks like and its setting: If you

---

48. http://www.kanga.nu/archives/MUD-Dev-L/

49. http://www.skotos.net/articles/

50. http://www.mudcompanion.com/

51. See also the Online World Timeline at http://www.legendmud.org/raph/gaming/mudtimeline.html, which gives further details with direct quotes from people involved, and Jessica Mulligan's more business-oriented recollections *Happy 30th Birthday, Online Games* in http://www.skotos.net/articles/BTHarchives/99.shtml.

want to role-play an interstellar pirate, you're not going to have a lot of luck in a Fantasy environment. Marketers and investors are more concerned with a product's longevity and its user demographics: They may not want to spend any time in a virtual world themselves, but they're keen to know about those who do. Finally, designers have their own, theoretical issues to resolve, in addition to understanding what the players and marketers think.

Having looked at virtual worlds from a historical perspective, the categorizations typically used present themselves fairly readily:

➤ Appearance

➤ Genre

➤ Codebase

➤ Age

➤ Player base

➤ Degree to which they can be changed

➤ Degree of persistence

Let's consider these in turn.

Appearance

Newbies tend to believe that the appearance of a virtual world is very important; old-bies are generally more concerned with other features.

Virtual worlds are typically characterized as being either text-based (*textual*) or graphics-based (*graphical*). The former use words to describe locations, objects, and other players, whereas the latter use pictures.

There is, however, quite a spectrum between the two extremes. To access a textual virtual world, a player needs some kind of software connection to it. This may be direct— for example, by running the game server from a console and typing at its prompts— or it may be indirect through use of a client. If a client is involved it may be *dumb*, *intelligent*, or *custom*.

Strictly speaking, a dumb client does nothing except input (the results of which it passes to a server), and output (which it does to whatever the server sends back). However, few clients are actually that dumb—even *telnet* can handle minor editing functions such as backspacing. It's deliberate that dumb clients don't do a lot, because that way they can be used for a greater variety of purposes.

Even when dealing with a dumb client—or no client at all—a virtual world need not merely consist of lifeless text. Individual letters, words, sentences, and paragraphs can be colorized by the server (usually using the ANSI standard understood by most PCs) to make the resulting display more attractive and meaningful.

Intelligent clients are intended for use with specific application types; in this particular case, that means textual virtual worlds. Such clients provide additional input functionality (such as macros or triggering) and tools for managing output (such as local logging and word-wrapping). Although these features could still be implemented at the server end and used with a dumb client, most modern server authors don't bother with this as they know there are now so many[52] good clients about that people will almost certainly be using one anyway.

A custom client works only for the small subset of virtual worlds that share its protocol (in practice, this usually means just one). The client sends packets of information to the server describing what has been input. The server sends packets back telling the client what to output. Although the input protocol is usually not all that sophisticated, the output can contain embedded codes that will cause the client to do things, such as switch fonts, play sound effects and music, or display pictures. For a textual virtual world, the pictures will by definition be static affairs, this being more akin to an illustrated book than a movie. However, it serves to show just how far a text-based world can go without being classified as graphical.

As a rule of thumb, first- and second-age virtual worlds used dumb clients, third-age used intelligent clients, and fourth-age used custom clients.

Fifth-age (graphical) virtual worlds also use custom clients, but display the information a different way. The packets received by the client contain information that can be used by the client to render a scene. This will be either 2½D (tessellated) or 3D

---

52. http://www.mudconnect.com/resources/Mud_Resources:Mud_Clients.html has a list of client resources.

(first-person), although doubtless "true 3D" (using some stereoscopic device to give depth to a scene) leading to full-blown VR isn't all that far away.

Thus, to a newbie who neither knows nor cares about the underlying mechanisms, the difference between a virtual world that has moving pictures and one that doesn't is fairly clear; indeed, it's probably what attracted the newbie to one rather than the other in the first place. To an oldbie, however, who understands that the fundamental machinery for implementing the virtual world itself (embodied by the server) is much the same whatever the client, the distinction between graphical and textual worlds is mainly an interface issue (albeit a not-insignificant one).

Genre

Another categorization that is important to newbie players but less so to designers is genre[53].

A newbie will look at a set of virtual worlds and say that this one is medieval Fantasy, this one is Cyberpunk Science Fiction, this one is dark vampire Horror, this one is Greek Mythology, this one is asexual Japanese Anime, this one is stylized Gangsters, and so on.

Again, though, from a design perspective most of the way a virtual world works is independent of genre. Sure, you're not going to need magic in a world based on Venice in the 16th century, and you're not going to need firearms in a world where all the players take on the role of fishes. However, most of the basic functionality isn't going to change a lot across genres.

Sometimes, though, there are serious implications of genre. Why are there so few Wild West virtual worlds? Because it's very hard to explain why Joe Newbie's character can't enter a shop, buy a loaded six-gun, and empty it into the back of a character that someone else has been playing for five years. They didn't call those things "equalizers"

---

53. I use the word to mean both the theme/setting and the content category (usually expressed in terms of suitability for children).

for nothing[54]! Fantasy, Science Fiction, and Horror worlds have fiction-preserving ways out of this, as do ones based another hundred years or more into the past. It's not the only issue, though—there are plenty more. Following are some examples:

➤ Crime fiction doesn't work well as a genre because players don't want to divulge clues to one another. This means they're discouraged from communicating; most designers would prefer to encourage them.

➤ Comedy flops as a genre. You laugh the first time something funny happens, but by the tenth time that same thing happens, it ceases to amuse you.

➤ Romance doesn't work for virtual worlds. Sex does, but romance doesn't. If you start out with the former, you rapidly end up with the latter.

➤ Lone heroes or heroines don't translate well into virtual worlds. It doesn't make sense to have 5,000 people running around who all act like Indiana Jones, Lara Croft, James Bond, or Dr Who. There wouldn't be room for them in the real world, let alone a virtual one.

These may look obvious to you, but they don't to everyone[55]. Even so, why would any business person want to fund development of an unproven (in virtual world terms) genre anyway? Surely they would go with what they know can be implemented?

Well, the chief importance of genres lies in their ability to attract players. From this perspective, the choice of genre becomes a marketing issue, rather than a design issue (although designers should, perforce, understand their market). Someone behind a glass desk realizes that millions and millions of people have seen the Batman movies and that's a good enough reason for them to press the issue—irrespective of whether Gotham City would make a good setting for a virtual world.

Fortunately, most designers can avoid the perils of a bad genre. There are plenty of perils of a good genre, too, of course, examples of which will become evident throughout this book. One in particular is the issue of licensing. Licensing is a big topic in the computer games industry as a whole. The arguments are

---

54. There's also the problem (noted by Damion Schubert) that the enemies don't get bigger. Aside from the real-life political problems that would arise from killing virtual natives and Mexicans, what happens when your character advances in experience? Do you kill bigger natives and Mexicans?

55. The only one of those mentioned above that I haven't encountered in my capacity as a virtual world design consultant is the Comedy genre. All the rest I've seen people try—some, more than once.

For:

> ➤ People know and trust the brand, so you will get more players.

> ➤ You gain the attention of the media and of your competitors.

> ➤ You receive free publicity from other license-related products.

> ➤ The design work for the overall concept has already been done.

Against:

> ➤ You have to pay an invariably large licensing fee and royalties, so your costs rise.

> ➤ The free publicity could be bad, or at least not helpful.

> ➤ Some accommodation may be needed by the license for gameplay purposes. These could annoy fans or (worse) license-holders.

> ➤ The overall concept is what designers like doing the most.

In terms of virtual worlds, the decision whether to license is generally made by someone other than the world's would-be designers. This imposes creative constraints, because designers have to fit the franchise. Although many license owners are fairly hands-off, others are particularly precious about their worlds and will not consent to anything non-canon no matter how much this stresses the constraints of a different medium. This can pose great difficulties for a designer. Sometimes, even things that *are* part of the fictional world can be out of bounds, for example the license for *The Lord of the Rings* would not necessarily cover material mentioned only in *The Hobbit*, even though they're set in the same Fantasy world.

Perversely, though, licenses can also be liberating—at least insofar as virtual worlds are concerned[56]. A sure-fire hit such as *Star Wars Galaxies* or *The Sims Online* can take risks that unlicensed games might avoid simply because if they do screw up, it's not going to kill the game. An innovation with a 75% chance of being a success could well be tried out by a licensed graphical virtual world when it would be left alone by an unlicensed one on the grounds that "There's a one in four chance this is going to burn a fifteen million dollar investment? Are you nuts?!"

---

56. For regular computer games, a license often amounts to a big sign saying, "Warning: Highly derivative product!"

For a competent design team, a world with a big enough license behind it isn't going to fail unless they set out to *make* it fail (for the time being, at least).

Codebase

Related to the idea of genre is that of codebases. To explain how the two are connected requires a short introduction to some principles of virtual world server architecture.

Codebases came about because much of the work that needs to be done to create a virtual world can be re-used when creating other virtual worlds. How much, exactly, depends on the codebase. Codebases are mainly associated with the third age of virtual worlds, although the codebase principle was used as early as *MUD1* and there are ongoing attempts to create similar solutions for graphical virtual worlds (*Asheron's Call* was designed with this idea in mind[57]).

The most basic part of the software that runs a virtual world is its *driver*. This has all the usual routines that appear in any sophisticated interpreter, handling things like memory management, parsing, and data structures. Coupled with these is more operating systems-like material such as input/output queuing, time-outs, packet handling, and so on. The result is that the driver can make two foundation concepts available to higher levels of the program: the existence of entities from which the virtual world is to be constructed (for example, objects) and the association of input/output with some of those entities (for example, players).

Above this layer comes what (for historical reasons) is known as the *mudlib*[58]. The mudlib defines the physics of a virtual world, which will include things such as mass/weight, timers, movement and communication, along with higher concepts such as (in a game context) magic and combat mechanisms.

---

57. The main open source 3D graphics engines in development are
    - *Crystal Space*: http://crystal.sourceforge.net.
    - *NeL*: http://www.nevrax.org.
    - *Quakeforge*: http://sourceforge.net/projects/quake.
    - *Worldforge*: http://www.worldforge.org.

58. For "mud library." *MUD1* had a mudlib, but it was an adaptation of the BCPL input/output library and therefore was at a lower level than today's mudlibs. The modern use of the term was coined independently by *LPMUD*.

The layer above the mudlib is the world definition. Using the model set up by the physics, world-specific concepts are added. New functionality is associated with these objects that is also consequent on the physics (although not necessarily defined directly by it). The world definition is fully descriptive: It can be used to create multiple incarnations of the world.

Finally, there is the particular instantiation of the world. Actual data items define this individual world, differentiating it from all the worlds that could possibly be defined.

Here's an example to show how this all hangs together. Suppose we have a world in which (among many other things) a silver key opens a silver casket. The driver defines the concepts of: discrete objects; actions that manipulate such objects; actors (that is, players) that can affect such actions. The mudlib defines the concept of objects that can contain other objects and the conditions under which this can occur. The world defines the concept of caskets and keys, and how using the right one of the latter on one of the former can cause that casket to open. The world instantiation includes an explicit representation for object32 (a silver casket) and object19 (a silver key); the state of a silver casket in the instantiated world depends on whether anyone has opened or closed it with a silver key.

Okay, so these are the various parts of the server:

➤ Driver

➤ Mudlib (physics)

➤ World model

➤ Instantiation

All codebases must implement these layers, but they don't have to do it all the same way. Typically, they use a combination of three techniques:

➤ Hard-code them using a real programming language such as C or C++.

➤ Soft-code them using a scripting language such as LPC or MUF (Multi-User Forth—used by MUCKs), which is interpreted by the hard code.

➤ Store them explicitly as data in files that are meaningful to the hard code, the soft code, or both.

How exactly they do this depends on the particular codebase.

Everything that is hard-coded constitutes the *engine*. For MUSHes and MOOs, the engine is just the driver; for LPMUDs it's the driver and the mudlib; for DikuMUDs it's the driver, the mudlib, and the world definition. The advantages of having an engine with higher-level functionality are ease of use and run-time efficiency; the disadvantages are inflexibility and a lack of expressiveness.

Everything that is stored to data files is the *database* (which may, or may not, be a third-party database with a formal query language and so on). This can be a little confusing, as there can be up to three completely different databases that make up "the" database:

➤ Scripting language code

➤ Templates

➤ Instantiations

Any or all of these could be used statically (for initialization only) or dynamically (consulted each use, on-the-fly).

Let's look at these different database forms a little more closely.

A *scripting language database* consists of the script files that the virtual world needs. For MUSHes, these scripts themselves define the mudlib, the world model, and the world's instantiation; for LPMUDs, they just define the world model.

A *template database* contains definitions for objects, from which a world can be constructed. With this kind of set-up, it's possible to do things like change the behavior of one of the virtual world's denizens by tinkering with the template from which it was stamped out—you don't have to change/recompile any code. DikuMUDs use a template database.

An *instantiation database* (more widely known as a *runtime database*) stores the state of the instantiated world, specifically those values that persist across server shutdowns and which can't be generated from either a scripting database or a template database. A good example is player character data, which is usually stowed in a database while the player is not present in the virtual world. Worlds that run continuously will periodically store their entire state in an instantiation database, so they can effect recovery in the event of catastrophic machine failure.

Note that it's possible for a codebase to incorporate these three databases into one. The object-oriented implementation of MOOs, for example, means that dumping all the data objects (that is, creating a runtime database) automatically dumps all templates and scripts as well, because they are defined as such objects.

Table 1.1 (based on Raph Koster's original at `http://www.legendmud.org/raph/gaming/book/6b.html`) summarizes these differences for a number of codebase families (and, for comparison, some individual virtual worlds). Each component level is described as being code (executed by the computer hardware), script (executed by the code[59]), or data (non-executable).

Table 1.1   Codebase Differences

Codebase	Driver	Mudlib	World Model	Runtime
DikuMUDs	Code	Code	Code	Data
MUD1	Code	Code	Script	Data
MUD2	Code	Script	Script	Data
Ultima Online	Code	Script	Script	Data
LPMUDs	Code	Code	Script	Script
MUCKs, MUSHes, MOOs	Code	Script	Script	Script

What does any of this have to do with genre?

Well, the way codebases are implemented has an impact on the virtual worlds that they themselves implement. Hard-coded functionality is less flexible but more powerful; soft-coded functionality is quicker to write but slower to run.

Thus, if you wanted a virtual world with a lot of action delivering an intense experience, you'd go for something that favored code (for example, a DikuMUD); if you wanted a virtual world where spontaneity and creativity were important, you'd go for something that favored scripting (for example, a MOO); if you wanted a codebase that had a detailed physics but in a nonstandard setting, you'd go for something that employed code for the mudlib and a scripting language for the world model (for example, LPMUD).

---

59. There is an argument that high-powered scripting languages such as LPC, which can be used for applications beyond virtual worlds (for example, writing WWW servers), should count as both code and scripting language. MUDDLE can even be compiled and run directly, instead of being interpreted.

Very generally, the major codebases[60] used for (textual) virtual worlds conform to the following stereotypes:

> ➤ *DikuMUDs.* Adventure-oriented, with a heavy emphasis on combat against computer-controlled foes. They are exciting experiences, but the worlds themselves tend not to change much over time. They mostly have a Fantasy setting, with Science Fiction in distant second place.

> ➤ *LPMUDs.* Also adventure-oriented, but with less emphasis on combat. They are often extended over time. Again, they're mainly Fantasy, but across a wider range; there are numerous Science Fiction, Horror, and mythological worlds, too.

> ➤ *MUCKs.* Socially oriented, heavily focused on role-playing. These are usually based on some specific work of Fantasy, Science Fiction, or Horror. Those that aren't often involve original, anthropomorphic animals (furries).

> ➤ *MUSHes.* Socially oriented, mostly focused on role-playing, but occasionally non-gaming in nature. MUSHes tend to have a Science Fiction setting based on books, comics, or movies, with Fantasy some way behind.

> ➤ *MOOs.* The least games-oriented codebase, responsible for more non-game worlds than all the other codebases put together. Those games it does produce are usually original (rather than derivative) Fantasy that are geared for role-play rather than adventure.

These stereotypes are reinforced by the historical heritages of each codebase. Although it's possible (for example) to program an exact replica of a MOO in LPC, people who wanted to write a "MOO-like" virtual world would probably just go for a MOO codebase instead. What's more, people just starting up an LPMUD would probably take someone else's mudlib as a starting point. Thus, the theme or genre connotations associated with a codebase will tend to be perpetuated as that codebase evolves, meaning that when new versions appear they will usually be refined for their preferred genres[61].

---

60. For further details and descriptions of derivative codebases, see the rec.games.mud FAQ parts 2 and 4:
    - `http://www.mudconnect.com/mudfaq/mudfaq-p2.html#q6`
    - `http://www.mudconnect.com/mudfaq/mudfaq-p4.html`

61. For an examination of the different codebases from both a player's and developer's perspective, see Andrew Busey, *Secrets of the MUD Wizards: Playing and Programming MUDs, MOOs, MUSHes, MUCKs and other Internet Role-Playing Games*. Indianapolis, Sams.net Publishing, 1995.

Codebases are a common way of categorizing free, text-based virtual worlds (of which there are several thousand); they are not, however, a lot of use in most other circumstances. Almost all graphical virtual worlds, for example, have their own, proprietary codebase. Other means of usefully distinguishing between the different natures of virtual worlds are therefore also commonly employed.

Age

How long does a virtual world typically last? What stops it from lasting longer?

To give you some idea of the longevity involved here, Table 1.2 lists examples of the oldest incarnations in existence of free, text-based virtual worlds.

Table 1.2   Ages of Extant Virtual Worlds

Virtual World	Birth Year	Codebase	Home Page URL
MUD1	1987	MUD1	`http://www.british-legends.com/`
Void	1989	custom	`http://void.greenfinch.com/`
DragonMUD	1989	TinyMUD	`http://www.dragonmud.org/`
BatMUD	1990	LPMUD	`http://www.bat.org/`
Medievia	1991	Custom	`http://www.medievia.com/`
Northern Lights	1992	AberMUD	`http://www.ludd.luth.se/mud/` `aber/northern_lights.html`
MediaMOO	1993	MOO	`http://www.cc.gatech.edu/~asb/` `MediaMOO/`

Textual worlds have the potential to last indefinitely. This isn't simply because the graphics never date and the bandwidth requirements are low (although those are factors); rather, it's that they can remain compelling for long enough that people want to stay. Those that fail to attract a critical mass of players tend to die after a few months, but beyond that a virtual world can last for years so long as there is someone around willing to host and administrate it[62].

---

62. Reasons why virtual worlds nevertheless don't all last for more than a few years are discussed in Chapter 3, "Players."

Graphical virtual worlds haven't been around for long enough to determine their individual chances of surviving into their dotage, but so long as the graphics are patched or otherwise updated so they don't fall too far behind the latest norms, the prognosis is good. Original estimates by publishers that virtual worlds would have around five years of life in them before the servers eventually had to be switched off were proven wrong (at least post-*Ultima Online*).

There's generally enough gameplay in a graphical world to last a player six to twelve months, which is less (by around half) than for most textual worlds. However, newbies are easier to attract to these larger environments, and therefore the shortfall isn't important[63].

When a free virtual world gets old, it may defy death for years because a rump of players stays with it; overheads would make this unlikely for a commercial virtual world. On the other hand, free virtual worlds rarely continue to exist after their original designers and administrators have lost interest, whereas commercial virtual worlds do. On the whole, it seems likely that commercial graphical virtual worlds have the potential to last just as long as free textual virtual worlds.

The reason age is an important consideration when looking at a virtual world is because it can be used as a measure of the success of that world. While acknowledging that failures can often be attributed to external factors, nevertheless good designs ought to survive and poor designs ought to fail. Age, as a measure of survival, is therefore a measure of success.

This is not a metric that can be applied in related industries. For example, the first computer game to be released on a CD-ROM came out in 1989: Activision's[64] *The Manhole*. Few people even remember it now, let alone play it, and yet *DragonMUD* was launched the very same year and has been played continuously ever since. The default assumption is that although regular computer games have a limited lifespan, virtual worlds (whether games-oriented or otherwise) could last forever. People don't ask why *Meridian 59* ran for four years, they ask why it *only* ran for four years[65].

---

63. From the point of view of the virtual world's healthy survival. Obviously a game will generate more money when paying customers stay longer, which is why retention is a big issue for commercial products.

64. The company was known as Mediagenic at the time.

65. Which perhaps explains why it was bought from 3DO and relaunched in 2002.

Player Base

The other way to look at the success or otherwise of a virtual world is by examining its player base. In theory, the better worlds will attract more players, and therefore those that have the largest player bases are the best. In theory....

Actually, there are many reasons why a virtual world may have a large user base (or a small one), with marketing and pricing not insignificant factors. From a designer's point of view, these have to be taken into account so the essential reasons for a *design's* success can be gauged.

The first thing to note, therefore, is that there are different measures of "size" here. If someone visits the same virtual world for three hours every night, should they carry the same weight as someone who plays for two hours every Saturday morning, or someone who only plays for two hours once every three months? Sure, there's a different business case for each usage pattern (hard-core players are more important for per-hour charging, whereas casual players are more important for per-month charging). However, that doesn't help when you're trying to figure out *why* a particular virtual world is popular so that you can adjust your own designs accordingly. Some of the best virtual worlds are free: Is being free one of the reasons they have a large player base, or would they have even more players if they charged a fee and could afford to advertise themselves?

For commercial games using the same business model, absolute subscriber numbers are an acceptable means of comparison. If game X has 300,000 subscribers and game Y has 100,000, and they both charge around $12 a month primarily to North Americans, it's not unreasonable to suppose that game X is "better" in some sense than game Y.

For virtual worlds that don't conform to these parameters, user base size comparisons are much harder. There are basically five approaches:

➤ Count the number of registered players. This assumes the world registers its players, of course, but not all do. Why is this? Well, when people want to try out a virtual world, filling out forms puts them off. Even asking for an email address can be annoying—who wants to end up on some mailing list when they're only looking to see whether they like the world? In other words, forcing players to register can be seen as a barrier to entry. You get more newbies into the game if you don't take down their particulars first.

➤ Count the number of characters. Every game keeps records of the characters belonging to players. Yes, there will almost certainly be people who have several characters, either attached to the same player account or ones belonging to false identities they've set up. The same applies to all virtual worlds, though, so the argument is that it ought to even itself out. The first flaw here is that actually, no, it doesn't even itself out. Some virtual worlds have entrance qualifications that make owning multiple characters or accounts very difficult—there are role-playing MUSHes[66], for example, that interview prospective players and have waiting lists for entry. The second flaw (which also applies to the "count the number of registered players" approach) is that some virtual worlds purge player records that remain dormant for a period, but others don't. A world which has been running for two years that doesn't clear out unused player records will be able to boast a larger user base than one that has been running for ten years which deletes records that haven't been accessed for 90 days.

➤ Count the number of players who access the world per day. This can actually be quite a useful measure, although a bad game with good marketing will get more suck-it-and-see players per day than a good game with bad marketing. Also, it depends on the day—weekends tend to be busier than weekdays.

➤ Count the number of simultaneous players. This measure posits that snapshots of usage throughout the day can give a good comparison of user base sizes across virtual worlds. Suppose two worlds each have 80 players in them at 7 p.m. and 120 players at 8 p.m. It seems fair to suggest that they have roughly the same degree of popularity. It doesn't matter that for one world half the players at 8 p.m. may still be playing from when they were counted at 7 p.m., and for the other some people have played for half an hour and missed being counted at all; indeed, this is entirely the point. Newbies who enter a game and see a lot of players in a world would think that world was popular, irrespective of how long those players spent per session. The main problem with using a count of simultaneous player numbers is that it varies so much depending on the time and the time zones where their players live. Worlds that have 700 players at 10 p.m. might have only 20 at 5 a.m. The figures are so skewed that the mean, median, or mode average is not of any use. Thus, when people do refer to the number of simultaneous players in a world, they tend to give the daily peak (which is better, but not *much* better).

---

66. Such as *GarouMUSH*, http://www.garoumush.org/.

➤ Count the number of player-hours. This is perhaps the best measure of the popularity of virtual worlds, but it suffers precisely because of this. Few administrators are going to publish details of how many player-hours are spent in their virtual world per day if this would make them look bad against the bigger games (and it would!). Incidentally, this and the previous measure are both susceptible to the inflationary effects of people who are logged into a virtual world but not actually playing it. Some textual worlds, for example, regularly have over half their players away from the keyboard while their characters remain unattended in full public view.

However it's measured, the size of a player base has big implications on the design of a virtual world. For example, the main differences between graphical and textual worlds from a designer's point of view are to do with the huge numbers of players that the former attract, rather than the fact they have pictures.

Size, as they say, isn't everything, though. Also important are the demographics of the player base—and not just so marketing people can sell to advertisers and sponsors. Those are *actual* demographics; when a game is being designed, the *target* demographics are important. The more designers know about the kind of players that are required, the better they can account for this in their design. A virtual world aimed at wealthy professionals would be different to one aimed at impoverished students. A virtual world aimed at children would be different to one aimed at bored homemakers. A virtual world aimed at everybody would be different to one aimed at just the design team (although many design teams don't yet seem to have figured this one out).

That said, demographics are only statistics, and they don't always tell the designers of virtual worlds what they need to know. It's clear that virtual worlds which are perceived as computer games—and most of them are—seem to attract different groups of people than their regular-game cousins; there is, however, wide disagreement among analysts over the actual figures[67]. The same overall trends are nevertheless present within

---

67. For example: What percentage of computer gamers are female?
   - 43% http://www.idsa.com/IDSATopTen2002.pdf (2001 survey by Peter D. Hart Research Associates and NPD Group)
   - 42% http://www.mediafamily.org/research/vgrc/2001-2.shtml (2001 survey by National Institute on Media and the Family)
   - 12% http://www.techmall.com/techdocs/TS000822-1.html (2000 survey by The Strategy Group for Ziff-Davis).

   Contrast these with the results of Nick Yee's *EverQuest* survey, which discovered that approximately 16% of that game's players are female. http://www.nickyee.com/eqt/demographics.html.

individual surveys (which compare like with like), and it's probably fairly safe to say that in general

- ➤ Virtual world players are older than console gamers, and cover a wider age range than PC gamers.
- ➤ Virtual worlds attract proportionately more female players than do console or PC games.

This information is normally interpreted in one of two ways: Designers should make their games more inclusive, so as to further appeal to the mass market; designers should make their games less inclusive, so as not to alienate their core audience.

Actually, though, it's possible to appeal to both groups of players. Whereas marketing people want to know *who* is playing, designers are more interested in *why* they are playing. Players' expectations and desires are more important to designers than their ages, incomes, and geographic locations; if designers can model how the different player types interact, and design their virtual world such that these interactions are both stable and intrinsically interesting for participants and observers, then demographic information becomes purely a marketing tool. If you want more female players, advertise to women; if you want more older players, advertise to senior citizens; if you want more teenagers, advertise to teenagers. It shouldn't matter who plays, so long as there are checks and balances within the virtual world itself to ensure that no one playing *style* can come to overwhelm the others.

Fortunately, models for representing playing habits independently of demographics do exist; they are discussed in Chapter 3, "Players."

Dimensions: Change and Persistence

So how do designers categorize virtual worlds? And why would they want to categorize virtual worlds anyway?

Categorizations make explicit some of the choices available to designers. It's all too easy to begin designing a virtual world having already made key decisions without even being aware of the fact. By laying out the options available to them, not only can designers be aware of what options *are* available to them, they are also forced to look at their solutions more analytically. Categorizations are particularly useful for seeing what the various combinations of design decisions imply about any resulting virtual world.

There are many high-level judgments that designers must make when considering the nature of the virtual worlds they wish to create—so many, in fact, that they merit an entire chapter of this book to themselves (Chapter 4, "World Design"). Most of these options are interdependent in some way, which makes them unsuitable as categorizations; others are so disjoint that they say nothing general beyond their own context.

Two, however, do combine to good effect: the degree to which a world can be changed by its players (sometimes called *player impact*); the degree to which changes persist over time. This model, originally devised by Raph Koster and Rich Vogel[68], elegantly exposes what is perhaps the most important question designers must face, which determines the very soul of their creations: Whose world is it?

The two dimensions—change and persistence—are natural progressions from some of the differentiators applied to codebases. Players of MOOs all have full *builder privileges*, meaning they can add to their virtual world almost indiscriminately (they have direct access to the scripting language, which controls everything above the driver level). Players of AberMUDs have no such capability to change their world. Similarly, in *Ultima Online* the entire world and everything in it persists indefinitely—you can drop an object in your house and it will still be there weeks later. In *MUD1*, everything except the player characters' details is periodically reinitialized.

The issue is one of *content*. Although developers throw around the term like everyone knows what it means, it's actually quite hard to pin down. Essentially, content is that which the world provides to hold players' interest. If players are consumers, content is what they consume.

As an analogy, content in virtual worlds is like what stand-up comedians call "material." They write a routine stringing together jokes, observations, and witticisms, which they then deliver to an audience. If they're really good, members of the audience may come back time and time again, but most won't. After all, if you've heard a joke once,

---

68. In `http://www.legendmud.org/raph/gaming/despat_files/frame.htm`. Their narrative cube, discussed in Chapter 7, "Towards a Critical Aesthetic," is a related idea.

it's not really as amusing when you hear it a second time; their material isn't *sticky*. For performances in a 2,000-capacity theater, a single routine can last a comedian for half a year; on television with an audience of 20 million, it's pretty well dead the moment it has been used.

Content in virtual worlds generally means giving people things to do, places to do it, and things to do it to. The mere presence of other players can be considered as a form of content, being as it is the primary reason most people play. Designers can't design players, however, just facilitate their interactions; this kind of content is therefore said to be *intangible*.

Virtual worlds have another major draw, however, that of the virtual environment itself. This, designers can change directly; it's *tangible* content. When designers talk about adding content to a world, they generally mean the tangible sort: that which can be coded or scripted, rather than that which emerges from interactions.

The combination of players and world gives rise to content so potent that people can be quite willing—indeed, positively enthusiastic—to repeat an experience over and over again. This makes virtual worlds incredibly sticky—much stickier than related leisure-time pursuits such as books, computer games, movies, and television. Only music is comparably sticky, with many people happy to listen to their same, favorite albums often and for extended periods[69].

Players do nevertheless (as individuals) consume content. So where does new content originate? In some virtual worlds, only from the interactions between the players: *MUD1* has had only minor changes to the virtual world since 1985, yet people still play it to this day. *MUD1*, however, is scaled just right for the number of players it attracts. For large virtual worlds such as *EverQuest*, there are far more people wanting to play than there are things for them to do. As players become increasingly practiced at the game and want to try out the more demanding challenges, there is greater demand for high-end experiences. Therefore, new tangible content (in the form of locations, monsters, treasure, and so on) must be added so that there's enough around for everyone to eat their fill.

---

69. Whether they would do so if they had to pay a monthly license fee to listen to them is another matter, of course.

This kind of content can be added in one of two ways: within the context of the virtual world (for example, a nobleman hires a gang of workers to build a castle) or without (for example, a player or designer inserts a castle using a development tool). The distinction is quite marked: Does the world make the changes, or do the players? Put another way, do players have to prove new statements from a given set of axioms, or do they get to add axioms directly?

Some virtual worlds allow only partial access to the full majesty of their scripting language (perhaps through permission restrictions, perhaps through the use of a separate "builder language" itself implemented in the scripting language like regular commands). You might, for example, be able to create objects but not locations, or locations but not commands. In practice, though, these are one step beyond the point of no return: Either you can change the world using independent meta-actions (which is called *building*) or you can't (in which case any changes must be through actions within the context of the virtual world itself). Thus, the measure of how much change a virtual world allows depends on the criteria that determine who gets to have the builder privileges.

For some worlds, for example most MOOs, everyone can build; for others, such as the heaviest role-playing MUSHes, only the world's guardian coders can build (even though the architecture is as open as a MOO's, and therefore anyone could in theory be allowed to build). In between these two extremes are worlds that allow changes by wider groups of coders/designers, by privileged appointees, by highly-experienced players, by players who have been playing for a certain time period, by players who pass an interview, by anyone who asks; it's not quite a spectrum, but it's close.

The other dimension under consideration here, persistence, is also more discrete than continuous. Persistence relates to the amount of a virtual world's state that would be retained intact were the whole system to be shut down and restarted. All virtual worlds have some degree of persistence (after all, it's part of the definition of the term "virtual world"), but exactly what they persist varies.

At the most basic end of the scale, all that a world persists is its initial state and the records for individual player characters. AberMUDs are like this. The next step involves persisting what the characters were carrying with them at the time

(DikuMUDs), certain classes of objects such as player characters' corpses (*EverQuest*), and so on all the way up to the entire world state (*Ultima Online*) and the entire world state plus all incrementally-added functionality (MOOs).

Persistence is more dependent on the available computer resources than is change. Put simply, the more you want to save, the longer it will take to save it and the more space it will take up. This is not, however, the usual reason why designers might prefer their world to have a relatively low degree of persistence. Adventure-oriented games in particular can have very complicated, inter-related tasks and puzzles that have far-reaching, gamewide effects; this makes them effectively impossible to disentangle from the state of the virtual world—you can't unlaunch a rocket or unexplode a bomb. Designers want to be able to reinitialize these puzzles, because if something has taken perhaps weeks to implement, they don't really want it to be single-use for the benefit of only a handful of players.

How can you reinitialize something that has all-embracing consequences, though? Reset strategies are discussed in detail in Chapter 4, "World Design," but for this particular problem the short answer is that you can't really reinitialize anything with such a large root system unless you initialize the entire virtual world. Full persistence in this situation would be a bad thing, because persistence is all about *not* reinitializing. Thus, designers of certain types of virtual worlds can have good reasons for not wanting to persist everything across reboots.

Okay, so let's see how these concepts of change and persistence interact. Table 1.3 shows a six by six grid, with persistence increasing left-to-right and access to content creation increasing top-to-bottom. Major codebases and a number of important individual worlds are positioned in the grid depending on how far they satisfy the persistence and change criteria listed at the heads of the columns and rows, respectively.

Table 1.3 Persistence Versus Change

		Persistence (what survives a reboot)					
		Map and characters	Property objects	Objects by class	Objects by location	Entire world	Functionality
Change (who gets to build)	Coders	*Shades*					(role-play) MUSHes
	Trained adminis-trators	*MUD1/II;* AberMUDs	DikuMUDs				
	Trusted players			*EverQuest*	*Asheron's Call*	*Ultima Online*	*MUD1/II;* Castle Marrach
	Experienced players	*MUD2*				LPMUDs	MUCKs
	Non-newbies					TinyMUDs	
	Anyone					*Lambda-MOO*	MOOs

The first thing to notice is that there's an apparent line running diagonally from the top left to the bottom right, with most of the virtual worlds appearing on or above it. What this says is that, in general, there's a relationship between the number of people who have the ability to build things in a virtual world and the persistence of their creations. Note that this alone doesn't say whether persistence implies building access or *vice versa*, just that the two go hand in hand.

Above the diagonal, fewer groups of people can build in the world, but what they build lasts just as long as for more relaxed regimes. Below the diagonal, more people can build, but what they build doesn't last as long as for more open architectures. Given that there are plenty of virtual worlds above the diagonal and few below, we can deduce that increased persistence doesn't really imply increased numbers of builders, but that increased numbers of builders does perhaps imply increased persistence. In other words, the more people who can add content directly to a virtual world, the more of that world will tend to persist.

Looking at the individual worlds in the grid, most commercial games appear on the horizontal line that indicates content can be added by trusted (because they've signed a contract) players but not automatically by anyone who happens to reach some world-defined level of expertise. Given that player-created tangible content is believed by many designers to be the future of virtual worlds, this reluctance to cross the line could present something of a problem. The topic is discussed at length in Chapter 5, "Life in the Virtual World."

Okay, we've learned something, but what has any of this to do with the soul of virtual worlds?

Let's examine Table 1.3 another way: as quadrants of nine squares each.

The top-left quadrant consists exclusively of adventure-oriented virtual worlds. The designers have created a world, and they're strict about who can add to it. Whatever content changes they do allow while the world is running will only persist across a reboot under very particular conditions. Everything in the world is how it is for a reason, and has been constructed to be immediately captivating. The virtual world is so rich and complex and its components so interdependent that players' changes aren't ever going to be able to do it justice. Sure, players can make changes to the world through their actions within the world, but those changes don't ever last for long because they disappear whenever the world is reinitialized. The world entirely belongs to the designers, like a movie entirely belongs to its director; it has little life beyond that of its own.

The top-right quadrant also emphasizes the integrity of the world. Only trusted people get to make changes. However, the world itself is more open-ended, and changes will persist for a long time. Whereas a volcanic eruption in a DikuMUD would last until the next reboot, in *Asheron's Call* it would lead to a more or less permanent change to the environment. Some of the things the designers put into the world are not immediately interesting, but like seeds they may grow into something special later (or they may not). Players can make changes through in-context actions that have lasting effects. The world still belongs to the designers, but when players start to live in it, it gets a chance to evolve in ways the designers hadn't necessarily considered.

The bottom-left quadrant is almost empty, with only *MUD2* making an appearance. The world design is so tight that little persists from one reboot to another, but in between reboots those players who are of sufficient experience to understand the design can create tangible (albeit ephemeral) content. The designers[70] allow certain players to take control of the virtual world in a major way, but they wrest ownership back with every reboot.

The bottom-right quadrant contains almost entirely socially-oriented virtual worlds (with LPMUDs being the only exception). These often have little or no "game" aspect, and building is considered part of the fun. The original designers only create the core of the world and the means by which it can be extended; thereafter, they hand it over to the players to do with as they wish (although there's a problem if what the players wish for is that the designers will take back control, as they famously did with *LambdaMOO*).

So, following this analysis we are at last able to answer the original question: Whose world is it?

➤ In the top-left quadrant, the world belongs to the designers.

➤ In the top-right quadrant, it also belongs to the designers, but players have a stake because the changes they make through their in-world actions can change the landscape.

➤ In the bottom-left quadrant, the world still belongs to the designers. Players are loaned world-changing powers, but come midnight their carriages turn back into pumpkins.

➤ In the bottom-right quadrant, the world belongs to the players.

When designers begin work on a new virtual world, the question of who is to own it should be uppermost in their minds: It really does encapsulate the soul of the world! Of course designers will have a vision of their world, and of course they will consider themselves to be better designers than are their players (not unreasonably so, despite what players[71] may think). Players are people, though, and need to be thought of as such. How much are the designers willing to trust them to add good new content?

---

70. Actually, because there's only one of me, this should be "designer."

71. The players who haven't read this book, that is.

➤ Not at all? Then go for low persistence and low change.

➤ A lot, if they stick to the rules? Then go for high persistence and low change.

➤ A lot, but not for long? Then go for low persistence and high change.

➤ Implicitly? Then go for high persistence and high change.

Perhaps the best expression of this difference is seen in the comparison between the early advertising slogans of Verant (makers of *EverQuest*) and Skotos (makers of *Castle Marrach*):

➤ Verant: You're in Our World Now.

➤ Skotos: Why Yes, I am God.

Skotos' games have only a fraction of the players that *EverQuest* has, but their slogan sells more T-shirts.

Influences on Virtual Worlds

Virtual worlds are not a self-contained phenomenon, insulated from the real world. Trivially, the hardware on which they run is part of the real world and therefore they themselves must be considered a part of it. However, there are other ways in which the real world can influence the virtual. From a designer's point of view, the most important of these are those that also involve the construction of imaginary—if not quite virtual—worlds. In practice, this means books, magazines, movies, television series, and (perhaps most importantly) role-playing games.

Printed Works

The single most important influence on virtual worlds from fiction is J. R. R. Tolkien's *The Lord of the Rings*[72] trilogy. Although it would be of huge significance merely for having established the genre of High Fantasy, its ultimate worth lies in its depiction of an imagined world. It's not the particular world it describes that is momentous (although

---

72. J. R. R. Tolkien, *The Fellowship of the Ring*. London, George Allen & Unwin, 1954.

Middle Earth is indeed classic source material for people writing new text-based games); rather, it's that creating a fully realized, make-believe world was shown to be actually possible. Prior to *The Lord of the Rings*, worlds of such depth were practically unknown.

The word "practically" is used because there were immensely detailed imaginary worlds before, but they evolved over centuries and had many authors. Folk tales, while perhaps originally having some basis in fact, nevertheless changed over the telling, drifting toward some popular shared setting that gave listeners a context. Individual stories had a place and time, so no background had to be given, and they in turn made a contribution to enriching the overall canon. These collections of tales set in what were to become shared fictional worlds gave rise to such well-loved anthologies as Britain's Arthurian Legends, the Middle East's *1001 Nights*, and China's *The Water Margin*.

The other great source of imaginary worlds is religion. This is a little trickier to discuss, because whereas few people today would disagree that the worlds of Greek, Roman, Norse, and Celtic gods were completely imaginary, the suggestion that there might be fictional elements in the Jewish *Torah*, Roman Catholic *Apocrypha*, or Hindu *Ramayana*—to name but a few—is just asking for trouble. The issue of real world religion in virtual worlds is debated in Chapter 8, "Coda: Ethical Considerations;" for the moment, it's sufficient to note that religion can be a source of imaginary worlds comparable in breadth and depth to those that are accepted myth, but you'd have to be brave or stupid to use a living one.

What J. R. R. Tolkien showed was that imaginary worlds did not have to emerge from amalgamations of the ideas of many people; it was possible for an *individual* to construct a believable world from first principles (although he did draw on many tropes from existing myth as part of Middle Earth's architecture). The sheer amount of vision he produced, maintained over six books in three volumes, is breathtaking. It's small wonder that the imaginative possibilities raised by *The Lord of the Rings* are as much an inspiration for designers of virtual worlds today as they were for the authors of *MUD1*.

That said, the actual content of *MUD1* wasn't drawn from Middle Earth. The game's terrain was English and the inhabitants were pure fairytale—it had "dwarfs" rather than "dwarves," for example, and no elves, orcs, nor hobbits whatsoever. There *was* a fictional influence, but it was due to the sword and sorcery of Robert E. Howard's *Conan the Cimmerian*[73] series rather than *The Hobbit*[74]. Long novels aren't as good as action-oriented short stories for evoking the heart-in-your-mouth style adventure that *MUD1*'s world was intended (among other things) to deliver.

Beyond *The Lord of the Rings*, the influence of fiction on virtual worlds is three types:

- ► *Direct.* The virtual world is an implementation of a familiar fictional world such as Robert Jordan's *The Wheel of Time*[75] or Terry Pratchett's *Discworld*[76].

- ► *Partial.* The virtual world is inspired by a particular work of fiction or a genre that is derived from one. It might have the same "mutant academy" idea of Stan Lee and Jack Kirby's *X-Men*[77], but let you create your own superheroes.

- ► *Indirect.* The virtual world implements or is inspired by some other work which itself is an adaptation of a book or comic series. A virtual world design team might decide to adopt the *Dungeons & Dragons* magic system without necessarily knowing that E. Gary Gygax and Dave Arneson (authors of *Dungeons & Dragons*) themselves adopted the idea from the novels of Jack Vance[78].

Given the choice, most professional virtual world designers would prefer to design their own, original virtual world. They have good enough imaginations that they don't need to steal from fiction (yet are regularly asked "where do you get your ideas from?" as if they couldn't just think them up unaided). Like a scriptwriter adapting a book for the big screen, designers working to a license might genuinely enjoy what they're doing but, deep down, they'd rather be exploring their own imagination than someone else's. For this reason, designers tend to approach novels analytically, deconstructing them for their form rather than their content.

---

73. Robert E. Howard, *The Phoenix on the Sword*. Chicago, *Weird Tales*, Popular Fiction Publishing Co., December 1932.

74. J. R. R. Tolkien, *The Hobbit: or There and Back Again*. London, George Allen & Unwin, 1937.

75. Robert Jordan, *The Eye of the World*. New York, Tor Books, 1990.

76. Terry Pratchett, *The Colour of Magic*. London, Colin Smythe, 1983.

77. Stan Lee (writer) and Jack Kirby (artist), *X-Men*. New York, *X-Men*, Marvel Comics, September 1963.

78. Jack Vance, *The Dying Earth*. New York, Hillman Periodicals, 1950.

There is, however, a fourth category of fiction that has subject matter *in itself* of use to designers. These are the books that are *about* virtual worlds; not in the pedagogical way that this book is, but far more speculatively. Books of this kind are of great interest to the designers of virtual worlds because they actually involve consideration of design issues. Suppose that all implementational and commercial problems have been solved, and people can physically visit invented worlds from reality: What might they find there?

In early examples of the genre, such as Larry Niven and Steven Barnes' *Dream Park*[79] and Vernor Vinge's *True Names*[80], the authors had not encountered virtual worlds[81] and were therefore writing from a position of pure conjecture. Nevertheless, they raised several issues about the design of virtual worlds that have proven to be quite prescient. *Dream Park*, for example, asks questions about narrative and ownership that were to be raised again some 20 years later when the debate about ongoing content provision for fifth-age graphical virtual worlds began in earnest. *True Names* made the distinction between player and persona (the real-world identity of an individual being a persona's "true name") and explored some of the consequences of identity masking that this enables.

When Cyberpunk brought new meaning to the term "cutting edge" in the Science Fiction literary scene of the mid-1980s, the future of virtual worlds immediately seemed laid out with neon clarity. In *Dream Park*, virtual worlds were glorified real-world theme parks; in *True Names*, they were stored in computers that people reached through electrode "portals" suckered to the head; by William Gibson's *tour de force* novel *Neuromancer*[82], access was through neural jacks making direct electronic connections to the brain. Surely this was to be the ultimate in imaginary experience made real? The notion of *cyberspace*—data represented as imagery within a shared virtual environment—burst into public consciousness. Virtual worlds were merely a manifestation of virtual reality; the interface not only brought the message, it determined it. The syntax shaped the semantics.

---

79. Larry Niven and Steven Barnes, *Dream Park*. New York, Ace Books, 1981.

80. Vernor Vinge, *True Names*. James R. Frenkel (ed.), *Binary Star #5*. New York, Dell, 1981. Full text available at `http://members.tripod.com/erythrina/index.html`.

81. Although *True Names* makes a direct reference to *Adventure* (*ADVENT*) and *Dream Park* does the same with *Zork*.

82. William Gibson, *Neuromancer*. New York, Ace Books, 1984.

It was easy to forget that Cyberpunk fiction was just that: fiction. It was predictive in the cautionary sense, showing how things *might* become, not how they *would* become. Part of Cyberpunk's agenda was to show that although technology offers a way forward, people could corrupt it for their own ends. That which has the potential to bestow liberty can be twisted to the cause of oppression or anarchy. Thus, it was in the interests of Cyberpunk authors to show cyberspace as a slick, high-tech victory of form over substance, hip and happening yet shallow and soulless but for its dark, in-shadow periphery. The cold, objective way that virtual space was depicted (as a network of freeform, three-dimensional statistical symbols) conveyed the impression that getting to cyberspace was more important than what was there when you arrived.

Many people find the neurotechnology envisaged in *Neuromancer* exciting, because (were it ever available) it would provide a means of entering a virtual world totally and completely[83]. It is unlikely, however, that any virtual world they did visit would look like a classic Cyberpunk vision unless the designers deliberately took such as their model[84]. This was acknowledged in William Gibson's later Cyberpunk novel, *Idoru*[85], which distinguished between network-as-medium and network-as-place by explicitly referring to virtual worlds as MUDs.

Cyberpunk teaches designers a number of valuable lessons about the sociology and psychology of players and the responsibilities of developers. Virtual worlds are not insulated from the real world; they can't be regarded as solely the purview of their designers, publishers, or even players. Their influence extends into the real world, and therefore the real world extends into them. Ultimately, though, the relationship is one-sided: The real world always wins in the end.

Cyberpunk was the evangelizing prophet of virtual reality, but, once the hype died down, other authors were able to look at the new reality and use that as their starting point for speculative work. Media darling *LambdaMOO* was an obvious first point of contact for people considering writing speculatively about virtual worlds, although in itself it was hardly representative of what was already out there.

---

83. Personally, I'd rather eat my own eyeballs than have a chip in my head.

84. A virtual world set in a fictional Cyberpunk milieu such as *Neuromancer's* "Sprawl" has, of course, been done many times—a fact sadly lost on the "kewl d00ds" who play games such as *EverQuest* as if merely being in cyberspace meant being in Cyberpunk.

85. William Gibson, *Idoru*. New York, G. P. Putnam's Sons, 1996.

Perhaps the most impressive of those novels first to be informed by extant virtual worlds is Tad Williams' *Otherland*[86] series. This monumental[87] work traces the fortunes of a number of disparate individuals accessing the "Otherland" virtual world of its title. Among the many things the series gets right that Cyberpunk got wrong are

- ➤ Client/server model dynamics. The gradual shift in importance from how powerful the client hardware is to how powerful the server hardware is.

- ➤ Multi-faceted worlds within worlds. This is typical of MOOs and other builder-centric codebases (such as the book's "Otherland").

- ➤ Inter-world object mapping, so that taking an object from one sub-world to another replaces it with a functional equivalent (an *analogue*). This is indeed how designers intend to handle transfers of objects and characters between virtual worlds.

- ➤ Player attitudes to gender-presentation betrayal. When people say they're something they aren't and get in too deep.

- ➤ Understanding of immersion (the sense of being "in" a virtual world). Cyberpunk mistook visualization for immersion: The two are not the same.

- ➤ Virtual worlds modeled on the real world. If what you see looks and behaves like reality, you feel you're "there" more than if it looks and behaves like a gridwork of platonic solids.

- ➤ Recognizing that people have expectations of degrees of reality within the virtual world. Fulfilling these expectations leads to increased immersion and denying it leads to decreased immersion. People don't want worlds to have anthropomorphic content merely because they feel more comfortable in them that way.

- ➤ The difficulty of distinguishing between computer-generated characters in the virtual world and ones under the control of human beings, and (more importantly) the consequences of not being able to tell. People have already been fooled into believing that virtual players are real ones for extended periods; many more will undoubtedly follow.

---

86. Tad Williams, *City of Golden Shadow*. New York, DAW books, 1998.

87. Four paperbacks weighing a total of 850g—about a pound each. I told you it was impressive...!

Of course, the series also gets some things wrong of its own account. The attitude that characters (in the first book) have to persona death, for example, is at odds with how people in the real world tend feel on the subject (real people are far less stoic). On the whole, though, it offers much for virtual world designers to ponder. Besides, no designer could possibly criticize a book that names a virtual mall after *LambdaMOO* and has the opening line:

> *It started in mud, as many things do*[88].

Film and Television

Most original fictional ideas appear in magazine, comic, or book form first, because these are far less expensive to produce than movies or TV series (or even stage plays). Many of the top-grossing movies, year after year, are based on stories or characters that first appeared in print.

Unsurprisingly, the influence of film and television on virtual worlds falls into the same categories as does that of books and comics:

➤ *Direct. Star Wars Galaxies* is set in the *Star Wars*[89] universe. There are textual virtual worlds based on *Buffy the Vampire Slayer*[90], *The Lion King*[91], *Battlestar Galactica*[92], and *Tron*[93]—to name but a few.

➤ *Partial.* There are virtual worlds derived from the concept behind *A Bug's Life*[94]. *Toontown*[95] is a graphical world set in the Disney cartoon universe.

---

88. I asked Tad Williams, and he confirmed that this really is a sly reference to *MUD* (that is, *MUD1*). Is that groovy or what?

89. George Lucas (writer and director), *Star Wars*. USA, 20th Century Fox, 1977.

90. Joss Whedon, *Buffy the Vampire Slayer*. USA, WB network, 1997.

91. Irene Mecchi, Jonathan Roberts, and Linda Woolverton (writers) and Roger Allers and Rob Minkoff (directors), *The Lion King*. USA, Walt Disney Pictures, 1994.

92. Donald P. Bellisario, *Battlestar Galactica*. USA, ABC network, 1978.

93. Steven Lisberger (writer and director) and Bonnie Macbird (writer), *Tron*. USA, Walt Disney Pictures, 1982.

94. John Lasseter and Andrew Stanton (writers and directors) and Joe Ranft (writer), *A Bug's Life*. USA, Walt Disney Pictures, 1998.

95. http://www.toontown.com

➤ *Indirect.* The original *Sailor Moon*[96] comic books were concordantly made into an animated series, which in turn was implemented as a virtual world (indeed, several of them).

➤ *Meta. The Truman Show*[97] says much about virtual world design, of narrative, and of the nature of reality.

Because of the crossovers between the media, the treatment of virtual worlds in film and television has paralleled that of novels, from the theme park beginnings of Michael Crichton's *Westworld*[98] to the neural implants of the Wachowski brothers' *The Matrix*[99]. Superficially, then, it appears as if books and movies will always tend to explore the same themes. This is not, however, necessarily the case.

It is the nature of books to *tell* and films to *show*. Thus, *Westworld* showed damaged robots being repaired for re-insertion into the virtual world (identifying what later came to be known as spawning), whereas *Dream Park* told what it was like to play (presaging the "it's just a game" arguments that still surface today).

By showing, a movie or TV series can present a situation in a direct manner, whereas a book (or even a comic) would take time to tell the same thing. If you see an image on a screen, it can convey in an instant what might take a minute to read. There are limitations on what can be shown, though, that don't apply to what can be told (you can't really "show" thoughts, for example, just the consequences of people having had them). Books are about imagination, whereas films are about sensory experience. Films concretize what books visualize. It's not an inconsistency of law that heavily pornographic movies are illegal but heavily pornographic literature isn't: With films, what you see is what you get; with books, what you get is what you see.

---

96. Naoko Takeuchi, *Bishoujo Senshi Sailor Moon*. Tokyo, *Nakayoshi*, Kodansha, February 1992.

97. Andrew Niccol (writer) and Peter Weir (director), *The Truman Show*. USA, Paramount Pictures, 1998.

98. Michael Crichton (writer and director), *Westworld*. USA, Metro-Goldwyn-Mayer, 1973.

99. Andy Wachowski and Larry Wachowski (writers and directors), *The Matrix*. USA, Warner Brothers, 1999.

For designers of virtual worlds, one of the most important tropes from film and TV that would not work as well in print is the *holodeck* from Gene Roddenberry's *Star Trek: The Next Generation*[100] and spin-offs (*Star Trek: Deep Space Nine*[101] and, in particular, *Star Trek: Voyager*[102]). The holodeck is a programmable environment with which real (in the context of the TV show) people can interact as if it were (their) reality. For example, a character might create and then enter a simulation of Victorian London, assuming the role of Sherlock Holmes. This works on the screen better than it does on the page because the world and the character's degree of immersion in it are immediately apparent; they require no unveiling. The situation is at once accepted, and the episode can progress to examining the issues it suggests. This can't happen in a book unless you're already familiar with the concept of holodecks from the TV show.

Holodecks, although occasionally used for serious purposes such as testing engine designs, are primarily viewed within the *Star Trek* universe as an entertainment medium. From this perspective, the main lessons to be learned from holodecks are

- ➤ They allow characters to express sides of themselves that they may not be able to do in reality[103]. One captain may play a low-life film noir detective; another, a romantic lead. The holodeck is a liberating, albeit temporary, release from reality.

- ➤ They distinguish between undirected and directed environments. A representation of a bar where characters can go to hang out would be an example of the former; an interactive "holonovel" to prevent a 1930s-style evil emperor from ruling the galaxy (while rescuing a feisty princess) would be an example of the latter.

- ➤ Creating virtual environments is in itself a fun activity.

- ➤ The representation of a living person without their permission is rude, but not forbidden. This is just as well, given that they *always* find out.

- ➤ They are a magnet for alien life forms unable to distinguish between the false reality presented by the holodeck and the true reality in which the holodeck exists. It's a metaphor for people who believe everything they see on TV[104].

---

100. Gene Roddenberry, *Star Trek: The Next Generation*. USA, Paramount, 1987.

101. Rick Berman and Michael Piller, *Star Trek: Deep Space Nine*. USA, Paramount, 1993.

102. Rick Berman, Jeri Taylor, and Michael Piller, *Star Trek: Voyager*. USA, Paramount, 1995.

103. "Reality" here is in the context of the *Star Trek* universe, not ours.

104. Or read in books, such as this one.

➤ They malfunction to the extent that they pose a greater threat to the health of crewmembers than a direct hit from a photon torpedo to the ship's hull with all shields down. This is as a consequence of *Star Trek* itself being subject to the same laws of drama that it imposes on its holonovels.

Many of the virtual worlds that exist today are, in some ways, more mature than *Star Trek*'s vision of the future; this is particularly the case with regards to the social norms that have evolved through their use. However, where the concept of the holodeck is most useful is in thought experiments: Were holodecks to exist, what new areas of narrative, performance, and self-awareness would they enable? Are these desirable or undesirable consequences? Could these new areas already exist—or be made to exist—in some form, using the technology of today?

The difference between showing and telling is not the only one between books and movies. Equally important is that, in general, movies will get more exposure (and will therefore be the more influential) than books. This means they will provide a greater cultural touchstone. Few people have read Philip K. Dick's short story *We Can Remember It for You Wholesale*[105], but the movie it inspired, *Total Recall*[106], grossed $119,394,839 in the United States alone in 1990[107]. The movie might cause virtual world designers to consider how to stop player involvement derailing prewritten plot lines; the short story won't, simply because few—if any—designers have read it.

In the same way that some worlds work better as books than on the screen (for example, C. S. Lewis's *Chronicles of Narnia*[108] series) and some work better as movies than in print (for example, George Miller and James McCausland's *Mad Max*[109] series), some virtual worlds work better in text than in graphics and *vice versa*. The reasons for this are explained in Chapter 4, but for now it's enough simply to note the fact because it leads to an interesting analogy (that most readers will doubtless have figured out already).

---

105. Philip K. Dick, *"We Can Remember It for You Wholesale."* New York, *The Magazine of Fantasy and Science Fiction*, Mercury Press, April 1966.

106. Ronald Shusett & Dan O'Bannon and Gary Goldman (writers) and Paul Verhoeven (director), *Total Recall*. USA, TriStar, 1990.

107. Source: http://www.boxofficemojo.com/y90.html

108. C. S. Lewis, *The Lion, the Witch and the Wardrobe*. London, Geoffrey Bles, 1950.

109. George Miller (writer and director) and James McCausland (writer), *Mad Max*. Australia, American International Pictures, 1979.

Basically, it can be constructive to regard textual virtual worlds as being like books, and graphical ones as being like movies. Books and textual worlds are cheap to create, more amenable to risk-taking, and they talk to the imagination; movies and graphical worlds are highly expensive productions, less inclined to experiment, and they talk to the senses. Similarly, few textual virtual worlds have the same profile as graphical ones, so when people see that *Star Wars Galaxies* has a hairdressing skill and think it's cool, they won't necessarily know that text-based games like *Castle Marrach* have had the same thing for years. They just think *Star Wars Galaxies* is better than *EverQuest*.

So it goes.

Books and movies, well known and respected art forms that they are, nevertheless rarely contain practical information that virtual world designers can actually use. They can suggest genres, directions, issues, problems, and (occasionally) solutions, but not in any great detail. It's like using a Canaletto painting of Venice as source material for a novel set in the city in 1740: You may get a great sense of *La Serenissima*'s atmospheric grandeur, and may in time be able to construct an impression of what everyday life there might have been like, what challenges the people faced; on the whole, though, a resident's diary would be far more useful for your purposes.

So is there an equivalent to the resident's diary for virtual world designers, for those times when realism is preferred to idealism?

Yes, there is: role-playing games.

Role-Playing Games

Role-playing games (RPGs) have always had an important influence on virtual worlds.

Role-playing is basically acting, and therefore has its roots in ancient history. It has many uses beyond theatrical expression (for example in psychology, education, and training), but it wasn't until the 1973 arrival of E. Gary Gygax and Dave Arneson's *Dungeons & Dragons* (*D&D*)[110] that the concept of role-playing games finally crystallized. *Dungeons & Dragons* was a fusion of traditional tabletop wargames and interactive storytelling, in which one player (the *referee*, later to be known as the Dungeon Master/Mistress (DM) or Games Master/Mistress (GM)) designed an imaginary world

---

110. E. Gary Gygax and Dave Arneson, *Dungeons & Dragons*. Lake Geneva WI, Tactical Studies Rules, 1973.

into which a number of players would go. The referee would describe what the players could see, hear, feel, and so on, and the players would explain what they (or, more correctly, their characters) would do. The referee would then roll a few dice to determine the consequences of these actions in the context of the imaginary world, which would in turn cause the players to try new actions, and so on. Virtual worlds are very close to tabletop RPGs except they have computerized referees.

Being games, RPGs need rules. Because the referee has to construct the imaginary world, these rules do not only describe how to play the game but how to create a game world—which may entail writing new, world-specific rules. Thus, these are actually *rule systems*. Although referees can and do create vast *campaigns* (as these worlds, or partial worlds, are known), it takes a lot of time to do so. For this reason, referees may use rule sets that have been adapted for their chosen genre (imperial Rome, horror, far future, wild west, whatever) and use these as a starting point. Others will acquire predefined *modules*, often written by professional games designers, which define a self-contained sub-world. These sub-worlds have explicit goals for the players and solution paths appropriate to the players' characters' abilities.

Some of the genre-specific information researched for these games can save valuable time for the designers of those virtual worlds that are set in the same place or period (which, as tabletop role-playing games tend to draw on the same fictional and historical influences as virtual worlds, is often the case). Indeed, the information they provide can be so well organized, accurate, and complete that it can benefit people not remotely interested in role-playing games or virtual worlds. Anyone wanting to write about, say, the golden age of piracy, should seriously consider buying a specialist rule set for that genre as a starting point[111].

Virtual worlds can therefore benefit from tabletop RPGs in four important areas:

➤ The basic rules of the game.

➤ The rules for creating an imaginary world.

➤ Rule sets for particular genres.

➤ Modules for actual game experiences.

---

111. Where else are you going to find out how many knots a 300-ton pinnace beating a 5-knot wind could make?

It is no coincidence that this reflects well the driver/mudlib/world model/instantiation breakdown of virtual world codebase architecture; the two systems really do have a lot in common. They even have branches at some of the same points: Steve Jackson's *GURPS*[112] system, for example, is LPMUD-like in that it provides common gaming and creation rules for different environments (feudal Japan, swashbucklers, time travel, you name it), whereas Kevin Siembieda's *Rifts*[113] system is more MUSH-like in that it ties multiple sub-worlds into a single coherent whole.

Virtual worlds borrow from RPGs at all levels. *MUD1*'s level system came from *D&D*, as a neat way to give players intermediate goals. The DikuMUD codebase draws heavily on first edition *Advanced Dungeons & Dragons (AD&D)* and Bioware's reincarnated *NeverWinter Nights* implements the 3rd edition *AD&D* rules very faithfully indeed. There are textual worlds set in environments designed for role-playing games, such as Mark Rein Hagen's *Vampire: The Masquerade*[114]. There are even virtual worlds based on specific game modules, for example city campaigns for Ed Greenwood's *Forgotten Realms*[115].

Although pencil-and-paper role-playing games can be used as a means to "dry run" virtual worlds, it is a mistake to believe that everything in the one is always transferable to the other. The two may be similar, but they are not identical; where they differ, the differences are profound.

The human referees of role-playing games have an intelligence that the computer referees of virtual worlds do not. They can create new content immediately, and are responsive to the needs of their players. What they lack, however, is speed, memory, and bandwidth. A human-moderated world may be more vivid than a computer-moderated one (because its level of detail can be tailored to the moment), but it doesn't *work* the same way as the real one and is thus ultimately less convincing[116].

---

112. Steve Jackson: *GURPS: Generic Universal RolePlaying System*. Austin, TX, Steve Jackson Games, 1986.

113. Kevin Siembieda, *Rifts*. Taylor MI, Palladium Books, 1990.

114. Mark Rein Hagen, *Vampire: the Masquerade*. Stone Mountain GA, White Wolf Games Studio, 1991.

115. See http://www.cc.jyu.fi/~tojan/fore/forefaq.htm for the *Forgotten Realms* story.

116. Computer-moderated worlds don't work the same way either, of course, but they act enough like the real world to merit the term "virtual." Note that this is to do with how a computer-moderated world handles multiple events in parallel in (near) real time, rather than the differences between speech, text, and graphics.

What's more, players of a human-moderated world can exert out-of-context influence over the referee and each other. If a squid picks up a sword and starts fighting with it, a player might say to a human referee, "Hey, squids can't do that!" The referee can reply appropriately to the situation. For example: "If you check the manual, page 54..." (correcting a misconception); "this one can" (mild hint); "perhaps it only looks like a squid?" (stronger hint); "some swords can control their wielders, you know" (misdirection); "you're right, its balance would be all wrong" (recognition of mistake); "you spot a thin wire attached to the sword" (taking the objection as an implicit command for the character to look closer).

If a squid picks up a sword in a computer-moderated world, well, the squid picks up the sword. The virtual world is as inviolate as the real one: Waving your fist at rain clouds while asking your deity of preference what you've done to deserve a soaking may make you feel better, but on the whole you're not going to get an apology[117].

So what developments in human-moderated worlds don't transfer to computer-moderated (that is, virtual) worlds?

> *Anything subjective.* Alignment does not travel well, because a computer can't quantify the concepts involved. Can a "good" character attack a player who boasts of being a thief? What if they've seen the character steal something? What if the theft was of an object that had itself been stolen from the thief? What if the thief originally bought the object from a fence, who got it from another thief? Human beings can make value judgments, but computers are hopeless at it.

> *Anything individualistic.* Most modern role-playing games are classless and skills-based. They let players decide the directions in which to advance their characters. Most virtual worlds have classes, races, and guilds to coerce players to band together. This helps players who don't know each other in real life to bond; it also serves as a means to introduce goals into player activities. It promotes role-playing[118].

---

117. Some heavily role-playing virtual worlds may be flexible enough to do this, and ones with strongly-managed storyline events (for example, *Achaea*) can do it too. It basically depends on whether there's an administrator on hand able to address the issue there and then; in this case, there effectively *is* a deity for you to wave your fist at!

118. Actually, it doesn't. The heaviest role-playing virtual worlds (MUCKs, MUSHes) have fewer constraints on characters, not more. This is a pet peeve of mine, which will become more evident when I harp on about it in Chapter 3.

➤ *Not everything theoretical.* Although the general principles of world design and role-playing have been analyzed over the years, and a good deal of what has been discovered is indeed applicable to virtual worlds, not *all* of it is. The danger here is that the studious virtual world designer will miss the boundary and go too far (for example, in creating believable non-player characters) or emphasize the wrong thing (for example, plotting over atmosphere).

➤ *Anything meta-interactive.* Players can interact with a virtual world[119], but they can't do so beyond its context. Builders can breach the context, but they can only act *on* the virtual world, they can't enter any kind of dialogue *with* it. Players of diceless role-playing games like Erick Wujcik's *Amber*[120], on the other hand, interact with the referee (that is, the world) the entire time.

So long as these distinctions are not important to the rule system, a transfer is achievable. Gary Gygax's RPG *Lejendary Adventure* is now being developed as a virtual world[121]. It is possible.

Transfers (and nontransfers) of expertise in the opposite direction, while perhaps important for the designers of role-playing games, are of little consequence for the designers of virtual worlds; they are therefore not considered here, except to note that there is a significant overlap between the "hard core" virtual world players, the players of single-player role-playing games such as Bioware's *Baldur's Gate*, and the players of pencil-and-paper role-playing games[122].

It should be mentioned that there is a third option for role-playing that calls on neither computers nor human beings to moderate the world. This is *live-action role-playing* (LARP), where people use the real world to model a fantasy world[123]. In *Dungeons & Dragons*, you roll dice to see if your arrow hits an enemy; in *Dark Age of Camelot*, the computer calculates the odds; in a LARP, the flight of the (safety-tipped) arrow through

---

119. Players for whom this is their defining activity are called "explorers." See Chapter 3.

120. Erick Wujcik, *Amber Diceless Role-Playing*. Detroit, Phage Press, 1992.

121. `http://di.gamepoint.net/lejendary/en/`

122. Newt Forager, a secondary character in Jolly R. Blackburn's *Knights of the Dinner Table* comic book series, got into role-playing games from playing MUDs. Aren't you glad that you read all these footnotes?

123. In practice, there do tend to be human referees too, but they're not essential.

the air is the only measure of success. Things the game wants to have that the real world doesn't are represented by symbols. For example, casting magic spells might be represented by throwing flour or birdseed at the target, or by passing a small token.

The influence of LARP on the design of virtual worlds has not been great, mainly because of the relatively small numbers of people involved. This is a shame, as there are many different LARP systems of potential interest to virtual world designers, offering practical illustrations that ground the mere speculation of, say, *Dream Park*. Virtual world designers are, on the whole, aware of LARP, but not appraised of it. They're consequently more likely to talk to actors rather than LARPers when they have their next brilliant idea to pay people to spend eight hours a day in character while role-playing personalities in their worlds. This is another shame.

Why isn't LARP more popular? Practical matters of organization aside, the main problem is that content in LARP is thinner and more expensive than in tabletop role-playing games or virtual worlds. If the referee of a tabletop game creates a village near a mine, it doesn't matter if the adventurers never visit it—the content can be used elsewhere, the next time a generic village is needed. For a virtual world, it matters only slightly less; players may not visit the village very often or for the reasons the designer intended, but they *will* nevertheless visit it in time. In a LARP, if the adventurers don't make an appearance it means several people have been sitting around in villager costume for an entire afternoon to no avail; for this reason, LARPs' gameplay is often more collect-the-plot-piece oriented than their cousins', with most of the fun coming from the deep role-playing involved rather than the adventuring. While role-playing to this degree is great fun for many people[124], it can be very hard to get into, particularly if you're shy or retiring (that is, actually likely to be good at role-playing).

One thing that these real world- and human-moderated worlds do show is that the role-playing experience can transcend any preconceptions of something being "only" a game. Role-playing is routinely used for non-game purposes, and appeals to people who would not (nor would they wish to) consider themselves as gamers. It's even used as a game by people who don't see themselves as gamers—*How to Host a Murder* is basically a mini-LARP. Many of the people who visit *EverQuest*, *Ultima Online*, and *Star Wars Galaxies* do not believe themselves to be gamers at all (which is only fair, given that they aren't).

---

124. Although it's not strictly LARP, I've seen re-creations of English Civil War battles that involved several thousand people (excluding ambulance staff).

Other Influences

The design of virtual worlds is influenced by printed works, film, television, and role-playing games. Individual worlds may draw from other fields, too; for example, there are text MUDs set in console game worlds like that of Hironobu Sakaguchi's *Final Fantasy* series, and there are scripting languages based on those used for military simulations. Anything requiring imagination can potentially be of value: These genuinely are "imaginary" worlds.

However, external factors are not the only ones at work here.

The greatest influence on the design of virtual worlds is (for better or for worse) the player base. Thus, anything that can influence existing or prospective players is itself an influence on the design of the virtual worlds they elect to play.

Some of this influence falls into the domain of marketing, which from the point of view of a designer can be viewed as a single pressure that is a convenient abstraction of the many other pressures the designer really, really doesn't want to know about. Further influence comes from customer service, which affects game designers more (in that they have to plan for it in their design), but again it can be viewed as a single pressure that is the summation of many other pressures off the designer's radar.

The remaining sources of influence are more direct, and should be consulted regularly:

➤ *Competitors*. Virtual worlds evolve by trying new ideas, yes, but also by taking ideas that work from other virtual worlds and by discarding ideas that have been shown to fail. Every virtual world has some innovation, and they shouldn't be ignored simply because they weren't written by you or they use a different genre.

➤ *Opinion-forming publications*. Reviews are important, as are regular columns: After all, even if a columnist were unilaterally to refer to virtual worlds as "MMO*s", sooner or later players would show up calling them MMO*s. However, a magazine's editorial policy matters the most, as it sets the tone for the articles. *Computer Gaming World* treats virtual worlds in a different manner than *Wired*, even though both are admirably responsible about the subject. Readers of one will get a different impression of virtual worlds than readers of the other.

➤ *Opinion-forming players.* Players listen to each other, whether it's in the virtual world, in an online forum, or at a rant site. Surprisingly for designers, not every word uttered by players is patent nonsense; surprisingly for marketers and customer service people, not every word uttered by players is blindingly insightful. Players can swirl into a great maelstrom of creativity, but few of them truly understand game design[125]. This is a theme that surfaces time and time again when considering the design of virtual worlds.

Designers should not delude themselves that they can manipulate any of the above. Your fellow designers will usually be only too happy to explain to you those advances of which they're particularly proud (it's not like these things can be kept secret once beta-testing begins), but they won't change their minds on your say-so. Similarly, although those journalists that your marketers allow you to speak to may seem wide-eyed and gullible, that doesn't mean they really *are*. As for manipulating players, the customer service departments of some virtual worlds prohibit designers from even speaking to them, so disastrous can the consequences be if they do!

These are sources that can influence designers; the only way to influence them in return is through the designed virtual worlds.

The Designer

The role of virtual world designer is fraught with paradoxes. You have to be imaginative yet realistic; deep-thinking yet practical; surprising yet dependable; an individual yet part of a team; a doer yet a listener. You have to know a lot about some things and at least a little about everything else.

This chapter has presented the context. If you didn't already, you should now know where virtual worlds are, how they got to be that way, and where they seem to be headed. Whether they actually *do* go in that direction is another matter. It all depends on people like you.

Subsequent chapters of this book lay out the choices before you, but only *you* can decide which to make.

---

125. Those who have read this book, of course, will be able to claim otherwise.

The options suggested are only that, options. If you look at them and think, "they wouldn't work in my virtual world," you could well be right; that isn't to say they wouldn't work in someone else's, though. Players are often quick to go to the specific when they should be staying at the general. "You can't have permanent death in *EverQuest*!" Well, of course not—*EverQuest* was designed not to have permanent death in it; adding the concept would be as misguided as placing a learn-to-play-golf feature in a Saturday night chat show. It doesn't fit the format. In an afternoon sports magazine, hey, it might work. In a new series targeted at the recently retired, it would make perfect sense.

You can taste ideas to see if you like them, but you don't have to swallow them whole. Besides, even if they're your favorites, they might not go together. Italian cuisine does not call for pistachio ice cream to be added to spaghetti bolognaise.

Question the paradigms, avoid stagnation. You have to *understand* a system before you can challenge it, but that doesn't mean you have to *accept* it. Just because you see a list of ideas here, that doesn't mean it's exhaustive. The virtual worlds people remember are the ones that are different, not the ones that are the same.

After the success of the *Harry Potter* series, children's book publishers went all out to find the next *Harry Potter*. Everyone likes plucky, magic-wielding youngsters! Well, up to a point: What they actually like is *Harry Potter*. Whatever the next big children's publishing sensation turns out to be, about the only thing you *can* say about it is that it *won't* look like *Harry Potter*. Those companies writing virtual worlds that are *EverQuest* clones are scrapping for crumbs from the high table.

Read, assimilate, understand. Then think for yourself.

Chapter 2

How to Make Virtual Worlds

KEY TOPICS

- Development
- On Architecture
- Theory and Practice

Virtual worlds are implemented using complicated pieces of software, but, contrary to what many developers would like to believe, they are by no means the most sophisticated programs in existence. Modern operating systems comfortably beat them, and they're dwarfed by major projects, such as air traffic control networks. When you read the following, therefore, remember that it could all be much, much worse.

This book is written from the perspective of a virtual world designer. The fun part of design is the creativity; the boring part is what you have to learn to inform the creative process. It's not surprising that many designers therefore omit this step. This is a Bad Thing. It is *not* enough to have played or even coded other virtual worlds; to do a good job, you have to understand how they *work*. For example, a college student putting together a textual virtual world might try out different codebases to see which is the most appropriate. Well yes, that sounds only sensible. However, it would be like someone who knows how to drive taking a selection of cars for a spin before deciding which to use as the basis for designing a car of their own. There is more to designing cars than finding something that suits your driving style; there is more to designing virtual worlds than finding something that suits your playing style. Before you can make a start you need to be aware of how virtual worlds function, what the components are, how they fit together, what can go wrong, and a whole host of other things.

A student building a virtual world from a kit has the excuse that in doing so they might actually learn some of the important design principles involved. The student's next world will consequently be much improved. Professional virtual world designers can fall back on no such justification. There are some things that they simply ought to know beforehand, whether they want to or not.

It's this background knowledge that this chapter is intended to impart.

Development

Design is just one part of creating a virtual world. Designers like to think it's the most important part, but is it?

➤ Designers have wild, airy-fairy imaginings.

➤ Programmers do the actual work of building the virtual world.

➤ Artists are the magicians who imbue it with form.

➤ Sound engineers determine the moods and emotions.

➤ Operations staffs are the engineers who keep it running.

➤ Producers provide the resources.

Anyone can have wild imaginings. Only people with specialist skills can program, or draw, or compose, or run networks, or manage a project. Why are designers so important?

Because, if a designer screws up, the consequences for the virtual world can be devastating.

A piece of code that doesn't work may be hard to track down, but once discovered it's usually easy to correct. An odd-looking yet crucial texture may need to be painstakingly redrawn, but it's still only a single bitmap. However, if a designer makes a seemingly minor misjudgment, the effects could be so pervasive that they might paralyze a world for weeks.

If you find that hard to believe, consider a virtual world in which non-player shop-keepers sell goods at fixed prices. What happens if there is inflation in this virtual economy? Pretty soon, you can have whatever you want for peanuts. What happens if there's deflation? Even trivial items cost so much that only the very rich can afford them. What factors affect inflation/deflation? Oh, just about all of them—in hideously intertwined ways as determined by the actions of the designer.

Broken economies are not pretty. At one point, *Asheron's Call's* currency became so worthless that players had to barter if they wanted to acquire goods from one another. This went on for months before it was finally brought under control; the debacle cost *AC* dearly.

So, that's why design is the most important thing about creating virtual worlds—it has the highest price of failure.

The Team

Design might be the most important cog in the machine that creates virtual worlds, but that isn't to say the other components are unimportant. Some are absolutely critical: If a server crashes, for example, every minute it stays down will be paid for in cancelled accounts. Designers have to know about these things, so they can account for them in their virtual world design.

Designers should have not only a realistic idea of their own place in the system, but also a sound knowledge of the roles of the other people involved in the creation process. Composers don't have to know how to play every instrument in an orchestra, but it's essential that they know how all the instruments sound; designers can't be expected to know how programmers or artists do what they do, but they must be aware of any limitations. If you want every wall of your virtual palace to have a stunning, original fresco on it, you can think again.

To create a virtual world is to create a piece of software. That's not all it is, of course—it's creating a community, a service, a place—but these count for little if there isn't an engine to run the world.

A typical software engineering company is organized along functional lines that cover the following areas:

➤ Company leadership

➤ Sales and marketing

➤ Finance and accounting

➤ Software development, support, and quality assurance (QA)

➤ Operations and information technology (IT)

➤ Human resources (HR)

Some of these may be split into separate sections, for example sales might be distinct from marketing; on the whole, though, the preceding list is fairly uncontentious. Note that normally there is no specific group responsible solely for product specification; the task falls to whoever sources the software, which in many cases could well be the customer.

A typical computer games development company is organized in much the same way, but with some games-specific differences:

➤ An art and animation section is added.

➤ An audio (music, sound effects) section is added (unless outsourced).

➤ QA is expanded, and is formally separated from actual software development.

➤ A (usually small) design group is added; its members will be paid less, but get more fan kudos, than their coworkers.

For developers of massively multiplayer, graphical virtual worlds, the games development model is used except:

➤ The design group is expanded.

➤ The operations group (which maintains and supports the hardware on which the system will run) is expanded.

➤ The support group (which deals with players, both inside and outside the virtual world) is greatly expanded, and is formally separated from actual software development. It will usually reabsorb the QA section.

Designers are only occasionally bothered by the company leadership, HR, IT, and finance/accounting people. They have a dialogue with sales/marketing that may be in balance or lopsided ("This is the kind of world we want you to design" versus "This is the kind of world we want you to sell"[1]). They tell the operations, artwork, and audio experts what needs to be done, but generally leave them to it. They interact mostly with

➤ The programmers (because designers are never specific enough about what they want, except when they're so enthusiastic that they try to tell the programmers how to program[2]).

➤ QA (because testers spot more design flaws than they do programming bugs and operations problems).

➤ Support (because players spot more design flaws than QA people).

➤ Each other (because although this book keeps referring to "the designer" of a virtual world, there's usually a *design team*, led by a *lead designer*).

When work on a new virtual world begins, a *core team* is assembled. For a small world, this could be a single individual performing multiple tasks; indeed, it might never get any bigger. For a large-scale world, though, it is merely the nucleus about which a full-blown development effort will form. A core team consists of the

➤ Producer

➤ Lead designer

➤ Lead programmer(s) (server, client)

➤ Lead artist(s) (environment, inhabitants/characters)

---

1. Marketing people consider themselves to have expert knowledge of what players like and dislike. They may indeed have this knowledge. The friction comes from when they try to tell designers what features should be added/removed/changed to exploit such knowledge.

2. It's particularly important that programmers don't feel that they can *ad lib* features of their own.

There may be two lead programmers because client programming is something best done by people with a background in computer games development, whereas server programming is best done by people with a background in software engineering. Programming is becoming a progressively more specialized field, and programmers expert in one area may need training to work in another.

There may be two lead artists because of the sheer quantity of artwork involved in a graphical virtual world (albeit not when development first starts). Strictly speaking, the "environment artist" is in charge of the concept art—defining the look of the virtual world. The "characters artist" is in charge of the technical side—interfacing with the programmers. Because this usually comes down to issues of animation, that's why they wind up being responsible for characters.

Increasingly, operations and customer service leads are being brought in to the core team, but because their work cannot begin until some time into the development process it's unusual if this occurs in a start-up company.

The Development Process

There are many steps to the development of a virtual world. For smaller worlds with fewer players and different functionality, some steps can be skipped or done in tandem with other steps. To highlight every aspect of the process, however, the description in this chapter is for a large, graphical world. Luckily, designers don't need to know every detail of this—that's the job of the producer—but they do need to have an idea of how it breaks down. Therefore, you'll be relieved to learn that only an overview will be presented here, rather than a how-to guide. If you want to find out more (and to understand why it is that producers are paid twice as much as designers), consult *Developing Online Games: An Insider's Guide*[3] by Bridgette Patrovsky and Jessica Mulligan (for virtual worlds) or *Game Architecture and Design*[4] by Andrew Rollings and Dave Morris (for games in general).

---

3. Bridgette Patrovsky and Jessica Mulligan: *Developing Online Games: An Insider's Guide.* Indianapolis, New Riders Publishing, 2003.

4. Andrew Rollings and Dave Morris: *Game Architecture and Design.* Scottsdale AZ, Coriolis, 2000.

The development of online games has four distinct phases:

- ➤ Pre-production
- ➤ Production
- ➤ Roll out
- ➤ Operation

Let's look at these in turn.

Pre-Production

Pre-production can last as long as six months. The aim is to do all the concept evaluation and project planning necessary to reduce risk in the later stages of development. It's undertaken by members of the core team, in close consultation with one another. In many ways, it's the most exciting part of the project, but it's usually done under time pressure with inadequate resources available, which rather dulls the edge. In particular, a number of important deliverables will have been prepared by the end, all of which will almost certainly have needed more work on them than they actually received.

These deliverables are

- ➤ A visualization document. This is produced first, by the lead designer. Although only a few pages long, it sets the tone for the entire endeavor, asserting the project's mission statement, its philosophy, its goals, its main features, and its look and feel.

- ➤ A design document. Because the designer(s) creates this, I spend much of Chapters 3 through 5 of this book addressing the kind of material that goes into it. For the moment, though, suffice to say it defines things such as the world's background, its architecture, its mechanics (including gameplay), its control mechanisms (how players interact with it), and its integral community support systems[5]. Specifics will be added constantly as development continues.

- ➤ A technical design review, assessing hardware and software requirements. What technologies are needed? What tools (both bespoke and middleware)? The technical design review is often folded into the design document.

---

5. In other words, it looks a lot like the strategy guide that will be sold when the product ships, except with the most boring parts removed.

➤ An art bible, describing the stylistic conventions to be used along with examples illustrating the range of material required. This is so that artists can produce work that is consistent with a single overall look[6].

➤ A production management assessment, which uses the other deliverables to gauge the project's demands. It will include a schedule (with milestones), resource requirement details and some risk assessment. The schedule will be continually updated in the light of how things actually proceed, as opposed to how they're supposed to proceed.

➤ Prototypes to provide proof of concept and to show that potential technical difficulties can be overcome.

Pre-production is primarily a planning phase, therefore the construction of (limited) prototypes might seem to be out of place. Prototypes are necessary partly for commercial reasons—they demonstrate to investors that the team can produce the goods—but they also benefit the team itself. They ensure standards for design, programming, and art have been set, and that source control works. They show that the basic principles will work, and (hopefully) can be integrated. For companies that produce a steady stream of material for different projects, assembly line style, the basic pathways for communicating with the various production centers will also have been tested.

The technical design review addresses basic issues, such as how the server code will be modularized, what network transport layer protocols will be used (TCP/IP versus UDP), how background content will be trickled to clients, and how multiple access options will be incorporated (PC/console, web browser, mobile phone). Additionally, it has to consider topics not directly related to the virtual world at all, primarily back-end systems for login, billing, and so on. The necessary software development tools (including ones for system testing and debugging) must be acquired at this stage, in addition to as many pieces of middleware as are suitable. In particular, even with the typically huge license fees involved, it is usually more cost-effective for a company to buy a database, 3D engine, and billing system than to write its own from first principles[7].

---

6. The artwork bible is often built up incrementally (and even informally) during the production phase, as it isn't always needed this early. This state of affairs isn't likely to last for much longer, though.

7. Programmers may resist using a third-party graphics engine, because every programmer who ever worked in the field thinks they can do it better than what's already out there. Strangely, this self-belief rarely extends to the less fun domains of databases and billing systems.

Whether or not you can acquire useful middleware for world creation and AI scripting is project-dependent, however, because it requires great flexibility. Developers usually like to have their own tame programmers available to make any necessary changes expediently, rather than having to rely on someone else's people to do so at short notice.

The production management assessment covers a wider brief than its name might suggest. The term comes from the computer games industry, where typical products don't need a great deal of support after they hit the stores; their management assessment therefore only needs to cover production. Virtual worlds (whether or not games) do, however, need to be managed after launch—immensely so! The production management assessment for them must also extend through the rollout and into the operation phase. This means it has to consider things such as quality assurance, live team management, community maintenance, content creation, and patching. It's also the place where the battle with the Marketing department starts over the handling of the product's launch.

Production

The *production* phase[8], which lasts between two and three years[9] for a large, commercial virtual world, is when the bulk of the programming and data creation takes place. Code must be produced for the client, the server, and for tools. It all has to be done in order, according to a production schedule[10] set by the producer. Tools are usually written first, because other activities are dependent on them and because some of the code can usually be re-used for the server or client. Tools are required for things such as world generation, artificial intelligence (AI) scripting, and customer service support. It's also a good idea to build some analysis tools, too, so that once the world is running it will be possible to determine what the players, the software, and the hardware are doing without having to ask.

The amount of server-side code needed depends on the chosen architecture. It includes driver functionality at the level of LAN networking (to connect the server to its peers) and communications modules (to connect the server cluster to the Internet). It usually

---

8. Also known as the *implementation* phase.

9. Or less, if the investment money runs out.

10. Or *pipeline*.

includes a mudlib layer, to support the world physics and AI system. Whether it includes a world model layer depends on what the scripting tools produce. If it is to run in multiple incarnations, it will not include any instantiation-specific detail (it would be too hard to make general updates otherwise).

The client-side code will be the home of a major 3D engine plus support for music and audio effects. Communications protocols to connect with the server are obviously necessary, as are software update mechanisms for when the client needs patching (which is an inevitability).

While the programmers are busy programming, the artists are busy creating object models (static and animated) and texture maps, along with other miscellaneous images (for example, for manuals, intro movies, and web sites). The volume of artwork required is so high that it will normally be stored in its own database so that the artists can keep track of it all. Scalability and maintainability issues also arise for graphics[11].

The world itself is constructed using the building tools that the programmers have created, to the specifications of the design document. There is a fair degree of creative freedom involved in this activity[12], which is why specialist designers usually undertake it rather than programmers; it's analogous to the way that animation is generally done by artists, even though programmers created the necessary tools.

Roll Out

Roll out is the most critical phase of development, when all the technologies and assets created are brought together to form a virtual world experience. It formally begins with the *open beta* (test), but has its roots much earlier in the development process.

Testing takes place all the way through development, of course. Programmers will test individual pieces of code, animators will test animations, even designers will run data through models to ensure that what they think will happen has a good chance of being what *will* happen after players are let loose in their handsome creation.

---

11. This is what's supposed to happen, anyway. Unfortunately, artists are often proudly nontechnical and will look for any excuse not to use such a system.

12. The task is known as *level design* in conventional games development terminology, but there's no real industry-standard name for it in virtual world creation. "World-building" is coming into fashion, but is somewhat ambiguous.

When enough of a virtual world is available as an integral environment, a *test server* can be set up and *alpha testing* can begin. This is undertaken by the designers, programmers, and artists themselves, looking for bugs mainly in their own areas of responsibility but also reporting anything else they discover that seems Somehow Wrong. Around now, enlightened developers might invite independent design consultants to take a look, but most aren't enlightened and don't. Folks, the opinions of knowledgeable people from outside the team who haven't been living and breathing it for two years *are* worth having, and worth paying to have. Of course, this does also assume that you'll listen to what they say rather than simply check the "hire consultant" box on the production schedule then move on.

Alpha testing is also the stage at which trained customer support staff can begin their learning process, subjecting the virtual world to the kind of punishment that real players are likely to mete out as they do so.

QA specialists may be brought in (externally or from elsewhere in the company) to perform platform testing—seeing whether the client runs on a representative variety of home computer configurations—but they won't hang around afterwards as virtual worlds are typically much greater in scope than regular computer games and take longer to play through. Given that customer service representatives need to have an in-depth knowledge of the virtual world anyway, it makes sense to provide them with enough QA training that they can perform this task instead, while building their playing skills.

During alpha testing, anything and everything goes as bugs are found, fixed, and their solutions reintegrated into the whole. Eventually, however (hopefully at a point previously scheduled by the producer), the world is stable enough to allow people into it who are not directly involved in the development process. In other words, players.

Initially, only a few outsiders are allowed into the virtual world. The first ones will be those the developers specifically ask to play, either because they are friends[13] or because they are influential yet responsible (or sounded that way on the community message boards). A few others will be signed up from a general call for play-testers, so as to disguise the fact that most of their peers get in through the back door. Thus begins *beta testing*.

---

13. Yes, developers have friends. The rationale for getting them into the beta is that honest opinions are needed from people who can be trusted. Trusted not to mind nepotism, this would be....

At this stage, it's a *closed beta*, because the world is invitation-only. As stability increases, player numbers can be gradually increased by letting in more wannabes from the general call (a technique known as *ramping*). When the barriers are lifted high enough that the testers begin acting like real players, the world is said to be in *live beta*; this may or may not coincide with the moment the world is officially opened up to all-comers for stress-testing—that is, when it enters *open beta*. Because this final stage of testing marks the point of no return, this is when the roll out truly begins.

Usually, computer games go into beta testing as late as possible. Virtual worlds, not really being computer games (despite what many of their developers seem to think), go into beta testing as early as possible. This allows for bugs and exploits to be discovered well before paying customers can leave over them, all the while forging strong community bonds between the beta testers. Some of these people may even come up with decent ideas for improvements[14].

Roll out ends after the launch, when its legacy is passed to the marketing department (which will have had considerable involvement in it already). Later expansion modules may have their own roll outs, of course, as they do the other phases of development.

To summarize, the aim of the roll out period is to launch a virtual world with

- ➤ A seeded community

- ➤ A primed market

- ➤ Balance

- ➤ No bugs

All but the last of these are possible.

Operation

The operation phase[15] begins when people start paying to enter the virtual world. It ends when people stop paying, or when the resources needed to support them would be better employed (that is, make more money) elsewhere.

---

14. They will, however, be minuscule in number compared to the vast hordes that *think* they've had a brilliant idea but are sadly mistaken.

15. Also known as the "commercial exploitation phase" in business school language.

During the operation phase, the original design and development team (the *dev team*) typically hands over control to a new set of developers (the *live team*). The rationale is that the battle-hardened dev team can move on to other projects (say, creating the next expansion), leaving the less experienced live team responsible for the maintenance and long-term improvement of the virtual world. This is not always the case, however; *Dark Age of Camelot*, for example, retained its dev team for the operation phase, rather than putting the very people who knew the project best to work elsewhere.

So what exactly does a live team do? Its tasks include the following:

> ➤ Customer and community support.
>
> ➤ Network and technical support.
>
> ➤ Feature development and enhancement.
>
> ➤ Maintaining overall quality of gameplay in response to player cunning.
>
> ➤ Keeping in step with technology (for example, new platforms, new video cards).
>
> ➤ Occasionally, marketing (the virtual world and its intellectual properties).

The size of the development team for a commercial virtual world varies; generally speaking, the further into the project, the more people are involved. Although some companies may claim that they can produce a world capable of handling 100,000 players with only a designer, a programmer, and a clip art package, the reality is somewhat different. As a rough idea, a year or so into the production phase there will typically be around 30 people in the dev team split 5:10:15 for designers, programmers, and artists/animators.

Why mention this now? Because the live team will be three to four times *larger* than the dev team! It'll have similar numbers of designers and programmers (maybe fewer artists[16]), but add a hundred or more people in customer and community support.

For virtual worlds, the work only *really* begins at the operation phase. Time and time again, this is something that developers fail to understand—especially if they have long-time exposure to the fire-and-forget approach of the regular computer games industry. Virtual worlds, despite their origins, are *not* regular computer games—or necessarily any kind of game at all (what they are instead is discussed in Chapter 6, "It's Not a Game, It's a...").

---

16. For non-3D virtual worlds, such as *Ultima Online*, this could mean no artists at all.

On Architecture

Chapter 1, "Introduction to Virtual Worlds," described the way that virtual world servers are constructed in terms of four different layers of functionality (driver, mudlib, world model, incarnation). This is the breakdown of most interest to designers. However, an understanding of how the rest of the system hangs together is required, at least at an abstract level. That's what's discussed next.

Overall Architecture

Actual architectures differ from developer to developer, but they can almost all be regarded as variations of a single generic approach that emphasizes reliability, scalability, and maintainability. Figure 2.1 illustrates this overall architecture.

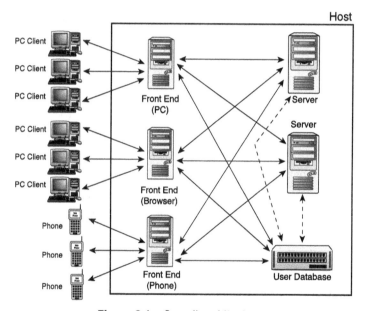

Figure 2.1 Overall architecture.

Here's how it works.

Central to the system is the *user database*. This is a powerful piece of software running on its own, fast machine with lots of storage. It contains records for all the players registered for the virtual world. Before anyone can access content, they must first log in; this means checking with the user database. Other parts of the complete system (not shown in Figure 2.1) for billing, customer service management, and patching also have access to the user database. It's a very important, industrial-strength system, and is therefore usually bought in rather than programmed in-house.

Players have a number of options for connecting to the virtual world. The main one is to use a client from a PC (or console or Macintosh or Linux box—the clients will all present the same interface, so the virtual world neither knows nor cares what operating system they're running under). Players may also connect to the host by using a browser, but not to the same extent as with a bespoke client; although there are text-based virtual worlds that do have good browser-based (Java) clients, no-one has yet been reckless enough to try the same kind of thing for a full-blown 3D graphics-based one. Similarly, mobile phones fall way short of being usable for actual play. However, both browsers and phones can be used to obtain information from a virtual world (for example, news, the virtual weather) or to make changes to standing orders (for example, training regimes, the prices of goods offered for sale). Phones and email can be used to inform players of unfolding events, but they don't usually offer the chance to participate in them.

When an incoming connection is established, it is handled by a *front end*. Front ends can communicate with both their target platform (client, browser/email, mobile phone) and the user database. Figure 2.1 shows the various front ends as separate entities because they're separate processes; however, in practice they may be consolidated onto a single machine or be split across several (for example, by real-world geography).

Individual incarnations of virtual worlds run on server clusters (also known as *shards*[17]). The architecture of shards is described in detail shortly, but for the moment a shard can be regarded simply as a unitary server entity. Having approved a player for access to content, the front end will either query the server to which the content relates (for browser or phone connections), or pass control to the server itself (for client connections). The server does not need to access the user database in order to support the virtual world, because servers deal with characters rather than players. Customer support staff, however, deal with players rather than characters, so they do need to be able to check the user database from within the virtual world. This is sometimes done using a

---

17. This term is an *Ultima Online* fiction to explain how come there are multiple copies of a supposedly single world. It's as if a mirror that reflected the world was shattered into a myriad of tiny pieces, each such shard reflecting the original world but in a slightly different way.

separate database tool that they can invoke while simultaneously using the regular client, but not always. In particular, if the client owns[18] the player's PC, a special *admin client* is needed with the database tools built in.

If this is so, then either the client has to be able to maintain two connections (one to the server, one to the user database) or—more easily—the server itself can issue database requests when required, passing the results back to the client.

Server Architecture

Server clusters implement instances of the virtual world. There may be programmed differences between them (attacking other players might be allowed on one but not on another, for example), but these are generally minimal in form if not effect. The number of servers present in a cluster varies from implementation to implementation, but it's usually around half a dozen or so. The number of clusters also varies, with more clusters being added as a product's popularity increases (*EverQuest* hit 40 server clusters in 2000, averaging around 1,500 players simultaneously on each one at peak time).

Figure 2.2 shows how a server cluster is typically configured.

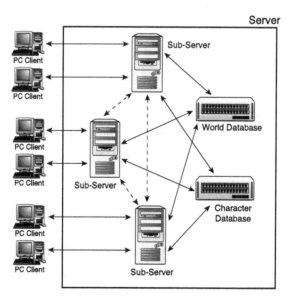

Figure 2.2   Server cluster architecture.

18. In the sense of allowing no other processes to run while the client is running, thereby making life difficult for hackers. It also makes life difficult for non-hackers, though, so clients may settle for merely owning the screen. Players still don't generally appreciate the gesture.

Individual clients are connected to individual sub-servers. Ideally, each sub-server does the same amount of work (which in practice means it handles the same number of players) as every other sub-server. Sub-servers have access to a shared character database[19] that stores the persistent data relating to players' characters on this server[20]. This may or may not be part of a systemwide accounts database for managing player access. For maintainability, a large-scale world generally keeps a separate database for environment data, which may be partitioned into a template database, a scripting language database, and an instantiation database (as described in Chapter 1).

Furthermore, whether these world/environment databases are shared (as shown here) or local to each sub-server depends on how load-balancing works. *EverQuest's* zoning system, for example, can get away with having smaller environment databases that are controlled by individual sub-servers; only the character database needs to be shared with the other sub-servers, for when characters move between zones. This is paid for in other ways, of course, which we will discuss shortly.

The hardware implementation of a server cluster is as a bunch of PCs or beefier hardware (typically running some flavor of Unix) connected over a LAN. Figure 2.2 shows the usual pathways between elements of the server, but in fact any sub-server can talk to any other sub-server should the need[21] arise. Thus, passing players between sub-servers can be achieved either formally (through the databases) or informally (by direct negotiation between machines). Individual sub-servers may also be in contact with the user database, as shown in Fig. 2.1 (but not in Fig. 2.2, so as to prevent its suffering from dashed line death).

I should point out that academics are experimenting with other architectures, particularly the distributed kind much loved by Science Fiction (*Idoru* and *Otherland* both use it, for example). These, and those involving multicast, are not, however, likely to be used beyond academia due to the security and liability issues they raise.

---

19. This was known as the *persona file* in *MUD1*.

20. For virtual worlds where characters can move between incarnations, a single-character database may be necessary that is shared among all virtual worlds (like the user database). On the other hand, if transfers have to be done manually then developers can reasonably charge for the service (this is *EverQuest's* approach; they'd made over a million dollars from it by mid-2002).

21. The precise definition of "need" here depends on the virtual world.

Load Balancing

Fortunately, the arcane subject of load balancing is not something with which designers need concern themselves directly. However, they do need to be aware of the consequences of whatever solution is adopted by the technical experts, especially because they are likely to be consulted on the matter.

Ideally, a virtual world would run on a single, very powerful computer. For textual worlds, this is already the case[22]. Graphical worlds may go the same way[23], but for the moment there are still plenty of things on which newly available computational resources could be spent at the server side:

> ➤ Increasing the number of players present in each incarnation (100,000 players on 50 servers is one thing, but 100,000 players on 1 server is something else).

> ➤ Increasing the level of detail at which the virtual world functions (for example, leaving footprints in the snow that fade as it melts or as new snow falls).

> ➤ Improving the AI of the virtual world's denizens (both in quality and quantity).

It is therefore likely that virtual worlds will soak up whatever additional computing power is thrown their way for quite some time. Inexpensive machines will still be clustered, because it will always cost less to use eight computers of power X than to use one computer of power $8*X$ (although management overheads degrade overall efficiency as new machines are added, which is why no one would use 64 computers of power $X/8$)[24].

So, given that distributed servers are here to stay, how does this affect the designer?

Well, the virtual world is too big to fit on one computer; therefore it must be partitioned over several computers.

---

22. Processor speed finally ceased to be an issue for *MUD2* when I replaced its 33MHz server with a swanky new 50MHz one.

23. *Meridian 59* has a single-server architecture, which limited it to 200 players per incarnation at launch. *Shadowbane* also has a single-server architecture, but runs on somewhat more powerful hardware.

24. Actually, no one has yet tried. Although this kind of parallel processing architecture frequently runs into problems for many business computing applications, it may be that for certain partitionings of virtual worlds it's fine.

Sort of….

If the virtual world were inert, that is, nothing ever happened in it, it wouldn't need any computers at all, it would just sit on a disk pack. It only needs computers when things happen in it. The issue is therefore one of ensuring that *activity* is spread across sub-servers such that they can all cope with the work they have; in other words, the computational load must be shared in a balanced way (hence *load balancing*).

The greatest source of activity in a virtual world is the player community. Every moment that they are in the virtual world, players are interacting with it. Merely moving from one location to another entails informing every other character that can (in the virtual world) see you do so. Yes, some activities are more of a drain on resources than others, but they tend not to be specific to particular playing styles. The issue is the sheer quantity of actions being performed, not the efficiency of individual actions. Load balancing in virtual worlds therefore generally means ensuring that roughly the same number of players is connected to each sub-server in the cluster.

The obvious way to do this would be to assign each incoming player to whichever sub-server has the fewest players. It turns out that it's quite difficult to do this without introducing big overheads, though. To update the instantiation database to reflect an action, records need to be locked to prevent other sub-servers from also changing them at the same time (for example, if two characters attempted to pick up the same object simultaneously). The sub-server needs to lock all records that it could need during an action, perform the tests to ensure that the action is possible, make any necessary update requests, and unlock the records. This is a lot of locking/unlocking. It would be really handy if there were some way to block-book records in the instantiation database for long periods without relinquishing control of them. Are there any types of records for which this could easily be done?

Statistically, most actions performed by players involve movement[25].

---

24. Actually, no one has yet tried. Although this kind of parallel processing architecture frequently runs into problems for many business computing applications, it may be that for certain partitionings of virtual worlds it's fine.

25. It's over 50% for *MUD2*; graphical virtual worlds have an even higher figure—90% or more—because players have to take more steps to get anywhere. This is changing with the arrival of click interfaces, in which you click where you want to go rather than point where you want to go.

The player wants to move their character from A to B, so the sub-server has to lock location B, check if it's empty, if so then move the player into location B, then unlock it. Location A must also be locked, so anyone wanting to do anything to the character that assumes it is in location A (for example, teleport it to location C) will not inadvertently screw up things. Many other common commands (particularly get/drop and those to do with communication) are also location-based.

For these reasons, servers typically partition responsibility for the virtual world along (virtual) geographic lines. A sub-server can lock location records in the instantiation database for extended periods; indeed, if the system is programmed correctly, it doesn't have to lock them at all—it has implicit control by mere virtue of the fact that none of the other sub-servers do.

To summarize the argument so far: We want to spread the players fairly evenly across sub-servers, but the obvious way would introduce too many overheads on database access; a far more efficient way to do it is to partition by geographical location. The question is: Would using this partitioning model give us load balancing?

The answer is that yes, it would. How, exactly, depends on the virtual world.

There are essentially two approaches: fixed load balancing and dynamic load balancing. The former, exemplified by *EverQuest*, assigns a predefined geographical location (a zone) to one sub-server[26]; the latter, exemplified by *Asheron's Call*, moves responsibility for geographical locations between sub-servers.

Fixed load balancing:

➤ Is easier to implement.

➤ Can partition the instantiation database and keep it local to the sub-server, for greater efficiency.

➤ Allows the client to figure out in advance what texture maps will be needed and preload them into graphics card memory.

---

26. It should be pointed out that sub-servers can handle more than one zone at once.

Dynamic load balancing:

➤ Has seamless terrain (you can see to the horizon[27]).

➤ Has boundaries that are not physical (monsters chasing you don't get stuck at zone edges).

➤ Balances the load better.

What does all this mean for design?

It's an example of where technology imposes constraints. For fixed load balancing, zones can be created with greater individuality: The 'physical' barriers between them allow for radical change. Players can cross from one to another and *expect* to see something different on the other side. For a seamless system, sudden changes have to make more sense or they'll seem out of place.

The fact that content such as monsters can't cross zone boundaries means that players will use different tactics in such a world than they would in one where there was always the possibility that a creature they had royally annoyed could pursue them relentlessly. Victorian London's police forces couldn't (legally) cross precinct boundaries: Jack the Ripper would commit a murder in one police district and then run into another where the police were not allowed to follow; if they could have followed, he would have had to rethink his getaway strategy.

Zoned worlds have something of a problem with *flash crowds* (people appearing instantly in the same vicinity in response to interesting news; the term comes from a 1973 Larry Niven short story[28]). Most of the time, each sub-server will be handling similar numbers of players. However, sometimes something happens that causes everyone to want to be in the same general locale[29]. Maybe it's a rare spawning of an impressive dragon, or a social event such as a wedding or guild rally. Whatever, all of

---

27. Invisible cross-server boundaries are also possible with tessellated worlds such as *Ultima Online* that have fixed load balancing. However, odd things may happen when interactions occur over server boundaries (for example, shooting arrows across them). In *Asheron's Call*, which has dynamic load balancing, characters that interact are moved to the same server so as to reduce interserver communication confusion.

28. Larry Niven, *Flash Crowd*. Larry Niven, *The Flight of the Horse*. New York, Ballantine, 1973.

29. If this is very focused, the same problem can afflict seamless worlds, too. It's less frequent than for zoned worlds, but because of this it can be harder to handle when it does happen.

a sudden more people want access to a server than it can handle. The designer has to decide what to do when this happens. Do they simply show a "zone full" message if people try to enter it? Do they let them in and leave Customer Service to handle the resulting complaints about lag? Do they organize the virtual world such that it would be counter to its fiction for everyone to want to be in the same zone?

Dark Age of Camelot partitions its player base into three "realms." Members of one realm can't enter territory belonging to members of another realm. They can enter a no-man's land between two realms, however, which is where realm versus realm combat takes place. The upshot of this is that unless there is a serious skewing of the *DAoC* player base, only a third of the players online will usually be present in any one realm. That's excellent for load balancing. What's more, realms are aggregations of zones, they're not zones in themselves. Each realm is made up of 13 outdoor zones (64K by 64K squares) plus five dungeons plus one city. There's no reason why a sub-server has to handle zones from only one realm; if (for some reason) 75% of the players are all in one realm, the sub-servers handling that realm will automatically have less load from the other (sparser) realms they're controlling.

Players of *EQ* notice how the sub-servers take responsibility for zones, but players of *DAoC* don't. Why not? Because of the latter game's world *design*.

Other Things Happen

Although players are the main source of the load on virtual worlds' supporting hardware, they are not the only one. Things can happen whether or not players are present. Some of it is mechanistic: The virtual world's sun rises and sets, its weather comes and goes, all irrespective of whether there are players around. For a highly detailed world, this could amount to considerable work (a breeze rustles individual leaves on a tree, one of which falls off to land in a stream that carries it lazily to a river and thence to the sea). Virtual worlds of this complexity are some way off at the moment, though.

What's more of an issue is the presence in the virtual world of virtual creatures. These are commonly known as *mobiles*[30] (*mobs* for short), and they represent the monsters and non-player characters that inhabit the virtual world. They are discussed in more

---

30. From *MUD1*, "mobile objects." I called them that because creatures moving in a controlled but unpredictable way are like the kind of "mobiles" that hang from ceilings. Well, I was in kind of a hurry...

detail in Chapter 4, "World Design," but what concerns us about them right now is that they need to behave in a believable manner. This requires artificial intelligence techniques, which gobble up computational resources like nothing else. Even simple path-finding is an insatiable consumer of CPU cycles. It would be great to have a virtual city with 100,000 virtual inhabitants, each making real-time decisions as to how to spend their virtual lives. We may have to wait some time before we get this, though.

If a designer wants more mobiles in the virtual world than the servers can handle, they have to offer solutions for managing these mobiles. The classic answer is to suspend processing of those mobiles whose actions would not be witnessed directly by players. What causes AI load is not the *number* of mobiles on a sub-server, but the number that are *active* at any one time.

Consider a group of goblins in a village. With no players in the vicinity, there's no point in having them do anything. Sure, a sub-server can move them around a bit when it's not unduly loaded, but players get priority. Only when a group of adventurers shows up is it time to activate the goblins so they can behave intelligently and give the players a run for their money. When the players leave, the dead goblins can respawn and wait for the next batch of adventurers.

Designers who want more mobiles than the programmers tell them they can have might be tempted to use this proximity activation approach. They have to realize, though, that every decision they make has consequences.

In this particular case, the consequences are on causality. If a tree falls in a desert, does it make a noise? Using proximity activation, it would never fall in the first place.

Consider a second goblin raiding party. It emerges from its camp, kills some villagers' sheep, and then returns home with the spoils. The villagers get angry and offer to pay players to kill the goblins.

It's an evening's quest.

It's an evening's quest that would never happen if the goblins stayed in their camp until a player happened upon them.

Yes, of course, plenty of ways around this instantly present themselves, but that's not the point: What's important is that the designer has to recognize that there may be a problem in the first place. Would your proposed solutions to the problem come with problems of their own? Would you have thought about that if I hadn't asked?

Virtual world design is about *consequences*.

The Client/Server Model

The server embodies the virtual world; the client translates it into a form the player can comprehend. Because the client is the player's window on the virtual world, designers have a lot to say about its look and feel. Much of this is a matter of taste and convention, though, and will therefore not be discussed here. Clearly, it does make a difference if your proposed spell-casting system is too complicated to be implemented for mouse and keyboard[31], but if this kind of thing isn't obvious to you, then you've no business being a designer anyway.

There are, however, engineering considerations specific to the implementation of virtual worlds that impact directly on the virtual world itself. These are unavoidable, and designers must be aware of them.

To illustrate: In theory, the same virtual world could be presented using different *skins*, so whereas one player might see a defense robot discharging an energy weapon, another might see a wizard wielding a wand. This is something that players would find novel, but it presents a major challenge to designers. Few genres map onto each other to this extent, so compromises would have to be made.

As it happens, this particular example is a red herring because the amount of artwork necessary to support just one genre, let alone two, is considerable. The benefits aren't worth the cost. Textual worlds are easier to reskin than graphical ones in this respect, of course, but have less reason to want to do it[32]. In practice, using skins for graphical

---

31. Well, only for spell-casters. There's no theoretical reason why different character classes can't have interfaces customized for what they spend most of their time doing.

32. Translation schemes for moving functionally equivalent objects between differently themed parts of a virtual world (and even between virtual worlds) do exist, however.

clients means altering the look and layout of the client's interface, not the look of what it displays of the virtual world. Hanging different curtains doesn't change the view through the window.

It turns out that there are only two issues relating to the client/server relationship that have concrete effects on the design of virtual worlds, but both of them are very important: synchronization and security.

Synchronization

It takes time for information to travel between the client and the server. It takes time for the server to execute commands. During this time, the client has to maintain its display of the virtual world. What it shows may not, therefore, be a true representation of what the server defines to be the current world state: The two aren't synchronized. In the real world, the sun might have spontaneously exploded 19 seconds ago, but you're not going to find out for another eight minutes. In a virtual world, someone may have quit four seconds before you loosed an arrow at him.

Lag due to server load can be addressed by buying in faster hardware and by optimizing code. There's little that can be done about lag due to communications, though. Even with a perfect connection, the speed of light through glass[33] is such that someone in Sydney playing in a virtual world with servers in San Diego[34] would experience a delay of over 0.06 seconds in each direction with a direct cable connection. The fact that their communication has to go through routers and isn't in a straight line brings it up to more like a third of a second. Throw in an analogue modem and you can add another third of a second. Lag happens.

Designers have to account for this by making nothing too time-sensitive. In a regular computer game, players can be expected to make timed runs through windmill sails or giant steam pistons or pendulum scythes, but in a virtual world there's no guarantee that when the player sees a gap on their client the server is actually implementing one. For this reason, players can never be called on to make reflex actions (although their *characters* can be), which means virtual worlds have little or no *twitch*.

---

33. Approximately 197,000 kilometers per second.

34. Approximately 12,083 kilometers from Sydney at sea level.

Timed actions are possible, but the window for success needs to be at least four seconds in duration or some players are going to miss it while believing they hit it. Nevertheless, improvements in Internet reliability have led to attempts to bring the kind of response times common in first-person shooters to virtual worlds: *Planetside*[35] is the best-known pioneer.

Precise timing issues aside, virtual worlds are fairly robust in the face of lag. The exact moment that a player initiates an action is rarely important; when players agree to do something "at the same time," they know it's a fuzzy concept. As long as designers avoid doing anything deliberately that requires speed, there's rarely a problem.

Although most of the lag that players endure is fairly constant across a connection, not all of it is. Sometimes, lag can be intermittent: Things can work fine then suddenly halt for no apparent reason. This kind of lag is actually due to bandwidth issues that cause a service provider to invoke some kind of resource allocation scheme. It doesn't matter how good your broadband connection is, if your ISP isn't sending you the packets, then you're not going to see them. This kind of lag can last several seconds, whereupon all the packets that are buffered up are dispatched at once and service resumes as normal.

Clients expect regular packets of data from the server to update their local state. Most of the time, these arrive in a timely manner. However, it only takes someone using the same router as you to start downloading copious quantities of pornography and packets will inevitably be delayed. What does the client do in such circumstances?

The easiest solution is to do nothing. Just sit and wait until packets arrive, then update them in sequence. The problem with this is that the virtual world effectively freezes for the player until the updates arrive. The player can try to do things, but gets no response until the packets start flowing again. This isn't always a problem in textual worlds, but it looks very disturbing in graphical ones.

Most graphical clients therefore use a predictive model, whereby they continue moving objects along whatever course they were taking the last time information was available. If a character is running east, the chances are that when an update packet finally arrives it will still have the client running east, so the screen will be right without ever having frozen. Predictive models work well when their predictions are correct, which

---

35. http://planetside.station.sony.com/

(fortunately) is most of the time. However, there are problems when they're wrong. If the character who was running east had stopped and turned north, there could be a serious discrepancy between their actual position and the position the delayed client is displaying them at.

To correct failed predictions, there are two approaches. The traditional way is to use the new information and just forget about the predictions. This results in an effect called *warping*, which originated in *Air Warrior*. Players would be on the tail of an enemy plane when suddenly it would disappear from their sights to rematerialize instantly a short distance away like it had made a hyperspace jump. Players even found ways to induce it, so they could plan the reappearance to gain a tactically superior position.

More modern clients apply gradual translations to the displayed position of an object so that it moves to its correct position smoothly (if a little more slowly and still looking highly suspicious).

For designers, this means that not only can't they use relative time (in three seconds) but they can't use relative space (dead ahead) either. The client might think a particular coordinate is slightly to the left of the player whereas the server knows it's slightly to the right. Commands that need coordinates therefore have to use absolute ones rather than relative ones. Again, when designers are aware of the problem and don't call for players to follow complex instructions in mazes or anything, virtual worlds are usually sturdy enough to cope; a little error in absolute positioning is fine. They do have to be aware first, though.

There is a special case, however, in that sometimes players want to do things to other players at a distance, for example, shoot an arrow at them. In this situation, not only might the archer's position be at odds with the server's definitive version, but so might the target's. The client knows that the player wants to shoot an arrow *at* a character, but doesn't know for sure that character's coordinates. The designer must decide whether the command is "shoot at a target" or "shoot at a location" (which hopefully contains the target). If the arrow has a timed flight (and if it's modeling a real arrow it certainly ought to), the potential for error increases even more.

Bleah!

Graphical virtual worlds are presented as being continuous. Although characters might actually occupy integral coordinates, they are animated such that they move smoothly between them, thereby giving the impression that they at times occupy the spaces "between" the coordinates.

Textual worlds can be continuous too, but they are usually contiguous. Locations can represent an area rather than a point, and several characters can occupy such locations[36] without causing an anomaly. Restricting horizontal movement to eight compass points means that using relative direction in such virtual worlds is a definite possibility. True to form, there are textual worlds that allow players to use both absolute (north, northeast, east, and so on) and relative (forward, ahead right, right, and so on) directions for movement, with the room description format (absolute or relative) also under player control. Graphical games can take relative coordinates from a client, but they have to transmit them as absolute ones.

A common mistake among inexperienced client authors is to take all this with a pinch of salt. So what if the client and server have slightly different ideas as to what is where pointing in whatever direction? There isn't going to be *that* much divergence. Okay, so maybe *occasionally* you see someone run through a solid windmill sail because there is a gap on their client, but that's hardly a show-stopper. Let the *client* decide if an arrow hits, rather than putting the burden on the server. There might be a few hits that should be misses and misses that should be hits, but it'll all even out over time.

This brings us neatly to the issue of security.

Security

Your client software *will* be hacked. For some virtual worlds (such as those with no game aspect to them), this won't necessarily matter. For the rest, it matters a great deal.

At the very least, it means that all packets sent from the client to the server have to be checked to see if they make sense. Error-correction at the hardware and transport layers should ensure that what arrives at the server is what was sent by the client, so why waste time checking for nonsense that isn't going to come? Well, the fact is that the server may not be talking to a *bona fide* client. It could be talking to a piece of code a

---

36. Which are called *rooms.*

player has written to masquerade as a client or to insert data into the client's packet stream. If the server receives nonsense but has no way of handling it, what happens then? Has someone acquired an ability to crash the server?

That's if it's even your server. Sometimes, groups of players will write their own server and persuade clients to speak to that instead. They can then design and play their own world in preference to yours—and all for free[37]!

Virtual world programmers don't have to make life easy for hackers—they can use encryption, own the screen, make very infrequent identity checks that packet-sniffing software may miss—but eventually their code will be reverse-engineered and people will figure out what's going on. Then they'll change it[38].

Important: Absolutely *no* decisions with regard to what happens in a virtual world can be delegated to a client. *No* decisions. That's *no* decisions.

Air Warrior's first client performed the necessary calculations to determine if a shot hit or missed. It was considered unfair for players to line up their sights exactly on a target, pull the trigger, but miss because their client was showing the target to be somewhere the server didn't think it was. All very laudable, until someone wrote a hack for the client such that whenever you fired, it sent a packet claiming you'd hit whichever plane was *closest* to your sights—irrespective of whether it was actually *in* them. Kesmai had to bring out a patch to fix it.

Programmers should *never* put world-critical code in the client. If they do, it can mean major, big-time fraud. Designers only need worry about this if they have to come up with a strategy for repairing the damage should it go undetected for too long (for example, groups of players giving themselves money and spending it in inflation-causing amounts).

Designers do have to worry about things such as automated play. Anything that requires similar actions to be performed repeatedly is usually easy to automate—it doesn't even need a client hack in many cases, as there are off-the-shelf tools that will

---

37. Examples include *EQemu* (http://www.eqemu.net/) and *EthernalQuest* (http://www.ethernalquest.com) for *EverQuest*, and *Sphere* (http://www.sphereserver.com/), *UOX* (http://www.uox3dev.net/) and *Epsilon* (http://www.epsilon.escend.net/) for *Ultima Online*. See *The Smithys Anvil* (http://www.smithysanvil.com/) for more.

38. This is what developers mean by the term *arms race*.

do it. *Ultima Online*'s craft system was so boring that players were overjoyed when they discovered macro software intended for typists that enabled them to save their index fingers from repetitive stress injury. Computers can generally issue commands faster than players, too: Someone wrote their own client for *MUD1* that stuffed commands down the line so quickly that 30 seconds after having started to play, the automated character would be standing with arms full of vicious weapons and other useful kit, while everyone else was still pretty well empty-handed.

Designers should therefore avoid calling for anything that involves doing something again and again and again with no respite (and that can include movement). If you really want an action to take a lot of time, let characters do it as a background task while their players are offline. If speed is occasionally important (for example, for dramatic reasons), insist that the server programmers institute delays between processing the commands from any one player[39]. If some level of searching or exploration is required (for example, for a puzzle), put in moving obstacles or traps so a program can't easily find a solution using a brute-force method.

People usually want to automate tasks that are tedious. If you design something that you think many players might like to automate, consider the possibility that it could be intrinsically uninteresting. For example, players will come to understand a virtual world far better if they make their own maps, so a designer might want to encourage them to do so. However, the actual mechanics of mapping are so mind-numbing that there are auto-mapping programs around (for textual worlds) that try every exit from every room until they have produced a complete map that can then go on a web site. If you were hoping to stimulate a climate of exploration by holding back on embedded mapping tools in the client, it didn't work.

There are other ways in which wily players can subvert a client to put themselves at an advantage. Consider the case of a character executing a 360° turn. The client must be in close, rapid contact with the server to ensure that the necessary information is at hand to display the world as the sweep progresses. If it weren't, then the player could be looking at a half-blank screen or seeing characters pop up in the middle of the view that weren't there an instant earlier. However, as was pointed out earlier, the client can't usually rely on a super-fast connection to the server.

---

39. Actually it's more fashionable not to enforce delays, but have the server—or even other clients—perform spot checks to see if someone is cheating. Needless to say, if clients get to report who is cheating, sooner or later they'll be hacked so as to accuse innocent players of doing it.

To solve this problem, the *EverQuest* server was configured to send the client more information than it strictly needed; if a player wanted to turn, then the positions of nearby objects would already be known and could be displayed without lag effects. To this end, the client was told the locations of all objects and players in the vicinity—not just those that character could "see"—along with other handy tidbits, such as what they were carrying and how many hit points they had. The geography also was kept permanently available on the player's PC.

This was an efficient approach, in that anyone could rotate or otherwise change the camera angle with impunity without suffering staggered images. However, a number of players soon realized that if the information was present, it could be displayed whether or not it was in actual use. They wrote programs to give radar-like readouts of everyone and everything in the neighborhood. No longer did mobiles attack them from behind; no longer did they need to guess which were carrying loot. One such program, *ShowEQ*, was so useful a tool that Verant felt compelled to ban its use (leading to one of its many public relations disasters[40]).

It doesn't even have to be the client that's hacked. *Ultima Online* used the PC graphics card to control brightness, which meant that opportunistic players could override the client (by turning up the gamma correction) to get full daylight when they were supposed to be in total darkness. Great for ambushes!

If at all possible, designers should be adamant that no items of data are sent to the client that convey any information beyond what the player's character is entitled to know. Client programming being the inexact science that it is, however, chances are some additional information will have to be sent in advance, even if it's only texture maps on a CD-ROM. Designers should be appraised of this in advance, so they can adjust their designs accordingly. If you know that players are going to figure out where all nearby objects are anyway, give that information to them officially and be sure it's never of much use. Have new mobiles that teleport in from nowhere, if you want to keep them on their toes.

---

40. Verant changed the end user license agreement to give them the right to search your home PC for programs that in their view could interfere with the proper running of *EverQuest*. The ensuing full-scale revolt helped them to reconsider.

Okay, so, your programmers assure you that nothing is in the client that should be in the server, except for a few elements that you can design around. That's the security issue sorted, then!

Aw, you know it isn't. Your design itself could have security problems.

For example, suppose (having decided that fixed prices are a bad idea) you make your economy determine the price of goods based on local supply and demand. Suppose also that it allows people to buy and sell in bulk at the price for a single item. Normally, this wouldn't be a problem: If there are 300 swords for sale, it doesn't matter whether you buy one at 20 UOC[41] or 10 at 20 UOC each. The price will rise the fewer swords are left, which is what you want—having bought 10 swords, the new price might be 22 UOC. You'd make the buy-back price be much lower than the sale price, so that anyone trying to sell back 10 swords they just bought for 200 UOC would receive maybe only 110 UOC for them instead of 220 UOC.

So far, so good.

What happens, though, for high-cost, low-production items? Maybe the local diamond mine unearths only five diamonds a week. When all five are available, the price at the diamond mart is 1,000 UOC; if only one is available, the price soars to 4,000 UOC. If none are available, the supply is exhausted. In that situation, how much could a single diamond be sold back to the diamond mart for? Even with a 50% mark-down on the purchase price, it would still be at least 2,000 UOC. So, if someone were to buy all five diamonds at once for 1,000 UOC each, then sell them back all at once for 2,000 UOC each, they'd make 5,000 UOC each transaction. Your design has given them an engine for generating however much money they like! Augh!

When something is allowed by the virtual world but the designers wished it wasn't, it's known as an *exploit*. Exploits—design bugs—can ruin a virtual world[42] overnight.

---

41. Units of Currency (UOC)

42. They can, of course, occur in any kind of simulation software, they're just at their worst in virtual worlds. I found an exploit similar to the diamond example in a single-player trading game (Ascaron's *The Patrician*) that finally allowed me to beat it after five years of trying. They took it out for *The Patrician II*.

Exploits aside, there are plenty of other ways that players can subvert a designer's well-meaning intentions. Identity theft—pretending to be someone else in real life—is fairly easy but is hardly the responsibility of the designer[43]. Character theft—pretending to be someone else's character in a virtual world—should not be easy, because it *is* the responsibility of the designer. In particular, if two players can use the same name for their characters then it's partly the designer's fault if one of them subsequently successfully pretends to be the other. This "name problem" is discussed in some depth in Chapter 3.

So, your design will have bugs. Players will find these and wring every advantage from them that they can. Even if they report them immediately, they'll feel you owe them for their honesty. So what do you do?

You can't prevent exploits, but you can take steps to minimize their number and impact. Detection and recovery are of critical importance. If possible, *log everything*. In *MUD2*, players would regularly complain that line noise[44] had severed their connection to the game and led to their character's demise. Instituting a "log everything" policy (player input/output transcripts and all server decisions) solved the problem at a stroke—90% of the time, players were exposed as having been active right up until the moment the dragon incinerated them or the wolf bit off their head or whatever, and therefore their impassioned pleas for resurrection amounted to cheating.

This degree of logging is not always possible for virtual worlds that use a lot of bandwidth, for example graphical game worlds. There are two approaches to it, but neither is particularly satisfactory: store events (from which exact circumstances can be reconstituted) or store client communications (which gives the player's actual viewpoint). Both of these create huge quantities of hard-to-search data. Customer service administrators may be able to *snoop*[45] on players as situations unfold, which can partially alleviate the problem, but if they arrive at a scene too late then the only alternative to logs is the presence of impartial witnesses (like there'll be many of *those*).

---

43. In 2000, I spent several months building a reputation in *EverQuest* despite not having played the game at any point during that period. Someone made out they were me, and other people believed them.

44. In the old days, modems did not have hardware error-correction. A crackly phone line meant crackly data.

45. Copy output from a player's screen to their own screen, not necessarily with the knowledge of that player.

Detecting possible bugs and exploits is important, but it isn't itself enough. When it transpires that something really has gone unfortunately wrong, the ability to correct the consequences of it should absolutely *always* be available (even if it means a whole-sale reinstallation of the character database from a timed back-up). An incomplete ability to discover when things are going awry is inconvenient; an incomplete ability to recover damaged data is incompetent[46].

Part of the satisfaction of virtual world design lies in seeing your creation evolving, with things occurring within it that you hadn't anticipated but which make perfect sense. One of the less fortunate consequences, though, is that some of what happens you'll almost certainly wish hadn't, and will have to fix. The more contingency plans you have in place, the better, but you'll never be able to cover everything.

Still, if you want the unpredictable, you can't complain when you get it.

Theory and Practice

How virtual worlds *ought* to be put together and how they *are* put together are two different things. You can spend 30 hours in a classroom learning how to drive a car, but fifteen minutes at the wheel is going to teach you a whole lot more.

At times, the practice is more useful than the theory.

This section discusses some of the things that look like they should be important, but aren't, along with those that look like they shouldn't be important, but are. It's a bit of a mixed bag, but is fairly representative of the kind of hidden depth (or lack of same) that only becomes apparent when you actually develop a virtual world. There are plenty more, but I'll leave them for you to discover them for yourself; as I said, you'll learn more by doing than by reading about it.

Modes

When you start up your web browser, what page does it point at? Surprisingly, for most people the answer is "whatever my ISP set it to when I installed its software." Their first view of the World Wide Web every morning is what their ISP shows them.

---

46. And if players realize you don't have accurate snapshots of events, that's when the problems *really* begin.

Virtual worlds have many ways to let players customize their experiences. In a textual world, for example, some people want full room descriptions the whole time, and some want short ones the whole time. There are commands that let players choose for themselves which of these to go with. However, one option will be the default, and that's the one that newbies will use. In *MUD1*, the first time you entered a room you saw its full description, and on later visits you saw the short version. This helped stop newbies from getting lost. Later, they would use exclusively verbose descriptions when making accurate maps and exclusively brief descriptions at all other times, but later is later. When they started, they got the default, and the default said, "Explore!"

Defaults set the tone of virtual worlds, because all newbies play under them. As they become more experienced, they'll inevitably customize some of the settings; most options, however, will stay at the default. Thus, the designer's choice of defaults can have long-term influences on how a virtual world is perceived. Defaults are more important than they look.

To illustrate this, let's take a look at *modes*, because in a sense they establish what the world is "about."

All virtual worlds assume a hardware device for entering freeform data; it's usually a keyboard. The player types some text, hits return, and—what? It depends on the current mode. In a textual world, the line is usually interpreted as a command.

```
open door
north
get book
```

This would be *command mode*.

In a graphical world, the line is usually interpreted as speech.

```
Follow me!
What happened? You were supposed to be following!
Hey! That's mine!
```

This would be *conversation mode*. Chat rooms usually default to conversation mode, too.

So where's the hidden depth here? It's not like you can't act in conversation mode or speak in command mode.

When a newbie enters a world for which the default is command mode, the message that the world is sending them is that this is a place where you can *do* things: It emphasizes freedom to act on the world. If the default is conversation mode, the message is this is a place where you can *communicate*: It emphasizes freedom to interact with other players. You might expect, therefore, that players of textual worlds do more and players of graphical worlds say more.

Actually, for graphical virtual worlds the default is to use the less-than-freeform mouse most of the time, forcing a greater distinction between limited doing and unlimited saying. If you want to talk or attempt anything complicated, you have to stop playing to do so. This is sound advice for crowd control, but somewhat dissatisfying for the individuals in the crowd so controlled.

The designer sets the default mode. The default mode shapes the style of play. The designer can therefore encourage or discourage a style of play by changing the default mode. Thus, a simple, almost throwaway design decision can have a long-term influence on a virtual world's ethos.

Note that although the main choice is between command mode and conversation mode, there are other modes used in virtual worlds. The convention has evolved that the first character in a line is used to switch modes for the remainder of that line. There will often be an option to turn a mode on/off until further notice, but no standard syntax for this has yet emerged.

Table 2.1 shows the most common modes in use, along with the (sometimes conflicting) options for the leading characters used to switch them on.

Table 2.1   Common Modes

Mode	Leading Characters	Explanation
Command	> / .	Input is a direct command to the server.
Conversation	' " `	Input is a parameter to the say command.
Coding	@	Input is a scripting language command.
Acting	; :	Input is a parameter to the pose/act/emote command.
Help	?	Input is a parameter to the help command.
Switch	/ \ $	Input is for the client or front-end, rather than the server.

Virtual Reality

Read a selection of Science Fiction stories about virtual worlds, and you'll soon discover that the following are inevitabilities:

> ➤ True intelligence will emerge from the hideously complex machinations performed by the virtual world engine, with unnerving consequences for human morality.

> ➤ Unscrupulous people will transfer their consciousnesses into hardware in order to live forever, muahahaha.

> ➤ Virtual worlds will be experienced through virtual reality interfaces so good that the virtual will be indistinguishable from the real.

The first two of these are not of immediate interest to the designers of virtual worlds, being somewhat distant prospects at the moment. Virtual reality (VR), however, while as yet nowhere near the quality envisaged in speculative novels, is far more accessible. Why not create a virtual world with a virtual reality interface? It would attract media attention, if nothing else.

For a virtual world with a closed user base, a VR interface is indeed a reasonable proposition. A small academic research community or a large industrial or military training establishment would be able to experiment with the idea and get fruitful, worthwhile results.

For an open user base, though, VR isn't yet an option. It's simply not value-added enough for developers at the moment, that is, the costs of putting it in outweigh the benefits. Until the technology improves[47] and the installed base reaches some critical mass (whether because of computer games, 3D movies, 3D video cameras, or something else), VR would be available to but a few, lucky or wealthy players.

There is an argument, though, that VR access to a major virtual world could *itself* be enough of a draw that people would be willing to acquire the necessary hardware to play. Of course, for this to happen VR would have to bring something quite special to the virtual world experience.

---

47. Minimally, it mustn't induce blinding headaches in its users.

So what would that be? It depends on the set-up, of course, but in the first instance the chances are that a basic VR kit would mean full-vision headsets with surround sound and orientation detection, plus gloves incorporating movement sensors and some degree of positive tactile feedback. Using such an interface, the virtual world could

- ➤ Let you see it in 3D[48]

- ➤ Let you hear it in 3D

- ➤ Tell in what direction you're looking

- ➤ Tell what your hand is doing

- ➤ Deliver sensation to your fingers

- ➤ Accept speech input

What advantages would accessing a virtual world through such a VR interface confer over the traditional mouse and/or keyboard approach?

There's some convenience in being able to control what you see and do by means of head and hand movements, countered only by the slight inconvenience in having to sport the equipment needed to support it. Nevertheless, it's unlikely that a player using a keyboard and mouse would be at a serious disadvantage compared with someone kitted out in the modest VR set-up described here, at least in terms of their ability to control their character in a virtual world.

Speech as an input form seems, at first glance, to be an attractive proposition. It wouldn't be all that great in command mode, because speech recognition software still has a long way to go before it could be of genuine utility. In conversation mode, though, it would be much more effective—but only if it could be completely disguised. Again, although voices can easily be distorted using today's technology, it's likely to be some time before they can be altered so well that they don't sound altered. But why is some form of disguise necessary anyway?

One of the main attractions of virtual worlds is the ability to be whoever you want to be; anything in the virtual world that anchors you to who you are in the real world is

---

48. Stereoscopically. As pointed out in Chapter 1, for virtual worlds the term "3D graphics" usually means that the graphics are displaying something that is 3D, not that the image so displayed is itself 3D. A VR headset could be expected to present separate images to each eye, giving a much truer sense of 3D than does a flat plane.

a disincentive. When you hear an elf in the middle of a sylvan wood speaking a New York accent, or a mighty-thewed, bare-chested barbarian who sounds like a school-marm, sadly reality is intruding a little too much. If voices aren't disguised, players aren't disguised, and then the virtual world is just another aspect of the real one.

3D vision and sound, and to some extent tactile feedback, are the real gold for VR. They make the virtual world more persuasive, which helps players immerse themselves in their (virtual) surroundings. The change won't be to everyone's taste—some people are always going to prefer text, for example, on account of how it speaks to the imagination rather than to the senses—but it'll help anyone who gets on well with graphics[49]. That said, flat images are already quite capable of immersing players into a virtual world, and they don't have to cut off great swathes of the real world to do it. Players *like* being immersed in virtual worlds, and will happily ignore negative cues if they get sufficient positive ones that they can will themselves to suspend their disbelief. You don't have to trick them into it; they'll go for it anyway. Giving them more 'realistic' visual and auditory stimulation will provide additional signals, but are they mere luxury? Designers can and do encourage immersion by many other means[50].

So, would VR merely amount to a marketing ploy to attract newbies?

Cynics might suggest that this is all that adding graphics to virtual worlds ever did, but even they would have to concede that it worked. The allegation is unfair anyway, in that a graphical interface to a virtual world does actually make a tangible difference. If, for example, in a textual virtual world you happened on a gathering of 50 characters, you'd have to read 50 names to see if there was anyone there with whom you wanted a chat. Spotting a friend from among 50 faces in a graphical virtual world is far, far quicker[51]. Would a VR interface add some genuinely useful feature that flat graphics and two-point stereo don't?

---

49. Well, almost anyone. If you only have sight in one eye, 3D visual effects aren't going to impress you. Similarly, if (like me) you can't tell where sounds are coming from, expensive 3D auditory set pieces are going to pass unnoticed.

50. Chapter 3 features an in-depth discussion of the concept of immersion in virtual worlds.

51. I should point out that long-term players of textual worlds can acquire the ability to do something similar—glance at a list of names and pick out a friend without having to read (or even speed-read) anything. It's a skill that comes only with time, however, whereas face-recognition is something humans learn in infancy (if indeed it's not already hardwired into the brain at birth). Of course, this point about facial recognition would carry more weight if people didn't all choose the same faces and outfits so everyone ends up relying on the names above characters' heads anyway.

Frankly, probably not. Unless the virtual world has very counter-intuitive physics (for example, the further away an object is, the bigger it appears), you're not going to learn much more about it from experiencing it in 3D than you can already figure out from the perspective and motion conventions of 2D.

Unless...

Unless designers can exploit the extra capabilities that a VR interface imparts. Instead of clicking where you want your arrow to land, you raise and point your bow, then release the string—with true depth to your vision, you can now judge trajectories. Instead of running to attack the lightly armed man, you flee—you can now see he's a giant. Instead of walking in the gaps between well-spaced trees, you push through dense forest—the tree trunks no longer merge to look like fences when they're close together. VR really does offer new prospects.

Unfortunately, virtual world design is not yet sufficiently developed to make the best of this. Game designers still have to make more use of sound as a gameplay element, so it seems unlikely that virtual world designers will successfully embrace VR the moment it becomes available. There may be some centerpieces that show off the technology, but that's likely to be all. When you catch a movie on TV and notice that people seem to be pointing or throwing things toward the camera a lot, pretty soon you realize you're watching an old 3D movie in 2D. Directors never really came to grips with 3D in movies. Will designers fare better when VR comes to virtual worlds? Or will it be a case of, "Aww, man, not the guys with pikes again!"?

The theory is good, but the practice may take some time to measure up to it.

Extensibility

Virtual worlds are designed such that they can be extended over time.

Why? To add content, to correct imbalances, to allow for more simultaneous players—there are lots of reasons.

Who extends the world? The live team.

Who created the world? The dev team.

Is the dev team a subset of the live team? At some point, the answer has to be "no."

For large-scale, graphical virtual worlds, the answer is usually "no" immediately, because the live team is a separate entity from the dev team. Even for small-scale worlds, or those for which the live team is built from the dev team, the original designers aren't going to be around indefinitely. Students who create virtual worlds eventually leave college; professional designers who create successful worlds are offered new opportunities[52]; people move, their circumstances change: Ultimately, no one lives forever.

The live team may therefore differ in attitude to the dev team[53] when it comes to assessing how the virtual world "should" work. There are many opportunities for divergence:

➤ The live team may fail to understand aspects of the design, seeing flaws where there are none.

➤ The live team may misunderstand the dev team's intentions, believing they're doing the right thing when they're not.

➤ The live team may have a different overall philosophy, and "correct" the design where it runs counter to this.

➤ The dev team's design might fail when exposed to real players.

➤ The dev team may have higher quality staff than the live team (or *vice versa*), with a consequently better handle on things.

Because the live team is in control, there is great scope for a virtual world to shift away from the designers' original vision over time. This isn't necessarily a bad thing—adapting to circumstances is how systems evolve, after all. Neither, though, is it necessarily a good thing—survival of the fittest is great when you're one of the fittest, but not so great otherwise.

---

52. It's quite a different story for professional designers who create unsuccessful worlds, but the effect is the same: They end up not working on the project.

53. Indeed, they may differ in attitude to the live team of a few months earlier.

At this level, it's a classic conflict between theory (what the dev team wants) and practice (what the live team gets). It's a little more complicated than that, though. The live team has to deal with players, every single one of whom believes they know just as much about virtual world design (if not more) than anyone in the live team—and are prepared to argue the point.

The bad news is that players know nothing about virtual world design. Nothing whatsoever.

Well, that's not *strictly* true. A very small fraction of them do[54], but these are generally indistinguishable from normal players except in the benighted eyes of people who actually *do* know about virtual world design. Message boards are full of erudite arguments by players able to put their opinions cogently, politely, and convincingly. That doesn't mean they're *right*, though. It's like listening to a religious discussion between people of a religion different than your own: They obviously know exactly what they're talking about, in great and profound detail, but from your point of view they're at least misinformed and at most completely misguided. Player discussions are frequently like that: Designers can recognize some truths in what is being said, but these are so mixed with dogma, rhetoric, and downright falsehoods that the conclusions they reach are often bizarre and irrelevant (whenever they reach conclusions at all, that is).

Yes, I realize I've just insulted about three million people, here.

It's not that most players *don't* know about virtual world design, but that their knowledge is too personal. As mentioned in Chapter 1, players tend to view all virtual worlds in the context of the one they "grew up" playing. If a new idea is suggested, many players will immediately consider how it would fit into their preferred virtual world, whether or not the virtual world for which it is intended is remotely similar. If the debate actually concerns "their" virtual world, they'll figure out the short-term repercussions of their own playing style and use that as a basis to decide whether they're for or against. They'll only refer to long-term effects or other playing styles when they're trying to win allies or to convince the live team that they are responsible people whose opinions should carry weight.

---

54 Hopefully, a fraction that will increase as more and more players read this book.

This is because actually playing a virtual world adds a *subjective* element to all discussion. Designers have to be *objective*. If you can play a virtual world for fun, it's very hard to be a designer; every decision you make is related to your own experiences as a player. Designers *can't* play virtual worlds for fun. When I enter a virtual world, all I see is the machinery, the forces at work, the interactions—it's intellectually interesting and can be artistically exciting, but it isn't *fun*. Other designers are the same: The price you pay for being able to deconstruct a virtual world is that of being unable *not* to deconstruct it. Magic isn't magic when you know how the trick is done.

That's why most players aren't good at design. They still sense the magic.

Unfortunately for the live team, that's not quite how the players themselves see it. Players want improvements made to their virtual world, and most of the time they are appreciative—even fanatical—of the live team's efforts. When they *aren't*, though, oh boy, do they ever let the live team know! The pressure can be phenomenal. It can reach the stage where it's more gainful to implement the change that everyone is screaming for than it is to answer all the emails they'd send if you continued to hold out.

At this point, the live team often surrenders. Top-down design gives way to bottom-up experiment.

Whether this fills the original dev team with pride or despair depends on the extent to which they'd planned for its occurrence.

Chapter 3

Players

The real-life human beings sitting at a computer and accessing a virtual world are its *players*. Players are distinct from the objects within the virtual world over which they exercise control; these are *characters*.

The difference between players and characters is absolutely fundamental to virtual worlds. Characters are conduits that enable players to act and interact with the world itself and with other players. Characters exist only within the virtual world; the decision to enter that world and to remain in that world is entirely the preserve of players. The aim of designers is to provide an experience for players, not for characters.

That is the concern of this chapter.

Who Are These People and What Do They Want?

As mentioned in Chapter 1, "Introduction to Virtual Worlds," the demographics of virtual worlds are important for two reasons:

> ➤ If you know who likes your virtual world (the *actual* demographics), you can use this to decide where to look for newbies.

> ➤ If you know who wants to like your virtual world (the *target* demographics), you can change the virtual world so as to appeal to those people.

Both of these are essentially marketing issues. In the former, the design group has the upper hand, delivering a product that the marketers have to sell; in the latter, the marketing group has the upper hand, selling a product that the designers have to deliver.

Demographics provide information as to the real-world make-up of your players (or intended players). What you do with that information is another matter, though. If there are relatively few men aged 30–45 in your user base, does that mean you should ignore that demographic (because they don't want to play) or pander to it (because you want them to play)? From the designer's point of view, demographics mean generalizations, generalizations mean stereotypes, and stereotypes mean problems. These problems are fourfold:

➤ Some stereotypes are over-independent. If you design a game for boys aged 12–16, that's all you'll get.

➤ Some stereotypes are over-dependent. If you want to attract heterosexual men aged 18–30 to your virtual world then you should try to pack it full of heterosexual women aged 18–30.

➤ Stereotyping is patronizing. There are few slogans more likely to put women off a computer game than, "Designed by women, for women"[1].

➤ Stereotypes force designers to embrace prejudice, whether or not they want to. All these examples, mild though they may seem, are offensive to one or another group of individuals[2].

Demographic information of this nature is not generally helpful to designers of virtual worlds. Designers need to know what players want to do in the virtual world—their *playing styles*, rather than their socio-economic profiles. Actually, designers need to know a lot of other things about players, too, as we shall see later in this chapter; their playing styles, however, are the most important thing[3], so that's what we're looking at first.

---

1. Especially if it's written in pink letters.

2. For those blinded by rage, I'd like to make the obvious point that I did not do this with the intention of offending anyone and do not necessarily hold any of the views implied myself. See how the mere mention of prejudice gets a designer worried?

3. This is only because at the moment it's the *only* one with a useful, proven, working theory behind it.

Of course, members of a demographic group might share a particular playing style, but this doesn't help unless you know what that style is; besides, not everyone will conform to the stereotype. If multiple playing styles can co-exist, so can multiple demographics, in which case actual demographics become less of an issue. This means that designers can focus on the practical matter of addressing what players of whatever background like doing, instead of what they believe players of a particular background will probably like doing.

Of course, this is useless unless you have a good categorization of playing styles.

Playing styles are defined by what players do; what players do depends on what they consider to be fun. The former can be divined from a statistical assessment of the demographic information and the latter from a psychological or sociological assessment. Unfortunately, the results of this kind of analysis aren't always very useful. It's all well and good knowing that some players are nurturing, helpful people, that others have problems with authority, that some like to collect objects, and so on; these may be valid playing styles, and may even be possible to address in terms of world design (introduce sick animals, quests for loners, coins with dates on them).

What such analyses don't necessarily say is how one playing style interacts with another. What would be the effect of filling a game with nurturing types? Or loners? Or collectors? Categorizations are also more useful if they're guaranteed to be complete. Is there an anti-nurturing type? Can an individual be both a loner and a collector? Can different virtual worlds be described in terms of their appeal to the various playing styles that have been categorized?

Players are all different, and they all behave differently. Nevertheless, there will be general playing styles that they adopt, and how these interact will have consequences on the success or otherwise of a virtual world. It would be very useful for designers if they had a demographic-independent theory of playing styles that could be used to predict the long-term future of a virtual world based on a sound categorization strategy. Armed with this, they could ensure that there were activities available for all playing styles (or be prepared to accept the consequences if there weren't); they could introduce checks and balances to make certain that if one playing style came to dominate, the other styles would be compensated so as to keep a healthy balance; they could alter the form or functionality of the world itself to force it back into equilibrium if circumstances favored or disfavored one style over another; they could implement design protocols to guarantee that new additions to the world are always checked for their overall consequences on different playing styles.

Yes, I wouldn't be banging on about this if it weren't the case that there is indeed a proven model for player categorization that has sufficient theoretical underpinnings to allow for a predictive analysis of individual virtual worlds.

Player Types

For almost two decades, virtual worlds had no theories of anything. There were theories of other things that were applied to virtual worlds (as will be discussed in Chapter 6, "It's Not a Game, It's a…"), but no theories of virtual worlds themselves. This changed in 1996, with the publication of *Hearts, Clubs, Diamonds, Spades: Players Who Suit MUDs*[4] in the first issue of the newly founded *Journal of MUD Research*[5]. Its author was Richard Bartle, that's me[6]; if that puts you off, please skip to the next section.

Rather than reproduce the entire paper here in full, I'll instead focus on its main points. Interested readers who prefer books to web pages are referred to Bridgette Patrovsky and Jessica Mulligan's *Developing Online Games: An Insider's Guide*[7], which includes this paper as an appendix.

The Nature of "Fun"

Why do people play virtual worlds?

For non-entertainment worlds, the answer may be "because they were told to." If participation is voluntary, though, the players must expect to get something out of their experience. This may be practical knowledge useful in the real world—playing a MOO

---

4. http://www.mud.co.uk/richard/hcds.htm

5. http://www.brandeis.edu/pubs/jove. It's now the *Journal of Virtual Environments*.

6. This explains why I get to write this book and you don't.

7. Bridgette Patrovsky and Jessica Mulligan: *Developing Online Games: An Insider's Guide.* Indianapolis, New Riders Publishing, 2003.

to learn to program or to aquire a foreign language, perhaps. For worlds with no pedagogical imperative, though, why *do* people play?

Isn't it obvious? To have fun!

At a superficial level, that answer is fine. When you start looking at it in detail, though, it starts to break down. Is having your character killed by a monster fun? Is waiting three hours for a dragon to spawn that may (but probably won't) be carrying a rare item fun? Is spending 40 minutes tromping across a desert without meeting a single fellow player fun?

Okay, then, perhaps people play because the *sum* of their experience is fun. When you finally kill the monster, or the dragon carries Rod of Bi'Gloot, or you reach the lost oasis, this balances all the pain you went through to get there. But surely in the end the rewards lose their luster, whereas the drudgery never gets any more interesting?

Well maybe people play because, though it might not be very fun, it's nevertheless more fun than not playing. People would have to have very sad lives for this to be the case, though, wouldn't they? Unhappily, it's entirely possible that they do—not everyone's real-world existence is an endless whirl of stimulating social engagements in exotic locations.

Whatever it is that causes a player to come back to a virtual world time and time again, there must be things happening that, on the whole, they find enjoyable or personally rewarding. This is what they call *fun*. There might not be a lot of it, or there may be a good deal of it, but it has to be there. Players enter a virtual world to have fun; other people could have different ideas about whether it's fun, but to that player it's fun. It's relative to individuals.

In a virtual world context, the word "fun" therefore has a slightly more specific meaning than in Standard English. It's the supreme emotional state that the player expects to experience as a result of playing in that world. It's a somewhat circular definition: Players play so as to have fun, fun being what it is they aim to feel when playing.

Perhaps by examining what players actually do in a virtual world, the notion of what constitutes "fun" for particular individuals could be broken down more productively?

Player Types

In 1989 and 1990, the senior players of *MUD2* got into a debate lasting several months to answer the question, "What do people want out of a MUD?" At its conclusion, I undertook an analysis of their replies, and summarized their ideas of what constituted "fun" for them as falling into one of four categories:

➤ *Achievers.* These people put the game-like aspect of the virtual world to the fore. They like doing things that achieve defined[8] goals, thereby progressing their character through the world's built-in ranking system.

➤ *Socializers.* People for whom the greatest reward is interacting with other people, through the medium of the virtual world. Some do it as themselves; others role-play behind a mask.

➤ *Explorers.* The ultimate delight for Explorers is increasing their knowledge about the way the virtual world works. Their joy is in discovery. They seek out the new.

➤ *Killers.* People who want to dominate others. The classic way is through attacking them or otherwise making life difficult for them[9], but it also can manifest in less overt fashion, such as politicking, rumor-mongering, pedanticism, or guilt-trip maternalism ("No, it's okay, you go and enjoy yourself. I'll just sit here by myself, waiting for someone to come along, I'll think of something to do...")[10].

These categories seemed correct empirically, but I couldn't be sure that they were exhaustive. Perhaps there was another category that I'd missed? I therefore needed a means of formalizing the player types such that each of them could be shown to be emergent from a more robust framework which *was* guaranteed to be exhaustive.

I quickly realized that as there were four player types, a two-dimensional graph (with four quadrants) would do the job. However, I needed to find the right axes.

I immediately saw that achievers and explorers were more interested in the game than in the players of the game, whereas socializers and killers were more focused on the

---

8. Defined by the virtual world; that is, getting points and rising levels.

9. In this context, they're generally referred to as *griefers*.

10. The word "killers" is perhaps unfortunate, given the misunderstandings that arise because of it; "dominators" is a less emotive alternative that some people prefer, although unfortunately it doesn't imply a desire to dominate people (as with achievers, who want to "dominate" the world).

players than any game aspects. This distinction provided one axis. What, though, did achievers and either socializers or killers have in common? Could the same partitioning work for explorers and either killers or socializers?

I felt confident that achievers and killers were active, in that they like doing things to other things (the game or its players, respectively). Explorers and socializers were passive, in that they liked things being done to them. I wasn't very happy with this, however, as it was clear that socializers did like doing things to other people (talking to them) and explorers did like doing things to the game (experimenting).

Over the course of the next few years, I refined my ideas. I relabeled the y-axis players/world instead of players/game, because only achievers regarded the virtual world primarily as a game[11]. I still had trouble with the x-axis, though. It wasn't until I wrote the whole theory as a paper and submitted it for peer review that I got the answer: Alan Schwartz, founding editor of the *Journal of MUD Research*, suggested that explorers and socializers both valued forms of interaction. This was exactly what I needed to hear, and everything immediately fell into place.

The resulting Player Interest Graph is shown in Figure 3.1.

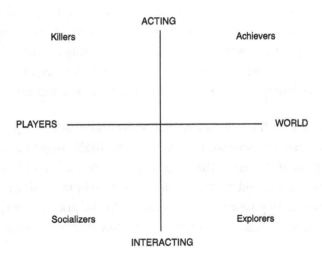

Figure 3.1   Player Interest Graph.

---

11. I also considered real/virtual, but didn't feel it was accessible enough. Players/world deals in the manifestations of these concepts, and it is much easier to get a handle on.

This graph describes players in terms of two (continuous) dimensions: How much they prefer acting on things as opposed to interacting with them; how much they prefer to direct their attentions toward the players or the world in which those players are present (as characters).

➤ Achievers have fun acting on the virtual world.

➤ Explorers have fun interacting with the virtual world.

➤ Socializers have fun interacting with other players.

➤ Killers have fun acting on other players.

Although other categorizations are obviously possible (and may well be superior), the use of opposing criteria for each of the axes in the Player Interest Graph shows that for this particular approach the categorizations are exhaustive.

As it stands, this graph tells designers quite a bit. If you want to increase the attraction of your virtual world to achievers, for example, you should include more content that involves acting upon the world; if you want to have more socializers, you should facilitate the capability to interact with other players, and so on. If you were to constrain the degree to which the world could be changed (for example by making areas out of bounds to certain groups of players), then you'd hit achievers and explorers but not socializers and killers. If you were to increase the capability to interact (for example by allowing players to keep notes on anything in the world they right double-click on), then you'd boost socializers and explorers but not achievers and killers.

It's possible to do this with other dimensions appropriate either to particular virtual worlds or virtual worlds in general. For example, a MUSH might have axes for story-telling/story-building versus theory/practice. Someone who likes to teach other people how to role-play would be in the theory/story-telling quadrant, whereas someone who likes constructing new content would be in the practice/story-building quadrant. Designers will use whatever categorizations they find most useful.

It's possible to do more with categorizations than merely state them and demonstrate them to be exhaustive, though. Having divided a set into four (or more) subsets, the question can be asked: What dynamics exist between the sub-sets? Are they independent (an increase in the number of people teaching how to build would have minimal impact on the number of people role-playing) or are there causalities (fewer people teaching how to build eventually leads to fewer builders)?

This is where it gets interesting.

Dynamics

In the wild, what effect does increasing the number of wildebeests at a watering hole have on the number of lions in the vicinity? Lions eat wildebeests, so the more wildebeests there are, the greater the number of lions that will turn up looking for a meal. However, wildebeests flee *en masse* when they so much as sniff a lion. The more lions that show up, the fewer wildebeest will hang around waiting to be eaten. This will lead to a reduction in the number of lions, which will cause an increase in the number of wildebeests, and so on, until equilibrium is reached.

Suppose we were talking about a virtual world rather than a watering hole. Substitute "killers" for "lions," "socializers" for "wildebeasts" and you get a reasonable approximation of the relationship between the two.

This is an example of the *dynamics* of player types. Increasing or decreasing the number of players practicing one playing style can affect the number practicing another. This in turn can have knock-on effects, and so on, until eventually the system finds some point of balance.

There are two ways that player numbers can change (they can rise or fall) and 10 possible pairings of types (A/A, A/E, A/E, A/K, E/E, E/S, E/K, S/S, S/K, and K/K). Some of these are free of dependencies—increasing or decreasing the number of explorers has no direct result at all on the number of socializers, and vice versa. Others have effects of varying degrees. Based on empirical observations, the dynamics can be summarized as follows:

- ➤ More achievers leads to
  - ➤ Slightly fewer socializers
  - ➤ More killers

- ➤ Fewer achievers leads to
  - ➤ Slightly fewer socializers
  - ➤ Fewer killers
- ➤ More explorers leads to
  - ➤ More explorers
  - ➤ Slightly fewer killers
- ➤ Fewer explorers leads to
  - ➤ Slightly more killers
- ➤ More socializers leads to
  - ➤ More socializers
  - ➤ More killers
- ➤ Fewer socializers leads to
  - ➤ Fewer socializers
  - ➤ Fewer killers
- ➤ More killers leads to
  - ➤ Fewer achievers
  - ➤ Slightly fewer explorers
  - ➤ Far fewer socializers
- ➤ Fewer killers leads to
  - ➤ More achievers
  - ➤ Far more socializers

Figure 3.2 shows these relationships.

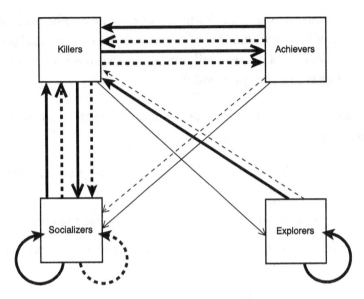

Figure 3.2 Influence graph.

Key: An arrow represents an increase (solid) or decrease (dashed) in the box from which it points. The effect on the box it points at will be either to increase (solid arrowhead) or decrease (open arrowhead) the contents of that box. The effect will be either slight (thin line), medium (medium line), or great (heavy line).

What Figure 3.2 shows is that most of the action concerns killers and socializers, where killer numbers are sensitive to those of socializers and socializer numbers are highly sensitive to those of killers. Explorers keep themselves to themselves, but have a mildly depressing effect on the number of killers; a virtual world can really only ever benefit by attracting explorers. Achievers and killers are in equilibrium, and there's a negative effect on the number of socializers if the number of achievers changes (up or down).

How can this be used predictively?

As an example, suppose that for whatever reason (advertising, a new patch, the closing of another virtual world) the number of killers increased dramatically. What would happen? Looking at the influence graph, it's clear that there would be a huge drop immediately in the number of socializers. Socializers are in an amplification loop with themselves—the more/fewer there are, the more/fewer will come/go. Thus, the number of socializers will drop even more until perhaps only a rump remains. Killers also have a lowering effect on the number of achievers. Lowering the number of achievers will reduce the number of killers. Either this will eventually reach some balance, or the numbers of both killers and achievers will drop so far that there are too few left to maintain a critical mass and the game will die.

By repeating this exercise for all player types, stable configurations can be discovered. It turns out there are four:

- ➤ *Type 1.* Killers and achievers in equilibrium, with hardly any socializers and explorers.

- ➤ *Type 2.* Socializers in dominance, with everyone else having only bit parts.

- ➤ *Type 3.* A balance between all four types, with enough explorers to control the killers.

- ➤ *Type 4.* An empty virtual world.

Of these, type 3 offers the best prospects for a world's longevity (types 1 and 2 will tend toward type 4 eventually). However, it is not clear that a large-scale virtual world, with its inherent community fragmentation, could ever attain this state. This explains why most virtual worlds are either social (typified by MUCKs, MUSHes, and MOOs) or adventure (typified by DikuMUDs, LPMUDs, and the big, graphical games). In practice, among the general public there are large numbers of socializers and achievers in comparison to explorers and killers, so it's just as well that types 1 and 2 are relatively stable.

After the underlying dynamics of a particular virtual world are understood, it's possible for the live team to influence that world's condition. If the number of socializers is dropping to the extent that the world is becoming "too" achiever-oriented, a simple solution might be to advertise the virtual world in a manner that would be more likely to attract socializers than achievers. Changes to the virtual world's design can also help, for example by heavily increasing the challenge to achievers (so as to persuade them to go around in groups, which socializers like) or by adding socializer goodies (such as letting them write their own in-world newspapers). There are plenty of ways[12] to do this. Solutions are easy to come by (if not necessarily easy to implement); you have to realize you have a problem first, though.

---

12. The original *Hearts, Clubs, Diamonds, Spades* paper lists over 30 examples.

Incidentally, there is a possibility that a virtual world can fake the presence of a player type without actually having players of that type around. The type most amenable to this is that of killers. Players can tolerate being inconveniently beaten up by mobiles more readily than they can by fellow players, and mobiles have the advantage of being controllable. Surprisingly, there is a lot to be said for this approach; although it doesn't replicate the effect of having killers exactly, nevertheless it can successfully approximate it to varying degrees. See the discussion on persona death in Chapter 5, "Life in the Virtual World," for more details.

General Observations

I noted in Chapter 1 that many players of virtual worlds don't consider themselves to be gamers, even if the virtual world is billed as a game. What's more, they're correct—they *aren't* gamers.

People sign up to large-scale commercial virtual worlds because these are advertised as games, but once there they don't necessarily want to play them as games; ironically, games have become the new "noble content." Players have different ways of amusing themselves. Applying the player types categorizations:

➤ Achievers see virtual worlds as games. Their aim is to improve, advance, and ultimately win (for some common, easily stated, world-supported definition of "win").

➤ Explorers see them more as pastimes, such as reading, gardening, or messing about in the kitchen. Reward comes from discovery and furthering understanding.

➤ Socializers see virtual worlds as entertainment, such as TV, clubs, or concerts. Discussion of the performance and behavior of themselves and others is their main draw.

➤ Killers see virtual worlds as sport. This is of the huntin', shootin', and fishin' kind, rather than the running the 100-meters or the marathon kind[13]. If the user base is large enough, some killers may treat virtual worlds as team sports—with themselves as captain or head coach.

---

13. Although that's a possibility too if they enjoy crushing the opposition.

It's interesting to postulate how pitching a virtual world as something other than a game might work. To attract socializers, for example, a world could be portrayed as a sophisticated chat room with built-in toys that players can do things with; in this context, achievement is a mere by-product that arises when people choose to use the toys to play games of their own devising. This approach would apply well to something like *The Sims Online*.

Of course, by focusing on only one notion of what a particular virtual world "is," there's a danger that people will believe it is not for them and will stay away. Would achievers bother with *The Sims Online* if it didn't at least nod in the direction of being a game? It's only because of the growing opinion that computer games don't have to be games (which was pioneered in part by *The Sims* itself) that non-gamers have come round to accepting them as noble content. However, if they entered a virtual world and found that it really *was* all game, they wouldn't hang around for long. Part of a designer's work is therefore to ensure that the philosophy governing what their virtual world is "about" is not too exclusive. If the design sends the wrong messages to players, it can alienate them.

On the other hand, there's a risk of going too far: That by trying to please everybody, a designer can end up pleasing nobody. It can be fine to tailor advertisements to particular audiences: The movie *Pearl Harbor*[14] was successfully sold as a war story in America and a love story in Japan, for example. However, there can be problems when groups with different expectations meet: Japanese moviegoers would not necessarily have enjoyed *Pearl Harbor* had they been sharing a theater with Americans cheering the U.S. counter-attack. In describing a virtual world, it's okay to tell all players the same thing; it's okay to tell them the same thing in different ways; what isn't recommended is telling them different things. There's a distinction between saying "this is a game for everyone" and "this is a game for you."

What designers tell players shapes the way a virtual world is perceived. "Tell" in this situation means through deeds rather than words: A world may be promoted as a place where basket-weavers are as respected as much as warriors, but when there are 25 different kinds of weapons and two different kinds of baskets, that's not what it's saying. This topic of how a design can (for better or worse) send messages to players is discussed in more detail in Chapter 5.

---

14. Randall Wallace (writer) and Michael Bay (director), *Pearl Harbor*. USA, Touchstone Pictures, 2001.

Using Player Types

Why use the player types model for virtual world design?

One purely pragmatic reason is that because it was the first such model, everyone knows about it; it therefore provides common ground for communicating ideas with other designers. This is by no means the only reason, though.

The model's main strength is its categorization of players into the four particular types: achievers, explorers, socializers, and killers. It has its roots in a consideration of what people find fun in virtual worlds, and is therefore attuned to situations that might impact on this: all big design decisions, in other words. If you're creating a virtual world and don't have an actual user base yet, categorizing it along the lines the model advocates will give you some idea of how the players might take to a feature (or not); if you're running a live game, the model will suggest how proposed changes might be received by existing players.

The dynamics that underlie the categorization are of less practical use to most designers. Occasionally it might be that a major, major alteration is planned, which will throw the balance so out of whack that some compensatory change will be necessary to stop a hemorrhage of players; this is not something that is an issue most of the time, though. When you add new functionality, it's useful to run through the player types to be sure it doesn't help or hurt any of them too much; it's less useful to wonder what the next level of knock-on effects will be. Dynamics are useful for consultants looking at virtual worlds that have either no user base or a very ill one; for day-to-day design, categorization is the handier tool.

You don't have to use this or any other model, of course. This one happens to have been applied successfully over the years to the players of a wide variety of virtual worlds, but that doesn't mean another model might not help designers more. The main problem is that there really *aren't* any other models to speak of right now; about the only other one in regular use categorizes players on the basis of their experience— "What will newbies make of this?" Perhaps the greatest service the player types model has rendered is to show that theoretical design aids can exist at all; if someone can produce a superior one, so much the better.

The player types model does have its limitations, of course, and designers should be aware of them. The main ones to watch out for are

➤ It doesn't address how players change style over time. The classic path is killer to explorer to achiever to socializer, but others are possible.

➤ It doesn't account for players who appear to play one style while actually playing another. If your achievers regard killing as achievement, it's bad; if your explorers see it as worthy of exploration, it's a calamity.

➤ If a virtual world is large enough that it can split into (geographical or social) sub-worlds, the model might apply separately to individual sub-worlds but not to the world as a whole.

➤ It assumes that players are independent. For virtual worlds with large numbers of players, this may not be the case. Killers don't often get along with each other, so in most worlds they play as lone wolves. However, in a large world where one of them can lead a gang of 50 impressionable achievers, their effect is somewhat magnified.

➤ It assumes that virtual worlds are independent. Players might have cut their teeth in a different virtual world before visiting this one.

➤ It can't account for poor design. If your world has too few socializers, the model can suggest means by which to increase the numbers, but they may not work. It has no way of knowing you're running a text MUD played using mobile phones and that people just can't be bothered to thumb in commands.

➤ It is open to misinterpretation. Players aren't always good judges of their own playing style: Many achievers seem to think they're killers or explorers; some killers mistakenly label themselves as socializers. Asking self-appointed representatives of one type what they think of a possible major change could lead to a questionable result.

Beyond this, the model may apply but still be of little or no use. Designers of worlds that people play for reasons other than having fun (for example, to learn creative writing) have no real need of it; designers of worlds that people can't have fun playing (for example, because the worlds are depressing or incomprehensible) have other problems they should solve first.

On the other hand, the model has been successfully applied beyond the confines of virtual worlds into domains such as online community management and tabletop RPGs[15].

---

15. Footnote addicts who looked at the *Knights of the Dinner Table* comic book series after I mentioned it in Chapter 1 may be amused to consider the following mapping: Bob/killer, Dave/achiever, Sara/socializer, Brian/explorer.

Although designers working in areas related to virtual worlds may find the player types model flexible enough to be of use, the further they are away from the subject then the less likely the dynamics are to work. They can use it to inform, but probably not to prescribe.

I should point out that although this research has been used on a number of occasions to "prove" that game-oriented virtual worlds "need" killers, this is not the case. The model is descriptive, not normative: It shows what will happen if the proportions of player types changes, but doesn't advocate one over another. If you want achievers but don't want killers, you can have them; you need to be aware that without intervention the achievers won't stay long, though. Similarly, if you design a game targeted at killers, it will require a major effort to stop the poor ones from quitting in frustration and the better ones quitting when there's no one left to bully.

It is important to remember that even if the player types dynamics are functioning and changes are being made with an eye to the categorizations, it may all be worth nothing. External influence can easily overwhelm the model. If the virtual world crashes the whole time, or the customer service representatives are unusually surly, or the price triples, then players have some reason other than lack of fun to consider not playing. If that's the case, designers should concentrate on high-profile changes of whatever nature they feel is appropriate—anything, so long as it will pull in *some* players after the problems are fixed. It's no use trying to balance a player base when there are no players to balance; recover the players, *then* balance it.

Most of these external effects need only be planned for as contingencies, if at all. There is one, however, with which designers do need to be concerned as it is the very life blood of their virtual worlds: the *newbie flow*.

The Newbie Flow

Imagine that your virtual world is a bucket, and players are water. There are holes in the bucket through which the water escapes. If you don't add water regularly, eventually it will all leak away. There may be a pool at the very bottom that isn't high enough to reach the lowest hole—that's you and your die-hard players. Eventually, even this will evaporate away, though.

All virtual worlds need a flow of newbies if they are to survive. It doesn't matter how wonderful your world is or how dedicated your players are: If you don't have newbies, you're in big trouble.

The flow does not have to be constant, just regular. As long as your bucket is big enough to accommodate a sudden wave of newbies should one arrive (for example, because school is out, or because of TV coverage), it's enough that the average inflow does not fall below the average outflow.

So far, so faucet/drain.

Designers don't get to control where newbies come from directly, although by designing an appealing virtual world they can do so indirectly (as players tell their real-life friends how great it is[16]). Newbies can sometimes show up on their own, having been looking for a virtual world that suits them and deciding to give this one a try. For small-scale virtual worlds, these two sources are often sufficient to keep everything ticking over nicely. Otherwise, if you want newbies, then you have to use marketing to entice them through your door.

Well, that's not absolutely true: There is another possibility that I alluded to in Chapter 1—the *newbie hose*[17]. This is where someone else has control of a flow of newbies and points it in your direction. The classic example is when a virtual world has links with a large portal that isn't ashamed of it, as with those on AOL in the mid-1990s. This is not the only way a newbie hose can arise, though. The buzz among the first players of *EverQuest* was so great that normal word-of-mouth became effectively a newbie hose; *Star Wars Galaxies* got one by virtue of its license.

The advantage of a newbie hose is that it doesn't matter how full of holes your bucket is, there's so much water going into it that it's always full. Hey, you can even add more buckets if you want. The disadvantage of the newbie hose is that sooner or later it either empties the tank or gets pointed elsewhere. When that happens, someone has to answer the very real question of where the newbies are going to come from instead.

The rate at which people leave a virtual community is called *churn*. It's expressed as a percentage of the user base that leaves over a set time period (a month is implied, but other periods are possible). Thus, if you have 100,000 players in your virtual world and every month 5,000 of them fail to renew their subscription, the churn is 5%. This

---

16. Hopefully not so great that they have lost all their real-life friends by the time they emerge from it.

17. The term comes from Clement Chambers, whose company On-line ran *Federation II* in the UK after CompuNet closed down. He also coined the prefix *massively multiplayer*.

would mean that on average players would last 20 months before quitting. In general, the aim is to keep the churn as low as possible[18].

Companies don't publish their churn rates, because the figures can affect share prices adversely. AOL, for example, used to run at around 3% churn, but when it was unable to reduce this it stopped releasing the data and emphasized absolute subscriber numbers instead; later, it advocated using the total time that users spent online as a measure of its increasing success[19].

Established virtual worlds have churn rates under 5%[20], which is considered excellent for this kind of product. A newbie hose masks churn, though. If a virtual world is growing by 3,000 players a month, everything looks rosy. However, that's a *net* increase. If 3,000 people signed up and none left, it's good; if 103,000 signed up and 100,000 left, it's not so good. An August 2002 article[21] quoting SOE stated that *EverQuest* players stayed with the game for eight months[22]. That means an average of one-eighth of *EQ* players quit every month—around 54,000 of them, in other words. Given that *EQ* was experiencing a net growth of around 2,300 players a month at the time[23], this suggests that they were signing up 56,300 new subscriptions. Attracting 56,300 new subscribers a month is very impressive; losing 54,000 is also very impressive, but for different reasons. A churn of 12.5% for a user base the size of *EverQuest's* makes them very reliant on a newbie hose, which perhaps explains SOE's decision to expand into the Korean market in 2003.

The importance of the newbie flow is so great that designers should put as little in the way of it as possible. It might be argued that those designers benefiting from the luxury of a newbie hose can concentrate on retention (that is, keeping people who

---

18. For non-commercial virtual worlds, churn is harder to measure because you can never be sure when someone has actually "left."

19. Actually, 3% churn isn't bad for an online service. A CompuServe executive once told me its churn ran at 10%, although that may have been part of a sob story to convince me to take a cut in the royalties for *British Legends*. If it was, it didn't work.

20. *MUD2's* is approximately 4%, for example.

21. Tim Green, *Brave New World*. London, *MCV*, Intent Media, August 30 2002.

22. I assume this does not include players who quit in the first, "free" month (for which churn is by far the worst).

23. According to SOE press releases, *EverQuest* had 400,000 subscribers in late June 2001 and 430,000 in late July 2002, which gives an average net gain of about 2,300 per month for that period.

have lasted a few sessions in the virtual world) rather than attraction; for the majority of virtual worlds, though, newbie-friendliness should always come before oldbie-friendliness. Most of the time, the two can exist in harmony anyway, with those problems that do arise only doing so because the designers forget one or the other. Sometimes, though, what interests oldbies can put off newbies entirely. Chapter 5 discusses an important example of this (the *trickle-down effect*) in more detail.

Player types can help with the newbie flow. They're no use for absolute newbies, who are often so confused or shy that they simply don't know what to do (therefore the first concern of designers is to persuade them to do anything at all!). However, once a player has found their feet, player styles apply. Many newbies will first want to ascertain the established norms of behavior (which can involve killer-style behavior), whereupon they will spend a period exploring the virtual world and their abilities within it. Having gained the necessary skills and knowledge, they can start to play "properly" as an achiever. Months later, when they have reached the top, they retire into the life of socializer. This is the killer to explorer to achiever to socializer path I mentioned earlier. Not all players follow this "main sequence," of course, and not all of them follow it at the same speed. Someone who is at heart a socializer will soon decide that exploring and achieving is not for them, and will reach the final stage early; someone who is basically a gamer will achieve everything they can do, then find there's little to do but chat or leave (so they'll leave).

Coming back to newbie streams, then, the things that designers should concentrate most on for inexperienced players are enabling them to find the world's behavioral boundaries quickly and providing plenty of interesting things to see and do that will help them develop their playing skills[24]. Support from customer service greeters can make some of this run more smoothly in practice, but that doesn't mean designers should shirk their responsibilities.

At this early stage, there's a possibility that designers can affect the future playing styles of impressionable or open-minded newbies. A player who is an achiever in other virtual worlds may discover the joys of being an explorer in yours, if you let them see what they're missing. If you want more of one player type than another, then making it

---

24. But not so many that the newbie is overwhelmed. With graphical virtual worlds, there is a case for providing special newbie-friendly client skins, so as not to expose newbies to the full majesty of what awaits. Textual worlds do this implicitly by only initially telling newbies about the commands they need to know—the rest can be found deeply nested in help trees or through conversation with more experienced players.

appealing to newbies is a way to achieve your goal. This is not to say that players should be given the hard sell: It's about presenting opportunities, not arm-twisting. *EverQuest 2* has a particularly impressive scheme for bedding in newbies (even though what they're bedded into isn't a whole lot different from *EverQuest 1*).

A balance of player types among newbies isn't important. After they jump off the main sequence and start to play in the style that best suits them, *that's* when they join the majority for which standard type dynamics apply. An overall balance among non-newbies is important, because balance leads to retention. Meanwhile, the next batch of newbies is beginning the process, and the wheel turns once more.

We'll be looking at the concept of "main sequence" in some detail later on in this chapter. It gets a Whole Lot More Complicated.

The Bartle Test

The final point to mention about player types is the *Bartle Test*.

I'm often asked about the Bartle Test, on the grounds that because it bears my name I must be responsible for it. Sadly, I'm not. The test is the brainchild of Erwin S. Andreasen and Brandon A. Downey, who wrote it in response to my player types paper so as to test the theory.

The Bartle Test is an online binary-choice questionnaire[25] that players of virtual worlds can take to discover what player type they are. As such, it offers potentially very useful information for designers. Are players mainly achievers and socializers, as empirical observation would suggest? Just how numerous are killers? Are there large numbers of silent explorers out there that no one knows about? How do the different codebases compare? Answers to these questions could provide solid figures that would help designers visualize the make-up of the user base they have or they want.

The result of having taken the Bartle test is a Bartle Quotient, expressed as three letters. For example, ASK[26] means you're foremost an achiever, then a socializer, and then a killer. The first letter in the result therefore indicates a person's primary playing style.

---

25. http://www.andreasen.org/bartle/

26. ASK is the rating you get if you answer all the questions with the first of the two options presented.

Of the 176,000+ people[27] who had taken the test by April 2003, 29% rated as explorers, 25% as socializers, 23% as killers, and 21% as achievers. Of the combinations, SEA was highest at 12%, followed by ESA at 10% and EAS at 8%.

These figures almost certainly do not reflect anything like the actual split among players. Reasons for this include

➤ Participants in the test are self-selecting. Most don't hear about it until they've played a virtual world for a while, therefore they are not representative of the general user population.

➤ It is clear from the nature of many of the questions what is being tested for, which means players can give the answer they believe will lead to a cooler rating (for example, explorer or killer) rather than the truth.

➤ There is no "neither" answer. A socializer being asked to choose between defeating an enemy and exploring an area may as well flip a coin to answer, given that they don't particularly care for either.

➤ Some answers favor two or more types. Killers and achievers would probably both prefer defeating an enemy to exploring an area, but the questionnaire can't disambiguate them.

➤ Ties aren't handled very well. If you choose achiever and socializer answers with equal frequency, you will be recorded as favoring A over S.

Just because the test is flawed, that doesn't mean it's useless, however. It helps players, for sure, because it lists the virtual worlds that most closely match each player type combination. So many people have taken the test that it has a large database of scores for individual virtual worlds (over 700 of them); if you end a test with a rating of ASK, you'll be shown a list of the five virtual worlds that have the most players also rating ASK, and the actual percentages involved. Alternatively, if you're a killer and want to find a game full of socializers to annoy, you can look at the overall statistics and find that out too. The figures may not be formally accurate, but they're pretty good in relative terms. If one virtual world scores fewer achievers than another, the chances are it really does have fewer achievers[28].

---

27. Their numbers grow by over a hundred a day.

28. This makes *MUD1*'s perennial placement in the bottom five for socializers all the more interesting.

For designers, the overall average scores aren't too helpful as they are skewed by the popularity of the virtual worlds from which the figures are derived. The ratings for individual virtual worlds are of more interest (see Table 3.1).

Table 3.1   Bartle Quotients by Virtual Worlds

Ultima Online	EverQuest	Asheron's Call	Dark Age of Camelot
SEA 11%	ESA 12%	ESA 12%	SEA 8%
ESA 10%	SEA 11%	EAS 10%	ESA 8%
EAS 8%	EAS 10%	SEA 8%	EAS 7%

This shows the three top-rated quotients for each of the first four virtual worlds to obtain results from 1,000 respondents. There are obvious similarities: None of these quotients involve killers[29] and none of them place achievers first. The actuality may be different, of course (*EQ* is achiever heaven, but you wouldn't know it from this set of data). However, as relative values they allow some conclusions to be drawn:

➤ *UO* and *EQ* are fairly similar, although *UO* allows a little more variety (its ratios are slightly lower).

➤ *AC* is heavy with explorers—exactly the kind of people who would be expected to like the idea of story arcs.

➤ *DAoC* accommodates playing styles less rigidly than the others (its ratios are much lower). This is perhaps because many of its players cut their teeth on *UO*, *EQ*, or *AC* but were unsatisfied; *DAoC* (with its RvR system) could provide a different experience, so they switched.

Bartle Test results don't allow designers to infer much about an individual virtual world in isolation. However, the relative effects of a major difference between otherwise similar virtual worlds (for example, ones sharing a codebase) *can* be judged. If a designer is considering such a feature for their own game, some indication of the possible effects on its user base can thus be derived.

---

29. This may be because killers tend to get banned from these virtual worlds.

For the record, I haven't taken the Bartle Test. This isn't because I object to it—I don't. Rather, it's because I can no longer play virtual worlds for fun, so I can't answer fun-related questions. Any responses I did give would depend solely on the player I was role-playing at the time, which would rather miss the test's point.

Other Categorizations

Although my player types categorization is perhaps the best known of those available to designers, it is not the only one. There are many others, of which three are of particular interest. Two of these are based on anecdotal evidence, and one on statistics.

Social Dimensions

One of the earliest systems to use a primarily graphical interface was *Habitat*, which appeared in the mid-1980s. Although not strictly speaking a virtual world (it was essentially a graphical chat room), it nevertheless did have close similarities and is regarded as an important milestone in the development of graphical virtual worlds.

The system administrator[30] of *Habitat* between 1986 and 1988 (during what would nowadays be called its beta-test phase) was F. Randall Farmer. In 1992, he wrote a paper describing some of his observations about the social dimensions of online communities[31].

Randy noticed that players behave in one of five different ways:

> ➤ *Passives.* People who want to be entertained without effort on their part. *Habitat* was only one of their online activities. 75% of players by number, but only 20% by connect time.

> ➤ *Actives.* Players for whom *Habitat* was their main online activity. They got involved as soon as they logged in, and used up most of the total connect time.

---

30. The *Habitat* term was *Oracle*.

31. F. Randall Farmer, *Social Dimensions of Habitat's Citizenry*. Carl Eugene Loeffler & Tim Anderson (eds.), *The Virtual Reality Casebook*. New York, Van Nostrand Reinhold, 1992.

► *Motivators*. People who make life interesting for the other players by organizing events, setting up institutions, opening debates. A good ratio is one motivator for every 50 passives and actives.

► *Caretakers*. Mature motivators, who may be employees of the developer. They helped newbies, mediated conflicts, noted bugs, and did other things that would today fall into the province of customer service.

► *Geek Gods*[32]. The designers and implementers who ensure that the virtual world works, and who make changes when it doesn't.

The categories here are quite vague, and two of them concern groups of people not normally considered to be proper "players" anyway. However, it's not so much the categorizations that are important as the fact that Randy noticed there was a pattern involved—what he called the *Path of Ascension*. Players started off as passives, then became actives, then motivators, then caretakers, then finally geek gods. People should be encouraged to move along the path in order to develop a vibrant, thriving community.

It may seem today that all this is fairly obvious. *Of course* you should try to get people more involved in the community! Did people *really* ever think differently?

Yes they did. Back then, players were frequently lumped together as an amorphous mass, especially by the big online services. There was a recognition that there were useful "mother hen" people who would do all your organizing for you happily and without pay, but no one gave any thought as to where these individuals might come from—they were just *there*. Randy pointed out how they got there, and how to get them there.

Unfortunately (for them), this had little influence on the big online services. The way they saw it, there were fewer people at each step of the path, so transition meant a loss of players. If 75% of the players were using 20% of the bandwidth, then any movement would reduce the overall number of players while increasing the bandwidth. Even with players being charged by the hour, this was too big a price to pay, so they kept the status quo. As a result, the community became sterile and unattractive to newbies.

---

32. It's a self-deprecating pun on Greek Gods.

The Path of Ascension concerns the development of players as they grow in maturity. As such, at least in its first three steps it ought to be related to the main sequence of the player types model; we'll see how, exactly, a little later.

A further refinement to the idea of progression came with the notion of "Circles."

Circles

Circles is the name given by then *Ultima Online* player Hedron to his 1998[33] description of how players advance through different states of maturity. Although it is not a particularly well-known approach, I shall describe it here because it makes some very insightful observations[34].

Hedron's vision is of virtual world players organized as concentric circles. They begin in the outer circles, and advance in their experience and attitudes through the inner circles; the analogy is (ultimately) the mandala of Buddhism, which adherents can use to symbolize conditions of spirituality that they desire to re-create through mental exercises.

From observation, Hedron postulates six circles, representing six increasingly higher states of being for players in virtual worlds:

➤ *First Circle—Survival.* Players begin as newbies. Their main concerns are acquiring the basic skills, stats, and items they need simply to survive.

➤ *Second Circle—Competence.* After players have sufficient expertise so that they can make progress, they begin to do so. The virtual world becomes more "fun."

➤ *Third Circle—Excel.* Having become "pretty good," players aim to become "very good." They seek out the toughest challenge that they can find in order to "beat" it.

➤ *Fourth Circle—Prove Mastery.* Having acquired technical mastery, players feel the need to demonstrate this to other players. They will typically do this either by helping/mentoring/leading or by attacking them[35].

---

33. http://www.falseprophecies.com/sixcircles.htm

34. You'll have to wait until Chapter 5 to discover just how insightful they are, I'm afraid!

35. When this article was written, *Ultima Online* still had problems with bands of roving killers.

➤ *Fifth Circle—Seek New Challenges.* Players feel that they have exhausted everything that the virtual world has programmed in for them to do. The only entertainment left is interaction with other players.

➤ *Sixth Circle—Everything Is One.* Players recognize all ways that people can play
the virtual world, and have a full understanding of the merits of them all. Players
accept and appreciate each other, the virtual world, and the way things are.

Hedron's article goes into some depth about the options available to players at the fifth
circle, at least one of which (leaving to play some other virtual world) does not necessarily lead to the sixth circle. There's no need to discuss that here, however.

All three of the approaches discussed so far rely on the observations of individuals for
their substance. There is a more scientific approach available, however: statistics.

Facets

The most extensive study of the player base for any individual virtual world is Nick
Yee's *The Norrathian Scrolls*[36]. This important survey is famed for both its extensiveness
and its statistical rigor. It considers the real-world and in-game demographics for
EverQuest, and correlates the two. For example, it provided concrete evidence that (on
the whole) male players tend more toward achievement than female players and that
(on the whole) female players tended more toward socializing. Its scope also considered other issues of use to academic researchers (for example virtual gender-bending).

Although *The Norrathian Scrolls* found differences among players based on their real-
world demographics, they were not strong enough to be of use to designers. Yes, on
the whole male players are more driven by achievement than female players, but there
are nevertheless plenty of female players who are achievers and plenty of male ones
who are socializers. Nick therefore decided to undertake a second survey to look for
more fundamental differences—ones that did not make reference to real-world
demographics.

In March 2002, he introduced the notion of *facets*[37].

---

36. Nick Yee, *The Norrathian Scrolls*, 2001. http://www.nickyee.com/eqt/report.html.

37. Nick Yee, *Facets: 5 Motivational Factors for Why People Play MMORPG's.* 2002.
http://www.nickyee.com/facets/home.html.

The point of Nick Yee's second study was to answer the question, "What do people want out of a game?"[38]. The methodology employed was to ask respondents a series of multi-choice questions concerning their motivation for playing in graphical virtual worlds[39], then running a statistical analysis on the results. The multichoice questions themselves were constructed so as to act as indicators for the four player types and a number of other relationships that Nick had noticed in his previous studies. The point of this was to see if the answers that players provided really did cluster toward the player types, or whether there were more "natural" motivational groupings.

A factor analysis of the responses discovered five significant motivations (the facets):

➤ *Relationship*. The desire to make meaningful relationships with other players in the virtual world.

➤ *Immersion*. The desire to become immersed in the virtual world.

➤ *Grief*. The desire to objectify other players for personal gain.

➤ *Achievement*. The desire to become powerful within the context of the virtual world.

➤ *Leadership*. The assertiveness and sociability of the player.

Immersion and leadership are qualities not addressed in the player types model. Relationship matches the socializer type well, emphasizing the formation of relationships as a primary motivation. Achievement matches the achiever type well, too, with evidence that the reason players like to achieve is so as to become powerful in the virtual world. Grief corresponds roughly with killers, although not to the extent that it covers the "interfering busybody" variety. Most interestingly, explorers don't appear to exist as a type at all.

Because of the lack of evidence for explorers, the survey was amended to promote those factors that would indicate their existence[40]. Nevertheless, the result did not change. Either: Explorers do not play graphical virtual worlds; explorers do not answer questionnaires; explorers subvert questionnaires; or, explorer is an insignificant type (if

---

38. But for using the word "game" rather than "MUD," this is the same question that my player types paper attempts to answer.

39. Of the nearly 6,700 respondents, the split was: *EverQuest* 5,486, *Dark Age of Camelot* 1,044, *Asheron's Call* 83, and *Anarchy Online* 68.

40. This "improved" questionnaire was answered by a further 500 respondents.

it exists at all). This is especially interesting because it seems to contradict the findings of the Bartle Test (which in turn contradicts my own empirical observations).

Of course, the study has its flaws, many of which are discussed in the paper itself. Among the most pertinent are

➤ The motivations suggested by the survey are implicit in the questions.

➤ Brainstorming motivations is as subjective as brainstorming player types.

➤ There is no guarantee that there are only five facets, just that there are at least five facets.

➤ There is no guarantee that the facets are all at the same level of abstraction. They might be like "orange, banana, lemon, lime, fruit."

➤ The labeling of the facets is not provided by the factor analysis.

➤ Some of the facets overlap, but some don't. Leadership could be an expression of an achievement, grief, or relationship facet, but not of immersion.

None of these flaws are show-stoppers at this stage of the research. More work needs to be done, of course, particularly in constructing an underlying mechanism to model the motivations, but already there are some interesting results. The nonappearance of explorers is perhaps the most significant of these, but a follow-up study[41] also suggested a number of others. From a designer's point of view, the big ones are

➤ Highly immersive does not mean highly addictive (and vice versa). Players can feel they are *in* a world without suffering withdrawal when they are absent from it.

➤ Immersion and addiction both imply retention. Players who experience strong feelings of presence in a virtual world, or who feel anxious when they are not playing, will keep their accounts for longer.

➤ Stickiness is strongest for relationships, then for achievement, then for leadership. If you want people to stay with your virtual world for longer, you should first and foremost try to foster relationships between them. It's more effective than locking them into an advancement system. It's more effective than locking them into a team.

---

41. Nick Yee, *Codename Blue: An Ongoing Study of MMORPG Players*. 2002.
   `http://www.nickyee.com/codeblue/home.html`.

These observations alone would make facets worthy of serious consideration by designers, and further research in this area is eagerly awaited. It's good to know *what* the correlations are, but it would be better if we knew *why* they are. If a model could be devised which was able to articulate the causalities that lead to these conclusions, we'd have a theory rather than merely data. Designers could then use it both predictively and quantitatively, backed up by actual numbers.

Facets have the potential to supersede player types as the *de facto* means by which players are categorized. More research is necessary, but for the moment the results are very promising.

Levels of Immersion

One of Nick Yee's facets is immersion. This is a concept with a long and distinguished history in role-playing contexts[42], and it has been mentioned a number of times already in this book. So what, exactly, is it?

Fundamentally, immersion is the sense that a player has of being *in* a virtual world. The more *immersive* a virtual world, the greater its ability to immerse its players. Some virtual worlds (particularly non-game ones) deliberately aim for low immersion, so as not to distract from their purpose; most, however, aim to be as immersive as possible.

Although players can experience many degrees of immersion, there are conceptual or emotional barriers along the way that players must pass if they are to proceed further. Immersion can therefore most usefully be described in terms of a series of levels:

- ➤ Player
- ➤ Avatar
- ➤ Character
- ➤ Persona

---

42. The first use of it that I can find with regard to a virtual world is an editor's introduction to an article I wrote for an early computer magazine: "Richard Bartle immerses himself in MUD." Richard Bartle, *Stuck in the MUD*. London, *Your Commodore*, Argus Press, March 1985. http://www.mud.co.uk/richard/ycmar85.htm.

The human being sitting at the computer, interacting with the virtual world, is a *player*. The player will be controlling an object within the virtual world that is associated with them. The way the player regards that object is a measure of their immersion. If they consider it simply to be a computer construction with which they don't identify (as they might, say, a document in a word processor), then they are not immersed.

Most players of virtual worlds easily identify with the object they control. At the very least, they regard the object as their *representative* in the virtual world. For them, the object is their *avatar*—a puppet that they control and the conduit through which they act. Players will refer to their avatars in the third person, but may flesh them out with a few personality quirks. "Alice has a thing about cats, so she won't go near them." On the whole, though, avatars are mere conveniences—ways to effect change in a virtual world.

The next stage is for players to stop thinking of the object they control as their representative, but rather as their *representation*. The object is a tokenization of the player. This is the *character* level, at which the majority of players are found. A character is an extension of a player's self, a whole personality that the player dons when they enter the virtual world. Players may maintain several characters, each a distinct and rounded personality, which the player treats as a friend. Characters are referred to by name; although a player might say, "I lost my sword last night," what they mean is more like, "Thorina lost her sword when I was playing her last night."

Avatars are dolls, characters are simulacra, but neither are people. The final level of immersion—the one which makes virtual worlds wholly different to anything else—is that of the *persona*.

A persona is a player, in a world. That's *in* it. Any separate distinction of character is gone—the player *is* the character. You're not role-playing a being, you *are* that being; you're not assuming an identity, you *are* that identity; you're not projecting a self, you *are* that self. If you're killed in a fight, you don't feel that your character has died, you feel that *you* have died[43]. There's no level of indirection, no filtering, no question: *You are there.*

---

43. Not that anyone could ever verify that this is what having died actually feels like, of course.

This is something that many people examining virtual worlds from the outside fail to understand. Avatars and characters are just steps along the way. Looking at characters to try to develop an understanding of why virtual worlds are so appealing is pointless except in the case of die-hard role-players. Sometimes full immersion is likened to an altered state of consciousness[44]; this is much closer to the truth, but still misses the mark (you can daydream while in a virtual world without leaving it).

It's about identity. When player and character merge to become a persona, *that's* immersion; *that's* what people get from virtual worlds that they can't get from anywhere else; *that's* when they stop playing the world and start living it.

I should point out that my use of some of the terms here is rather technical. In my explanation of the different levels of immersion, I was at pains to refer to the object that the player is associated with as just that, an "object." In everyday use, designers will use the terms "players," "avatars," and "characters" almost interchangeably. Even at the technical level, there can be differences: Some designers, for example, use "avatar" to refer strictly to what I have called "character," preferring "puppet" for what I have called "avatar;" others use it to refer to the graphical representation of a character as rendered on a screen (as opposed to the in-world object itself). There's also a possible additional level between player and avatar, *subordinate*, whereby the player treats their world object as an independent agent able to obey commands but capable of autonomous action; in practice, though, virtual worlds are set up such that almost every player skips the stage entirely.

Immersion is connected to the computer-mediated communication (CMC) idea of *presence*—the illusion that a mediated experience is not mediated[45]. Presence manifests in several forms, of which two ("presence as immersion" and "presence as transportation") together correspond well with what virtual world designers mean by "immersion;" others, particularly "presence as realism," can help effect immersion.

---

44. Bromberg, Heather. *Are MUDs Communities? Identity, Belonging and Consciousness in Virtual Worlds*. Rob Shields (editor), *Cultures of Internet: Virtual Spaces, Real Histories, Living Bodies*. London, Sage, 1996.

45. Matthew Lombard and Theresa Ditton, *At the Heart of It All: The Concept of Presence*. Los Angeles, *Journal of Computer-Mediated Communication*, University of Southern California, September 1997.
   http://www.ascusc.org/jcmc/vol3/issue2/lombard.html.
   For a description specific to virtual worlds, see John Towell and Elizabeth Towell, *Presence in Text-Based Networked Virtual Environments or "MUDs."* *Presence: Teleoperators and Virtual Environments* Vol. 6 (5). Cambridge MA, MIT Press, October 1997.
   http://www.fragment.nl/mirror/various/Towell_et_al.1997.Presence_in_MUDs.htm.

In a CMC context, transportation concerns the sense a user has that something is elsewhere from where it really is; for virtual worlds, the "something" is the player and the "elsewhere" is the virtual world. The CMC idea of immersion does not rely on transportation, but is otherwise quite similar to what virtual world designers mean by the term. The main difference is one of emphasis: CMC researchers view "perceptual immersion" and "psychological immersion" as equal partners; virtual world designers view psychological immersion as paramount, considering perceptual immersion to be merely one of many possible means to achieve that end.

Immersion is also connected with the psychological concept of *flow*[46]. Indeed, some designers see the two as equivalent. Flow is an exhilarating sense of control and mastery that can arise from pursuing a focused, goal-driven activity; it's a deep involvement that transcends distractions and sense of time, leading to an ecstatic state of peak productivity. However, although flow regularly occurs in virtual worlds, it's not the kind of immersion that I'm talking about here. Players can be fully immersed without any sense of ecstasy—indeed, they could be quite miserable. Flow and immersion (as I mean it here) can play off each other, but neither is dependent on the other.

Immersion is an important concept in virtual world design, because it plays so much a part in conveying the entire virtual experience. Without immersion, there is a fence between player and virtual world; with immersion, the barriers are lifted—players can concentrate on doing what they want to do, on being what they want to be.

That said, the role of immersion is often misunderstood. It's an important facilitator, but that's all it is: Although players intensely enjoy being immersed, imbuing immersion is not itself the ultimate aim of virtual world design. It does lie on the right path, but a little further back than many designers suppose.

I'm getting increasingly philosophical here, but it's not immersion itself that is intoxicating; rather, it's what immersion helps deliver: identity.

---

46. Mihaly Csikszentmihalyi, *Flow: The Psychology of Optimal Experience*. New York, Harper & Row, 1990. For a description specific to virtual worlds, see Katelyn McKenna and Sangchul Lee, *A Love Affair with MUDs: Flow and Social Interaction in Multi-User Dungeons*. http://www.uni-koeln.de/~am040/muds/ipages/mud.htm.

The Celebration of Identity

I have a story to tell.

Polly's Tale

So it's a weekend in 1980. I'm in a computing laboratory with 15 students, all of whom are playing my game, *MUD*. This being 1980, and this being a computing laboratory, and this being a weekend, everyone here is male. The female computer science undergraduates have better ways to occupy themselves (mainly concerning male non-computer science undergraduates).

I look around at my friends and realize that chances are not one of us has ever had a girl-friend[47], nor have we any prospect of ever finding one. We regard all the female students on our course as people rather than as girls, and we'd no sooner hit on one of them than we would on each other. We're desperately short of social skills. The non-computing girls on campus are split between those who shy away in horror and those who laugh in our faces. It's pointless even trying: We're inexperienced and out-gunned.

None of us is happy with the situation, but we're resigned to it. We suffer in silence together. Here we are on a beautiful weekend, sitting around computers writing and playing games.

It's so sad! I see decent, honest, likeable guys becoming more and more set in their defensive, insular ways. They're not bad people, but they're hiding themselves away! They need to *grow* their personalities, not retreat into them! Yet how can they do so, knowing that every attempt to change will inevitably end in humiliation? There ought to be some means by which they could behave in ways that they wouldn't ordinarily, yet be safe from the consequences of failure. If they could experiment, could make adjustments, could see themselves succeeding, could discover and emphasize those aspects of themselves they most admired; might this not equip them to behave a similar way in real life?

Then I look at my screen, and a thought occurs to me.

(To be continued...)

---

47. Or boyfriend. Essex University was politically correct years before the term came into vogue.

To Be, or What to Be?

The celebration of identity is the fundamental, critical, absolutely core point of virtual worlds.

Yes, that is quite some assertion.

Except for those worlds that people play for purely practical reasons (such as virtual classrooms), everything that players do ultimately concerns the development of their own identity: who they are. It's why achievers achieve, explorers explore, socializers socialize, and killers creep up from nowhere and batter you with a stick.

You can't design for it, because everything affects it; yet for the same reason, you can't *not* design for it—it touches everything you do. It's portable, so it's beyond a designer's reach—it can be used across many virtual worlds[48]. It's unquantifiable—you can't rate for "identity" the actions, objects, structures, or anything else that's programmed in. You can design for certain expressions of identity, and you can design ways to channel these expressions, but you can't do so systematically. Identity flowering is an inherent property of virtual worlds; if you control it or repress it or subvert it, the changes you'd have to make to do so would leave you with something that was no longer a virtual world.

Okay, you've let me babble on about this for a couple of paragraphs, but enough is enough. Ask a dozen players why they play virtual worlds, and you'd be lucky if even one gave an answer that even hinted at "the celebration of identity." They usually reply in terms that categorize them as being an achiever, explorer, socializer, or killer (which is how I derived those types in the first place). To convince you that identity really is the fundamental, critical, absolutely core point of virtual worlds, I'm going to have to provide some evidence.

Fair enough. Let's start with some empirical observations.

Observation 1: Players of virtual worlds often notice that they behave differently in the virtual world than they do in real life. They may be more (or less) assertive, talkative, flirtatious, argumentative, pensive, creative—the list just goes on. For some people, the changes are more dramatic than for others, but most players would concede that they

---

48. And beyond. Many players like to write fiction about their characters, for example.

do seem to have a virtual personality that's different from their real one. Generally, they like their virtual personality more than their real one, but not always. Reflecting on this difference will cause them to make judgments about themselves, therefore their personality (virtual or real) will either shift[49] or the two will remain in conflict until the issue is resolved.

Observation 2: Most players maintain several characters in a virtual world (if that world allows it). Some may be for specific purposes (for example *mules*, to do drudge work for the main character) and others may be the result of failed experiments ("Hmm, so elven thieves don't really work"). There are often two or three, though, that the player uses regularly, depending on their mood. If they're depressed, they may choose their dark, brooding magic-user; if they're angry, they may select their barbarian warrior to let off some steam; if they're wistful, perhaps their bard would suit best. In these situations, the players are using their various characters in the virtual world to work through their real-life issues. They'll grow as people because of it.

Observation 3: Suppose you had poor social skills, and found a social environment where this didn't matter. Merely by interacting in that environment, your skills would improve. In real life, you might be shy and awkward, but if you found a place where wild self-expression was not only permissible, but also positively encouraged, you could suddenly bloom. In becoming accustomed to this virtual personality, you might gain sufficient confidence to be able to maintain it in real life. You wouldn't necessarily even have to think about it, it could just happen. Wouldn't that mean you'd developed as a person?

So, after those three cod-psychology examples we can probably agree that it's possible—common, even—for people to exhibit different behaviors in a virtual world and in reality. This was noticed by academics early in research into virtual worlds. Amy S. Bruckman's groundbreaking paper on the subject[50] was published back in 1992.

What does this have to do with identity, though?

---

49. This is called *slippage* in psychology literature.

50. Amy S. Bruckman, *Identity Workshop: Emergent Social and Psychological Phenomena in Text-Based Virtual Reality.* MIT Media Laboratory, 1992. `ftp.cc.gatech.edu/pub/people/asb/papers/identity-workshop.rtf`.

Well, in the examples I gave there is a separation between the player and the character. This is immersion at the character level. If it stays that way, the player isn't really going to mature. However, for virtual worlds it's almost unavoidable that the character and the player will tend toward each other. If you like your virtual self, you'll take on its characteristics; if you keep mood characters, you'll gradually stop playing all but one; the social skills you acquire will become skills that you use. Ultimately, you advance to the final level of immersion, where you and your character become one. One individual, one persona: identity.

Okay, so players can create separate selves, and over time unify the best aspects of them into a single identity. That doesn't mean it's inevitable, though. This phenomenon of a separate "online self" appears in many other computer-moderated activities, from email to chat rooms to forum postings. Why can't *they* raise identity issues if virtual worlds can?

The answer is that they do, but nowhere near as well. Virtual worlds, armed with a potent combination of environment and fellow players that's unavailable to other online applications, are able to present people with a stream of challenges; an individual's response to each challenge helps define that individual. The challenges of email, chat rooms and forum postings are much narrower in scope, weaker in intensity and rarer in frequency.

This reaction to challenges is how most identity development occurs. Although mood characters and the like make good, neat, psychology parcels to show to cynics, they're overt; the main identity action is covert. Things happen, which present challenges; your reaction to these causes you to acquire insights, which in turn lead to minor readjustments in your understanding of yourself (that is, your identity). Examples: Dealing with responsibility, relationships, unfairness, success/failure, betrayal, strangers, and so on.

These aren't personality change issues. It's not that you stop being a shy loner and are suddenly compelled to transform into an outgoing extrovert; rather, it's that you were always an extrovert, you just didn't realize it. The virtual world lets you try being one, and your opinion of yourself changes as a result of how it works out. If you weren't an extrovert at heart, then you wouldn't make the change; the extrovert virtual you would drift toward the introvert real you, rather than the reverse. It can't make you something you aren't.

Virtual worlds enable you to find out who you are by letting you be who you want to be.

Not everyone necessarily wants to find out who they are, of course. Others do, but don't like it when they learn the answer[51]. Not everyone wants to change, and not everyone likes challenges. Some people may thus be attracted to virtual worlds by the promise of identity freedom, but become increasingly angry and frustrated—unable to leave, but unwilling to do what is necessary to stay. It's particularly sad when an individual takes a harsh lesson but doesn't learn anything—continually acting out rather than working through a difficulty. Fortunately, this doesn't happen very often, but when it does it can be somewhat disruptive.

Incidentally, if you are at all interested in the psychological and/or psychotherapeutic value of virtual worlds, you should look at *Life on the Screen*[52], by Sherry Turkle (if you haven't already). Chapter 7 in particular is directly relevant to the subject, and includes a number of interesting case studies.

So, to summarize: For the great majority of players, virtual worlds encourage them to present different sides of themselves in a safe environment; challenges arise in the virtual world which enable them to reflect (consciously or otherwise) on their responses to those challenges, leading them to develop a greater understanding of themselves; over time, this brings about a gradual merging of the virtual side and the real side, as the player becomes increasingly attuned to their persona.

The persona level of immersion isn't the end of the journey. You've reached the top of a hill, but there may be another one that's higher: There may be a better you. Thus, people will always create new characters and try out new ways of self-expression. Besides, self-affirmation is good, too.

Hey, you're an Eastern mystic, and you didn't even know!

Identity and Identification

Players play virtual worlds in order to be themselves.

Well, perhaps not quite *all* of them do, but it's true of those who play for fun. Even in game worlds, some people will be there for specialist reasons (play-testing, customer

---

51. Some people really *are* total jerks.

52. Sherry Turkle, *Life on the Screen*. New York, Simon & Schuster, 1995.

service, spying from some competing game); none of these individuals would necessarily have any inclination to become immersed, and those that do would be professional about it. There will also be a few people who are in the process of "getting" what a virtual world is about; these will mainly be insufficiently immersed newbies, but occasionally there are individuals who never "get" what virtual worlds are about but play nevertheless (generally, to the irritation of everyone else). Most of the players will be there because of the freedom to be themselves that the virtual world offers, though.

People who don't play virtual worlds (but have tried them) find other ways to be themselves. It has been argued that one of the reasons more men play virtual worlds than women could be because in modern society men have less opportunity to experiment with their identities in real life[53]. For players, though, virtual worlds afford an unmatched ability simply to *be*.

Let's look at this a little more analytically, and see if there's anything that designers can do to make this salute to identity any easier.

We should begin by noting that identity is not the same as identification, although the two are related. Identification is the modeling of the self on some ideal. For players of virtual worlds who might sense the possibilities of identity exploration without really understanding how to invoke it, the provision of ideals can help. This is why many virtual worlds have a class system.

The idea is that the individual takes on board those aspects that define the ideal, because these are what the individual admires. They provide a target—something to shoot for. If a proposed role model exhibits other features that conflict with an individual's sense of self, that role model is not suitable as an ideal. It's therefore easier to identify with an abstraction rather than something concrete, because abstractions present fewer features; you can flesh out what isn't mentioned without hitting contradictions.

This would imply that the lower an ideal's detail, the better. Sure enough, many virtual worlds have dozens of classes for players to peruse. The disadvantage of this approach is that the fewer qualities an ideal presents, the less rounded it is, and therefore the flatter it makes those people who aspire to it seem. An ideal with a single outstanding feature leads to players who are defined by that single outstanding feature, that is, who

---

53. How many men in make-up have you seen today?

are one-dimensional. One-dimensional characters don't make for riveting movies, and neither do they make for enthralling virtual worlds. Many virtual worlds with character classes therefore also have character races, to provide another dimension (although there tend to be specific class/race combinations that work better than others, so in practice the choice isn't quite as wide as it may appear).

Whereas identification is about projecting your self-image onto some ideal, identity is about projecting it onto yourself. The former can help the latter, but has neither its extent nor its fidelity. If it goes too far, it can be counter-productive. Identification is allowing yourself to be defined by an image[54]; in excess, it can therefore lead to a conflict between personal identity and that perceived of the ideal. A painting doesn't change, but an artist must. If a virtual world commits a player to identifying with a fixed set of ideals, there will be problems when those ideals are no longer appropriate.

Identity is a product of thought, manifested by expression (actions, words). It has to be flexible, so it can wander, focus, be reborn. It also has to be true. A false image may be projected for the benefit of other people, as a way to influence them; individuals can't lie for long to themselves, though—that is, if they can *see* themselves. In the real world, this can be difficult.

Virtual worlds provide people with a mirror. In a virtual world, you *can* see yourself. You only see what you show to the mirror, which may not be what everyone else sees, but it's more than enough. With identity, the question is how much you like your reflection; with identification, it's how much you believe it.

Virtual world designers have some control over this. They get to provide the ideals; they get to make the mirror. As I said earlier, though, they can't do this systematically. You can't draw a graph with an "identity" axis and place players at various places along it. The best you can do is to assess the likely consequences of their progression to greater maturity. To do that, you need to know the course that progression takes.

---

54. Do people who wear the same make-up every day do so because of what other people think about them, or because of what they think about themselves?

Progression

I mentioned earlier the *main sequence* that charts player type drift. This gets its name from the main sequence of star development used in cosmology[55]. Players typically start off testing the immediate bounds on their behavior (killer) then begin to acquire knowledge of their environment (explorer); following this, they apply their knowledge (achiever), in the course of which they forge bonds with other players; finally, they retire and spend their time chatting with their friends (socializer).

Sometimes, people stay in one area. Long-term killers will often be youngsters who have feelings of inferiority[56] and need constantly to validate their worth to themselves. Long-term explorers know they have the ability to apply their knowledge, and feel no urge to demonstrate the fact to others. That said, a good many people follow the main sequence the whole way.

There's a flaw in this argument, though. As people grow in virtual worlds, their real selves and their virtual selves gradually become one. Because socializer is the last step on the main sequence, all socializers should be immersed to persona level. They're not. You can start as a socializer, socializing effectively while being barely immersed to avatar level. Your development is due to social challenges rather than environmental ones. This rather undermines the use of player types in predicting the effects of growing maturity, doesn't it?

As it stands, yes, it does. There is, however, an interesting solution.

My original work for *Hearts, Clubs, Diamonds, Spades: Players Who Suit MUDs* evolved from summarizing a discussion among the players of *MUD2* that ran from November 1989 to May 1990. The paper as finally presented concerned only the actions and interactions between *mortals* (that is, normal players); it did not make particular reference to *wizzes* (that is, players trusted with administration powers—this is *MUD2*'s *elder game*). Wizzes[57] had already played the game in its entirety, as that was the qualification to be a wiz; therefore, they were on the whole no longer concerned with the

---

55. The Hertzsprung-Russel diagram: Map absolute visual magnitude against spectral type. The main sequence, on which most stable stars lie, runs roughly diagonally from high luminosity/low temperature to low luminosity/high temperature.

56. "Ha! You call *that* an inferiority complex?!"

57. The term is gender non-specific, meaning "wizards and witches."

virtual world *per se*, just in its inhabitants. There were a few explorers who made wiz better to aid their exploring, and a few achievers who regarded building as a competitive act; the majority, though, were either socializers or killers.

In separating wizzes from mortals, I noticed that there were some very distinct behavioral differences between the wizzes themselves. Wizzes were keen to articulate their beliefs about what they and their peers should and should not do to manage the game, as there were particularly strong conflicts between certain groups. Therefore, at the same time I constructed the player interest graph (refer to Figure 3.1) for mortals, I constructed a similar one for wizzes. The players/world axis was not relevant here (because nearly all wizzes were at the players side); in its stead was a different axis that rated the degree to which wizzes did things in an explicit or implicit[58] fashion. Explicit wizzes favored the known over the unknown, realism over idealism, the overt over the covert, expectation over surprise, and order over disorder.

Note that "explicit" here is meant in the general sense of the word: leaving nothing implied. It's not intended to have any "explicit photographs" style overtones. In computer language semantics, explicit means data, implicit means code; in AI terms, explicit means examinable, implicit means executable. That's how I mean it.

There were a number of conflicts suggested by this implicit/explicit analysis, which led to some interesting underlying dynamics (and alarming consequences for inter-wiz balance). However, as the graph was specific to the relatively small set of administrators in a game-oriented virtual world that selected them by unusual means, I felt it would have distracted from the main thrust of my player types model had I presented it in my paper. I therefore left it out.

Perhaps, though, it doesn't just apply to wizzes?

What would happen were we to incorporate this implicit/explicit dimension[59] into the basic player types model? Specifically, would it help us differentiate between sub-types of the player-oriented styles, killer, and socializer?

---

58. For *MUD2*-specific reasons to do with the nature of the wiz invisibility command, the original axis labeling was *open* (explicit) and *closed* (implicit).

59. Readers of Michael Moorcock and players of *D&D* can use law/chaos if they really must, but it's not quite a match.

Yes, it does[60]. We get:

➤ *Politicians*. Players who act in an open fashion on other players. Whether you view them as inspired, visionary leaders or interfering, self-serving busybodies depends on how gullible or cynical you are.

➤ *Networkers*. Players who interact openly with other players—even complete strangers—on any and all subjects. Less charitably, gossips.

➤ *Friends*. Players who interact primarily with people they have known a long time and with whom they have deep bonds (often forged through adversity). They do not feel bound by the conventional rules of interaction, because they understand each other so well.

➤ *Griefers*. Bullies prepared to use force or other unpleasantness to get their way or be noticed.

Figure 3.3 shows this as a graph.

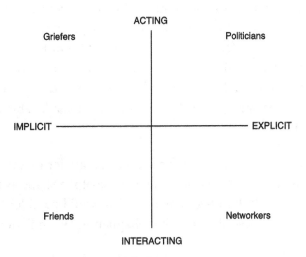

Figure 3.3 Players-oriented Player Interest Graph.

If this served only to clear up some of the confusion about the different varieties of the killer type (griefers and politicians) it would have done its job. However, it's not quite a one-trick pony.

---

60. Unsurprisingly, as obviously I wouldn't have mentioned it otherwise.

What happens when a player-oriented newbie enters a virtual world? The first issue many of them face is coming to terms with the fact that they are part of a community. Some will immediately comprehend the situation, but not everyone. Those that don't will objectify other players, treating them as helpdesks, servants, gophers, and sources of experience points or kit. The reaction of the other players to this approach will cause all but the most mule-headed newbie socializer to understand fairly rapidly the social mechanics of the world. They can then move on to the business of getting to know people. To make friends with someone, you need to meet them, which means you have to network. Some people you won't like, and some won't like you, but after a while you'll find you hang out with the same, relatively small group of people most of the time and be acquainted with many more.

Your group will almost inevitably experience conflicts, both internal and external. Perhaps several people want to be leader, or don't like where the leader is taking them. The group may grow too large, or too small, or otherwise become dysfunctional. Environmental changes could trigger problems—a change in the way the virtual world works, for example, or a loss of group status. Ultimately, everyone in the group has a view and will at least some of the time want to impose it on the other members—even if it's only as a form of self-defense. The trials that result put big stresses on relationships, some of which may break down irrevocably. Eventually, though, players will come through with a fuller understanding of themselves and of their friends. Their earlier ties will have been strengthened, and they will at last be able to settle down and appreciate one another.

What we have here is a main sequence for socializers: griefer to networker to politician to friend. Drawn on the graph[61], it's the same reverse-alpha shape as the standard main sequence, which is nice. Back in two dimensions, it would be killer to socializer to killer to socializer, but it's less obvious what's happening when flattened that way.

At this point, we can see where F. Randall Farmer's Path to Ascension fits in. This is perhaps unsurprising, given that *Habitat* was a socializer-centric system. Ignoring the "non-player" caretaker and geek god roles: Motivators map onto politicians; actives and passives both map onto networker (actives being more immersed than passives)[62].

---

61. For the record, this also works on the original, wiz-specific graph.

62. This suggests that at least in some cases, refining the model to account for gradations of immersion may be useful.

So, having added an extra dimension, the obvious question to ask next is: What—if anything—does adding an extra dimension buy us concerning the world-oriented players (achievers and explorers)?

Well, the subdivisions are relatively easy to construct:

➤ *Planners*. Organized achievers, who decide what they want to do then go off and do it.

➤ *Scientists*. Explorers who experiment in a thorough, methodical fashion.

➤ *Hackers*[63]. Explorers whose understanding of the virtual world is such that they can proceed purely by intuition.

➤ *Opportunists*. Achievers who go where their fancy takes them.

Figure 3.4 shows the resulting 3D graph.

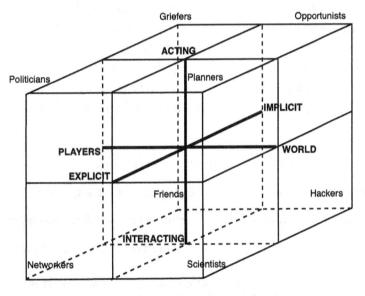

Figure 3.4 3D Player Interest Graph.

---

63. This is in the traditional sense of the word, not the break-into-your-computer-and-erase-your-data one.

Whether this is of tremendous use is another matter, of course[64]. Instead of four player types, we now have eight: opportunists, planners, politicians, griefers, hackers, scientists, networkers, and friends. The conflicts between some of the eight are meaningful (for example griefers versus planners), but for others the old types work just as well and are better at encapsulation (for example socializers versus achievers).

If having more categories doesn't deliver more tools for designers, there's little point in designers using them. Mere categorization doesn't itself guarantee utility, even if it can be shown to be inclusive (as this one can) and is easy to validate empirically (as this one is). After all, adding a dimension for the time of the year in which a player was born would be inclusive and verifiable, but designers would find it of very little general efficacy[65].

Concerning our current discussion on player type progression, though, the addition of an extra dimension does have an effect for world-oriented players: It gives another sequence—opportunist to scientist to planner to hacker. We also can "unflatten" the main sequence (killer to explorer to achiever to socializer) from 2D into 3D, giving griefer to scientist to planner to friend. Tempting though it is to look for a sequence matching this of opportunist to networker to politician to hacker, this can't be validated empirically: People simply don't follow that career path. However, there *is* a minor fourth sequence, for opportunist achievers who learn by networking rather than by experimentation. This gives us

➤ Griefer to scientist to planner to friend (main sequence)

➤ Opportunist to networker to planner to friend (minor sequence)

➤ Griefer to networker to politician to friend (main socializer sequence)

➤ Opportunist to scientist to planner to hacker (main explorer sequence)

At last we're getting close to a model good enough to use for something. If designers can assess how players are likely to mature, they can account for their progress in their game designs. We're not quite there yet, though.

---

64. Tools are only objects if they have no use. What's more, it's far better if the tool is designed to fit the problem than if the problem is designed to fit the tool. I don't want to be a man with a hammer looking for things I can nail.

65. Sorry to break the bad news to any astrologers among you.

Development Tracks

The thing is, those sequences overlap. People can switch paths, if they have some moment of epiphany. Someone could go griefer to scientist (main sequence) to planner to hacker (explorer sequence). They could go opportunist to networker (minor sequence) to politician to friend (socializer sequence). They'll tend to keep to whatever path they began on, but sometimes they decide to go a different way when they meet a fork in the road[66]. Writing the sequences out linearly gives Figure 3.5.

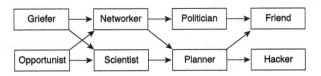

Figure 3.5   Player development tracks.

From Figure 3.5, we can make a number of observations. It's immediately apparent that there's an oddity with politicians. Although people can become planners by applying knowledge they learned themselves (as scientists) or from others (by networking), for politicians only networking works as a qualification. Similarly, although planners can go on to become friends (forged through adversity) or hackers (understanding the world almost spiritually), politicians only ever go on to become friends. Designers can therefore be fairly confident that their world's politician-friendly features should not be deeply hard-coded (because no one who experiments with them is going to use them) and that politicians should not be given too much ability to affect the physical structure of the world (because they're never going to be attuned to it).

Another point that the development tracks show is that the elder game[67] (that is, what they do having played through the virtual world) would work best if it aimed at providing tools for people to tinker with the world or to enjoy one another's company. Many textual worlds allow players to become builders once they've "won"; others provide private gathering places where players can sit and discuss the issues of the day. It's certainly possible to have an elder game of a different kind, for example by

---

66. Alternatively, they could completely hit a wall and bounce right back to the beginning again. Instead of developing in the face of a crisis, they could, for example, regress to some vengeful griefer state. This is, needless to say, not really what we want to see happening.

67. This is another one of those terms that has come from game-oriented virtual worlds that doesn't really have a non-game equivalent.

allowing players to repeat their time as a planner or politician in a different manner, but it's less satisfactory for individuals that way[68]. Only if the elder game is radically different from what went before will players begin development from scratch again.

Designers can take advantage of the fact that immersion is related to how far a player has proceeded in their development. Most networkers will not be deeply immersed, for example, therefore a designer could argue that it's okay to put in immersion-breaking communication systems that facilitate networking. Most planners are immersed, therefore a designer might decide that statistical information regarding the operation of the virtual world is not available from within it: Players might know from a web site that their sword is a hackmaster +12, but when they bring it up on their inventory the number is represented descriptively or graphically instead.

As a more general comment, Figure 3.5 shows that identity paths progress in the same way; furthermore, this links directly to the 3D player interest graph (refer to Figure 3.4). The original 2D player interest graph (refer to Figure 3.1) is the same as the 3D graph (refer to Figure 3.4) with the implicit/explicit axis removed. If we take out the players/world axis instead, we get Figure 3.6.

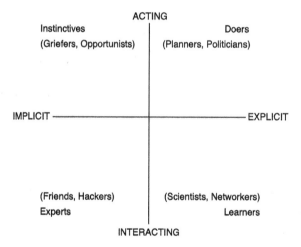

Figure 3.6 Flattened Player Interest Graph.

The player type labels for Figure 3.6 aren't particularly important; more interesting is how players change from one to the next.

---

68. This isn't to say it wouldn't be better for the health of the virtual world itself, of course.

When a player arrives in a completely new situation, they have to act on instinct—there's little else they *can* do. A player's first aim is to determine the parameters that govern what they can do, which means trying everything they can think of to discover what basic actions are available. Having bootstrapped to a level where the player can reliably perform individual "primitive" actions, the next thing to do is to go about discovering sequences and combinations of these actions. The player does this methodically in a data-gathering phase, until they become thoroughly acquainted with the options available to them. Following this, the player applies what they have learned intensely, until eventually mastering it and it becomes second nature.

Baby arrives in the world. Baby flails about, until baby realizes how to move its legs, its arms, its feet, and its hands. Baby combines individual movements into sequences, some of which work and some of which don't. Baby sits up. Baby toddles. Baby toddles more and more, until eventually baby can walk and run. Now, for baby, running is effectively a primitive action.

Locate, discover, apply, internalize. From acting on instinct, acquire knowledge, use that knowledge, and become able to interact on instinct.

I mention this feature of the 3D Player Interest Graph only to show how the player development tracks (refer to Figure 3.5) fit into the overall scheme. In practice, the tracks themselves are of more use to designers than the flattened graph (refer to Figure 3.6), although we'll see later that there's an interesting analogy that can be drawn from it.

There remains the question as to whether flattening the graph by removing the acting/interacting axis gives a useful new perspective, but it's easily answered: No, it doesn't. This may indicate that there are better choices for axes available which have yet to be discovered.

With that, we reach the end of this discussion of identity. There are some follow-up topics we need to look at, but we're done with the central issue. The question might now be asked: Was it worth it? Although this analysis has produced some results of tangible use to designers, has it all *really* been necessary? Isn't it, beneath the surface, just a lot of pseudo-psychological nonsense? What has it to do with design?

Directly, it contributes only in a few areas. Indirectly, it pervades everything. If you don't understand the nature of what you're designing, how can you design it?

People play virtual worlds to celebrate their identity. Designers must understand that.

It's a freedom thing.

Anonymity

Good simulations allow people to do whatever they want to do; good virtual worlds allow people to be whatever they want to be[69].

Anonymity is itself a neutral concept: You can use it for good or for evil. In practice, *someone* has to know who you really are, so you can be called to account should you cause pandemonium. In virtual worlds, this will be the administrators; other players don't get proof of who you are unless (through your behavior) you give it to them.

Reduced consequences for actions makes for the disinhibition that so characterizes virtual worlds. Anonymity is central to this, because only through anonymity do people have the freedom to change. If you make a mistake in the virtual world, you can restart; it's okay to experiment, to take risks. However, if a real-world friend finds out about some virtual-world mistake, restarting will not erase it. Contact with reality collapses virtual identity like observation does a quantum wave.

Life with a Backspace

Starting a new character is like backspacing over your identity mistakes and retyping them a different way. It's only possible in virtual worlds[70].

Anonymity separates the real you from the virtual you. This has three effects:

> ➤ People in the virtual world won't prejudge you on superficialities.

> ➤ Your real-world friends won't judge you by your virtual-world actions.

> ➤ Your virtual-world friends won't judge you by your real-world actions.

---

69. Contrast not-so-good virtual worlds, where you can be whatever the designers want you to be.

70. And witness protection schemes.

Without anonymity, your virtual actions have real-world effects and vice versa. If no one knows you're the U.S. president, you can be yourself; if they do, you're back to being the U.S. president.

It doesn't usually take long for newbies to realize that anonymity means they can restart if they screw up. It's pretty obvious. However, in practice it's not actually as important as people often think. The longer you play a character, the more attached to it you become, and the more people come to know that character. You soon reach the stage where you've invested so much in that character that if you do screw up you would be very reluctant to throw it all away. Instead, you ride out the storm (and are perhaps a better person because of it).

This can lead to an extra level of anonymity. If you decided to create a second character, you might not want it to be associated with either your real self or your first virtual self. Anonymity lets you branch. Thus, we should think of anonymity[71] as acting as a buffer between all your separate identities, not just the real and the virtual. When you start a new identity, your primary concern is to keep the old identities intact and separate. Therefore, the main advantage of anonymity is not that your new friends won't find out about your other selves; rather it's that your other friends won't find out about your new self. It can be the other way round (for newbies and U.S. presidents), but mostly it isn't. The virtual girl who doesn't want her friends to know she's a real-life guy has less to lose than the real-life guy who doesn't want his friends to know he's a virtual girl[72].

It turns out that maintaining separate identities in the same virtual world can be quite difficult. Experienced Wild West telegraph operators were able to tell which of the other operators on their line they were communicating with from nuances in the way they tapped out the Morse code[73]; it's unsurprising, therefore, that players in virtual worlds can often detect other players by subtleties in the way they act and speak. If you always misspell a particular word, for example, people will notice. This means that anonymity across characters can't always be relied upon. There are ways to succeed,

---

71. Because virtual identities are named and can be referenced, the term *pseudonymity* is preferred by some researchers in this context.

72. As people spend more and more of their time in virtual worlds, this could change. When they spend most of it there (as in *True Names*, for example), people may want to protect their real-world identities the most.

73. Their styles were known as their "signatures."

which I'll discuss a little later; on the whole, though, people who feel they need anonymity should switch to either a different virtual world or a different incarnation of the same one.

An interesting side issue here is that although players will often mature quicker if they regularly start up new characters, most of them are reluctant to do so because of the time they have invested in their old ones. They therefore find themselves facing the same challenges as before, responding in the same ways, and generally not getting much out of the experience. Were they occasionally forced to change character (for exmple, by its erasing following virtual death), would this not perhaps lead to greater enjoyment for them in the long term? Probably, yes; however, if they knew that characters could die dead-dead after months of playing time, players perhaps wouldn't sign up for a virtual world in the first place. This is the great tragedy of persona death in virtual worlds, which causes more problems than any other for designers. It is discussed in considerable depth later in this book.

Returning to the topic of anonymity, then: What are the implications of all this on virtual world design?

Well firstly, a certain degree of anonymity must be guaranteed. Clearly, the live team needs access to the real-world details associated with a character, but this information should be considered private. If there is any way that a regular player can uniquely identify another regular player without the latter's permission, it's not good. *You* might think that associating email addresses with every character is beneficial for community development, but that's not how the majority of players will see it.

Secondly, it shouldn't go too far. People want to have separate identities, not no identity. If every character looked the same, that would lead to anonymity. If you can't tell people apart, everyone could be anyone. Identities should be constructible to as great (or shallow) a level of detail that a player wants. Anonymity is relative, between characters; it isn't absolute for individual characters.

Finally, players should be able to start up new characters with relative ease. Players won't grow if they can't occasionally experiment, and they'll eventually lose faith in the virtual world unless once in a while they can start afresh. This does not mean that they should be offered new accounts at a cheaper rate; rather, there should be several slots on their existing account so they can maintain several characters simultaneously (in practice, the absolute minimum is three, but five is normally enough for most people).

Well, that's the traditional point of view.

There is another argument that says players should only have one account with only one character on it. In game worlds at least, most people use secondary characters either as mules (which screws up game balance) or as griefers (so they can act like jerks without fear of reprisal). In both instances, the virtual world would be better off without them. Furthermore, in a commercial setting you can check names, addresses, credit card numbers, and computer registry settings to ensure that people don't simply buy a second account to use for their mule or griefer activities[74].

This is the approach adopted by *Star Wars Galaxies* (although their hands were somewhat tied by the fact that the huge amount of data they store for each character is such that it would exceed their database's capabilities to allow more than one character per account—well, that's the official line anyway).

As it happens, none of these are particularly thorny issues for designers (although the number of characters per account may yet become so). The immediate problem with anonymity is practical rather than theoretical: It must be possible for characters to be referenced. This means they need a name. In a virtual world with half a million players, that's a lot of names.

The Name Problem

In a virtual world, you are represented by, represent, or are an individual. The world fiction may pretend otherwise, for example, by allowing hive minds (such as ant nests) or shared-mind couples (such as Tweedledum and Tweedledee), but these are mere conceits. You are associated with a single, sentient game object: your character[75]. So that people can refer to your character in conversation and commands, that character must have a label; in other words, a *name*.

---

74. CompuServe allowed one character per account on *British Legends*. Some players therefore accumulated several accounts—a dozen or more in some cases—so they could have multiple characters in the game. Needless to say, these accounts did not come at a cheaper rate, either.

75. Or avatar or persona, but these generally lose out to character in discussions for which immersion is not an issue.

MUD1 originally allowed players to have the same names, as long as they weren't logged on at the same time. This rapidly led to problems of mistaken identity (and, to a lesser extent, impersonation). Permitting only one person with a particular name to be in the virtual world at any one time was no help: Players could find themselves locked out that way. The solution adopted was to allow only one instance of any name in the entire virtual world. There were still occasional problems when a character was killed and someone stole its name before the original player had recovered enough to return, but these were only isolated incidents that could be handled by administrators on a case-by-case basis.

On the whole, this is how virtual worlds are still designed today. There are implementational reasons why two characters[76] with the same name should not be allowed into a virtual world at the same time (it makes parsing and communication *so* much easier), and disallowing name clashes[77] for offline characters, too, is essentially a customer relations requirement (although there are other benefits to do with helping engender a sense of identity).

Virtual worlds with large numbers of players rapidly run out of decent names. It's not a problem that dogs only virtual worlds, of course—it's far worse for URLs, AOL account names, and Hotmail email addresses—but that doesn't mean it isn't an issue. The designers of *Ultima Online* anticipated that names would be in short supply, so they took the decision to allow them to be non-unique. To stop lock-outs, people with the same name could both play at the same time. Impersonation and communication evils ensued. Both were fixable while retaining non-unique names, but only with immersion-breaking solutions. The graphical virtual worlds that immediately followed did not make the same mistake, and used unique names from the beginning.

This still meant that there was a shortage of supply, of course: If you have 400,000 players, they need to have 400,000 names (and more if they have multiple characters). An obvious compromise is to limit uniqueness to server cluster (that is, to an individual incarnation/shard). With 40 servers, players' imaginations need only stump up 10,000 different names, which is far more tractable. Sure, some other guy might be using your name on a different server, but your friends are all on this one.

---

76. It's actually stronger than this: No two *objects* should have the same name (identifier).

77. Names don't have to be exact to "clash," just similar enough that at a glance you could mistake one for another.

How to choose a name? Players identify more with their characters if they get to choose the names themselves; name selection is the first and arguably most important decision concerning their virtual identity that a player can make. Giving them a free hand, though, can be tiresomely fiction-breaking (Robinhood the elf is here). It's a problem: Randomly select any virtual world with a policy of free naming and the chances are there will be *someone* called "Gandalf"—irrespective of the genre.

One solution, hinted at previously, is to use a restrictive naming policy. Administrators vet prospective names. This is practical and very effective in virtual worlds with strong role-playing elements, because in explaining why their character has the name it does, a player must necessarily flesh out that character. It's a barrier to entry, though: If someone tries to play your virtual world and finds there's a 10-minute delay while you okay the character name, they'll go somewhere else that doesn't have a 10-minute delay. It's also way too expensive to implement for virtual worlds that have thousands of newbies arriving every day.

A way to preserve an element of choice, while limiting the freedom to choose something unfortunate as a name, is to use *name lists*. The idea is to present players with a list of, say, 10 or 20 available names, and let them pick which one they want. If none of them really suit, another list can perhaps be presented, until all possibilities are exhausted. Players could still be given the option to enter a freeform name and wait for it to be vetted, but they wouldn't *have* to do so.

There are a number of ways that name lists can be generated. The most obvious one is to do it randomly. This has to be good to work: *EverQuest* tried it, but it wasn't and it didn't.

Another way is to use the context of the virtual world to present possibilities. This is used sometimes in pencil-and-paper role-playing games. The idea is that the character's name is built up from syllables that have a meaning in some ancient language supposedly spoken by the character's people. A typical arrangement is to have an opening syllable, one or more middle syllables, and a closing syllable. An elf might thus choose "Ard-la-shi-sa" meaning "tree-of-silent-spirit," whereas a dwarf (using a different set of syllables and ostensible meanings) might pick "Khad-rak-uz" meaning "Stone-strong-beard." These are fun for designers to design and for players to play with, but you have to be careful—I once managed to get Fu-qu-az-ole out of one of these.

Using such pseudo-cultural definitions for names, it's possible to re-introduce a modicum of non-unique naming. If players are given a surname based on their character's race/class/gender/whatever, then they might be able to choose the same first name as someone else with a different surname. If Urk Wolfhead and Urk Sharpspear play at the same time, either can be referred to as Urk by other members of their tribe or by people in the same general location as they. Only when someone from a different tribe wants to reference one rather than the other does the surname also have to be used (adjectivally). This is a neat solution that allows for some degree of choice while preserving the decorum of the virtual world.

Names are referents, but they are not the only ones. Hey, you know that charismatic, short, French general who conquered half of Europe in the early 1800s? Well yes, of course you do—it was Napoleon Bonaparte. I didn't have to give you his name before you knew who he was, though, did I[78]? There is an argument that virtual worlds should allow this kind of relative description for characters, and that it should be preferred until you've actually been introduced to someone (or told who they are by someone who already "knows"). The rationale for this is that in the real world people don't walk about with their names tattooed to their foreheads, and therefore neither should characters in virtual worlds. The counter argument is that having to refer to someone as "The Tall Stranger" the whole time gets in the way of interactions—even if it eventually encourages people to interact by asking each other their names. As with many real-versus-virtual arguments, both sides have a point, and it's ultimately up to designers to decide how they want to handle the situation in their own virtual world. Most of them go with the see-the-names approach, because it's easier on newbies. If people complain, they can always produce some fiction to explain it away ("All player characters are by definition heroic, therefore they're also famous, therefore everyone knows who everyone else is already").

Relative names illustrate a point that game designers often forget: Names are owned by an individual, but used by everyone else. If "The Tall Stranger" won't tell me his name, I may just decide to call him Lanky: I can invent names for other people. In *MUD1*, killers would give themselves hard-to-type names like Mmnmnnmn so that people would have a hard time casting spells on them, stealing goodies from them, and so on. I got round this by using pronouns, although this was not itself without problems. In particular, you might type something like "sleep him." Then just as you were hitting

---

78. If I did, you should have paid more attention in history class.

return a friend would appear and change the binding for "him." *MUD2* added the ability to create synonyms for players and objects, so that once you (or anyone else) had typed "syn Mmnmnnmn as 'Mm'," you could thereafter refer to Mmnmnnmn as Mm.

Why stop there, though? Why not allow players to annotate one another? Most people see, "Jay says, 'hello';" you see, "Jay the boring creep says, 'hello'."

This raises the issue of how players annotate themselves.

Image

Traditionally, virtual worlds make a distinction between stats (short for "statistics") and knowledge. Stats are what characters have (strength, dexterity, magic points, and so on); knowledge is what players have (how to bring down a dragon, the route to the citadel, that player B is an idiot, and so on). The virtual world knows everything about stats and nothing about knowledge; for this reason, the terms *tangibles* and *intangibles* are used when referring to attributes of characters[79] as opposed to attributes of players. A player's knowledge of tangibles is itself intangible, of course.

Only tangibles are meaningful to the virtual world, but both tangibles and intangibles are meaningful to players. Virtual worlds generally have no way even to know that player A thinks player B is an idiot, let alone to model the fact. Players, however, do like to know this stuff, and are excellent at assimilating it. Many virtual worlds therefore provide what are essentially bookkeeping facilities for players, wound into their own context to maintain a degree of immersion. However, they don't actually use any of it to introduce goals for the players—they have no access to the content of the information, just to its form. There is therefore no gameplay reason why a player should be able to make a private annotation to another player's character; it just adds to their enjoyment.

The most important intangible is a character's name. Unless the name is constructed from components that the virtual world knows about, it has absolutely no handle on what a name might "mean." Players will hazard a guess that Cupcake and Hardcore might have different personalities, but the virtual world doesn't know. Names that are names in real-life are especially potent: Anyone picking such a name has some *reason* for doing so (typically to do with role-playing or real-life self-image).

---

79. These terms extend to the virtual world in general (as described in Chapter 1).

There are plenty of other intangibles, however. It costs a virtual world practically nothing to allow characters to have different color clothes, hair, weapons, and so on, but it allows people to individualize themselves and make personal statements. This is made easier by the fact that these are *recognizably* intangible: At character-creation time, players aren't going to worry about the gameplay effect of having blue eyes, whereas they might for having a particular weapon or skill. They can concentrate on their image. Purists often sneer at such distractions from what a virtual world is "about." Why would anyone in their right mind want to wear a suit of crimson armor if there are cheaper regulation gray ones that offer a better defense? Shouldn't designers be investing their time in extending gameplay rather than adding yet more eye candy? Some designers do go overboard in this regard, it's true, but then some non-gameplay features can be absolutely critical. Strictly speaking, for example, communication between players is rarely necessary for gameplay reasons, yet take it away and you don't have a virtual world.

That said, the purists do have a point in that although there's no reason why a suit of crimson armor should have any gameplay differences from a regular suit of armor, there's no reason for it not to, either. If someone has gone to the trouble of collecting all the various crimson parts (breastplate, helmet, gauntlets, epaulettes, grieves, and so on), it doesn't hurt to make the parts or the suit as a whole give more protection against, say, fire than a standard-issue suit; what's more, it makes it a little more interesting for achiever types. Even someone who is wearing it only because it makes them look good might feel more satisfied if they can convince themselves there is a "legitimate" gameplay reason for sporting it[80]. Note that this does not apply for customizations that players pay for. There is money to be made in selling players one-off character modifications or pieces of customized kit, but *only* if it doesn't affect gameplay. It's okay to replace a shield with a functionally equivalent one that looks different, but it's not okay to replace it with one that acts different; otherwise, players who can't afford to pay for such a change will complain bitterly that they are disadvantaged[81]. Changes to intangibles are acceptable, but changes to tangibles aren't.

---

80. The same applies for role-playing props. If there's a gun on the wall then you ought to be able to fire it, even if laser weapons are better (apologies to Chekhov).

81. There is an argument that this doesn't apply for virtual worlds (or particular instantiations of them) that are designed to use charging for gameplay-significant objects from the beginning, advertising it as a main feature of their business model. Of course, such worlds might not attract many players, but hopefully they'll get more money from each one. The main standard-bearer of this approach is *Achaea*, where player expectation is so geared up for it that they sell over half a million objects with tangible properties a year—a phenomenal figure!

Tangibles mainly interest achievers. It therefore comes as little surprise to learn that intangibles are particularly important to socializers. Therefore, designers who want to make their virtual worlds attractive to socializers usually incorporate a number of intangible-friendly tools in their worlds. As the celebration of identity lies at the very core of virtual worlds, chief among these will be the means made available to players for determining their appearances in the virtual world.

The mechanisms for creating a basic character differ between textual and graphical worlds, and the various options are discussed fully in Chapter 5, "Life in the Virtual World." For now, though, we'll assume that a new character has been created: This new character is the player's opening statement. Customizations subsequent to it are modifications to that statement and can say important things about the way individuals view themselves. It is therefore in the best interests of designers to make customization easy, so that people can go where they want to go. The simplest method is to allow players to make freeform notes about themselves that other players can read as an adjunct to their name, but this is just one of three general approaches available:

➤ *Tangibles real for the virtual world.* A character can remove a suit of armor and give it to some other character who will benefit from its protective attributes.

➤ *Intangibles real for the virtual world.* Your character can dye their hair yellow and their hair will thenceforth be reported as being yellow—even if hair color is transparent to the mechanisms of the virtual world.

➤ *Intangibles virtual for the virtual world.* You can annotate yourself with a publicly readable note that says dogs adore you, but the virtual world would take no account of it were you to encounter one.

Players can therefore use a combination of methods to make statements about—that is, to express—themselves. They can write their description such that when someone looks at them they're told they see "a mighty knight;" they can wear some impressive-looking armor that makes them appear like they're mighty knights; they can wear some top-of-the-range plate mail that makes them *be* a mighty knight.

Freeform descriptions aren't as important in graphical worlds as they are in textual ones, because people go by looks in the former and by "look" commands in the latter. Most MUDs have freeform descriptions, and they're considered the main way (other than by name) to flesh out a character. There are two problems, however, neither of which is immediately apparent.

The first is practical. On the face of it, it might be thought that there could be trouble with hugely unsuitable descriptions[82] if people are allowed to depict their characters however they see fit, but this is only the case for griefers (who are trouble anyway).

Other players may inflate their status, but it's easy to spot and only makes the perpetrator look foolish (well, not quite "only"—it spoils immersion for others, too). No, the main problem with the content of personal descriptions is that they are often either touchingly illiterate or irredeemably clichéd. There may be a thousand ways to say that a character is tall, dark, and mysterious, but if every male character you meet is basically tall, dark, and mysterious then they all kind of merge into one. They even have eyes that seem to pierce your very soul the same way[83]. Female characters are green-eyed, flame-haired, pale-skinned, beauties who move with the catlike grace of a dancer while wielding matching swords. Oh, and they have heaving breasts, too. There must be a factory somewhere manufacturing them.

The second problem is less easy to fix by taking someone aside and having a quiet word. The thing is, it's an act of will to change a description. The player may change, but unless they notice it their character's description won't. Even if it does, there are limits; "tall, dark, and mysterious" may mean a player feels out of place and misunderstood yet possessing of hidden depths, but if they later feel at home, at ease, and gregarious, how do they change their description to reflect that? Their character shrank a few inches and went blond overnight? Worse, will they even effect a change if every time they meet someone new they're treated like they were tall, dark, and mysterious? Freeform descriptions can anchor players too much; in graphical worlds, the same applies to their character's visual appearance. I didn't implement character descriptions in *MUD1* precisely for this reason: Players can explore their identities more freely if they aren't tied to some image[84].

---

82. If they're descriptions at all—web site addresses sometimes feature, for example.

83. Which can still happen when they're asleep, unless the virtual world provides facilities to switch descriptions depending on character states, which most don't.

84. This is an example of where virtual world designers don't always understand their virtual world's design. Why do most textual worlds have free-form descriptions in them nowadays? Well, it's because someone way back when added the facility to an ancestor world and they've simply inherited it. Why was it added in the first place? Was it because the designer who did it knew what they were doing or because they didn't know what their own "parent" world's designer was doing? In either case, how can the designers of today's worlds be sure it's the right thing for *their* world? How many of them even consider that the feature might be optional?

There are two basic mechanisms for getting around this.

The first one is to have characters die occasionally, so players have to create new ones. This gives players the opportunity for some redefinition. Persona death has other implications, however, so this is not necessarily an option for most designers.

The other approach is *profiling*. The idea here is that characters have computer-generated descriptions based on their actions. It's not as expressive as freeform text you've written yourself, but at least it gets updated. Its most basic form is to tag a character's name by some epithet based on some combination of that character's level of experience, class, race, and gender: "Felice the heroine" rather than just plain "Felice." Special titles and epithets, for example "Felice the giant-killing heroine," can be added for particularly exemplary deeds, either automatically or by admiring administrators.

Longer biographies can be built up separately, for anyone to access if they want to know more about a character's actual deeds. This allows people to form an opinion about a character, which is particularly useful in virtual worlds where characters never really "die." The half-life of these descriptions should depend on their importance. "Felice vanquished the maiden and saved the dragon" might be a big deal for a relative newbie, but not worth a mention after a couple of weeks. "Felice beat seven kinds of hell out of Tommy and took his shoes" would probably hang around to stain Felice's reputation for somewhat longer.

Profiling also can be used as a more general tool to provide information for other parts of the system. For example, if a group of players finally destroys the demon lord after two months of trying, the server could automatically generate a newsflash (for a login message, for a web site, for a mobile phone message, for email) to inform everyone what's happened. Done right, it may even be possible to create faux articles for the virtual world's virtual newspapers.

It's therefore not only individual players who can benefit from a virtual world's acceptance of intangibles: the whole community can.

Role-Playing

I have a story to complete....

Polly's Tale (*Continued*)

Why won't they role-play?

Everyone is in the same real-world room. Everyone can see each other in real life. They're in *MUD*, but only shallowly; they're still connected in Reality. Everything they do in the virtual world is subject to the same peer pressure as in the real one, because they still feel like they're their real selves. They're constrained.

Yet I've played *D&D*. I know that people can be connected in the real world and still role-play. *MUD* offers even more opportunity to experiment with identity—precisely what my friends seek. So, why won't they step over the line?

They need *permission* to role-play.

As *MUD*'s programmer and the group's overall leader, I'm the obvious choice to give them this permission. Yet how can I do that? And how will they know what to do when I've given it anyway? They won't take direction—I can't say, "Pretend to be someone a little more tolerant than you are," and expect them to go with it. The best I can do is to demonstrate role-playing in action.

Yet even then, there's a strong pull back to reality. I can create a character and pretend it's a pirate or a monk or an enthusiastically chivalrous knight, but they'll still identify the character with me. That could be tricky, as there's no shielding context: Pretending to be an upper-class twit is fine if you're acting in a play, but bizarre if you do it while playing chess. Somehow, I have to show that *MUD* is a shielding context.

If I'm going to break the mold, I'm going to have to hit it hard.

I formulate a fiendish plan.

I create a character called Polly. Polly is a secondary character I use for testing things in the game. I say that I chose the name because Polly is like a parrot. Everyone knows Polly is my debug character.

When I inherited *MUD1* from Roy, it didn't implement gender. This was entirely due to Roy's rush to write as much of the program as possible in the short period of time available to him; he felt that gender could easily be added later, whereas things such as communication had priority[85]. As far as both Roy and I were concerned, gender was merely a linguistic issue forced on us by the English language; the only changes it meant for the virtual world concerned personal pronouns in event descriptions.

Polly may be the stereotypical name for a parrot, but it's a female name. This gives me my excuse. I add gender. Players are asked, "By what name shall I call you?" then "What sex do you wish to be?" Naturally, I use Polly to test my new code.

So Polly is no longer a parrot. Polly is a cheerful yet feisty girl who likes helping people but gets cross if they patronize her.

If I'd added gender to *MUD* and not created Polly, what would have happened? The chances are, people would not have played with switched gender, afraid of the disparaging remarks about their sexuality that doing so would attract.

I run that risk, of course, but I'm confident that I've designed Polly well enough that no one is going to see her as a sexual object, just as an ersatz sister. I also have the advantage of not actually caring if people say I'm a transvestite behind my back.

Luckily, Polly works.

People know I'm Polly, but they also know I'm not Polly; I thereby illustrate the massive gulf it's possible to create between player and character. As *MUD*'s programmer, my kudos is sufficiently strong enough that I pull it off. People think, "If Richard can have a female persona, maybe I'll try it myself."

They do. The gates are open, and new lands await. Players laugh and joke about having female characters, but their other characters also begin to act in smaller, more incrementally different ways. Players have a freedom that they couldn't have in real life.

---

85. This was nothing to do with the fact that we had no female players. Roy was, and is, against blind prejudice of any kind.

I'm ashamed, because I've been manipulative, but I believe that overall I did the right thing.

Besides, I'm rather fond of Polly.

Postscript

Did any of this help my friends?

To be honest, probably not—it was by then too late for most of them. It did help de-nerd those that followed, though.

It also set a lasting precedent: Virtual worlds are still seen as acceptable shielding contexts. To this day, playing a character in a virtual world with a gender different from your own does not suggest anything about your sexuality—just your readiness to spread your wings and fly.

I'm rather proud of that.

On Being Others

I told Polly's tale for three reasons:

- ➤ To illustrate the importance of identity exploration in virtual worlds, and the emptiness of a world without it.

- ➤ To demonstrate how something that many designers take for granted as part and parcel of virtual worlds has a real-world beginning.

- ➤ To counter the popular notion among some researchers that *MUD1* was written by a couple of one-dimensional hackers whose only aim was to provide a medium for adolescent males to live out fantasies of bloodthirsty violence[86].

Crossing gender with Polly was not done as a means unto itself: I was attempting to show what role-playing enabled, and that it was okay to indulge in; gender was just the mechanism I used to do this. The fact that researchers almost invariably write about

---

86. Yes, Dale Spender, author of *Nattering on the Net: Women, Power, and Cyberspace*. Melbourne, Spinifex, 1995. I'm talking to you.

crossing gender in virtual worlds as if it were something amazingly special is slightly off the point. It is important, but no more so than any other severe disjunction between player and character. Maintaining the impression that you're a 90-year-old ninja elf is far more difficult than acting as if you're the opposite gender[87].

Pretending to be your non-biological sex in a virtual world has a higher profile than other forms of identity dislocation because it's the only "physical" identity cue that players have to specify in virtual worlds. However, it's just one of many dimensions. If virtual worlds asked players to specify a real-world race for their characters, whether instead of a fantasy race or in addition to one (a Jewish elf, a Chinese troll), then this would be high-profile too[88]. As it is, almost every textual world avoids real-world race; graphical worlds use skin tones and identikit face construction to allow players to present whatever look they want, but it's never referred to as race or ethnicity. It's just a look, which is forced on a graphical world in the same way that language forces gender on textual worlds[89].

MUD1 didn't have race, age, class, weight, or any other physical identity cues except for gender; it wouldn't have had that either if English was up to the job. Players could have still pretended to be the opposite sex had that been the case, of course, but they wouldn't have been forced to instantiate to either. Constraints diminish opportunity.

Playing a character of a gender opposite to your own should therefore be regarded as merely one of a number of ways that players can choose to explore their selves; it is discussed in greater detail in Chapter 6, "It's Not a Game, It's a...."

For the moment, however, one of the consequences of this kind of identity experimentation is of more pressing interest.

As a man, there's nothing incompatible with having a female persona (nor *vice versa*): Although men can't be women in real life (without a series of very unnerving operations, anyway), they can be women in virtual worlds. Your persona is you, in the virtual world: You can be female there, whatever your real-life gender.

---

87. Assuming, of course, that you aren't a 90-year-old ninja elf in real life.

88. For a discussion of race (or lack of it) in virtual worlds, see: Beth E. Kolko, *Erasing @race*. Beth E. Kolko, Lisa Nakamura and Gilbert B. Rodman (editors), *Race in Cyberspace*. New York, Routledge, 2000.

89. Most languages, this is. Some languages, for example Chinese written in pin yin, can be gender nonspecific.

When you're starting out, though, you have to play a role. You have to decide how you think a character of the opposite sex would act, and stick with it. Your own identity can adapt toward that of your character's, but your character's can't (at this stage) shift much toward your own. It's locked in place.

This brings us to consider the nature of role-playing.

The Role-Playing Paradox

Experienced players will sometimes speak of "wearing" a character, like they might wear a mask. The freedom of revealing less of their outer selves can lead them to reveal more of their inner selves. They can, therefore, learn more about their inner selves, and change their character so it fits more comfortably. Ultimately, their inner and outer selves line up, and character becomes persona.

This is often described as *role-playing*.

It is not.

Role-playing is about assuming a role and maintaining that role. The role doesn't change; if the character changes, it's only for reasons that make sense for that character, not for the role-player.

An actor on a stage is playing a part. Actors might put more of themselves into a part as they come to know their character, but they can't change the part. A theatergoer might notice a distinct difference between performances six months apart in a run, but actors and their characters remain separate. Spending every night playing a poisoner may give an actor insights into the mindset of such a person, but it's unlikely to turn the actor into a poisoner; crucially, it most definitely won't turn the poisoner into an actor.

Players can adapt their characters. Role-players determine not to. Role-playing is therefore a sub-class of playing. Both are paths to fulfillment, and both have the same overall goal: Being someone else in order to become a better you. Unfortunately, the term "role-playing" is widely applied to all kinds of playing in virtual worlds—it's even incorporated into the acronym MMORPG. Properly, though, it should only be used to describe fluid-player-to-set-character play. Much confusion flows from this.

I should point out that putting yourself in someone else's shoes is a perfectly valid way to learn more about yourself; I'm not about to disparage role-playing here. What I am about to disparage is the misunderstanding of what role-playing is, and the design paradigms this misunderstanding has promoted.

Role-players map themselves onto a character. They don't map the character onto themselves. In so doing, they can come to an understanding of what makes their character tick, which enables them to reflect on their own attitudes, beliefs, and ways of thinking. The key is that *they* change, but the character *doesn't*. The default for virtual worlds is for *both* to change. As a role-player, you can only learn about yourself as you *approach* a character; once you *reach* the character, you can learn no more from it. You have to take another role if you want to go in a different direction.

This, then, is the *role-playing paradox*: As a role-player, you try to become your character; however if you succeed then you're no longer role-playing.

In other words, the journey is the point of the exercise, not what you do when you get there.

So role-playing sets up the necessary conditions for immersion, but the harder you role-play the less immersed you get: Thinking about your character as a separate entity breaks immersion. The more you think about a line to decide whether it's right for your character, the greater the distance you put between yourself and that character. The conscious post-editing of your character's words means the subconscious separation of you and your character.

This isn't how players and designers of virtual worlds usually see it at all.

Soft Role-Playing

Role-playing in virtual worlds is one of those concepts that is inherited from "parent" virtual worlds without a great deal of thought as to its nature. Consequently, over the generations it has become less understood. There are honorable exceptions—particularly among TinyMUSHes—but for the most part virtual worlds have a fairly relaxed idea of what constitutes role-playing.

One of the tenets of role-playing is that role-players must have a role to play. It doesn't matter *per se* whether these roles are created by individual players or they're assigned by some referee. Players usually like to create their own characters, but in practice most settings have constraints on the roles people can play (no cowboys in the court of Louis XIV). A midway position is therefore usually adopted where a number of scenario-specific templates are provided (musicians, advisors, guards, courtiers) and players get to choose which one they want. They can customize their character further if they so wish, so long as they stay within the character's (and scenario's) stated parameters. There will be limits on specific roles (only one person gets to be Louis XIV) and balance issues between generic ones (guards are needed—not everyone can be a courtier). These are rarely hard to resolve, though.

Although this template scheme works for role-playing in general (historical re-enactments, Murder on the Luxor Express dinner parties, theatrical productions), why does it appear in virtual worlds? In almost every virtual world, one of the major decisions players have to make when they create their characters is what *class* they have to be. Why is that?

Early MUDs did not have character classes. Some second age virtual words introduced them, but it wasn't until the third age that they really took off. Character classes[90] were absorbed from *AD&D*, which ultimately got them from the miniature wargames (that is, wargames using toy soldier "miniatures") that gave rise to *D&D*.

In a miniature wargame, units are categorized much as they are in real life: A Napoleon-era general might think in terms of cavalry, infantry, and artillery units, each with its own particular strengths and weaknesses; a player in a miniature wargame will also look on their units this way, with perhaps special miniatures to represent major individuals on the battlefield (for example, Napoleon). If the battle were in a fantasy setting (say, the Battle of the Five Armies from *The Hobbit*), there might be units representing monsters (wargs, orcs) and specialist troops (elven archers, dwarven axe-wielders), plus a few for individuals (Bilbo, Gandalf, Beorn, Thorin) and wild cards (eagles). A more generic fantasy setting might have units for magic-users, fighters, holy men, and so on, their powers on the battlefield defined in terms of a quick-and-easy *level* rating.

---

90. Traditionally these are all variations on *fighter, magic-user, cleric, thief*; as these are fantasy-oriented, though, players and designers will sometimes speak of *tank, nuker, healer, rogue*.

Taking these characters out of the battlefield and into the dungeon, their classes and levels were already set; their abilities could be defined in terms of those classes and levels. Thus, when role-playing evolved as a concept in gaming, character classes were already there. However, role-playing meant taking on the *role of an individual* (as opposed to a unit comprising several individuals), not the role defined by a class.

This traces how character classes came to be a part of virtual worlds, but it doesn't explain *why*.

Well, there are four reasons:

➤ *Expectation*. Virtual world designers had played *AD&D*. *AD&D* had levels and classes; virtual worlds had only levels, therefore they ought to have classes, too.

➤ *Individuality*. Players like to feel unique. If a virtual world isn't richly featured enough for players to differentiate themselves by their deeds, give them one that enforces differentiation.

➤ *Balance*. If one playing style leads to greater success than others, most people will adopt it. By deliberately partitioning the player base such that there are several styles, each of which is dependent on the others for success, a virtual world is much more interesting. Adventuring groups form social bonds, too.

➤ *Direction*. Not everyone knows who they want to be. If you stand at a crossroads, can you decide which road to take if there are no signs? Classes provide signs.

Note that none of these have much to do with role-playing. Somewhere, players and designers alike lost sight of what it meant. Instead of class being an aspect of an individual, individuals were aspects of a class. Role-playing meant being a thief or a healer, not being Knuckles or Justina.

Thus, we have two paradigms for role-playing in virtual worlds: *classless* and *classbound*[91].

I much prefer classless. Here's why.

---

91. Because the early (classless) MUDs were British and the tabletop (classbound) standard came from the U.S., these were originally called the *British* and *American* styles of role-playing. I prefer classless/classbound, however, because it's more accurate and doesn't carry connotations of nationalistic bias.

Let's consider that list of reasons why classes appear in virtual worlds. The first one, expectation, is not really an issue. Nowadays if players see a virtual world with no classes when they were expecting classes, they might want to know why classes are missing—that's okay, we can tell them. They're not going to ignore a world through some sense of "incompletion," though, if indeed they ever were before.

The next reason, individuality, is a consequence of a world's lack of depth. If your world is so shallow that players can't do different things unless you give them different tools, you need classes. Today's virtual worlds should not be this shallow, though. Modern tabletop role-playing games use skills systems rather than classes; this build-from-pieces approach offers far greater variety than the cookie-cutting land of classbound systems.

Balance can be an issue. If there is no explicit fence keeping abilities separate, what is to stop someone from maxing out in fighting skills, magic, and healing, and becoming invincible[92]? Won't everyone end up looking and acting the same? Again, this assumes that your virtual world is so impoverished that it can only offer players one overarching goal (normally "kill things to get stuff so you can kill more things"). However, at a practical level balance is dependent on how advancement works. If it takes you the same time to become a level 20 fighter/magic-user that someone else takes to become a level 40 magic-user, you have the worst deal—they'd probably beat you easily in combat. People can still take different career paths and parties of specialists will still be formed. To stop getting maxed-out killing machines, either introduce permanent death into your virtual world or take off the level caps.

The final reason for having classes is to give players a vision of the future. They choose a destination, board a train, and know where they're going. The same can be done with character kits, though—skill sets optimized for a particular playing style template. Chapter 5 gives a few other ways to do it. Players seeking direction want to know that fighter and magic-user are careers it's sensible to pursue; they don't care whether these are implemented as classes or as kits.

Okay, so a classless "role-playing" system can be tweaked to do what a classbound one can. There are a few other minor reasons for using classes, but solutions to those can be hacked together, too. This doesn't explain why anyone would *want* to use a classless

---

92. Such characters used to be called *tanks* or *tank mages*, but now the term "tank" is used to apply to any out-in-front fighter character.

system, though. Classes are easy to implement. What does a classless system offer that a classbound system doesn't?

It offers change.

People play virtual worlds to explore their identities: You pretend to be someone else in order to become a better you.

In classbound role-playing, you begin your journey of self-improvement with a definite goal in mind. If you want to be mysterious, aloof, singular, and powerful, you become a mage; if you want to be quick-witted, spirited, independent yet lovable, you become a rogue; if you want to be strong, noble, valiant, and victorious, you become a fighter. Or you pick one of the many sub-classes that make this virtual world different to the one next door.

It's aspirational. You decide where you want to go, then you board the train and the virtual world takes you there.

But it's a train. It runs on rails. You can't get off. You have to start with another character and board a different train if you want to go somewhere else. There may be a branch line for "fighters who do some healing" or "thieves who thieve for good," but they're still lines. Between the lines is a whole continuum of experience that you can't ever reach. You may get the occasional glimpse through the window, but you can't ever visit it no matter how much you like the scenery.

In a classless system, you can go where you want. You may start out intending to be a fighter and have your character take a job guarding a merchant caravan. From there, you may try some minor trading yourself so you can improve your weapons and armor, but discover that you prefer the trading to the fighting so you switch to being a merchant full time. Or maybe the bandits who raid the caravan are fighting for freedom from a tyrannical ruler, so you join up with them, rising through the ranks until you find yourself a major revolutionary figure who is given the job of reconstructing the country when peace finally comes. Now if at character-creation time you'd been offered the chance to become a merchant or an aid worker, would you have taken it? No, because you wanted to be a fighter. In a classless system, you can still start off as a fighter; you can still stay a fighter, if that's where your calling lies. However, you can also veer off and become something else if the muse takes you.

In a classbound system, you can only be what the designers determine you can be. In a classless system, you can be something that the designers haven't even dreamed of.

It's possible to tinker with class systems to allow some degree of lateral movement. *EverQuest 2* has a funnel-like system, which doesn't force newbies to make any major decisions as to what class they want to be. As they go up levels, however, they have to specialize more and more, until they become locked in to their chosen career. This is a great way of helping newbies settle in, and by the time they commit themselves to a single class they're pretty sure it's the right one. Unfortunately, it's still only the right one of those available; it's still only the right choice for now.

The same argument that applies to classes also can be applied to character races. Just as magic-users differ from fighters, so magic-users that are human differ from magic-users that are elves[93]. If you take on the role of a blue-skinned, triton-waving, lizardoid fighter then you probably will find things about yourself that you wouldn't if you didn't, but it could well be an unsatisfactory experience. It has the same dual player/character drift that you get in classless systems, but the character is constrained; when it reaches the boundaries of what the virtual world allows, the player still wants it to move, but it can't.

This is soft role-playing: The character can change, but not always by enough to supply the player's needs. In hard role-playing, the character remains fixed, which sounds like it should be even worse; however, the player changes willfully, and can therefore be more systematic about challenging their attitude and behavior. After the hard role-player has wrung a role dry, they drop it and choose another; soft role-players have no such option, which can make for a frustrating time.

As a virtual world identity-exploration experience, role-playing works. Staying with one role the whole time is inherently limiting, of course, but it can be more intense. Unfortunately, hard role-play immersion is only ever ephemeral. Nevertheless, done right it can be very rewarding for players: MUSHes in particular are often entirely role-play in nature, with no one playing out-of-character (OOC). Role-playing also is

---

93. Gender differences don't generally apply, though. Hey, virtual worlds are progressive places, they don't want any sexism. Institutionalizing abstract racism seems to be fine, though. See Chapter 8, "Coda: Ethical Considerations," for a further discussion of these issues.

perfectly compatible with virtual worlds in which the majority of players are not role-playing; most of the time, it's only a problem if people try to use it as a shield ("That wasn't me who insulted your mother, it was my other character." Yeah, right.).

That's *most* of the time....

Very, very occasionally, over-enthusiastic role-playing can lead to problems—problems that provoke some of the most profound, negative emotions that players in virtual worlds ever have the misfortune to feel.

Masquerading

Role-playing a character is one thing; role-playing a player is something else.

Suppose you're male in real life, playing a female character. Some other player asks you whether you're female in real life. You have three options:

> ➤ Tell the truth. Everyone knows you're a real-life guy, but who cares? Most people will happily play along with the fiction.

> ➤ Don't answer the question. Everyone still knows you're a real-life guy, but they respect the fact that you're role-playing and want to keep in character.

> ➤ Lie. Now you're not role-playing a character, you're role-playing a player (an *alter ego*) who is playing a character.

Why do people lie about player/character mappings?

It may be because they have a real-world reason for it: They are an administrator for the virtual world trying to get a sense of the "the word on the street"; they are famous and want to take a break[94]; they are parents checking out that a game is suitable for their children. In this sort of situation, they are said to be playing *incognito*. Usually, they'll be happy for the administrators of the virtual world to know the score, just so long as other players don't find out.

---

94. Even Superman had to be Clark Kent some of the time.

For the majority, though, there usually isn't any premeditated reason to lie. They do it because they can, or because it gives them a frisson of excitement, or because they like the way people treat them, or simply to see what happens. Almost always, they don't think it's all that big a deal to start with; they will nevertheless try to keep their activities a secret from administrators just as much as from other players. Role-playing a person who is playing a character is called *masquerading*.

The problem with masquerading is that deep relationships are formed between people, not between characters. Characters can have virtual relationships (a player can cause Tommy to act like he loves Tammy), but players have real ones (the player playing Tommy really does love the player playing Tammy). The longer and more convincingly a lie is sustained, the more meaningful the relationships formed become; when the lie is finally exposed, the emotional effect can be absolutely devastating. Finding out that the 20-year-old, wheelchair-bound ex-athlete you've been getting to know over the course of two years is actually a 40-year-old company lawyer from Chicago could represent for you a betrayal of trust at a profound level. All that time you were building up an emotional attachment, someone was playing you for a fool. Everything was a lie, from beginning to end.

I've seen it happen several times, and it really is very, very upsetting for all concerned.

So, how do you spot it?

Most of the time, it's easy. People will often realize what's happening in time and stop before things get out of hand. Of those that don't, many are found out early because of flaws in their role-playing ("How come you type so fast if you have two-inch long fingernails?"). For the remainder, it's harder. Nevertheless, because most people don't plan on masquerading (they just fall into it), there are a number of common themes.

Players will

- ➤ Claim their *alter ego* is physically attractive or of high status.
- ➤ Give their *alter ego*'s character the same valid real-world name as their *alter ego* (especially when crossing gender).
- ➤ Invent some reason why their *alter ego* can't go to real-life meets (disability, phobia, lives in Saskatchewan).

➤ Never give out their phone number (or, if they do, will always insist on talking in the virtual world whenever you call).

➤ Avoid players who really are what the player is only pretending to be (men playing women will avoid real women).

➤ Bring in "friends" their *alter ego* knows "in real life." These friends never become regular players.

➤ Have their *alter ego* take on high-profile roles, usually for the good of the community.

➤ Have their *alter ego* succumb to injuries or ailments that lead to absences or promised absences.

Of these, the saddest sign is perhaps the last one. The player feels guilt over their deceit and has genuine fondness for their virtual world friends. The player knows how distressing it would be were the truth to come out, so they try to provide an exit. They stop playing for no reason, but have to come back because there's no closure, which means they must explain why they went missing. They set themselves a deadline for when they will quit and invent a fiction for it so everyone knows they'll be going at that point, but the fiction makes their bonds even stronger and they still can't leave.

Ultimately[95], something has to give. If a player becomes a persona but that persona can't become the player, there is a tension that can never be resolved. Either the player feels they have to tell someone, or they make a series of errors so glaring that they are certain to be found out, or they contrive for their *alter ego* to leave in such a manner that return is impossible.

The single greatest cause of sudden death among beautiful, young, female players is that the guy who was role-playing them wanted an irreversible out.

So could you ever masquerade and get away with it?

Well yes, you could, but you *really* ought to think about why you'd want to. It's more appropriate to ask whether you can play incognito and get away with it. The answer here is that it's relatively easy in the short term if you obey a few simple rules:

---

95. Generally, 18–24 months after having started to play.

➤ Don't get attached to your *alter ego*. It isn't going to last.

➤ Don't get into relationships with other players beyond politeness.

➤ Keep your head down. High-profile characters attract attention.

➤ Abandon the exercise the moment anyone smells a rat.

➤ When you abort, don't immediately restart.

For this level of playing incognito, you generally don't care if you're caught. This is probably just as well, because if you're a long-term player of the virtual world, then people will notice your idiosyncrasies sooner or later anyway. After all, if telegraph operators can be identified from tapping out Morse code, what hope do you have?

Well, you can take precautions. You can run a spell-checker over a log of your communications and find out what words you consistently misspell, then resolve not to use them. You can think up a few catchphrases like "I guess" or "you know" that you don't normally use and sprinkle those into your speech. You can use meticulous capitalization or sloppy abbreviations—anything to disguise your underlying speech patterns. I once played a character incognito whom I decided wouldn't use nouns that began with vowels; nobody noticed, but it meant I post-edited every line he said and was thus better able to keep in character.

This kind of thing leads to a more serious level of playing incognito. In essence, what you're doing is designing a player in the same way that a normal player would design a character. You'd give your *alter ego* a number of superficial differences in playing style to your own, some knowledge (and misconceptions) of the virtual world, enough to throw anyone suspicious off the scent. "That can't be Mike, he spends all his time killing undead with a sickle;" "Jo never plays this early in the evening;" "It's spelled LOSE, not LOOSE!"

Using this approach you can play for several weeks or months without detection, although I'd recommend getting an accomplice to help you every once in a while so both your regular characters and your *alter ego*'s characters can be seen hanging around doing sensible things at the same time.

If you plan on playing incognito in the same virtual world for a year or more, it starts to look less like playing and more like espionage. It's hard, but not impossible, to escape detection, as long as you're well prepared in advance and have reasonable acting skills. Here's what to do:

➤ Be sure you have a very good reason for embarking on this task. "To have fun" is not a very good reason.

➤ Ensure you can spare the time. This will really gobble it up.

➤ Design your *alter ego* from the ground up. What makes it tick? What are its goals, background, fears? How intelligent, articulate, extrovert is it? Do some personality tests in-character, make sure it's all consistent.

➤ Give your *alter ego* a history. What has it done in life? Who are its friends and relatives? Why are they playing this virtual world? Be sure to come up with some reason why no one can phone you (paranoia only works as an excuse for four months or so before it starts getting harder to justify).

➤ Give your *alter ego* an online history. Six months before you need your *alter ego*, create a web site. Illustrate it with photos of a friend who is not stunningly good looking. Hand-code the HTML so it looks different from your own web site. Later, create web sites for "friends" and put links between them. Make some Usenet posts. Tell nobody about these—it'll look suspicious. Let people find you through search engines.

➤ Don't give your *alter ego* skills or knowledge you don't have. If their favorite music is classical, be ready to answer questions as to whether Mahler's use of strings is sublime or over the top. If your *alter ego* speaks German, you'd better speak it too.

➤ Dry-run your *alter ego* on other virtual worlds and in chat rooms. Make sure it works coherently and you can keep it up.

➤ Either use an accomplice or never go on vacation. Your accomplice plays *you* when you're away, not your *alter ego*.

➤ Use a separate PC for your *alter ego*. Firewall it. There's just too much risk of detection from cookies, misdirected emails, and slips in concentration otherwise.

➤ Locate your *alter ego* somewhere remote, so meeting anyone in real life is impractical. Important: You should have been to this place in real life; keeping a guide book or a web site at hand isn't enough.

➤ Have an out from the beginning. Absolutely the best is the main reason most people leave—to play some other virtual world instead. However, if you do this, then you may be tempted to return. You might therefore prefer to choose some life-changing event in advance that will enable you to leave your friends behind without causing them any worry—your *alter ego* is going to college, or is getting married, or is doing voluntary service overseas.

➤ Leave false clues that you are someone else, preferably someone in a position of power in the virtual world. If anyone suspects your *alter ego* of being someone playing incognito, they won't think it's you.

➤ If you plan on doing this several times, build more than one false identity and overlap playing times. If *alter ego* X is due to leave in a few weeks, introduce *alter ego* Y now.

➤ Do not form deep relationships. Playing incognito is deceitful, and no matter how good your reasons for doing it, you have no right to trample over people's emotions. Have a barrier in place from the very beginning—inventing a steady real-world boy/girlfriend is perfectly acceptable.

➤ The instant you are suspected, stop playing. If you don't, things will only get worse than they are already.

I've listed this sneak's charter for two main reasons.

The first is to continue the discussion on role-playing. If people can go to these lengths and play incognito for two or more years at a time, shouldn't this have weird side effects on their sense of identity?

It's quite possible it could have, yes. This really is something nobody should attempt unless they know what they are doing! That said, some people can play this way successfully for long periods—years—without ill effects. This is because it enables the separation of immersion from identity. You don't feel that *you* are in the game, you feel that the player you've created is. Identity drift can still occur between character and invented player (or even you), but rarely between invented player and you except by explicit reflection. This is because immersion in a real-world invented *alter ego* is overwhelmingly more difficult than it is in a virtual character, if indeed it makes sense to talk about the concept at all.

The lesson we can learn from this is that although immersion and identity are strongly interdependent, they're not inseparable. One of my hobbies is taking 3D photographs, which consist of two 2D images taken from slightly different angles, viewed side-by-side. If I cross my eyes, I can make it appear as if there is only one image, but it's out of focus. I have to bring it into focus while keeping my eyes crossed; this means decoupling the eye's focusing mechanism from its directional mechanism. After years of experience, I can now do this easily, but it took a while to learn the technique. So it is with immersion and identity: Although normally they work together so closely that it's as if they're a single system, actually we can now see they're not. Immersion may help bring dimension to identity, but it's only the default way to do it. You can be immersed through the medium of a constructed player without its greatly impinging on your sense of self. From this, we can deduce that it isn't immersion that drives the celebration of identity, but something else of which immersion is an aspect. We'll return to this topic later in this chapter.

My second reason for describing how someone might go about dishonestly deceiving players as to their real-world identity in this underhanded fashion is that unfortunately it's *really useful* for designers on the live team to be able to do this. Data-mining can only go so far[96]. By actually playing a virtual world as a real player from beginning to (nominal) end, designers can get an unparalleled understanding of what it "feels" like. They don't have to rely on the outpourings of players on rant sites to tell them what's wrong, they can see it with their own eyes—and they can also see if a problem is non-existent or is being exaggerated out of all proportion. It really does give them an understanding they simply couldn't get any other way.

Whether they have any moral defense for these actions is another matter, of course. It's not unprecedented in the real world: Henry V of England dressed as a common soldier and wandered among his men on the eve of the Battle of Agincourt; the Russian emperor Peter the Great traveled Europe incognito as Sgt. Pyotr Mikhaylov, spending four months as a carpenter in the shipyard of the Dutch East India Company at Saardam before working in the Royal Navy yards at Deptford.

For a game designer, well, it's up to you. If you don't like it, don't do it.

---

96. David Kennerly, *Better Game Design through Data Mining*. San Jose, *Proceedings of MUD-DEV Conference*, 2003. http://userwww.sfsu.edu/~kennerly/game_design/Data_Mining_files/frame.htm.

From a purely pragmatic point of view, it would probably be more useful for a large-population virtual world than for a smaller one. I've done it several times for both *MUD1* and *MUD2*, and feel that on the whole it's worthwhile as long as you really *are* finding it useful. If you're not, stop. If it becomes an obsession, stop. If your *alter ego* falls out with your friends, stop. Especially if other people start investing in emotional relationships with you, stop.

Players may take issue with this. The live team stomps on people's feelings? And because it's for the long-term "benefit" of the virtual world, that somehow makes it okay? Don't players have rights?!

That's actually quite an interesting question.

Player Rights

Players do have rights. Players are real people, real people have rights[97], therefore players have rights.

Characters, on the other hand, have no rights whatsoever.

For example, it makes sense to say that players have a right to exist, but no sense to say that characters share that right. Characters can—and do—get killed regularly in game-style virtual worlds. Characters don't even have to have a human being controlling them.

When players become so immersed that they merge with their characters, they still have rights. Their characters (personae) now have rights too, but only in the sense that players do. Killing a persona does not kill a player; it might cause a player severe emotional distress, but any system of rights embodying "the right not to be made very upset" would be wholly impractical ("You mean I can't dump my girlfriend?"). Systematically persecuting a player through the vehicle of their persona, on the other hand, does border on oppression (if not exactly torture). It's still the player that suffers, though, not the character. Just because someone puts your character on a rack, you can't claim it's "just like" you were put on the rack yourself. It isn't.

---

97. In theory, if not always in practice.

There is, however, an often-supposed notion that players nevertheless have rights in a virtual world beyond those granted by the real world. There are two arguments as to why this should be the case.

The first argument is that the players of a virtual world make up a population, and populations determine for themselves what rights they have. Who gave the citizens of the United States their rights? "We, the people." Unfortunately, for virtual worlds the populace does not have sovereignty. The people who write the code and run the hardware have sovereignty. The counter-argument is that with this power comes responsibility. That's true, it does, but responsibility doesn't mean rights.

The second argument is more pragmatic. Rights are granted by those who have power. Administrators have power because they can turn off a virtual world. However, players also have power because they, too, can turn off a virtual world—they can stop playing. By constructing a virtual world and inviting people into it, administrators are conceding that they have a need for players. Players are therefore in a position to insist on guarantees from the administrators, enshrined as a constitution, otherwise they'll go play elsewhere. Players have rights because in the end it is they who wield the most power, not the administrators.

As a thought experiment, Raph Koster constructed a *Declaration of the Rights of Avatars*[98], based on the French *Declaration of the Rights of Man and of the Citizen* and the American *Bill of Rights*. On the face of it, the result is way too unpalatable for most developers to swallow, however it loses a lot of its bitterness when rewritten in plain English as "advice to virtual world administrators" rather than "rights of avatars." What it then amounts to can be summed up pretty well as

➤ Ultimately, someone has their finger on the power button.

➤ What this someone says, goes.

➤ If this someone doesn't provide a code of conduct for their virtual world, then anyone playing in it deserves all they get.

➤ If this someone wants to change the code of conduct, they should consult their players, but they can ignore whatever they are told.

➤ Codes of conduct should be fair and should be applied fairly.

---

98. `http://www.legendmud.org/raph/gaming/playerrights.html`

Codes of conduct are basically sets of laws. Although the *Declaration of the Rights of Avatars* assumes a U.S. perspective (anything not prohibited by law is permitted), this isn't to say that alternative forms aren't valid (in much of continental Europe, what is not permitted by law is prohibited). It's just one example of what a constitution might look like.

There are two areas of confusion, however: Between players and characters and between real and virtual worlds. The following argument illustrates both.

Let's accept that people have rights to liberty, property, security, and freedom from oppression. This does *not* mean that their *characters* have any such rights. If my character locks your character in a room and steals your stuff, that affronts no inalienable rights. Its rightness or wrongness is determined entirely by the context of the virtual world. Some virtual worlds may be constructed so that this is intrinsic to them. If I were playing in an "escape from Colditz[99]" virtual world, I would be disappointed if my character could walk out of the front door simply because some right to virtual liberty was being infringed. I would expect the guards to destroy my character's digging tools if they found them—it would spoil the game if my character's property rights made this unconstitutional.

Even if you were to buy a virtual object with real-world money from its real-world owners[100], that still would not mean your character had any "right" to it. My character would not be prevented from stealing it from your character if that's how the virtual world worked. You'd still real-world own the object, but that would not mean you could demand that it be changed in the virtual world unless you'd also bought some sort of explicit servicing agreement. You could conceivably argue that changes due to bugs in the code be reversed, and you *may* have a case if your object were destroyed. However, if in the real world you own a piece of a virtual world, you can't extend this to say your character owns it in the virtual world.

The implementation of the virtual world alone determines the meaning of ownership—and everything else—within that virtual world. If you know this when you buy your virtual object, you can't complain. It would be like taking a bicycle back to the shop

---

99. Nazi Germany's highest security prisoner of war camp, a converted castle.

100. This will originally be the developers, no matter how much players would like to believe otherwise.

because it didn't turn to gold when you sat on it. The laws of physics don't work that way in the real world. In a virtual world, everything tangible is subject to the laws of that virtual world's physics. That *includes* concepts that are nonphysical in the real world, such as that of ownership.

Virtual worlds don't work the same way that the real world works. It is a mistake to assume that they do.

So what can we say about players' rights?

- ► Players have rights in the real world, of which the virtual world is a part.
- ► When considering rights, virtual worlds should only be thought of in terms of being a part of the real world.
- ► Administrators can take their ball home if they like.
- ► Players don't have to play ball if they don't want to.

For designers, the only impact of this is that they should always remember there are real people attached to virtual characters. These people can be affected in the real world by events in the virtual world. If the way these people are affected breaches their rights (or the laws that express these rights), then the designer is errant. Fortunately, the context of the virtual world normally provides enough cover that even when designers do slip up the damage is not normally too great. In the same way that someone who deliberately visits a museum of slavery can't complain if the accoutrements of enslavement exhibited within give them nightmares, so a player who signs up to an "escape from Colditz" game can't legitimately complain if there are images of Nazi regalia everywhere. They could, however, complain if their character escaped from Colditz and encountered a starkly realistic depiction of a concentration camp. They didn't sign up for that, and suddenly the game is not a game any more.

Most problems of this nature will come from misjudgments rather than from deliberate flouting of the law. It's quite difficult, in fact, to conceive how a designer *could* contravene a player's fundamental rights in the real world by means of constructs in the virtual one.

That said, this is not actually hard-and-fast[101]. I'm not a lawyer, none of what I have said here has yet been tested in a court of law; it might turn out to be complete hogwash. So young is the debate that its parameters are still being set. The first legal battleground to determine the place of virtual worlds in the real world is likely to be in intellectual property law; whether this will turn out to be robust enough to settle all outstanding issues depends on how the lawyers and judges slug it out, but it seems doubtful. In all probability, it will be some time before a working legal and constitutional understanding of the place of virtual worlds is reached.

It would be easy to conclude this analysis of players' rights by stating that designers have very little to worry about on the subject, so all is well. It has, however, exposed an issue that really should be of come concern to them. In the concentration camp example mentioned previously, it was clear that occurrences in a virtual world can have such deep real-world implications to a player that it can break that player out from the deepest levels of immersion and make them think, "whoa!" This is something that can't *but* concern designers. Unless you're trying to make some kind of provocative artistic statement[102], it's not supposed to happen. Players want to be immersed and designers covenant with them to deliver this immersion; if something within the virtual world shakes them out of their immersion, it's cause for concern.

If a player loses immersion like this, it's because they have a problem with something in the virtual world. The virtual world falls short of the standards the player expected of it. Those standards could have to do with the world's physics, appearance, or performance, but in the concentration camp case it's far worse: It's an ethical issue. Bugs just show incompetence, and can quickly be fixed; poor ethics show poor principles, and they aren't so easily forgotten.

Ethics are so important that they get a whole chapter of this book to themselves, Chapter 8, "Coda: Ethical Considerations." Don't expect answers—ethical issues are all questions.

I'll wrap up this discussion about the intrusion of reality into virtual worlds with a celebrated and oft-republished story from *LegendMUD*.

---

101. There are philosophical arguments that suggest avatars (in addition to players) *should* have rights, although that's not to say that they *must* have them or that they should all have the *same* ones. See Wesley E. Cooper, *Wizards, Toads and Ethics: Reflections of a MOO Administrator. CMC Magazine*, January 1996. http://www.december.com/cmc/mag/1996/jan/cooper.html.

102. Which for most virtual worlds would run counter to what the player was expecting so much that merely making such a statement would itself be a statement.

A Story About a Tree

A Story About a Tree[103] is an eloquent rebuttal by Raph Koster of the suggestion that a virtual world is "just a game." It concerns a player called Karyn.

In real life, Karyn was from Norway, but she found a virtual home in *LegendMUD*. She soon made friends, and would sometimes bring friends of her own along (although their English wasn't always all that good, and she often had to translate). After a while, she set up a web site about *LegendMUD*, on which she posted a few pictures of herself (she was very photogenic; unsurprisingly, as she was a former Miss Norway).

She became more and more integrated into the virtual community, until eventually she started a guild, "the Norse Traders." With much effort, she built up this into one of the most popular and well-known guilds in the whole game. The ties between its members were strong, and so were the friendships that developed.

One day, some of her friends realized they hadn't seen her around for a while. They checked her web site, and found to their dismay a message from her parents. Karyn had died two months earlier in a head-on collision while test-driving a new car. There was a copy on the site of a news item (in Norwegian) describing the accident.

There was an immediate outpouring of grief in *LegendMUD*. Emails were dispatched, players who hadn't been around for months logged in to share their sorrow. A memorial service was held, and a garden or remembrance created. In that garden was planted a tree, bearing a plaque: "In memory of Karyn."

Two things disconcerted the players.

Firstly, how could they feel a genuine sense of loss at the death of someone they had never actually met? Many of them found it hard to articulate their reasons, but eventually it was recognized that Karyn hadn't been just someone they "gamed with," she'd been a vibrant part of their *community*.

---

103. The original essay is at `http://www.legendmud.org/raph/gaming/essay1.html`.

Secondly, the grief came at the wrong time. "The Norse Traders" had fallen apart two months earlier, and no one had thought why. It was obvious now, of course—its heart had been torn away. The community had felt Karyn's loss when she stopped logging in, but only now understood it.

Karyn's tree stands in *LegendMUD* to this day. It stands there as a memorial to a much-loved human being, but that it was erected at all is a testament to the realization among the players—as individuals—that they weren't merely "playing a game." The grief they felt was real; virtual relationships are real; virtual communities are real. Virtual worlds are not "just games."

A Story About a Tree is not unique. In *MUD2* there is a Dally Lane, named after the man responsible for bringing it out of academia and into the real world, Simon Dally. Simon was popular not only as an administrator and a player, but also as a human being. When he suffered from a bout of manic depression and committed suicide, the grief felt among the players of both *MUD1* and *MUD2* was as intense as that for Karyn in *LegendMUD*.

So why did I present *A Story About a Tree* here when I could have written *A Story About a Road* and not have my abridged prose suffer in comparison to Raph's powerful original?

Let's look at that opening paragraph again and compare it against the classic indicators for masquerading that I listed earlier:

> *In real life, Karyn (BONG!) was from Norway (BONG!), but she found a virtual home in LegendMUD. She soon made friends, and would sometimes bring friends of her own along (BONG!) (although their English wasn't always all that good, and she often had to translate). After a while, she set up a web site (BONG!) about LegendMUD, upon which she posted a few pictures of herself (she was very photogenic; unsurprisingly, as she was a former Miss Norway (BONG!)).*

That's a lot of BONG!s. Add the guild and the violent death, and Karyn starts to look more than a little suspect.

Before any angry players of *LegendMUD* email me[104] to say that they met Karyn in real life and know for sure she was a real person, I should mention that it's only the abstract principle I'm concerned with here. The events of *A Story About a Tree* happened in 1998, so people have had plenty of time to check the facts[105]. The point is that even though Karyn almost certainly was whom she said she was, it's easy to see how, in some *other* virtual world, someone with her story might *not* have been real. There could be some unKaryn in some un*LegendMUD* who was truly a fictional construct.

I wouldn't doubt that the grief felt by these un*LegendMUD* players was real. I wouldn't doubt that many of the people who experienced that grief would be deeply offended by the mere suggestion that unKaryn might have been bogus. It doesn't undermine the basic point, though.

I've seen players fall in love with other players who turned out to be inventions. I've seen a player get close to another player who was the creation of two people playing together because they could only afford one account (fortunately they aborted when they realized what was happening). There are complex factors at work here.

A Story About a Tree shows that players can have real relationships with people whom they have never met. The masquerade corollary shows that it's also possible for players to have real relationships with people who are imaginary.

In virtual worlds[106], people are constructs in the minds of other people; relationships between people exist only in the minds of individuals.

In the end, creating constructs in the minds of players is what a designer's job is all about.

---

104. Richard@mud.co.uk

105. I ought to mention here that I'm not one of those people. All I know about Karyn is *A Story About a Tree*.

106. Heavy-duty philosophers and their followers might argue that this applies to the real world, too.

Community

So far in this chapter, I've been talking about players as individuals, at a "psychological" level. Now it's time to look at collections of individuals, at a "sociological" level. The object of study increases in size from individual to group to community to society. In virtual worlds, it's most important to understand individuals and community first; groups have elements of both in them, and society implies large numbers of diverse but interdependent communities that just don't exist in virtual worlds (yet).

Beginnings

When the Internet hit the headlines in the mid-1990s, there was much talk about how important "community" was. Community meant retention: If you had community, people would keep coming back. I attended numerous conferences where "community" was hailed as if it were an amazing new discovery. Big name executives of games companies' newly formed online divisions drummed in the idea that community was IMPORTANT. They didn't know anything *else* about it, of course, but they knew it was IMPORTANT.

They were right, of course: Community *is* important. So is money, but my knowing that doesn't help me get it into my bank account. Identifying a problem doesn't solve it.

Back then, community was looked on as some kind of commodity. "Why won't people buy our sheds over the Net? Our web site really needs some community." Times have changed, of course, and business people now have a better understanding of when community can be used and what it delivers. However, it can still sometimes be seen as a commodity.

Virtual world developers are pretty good in this respect, as it happens, because most of them have played virtual worlds themselves and have first-hand experience of what membership of an "online community" implies. They partition community/customer relations/service/management into a separate division and try to staff it with people who know what they're doing[107].

---

107. Even at the height of its community management problems, *EverQuest's* players had few complaints about individual, street-level representatives. They just hated the guys at the top who made all the bad decisions. Indeed, there's a growing feeling among community management teams that having a thick-skinned individual to take the flak for screw-ups is a good idea, as it gives players a name at whom to vent their emotions but keeps the relations with the rest of the live team good.

The big issues concern responsibility: If the community managers want a change made to the way that the virtual world works (perhaps to correct some perceived imbalance by the players) but the designers don't want to make it (because they feel it undermines the integrity of the virtual world), then who wins? In theory it should be the designers, because they are the only people able to account for the virtual world as a whole; in practice, it's often the community managers, because they can show company high-ups actual short-term data to support their arguments (designers can only really say long-term "trust us"). Experienced developers have policy documents in place to ensure that a balance between knee-jerk compromise and grandiose vision is achieved.

So, what is community? Interesting though this question is, it doesn't actually matter to designers—community is what they get, whether or not they like it! The more pressing questions are what kind of community should the virtual world have, and how should designers set about ensuring it has it?

Unfortunately, communities are 20% nature and 80% nurture. Designers set up the nature—the conditions that allow a community to develop along certain lines. The members of the community (influenced to varying degrees by the community management team) perform the nurture—how the community develops. Even identical incarnations of virtual worlds will usually end up having recognizably different communities.

For many small virtual worlds (such as college MUDs), communities are already there at the beginning: A bunch of people from an existing virtual world decide to set up their own, or an enthusiastic individual does so and calls on real-world friends to take a look. The community that develops is sufficiently small that administrators can directly influence its disposition. For a large-scale virtual world, however, it's a different story. Complete strangers will be coming together. How will this community develop?

Here's how it works.

The virtual world reaches a point where it needs to be beta-tested. Invitations to the closed beta are sent out, and a small group of players signs up. The primary aim is for them to test for balance and bugs; the secondary aim is to create a marketing buzz about the virtual world so people will be eager to try it. As time passes, more people are admitted into the program, eager to see the virtual world and put it through its paces. The world goes into open beta, accumulating yet more players; thus, when it finally launches, the developers can be fairly sure that everything will work and that there'll already be an established player base[108].

So where does the community originate? You can't simply "create it;" it has to grow from relationships formed between players. Which players? The beta-testers: They are the ones who will establish the social norms, the culture, and the ethos of the virtual world; they *seed* the community[109]. It would make sense, therefore, for a virtual world to pack its beta with responsible individuals who exhibit the kind of mature attitude that will lead to a vibrant and prosperous community. Gung-ho, hard-core, hit-it-till-it-breaks beta-testers are therefore perhaps not the best choice from this perspective.

Here's how to seed a community badly, which happens to coincide with the industry standard model for graphical virtual game worlds:

➤ Recruit the hard-core players of other games as beta-testers, so you only get the ones with low product loyalty who'll leave your game the moment a newer one comes along. Go for guild leaders who might bring their whole guild with them.

➤ Enthuse them to create a buzz about your game on super-critical fan sites read mainly by people who need reassurance that the game they play is no worse than any of the others.

➤ Create a web site for your own game that won't be read by any of the people who'll eventually play it.

➤ Listen to the beta-testers, so as to make your game exactly like the games they first played against which all others pale in comparison.

➤ Hey presto! You have a virtual world primed with just the kind of players you don't want!

---

108. Small virtual worlds often have problems attaining a *critical mass* of players. If a prospective player arrives and finds the world empty, they'll perhaps potter around for a few minutes but then leave. A second prospective player arriving five minutes later will do the same thing. Critical mass means that there are enough players for prospective players to feel the world is alive. Exact numbers depend on the nature of the virtual world; the longer prospective players can be persuaded to hang around on their own before meeting someone, the smaller the critical mass for that virtual world will be.

109. Seeding is also known as *preloading*.

Designers can't do a lot about how a community is born, or even how it is fostered, but they control its environment. They can encourage and discourage particularly desirable or undesirable activities, and although their ability to force an issue is limited, nevertheless they do have a considerable part to play.

If they're to do it right, of course, they need to have a reasonable analytic model of how communities work.

Levels of Community

Joe Newbie arrives at a virtual world. He's not there alone—people are busy, they come and go, the whole place looks vibrant. He quickly picks up the basics of the user interface he's using, and feels a little awkward. He's new, he doesn't know the ropes, he doesn't want to make a fool of himself asking a dumb question. Yet he's eager to participate, to let people know he's there. What does he do?

Well, perhaps emboldened by the realization that no one knows who he is, and that character creation wasn't so painful that he'd hate to do it again, he makes the first move and regales a passer-by. Or perhaps a community representative is on greeter duty and comes over to break the ice. Or perhaps there's a newbie hose and suddenly standing right next to him is Joanna Newbie, whom he can speak to because she's in exactly the same situation as he is.

The ability to communicate is the entrance qualification for a community. Everyone who can communicate shares a (very loose) community with everyone with whom they can communicate.

As to what they communicate *about*, that depends. In the first example here, Joe Newbie just wants to communicate, period. In the second example, he may have some procedural questions he can ask of the community management rep, but it'll be at the level of polite conversation; to the rep, Joe is just the latest in a long line of newbies, and it's impossible to form strong ties with all of them. In the third example, though, Joe and Joanna share a context. Both are in an enticing new world that they want to explore but don't fully understand, while surrounded by people who know a lot more than they do. It's daunting, but it'll be easier if they team up. They have a shared interest: Joe can talk to Joanna because they're both in the same boat.

Greeters have three aims: to reassure newbies; to ensure they understand the basics of how to play; to introduce them to the community. If they can hook them up with another newbie, so much the better. What happens thereafter is up to the players themselves.

A lot of work has been done on the notion of community in the real world. It's important to architects, anthropologists, aid workers, ad companies (and those are just the A's). Unlike most of the topics important for virtual worlds, the study of community has a solid body of work behind it. For designers, the problem is therefore the pleasant one of distilling salient points from a wealth of theory.

Here are the basics of community.

Communities are groups of people who

➤ Have the means and opportunity to communicate with one another.

➤ Have some reason for communicating with one another.

➤ Share a cultural context.

➤ Can choose the degree to which they participate in the community.

➤ Can be in other communities at the same time.

Members of communities have to have the ability to communicate (to talk), the chance to communicate (they're in the same location as someone who can hear), and some grounds to communicate (to find something out)[110]. They must share a cultural context, so what they say will be understood (they have to speak the same language). Communities have voluntary participation—you can put as much into them as you want to—and their memberships overlap.

Virtual world designers have understood all this for some time, at least at an intuitive level, and they routinely look for ways to further it in their games. They add new communication commands, new management tools, new ways to enable friends to find each other, and new dimensions along which players can group.

---

110. Or "means, motive, and opportunity" if you're into detective fiction.

These criteria outline what a community is; all communities must have them to some extent. There are other features that communities *often* have, but that they don't necessarily *have* to have; the more they do have, though, the stronger the community is. From a virtual world perspective, the most important of these characteristics are

➤ Members have a shared pool of knowledge.

➤ Members adhere to common practices.

➤ The community has a history.

➤ Members share a vision of the community's future.

➤ Members work together on projects that are for the benefit of the community.

This list is more useful from a designer's point of view, because it suggests concrete ways to encourage communities to be strong. We'll look at some of these shortly.

Strong communities are desirable because the stronger the bonds between people, the less likely they are to want to break those bonds (for example, by going off and playing someone else's virtual world). It may therefore appear that pushing community heavily is an indication that a virtual world doesn't have enough gameplay to sustain it, however this is not the case: Community is a good thing to have no matter how compelling the content of a virtual world is. That said, when community-friendliness extends to significantly undermining gameplay, that *is* a warning sign that a virtual world is in trouble.

Community "strength" is described in terms of *levels of community*. How many levels there are depends on what you want to use them for, and some levels are more important than others for particular applications. For the purposes of virtual worlds, however, there are five levels, the first of which is trivial but I'll mention it anyway.

In increasing strength:

➤ Communication

➤ Community of interest

➤ Community of practice

➤ Community of commitment

➤ Spiritual community

You get *communication* by default in virtual worlds; merely by showing up, you're communicating *something*. The first "proper" type of community is the *community of interest*, wherein people with the same individual goals and interests group together as a means of furthering those aims. Mechanisms for pooling and sharing knowledge and information develop, leading to a *community of practice*. An important emergent property of this is that members start to view the community as offering more than simply a means to an end, but of having intrinsic value itself. Community members then begin to work together on projects that are important to the aims or shared vision of the community, investing significant time and effort for the benefit of the community as a whole: This gives a *community of commitment*. The final stage, the *spiritual community*, arises when individual members understand and trust each other so implicitly that they can communicate almost intuitively. At this level, the personal bonds between members are supremely strong. Most communities never reach this level.

For example, suppose after sitting down playing computer games for too long, you decided it was time to get into shape. You go to a gym and sign up. Even if you were there to clean the floors, you'd be able to talk to anyone and they to you, so at the very least you're in a communication community. The instructors show you and other newcomers the pieces of apparatus available, and you set to work. Everyone else there wants to get fit or keep fit, so they have the same goals as you: You're in a community of interest. The instructors and some of the longer-term members give you tips on how to tone up your abdomen or whatever, and warnings if you're doing something wrong. In so doing, you form friendships with some of them. This puts you in a community of practice. One evening, at a dinner party with a few of your friends from the gym, someone mentions that the gym isn't really used much during the day. Someone else says there must be schools or charities that could make use of the facilities; after all, helping people become fit is always a good thing. Someone on the gym's management committee suggests a feasibility study. You volunteer to contact the nearby hospital's physiotherapy unit to see if it would be interested, another friend says they'll look into any potential problems with insurers, and pretty soon everyone is involved. It's now a community of commitment. In the months of fighting local bureaucracy that follows, the team suffers several major setbacks; individuals rally to the support of each other, though, which serves to strengthen their relationships further. Eventually, when the first of many batches of underprivileged teenagers arrives for their session, you know exactly how everyone who helped organize it is feeling—it's as if you shared emotions. You have a spiritual community.

It's clear from this example that not only can a community be at different levels, but that it can be at different levels at the same time. While long-term members of a community of commitment are out there doing their bit, newbies are arriving who have some definite personal reason for being there that has nothing to do with any grandiose schemes for advancing the community's aims. To be strictly accurate, of course, the broader community consists of a number of smaller communities that constantly shift, change, and overlap. Whether you treat these sub-communities as distinct from the community as a whole or not is up to you: It makes sense to view communities both ways, depending on the context.

Looking just at community levels, virtual world designers are presented with a number of opportunities to strengthen the bonds between players. The boundaries between the different levels of community are particularly fruitful.

For example, for people to join a community of interest, they must find other people who share that interest: A matchmaking service to connect players who are looking for a group with groups who are looking for new members is one way of doing this. Allowing groups to own property, keep archives, and institute a formal structure will encourage the development of communities of practice. Communities of commitment will arise if groups are afforded goals that are distinct from the goals of individuals. Spiritual communities will evolve if groups are put under immense emotional pressure.

There are two important points to bear in mind if you want to try this sort of thing.

Firstly, remember that participation in groups is a voluntary thing. If players can't get anywhere unless they're in a group, you're effectively forcing them to join a group. Players should be able to spend time on their own if they feel like it. Explorers may want to discuss what they've found out after a hard day's experimenting, but they probably won't want to have to hook up with six other people just to do the experimenting.

Secondly, the order is important! Putting a community of interest under severe stress is only going to scatter it most of the time. Use smaller conflicts as filters so that the riskiest situations are only available for those groups mature enough to handle them.

Even in the right order, stress might have unacceptable consequences. A community of commitment is usually strong enough to stay together for the most part when the going gets tough, but there *is* fallout; it's in repairing the emotional damage that spiritual communities can arise, but if that means some players fall by the wayside and quit, is it really worthwhile? In the real world, army units often form spiritual communities under fire[111], but no sane army commander is going to bomb their own troops just to build a sense of camaraderie.

Levels of community reflect the relationships between community members. Ultimately, therefore, they depend on the individuals concerned. No matter how much designers or community relations staff might encourage players to form stronger bonds, some people (perhaps most people) are just too independent. Communities of practice are relatively easy to achieve, but as soon as players have to commit to doing something for the community (rather than for themselves), many will balk. Some players relish the opportunity to organize others, but a good many more don't—and some of these will only reluctantly agree to be organized by anyone at all.

When designers are designing for community, they are really designing for relationships. In *Dark Age of Camelot*, players who want to join a group can flag themselves as being available. In the real world, people who don't want to find a partner can flag themselves as being unavailable (by wearing a wedding ring). The defaults are different, but the purpose is the same: to signal availability or otherwise to prospective suitors.

Groups emerge from the interactions of people; communities emerge from the interactions of people in groups; societies emerge from the interactions of people in communities. Interactions are at the heart of all this. Communities are a very useful conceptualization for virtual worlds, just as long as the fact they're made up of people isn't forgotten.

It's a friendship thing.

An Analogy

The reason that virtual world designers find viewing the player base in terms of communities useful is fourfold:

➤ Community ties rank among the most powerful reasons for players to stay with a virtual world. They generate intangible content, but can be aided in tangible ways.

➤ The sheer number of players in some virtual worlds makes it impractical to consider players at a personal level. It's easier to reach communities than individuals.

---

111. As Jessica Mulligan (a former U.S. Ranger) once put it: A guy who charges a machine-gun nest isn't doing it to win the war; he's doing it because otherwise his buddies are going to get machine-gunned.

➤ Players frequently act in groups. If you look at them as individuals the whole time, you miss what's going on ("you can't see the woods for the trees").

➤ Communities act analogously to players. Many of the things designers know about players can be applied to communities.

We've looked briefly at the first of these, and will look at it some more. The second item is purely pragmatic—we have to live with it, but it doesn't really tell us anything. The third makes a good point; furthermore, because there is an existing body of work on this subject, designers can adapt and apply what has been learned in other fields to virtual worlds. The fourth item, which I'll address now, is a way that designers can use work in their own field to think about communities.

Put simply, levels of community are analogous to stages of player progression. Look back at Figure 3.6:

➤ Players start as instinctives. They go in all directions at once to find the limits of what they can do. A community of interest behaves the same way, all members pushing their own interests to determine its boundaries.

➤ Next, players become learners. They embark on a process of discovery to find out more about what interests them. A community of practice is similar, its members pooling what they know to increase the knowledge of the community as a whole.

➤ After this, players become doers. They apply what they have learned to better themselves. This is like a community of commitment, where members work together on projects for the benefit of the community, rather than for the (immediate) benefit of themselves.

➤ Finally, players become experts and communities become spiritual. Both have fully internalized their experiences.

This is only an analogy: Communities resemble players in some respects, but are very different in others. The two aren't tied together, either—it's perfectly possible to have scientist-type players in a spiritual community and hacker-type ones in a community of interest, for example. Communities may be defined by their members, but the reverse does not apply.

Knowing this connection between community development and player development, though, it's possible to look at both with more enlightened eyes. Player development tracks, although they do show how players progress over time, are because of their origins more focused on what players want at each stage (rather than what should be provided for them to advance to the next stage). In contrast, levels of community are mainly to do with development—how to take the next step toward a spiritual community (rather than how to provide for players who are going to remain within a community at the same level for some time). Thus, designers should be aware that they should accommodate the stages and transitions between those stages, whether considering community or player progression or both.

There's one final observation we can make (if not actually use).

Player progression is closely connected with deepening immersion. Progression of communities through increasing levels should therefore, by analogy, be closely connected with immersion of the community (as an entity). How, though, can a virtual community be said to exhibit immersion? In what sense can a spiritual community be more "in" the virtual world than a community of interest? It can't; but it can be said to be more in the *real* world than a community of interest, because it forms real bonds between real players.

Immersion puts the real world into the virtual; community puts the virtual world into the real.

That's enough community theory for the purposes of this book, but there are plenty of places you can look if you want to learn more. For a short introduction to levels of community, read ethnographer Arian Ward's succinct article, *What is a Community?*[112]. For a longer one, which discusses virtual world communities in terms of community studies in general, Chapter 6 of Lynn Cherny's *Conversation and Community*[113] is invaluable. For a psychological perspective of virtual communities (with particular reference to virtual worlds), explore John Suler's superb ongoing hypertext book,

---

112. Arian Ward, *What is a Community?* http://www.workfrontiers.com/what_is_community.htm.

113. Cherny, Lynn, *Conversation and Community: Chat in a Virtual World.* Stanford, CLSI, 1999.

The Psychology of Cyberspace[114]. To learn more about managing virtual communities in general, consult Amy Jo Kim's *Community Building on the Web*[115] or Jenny Preece's *Online Communities*[116], both of which make reference to virtual worlds. If you just want a broad but thought-provoking overview of what virtual communities are, Howard Rheingold's *The Virtual Community*[117] is still required reading.

Now let's see if we can apply some of what we've learned here.

Influence Through Design

Virtual world design is about consequences. Every decision that a designer makes will have effects; some effects will be desirable, some will be undesirable, and some will be unforeseen. The direct consequences of a design decision can often be made with a high degree of certainty: If you give players lock-picking skills that go from 0 to 100 and create certain locks that require a skill of 110 to pick, you can be fairly sure that the integrity of those locks will not be compromised unless someone gets hold of the key you've given to the boss mobile. The indirect consequences may be trickier to predict: Will thief-class characters ignore lock-picking skills and max out pickpocketing instead so they can steal the keys they need?

Making judgments about the likely reactions of players is difficult, even with behavioral models to help. Designers have total control with regard to the tangible aspects of a virtual world, but with intangibles they can only hope to influence players, not to force them (which is probably just as well). Thus, designers present their most favored options favorably and their most unfavored options unfavorably, but ultimately players decide for themselves what to do.

Immersion and community are the great intangibles. How can designers influence them?

---

114. Suler, John, *The Psychology of Cyberspace*. http://www.rider.edu/users/suler/psycyber/psycyber.html, 1996 (orig.).

115. Kim, Amy Jo, *Community Building on the Web*. Berkeley, Peachpit Press, 2000.

116. Preece, Jenny, *Online Communities: Designing Usability, Supporting Sociability*. New York, Wiley, 2000.

117. Rheingold, Howard, *The Virtual Community*. London, Secker & Warburg, 1994.

Churn, Sink, and Drift

Churn is the rate at which people leave a virtual community. The greater the level of community, the lower the churn, because the stronger the bonds that hold the community together. Most churn occurs in a newbie's early days: They play, decide they don't like the virtual world, and leave. This cause of churn is called *sink*: Newbies show up, play a little, don't like it, and sink without trace. They may flit into a few communities, but none of these gain enough of a hold. (Indeed, they may loosen them: The virtual world itself might be compelling but have thoroughly obnoxious players.)

If players take a bite of a virtual world and decide they like the taste, they'll stay longer. For most commercial virtual worlds, there's a formal start to this: When their free suck-it-and-see starter period runs out and they have to commit to paying a monthly fee. From this point, they'll only leave the virtual world if there are real-world reasons (perhaps they get married) or because they lose interest in the virtual world. This cause of churn is called *drift*.

Contrary to what many players and some community managers believe, most established players do not leave after blazing, public rows. Most of them simply disconnect and drift away. Players who complain the loudest care the most; they're complaining because they see faults that they perceive as a threat to their world and their community, so of course they're not going to leave! They may *threaten* to leave, and may even act on that threat, but in most cases they're back within two weeks if they do.

No, most players—the "silent majority"—simply drift away without a word. They appear less and less frequently, until eventually they don't appear at all. For a commercial virtual world, players may have to cancel their subscription explicitly for a break to become formal—a decision they're often reluctant to make because of the investment they've made in their characters (it amounts to killing them). However, eventually the bonds fade so much that even this is not important any more.

Virtual world designers usually want to do as much as they can to minimize both sink and drift. Much sink is often impossible to address, being the result of marketing (direct, indirect, or viral) that draws to the virtual world people who simply aren't ever going to like it. Beyond that, the more barriers to entry there are, the fewer people will care to surmount them; a virtual world with a beautiful character creation system still needs an "auto" button so that people who just want to *play* have the opportunity to do so.

Strategies for inveigling players after they've made it through the door include giving them a mentor the moment they've caught their breath, showing them "wow!" environmental effects within five minutes and rewarding them for absolutely anything they do. Good help facilities, easy early goals, and gentle hand-holding will increase the chance that they'll make the decision to stay for a while; I'll mention a few others later in this book.

For most virtual worlds, the newbie experience is not all that great, however. It can be argued that this may be good in the long term, as it means that those players who persevere really *do* like the world and are therefore worth investing time in; unfortunately, if three times this number of newbies are put off who would have grown to like the world had they spent longer in it, filtering in such a manner isn't necessarily a wonderful idea.

Sink is about why people want to play virtual worlds; drift is about why they stop wanting to play them.

Immersion and community are the hooks that pull people in and the anchors that keep them there. Both can be used to address sink and drift. Remember, though, that they aren't *themselves* the core issues, they're just expressions of them. Immersion is a freedom thing; community is a friendship thing. Freedom and friendship are what designers should *really* be concerned with; immersion and community are convenient visualizations that can be used to overlay structure on the two more fundamental concepts.

With that in mind, we can look at specific ways for designers to influence community development and individual immersion.

Influencing Community Development

The first decision that designers must make in looking at their virtual world in terms of community is how large they want their community to be. The rule of thumb here is that beyond 250 members, a community of interest is going to fragment into sub-communities of sub-interests no matter what you do (and the majority fragment much sooner[118]). Most

---

118. An analysis of community sizes in reality suggests that 150 is the maximum, but it could be that virtual worlds (in which people aren't always present) have a wider penumbra. For an in-depth discussion of groups in virtual worlds, see Raph Koster, *Small Worlds: Competitive and Cooperative Structures in Online Worlds*. San Jose, *Proceedings of Computer Game Developers' Conference*, 2003. http://www.legendmud.org/raph/gaming/smallworlds_files/frame.htm.

communities will be communities of interest and/or practice, with overlapping sub-communities of commitment. Few spiritual communities will exist, and when they do they'll be very small (just a handful of players).

If you're looking at a large user base, therefore, the question becomes: How large do you want your basic communities of interest and practice to be?

Large communities are

> ➤ *More robust.* In times of stress they can spin off smaller communities instead of shattering.

> ➤ *Easier for newbies to join.* They have more people out recruiting.

> ➤ *More accommodating.* There's always "room for one more."

> ➤ *Fewer in number.* You don't have to provide so many interests about which they can form.

> ➤ *Easier to merchandise to.* Sell 50 baseball caps instead of 5.

> ➤ *Easier to link to reality.* People visit their web sites and attend their meets.

> ➤ *More powerful.* Therefore their actions are more dramatic.

> ➤ *Inclusive.* Socializers and achievers prefer them.

Small communities are

> ➤ *More intense.* Someone who is 10% of a community has a bigger say than someone who is 1% of it.

> ➤ *Quicker to develop.* Fewer people make for a more streamlined passage through community levels.

> ➤ *Friendlier.* Newbies are treated by all members at a personal level.

> ➤ *Less fractious.* If a small community erupts into civil war, fewer people are caught in the crossfire.

> ➤ *More diverse.* The special interests are more special.

> ➤ *Exclusive.* Killers and explorers prefer them.

Of course, you'll get a range of community sizes whatever you do; your influence comes in pushing the bell curve toward larger or smaller communities.

You can do this in two ways: By providing or failing to provide in-context community management tools for the players (bigger communities need more tools, therefore if you don't give them these tools it's harder to keep such communities coherent); by setting the natural lines of partition. In general, failing to provide tools for no reason other than you don't want players to use them is a bad idea. Partitioning is therefore the favored approach for determining average community size.

Lines of partition vary. The most obvious (because of the way basic communication works in virtual worlds) is to use geographic partitioning. Players who are in the same communication space, with access to the same kind of resources and experiences as other people in that space, will find it easier to form communities with one another than with people in spaces that are remote. Therefore, by providing boundaries to spaces a designer can foment community within the population penned in by the space.

Examples of geographic boundaries (in decreasing strength) are

> ➤ *Physical.* Walls, impassable mountains.

> ➤ *Resource-based.* Expensive boat rides, hard-to-find single-use keys.

> ➤ *Mental.* Tiresome-to-cross forests and deserts.

> ➤ *Relative.* Your magical powers diminish as you move further from your mana source.

The most popular[119] way to effect partitions is by functionality. This comes in two flavors: Those who have similar functions (mages all join the mages' guild) and those who have complementary functions (someone to take damage, someone to cause damage, someone to repair damage). The former tends to lead to large, clearing-house communities of interest that then form sub-communities (while remaining part of the community as a whole); the latter will lead to smaller communities of commitment fairly rapidly.

---

119. Because it's a by-product of other design decisions that designers often make.

In theory it's possible to take any tangible property of a character and use it as a basis for forming a community. It's conceivable to have communities based on character gender, character race, character strength, color of character's hair, whether the character's name begins with J—the list is endless. In practice, though, only character experience happens often enough to be significant: Relative newbies will often join with other relative newbies on the basis that they can't join up with anyone else. Although mixed-ability groups are possible, providing mixed-ability content for them is awkward, so many designers prefer players to hang out with their peers anyway.

These are communities formed about in-context interests, of course. Many communities form for out-of-context reasons. There may, for example, be communities of real-life friends, of people who speak some foreign language, of fans of some TV series, or of people who share the same real-life gender[120]. There is little that designers can do to stop such communities from forming, even though they can spoil immersion for non-members (and for members, too).

Partitions can be *formal* or *informal*. Formal partitions are ones that the virtual world provides itself, hardwired in. Most geographic partitioning is formal, although the weaker ones can be informal. Functional partitioning can be both. Typically, a virtual world will come with some prefabricated placeholders for communities that the designer wants or that the fiction demands. For example, all villages may be defined to have a "leader" office, the holder of which is responsible for setting local tax rates and deciding on what to spend the resulting income. The purpose of this role might be to give politician-type players something to shoot for, but because leaders are elected by other players[121]
a "natural" pressure for a geographic community of interests exists. This would be a formal partition. Alternatively, a group of players may get together and become bandits, raiding plump wagon trains. They, too, will choose a leader. This would be an informal partition. The designer may have deliberately created plump wagon trains with the intention of inciting players to become bandits, but unless there's a tangible, bandit-specific construct involved, the community of bandits is informal.

---

120. Interestingly, although groups of female-only players aren't a staggeringly unusual sight, groups that deny entry based on real-life ethnicity are as rare as fish feathers.

121. Non-player characters are usually either disenfranchised or statistical aggregates.

Communities made up of members with complementary functionality are generally informal, but there is often a "winning formula" that ensures they gravitate toward a common make-up. By careful composition of gameplay elements[122], designers can pre-define roles without necessarily hardwiring them. The fighter/magic-user/cleric triple may be classic, but it's not the only possibility even for combat (the real world's traditional infantry/cavalry/archer triple is arguably better for gameplay purposes, as it's more stone/paper/scissors). The point, though, is that by engineering a need for team play at this level—whatever the roles involved – designers can encourage players to seek out members to complete their team. This means unattached players are actively sought out and brought into communities, rather than left to mope around until someone takes pity on them. Once the team is formed, the barriers go up and its members are relatively insulated from social contact with members of other teams; this usually leads to the speedy formation of a community of commitment. The approach can work spectacularly well (see *EverQuest*), but suffers in that not everyone wants to play as a team the whole time.

Another decision that designers need to make concerning their groups is how modular or intertwined to make them. If players can be members of more than one community, that gives them multiple possibilities for finding the one that's right for them. More cynically, it gives them multiple reasons for not leaving. If communities are modular, the argument goes that they provide a hot-house atmosphere, with nowhere for players to go to cool down, therefore disputes come to a head and are resolved rapidly instead of brewing for weeks. Thus, they will grow to a spiritual level that much more quickly. Unfortunately, if a community is modular then it can leave a virtual world as a module if its members so decide, setting itself up in some other virtual world instead.

To entwine communities is fairly easy once you've made the decision to do it: You simply provide orthogonal interests that some members of a community might share but that others won't. A player may bond most tightly to their regular party members, but also have friends in the fighters' guild, the army, the swordsmith co-operative, the Northlands expatriates club and the glove collectors' society. If you want to encourage some of them further, build formal hierarchies that have preconfigured cross-links ("Sorry, we only buy old swords from members of the fighters' guild").

---

122. Or, more usually, by evolution based on blind chance discoveries.

To modularize communities is easier in one sense, in that it means less design work overall, but it's quite hard to achieve in practice because of the constraints it imposes on the rest of the design of the virtual world. The *DikuMUD* paradigm of party roles (as exemplified by *EverQuest*) is one way, and the fealty hierarchy of *Asheron's Call* is another. The key is to stop players from "leaking out" of their tight little groups without stifling them to the extent that they feel they've joined some weird mind-control cult. Unfortunately, the more variety a designer provides, the greater the urge players have to pursue disparate interests. *EverQuest* overcame this by having one overarching interest (kill things to get stuff so you can kill more things). *Asheron's Call* attempted it by not providing mechanisms for players to organize outside the central hierarchy, but found to its cost that this caused frustration and resentment. It's one thing to provide only carrots to eat, quite another to provide a variety of food but only let people eat the carrots.

Big communities will hold together better if they have structure. Structure will also help formal communities come into being, as it gives them a framework to flesh out. On the other hand, structured communities can't always form in an impromptu fashion and their overt lack of equality is a barrier to achieving spiritual level. Designers realize that structure is important for communities and will often provide a number of methods by which groups can be formed, merged, and unformed, by which positions can be created and players promoted, demoted, or shifted sideward, and by which members can be admitted or expelled. Communication channels, group ownership of property and bank accounts, group-specific iconography—all these can be added to help structure. The only caveat is that it should still be possible for groups not to have structure if they don't want it. A bunch of mages who meet in a pub and decide on the spur of the moment to go off and try to take down some trolls without a tank, just for the hell of it, don't want to have to buy a guildhouse in order to get a private communications channel to use.

Chapter 5 discusses different ideas for formal and informal hierarchies and other social arrangements that can be used to help crystallize communities about them. For now, though, we'll conclude our look at communities by considering ways to promote community in general.

Ways to Promote Community

Having ways to shape communities is all well and good, but you need to have communities in the first place. Communities will form whether or not you want them to, of course, but except in very particular cases (for example, psychological or anthropological studies) you should do everything you can to promote them. Note that's "promote," not "force."

Here are some suggestions.

Communication

The more that people communicate, the more they will develop relationships. The more relationships that develop, the stronger the community becomes. Remember that it's individual friendships that are important: Community is just an emergent consequence of these friendships.

Provide channels. Let people receive messages by their names, their locations, their character's properties, the groups they're members of, by topic—the more the merrier. Let them do it using real-time typing, through message boards, through email—however you can. Let them opt out of channels that don't interest them so they can focus on the ones that do. If none of this fits with the virtual world fiction, change the fiction. It's that important.

Supply ways for them to exhibit non-verbal cues. Studies of real life communication always show the importance of body language, facial expressions, tone of voice, and so on at conveying meaning. People will use gestures while on the phone, even though the person at the other end can't see them, because it helps them express their thoughts. You can't take such things into the virtual world, but you can provide substitutes that allow for players to articulate themselves without using words. Use "smile," "weep," and every expression of emotion in between that you can find in your thesaurus. If they need tangible effects to support them, add these. Include parameters, so you can "annoy Gilead" or "praise Gilead." Allow adverbs, "say 'hi there' sarcastically." Put in freeform emotes/poses: It doesn't matter if your graphical world can't depict "emote bares his fangs in a gesture of territorial defiance," just let the guy type it. *MUD2* has used emoticons, :-), as commands for years. Look at other people's virtual worlds for ideas.

Filtered Communication

This isn't as important as communication itself, but by allowing communication itself to be a topic of communication, further communication can be stimulated. Communication filters are fine if they don't remove too much meaning from the message and don't become the default. If your virtual world has a "say" command, add "lisp," "stammer," "stutter," and anything else you can think of. If characters drink 10 bottles of ale, replace all occurrences of the letter "s" in their speech with "sh." It's only a diversion, but if it prompts only one conversation in 10,000 it's worth it.

Be very careful about adding barriers to communication. These *can* be unifying if done carefully, but they also can be counter-productive. Players communicate with one another in (usually) English, but their characters might theoretically be speaking Elvish. Therefore, if another character comes along who doesn't speak Elvish, they shouldn't see the English ("Thorina says something in Elvish"). Thus, the players with characters who can speak Elvish can operate as a community closed to those that can't; it gives them an in-context secrecy filter that works naturally as a community boundary.

Providing a "common tongue" that all players can speak (in addition to one or more other in-context languages) is a way to enable communities to form across these language barriers; allowing characters to learn other languages is another way. If you do decide to use language as a community partition (as *Dark Age of Camelot* does between its three realms), you have to be confident in advance that you'll have a player base large enough to withstand such partitioning.

Mutual Dependencies (Characters)

If characters are dependent on other characters to succeed, then players will come to trust those characters who don't let them down. Bonds will be formed, and (if these are reinforced often enough) communities will arise. All members of an adventuring party should depend on one another to some degree, but there are plenty of other ways to promote mutual dependencies. Simple economic need is a favorite: Miners need blacksmiths to buy their iron, and blacksmiths need miners to provide their raw materials. This can be extended in different directions, for example temples may need worshippers to cause deities to give their priests powers, and worshippers may need those priests to cure diseases, purify water, and vaporize undead.

There's a danger of going too far and forcing players to maintain such a web of contacts that they never get anything done. If you need to source 50 components to make a cart, you're not going to make any carts.

Remember that the idea is to *promote* dependencies, not to enforce them. Some people like being independent, and will resent being made to rely on others. If blacksmiths want to dig their own iron ore, it should be possible for them to do so.

The dependencies here are gameplay ones. It's possible to create social dependencies, but these always seem "forced;" besides, socializers will group together anyway without prompting. The exception is when the dependencies are between community newbies and community oldbies. For example, suppose characters lose status for living in a dirty city, but lose even more status if they sweep the streets clean. Newbies, who have no status, can clean the streets without losing status, for the benefit of the community. It's therefore in the interests of oldbies to attract newbies to their city, so they don't lose status. The oldbies depend on the newbies (which is the reverse of the normal state of affairs).

Coupled with the idea of dependencies, find ways to allow players to do each other favors. Player A may not depend on player B to achieve some goal, but player B can make it a lot easier for player A by helping in some trivial way. Acts of kindness are the currency of friendships.

Mutual Dependencies (Communities)

As well as dependencies between individuals, create dependencies between communities. Again, the simplest way to do this is economically: The elves make the bows and arrows that the humans use to hunt boar so they can sell the meat to the elves. It doesn't have to be this clear cut, though: The sorcerers and the necromancers keep apart so as not to contaminate each other's magic wells.

Dependencies that are threatened can give cause for conflict. If humans cut down trees to make fires on which to roast their boars, this may impact on the elves. If there are so many sorcerers that a single magic well is not enough, they may need to set up a second well nearer the necromancers.

Dependencies are about resources. Although some won't be physical ("the secret of fire"), most will be. Miners convert land into iron; blacksmiths convert iron into swords; soldiers convert swords into land. Characters can be resources: Priests convert worshippers into powers[123].

Economics and related issues are discussed in Chapter 4, "World Design."

Reconnection

If you miss a session in the virtual world because your cat was ill, the rest of your party may have moved elsewhere. How are you going to find them? Even if you know exactly where they are, it's not really pleasant to spend half an hour trekking through swampland to hook up with them.

If people are members of a community of interest, they need to be able to communicate with one another; if it's a community of practice, they need to be able to access one another's data; if it's a community of commitment, they need to be able to act in concert with one another; if it's a spiritual community, they just need each other. The domain in which these proceedings take place is the *community space* for that community. For mages passing spell sequences between each other telepathically, all action and interactions takes place through the telepathic network, therefore that would be the community space. In most cases, though, the virtual world's geography is the community space. In order to participate in a community, members need to be proximate to the rest of the community in its community space; for virtual worlds, therefore, this means that characters must be able to reach the same (virtual) physical location as other members with relative ease. In other words, they have to be able to teleport to them.

There are two main problems with this. First, it's often fiction-breaking. If it took eight of us five hours to reach the oasis and it took seven of us another five hours to reach the pyramid, how come it takes one of us only five seconds to make the second half of the journey? Magical explanations are always possible, of course, but the players will view them as the cop-out that they are, spoiling immersion. The second problem is that if characters can appear anywhere at a moment's notice it makes everywhere local to everywhere else; this plays merry hell with economic systems.

---

123. This brings new meaning to the phrase, "preaching to the converted."

Fortunately, there are ways to promote connection without screwing either the fiction or the economics too badly. These are discussed in Chapter 5 in some detail, but they essentially involve finessing everything through the medium of offline action. When you're not playing, your character is still active. When you restart, you decide where your character traveled during your offline period and appear there.

Jargon

Jargon consists of new (or specialized meanings for old) words, terms, and phrases; it comes with communities of practice. Although often seen as a barrier (if you don't speak the language, you're not ready to join), jargon can be a very effective way of making players feel they really are part of something. It serves to draw in people: You hear someone say "rotate aggro" and you want to know what it means[124]. Acquiring the vocabulary gives you a badge that says, "Hey, I'm one of you."

Don't consciously create your own jargon—let it evolve. That way, you'll get terms that fill a genuine need. The important thing is to record anything that sticks, and make the record available to players. Journalists called the jargon used by *MUD1* players *MUDspeke*, so for *MUD2* I compiled the *MUDspeke Dictionary*, accessible from within the virtual world itself as an out-of-context command[125]. People look up what words mean, and can use them themselves. It helps them become accepted; it makes them part of the club.

Don't dismiss jargon as unimportant. Try speaking to a fellow designer without knowing what PvP, PvE, RvR, PD, and PK mean, and see how far you get....

Communal Activities

Sadly, players can't gather round a camp fire and have a good sing-song; lag, if nothing else, prevents players from acting in concert to this degree. Nevertheless, there are things that players can do together as (virtual) leisure activities, and designers should support them.

For example, players like to tell stories. This doesn't mean that there should be a bard class and everyone should be obliged to listen politely to their excruciating poetry. It does mean that there should be venues and situations conducive to storytelling and

---

124. It's *EverQuest*ish for "take it in turns to become the subject of the attacking creature's aggression."

125. It's also available at `http://www.mud.co.uk/muse/speke.htm`.

suggestions as to how to go about it. A somewhat overt approach would be to have a Storyteller's Hall, for example, containing a variety of atmospheric rooms, each with a Storyteller Stone that bears the legend "tell your part of the story, then pass me on." It's crude, but it works.

Another example: Provide players with musical instruments. When someone plays the instrument, generate music. It doesn't have to be complicated (although you can allow some MIDI-style composition if you wish). Playing an instrument is tangible: If someone else in the vicinity plays another instrument, you can lock it in to the same time and rhythm as the first player, lag or no lag. It's possible to build up bands and orchestras this way. Other players can dance to the music. They're communal activities that serve no gameplay purpose (although one could be devised). They're popular because they bring people together. *Asheron's Call 2* features the playing of musical instruments precisely for this reason.

When people have done something exhausting, they want to relax. In the real world, that can mean going to the virtual world for some fun. Sometimes, though, the nature of this fun can itself be exhausting, and players need a way to relax *within* the virtual world. Give them ways to do it, or they'll log off and find a real-world alternative.

Stake-Holding

Members of communities act and interact in community space. If they own some of that community space, it can help them feel like they're a permanent part of that community. For virtual worlds, that generally means they should own some virtual place of residence. It shows they care for the community space, and therefore (by extension) for the community.

Textual worlds introduced the idea of owning property; indeed, building their own house was a major preoccupation of players of TinyMUDs from the very beginning. Many MUDs using codebases that didn't let players access content-generation tools also allowed characters to own houses, although the practice was not widespread. Its importance was only really highlighted by its inclusion in *Ultima Online*, where it proved a galloping success[126].

---

126. Interestingly, it almost didn't happen. The development team worked all weekend to implement it, having got word that Origin's upper management planned to include it in a deadline-beating feature-cut the following Monday.

Stake-holding is good for other reasons, too. Like any property, players see housing as an investment. If they spent weeks collecting the necessary resources, found the perfect plot and designed exactly how they wanted their building to look, they will be loathe to quit and leave it to decay.

From the live team's point of view, property can be a useful indicator of a community's well-being. If the area where all the bards congregate is run-down, with few people on the streets, something is wrong in bardland and it merits investigation.

I'm talking about stake-holding in terms of housing here, but it doesn't have to be just that. Players who create in-world works of art, or who have acquired some (other) unique piece of content, will often feel that they have more of a stake in the virtual world than those who don't.

There are no major reasons not to have housing (or some equivalent) but plenty of major reasons to have it. Unless you have a compact or highly content-driven virtual world, put it in.

Things to Demote

Some things are generally good for communities, and some things are generally bad. There are any number of real-world reasons you wouldn't want these anyway, but players being players they'll sometimes occur. Designers should make every effort to prevent this from happening unless explicitly trying to make some kind of point or working with precisely controlled gameplay mechanics.

The main ones to watch out for are

➤ Xenophobia

➤ Prejudice

➤ Oppression

Xenophobia can cause an individual community to become stronger within itself, but it will be isolated from the rest of the virtual world in a way that other communities aren't. In some virtual worlds, modular communities often have no motive to interact with other communities, but that's quite different from having a motive *not* to interact with them. A party of *EverQuest* adventurers might keep itself to itself, but if some other party asked to team up for a while to tackle a particularly tough monster, they'd generally give the suggestion a fair hearing. A system that made it easy for the second party to slaughter members of the first party once they'd gained their trust would cause these communities to become more tightly woven (which sounds good) while treating every other community as a threat (which may also sound good, but is most certainly not). People don't like having to be on their guard the whole time. Under this kind of pressure, modular communities will emigrate to some other virtual world where they're not going to have to watch their back.

Prejudice is another problem, and one that is harder to deal with as it relies on real-world points of view. An adventurer might consider all socializers to be lazy cowards and a socializer might consider all adventurers to be one-dimensional primitives. Making socializers and adventurers have some mutual dependency would help if done well, but done badly it could cause resentment and make matters even worse. You have to be very careful, but it's tractable.

When prejudice is based on the real-life attributes of players ("She's a real girl, they're unreliable") there's very little that can be done; when it's perceived as a response to prejudice ("We don't want your male prejudices in our group") there's even less. The only strategy available is to make the virtual world sufficiently engrossing and immersive that people leave their real-world prejudices behind; if they form new ones in the virtual world, well, at least your community-promoting strategies are there to address it.

Prejudice is bad because it uses the community-promoting tools to undermine community. What causes bonds can be used to break them. Communication is good, but not when what is being communicated is an ill-judged message not to communicate with someone else. Some people really are detestable, of course, and deserve their fate; prejudice metes out the same fate on those who don't deserve it. Again, this could strengthen a community under attack, but it can provoke xenophobia while doing so and drive the members out.

Finally, oppression is not to be encouraged. Again, some idealistic designers might see it as the ideal way to fuel community. Under the heel of the despot, the players form tight, close-knit groups as they plot the revolution. Then, suddenly, they rise up as one, depose the tyrant and form a spiritual community that lasts in perpetuity.

Unfortunately, players intensely dislike being given orders by other players or having to hand over their property. The only reason they'll put up with it for extended periods is if they figure that at some point they'll get to have a slice of the oppressor's power themselves. In the real world, oppressed peoples have no escape except revolution or liberation; in virtual worlds, they just go somewhere more conducive to having fun. Thus, designers should strike out anything in the virtual world that allows any player unfettered access to mechanisms by which they can make the lives of other players a misery. Always have checks and balances.

Influencing Immersion

People want to be immersed. Designers want them to be immersed. Therefore, designers and players can collude to make immersion happen. In this sense, immersion is easier to design for than community, because it mainly involves telling players what they want to hear. You don't have to worry about how much immersion you want, or how quickly to deliver it—just give them as much as you can as quickly as you can, and they'll do the rest.

The key to immersion is *persuasion*. The more persuasive an environment is, the easier it is to become immersed in it. The biggest weapon in the designer's armory of persuasion is familiarity. You might at an intellectual level know you're in a virtual world, but if everything acts just like it would in the real world then you gradually find yourself treating the world as if it were real while knowing it isn't. Because you do know it isn't real, you can still behave as an individual in ways that you wouldn't if it were the real world, yet because it feels real you can nevertheless believe you're in it. When knowledge and belief coincide, that's immersion[127].

Although similarity to reality is a good way to influence immersion, it suffers from the fact that at first glance players don't *want* reality; if they did, they could have it by default for free—they wouldn't be in the virtual world. Historical, magical, and futuristic virtual worlds by necessity must differ from reality; however, that doesn't mean they don't intersect with reality. Players can still be given a strong sense of familiarity, which will smooth their path to immersion just as much as it would in a present-day setting.

---

127. In viewing the presence of individuals in virtual worlds as *participatory theater*, that is, as hard role-playing, the concept of immersion stops short of this. There's a discussion of this kind of immersion with respect to text-based virtual worlds in Chapter 4 of Janet H. Murray, *Hamlet on the Holodeck: The Future of Narrative in Cyberspace*. New York, Free Press, 1997.

This "similarity to reality" approach to inducing immersion seems to suggest that graphical virtual worlds have the edge on textual ones, because they have pictures (like reality) whereas textual worlds don't. Although in the short term they are indeed patently more like reality, in the long term the situation is not so clear cut. The constructs that designers are creating exist only in the minds of players: Graphics put it there through the senses; text puts it there through the imagination. Text can convey nuances that graphics can't; indeed, it can convey nuances that reality can't except through language. Text is also harder to deny. It is not, however, anywhere near as immediate as graphics. On the whole, therefore, text gives the more immersive experience, but it starts too slowly for many people. With graphics, you can still reach immersion, and you start off halfway there already.

The more that players don't have to think about interacting with their environment, the less they *will* think about it, and therefore the more immersive their time in the world will be. As an example, consider gravity. There's no inherent reason why a virtual world should have gravity pulling people down—it could just as easily pull them clockwise around the planet. If it pulls them down, though, players take it for granted. They know what will happen when they drop something. They know what will happen when they jump off the ledge. They don't even have to think about it, as it matches their model of real-world physics. It enhances immersion.

If they know it, they don't have to learn it; if it works like reality, it seems more real; if functionality is transparent, it won't be seen. When players say that a virtual world is *unrealistic*, they're complaining that it is breaking their immersion[128]. Magic doesn't happen in real life, but in a Fantasy virtual world it's not unrealistic; if it appeared in a Cyberpunk setting, that would indeed make it unrealistic.

Let players use their intellect to operate within the context of the virtual world; don't force them to use it to maintain the illusion of reality for themselves.

---

128. Ironically, many breaks in realism occur for playability reasons. This is a trade-off common to all games that have some form of reality simulation in them. For a clear and relatively concise assessment of the issues, see Steve Jackson, *Realism versus Playability in Simulation Game Design*. Proceedings *Joks i Tecnojocs* conference, Barcelona, 1991.

Ways to Promote Immersion

Immersion will happen almost by default in a virtual world eventually. Nevertheless, designers shouldn't take this for granted. Here are some ways by which to promote immersion. Again, note that's "promote," not "force."

Control

The more immersed a player is, the less the virtual world can dictate to them. In particular, it can't treat their characters as if they weren't people.

If my character waves and the feedback is, "You wave enthusiastically," that takes control away from me. I didn't "wave enthusiastically;" what I did was "wave." Virtual worlds should not presume to control my character for me.

The only exception is if I give my consent. If my character consumes alcohol, I'm explicitly relinquishing some degree of control. Loss of control is a well-understood property of alcohol. Therefore, if my character suddenly staggers off involuntarily in some direction after consuming a bottle of port, I've consented.

There is an implied consent to submit to environmental effects, but only in moderation. Your character may sneeze from dust, laugh when tickled, catch a bad cough—all these are acceptable if done infrequently, and help sustain the impression that the virtual world works like the real one. It's just about okay to let characters faint if they spend too long near a powerful heat source. It's not okay to have a mind-control spell go off that makes them attack their friends.

There's a gray area covering the situation where players try to do something really stupid. If a newbie runs up to a cliff edge and doesn't stop, what should the virtual world do? Let them continue running and fall to their doom? Or put some self-awareness into their character and have them pull up? If a newbie wants to attack a dragon alone, should the virtual world let them or should it point out they stand only a one in 20 billion chance of winning?

The best (albeit still not ideal) solution is to allow players to set a safety switch. If they decide at character-creation time to be prudent, then an attempt to jump off a cliff would be blocked ("You don't think this would be prudent"). A reckless character would make the jump; a paranoid character wouldn't drink an unlabeled potion. Later, the player could change their safety setting if it started getting in the way of play.

Another example of taking control from players is giving them goals they don't have. This most often happens in training programs for newbies, where designers are trying to teach new players the ropes. New characters aren't necessarily new players, so there should always be a way to decline a quest. "The first thing you need is a weapon. There is a shop…." No, the first thing I need is a teleport ring from a guy who owes me one, so I can meet my buddies up on the mountain where we're tracking werebears.

Detail

More detail makes for more persuasiveness. There are two caveats: Detail should be non-contradictory, and it should be at a consistent level. Contradictions usually only arise when two different designers working on disjoint parts of the virtual world independently specify content that clashes; this problem is almost always easy to fix. Inconsistent levels of detail are another matter, though. They arise because designers focus on one feature without following through the implications. For example, it may be possible to fell a particular tree to expose a hollow core that you can climb down through, but not be possible to fell any other trees, even saplings. Players would accept the same level of depth throughout (that is, no fellable trees) but if one tree can be chopped down and others can't, they're reminded that they're in a virtual world. Furthermore, it's an incomplete one (from their point of view) because felling trees isn't fully implemented. Better you can fell no trees than just one.

Detail in the virtual world is in terms of both depth and breadth. This means lots of things working in lots of ways, arranged together in an integrated fashion. Initially, everything in the virtual world should make sense. Alchemists making fire bombs wouldn't live in crowded areas, loggers would have their depot next to a river, forest creatures wouldn't all be carnivores. If players come across something out of place, it's either out of place for a reason ("This tower is miles from civilization, how did they build it? Unless…") or it's because some player did it.

Critical to this is the sense that the virtual world has a past—that it was fully functioning before players came along. Most virtual worlds have a backstory to explain how and why things came to be the way they are. This serves two purposes: to introduce gameplay concepts that wouldn't make sense otherwise; to set the context so that newbies know in advance what kind of world they're entering (it may even attract some of them, especially if it's a big license).

Backstory isn't history, though. You may assert that in the time before the coming of the humans, elves, and dwarfs roamed the lands, but that doesn't tell you which parts of the land they stalk now, and why that makes sense. A handy tip is to run a board game simulation[129] of the virtual world's history that can provide the necessary explanations. Use what the simulation implies in the virtual world: Why this area has a sizeable minority population of dwarfs; why that area has ancient reptilian monuments; why in those areas the humans speak Elvish. It all adds to the veracity of the detail that will enable players to buy into the world.

Detail is important. Having greater detail is one reason that textual virtual worlds can be more immersive than graphical ones.

Freedom of Choice

Designers decide what options to provide to players and the manner in which to provide them. This is how design influences players.

For promoting immersion, it's slightly different. The whole point of identity play is that you're free to make choices. Designers may suggest directions that you hadn't considered, but they have to stop short of actually recommending any of them. It's for you to make up your own mind.

Virtual worlds should be as open-ended as possible. Players should be able to try anything. They don't have to succeed (there are too many killer-type players for that), but they do have to know they could have tried. The decision not to do something can be as life-changing as the decision to do it. Let players take their own path.

This particular way to promote immersion is one with which many designers feel uncomfortable. They don't like giving players the freedom to make major decisions because, all too often, they make the wrong one. They then refuse to accept it's their fault, sulk, and quit. The counter-argument is that these are the players who were going to quit after a short while anyway, so why pander to them? From this point of view, the question boils down to: Do you want their business for a couple of months or don't you?

---

129. Just choose some existing board game that you think will work and use your own map. Half a day playing *Diplomacy* is fine if it gives you concrete reasons for why the elves ended up scattered to the four winds and the dwarfs remained stuck in their mountain redoubt.

It's actually a broader issue than that, though, involving concerns such as narrative, content, and (of course) community. Choice of action has implications beyond immersion that must be considered.

Choice promotes immersion. It's up to individual designers to decide whether to act on the fact, though.

Self-Expression

Self-expression is another way to promote immersion. By giving players freeform ways to communicate themselves, designers can draw them more deeply into the world—they feel more of a part of it. Communication and stake-holding help players to exhibit self-expression in addition to being ways to promote community; the decision to have them therefore looks trivially easy.

Self-expression allows players to discover more about themselves, which is almost a definition of the goal of immersion. It also, to a lesser extent, lets them find out more about the virtual world; this, too promotes immersion.

The only real reason to curtail self-expression is the impact that it can have on other players. However, that is a *very* powerful reason. One person's self-expression can be someone else's "limbo dancing wasn't a feature of life in ancient Rome." The appearance in a recreation of Victorian London of a character called Ladyboy is going to unimmerse even those players who smile when they see the incongruity of it. It can undo hours of work: A designer may have agonized over the exact positioning of a field to create just the right sense of rural idyll from a neighboring hillock, but if someone has planted potatoes in it in the shape of a smiley face then it's all to waste.

Self-expression will find a way, but promoting it will increase its prevalence. It helps immersion for individuals, although it can reduce immersion for other players. Whether this becomes a problem depends on the maturity of the player base and the vigilance of the community management representatives.

Things to Demote

The twin enemies of immersion are reality and sterility.

If players are continually reminded that they're in reality, it will disrupt their sense of immersion. You can't stop someone's significant other from bringing them a mug of coffee, but you can stop your virtual world's interface from being intrusive and you can prevent references to reality from sneaking in. Keeping reality out is why commercials are unacceptable in virtual worlds, but product placement is comparatively okay.

Demoting reality can be tricky because designers often want to provide mechanisms to support other features (particularly community) that involve reference to it. Immersion usually loses out in these conflicts, because returning to it is relatively quick. When it does become necessary, designers must first consider whether they can hide it within the virtual world's fiction. If they can, that's fine; if they can't, they should formally take it out of the virtual world in some way—a separate window, a different color of font—so that players perceive it as being distinct from where they were. When the screen returns to normal, they can then (hopefully) dive right back in where they left off.

Sterility is counter-immersive because it induces ennui. While they're having fun, players are working toward immersion; when they become bored, the direction changes and they work away from it. Note that this does not happen in the face of unpleasantness, unless the unpleasantness is relentless; players accept change while immersed, but not fossilization. It's as if you're watching a movie and suddenly the projector locks in freeze-frame: You may not have been enjoying the movie, but at least you were absorbed by it; now, you're out of it.

Of all the ways to kill a virtual world through bad design, boring the players is the one most guaranteed to succeed.

Chapter 4

World Design

KEY TOPICS

- Scope
- Major Decisions
- Geography
- Population
- Physics
- Reset Strategy

The scientific view of the real world is that human beings and other organisms are under constant evolutionary pressure from the environment and from each other. The environment was not designed for humans, and neither were humans designed for the environment; this is because there *is* no "design." Things got to be the way they are through complex combinations of chance events.

The religious view of the real world is that one or more deities created it. Normally, the deities put the world together before introducing humans into it (rather than creating both at once or the humans first). However, from the beginning, the deities intend to populate the world, and therefore design it with the humans who will live there in mind.

For the real world, you should decide for yourself which of these views is the more correct. For virtual worlds, discount the first one. Deities create virtual worlds; designers are those deities.

You know, when you start designing your virtual world, that it will have players. These are the people for whom you are designing your world. They won't spend millions of years evolving to fit it; you have to create the world to fit them. The more you know about them, the better you will be able to do this. Therefore, you should look at players first; only then can you look at worlds.

We spent Chapter 3, "Players," looking at players. Now we can look at worlds.

Scope

The nature of a virtual world's design is determined by three factors:

> ➤ *Business*. What will it cost? How will it be sold?

> ➤ *Technical*. What can be implemented? How long will it take?

> ➤ *Gameplay*. What will people do? How will they have fun?

These are general terms. "Business," for example, doesn't necessarily mean commerce: Even a free, stock, textual world will need an investment of time, and its players still have to come from somewhere.

Using Chapter 2's, "How to Make Virtual Worlds," model of a massively multiplayer games development house, "business" covers company leadership, sales/marketing, finance/accounts, and HR; "technical" means software development, operations/IT, art/animation, and support/QA; gameplay is the design team.

This chapter concerns only gameplay.

Typically, business will want the virtual world to have certain features that it considers prerequisites for its success. Some of these just won't work in a virtual world, and others will be unimplementable. Technical will want heavily over-specified kit, on which it will implement everything in experimental, beyond state-of-the-art ways. Gameplay wants a world that won't sell, and that would need more computers than there are atoms in the universe to support it.

There will thus almost certainly be criteria from the business and technical sections to which the designers must adhere. These will vary on a case-by-case basis, but the ones that are most frequently "a given" are

> ➤ Genre

> ➤ Platform

> ➤ Unique selling point

Designers of virtual worlds have very little influence on genre unless they had it explicitly written into their contract when they signed up. Designers of free textual worlds effectively run their own company, so in theory can do whatever they like; the availability of a suitable codebase may force their hand, though.

Nevertheless, within a genre there can still be a lot of leeway. Fantasy and Science Fiction are very broad areas, for example. Even within a license there can be freedom, although as noted in Chapter 1, "Introduction to Virtual Worlds," some licenses are pickier than others.

Related to genre is the user base. Designers can't choose where their players come from. Often they have to address a particular market. A virtual world expected to be played primarily by adolescent boys will be different than one aimed at homemakers. An inclusive virtual world that welcomes everyone has balance issues that a world for children aged eight years and under doesn't. Designers can hope to expand beyond their core player base, but the core itself is often determined from the outset.

The technical platform of both server and client is also a given, although the client more so than the server. This isn't too bad: Designers look on technology as physics that they can't do anything about, so they accept it. It's only an issue if programmers push their luck and claim that things can't be done that can.

Architecture, however, is a technical consideration that may be imposed for business reasons. Designers are told whether the virtual world will be textual or graphical, and, if the latter, what sort of graphics they will be (2½D, 3D). From a purely gameplay point of view, text is better for intimate, intense, imaginative worlds where thought is more important than action and individuals are preferred over parties or clans. Graphics are better for gregarious, large-scale, beautiful worlds where action is more important than thought and clans and parties are preferred over individuals. Designers have no say in which they get.

A unique selling point (USP) is a Big Idea that marketing people feel will attract players and interest to the virtual world. Examples are: "Inter-clan warfare!," "Pay real money for game money!," and "A five-year story arc." Most of these aren't as unique as the people who think them up like to imagine, and they're often of dubious worth as selling points, too.

Designers can have a big idea, just the same as anyone else. Be *very* careful if you do, though. A big idea completely dominates a project, with everything becoming subservient to it. This makes the virtual world one-dimensional, preventing people from having multiple big ideas.

Sometimes, though, a big idea can lead to a paradigm shift. *EverQuest* may have been dominated by the big idea of having first-person graphics, but benefited because this really *was* a big idea (albeit one pioneered by *Meridian 59*).

So, designers will have constraints on what they can design. For the most part, these will be beyond their control, and represent a non-negotiable starting position. Within such parameters, however, designers have absolute dominion. It is here that the virtual world is shaped to their will.

This is the context that the remainder of this chapter assumes.

Major Decisions

Designers can't leap right in and start work at the nuts-and-bolts level. Although such a "bottom-up" approach may work for smaller tasks, virtual worlds are too complex for this. If you were designing a cruise liner, you wouldn't start by specifying the décor for cabins. Yes, at some point you *would* need to do it, but there are other things that are more important; some are even so important that they impact on it (the cabin's dimensions, its window sizes, furniture access, and so on).

So it is for virtual worlds. Some things have to be decided first, because they affect what is decided later.

Most of these have already been introduced in this book, so now let's look at them in detail.

Ethos

What kind of a virtual world do you want?

To a large extent, it depends on the players. Where will they come from? What will their background be? What player types will dominate? Why will people eventually leave?

Players bring aspects of their real-world community—their culture—into the virtual world with them. Part of the point of virtual worlds lies in being able to pick and choose what you leave behind. Culture is that which is passed from generation to generation without being inherited; virtual worlds let you rethink what you've been taught at every level.

One player may find this a liberating experience and take a more progressive attitude in real life; another might despair of the superficial values and reaffirm their real-life cultural anchors. It doesn't really matter which: The point is that players must have the *option* of stepping out of their culture; whether they stay out or step back is irrelevant.

If players do step out, though, what do they step into? It can't be a wild maelstrom of anarchy, because otherwise players could only interact transiently with one another and the virtual world would not survive. The virtual world must *itself* have a culture— one supported by its community in general. Sure, it's not as deep as a real-life culture, but it's a culture nonetheless.

How does this culture arise? It emerges consensually from the player community. As noted in Chapter 3, this is something designers can shape but can't control.

The theory works as follows:

➤ The designer determines an ethos, and fixes the virtual world to reward activities that exemplify this ethos.

➤ Players who share the designer's ethos seed the virtual world.

➤ The virtual world's design attracts players hopefully compatible with its ethos.

➤ Thereafter, it's mainly self-selecting (newbies either take the ethos on board or don't like the atmosphere and leave).

➤ The live team can reinforce or undermine the ethos by example.

In practice, designers are often cheerfully unaware of the extent to which they set the tone of their virtual world. They seed it with people whose shared ethos is to find ways to exploit or otherwise abuse the virtual world. Cynical marketing techniques attract players to an image of the virtual world that doesn't necessarily match the product. Newbies who don't like the culture damage it before they leave. The live team spends all its time firefighting and doesn't have the staff to do anything more cerebral[1].

That said, the exercise isn't entirely pointless. There may be obstacles piled at the window, but if a single shaft of light gets through it can be enough to see by. A virtual world drawing players from advertisements on first-person shooter web sites will be different from the same software drawing players from advertisements on chess web sites, but some attitudes may prevail in both.

As to what ethos to adopt, well that's really up to the designer. Be sure you do have one, though; if players can't sense how they should behave, the law of the jungle applies, and as with any question of morality, different people have different ideas. However, there are some things that are more conducive to the prosperity of virtual worlds than others. Many of these occur in multiple philosophies[2] and will usually appear in some form by default anyway. Of those attitudes that don't, you should probably consider promoting some or all of the following:

➤ Reality is another place.

➤ A virtual action with real-world effect is a real action.

➤ Yours is just one way of many to play.

➤ There's no stigma to role-playing.

➤ Newbies aren't children.

➤ Evilness is not a winning strategy.

➤ It isn't rude to say hello.

---

1. Sometimes, the customer support staff develops its own rogue culture independently, which then becomes embedded in that of the virtual world. If the staff has a lax attitude to its responsibilities (for example, fixing bugs), players will develop lax attitudes to theirs (for example, behaving civilly).

2. Hinduism: "Do naught to others which if done to thee, would cause thee pain." *Mahabharata 5:5-7*. Zoroastrianism: "Whatever is disagreeable to yourself, do not do unto others." *Shayast-na-Shayast 13:29*. Buddhism: "Hurt not others with that which pains yourself." *Udana-Varga 5:18*. Confucianism: "What you do not want done to yourself, do not do to others." *Analects 15:23*.

Unending or Circular?

In a single-player computer game, when a player makes a mistake it means a restart from their last save. In virtual worlds, this is impossible—a restart for one player means a restart for all of them. How, then, can a player learn from their mistakes? Do similar situations arise regularly? How about the same situation? Does everything repeat in time, or does the world evolve?

This is basically a change and persistence issue.

Players consume content. There is certain content that they like, and which they are not averse to consuming several times. Other content they can only really consume once. On the other hand, just because one player has consumed something, that doesn't mean someone else wouldn't like to try it. How can these differences be reconciled?

Well, that's what you have to decide. In practice, you can't have them all at once: It's a sliding scale from low change/persistence (circular) to high change/persistence (unending). A fully circular approach reuses content but has nothing new; a fully unending approach abandons used content but offers fresh experiences.

Virtual worlds that don't change much and don't persist much have to be sufficiently broad and deep that players take an age to explore them; otherwise, only the activities of other players will provide novel experiences. Virtual worlds that do change or persist will retain players' interest[3], but be costly (because new content has to be created[4]) and wasteful (because old content isn't reused). Furthermore, virtual worlds need checks and balances to ensure that all new content is in keeping with the virtual world as a whole.

---

3. Unless there is so much change that it renders large chunks of players' knowledge unusable.

4. It's a never-ending commitment, too. Once you begin adding content regularly, players will come to expect it regularly, irrespective of whether the virtual world actually needs it.

Virtual worlds that don't introduce content are called *fixed*. Whether virtual worlds that do introduce content are fixed depends on whether the content is fixed. A predetermined storyline is not new content; it's old content that hasn't been added yet[5]. Players have no more ability to change the future than they do in a virtual world that resets every two hours. If storylines are reactive or emerge from player actions, that means the virtual world is not fixed.

Note that by "virtual world" here I don't mean just its physical geography; anything from its social structures and mobiles to its economy and combat systems can be changed. *Asheron's Call* and *Anarchy Online* both have basically fixed storylines, but the former's can involve the leveling of entire cities whereas the latter's (because of how it's implemented) can't.

Does the virtual world have a future? If so, who decides it?

You get to choose.

Hands On or Hands Off?

Intangible content in virtual worlds will arise naturally through the interactions of players. Designers can and should assist these interactions, by providing tangible means of support and encouragement. How far should they go, though? In particular, should they be proactive to the extent that they provide for live team "leader" players to catalyze these interactions?

In traditional tabletop role-playing games, the referee not only designs the game world but can lead the players through it. Players perceive a highly detailed world because the referee can resolve everything they do, to whatever depth. Referees don't have to think up everything in advance; they can create some of it in response to the actions that players take.

---

5. Players may perceive this as new content, because they haven't seen it before. From a designer's point of view, though, it isn't new. What constitutes "new content" varies from virtual world to virtual world: It usually means new monsters and areas, but it could also include additional skills, spells, classes, or even races. Basically, if "content" is stuff that holds the interest of players then "new content" is stuff that does this which wasn't there before.

In a virtual world, the designers have to put everything in to begin with. There's a bedrock level of detail beyond which players can't descend. This is most noticeable in the behavior of mobiles, none of which have remotely convincing artificial intelligence[6]. There is, however, something that can be done about this. People could be allowed to play on the same "side" as the virtual world, as an adjunct to it. There is already a community management team; why not allow specialized members to participate in the virtual world in character?

There are several levels at which such characters could operate:

> *Undercover*. Nobody knows they're part of the live team, but they make life interesting for other players through what they do. They're like audience plants who "volunteer" to help magicians[7].

> *Entertainer*. Everyone knows these people are part of the live team, but by their ready wit and repartee they manage to make the world more fun.

> *Performer*. Players in a *Lord of the Rings* universe will want to meet Gandalf—he's part of the package. The live team therefore hires an actor to play the role.

> *Guide*. "So you guys have never visited the caves of Drachen, huh? Stick with me and just maybe you won't get hurt *too* bad...."

> *Referee*. These are guides that have out-of-context world editing abilities. If a player on a quest decides to do something inventive that wasn't planned for, the referee can produce a tangible response.

> *Unseen referee*. The quest is managed behind the scenes. Players don't know that the reason there's a key lying in front of them is because they didn't search the body of the troll and find it earlier.

The hands-on approach is used mainly for manufactured quests. It had been applied for other purposes right from the start: *MUD1* had organized events called "spectaculars" that involved much hands-on activity by a wiz-level administrator. Only with plotted quests, however, were the virtues of participant management to become fully

---

6. If they did, how could developers hope to control them (both practically and morally)?

7. The irony with these is that to succeed, players must not recognize them for what they are. This means that when the live team sets up large-scale events, players don't credit them with having done so. In *Ultima Online*, players were found to express disappointment at never having participated in an organized event when at that very moment they actually *were* participating in one!

apparent. *Avalon* pioneered this idea commercially in the early 1990s, and it became formalized in *Achaea* circa 1996. Nowadays, some of the products of the innovative textual world company, Skotos, rely so much on the activities of highly experienced referees (which it calls *storytellers*) that they would be almost dead without them; with them, however, they are profoundly alive.

If a hands-on style can deliver this degree of immersion while fostering community, why would a designer *not* want it?

Firstly, it's expensive. There may be players willing to do it for free, but quality control and time management are difficult to maintain. Also, developers are sensitive to accusations that they are exploiting their player base, and therefore prefer to have people on their payroll[8].

Secondly, the deeper levels of event management only really work in smaller virtual worlds. If there are 2,000 players milling around and 40 referees running quests, it's harder for them not to tread on each other's toes than if there are 100 players and 4 referees (despite the latter's greater density of referees to players).

Thirdly, the players don't all like it; specifically, the players who don't get to participate in organized events don't like it. To an achiever, seeing someone (particularly someone else) go up levels after being "walked" through a quest is galling. Getting help from community management—it's like cheating! Socializers may view intervention as patronizing. It's a virtual world, not a theme park. Skotos targets its games at players who do like this degree of personal touch; virtual worlds that don't may not have the same results.

Fourthly, it's very difficult to test quests and events prior to running them. There may be unwanted effects (such as bugs) or side effects (such as characters getting frequently killed). Occasional events with wide coverage can be very popular, but they tend to have a greater chance of going wrong, too.

Finally, no matter what spin you put on it, using real, live people to make your content interesting is like an admission of defeat. It says that a virtual world is neither sufficiently compelling to be interesting in its own right, nor sufficiently rich to enable

---

8. The fact that developers risk being taken to court under minimum wage legislation if they don't is perhaps another factor.

players to make it interesting themselves. Of course, it could be argued that no virtual world is so compelling, but that's not how designers see it. Besides, professional mourners can spoil a funeral, rather than enhance it.

Categories

Another major decision designers have to make is whether to categorize players or not. In many cases, the question they actually ask themselves is *what* categories to have, which rather jumps the gun. The categorization of players is not a fundamental component of virtual world design.

Chapter 3 described the differences between classbound and classless systems. There, I argued that a classless system can fake up a classbound one while offering more. Because some players (particularly newbies) can benefit from the provision of predefined character types, I suggested a "character kit" approach to allow them to choose a pseudo-class while retaining the overall flexibility of the classless ideal. Ironically, this means that even if a designer decides against a classbound regime, they could still have to produce something that looks like a list of classes (if only to placate newbies who are expecting to see one).

So what are the usual lines of partition?

The first one is, inevitably, gender. Textual worlds are hamstrung by language in this respect, and graphical worlds by images. Although it is quite conceivable to create a virtual world in which all the characters are of the same gender, it's nigh impossible to create one in which characters' gender is merely unspecified without convoluting the language[9]. Gender is probably the only categorization that virtual worlds are stuck with.

Gender is a physical difference, although in virtual worlds it is usually presented as a cosmetic one. The reasons for this are given in Chapter 5, "Life in the Virtual World," but the basic explanation is that designers don't want to offend anybody.

---

9. This is in Indo-European languages; it may be easier in others. As I alluded to in an earlier footnote, the Mandarin Chinese word for "he" and "she" is the same—*tā*—although they're written using different symbols.

Another physical dimension for partitioning players into groups is by race. Given the way that virtual worlds are so politically correct about gender, one would expect that race was also a purely cosmetic issue, but that's not the case: Races are presented as being fundamentally different, with significant strengths and weaknesses. The reason for this is that what virtual worlds call race, the real world would call sub-species; what the real world calls race, virtual worlds call nothing at all and do treat as a merely cosmetic aspect of a character. Some of the moral implications of this are discussed in Chapter 8, "Coda: Ethical Considerations."

Races follow stereotypical lines. The short, stocky, bearded axe-wielders who live underground hate the tall, slender, pale archers who live in the forests, and vice versa. Scaled-up humans have more strength than brains, whereas scaled-down humans have more brains than strength. Nobody likes a lizard.

There are common sub-races, too, which also run along stereotypical lines. Fantasy worlds have half-elves and half-orcs, but never quarter-elves or half-dwarfs[10], and there isn't even a word that means the progeny of an orc and an elf.

Because races have physical differences, designing kits for them is tricky. It's easy enough to make height, musculature, skin tone, ear and eye shape, hirsuteness, and so on be parameters that can be adjusted at character creation time, but this would allow players to customize races of their own—giant, puny, hairy lizards, for example—that didn't make sense. Representing these graphically may introduce unnecessary complexities, too. For this reason, virtual worlds that must have races (because of their fiction) almost always have to hardwire them in. It's limiting, but it's a necessary compromise. Although people who start off as farmers may become politicians, nobody who starts off as a troll is going to become an elf[11].

Related to race is the notion of nationality, or, more accurately, country of origin. This is a less frequently used way to categorize characters, combining them by geographical proximity. The reason it's not so popular is because players want to move around as

---

10. Most virtual worlds that have them refer to "dwarves" rather than to "dwarfs." This is either because their designers are following Tolkien's lead or they're illiterate.

11. Yes, I know, in some enlightened virtual worlds race can be changed through magic or whatever. On the whole, though—especially in graphical worlds, where identity is bound tightly to appearance—race is pretty well inviolate.

their characters progress, to be close to the facilities they need (and things they want to kill). The result is that nations are often only nations of NPCs, as PCs are spread about all over the place.

Although one race may dominate a region, others are not excluded; also, the same race may dominate more than one region. Nationality is best used to engineer social conflicts between large groups of players, and in that sense it doesn't necessarily play a part in a player's sense of their character's identity. However, when nations are typecast it can become a constraining influence. The cultures of the three realms in *Dark Age of Camelot* are quite distinct.

Beyond the physical and geophysical, categorization becomes harder to justify. The dominant approach is that of character classes, which derives from the old tabletop role-playing paradigm. Skills systems are usually grafted on to this, rather than being independent of it, which is rather a shame.

Both character classes and skills systems are fairly arbitrary: Depending as they do on the nature of the virtual world itself, there isn't really a systematic way to determine which ones you "need." I'll describe the various ways to organize skills in Chapter 5; only in creating the skills will designers get a feel for what character kits might be appropriate. Thinking up the kits (classes) first and then imposing them on the skill set is the wrong way to go about it. I won't be listing any skill sets or classes here, but if you want ideas you should look at other virtual worlds[12].

The final common way to categorize characters is by alignment. This, too, is an old tabletop role-playing game concept, intended as an aid to role-playing. The idea is that players decide in advance how their character is to behave, and stick to it. If they step out of line, the referee penalizes them. The traditional alignment dimensions (from Advanced Dungeons & Dragons) are law/chaos and good/evil, with the crossing point of the two axes labeled "neutral." A lawful good character is benevolent and just; a lawful evil character plays by the rules but is without mercy; a chaotic good character is a rebel with a conscience; a chaotic evil character is a self-serving bully who'll do anything to further their ambitions. There are another five combinations involving the concept of neutrality.

---

12. Textual worlds are particularly fruitful in this regard.

Alignment is a useful concept for soft role-players because it's moveable. By saying that your character is lawful neutral you're making a statement about how you intend to role-play that character. If you consistently act good in situations where you could equally well act neutral or evil, eventually your alignment will shift to lawful good. Some actions may be outlawed altogether—paladins don't get to douse beggars in burning oil no matter how bad they smell.

In tabletop games, the referee determines when alignment violations occur. In virtual worlds, much of what is good or evil, lawful or chaotic, is intangible; it can't be tracked by the virtual world, therefore it can't be enforced. If I attack another player, am I being good or evil? What if they had stolen something from me? What if it was theirs in the first place? What if they had attacked me in the past? What if I'd attacked them beforehand? What if I attacked because they'd killed a friend? What if the friend had started the fight and I only *think* they were innocent?

There is no point in trying to get the virtual world itself to track alignment.

So is attacking another player good or evil? If they're evil, it's good; if they're good it's evil. Put this way, good and evil are just badges. Players will say they're evil without understanding in the remotest sense the depths of cruelty that this implies; players will say they're good without ever having exhibited the slightest tendency toward compassion. They're just labels: They may as well be green and yellow.

It may be possible to define an intangible concept like alignment[13] by asking other players to make judgments in a tangible fashion (for example, by voting). This isn't without its problems, though: It's immersion-breaking, it depends on player goodwill, and it's too easy to subvert.

On the whole, alignment in virtual worlds works only as another shallow, artificial way to partition players into smaller communities. Unless it's an important part of the virtual world's fiction, it's probably not worth having.

---

13. Reputation systems, which are discussed in Chapter 5, are closely related to this idea.

Intimate or Grand Scale?

Virtual worlds imbue a sense of size. Players have very definite views on how large the areas they cover are. *Asheron's Call* feels bigger than *EverQuest*.

Size is affected by many factors. The most obvious is the number of discrete points that a character can occupy: A text world with 20,000 rooms will generally feel larger than one that has 500; a graphical world measuring 32K by 32K will feel smaller than one measuring 256K by 256K. Speed of travel affects size: If it takes you half an hour to traverse one virtual world and two hours to traverse another, the former may appear to be smaller than the latter even if it isn't; if you can teleport anywhere, the world will feel smaller still.

The abstract size of the world being modeled is significant, too, especially in textual worlds. One room may only be 50 moves away from another, but if the locations in between are written to convey an impression of vastness and fraught with dangers and dead ends, players can be left with the feeling of having undertaken an epic journey.

As well as the physical size of the world, there are other features that can indicate its scale—the number of independent organizational substructures (dukedoms, countries, planets, and so on), for example. The reach of these can help convince players how big the virtual world is: If the non-player characters (NPCs) change language or religion, or the currency no longer works, or the buildings have onion domes instead of towers, it reinforces the notion that a place is remote.

Virtual world designers like the idea of creation on the grand scale. The more there is to design, the more designing they can do, and therefore the more fun they'll have. Big worlds have interesting interactions that small ones don't; a big canvas makes for more detail.

Unfortunately, virtual worlds can be *too* big. Scatter 100 people around a regular house and it will seem crowded; scatter them in the Sahara desert and they'll never find each other; put them next to each other in the Sahara desert and they won't see more than a fraction of the rest of it.

Virtual worlds have to be of a size appropriate to the number of players they attract. In textual worlds, a rule of thumb is to aim for a *rooms per player ratio* of about 40; 20 rooms per player is crowded but bearable; 60 rooms per player is sparse but you can still bump into people by accident. It's possible through design to influence how crowded a virtual world feels—for example, by introducing honeypot rooms or thoroughfares to attract players to the same location, or by starting players near to one another or far apart when they enter the virtual world. In *MUD2*, I have self-contained flood-control areas that only open up when a certain threshold of players has been reached. On the whole, though, it's better if you just get the size right to begin with.

Another problem with having a large virtual world is that it needs content. More content means either more designers or more time for them to design in, both of which are expensive. Players would rather play in a world that is small yet packed with interesting things than a world that is large but empty.

As I remarked, actual size does not have to coincide with apparent size. A small world can seem large, and a large world can seem small. A seemingly expansive world will impress relative newbies and give them the urge to explore new vistas; a seemingly cozy one will feel more secure to them and make conversation easier. Designers will therefore use a hybrid approach sometimes, whereby newbies are initially presented with an intimate[14] environment, then see things on the grand scale when they emerge from it.

The apparent size of a virtual world helps contribute to its atmosphere. The actual size is important to ensure that players meet each other serendipitously often enough to form relationships yet not so often that these turn sour. Ideally, a designer can find such a balance. Sometimes, though, their hand is forced. In particular, if they are writing to a license, they could have problems. The licensed world may be impractically large (for example, Middle Earth) or impractically small (for example, Hogwarts School) for the numbers of players expected[15]. Designers then have to decide how faithfully to honor their virtual world's sources. "Inspired by" can work: *Dark Age of Camelot* isn't an authentic retelling of Arthurian myth, but is close enough in spirit not to disappoint newbies. However, *DAoC* didn't pay money to use its sources; had it done so, the pressure to use the entirety of what it had bought would have been great (not least from the license holders wishing to protect the integrity of their universe).

Size doesn't just pop out of a design. You have to think about it from the beginning.

---

14. Hopefully, not claustrophobically so.

15. That said, textual worlds are much better at dealing with this kind of thing than graphical ones are.

Purposeful or Decorative?

You look at a wall. Hanging on the wall is a picture. You go up to the picture to remove it and find it's actually part of the wall. In a textual world, it would be embedded in a room description; in a graphical one, it would be part of the texture for the wall. It's purely decorative.

Some objects are in virtual worlds for tangible reasons; others are there for intangible ones. Should you give even the intangible ones some tangible purpose, or keep them as the props they are?

It might seem a little premature to decide at the very beginning of a virtual world's design whether to assign meaning to everything. Surely you can figure all that out later, once the really important things have been done? Well yes, you can, but by that time you may discover that the decision has been made for you: It would be simply too much work to give everything meaning. This is why so many virtual worlds have windows that don't break, chairs you can't sit on, grass you can't pull up, trees you can't chop down....

If you know from the beginning that objects will all have tangible functionality, it means you can design for this from the beginning. If you know they won't, you immediately increase the range of what you can design. You'll have longer to do it, too: Depth eats into design time, but if it's there from the start, it won't eat anywhere near as much as it would if you added it later.

An example: Are clothes just costume or are they fashion? It's possible to analyze what characters are wearing statistically and determine what is and isn't in fashion. If you wear fashionable clothes, your status goes up; if your status is high, what you wear is fashionable until everyone is wearing it. Non-player characters will treat high-status characters in a tangibly different way than low-status characters. Should this gameplay element be added to push players into making choices about how their character looks? Or should they be free of such tyranny and be able to wear whatever clothes they like? Even those of the opposite sex?

Another example: Should coats of arms be regimented or freeform? Real coats of arms are steeped in symbolism. Should players send their characters to a college of heralds to compose their device from templates? Or can they scan a photo of themselves and use that? In the former case, NPCs could be expected to "read" the meaning and react appropriately (farriers may give a discount to a knight whose shield features a horseshoe; bandit rebels may decline to attack a character whose shield bears a holy symbol[16]). Uploaded images are meaningful to players, but meaningless to NPCs.

In general, designers do want a gameplay meaning for everything in their virtual world, because it makes the world more immersive. If they don't determine this from the outset, though, they may be unable to have it when they're at the point they need it (fleshing out the details after the framework has been implemented).

There's a second issue here, though, which is more contentious. What we've been asking so far is whether things that are needed for out-of-context reasons should be given some contextual meaning. However, what about things that are needed for contextual reasons that have out-of-context meaning we don't want? "I was lying across the tracks when the train ran over me: Why am I still alive?" "Because we thought you might stop playing if you died."

This tension between what is good for tangible reasons but bad for intangible ones has claimed many victims in the past; it's sure to claim more in the future. It isn't only manifested by permanent character death (the virtual economy is the other big loser, and there are many smaller ones), but that's where the battle lines are drawn[17]. The problem is that some things are really, *really* desirable for tangible, gameplay reasons and really, *really* undesirable for intangible, business reasons. If gameplay wins, business suffers; if business wins, gameplay suffers (and then business suffers).

The general policy with regard to whether gameplay or business imperatives have priority should have been decided when the parameters of the design were set out. For a well-known issue such as permanent character death, this will almost certainly be the case. However, there will undoubtedly be other instances where friction will occur. Be sure that the procedures for dealing with the resulting disputes are in place; you'll need them.

---

16. Or, of course, they may attack if it's the wrong holy symbol. This won't go down well with players who only carrying the shield because "it looked cool," but that's the price of vanity.

17. The arguments both for and against permanent (character) death are considered in Chapter 5.

Closed or Open Economic Model?

The first question you should really ask is whether your virtual world needs an economy at all. They don't have to have one. If, for example, characters can take nothing with them between playing sessions, not only is an economy unnecessary, but you can't have one anyway. The more persistent a virtual world, the greater its need for a means to facilitate the efficient transfer of goods between players, but even then this doesn't imply the worlds need a formal currency. That said, the real world has money and therefore virtual worlds that want to seem real will have money too.

There are two ways to run a virtual economy: The one that designers want to have, and the one they end up having. The former is the *closed economy*; the latter is the *open economy*.

A closed model is internally consistent, with inbuilt defenses against abuse. It's a cycle. Resources are taken from the virtual world at the rate they are returned to it. There is a set[18] amount of money and a set amount in circulation, although the goods that can be bought with it may increase or decrease in number (that is, the economy can grow/shrink). On the whole, cash retains its value.

An open model is not internally consistent. It's *faucet/drain*. Resources enter the system and resources leave the system, but there is no prescribed relationship between the two. If the cash sinks aren't big enough, then players can hoard money, which therefore decreases its value; if the cash sinks are too big, then players have to spend money, which therefore increases its value.

The closed model is desirable because, done properly, it delivers many benefits[19]. There is no inflation; market forces control the price of goods; it allows for economy-driven gameplay. On the other hand, it's very hard to balance, highly sensitive to bugs, not accepted by players, and (most devastating of all) too easy to gouge. Players will attempt to break it, and will invariably succeed.

---

18. This may be pegged to some indicator—for example, the total number of players. In theory, you can instead fix the number of goods available and make the money supply variable, but that's not a popular solution.

19. I suspect, however, that none of the benefits I'm about to list are the real reason many designers want a closed economy. The thing is, a closed economy is just *so* much neater.

The open model could, in theory, be balanced. In practice, though, it's much easier to give characters money than it is to take it from them; rampant inflation is the result. Virtual money rapidly becomes worthless, and players adopt a barter economy instead.

Designers therefore have three options:

> ► Create an unbreakable closed economy. No one has done it yet for large-scale virtual worlds, but that doesn't mean it's impossible. The global economy of the real world taken as a whole is closed.

> ► Create a managed open economy. Put in checks and balances that will regulate both the flow of the faucet and the outflow of the drain such that if the two aren't reasonably close to equilibrium then measures to correct it are taken. No one has managed this yet, either.

> ► Don't have a formal currency. Players are going to end up bartering anyway, so throw in the towel and build for a barter economy from the beginning. Perhaps have a throwaway currency that newbies can use, but accept they'll rapidly be measuring their wealth using floating-point numbers and will then switch to the formal barter economy.

We'll discuss these particular ways of handling virtual world economies later in this chapter.

There are other ways to look at economies, of course. Some, such as gift exchange, are promising but as yet unproven; they may work as part of a more general economy, but don't seem strong enough to work alone.

A perennial favorite is to integrate the virtual economy into the real one. This does have merit—it works for the textual world *Achaea*[20], for example—but there are limits. Few players will object to another player paying real-world money for an item to be given properties that have no gameplay value. For example, a rich player could pay several thousand dollars to have a customized sound played whenever they unsheathed their sword. Other players may find it amusing, tacky, or "unfair" (that is, they're jealous that they can't afford something similar). However, if the sword doesn't do any extra damage or convey any tangible benefits it didn't have anyway, that's fine.

---

20. `http://www.achaea.com/`

Intangibility is the domain of the real world; paying real money for something intangible is justifiable. Paying real money for a tangibly better sword is another matter entirely, though; virtual worlds hoping to use exactly this as their business model should pay very close attention to the likes of *Achaea* to see how to do it—it requires some very careful balancing and only attracts a certain breed of player. Designers intending to extend the model by letting players take real money out of the virtual economy (*Project Entropia*[21] is the trailblazer here) have considerable cause to worry—even if they do by some miracle manage to get their virtual economy to work.

The final point to make about a virtual world's economy is that at an abstract level ecologies work the same way. If you have a closed economy and open ecology (or vice versa) you should ask yourself why one works in closed form and the other doesn't.

Information Versus Immersion

Which is better: to tell a player they hit a troll really hard, or to tell them they did 25 points of damage? The former is what the character would see; the latter is what many players want to see. If they do see it, though, it works against immersion: In the real world, you don't see numbers appearing every time you hit something with a hammer, so why should you in the virtual world?

The last of the major decisions that designers have to make about their virtual world is the degree to which immersion should be sacrificed for the benefit of players' spreadsheets. It's easy enough to say, "Oh, let the players themselves decide," but there are limits. Also, designers get to determine the default; what newbies see can have a lasting impact on the culture of a game.

The trade-off between information and immersion uses a sliding scale that can be split into three zones:

> ➤ *Immersion always wins.* Players don't get to see the code that dictates mobile AI, and that's final.

> ➤ *Players choose.* Some will see it as "the red bag," but for others it's "bag002."

> ➤ *Information always wins.* You're told the name of the nearby character, whether or not your own character has ever met them before.

---

21. http://www.project-entropia.com/

Designers set the boundaries. Although the middle zone allows for multiple settings ("I want to know how much I've been hurt, but not the true names of objects"), in practice it works fine as a single, binary setting.

Again, the reason that this seemingly mundane decision assumes unusually high significance is because by the time it becomes an issue it's normally too late to do anything about it. During testing, everybody wants as much information as they can get; the capability to switch it off can be left almost as an afterthought. It needs to be determined right at the beginning.

Players want to see numbers (or stats bars or labels) because it helps them play. Information given in more circumspect ways is an unnecessary encoding. Everyone is eventually going to get the data they want anyway, so why try to hide it? Once numbers are accepted as part of the virtual world then surely they won't thereafter disrupt immersion? In the real world, some objects *do* have numbers on them: If I buy a bag of sugar, its weight is written in bold letters on the side; if I buy a car, it has a license plate that identifies it uniquely. Freedom of information is good. Isn't this obsession with "immersion" just pretentious nonsense?

In some respects, a designer's decision of whether to favor information or immersion is a partial statement of their design philosophy. Players want information for achievement and killer purposes (explorers like it too, but then they also like deducing it when it's not provided). If you give numbers to newbies, you're telling them that this is a virtual world that they should take by the scruff of the neck and make their own; if you don't, you're saying it's a mysterious, perhaps dangerous place, where knowledge reveals itself only through experiment or the experience of others[22].

Decide what you want to tell them and why. Then tell them.

---

22. In large-scale games, players will eventually need to be able to switch on the numbers even if they start out being unable to; this is for the simple reason that if they can't, they'll generate huge numbers of false bug reports because the virtual world is not behaving exactly how it should (according to their empirically derived definition of "should").

Geography

Authors of epic Fantasy novels often start with a map. Similarly, designers of virtual worlds often choose a map as the first concrete realization of their dreams. In any venture that has place or travel at its core, a map is the natural starting point. In constructing a map, not only are ideas given form, but new ideas are suggested. It's unlikely that a designer will create a map only to go back and change it later to account for details that have arisen from fleshing it out. The design process rarely backtracks over maps, and therefore they're an excellent way to begin developing content.

Virtual worlds have a more practical reason for doing maps first, in that there are technical constraints in operation. If the programmers insist on a zone-based approach, for example, that directly affects the topography of the world; if the designers want 200 zones, that affects the topography of the network the operations team has to support.

Geography is therefore where designers usually begin to turn their concepts into (virtual) reality.

Geographical Consistency

Throwing paint at a blank canvas does not create the geography of a virtual world. To be immersive, everything should be where it is for a reason. Much as a designer might relish the prospect of creating their planned Magic Shoppe that's bigger inside than it is outside[23], at this stage it's only ever going to serve as a prototype to demonstrate the principles involved. Although not a bad thing in itself (actually, it's quite a good thing—I usually recommend it to newbie developers), piecemeal development of individual structures is not the way to get a whole world. For that, you have to take a more top-down approach, through various levels of abstraction.

These levels (from most general to most specific) are

- ➤ The world
- ➤ Zones
- ➤ Regions

---

23. Or, to be more original, bigger outside than it is inside.

> ➤ Areas

> ➤ Rooms

Although in technical terms there may be a multiverse of parallel worlds (that is, different shards/incarnations), this is not something that directly affects the geography of a single such world.

The layout of a world depends, naturally, on its genre. A "world" for a space opera might consist of several planets; one for a prohibition-era gangster game could be a single city. At this level, the main geographic features are placed so as to make sense. Depending on the scale, this can mean suns, moons, oceans, continents, rivers, mountains, deserts, forests, parks, freeways, roads, and so on. The main aims of the designer are

> ➤ To create a believable overall map. Rivers run from mountains to seas; forests don't appear in deserts; cities aren't built on glaciers.

> ➤ To partition the world so that it can cluster players. The world may be huge, but you still want people to meet up (but not so much that they never go anywhere).

> ➤ To allow for the world to be extended, both internally ("Where can I put the new sponsor's coffee shop?") and externally ("Where do I put the expansion set?").

> ➤ To have room for some ideas you want to put in. "I'd like a city on the edge of a desert, so I guess I'll need a river or a major oasis or no one would have built a city there."

> ➤ To provide for a meaningful ecology and (through resource placement) economy.

> ➤ To be attractive to more than one player type. Just because a place is a slug-fest, that doesn't mean interesting flowers can't grow there.

> ➤ To give themselves ideas. "Hey, that mountain lake would be perfect for a mystic kingdom of martial arts experts!"

Interestingly, these same aims (apart from external expansion) apply at all the other levels of abstraction, too. "Hey, that ox-bow lake would be perfect for a rowboat-leasing facility!"

Geographical consistency can be achieved in a number of ways. If spending a few hours learning about plate tectonics will help you place mountain ranges and volcanoes accurately, do so—your players will appreciate it. If something doesn't make sense, there should be a very important reason for it not to do so. A player who wonders why there is a perfume factory in the middle of a quiet residential area[24] should be able to figure out it's a front for a bootleg distillery, rather than sloppy work by a designer. If something doesn't make sense, it should fail for a reason that does make sense.

An obvious way to get guaranteed geographical consistency is to replicate parts of the real world virtually. This is particularly useful for non-game applications, where teaching or exploring a real location might be a primary aim ("Welcome to Virtual Venice!"). Fictional worlds that use real-world settings are more problematical. It can be argued that depicting an environment with which players are already familiar is good for immersion (players already know and understand it); however, unless the depiction is highly accurate, it could be bad (incorrect or missing details will jar against the player's knowledge of reality). There are problems of data-gathering and data-maintaining, both of which are expensive, and if recognizable real-world buildings appear, there could be legal issues (a virtual bordello set up in a virtual building, the real-world twin of which is occupied by a mosque, would bring all kinds of real-world laws to bear). Another problem of using the real world to give authenticity to the virtual world is that it may not be authentic in the context: A post-apocalypse Washington, D.C. would be unlikely to contain many of its most famous monuments, for example.

Unless the designer is trying to make some kind of artistic point, replicating recognizable parts of the real world in the virtual world is usually a bad idea. As a rule of thumb, keep real-world proper nouns out of virtual worlds.

If you want geographic consistency, use the levels of geographic abstraction.

Levels of Geographic Abstraction

Geographers have many different ways to look at this and other real worlds. They're experts, after all. Most players of virtual worlds are not geographers, however, and they're only going to notice more obvious errors. A degree of knowledge beyond that of the average player is always a good thing for a designer to have, of course, but as soon as players stop noticing what you're doing you can stop doing it. Immersion is

---

24. This assumes that at least one of your world's settlements is extensive enough to have a "quiet residential area." A town in *EverQuest* is considered by the players to be "large" if it has 20 buildings.

about not busting players into reality; it isn't about teaching them erosion patterns for sedimentary rocks[25]. From this point of view, the levels of abstraction listed in the previous section are sufficient to give a virtual world all the geographic consistency it needs. Let's look at them in more detail.

Zones are a functional partition of the virtual world, imposed for technical reasons. Not all virtual worlds will have them. Their usual impact is to consolidate geographical features into zone-friendly blocks. The mountain range will stop short of a zone boundary, rather than poke a couple of foothills across it; the river will run through a zone, but not weave over zone boundaries and back; the peninsula will jut out just far enough that it won't entail a zone change to reach the end of it.

Zones are like the pages in a road atlas, except that you get to change the geographic features so they're a tidy fit.

Regions are large swathes of territory that have distinct, thematic differences at the strategic level. "The north," for example, may be cold, populated by hardy, hairy, expansionist barbarians; "the isles" may be beautiful, lazy paradises whose inhabitants have a penchant for human sacrifice; "Westside" may be a neighborhood full of big houses with pools and long driveways, populated by rich people who have nothing but contempt for those born across the river.

Regions fit natural geographic boundaries. If they spill across such a boundary, it's a cause for conflict. In worlds that have zones, the two often coincide; this is because players feel zone boundaries with the same (if not more) intensity that they feel purely geographical ones. The zone/region relationship is not necessarily one-to-one—you can have several zones to a region or several regions to a zone—but it's usually integral; you won't find 1½-region zones very often.

Areas are subdivisions of regions that, while thematically similar at the strategic level, are thematically distinct at the tactical level. "The north" may consist of "the mountains," "the valleys," "the frozen waste," "the isle of the gods," "the lava pits," and so on. It's often the case that areas are specified fully by individual designers, to ensure an atmospheric consistency within each area.

---

25. I guess this statement wouldn't apply to a geology-focused educational virtual world, though.

Areas are made up of rooms. This is the level at which players experience the virtual world. The definition of what constitutes a "room" depends on the way the virtual world is displayed to players. The options are

➤ Nodes

➤ Coordinates (tiles)

➤ Coordinates (polygons)

Nodes are points with (potentially) unlimited connections to other points. These are the dominant paradigm for textual virtual worlds, although some also use coordinate systems. Normally, a single node represents the smallest unit of position that players can share, which (in buildings) would be a room—hence the name.

Formally, tiled coordinates are nodal systems that enforce a rigid relationship between the nodes; you can, in theory, represent them as freeform nodes. In practice, though, tessellation is used because it can be implemented easily with an array. There are often other contributory reasons, but its mapping to a fast, random-access data structure is the main one. Arrays allow for automatic content generation for speedy, shortest-route path-finding and (most importantly) for display as (2½D) graphics.

Textual virtual worlds that use tiled coordinates will usually give the tiles the same status as other nodes—that is, treat each as a room that more than one player can potentially occupy. Graphical virtual worlds go for a smaller granularity, with a tile representing the space that an individual character takes up; for this reason, they are single-occupancy only, and a subjective "room" consists of contiguous tiles bordered by ones that contain walls, doors, windows, and other architectural features.

Both the nodal and tiled approaches define a virtual world in terms of space. Polygons define it in terms of enclosures. Characters do occupy coordinates, but their world is defined in terms of barriers—planes through which they cannot move. As an analogy, consider a piece of graph paper: Nodes define the lines by numbering the squares; polygons define the squares by numbering the lines.

Virtual worlds that use coordinate systems can be displayed graphically. The resolution of the coordinates in a polygonal system is yet smaller than that in a tiled system, because characters themselves are made up of polygons. The concept of a "room" still exists, as an enclosed space that many characters can occupy, but it's not atomic: Characters can be between rooms, in some kind of transition state; for a nodal system this location would itself constitute a room.

Of the three, a tessellated system is the least flexible. It doesn't have the resolution to handle details; in particular, it doesn't get along well with curves. Carefully drawn texture maps can create illusions of curves, but they're exposed if players ever do anything to them (for example, walk on what looks like a gentle curve but is actually a step).

When 2½D is used, it's normally because it's relatively easy to implement, to animate[26], and to upgrade[27]; it's often the first choice for hobbyist graphical worlds such as *Furcadia*[28]. This may change as cheap or free full 3D engines become more available[29], but some people prefer the "pieces on a board" look and the clear demarcations of space it offers; the 2½D approach is therefore unlikely to go away.

A world made of polygonal planes better represents different facets of an environment, because of its higher level of detail. You can easily rotate large objects through arbitrary angles, not just 90 degrees. Curves still have angles, but these are small enough to hide behind texture maps without looking fake[30].

Node-based systems are the most flexible of all, because they allow for non-Euclidian geometry. In a nodal world, you can exit a room to the north to enter it from the east; you can walk into a wardrobe and find Narnia there; you can be inside a room that contains itself; you can have multiple exits leading to the same entrance; you can reconnect or destroy nodes, leaving a sealed void.

The most immediate benefit of a nodal approach is that you don't have to use a constant scale. A journey to the top floor of a tower can take as long as the journey across a mountain range. Important details can thus be given close attention, whereas

---

26. Assuming some degree of artistic talent.

27. Updating animations can, however, be more expensive than for a 3D approach.

28. http://www.furcadia.com

29. *Ultima Online* now boasts both a 2½D and a 3D client for its virtual world.

30. There are limits, though. In a demonstration of a new role-playing game at a computer show, I found I could hide my character completely in the texture map of a tree that overflowed the space that the tree formally occupied. Great for ambushes!

unimportant ones can be dismissed as part of a broad sweep. The world can focus on what matters, matching the way that a cognitive map built up in a player's mind works. Worlds founded on a coordinate system are limited to real-world physics, and don't have this level of refinement. On the other hand, they can be represented graphically, which can't be said of an unrestricted nodal system.

An issue affecting all these approaches is what to do at their edges. If you keep walking east what happens? There are a number of tried-and-trusted ways to deal with this situation:

➤ *Wrap around*. If you go east forever, you end up back where you started—just like with the real world.

➤ *Physical boundary*. There's an unclimbable cliff, unswimmable river, unnavigable ocean, impassable forest in the way.

➤ *Big stick*. If you walk too far into the desert, the sun is going to bake you dead no matter how well-prepared you thought you were.

➤ *Emotional boundary*. Your character "doesn't want" to go any further. You might, but you don't control your character.

➤ *Notice*. If you try to go too far, you're given a polite message explaining that the designers have failed to provide the necessary content.

➤ *Invisible wall*. There's no explanation, you just can't move off the board.

Of these, the physical boundary is the most popular as it's within the context of the virtual world and leaves open the door to further expansion. Unfortunately, it's so popular that its expression can lead to cliché. "Hmm, the sea. Looks like I've reached the western edge of the map, then." There is a great opportunity for imaginative solutions here.

Terrain

Terrain is what geography is made of. It also has levels of abstraction, matching the needs of the thematic levels. Someone designing a region might decide to place a forest; someone designing an area might decide to place a wood; someone designing a wood might decide to place a tree. Terrain is the paint that depicts the image a designer wants to convey.

The different types of terrain that are available to a virtual world depend on that world, of course. Swampland isn't necessary for a virtual world set entirely indoors, for example. Tempting though it is to go straight to an atlas and look at the symbols it uses, there are more scientific ways of determining terrain that allow for more realistic tangible effects. For a generic, outdoors, continent-scale kind of virtual world, the following dimensions are likely to be most useful:

- ➤ Elevation
- ➤ Surface geology (rock, soil, water, sand…)
- ➤ Vegetation (none, grass, scrub, cultivation…)
- ➤ Cover (none, snow, ash…)
- ➤ Volume (air, water, mist…)

Thus you can have a hill, a forested hill, a snow-covered, forested hill, and so on. The particular types of forest would depend on the level of abstraction (jungle, mangrove swamp, pine, oak, whatever).

Explicitly representing each layer allows for a virtual world to give different terrains different properties. Graphical worlds benefit the most from this as they need the texture maps, but they can use them for other things, too (movement speed, footprints/footfalls, ambient sounds). However, even textual worlds can profit from giving rooms a terrain property: Trivially, if you drop a glass bottle on a paved road, it'll shatter; if you drop it on a sandy beach, it won't. Multi-layered terrain will also allow you to spot incongruities, such as underwater snow, but to be honest anyone stupid enough to do something like that is going to be too stupid to check for it anyway.

Ah, yes, weather….

The first time I went to San Diego, U.S. customs hauled my bag out of the X-ray machine and made me open it because they couldn't figure out what I had in it. The object perplexing them turned out to be my umbrella.

I'm from England. We have weather in England. Weather affects terrain. Calm seas can become rough, trees in forests can sway, snow can turn to slush, grassland can become marsh, streets can turn to rivers, hail stones the size of golf balls can appear with no warning in mid-July and set off the alarms of every car parked within a square kilo-meter[31]. A persistent world with a climate appropriate to its geography is more believable than one that's the same the whole year round[32]. You don't need a sophisticated model to decide the prevailing winds, the temperature, and therefore the cloud cover and likely precipitation. Just because it's always blazing sunshine where you live, that doesn't mean it should be like that in your virtual world. Those lush green pastures have to get their water from somewhere.

The second time I went to San Diego, I left my umbrella behind. It rained so hard it stripped the paper off billboards. The locals were unfazed, as it had been forecast for two weeks. Augh!

Using a systematic approach to terrain makes moderating the effects of weather much easier. It has another, equally nice feature, which although not yet used a great deal could nevertheless be the answer to some designers' prayers: implicit terrain.

In *Lord of the Rings*, all the action takes place in just a few regions. Vast swathes of Middle Earth are not affected by the conflict to any great degree. If you were designing a virtual world in this setting, you'd want to ignore those places the players weren't going to be interested in and concentrate on those they were. Unfortunately, the result would be rather patchy. In players' minds, maps should at the very least be rectangular; if they've read *Lord of the Rings*, they'd expect the virtual world to match the maps in the books, too.

Content costs money. Even mundane content costs money. There may only be one or two sites of interest in the Misty Mountains, but if the entire map were being represented virtually, then some designer still has to place every tree on every slope leading to every jagged peak in the whole range. That's a lot of effort, just to pacify the occasional player who wanders by.

The overall map shows what the general terrain in a region is, even down to the area level. It's only when the map has to be realized as actual polygons that its creation becomes tedious. This is where implicit terrain comes in.

---

31. Not that I'm speaking from personal experience or anything.

32. Even if it's not entirely believable, the players will like the variety it offers. The lakes in *Asheron's Call 2* freeze in its winter, allowing characters to walk across them.

Implicit terrain uses a guiding terrain type (that of its area) plus a random number seed (based on its coordinates) to generate actual terrain on-the-fly. When a player enters an area, only then is the content for it created. Any changes made by the player (for example, burying treasure) are recorded so as to supersede the implicit definition, but everything else can be discarded after the player leaves. It's less efficient in implementation terms than an explicit representation, but more than makes up for this in designer efficiency. Random mobiles can be created for an area to spice it up, but on the whole they are only there because players are passing through and would notice if they weren't. Having terrain that's defined in layers makes for easier fractal area generation than terrain that's defined by natural language terms[33].

Most designers won't have this problem of a map that's too big. However, that doesn't mean implicit terrain can't be of use to them. In particular, it can step in to generate content whenever a player walks off the map. Players can be dissuaded from going too far by including ever-tougher mobiles, but then it doesn't really matter if they do go on forever— the geography can always be generated for their coordinates. It won't be *compelling* content, of course, but it removes the problem of clichéd boundaries. If you're doing a virtual world set in space and you want an infinite universe, well, you can have one.

Movement

Movement in virtual worlds is, strictly speaking, merely a specific form of object state transition. Because it's the tool that players use to construct their cognitive map of the environment, however, it has enhanced significance—at least in the minds of players (which is what designers are designing for). The geography of virtual worlds must account for how players will build it in their heads, which depends not only on what they see but also on how they see it. Because virtual world geographies are too big to experience in a single event, movement heavily influences both.

So, let's take a brief look at the various ways to move through virtual worlds, and consider the geographical[34] implications.

---

33. *Star Wars Galaxies* has a terrain-generation tool that fleshes out a basic model explicitly, allowing the designer to concentrate on placing only the gameplay-specific features of interest.

34. And, for towns and cities, architectural.

Basic movement occurs between contiguous locations. These locations will either be nodes or points. To transfer from one location to another, players must issue a movement command (or, in rare instances, fail to issue a cease-movement command). There are four main ways to do this, none of which are mutually exclusive (that is, you can have them all if you want):

> *Absolute directions*. These are the classic ones that use the points of the compass. North, northeast, east, and so on.

> *Relative directions*. These treat the character as the point of origin, and align with their line of sight. Left, right, forward, and so on.

> *Contextual directions*. Commands have different meanings depending on the context. In, out, back, and so on.

> *Landmark directions*. These move you toward a location that contains a major feature. Swamp, tower, shop, and so on.

Most textual and 2½D graphical worlds favor absolute directions. Most 3D graphical worlds favor relative directions.

Absolute directions are preferred in textual worlds for three reasons:

> Room descriptions don't have to take into account the point of view of each character. Note that if this is why you want absolute directions, you can't simultaneously have relative directions.

> Absolute directions are much easier for players to map with than relative directions. Players prefer them, when given a free choice of which to use.

> In English, the four main compass points have unique, single-letter abbreviations; the four intermediate points have unique, double-letter abbreviations. None of these clash with other abbreviations for common commands. Abbreviations for relative directions are clunkier ("sl" for "slide left") and they do clash with other common commands ("l" could be either "left" or "look").

2½D virtual worlds use absolute directions because they present a fixed view of the virtual world. They may allow 90-degree rotation, but it's always clear which way is north. 3D virtual worlds present the player with a character's eye view of the environment, therefore all movement is relative to the character's line of sight. Absolute direction may be determined from a second, "radar scan" panel, but then again this could use relative directions too.

It's possible to track absolute directions from relative ones, of course, but it's tedious. Given that most players prefer absolute directions so that mapping (real and cognitive) is easier, absolute directions should usually be provided as a convenience[35]. Yes, relative directions are the more realistic (no one has a compass stapled to their nose), but if you insist on having them then expect players to get lost.

Getting lost is the main issue that virtual geography must address. Although occasionally losing your way isn't necessarily a bad thing (especially if you're exploring), if it happens often it means that players haven't been able to build a working model in their heads of how the virtual world is laid out. Such confusion causes frustration (which is bad enough) and further it suggests to newbies that the whole system is confusing (which is worse). If a virtual world is so badly designed that you can't even walk from A to B without getting lost, what chance is there you'll be able to figure out spells or combat or the manufacture of crossbows?

In order not to get lost, a player needs to measure two things: distance and orientation. In nodal worlds, distance is a problem because it's measured in rooms, not in unit lengths. It's possible to go north, east, south, and arrive at the same location as if you'd gone east five times. Worse, you could go northeast and southwest and not end up where you started. For this reason, contextual and landmark commands are used, so that players can get back to somewhere they know relatively easily. Most landmark commands are hardwired into the virtual world, but actually there's no reason why players shouldn't be able to create their own. Route-finding algorithms are fast and efficient, and as long as they don't check things a player couldn't know (such as whether an intervening door is open or locked shut) it should be fine to allow potentially any static geographical feature to be used as a landmark.

Graphical worlds satisfy the distance criterion for not getting lost, but they don't deal with the direction one very well. Furthermore, they don't normally have the interface

---

35. This isn't to say that players will use them properly. Over the years, I've encountered several players with "east-west dyslexia," a condition whereby they have a completely accurate, functioning map in their head that is a mirror image of the one in every other player's head. Making pictorial maps available to newbies got rid of the problem.

to allow explicit lost-busting contextual or landmark commands, relying as they do on mouse and arrow keys[36]. If they want such commands, they have to provide them implicitly in the environment. Players go "into" a room because there's a single door. The tower is a "landmark" because it's the tallest structure for miles around.

Landmarks are important because players use them as reference points[37]. Not all reference points are landmarks in the "being highly visible" sense, though. Inns, underground caves, shrines, sunken oases—people may well regard these as points of reference, but not see them until they're close up. In this event, graphical virtual worlds should provide players pointers to show directions: Roads, rivers, and (of course) signposts can help in this regard.

Some environments are more likely to get players lost than others. The main culprits are

- ➤ Featureless landscapes, such as deserts.

- ➤ Landscapes packed with similar features, such as forests.

- ➤ Landscapes that frequently change. "The hills *are* alive!"

- ➤ Deliberately disorienting "crazy angle" vistas designed to convey alienness.

- ➤ Landscapes you have to traverse at speed with sudden, arbitrary direction changes. "Velociraptors! Run for your life!"

- ➤ Twisting, turning, irregular passageways. Mazes you can't steer clear of are *not* fun.

If you don't want people to get lost, avoid these. If you can't, then be sure that entering them is optional.

So far, I've only discussed contiguous movement. Characters also regularly travel using discontiguous movement—that is, teleporting. This is like moving using landmark directions, except movement to the landmark is instantaneous. Teleportation has implications for several aspects of virtual worlds (particularly the economy), but we'll just look at the geographical ones for now.

---

36. There are other devices, of course, such as joysticks and VR rigs, but they have the same problems.

37. Some virtual worlds give players access to the coordinate system so they can associate explicit reference points to positions.

One of *MUD1*'s most influential early players, Mark Longley, used to go to London by train fairly regularly. On arrival, he'd take the underground to the stop nearest whatever museum, exhibition hall, or Science Fiction bookshop he was visiting, walk the short distance to his destination, then return the same way. He once explained to me that his geographical knowledge of surface London consisted only of disconnected small areas within a short radius of underground stations, and it was quite a surprise when he looked at a map and discovered just how close some of the stations were in real life.

Virtual worlds with teleports are like Mark's version of London. They may be huge and packed with interesting things, but if people can use portals, then they'll never see anything any distance from one. The fact that most virtual worlds (unlike London) rarely have anything worth seeing on the walk between portals only compounds the problem. It's not so much a virtual world as a collection of virtual sub-worlds.

This may be okay with some designers. Content can gravitate toward portals in the same way that burger restaurants gravitate toward road intersections. It does, however, mean that much cohesion is lost, and it can greatly reduce the sense of awe that players experience on visiting a place for the first time. Atmosphere relies as much on anticipation as it does delivery; enchantment is enhanced by surprise, not by guide books.

These problems can be alleviated to some extent (at least in graphical worlds) by the use of better fiction that makes travel faster but not immediate. If characters can increase their speed by riding on a horse or taking a boat ride, they get to see the local terrain and will arrive at their destination with a better idea of where it is. Failing that, travel could proceed while the player is offline: Tramping across salt flats is boring, but if your character does it while you're asleep in the real world, what's it to you? Travel this way doesn't have to be dangerous—it effectively works by "slow portals"—but at least it gives an idea of how far you've traveled (if not exactly where to).

So, when designing your virtual world's geography, remember that people will have to experience it. Give them landmarks, give them maps, give them coordinates if you must—just make sure, however you do it, that they know where they are. Then, they can decide where to go.

Settlements

Many virtual worlds contain virtual buildings. Although some of these may be isolated (farmhouses, cottages, wizards' towers), worlds created to a bigger scale will want settlements.

Settlements in this context are collections of buildings (or one huge building with lots of rooms—a castle, say, or a space station). Most of the time they will be occupied, but ruined settlements are also possible.

It should go without saying that settlements are positioned where they are for a reason. Virtual worlds are more believable if their settlements are built in locations that make sense. A town with no access to fresh water or no trade routes to other settlements will cause anyone who gives them a moment's thought to raise an eyebrow. Unfortunately, many designers are oblivious to such formalities. They're quite happy to put a ruined city on the side of a mountain and say it's the site of a massacre of humans by dwarfs, but they're less concerned about what the humans who lived there would have eaten.

There are many reasons why large-population cities in the real world are built where they are. Most grow from smaller settlements, although some are founded by rulers (for example, Baghdad, Munich, St. Petersburg, Washington D.C.). To prosper, all of them need

- ➤ Plenty of level ground
- ➤ Access to food and water
- ➤ Nearby building materials
- ➤ A non-threatening climate/geology/geography
- ➤ Communication links
- ➤ A population

If they are close to natural resources and are in an easily defensible position, so much the better.

Note that for many virtual worlds, some of these criteria are *not* necessary from a strictly gameplay point of view. Food and water are only needed if characters need to eat and drink; characters are generally impervious to the effects of climate;

communication is often instantaneous. Indeed, people may only want to have a house at all so they have somewhere to store their stuff. That's not how real-world settlements form.

For virtual worlds designed under license, settlements have to appear where the map says they do. Even so, it doesn't necessarily hurt to put roads, springs, forests, and cornfields in the vicinity. Designers of other virtual worlds have more freedom to put cities where they want, but more responsibility to put them somewhere non-idiotic. As with many aspects of virtual world design, the key is to do your research: A few hours spent skimming through a textbook for first-year Town Planning undergraduates will give you the rudiments of settlement organization (which are all you need). With a virtual world, you don't only get to place a settlement where you want it in relation to other settlements, but you can change the geography to accommodate it. There really is no excuse for carelessness. The usual rule of rule-breaking applies: If a settlement is in a place you wouldn't normally find a settlement, there's some in-context *reason* it's in such a place (for example, the religious inhabitants don't want contact with outsiders).

Note that smaller virtual worlds, especially ones that don't have a high degree of persistence, may use social places, such as inns, as hubs (rather than resort to full-blown settlements). The placement rules for these will differ, but they'll nevertheless still exist; don't just plonk them down anywhere.

Given these basic laws for positioning settlements (or whatever), the next issue is applying them to derive the configuration that designers want. Settlements invariably serve some gameplay purpose; they're not there merely to provide yet more background color. Although some locations are so natural that a settlement just *has* to occupy them (the estuaries of major rivers, the heads of deltas, the desert oasis on a major caravan route), the positioning of the rest depends on what designers want out of them—in particular, whether or not they want players to visit them. Often, settlements will be centers of trade, where players can go to sell their stuff and buy better stuff. They're also frequently places where players get quests. Thus, they act as focal points and can foster a sense of community; in worlds that allow for property ownership, they can become the physical embodiment of communities.

If there are too few settlements, players will crowd out the ones that do exist. It's less of a problem if there are too many, as players will gravitate to just a few and leave the others as testimonies to designers' wasted time.

Ideally, settlements should fail or flourish by a process of survival of the fittest. At a superficial level, this looks easy: The ones that players frequent should expand to offer new opportunities and services; the ones that are forgotten should atrophy away to become ghost towns. Unfortunately, this is easier said than done: The majority population of most settlements consists of non-player characters, who won't necessarily be easy to move (even from a purely implementational point of view). More worryingly, they could look useless but perform an important function indirectly. For example, players may never visit the mining town but if it produces all the iron that the artisans in the big city use to make armor, closing it down would be a mistake. In a sophisticated virtual world with interlinked economies, ecologies, and communities, measuring the success of a settlement merely by the number of player-occupied houses is not enough.

Should players be able to build their own settlements? This would allow for them to appear spontaneously where designers (deliberately or otherwise) left a hole. *Ultima Online* allowed it from the beginning, but other virtual worlds can have technical reasons for not permitting it: *Asheron's Call* only lets players buy prebuilt housing, for example, because its long-term story arc could suddenly call for a volcano to appear beneath a shanty town otherwise. On the whole, though, player-built settlements are simply too powerful a retention tool to dismiss; for long-term persistent virtual worlds, if player-created settlements make any kind of sense at all then designers should aim to facilitate their creation.

This isn't actually as easy as it sounds. Virtual worlds need virtual inhabitants as well as real ones. Settlements that don't have NPCs in them won't be as functional as those that do. From where do they acquire their denizens?

There are three main ways to do it:

> *Sleight of hand.* When the settlement reaches a certain size, NPCs appear. Other than in defining the boundaries (and therefore size) of a settlement, the only disadvantages of this to speak of are that it isn't exactly convincing and it can lead to NPC inflation (that is, the more NPCs there are, the less the value of each one).

> *Bought in.* With these, buildings that operate services come with their own staff. If your community clubs together and funds the construction of a cobbler's shop, it comes automatically with a cobbler. This is marginally more realistic and allows

for a greater variety of towns, but can still lead to NPC inflation. If every town builds a cobbler's shop, how does this affect the price of shoes?

➤ *Economics.* NPCs periodically look at how their business is going, and if it's poor, they move to somewhere else where it won't be poor. This is the most realistic solution of all, but it needs a good economic model to underpin it—one that can be used predictively so NPCs can speculate where a good market may be[38].

Construction time is another issue. If major buildings can spring up overnight, then it doesn't bode well for a sense of realism. Unfortunately, if it takes a realistic time, then it doesn't bode well for community management: Impatient players will complain if it takes a whole week to build an entire castle, let alone a modest dwelling (although this can be alleviated if you make them build in stages). There's a case for having some delay, even if the fiction can support instant houses ("Just plant the house seed where you want it to grow, then water it and stand back"). A wait can heighten the anticipation, especially if progress is visible. Too long, though, and it becomes frustrating[39]. It's up to you where you draw the line.

Perhaps the most noticeable thing about the settlements in virtual worlds is that they aren't actually all that large. *EverQuest's* largest towns have perhaps 50 buildings in them—they're mere hamlets. Big textual worlds can have many more, but they suffer from not "looking" big. If graphical worlds had 5,000 buildings, *that* would be more like it! Unfortunately, this would depend on their having a capability to support significant numbers of NPCs that most of them severely lack (because of the degree of AI needed to control the little dears). Also, many designers see little point in having large numbers of pretend people in a virtual world that can boast several thousand real ones[40].

Nevertheless, I look forward to the day when I can visit a virtual city populated by tens of thousands of virtual players, each of whom has their own life to live and their own place in their virtual society. That would really be quite something.

---

38. It won't be able to account for intangible effects, though. A community of pacifist players who don't buy weapons would attract NPC weaponsmiths to set up shop because all they see is a large population of characters who don't have weapons—exactly what they're looking for!

39. "God should have made the gestation period for humans six months instead of nine": discuss.

40. This situation is likely to change under pressure from epic-scale, single-player role-playing games (Bethesda Softworks' *Morrowind* set the alarm bells ringing).

Population

Let's take a closer look at the inhabitants of virtual worlds. Basically, there are three sorts:

> *Characters*. These are run by players.

> *Non-player characters*. These are run by the virtual world. They look like players' characters, and would think they were the same if given the AI.

> *Monsters*. These are run by the virtual world, but neither look like nor think they are players' characters.

We'll start with the effect that NPC population has on the fabric of the virtual world because it raises issues important to the other two. Note that there is also a shadowy fourth sort of inhabitant, *non-player players*, which accounts for people who need to visit the virtual world but not play in it; I'll consider these separately last.

Non-Player Characters

What are non-player characters for? They

> Buy, sell, and make stuff.

> Provide services.

> Guard places.

> Get killed for loot.

> Dispense quests (or clues for other NPCs' quests).

> Supply background information (history, lore, cultural attitudes).

> Do stuff for players.

> Make the place look busy.

In buying, selling, and making stuff, they're normally just fictional conveniences; they may as well be vending machines. Similarly, in providing services (training, repairs, healing spells, and so on), they are interface conceits: Designers want the players to be able to obtain the services in question, and NPCs are the mechanism that has evolved to dress up what's happening so it fits in context. Their being player-friendly helps; they don't *look* like vending machines.

Guards exist for the same general reason: They're the way designers traditionally choose to enforce a range of gameplay elements that require some justification if not to seem arbitrary. For example, suppose players are to be prevented from attacking one another within a city's walls; one way to effect this would be simply to tell them that they can't. This is unsatisfactory because it's out-of-context—*why* can't they? Furnishing an explanation along the lines of "you'd never get away with it" is slightly better, but still not ideal: Let players be the judge of whether they'd get away with it, not some invisible commentator. By introducing guards, players can find out for themselves that they indeed won't get away with it. Guards are almost invariably unbelievably tough. Characters that routinely hew down hordes of rampaging giants remain impotent against guards. This is because guards that are unable to guard might as well not be there. Guards that are regularly beatable are meant to be regularly beatable, and therefore aren't guarding any location or state of affairs that the designer really doesn't want to be violated. These "guards" therefore fall into the "get killed for loot" category. NPCs of this sort are basically just regular monsters that look like player characters (PCs). They may be slightly smarter than their monster brethren, but essentially they're there to be hacked and slain. Rarely do these NPCs have names.

NPCs that dispense quests may double up as one of the other kinds of NPC, but in general they have a special status. Indeed, they may be so special that they're elevated to having their own, distinct personalities. Even so, they're still principally a front to allow players to communicate with the virtual world without feeling silly. Their job is to give players things to do and then to remunerate them once they have done it. Beyond that, they're mere flavor text.

Quest dispenser NPCs get players to do things for them. With sidekick NPCs, it's the other way round: They do things for players. Although nominally independent, sidekicks are in essence mere extensions of the player's character. Though presented as henchmen/henchwomen, servants or familiars/pets[41], they're really just a way to extend the powers of a player. Too many objects to carry? Employ a porter or pack animal. Can't find someone to heal you after a fight? Hire the necessary skills in the form of a cleric. Sidekicks aren't usually used in larger games, as players themselves are intended to undertake the necessary roles. Besides, if a group of 25 players and their 25 sidekicks were trying to act in concert all semblance of organization would rapidly disappear. Players do still need mules, but in those situations they create secondary player characters instead.

---

41. A *DikuMUD* favorite that has since become standard in graphical worlds.

Lore providers are like online manuals. Players can consult them to find out things they want to know, or be accosted by them to be told things they don't want to know but, dammit, it's for their own good that they do. Lore providers can be standalone, but they will often have some other function too (for example, quest dispenser).

The final type of NPC is the extra. These wander around as part of the background. Any attempts by players to bring them to the foreground (for example, by communicating with them, stealing from them, shooting arrows at them) are rewarded with a canned or inert response. Extras don't feature highly in virtual worlds; because players can routinely interact with one another, they are disappointed when confronted with NPCs that have no obvious reason to exist.

Okay, so I admit that this summary of NPC types is perhaps a little cynical. There are plenty of virtual worlds where even the monsters can have personalities[42], let alone the NPCs. The problem is that there are too few such worlds. When a virtual world is alive with real players, designers don't feel the need to make NPCs more than ciphers for interacting with the virtual world. Players objectify NPCs in a way that only killer types objectify PCs.

Again, though, things are changing. Virtual world technology is driven by the big, graphical games, which in turn are driven by their hard-core players. The hard-core players play other computer games, particularly single-player role-playing games. When they see NPCs in these games that are above and beyond what they encounter in virtual worlds, they perceive virtual worlds to be behind the times.

They have a point, too. Virtual worlds have a much longer lifespan than ordinary computer games. A game from five years ago will look very dated by current standards, of course, but it isn't just a graphics issue: Gameplay that was cutting edge five years ago can seem dated, too (albeit less so). Virtual worlds have to adapt and evolve if they are to keep up with the times. There is an argument that textual games don't become dated because people's imaginations don't become dated[43]; in her *tour de force* 1994 exploration of the Internet[44], J.C. Herz asserts that no graphical virtual world could ever

---

42. *MUD2* has a baby dwarf that players are strangely reticent to kill, at least until it howls and alerts the other 50 dwarfs in the vicinity.

43. There is another argument that suggests they don't become dated because they're dated to begin with.

44. Herz, J. C., *Surfing on the Internet*. New York, Little, Brown, 1995.

match the imagery present in LambdaMOO—a sentiment with which the players of many textual worlds would agree. This may be true of the imagery, but it's not (yet) true of the gameplay.

NPCs embody gameplay elements; therefore, if gameplay seems dated, then its associated NPCs will seem dated, too. Players don't want dated content.

Just because players want something, that's not a reason to give it to them, of course. Design is about consequences, and players don't always accept them. Creating a fully rounded personality for a non-player character has been demonstrably possible since the days of Floyd from Steve Meretzky's *Planetfall*[45], but it takes a lot of effort. In a graphical virtual world, there's also the issue of animating different personalities. Slimy, sycophantic advisors have different body language than confident, cruel despots. Animating such differences is a painstaking art. Motion capture can help, but it doesn't work for dragons.

In other words, creating fully rounded NPCs is an expensive business, especially in graphical worlds, and very especially if you want 10,000 of them. Players who require intelligent NPCs can expect to have to pay more to get them.

Yet the same applies to many single-player role-playing games. *Baldur's Gate II*[46] has several hundred NPCs; some of these are so rounded that they can (act as if they) fall in love, but most are there either as plot hooks or local color. Nevertheless, it's possible to speak to all of them, even if they don't actually have anything meaningful to say. The mechanism for interaction is simplistic—the same, select-response-from-a-menu deal that the original *Ultima* series used—but it's better than the nothing you get from unidimensional virtual world NPCs. Textual virtual worlds sometimes implement a similar approach that masks the actual number of choices available (you might have to "ask guard about prisoner" rather than selecting it as an option from a list), but only for a few specific NPCs. Beyond that, there are pattern-matching schemes[47] based on

---

45. Steve Meretzky, *Planetfall*. Cambridge MA, Infocom, 1983.

46. James Ohlen and Kevin Martens (lead designers), *Baldur's Gate II: Shadows of Amn*. Irvine CA, Black Isle Studios, 2000.

47. Formally, these are known as "case-based reasoning."

Joseph Weizenbaum's classic *Eliza*[48], and hugely sophisticated bots like Michael Mauldin's *Julia*[49] (although these don't have a gameplay role).

Artificial Intelligence research is ever-advancing. It's unreasonable to expect virtual world designers to ask programmers to endow NPCs with the latest technology, but even a few 20-year-old ideas would make a big difference. So why don't virtual worlds contain more intelligent NPCs?

The usual explanations are as follows:

➤ They don't need them because they have real players instead. (Yet they do need dumb NPCs?)

➤ Smartening up NPCs would be too expensive. (So how do single-player role-playing games seem to manage it?)

➤ It takes too long to add AI to NPCs in virtual worlds. So much other stuff has to go in beforehand that it's just unnecessary icing on the cake. (But a small team of AI experts couldn't work on it from the beginning?)

➤ Artificially intelligent NPCs are never convincing and always spoil immersion. (More or less than artificially unintelligent NPCs do?)

➤ Neither the designers nor the programmers are familiar with AI. (And they can't ever become familiar with it[50]?)

➤ Players don't like NPCs that are too clever. (So don't make them *too* clever[51]?)

➤ It's inappropriate for this particular virtual world. (Finally, a valid excuse. You may have a fiction that explains why NPCs are stupid—time travel to Neanderthal times, for example.)

---

48. Joseph Weizenbaum, *ELIZA—A Computer Program for the Study of Natural Language Communication between Man and Machine.* New York, Vol. 9 no. 1, *Communications of the ACM,* January 1966.

49. Michael L. Mauldin, *Chatterbots, Tinymuds, And The Turing Test: Entering The Loebner Prize Competition.* Menlo Park CA, Proceedings AAAI 12, 1994.

50. I did a Ph.D. in AI because of its applicability to virtual realities, although I wouldn't necessarily recommend this degree of enthusiasm to everyone.

51. I put a simple expert system into *MUD2* to control mobiles in fights, but toned it down because it turned out to be better than many players. It's merely a question of balance.

In most cases, the reasons that virtual worlds don't have intelligent NPCs are to do with complacency, inexperience, and (for free virtual worlds) lack of resources. However, there is also a view of "if it ain't broke, don't fix it." There may be only scant justification for not making NPCs more rounded, but that hardly amounts to an incentive to unflatten them. Why *should* virtual worlds contain more intelligent NPCs?

There are only two reasons.

The first reason is that even minor personality quirks in an NPC can give players some reason to care. Players can anthropomorphize NPCs very well, and are happy to do so in a virtual world. It's not that NPCs have any intrinsic meaning, but that players can invest them with it.

As an example, suppose that the NPC mother of a young NPC boy asks for your help to get a saucepan off his head. It's just a little quest. Next time, she asks you to get him down from a tree he's climbed. Maybe she hits him when he's rescued, maybe she hugs him and cries with relief; it's still just another little quest. The time after that, he's got his head stuck in a fence; the time after that he's locked himself in a cellar. You come to know the two NPCs—the reckless child and the self-critical mother—and if you need a small filler quest you'll often pay them a visit. Then, one day, the mother comes running to you. Her son was dragged off before her eyes by some kind of red-eyed demon. She's hysterical. He kept crying, "Mommy!," she tried to save him but the beast hit her, by the gods, please, can't you help?

Now the situation has meaning. You and the NPCs have a history. The mother didn't go to any other PC, she went to *you*. Are you going to leave her son to be eaten alive? No way!

So that's the first reason: It enables players to form emotional attachments to objects in the virtual world; these relationships can then be stressed to add drama and give players cause to ponder their own actions. The relationships aren't anywhere near as strong as between real people, naturally, but they're there. They give the player a reason to feel a part of the virtual world.

The second reason, you'll either comprehend instantly or it'll take an epiphany. It's this: *Imagine it!* Imagine a virtual world with thousands of virtual people living virtual lives—each with their own goals, their own relationships, their own existence. A living, breathing, self-sustaining creation! Doesn't that fill you with awe? Don't you want to *go* there? Don't you want to see what they'll do, and do it *with* them? Wouldn't that *truly* be a virtual world?

If so, you get it: I don't have to explain further. If not, there's little point in my trying to explain! All I can do is pose the following question: Should those lacking a god's motivation assume a god's powers?

There are other reasons why having intelligent NPCs is good, but their effects can be achieved using other mechanisms. The most important of these concerns the fact that even the biggest virtual worlds don't have enough PCs to sustain their systems and, even if they did, few players would want to do the mundane things that occupy NPCs. Who craves a career as a city guard? Players visit virtual worlds because they offer experiences that they don't get in the real one; they don't want a "real life" in a virtual world. NPCs, on the other hand, live in the virtual world, so their "real life" consists of doing the kind of things players would do in their real "real lives."

For example, some people want power. In this context, "power" means power *over* someone. Players won't tolerate being under other players' thumbs for long, therefore NPCs are needed to fulfill the roles of functionaries and foot soldiers. Similarly, players don't buy or sell enough objects to sustain an economy, therefore NPCs should engage in commerce to ensure that prices rise or fall appropriately. The collective behavior of NPCs can be used to regulate reputation systems, consequences for high/low status/fashion, rumor propagation/decay, the growth/decline of settlements, elections to office, and many other useful "background" tasks that contribute prominently to the experience of players but in which players themselves are loathe to get involved. If NPCs report their feelings when asked, this can add even more: I might not care that the NPC wants to tell me about the nearby ruin I already visited five times, but I'd certainly care to know whether that NPC was thinking of voting for me in the upcoming Guild of Mercenaries elections.

Giving individual NPCs more capacity for self-determination is one way to implement these behaviors. Another way, though, is to model the actions of NPCs as a whole, rather than individually. For example, instead of each NPC deciding when they need to buy a new gown and the price they're willing to pay for it, a general model of NPC buying habits can be used to calculate the overall demand curve for gowns and the impact that this has on price. This is easier to engineer, less expensive to program, and simpler to fine-tune than its micro-economic counterpart, although it's also more predictable and not as robust. It's a viable alternative to using hordes of independent NPCs to obtain the same effect. If you have those hordes for other reasons, though, it makes sense to arrange for their collective behavior to emerge from their individual actions, rather than simulating it and having the two diverge.

It could be argued that if a virtual world needs intelligent NPCs, making them artificially intelligent is the wrong route to take. Why not employ actors to control NPCs, and get intelligence of the natural variety? Set up an office in Hollywood where wannabe actors are endemic and it wouldn't even be all that expensive.

I have two objections to this, one practical and one philosophical.

The practical objection I outlined earlier. Going hands-on works for small, intimate virtual worlds, but not for ones with large numbers of players—it's hard to maintain non-superficial relationships with 200 people. Players are deeply suspicious of vendettas, favoritism, and other imagined ways to cheat; if they find that you sent one more monster against them than you did against some other group, they will whine incessantly[52], no matter how much fun they had. They don't generally like talking to patronizing, in-character, support staff at the best of times. Besides, it *would* be expensive to hire actors in quantity, even in Hollywood.

The philosophical objection is that one of the major goals of virtual worlds is self-reliance. Computers, not minds, model the physics; the same applies to the virtual inhabitants. If your virtual world design relies on people as components, it may be ahead of its time but it nevertheless crosses a boundary that stops it from being a virtual world. Players are necessary; community managers are acceptable; PC NPCs are a contradiction in terms.

Designers will determine the numbers and population density of NPCs depending on the roles they need them to fill. This raises a question: As a general rule, should it be possible for PCs to do anything that NPCs can? With some minor qualification for the virtual world's fiction, the answer should be yes; it ensures flexibility in design. That in most virtual worlds it isn't true shows just how inflexible designs are. The question

---

52. Never underestimate the whine factor!

also can be turned around: As a general rule, should it be possible for NPCs to do anything that PCs can? Again, the answer must be yes. Why yes? Players will usually have no trouble telling other players' characters from NPCs, but that doesn't mean NPCs also should be able to: If one NPC offers a quest, there's no theoretical reason why some other NPC shouldn't be able to undertake it. This can only add depth and variety to a virtual world—both good things.

From the foregoing discussion, it should be pretty obvious where monsters fit in to this equation: They're simply NPCs that operate under different AI rules[53]. What about players, though? Are they merely NPCs controlled by natural rather than artificial intelligence?

Would that it were so....

Player Characters

Players are the best things and the worst things about virtual worlds. They're contradictions.

Players want an immersive experience. They want a virtual world that looks and feels like how they expect it should look and feel. They want to share it with thousands of other people. They want fully integrated, working systems that support a rich, eclectic mix of activities in a balanced way. Only when they have it do they change their minds.

Players' desires completely overwhelm a virtual world. You could have a smooth-running, functionally luxuriant virtual world of 50,000 NPCs that would collapse if 50 players entered it (think Aztecs and Conquistadors here). There's a conflict between what players want and what has to be true for them to have it.

For example, they like a huge playing field. The early textual worlds often advertised themselves in terms of the number of rooms they had, the bigger being implicitly the better[54]. However, when it comes to moving around in such a virtual world, suddenly

---

53. Usually, they also operate under different environmental conditions: Monsters are subject to an ecology and NPCs are subject to an economy. As we'll see later, these (like monsters and NPCs themselves) are really just two sides of the same coin.

54. Sadly, some still do this, even to the extent of using the same, tired old techniques of yore (for example, coordinate systems) to inflate their numbers and disappoint their newbies.

distance becomes an inconvenience. Players want to be able to get where they want to go quickly. Why should the first half an hour of a session involve moving through uninteresting territory to where the action is? They want teleportation, portals, high-tech transporters—anything, so long as it bypasses the points between start and destination.

So they want a big world, then they want to shrink it.

A common outcome of players' insistence on such luxuries is that only player characters get to use them. Mobiles don't. There may be a public-transport teleport gate in the middle of town, convenient for all amenities, but NPCs saunter right past. Those NPCs who want to go anywhere have to walk. The same applies to many other situations: player characters might get better after they've been killed, but monsters certainly don't—they're well and truly *gone*[55].

This special treatment for players is not in itself necessarily bad. It only becomes bad when it subverts systems, such as the ecology or (especially) the economy. Here's an example of what I mean.

In medieval times, wine was a drink for the peasants in France but for the nobility in Scotland. Why? Because grapes grow in France and they don't grow in Scotland. French peasants harvested the grapes and made it into wine. They kept some for themselves and handed the rest over to the local feudal lord, who would retain some and sell the excess to merchants. Those merchants would transport the wine to the coast, put it on a ship, and dispatch it to (among other places) Scotland. There, it would be unloaded and sold to another merchant, who would trade it to the nobility because no one else could afford it. The cost of transporting the wine from France to Scotland is what made it so expensive there (well, that and the import duty levied by the Scottish monarch).

Now assume that the people in Scotland could have materialized in France, undertaken some transactions, and then rematerialized back in Scotland. What effect would this have had on the price of wine in Scotland?

---

55. There may be unkillable NPCs. Some of these vaguely make sense in context (for example, guards) but others don't. A clan of 100 players can wipe out a clutch of red dragons but find itself powerless against the might of a shopkeeper who doesn't want to lose his stock.

It would have fallen, obviously. Scots could have bought the wine at source. In fact, they could have done better: They could have bought the grapes at source and then made their own wine. If everywhere is local to everywhere else, this is exactly what happens. Nowadays, transport is much less expensive (although taxes are just as high), so the price of wine in Scotland is comparable with that of the local product, whisky. If transport were free and immediate, the only reason to make wine in France would be because that's where the winemakers wanted to make it.

Now imagine you're back in medieval times and you have access to a teleporter. You can buy wine in France and instantly sell it in Scotland at a far lower price than regular merchants can while making a far greater profit. At a stroke, you have completely wrecked the economy as it stood.

This leaves designers with a problem. NPCs have to use the same economy that players do. With instantaneous travel, there's no such thing as a local market: Prices for goods are the same everywhere. Therefore, the virtual economy should at least simulate the ability of NPCs to use teleporters. Yet, defiantly, players don't want this. They want tin to be cheap near tin mines and expensive elsewhere, just like in the real world. They want silk to come from China, wood to come from Scandinavia, spices to come from India, gold to come from Central America: That's what they learned at school and that's how it should be. If diamonds the size of tennis balls can only be mined on the planet Eebagum, then they should cost less in the gem markets of Eebagum than back on Earth. It stands to reason. Thus, when a player teleports from Eebagum to Earth with a sack full of diamonds and sells the lot, the price shouldn't drop. Then, a month or so later, they can wonder why their immense wealth won't buy them anything from other players.

The subject of player perversion of virtual economies is a big one. However, it's something designers really need to know about, so let's make a start.

Economics

Economics is a huge subject of immense importance. In the real world, it touches on absolutely everything that people do. Daily it occupies some of the finest minds on the planet, and yet still the mechanisms by which it functions aren't completely understood. Even top economists can't agree on everything.

Is it any wonder that it scares the willies out of virtual world designers?

As part of their trade, the designers of virtual worlds must accumulate a wide range of knowledge covering many specialist subjects; some of these they'd perhaps rather avoid, but none of them are truly avoidable. Economics is one such specialist subject. Unless it's your own specialist subject, you're in bother.

My advice in such circumstances is to visit your local university. Head for the bookstore and buy whatever book entry-level students are buying. This applies whether you want to know about economics, psychology, artificial intelligence, sociology, anthropology, astronomy, whatever[56]. Read the book you buy. If half of it or more makes sense, you probably have enough of a grounding to be able to apply your newly acquired knowledge to virtual world design. Complex though they may be, virtual worlds are nowhere near as complex as the real one; you may only have the gist of the subject, but when you're working with something that's only the gist of reality, well, that's usually sufficient.

If you don't understand even half of the book, hire a specialist. No sense in burning out your brain.

So, what, fundamentally, is economics about?

It's about resource allocation. Resources are anything that people need or want for any purpose—land, food, labor, sports cars.... When resources are scarce (as they usually are), they can't be allocated to satisfy every need or want, therefore some system of resource allocation must pertain. This system is the economy.

Some economies are more efficient than others. In a barter economy, I might raise chickens and buy the things I need using eggs. Other egg farmers could do the same. If two of us wanted to buy the miller's last sack of grain, the one of us who was prepared to offer the most eggs would probably get it. If we both wanted the same Stradivarius violin, however, it would be more problematical: We might not have enough eggs, the seller might not have a use for that many eggs, and we could be up against someone else who wanted to pay in shoes. It's likely that none of us will get the Stradivarius, even though we all want to buy it and the owner wants to sell it.

---

56. To anyone who bought this book with the aim of studying virtual worlds from the perspective of some other discipline: Hi!

Most societies use currency to make transactions more efficient. I can convert my eggs into coins. I can save these up to buy a Stradivarius[57], and the person from whom I buy it can use the coins to buy other things. Currency facilitates transactions.

The example with the eggs, although it uses a barter system, follows the principles of a free market economy. Prices fluctuate depending on supply and demand. If the miller had many sacks of grain, I could have got a sack at a lower price; if I had many spare eggs, I could have afforded to pay more eggs for a sack.

For virtual worlds, a free market is not the only option available. There are basically four types of economy you can have:

➤ None

➤ Fixed prices

➤ Free market

➤ Faddish

Having no economy is fine for worlds with very low persistence. It isn't that there's no economy at all, of course, just that there's no *formal* economy. If you can't save objects across sessions, for example, there's very little reason to buy things; informal bartering is enough. It's possible that there could be a service market ("I'll train up your strength if you give me 400 units of currency, which I can save up to spend on improving my fishing skills") but even this is amenable to simple barter.

Heavy role-playing-style textual worlds often have no formal economy (although some older custom codebases[58] omitted it, too). In these, it's common for people to give things away that they don't need, thereby encouraging a community-strengthening favor reciprocation system. The more persistent a virtual world is, though, the greater the need for a formal economy; otherwise, players wanting to exchange goods and services get very frustrated if their favors are not returned.

---

57. Sadly, I'm only talking hypothetically here.

58. Although the idea of putting money into *MUD1* was suggested many times by its players, I always resisted because I didn't feel it could have coped with inflation. Given that its economy would only have been small and therefore very susceptible to player exploits, on the whole I'm rather glad I did.

The fixed-price approach also works in low-persistence virtual worlds. If you can't take your cash with you when you quit, fixed-priced objects retain their worth. If you can take some money, but only up to some moderate amount, that also can work. If you can keep arbitrarily large amounts of money, fixed pricing eventually equates to "free." I'll explain why shortly.

Prices in a free market change to reflect how much people are willing to pay and how much people are willing to be paid for particular goods or services. This is the approach used by most virtual worlds. It ought to work—it does in the real world—but there are a few problems that virtual worlds have which the real one doesn't. Again, I'll come to these shortly (after I'm done summarizing economy types).

The final common type of economy is whatever fad idea enthuses the designers enough that they decide to use it. Although the designers will thus be 100% committed to it, prospective players will generally be 100% the opposite. It may well work in practice as well as in theory, but the chances are it will do neither.

Most virtual worlds aim for a free market economy. There has yet to be a successful large-scale implementation of this, however. There are two reasons for this: Designers don't make the economy as free as they think they're making it; players beat it to a bloody pulp.

Let's see how these situations develop.

Wealth enters the system: The main sources of this are monster drops, quest rewards, farming/mining, and newbies' grubstakes. Characters accumulate wealth. By their efforts, they may create more wealth by adding value to items or by performing services. Wealth leaves the system: In a closed economy, what leaves goes into some simulation (for example, of the activity of unseen NPCs) to return in some form later. In an open system, what exits the system has no effect on what enters.

What happens when, because of players' industry, wealth appears at a faster rate than it disappears?

In a closed system, the rate at which recycled wealth enters falls to compensate. There are fewer monsters and quests, or the rewards for success are lower. Players find they are receiving less money, so are more inclined to keep what they have ready for when they really need it; this means that the amount of wealth leaving the system falls again, leading to a fall in the amount entering. It's a vicious circle, which guides the economy to a grinding halt. All it takes is for more people to hang onto their wealth than the designers had allowed for, and it's guaranteed to happen. Given that organized griefers will figure this out and deliberately save money just to watch the whole edifice tumble, closed economies can always expect to dry up eventually[59].

Most virtual world economies are open. If more wealth comes in than goes out, then players accumulate wealth and can buy more things; if less wealth comes in than goes out, they go broke and can buy fewer things. This doesn't matter in a truly free market economy, because prices can rise or fall to match income—even inflationary income. If today the average wealth of a character is 500 UOC and a new helmet costs 10 UOC, then in six months when the average wealth of a character is 5,000 UOC the price of a new helmet will be 100 UOC (if supply and demand remain constant). Thus, although absolute prices may change, relative prices only change when supply or demand changes.

In a fixed-price economy, this doesn't happen. A 10 UOC helmet costs 10 UOC whether people have nothing in the bank or millions. It's normally the latter; this means that after a while helmets are basically free—great news if you want a helmet, but terrible news if you're a player whose character manufactures helmets. In any system with fixed pricing, inflation hurts everyone who crafts goods for which fixed prices pertain. It doesn't matter if you can raise or lower your *own* prices: If NPC vendors buy and sell at fixed prices, you're screwed.

The obvious solution to this is to have variable prices—that is, a fully free market. The problem is that unless *all* prices are variable, this doesn't work. One consequence of this is that quest rewards and mobile drops should be variable, too. Who'd want to risk life and limb for 20,000 UOC if it wasn't enough to buy an arrow? Yet how do designers make these price rises occur rationally in such a way that unscrupulous players[60] can't screw over the system?

---

59. This assumes that players can keep their money in complete safety. If they can't, they will be less likely to hoard it (because it could be stolen). If they can, but that place of safety is a bank, that helps too because money can be loaned from it and thereby re-enter the system. Needless to say, this is not what tends to happen in virtual worlds.

60. Some designers might suggest that the term "unscrupulous players" is a tautology. Even though this is perhaps unfair, it can certainly help to look on them that way occasionally.

Actually, it's surprisingly doable. The trick is to give *goods* rather than cash as rewards. Goods get their value from the free market; therefore their value varies in keeping with supply and demand. If you get a wolf pelt for killing a wolf, then the sum total of the wealth of the virtual world increased to the tune of one wolf pelt. The amount you can sell this for depends on the demand for wolf pelts at the time. If demand is low, you get a smaller return than if demand is high, therefore you go off and kill something else instead of wolves. This will lead to a drop in the supply of wolf pelts until there's a shortage of them, whereupon prices will rise and you might think about killing wolves again. It all works very neatly.

Unfortunately, there are some consequences of the free market economy that require players and designers to accept some as-yet unpalatable truths.

Designers first. A free market economy operates using what Adam Smith famously called an "invisible hand"[61]. Individuals work to promote their own self-interests, but in so doing promote the interests of society as a whole (generally unintentionally). Farmers sell us food because it's in their interest to do so, not because we'd die if they didn't. If all players act in their own best self-interest, the free market economy will flourish.

Unfortunately, in virtual worlds players' best self-interest may be to make your economy collapse—and that's not even the worst of it.

In the real economy, you have to participate because there's nowhere else to go. Everyone can't be rich; some people have to be poor. In virtual worlds, you do have somewhere else to go. If you're poor, you can emigrate to some other world where you can be rich. In the real world, if no one buys the helmets of which you are so proud, you have to make something else instead; in the virtual world, you quit and go where helmet-making is valued. Helmets, potions, laser rifles—it applies to all crafted items.

Also, the free market model says that if a bunch of players want and can afford quality swords and there's no one making them, the demand will prompt someone to get into the quality sword business. Unfortunately, that reasoning only applies within the context of the virtual world. The demand also can be satisfied by frustrated fighters decamping to some other virtual world where there is no sword shortage. No matter

---

61. Adam Smith, *An Inquiry into the Nature and Causes of the Wealth of Nations*. London, W. Strahan and T. Cadell, 1776. Full text available at http://www.adamsmith.org.uk/smith/won-intro.htm.

how much a designer might want it, his virtual world's economy can never be truly closed because players are a part of it and players can come and go. The free market does work here—supply, demand, and prices do achieve equilibrium—but it works in a way that hurts your real-world profits.

It may be that a free market has unpleasant consequences on the virtual world itself, too. Take the example of bakery wars: A big guild with deep pockets sets up a bakery in a town that already has a bakery. The established shop has a loyal customer base, a long-standing reputation, and it makes tasty bread. The guild shop starts to give away free bread. People go to the guild for their free bread.

What does the local bakery do? It can give away bread for free too, but it still has to pay for the raw materials and it therefore takes a loss on every loaf (so does the guild, of course, but the guild is rich and can afford the loss). The bakery can continue to charge a fair price for its bread, but people won't buy it because they can get something fairly similar for nothing from the guild. Eventually, the original shop is going to have to face facts and shut down. The guild will then hike the price of its own bread sky high so that it not only covers its losses but it becomes even richer. Do you, as a designer, allow such monopolistic bullying[62]? It'll cost you at least the local baker and perhaps some of the people who used to buy their bread there. If you thought about it in advance you can devise ways to stop this sort of thing from happening, but what about the ways for players to turn over your economy that you haven't thought of? What checks and balances do you have in place to defend against unforeseen attacks?

Another example: pelt hoarding. Suppose a guild seals off the forest where the snow wolves live. No one goes in or out of the forest unless the guild guards get out of the way. If there's a constant demand for snow wolf pelts (they're used for making frost storm spells or something), then the price of snow wolf pelts will rise. Ordinarily, it may be that the forest spawns 20 snow wolves a day and the pelts fetch 50 UOC each. Now, it's still spawning 20 a day but if the guild only kills two of them, then each pelt may fetch 1000 UOC. That means they double their profits. This is how cartels operate: By restricting supply, demand is artificially inflated and prices are kept artificially high. Do you have your world react to this, for example by spawning snow wolves in more places? If not, the players who need the pelts will wail about how your crock of

---

62. It may be comforting or otherwise to know that real-life governments have to wrestle with these exact same issues, too.

an economy allows this kind of abuse to occur. But if so, the cartel will flood the market with snow wolf pelts until your spawning stops, then repeat—all the while complaining bitterly about your interference.

This brings us to the second group of people who have problems with a free market economy: the players.

Players will produce spreadsheets covering your economy. They will then gouge it. They will expect to gouge it, regard it as perfectly natural behavior, and be outraged if you make any attempt stop them. Everyone else, on the other hand, they regard as having no right to exploit the economy in any way remotely detrimental to their own well-being. This is true in the real world, of course, but you can't quit the real world; you can quit virtual worlds.

In a free market economy, the activities that people undertake will sometimes be rewarded poorly. This acts as an incentive for those people to do other things that are better rewarded instead. Unfortunately, for a player of your virtual world, "better rewarded" might mean playing some other virtual world rather than yours.

Suppose you, as a player, like making clothes. It's a big creative thing with you—you enjoy seeing characters walking around wearing your designs. Your entire aim when selecting a virtual world is to have your character be a tailor. So, you sign up to a world that lets you be a tailor, and start to churn out jackets and skirts and coats with which you're immensely pleased. What happens if there are so many other tailors around that nobody wants to buy your clothes, no matter how much you advertise them?

In the real world, you would lose money to the extent that eventually you'd have to face facts and stop making clothes. In the virtual world, you would scream and scream and scream until the world was "fixed" so that there were always NPCs willing to buy your garments. If it wasn't "fixed," you'd eventually leave in disgust at its betrayal. Again, the virtual world's free market economy is working, but the real world's free market economy is also working; of course, the real world always wins.

Players want an honest day's pay for an honest day's work. If you don't reward them, they feel cheated. If you set up yourself as a snow wolf hunter and make 50 UOC per pelt profit, you're happy. If other people find that killing snow wolves is profitable, they'll join in. With the resulting increase in supply, you'll find you can't sell your snow wolf pelts unless you drop the price. Now you're making only 40 UOC per pelt[63]. What do you do? Either you accept the realities of the free market or you dash off an email to the community service team screeching, "Your STOOPID game NERFED snow wolves!!!"[64].

Players like it when the free market works in their favor; they don't like it if it doesn't. This may be a problem that, in time, the maturity of players cures. Then again, if enough precedents for pandering to players are set then it may never get the chance to be tested. Players will complain—and get a hearing—if they do things that are blatantly stupid.

> Player: "You killed my chickens!"
>
> Community manager: "You built your chicken farm in a forest full of wolves. Didn't you expect maybe they'd eat your chickens?"
>
> Player: "Are you hearing me? YOU KILLED MY CHICKENS!"

Telling players that the miserable time they're having is all their own fault will not endear you to them. If they spend four hours hunting wolves when the price of wolf pelts is rock bottom, they don't like being told to hunt something else instead. If they're told that hunting itself is an over-subscribed activity (having designed their character to be a hunter), they will be absolutely livid. Players *will* spend a lot of time being miserable if the reward is high enough. They'll mindlessly click on the same "mining" icon for three hours, hating every moment of it[65], if the result is that they find the diamond they need to give them an arrow of dragon-slaying. It's when they make themselves miserable for no reward that the problems come. They want an honest day's pay for an honest day's work; they've done the honest day's work, so now they want the honest day's pay. It's immaterial to them that what they've done is as useful as counting buttons.

---

63. Or, if things get as bad as they did in *Ultima Online*, one UOC.

64. To *nerf* means to adjust the tangible effects of a virtual world element downward. Although nowadays it can apply to everything from skills to classes to races to spells, it's traditionally used for objects. It comes from the Nerf brand of safe-play toys. A Nerf gun does less damage than a real one.

65. It's easy for designers to mistake what people *do* for what people *enjoy* doing. The chances are if players tell you they don't like doing something, they're not lying—no matter what the data mining results say.

It's because players are frequently unwilling to accept this consequence of a free market economy that virtual worlds will guarantee prices for crafted objects. This assures a market, so players stop complaining, but then there's no incentive for them to change to making something people really want. Besides, players have other requirements, too: Someone who makes clothes that no one buys may be temporarily pacified by being able to sell them to NPCs, but unless NPCs actually wear those clothes they're still going to feel unfulfilled. Even then, NPCs aren't PCs. Surely, PCs would buy your clothes if only their existing clothes wore out quicker? So it's complain-to-live-team time yet again.

Note that designers don't have to guarantee fixed prices, just decent prices. It's perfectly within the power of the live team to change prices manually or to force a change by (again, manually) altering supply and demand—creating and destroying virtual goods is free for them, after all. In the real world, the social costs involved in doing this are too high for it to be successful; as economist Edward Castronova has pointed out[66], however, these costs are absent from virtual worlds and therefore price-fixing could be considered a viable strategy in such an environment. However, as I've just illustrated, there would remain other undesirable effects to do with concepts of fulfillment and self-worth. So although live teams could indeed attempt to control prices, they'd have to know *exactly* what they were doing to succeed (and be ready for the inevitable accusations of bias and favoritism that would follow).

Fixed prices aren't in keeping with a free market, and neither is fixed income. If all newbies get a grubstake of so many UOC, the purchasing power of that grubstake depends on prices. It's better to give them a range of kit, but even that can lead to perceived unfairness if the exchange value of what today's newbie gets is more (or less) than it was two months ago. It's more palatable than giving inflation-adjusted grubstakes, though.

Similarly, if monsters drop a (relatively) fixed amount of coin when they die, what it will buy depends on current prices. Again, it's better if you make them drop some resource that can be traded instead of raw money, even if the money is inflation-adjusted—players will moan if "last week I only got 600 UOC but this week my friend got 650 UOC, so you owe me 50 UOC." You can still get a form of inflation with this, though: A mobile dropping a +1 sword is dropping nothing if everyone already has a +1 (or greater) sword.

66. Edward Castronova, *On Virtual Economies*. CESifo Working Paper 752, 2002.

Fixed prices and incomes are bad for an economy, as eventually either everyone can afford everything (inflationary world) or no one can afford anything (deflationary world). Fascinatingly, this same argument can be used to justify assigning constant experience point values to mobiles: The more experience points you have, the less the value of an "easy" mobile is to you. Therefore you have to go for the tougher mobiles that give higher returns (leaving the easier mobiles for relative newbies). A consequence of this "level inflation" is that eventually no mobiles are worth enough. Without sufficient sinks (that is, ways to lose experience points), new content must be added somehow, either by the live team or designed-in as an elder game.

Of early virtual world economies on a massive scale, *Ultima Online*'s was the best. It *almost* worked. The economy and ecology were interlinked and interdependent. It began as a closed system, but it soon became apparent that the sum total of the world's wealth wasn't large enough to go around. It switched to a faucet/drain economy, which held up for a long time despite having some fixed prices (for crafters) and periods of inflation due to bugs. What finally broke it was the lack of sinks: People didn't have enough to spend their money on, so it simply accumulated.

Following on from *UO*'s complex economy, there was a backlash. *EverQuest* and *Asheron's Call* both had much simpler economies. Both of these suffered from inflation, although in *EQ*'s case the vast numbers of newbies entering the world managed to soak up the excess to some extent and eventually the economy became relatively stable. *AC* rapidly achieved hyperinflation (it wasn't helped by some money-duping[67] bugs that effectively gave players their own mints) and its economy never really recovered. Unsurprisingly, most of the *EQ*–inspired graphical worlds went for the *EQ* approach rather than the *UO* one, although *Star Wars Galaxies* sees the pendulum swinging back to a system that doesn't require a newbie hose to sustain it (ironically, because *SWG* does have a newbie hose).

The interesting thing to note about formal economies is that when they do break, an informal economy will normally emerge to replace them. *AC*'s informal economy, based around gem shards (needed to make kick-ass armor), certain keys (giving access to spell scrolls and other kick-ass armor), and writs (required to lease a house), became

---

67. *Duping* is short for *duplicating*. It means creating copies of objects (or whatever), normally as a result of programming errors. Virtual worlds implemented using a template system for object creation are particularly prone to it, and stackable objects (such as coins) are their weakest point.

highly robust and stable; the formal economy was only used for interactions with NPCs. It's to the designers of *AC*'s credit that although the economy they originally put together fell apart, their virtual world was sufficiently deep that the informal economy that replaced it became something of an exemplar.

Interference in Economies

How much should you interfere with how an economy "should" work to facilitate its smooth operation?

Let's start with something relatively mundane. Players don't like being ripped off; if they want to trade, should there be a secure trading system whereby goods can be exchanged with no danger that anyone will take the money and run? It's not very immersive, but players are accustomed to the idea and will accept it without thinking (in the same way that they accept slow scene dissolves in movies as a signal for the passage of time). The easier it is to trade, the more likely players are to engage in trade.

Trading, though, is tangible: Coins and objects are things the virtual world can track. Services are intangible: If I want to pay you to guard something, how can the virtual world track whether or not you did it? Similarly, although it's possible to contrive a trade screen whereby I cast a heal spell if you give me money, it's not so easy to do it for more complex arrangements (such as casting heals on you "whenever you need them," in exchange for "a share of an expedition's profits").

There will always be unsecure trading, because designers can't hope to model everything that players may want to trade. Given that they can't model everything, the question that then arises is whether they should model anything at all?

The answer must be yes, because it's the only way for low-AI NPCs to trade. Given that it's therefore there already, allowing it for instant interplayer trade isn't really going to hurt any. For transactions that take time, though, it's trickier. If I pay an NPC to train me to use a crossbow, I know that the NPC is not going to disappear with my cash; with a PC, I don't know that. This *can* be shoehorned into a transaction system, but the more complex transactions become, the harder it gets. There comes a point where to continue would be ridiculous, even if it's short of what NPCs can do. Automated transactions are okay if they don't stretch convention too far, but beyond that they hurt immersion.

If a smooth-running economy were the only aim here, this model could be further extended. For example, players could be allowed to trade with one another without being in physical proximity. Goods could be teleported immediately from point of sale to point of purchase, with the two not necessarily coinciding. This would greatly facilitate the exchange of goods, leading to greater satisfaction for all. In a Science Fiction virtual world, it may even make sense within the fiction.

Whether it would be any fun is another matter, though. One of the things about an imperfect economy is that it takes time for production and demand to fall into step. During that time, profits can be made. If response is immediate, this smoothes out the creases that make commerce interesting.

In some virtual worlds, the mobiles you fight are tuned to your combat abilities. In other words, no matter what you attack, it will adapt to be commensurate with your abilities to defeat it. The design thinking is that you'll have a more exciting time if you're pushed close to defeat but still manage to win. It's flawed, though, because nearly-losing-but-then-winning is only exciting if there exists the possibility that you could actually lose. Because mobiles are bent to fit your abilities, there's actually no real danger of this. Combat is ultimately dispiriting.

A similar thing applies to over-smoothed economies. If as soon as players think of something clever to do, checks and balances come into play that dampen the effect, in time people are going to wonder what the point of it all is. There has to be enough opportunity to make a success of something before the bandwagon arrives, otherwise it's just not worth trying.

Interference in the low-level workings of an economy can thus be counterproductive: The easier you make it for people to trade goods and services, the less interesting it becomes. On the other hand, if you don't interfere then the economy might not work at all. You have to achieve a balance.

There are other ways to interfere that could help.

National governments use interest rates to control their economies. Low interest rates cause people to spend; high interest rates cause people to save. If you have a virtual world where players are spending or saving too much, it shouldn't be too hard to create a mechanism that corrects the problem (for example, by making NPCs change their prices, or by taxing PC bank accounts).

Regrettably, this isn't as straightforward as it sounds. The problem is not the implementation, but players' perception of it. Unlike with a secure transactions system (which is a transparent process), they don't see the workings of the economy's carburetor, just the effects. It's very difficult for them to trust what's going on. Even if you completely automate the checking and balancing, there'll still be a deep suspicion that actually it's the live team that makes all the decisions, with some "nerf knob" they can turn to make prices rise or fall.

It's an issue of trust. If you must have a nerf knob, you might want to give control of it to a committee of players rather than automate it. They may screw up, but at least they'll get the blame, not you!

Tips for a Successful Virtual Economy

I'll wrap up this discussion of the economies of virtual worlds with a few tips to help you design one that works. Rather than merely repeat what I've already said ("Don't use fixed prices, you idiot!"), I'll concentrate on ideas that might not be immediately obvious. Not all of them apply to all virtual world economies, but hopefully they'll spark a few ideas.

Have Stuff Wear Out

The normal problem in virtual worlds is inflation. The effects of this are alleviated somewhat if players have many ways to be separated from their cash. The easiest way to do this is to have stuff wear out so that replacements have to be bought. This hands money to NPC vendors or (if goods are bought from PCs) to NPC miners/farmers. If PCs do all the mining and farming too, it's still of some use because it encourages trade; it's best as a money sink, though. It helps keep scarce items scarce.

Players see it as a money sink, of course, which makes them suspicious. It's basically a tax on action. However, as long as you make it "realistic" you can get away with it: Shields used in combat really do receive a battering, but you'd be hard-pressed to justify why a ring wore out.

Charge for Services

Players don't like it when you take money from them, but they don't mind so much if they think they're spending it. They are quite happy to pay for things that reduce the amount of work they have to do.

For example, consider teleportation. When a player wants to go from A to B, the cost of teleporting compared to the time cost of walking should really be an issue. Players ought to have to *think* about whether they need a service enough to pay through the nose for it. Naturally, they'll complain that teleporting is "too expensive," and they could well be right. With a pricing structure that rises and falls depending on how many people use a teleporter, though, a balance should be achieved.

In considering services that can be charged for, anything that satisfies these three criteria is suitable:

➤ Player characters can do it.

➤ NPCs or the virtual world itself can do it for them.

➤ Players don't like doing it.

Have Multiple Currencies

In the real world, there are many currencies. If a price is quoted in one currency and you want to pay in some other, you have to sell some of the latter currency to get some of the former. I can't give a taxi driver in Paris dollars and I can't give a taxi driver in New York euros[68].

Exchange rates between currencies fluctuate. In theory, this happens because of trade: If a country manufactures goods that lots of other countries want, those countries will have to acquire the currency of the first country in order to pay for the goods, which will lead to a rise in the exchange rate in the first country's favor. If a country needs more capital to invest in its industry and infrastructure, it can raise interest rates, thereby attracting investors who want a guaranteed return; this will also lead to an increase in the exchange rate.

A virtual world can have multiple currencies, and exchange rates between them. This can act as a form of trade tax (because converting currencies will almost inevitably incur a commission charge) and it's also good for limiting the spread of inflation (the more money of one kind there is in circulation, the less money of another kind it is worth). The number of currencies doesn't have to be high: Gold versus silver coins can work; Simutronics' game *DragonRealms* successfully runs three "local" currencies.

---

68. Well I can, but they're not going to let me out of the cab if I do.

In practice, real-world currency markets are dominated by speculators. In virtual worlds, the fact that you can tax each and every currency transaction would immediately put a stop to this (assuming you wanted to).

Give Money Weight

This is a great tip for virtual worlds with a pre-Victorian era setting.

If you have 100,000 gold pieces, that's a lot of gold. Post-1982 U.S. 1 cent coins (pennies) weigh 2.5g; 100,000 of them would weigh 250kg, or about 550lbs. Coin quality gold is about 2.5 times denser than electroplated zinc. Moving that kind of mass is not easy without cheating physics.

When coin has weight, the act of transporting it is non-trivial. Someone who is rich in one city is not so rich in another. A local economy can therefore flourish because players can't easily transport enough coin there to undermine it. It leads to a more stable overall economy. Objects genuinely do have different values in different places, and a career as a merchant suddenly becomes a possibility. Although giving coin weight gets in the way of trade, it also makes trade more interesting; it gives it gameplay elements that it didn't have before.

Players can carry high-value items such as gems instead of coin, of course, but gems are like multiple currencies. Rubies are worth more in places far from ruby mines, and then only if PCs or NPCs actually have a use for them. You might be able to convert from coin to gems, but where you're going you may find you can't convert back, or that if you do you get a different amount of gold[69].

A corollary to this is: No banks, no banknotes. For any world in a prerenaissance setting, this is historically accurate; for any other world set prior to about 1900, it's inaccurate for the very wealthy but is fine for the general population (who never saw banknotes nor visited banks). In Fantasy virtual worlds, banks are basically there as a convenience for players, acting as money teleports: You pay cash into one and withdraw it out of another. They're effectively ATMs, and as such are somewhat out of place. It's hard to imagine Gandalf visiting a bank in *Lord of the Rings*; likewise, it's hard to imagine Elrond paying for a horse with a banknote.

---

69. If you're lucky, this could be more than you originally paid for the gems, of course.

Multiple Uses

Elves draw magical power from the number of trees that exist within a certain range. Humans in the nearby town want wood for housing. This is conflict. Economies can drive conflicts. Conflicts can also drive economies. Dwarfs need elf skins to enchant their forges.

Conflict like this is good for gameplay (if not overdone), and having multiple uses for resources is a neat way to introduce it. The same technique can be used to enhance trade (by driving up volumes) and challenge monopolies (because the opposition to them will be greater).

Similarly, having multiple resources for the same use[70] can keep a virtual economy from being mugged. In practice, goods are usually implemented as being similar but not exactly equivalent, so a snow wolf pelt might have a slightly higher warmth factor than a snow bear pelt, but get mangy quicker. Nevertheless, if there were a sudden shortage of snow wolf pelts, people who made clothes out of them[71] could switch to bear pelts. When people have choices like this, meaningful decisions must be made; meaningful decisions are at the heart of gameplay.

Charge for Advancement

Players are so pleased when their character has gained enough experience for them to advance a level or skill that they are quite happy to pay virtual coin to seal it. Whether this is through "training" (which for some reason only NPCs seem able to provide) or the acquisition of some expensive item (mithril cross, ebony staff, engraved armor) is not the point: The point is to provide a money sink.

Some designers adopt a "charge for everything" view and make characters pay to enter cities, to cross bridges, to speak to officials, and so on. This can backfire if people find it too tiresome or depressing. By charging for things that don't happen all the time and that the player is happy about, these negative effects are greatly reduced. Charging for advancement is the perfect example of this idea in action.

---

70. These are known as *substitute goods*.

71. See Chapter 8 for a general discussion of doing things with your character that you might disapprove of in real life—wearing fur coats, for example.

Personally, I don't like charging for advancement; it's a little too cynical and opportunistic for my tastes. However, with plenty of players trained to accept it by existing virtual worlds, that's no reason for you to overlook it.

Charge for Abstraction

Should player characters have to eat? If they do, should the food work its way through their digestive system or be beamed out of them at the last moment as seems to happen in *Star Trek*? If nature proceeds like it does in real life, are there consequences for not washing your hands afterward? Or is this all a level of detail too far?

Some textual virtual worlds have eating. Every so often, characters will feel hungry. If they eat, the hunger goes away; if they don't, their attributes degrade increasingly until they do. Some foods are better at restoring attributes than others, but basically, eating remains a background maintenance task that adds authenticity but little gameplay.

Players deal with this by using clients that trigger on key phrases. When the "you are hungry" line arrives, the client automatically issues commands to remove a food item from the character's backpack and eat it. The original message, the commands to address it, and the messages confirming those commands are all stripped out. The player doesn't know the maintenance has taken place, except that the backpack needs restocking with food occasionally.

If players routinely automate responses, why bother having the events that trigger the responses at all? They're just hoops that players are being made to jump through. It may add realism, but the use of trigger code to make them transparent shows that it's realism players would rather do without.

So players shouldn't have to eat, then? In that case, what are all those NPCs doing working on the land? Only NPCs have to eat?

One solution is to make eating improve your character on a temporary basis. If you don't eat, your stats stay low. This is actually pretty much the same as using eating to maintain your (higher) stats, with failure to eat incurring a penalty. However, when phrased so it sounds like it's giving players something for performing an action (rather than taking something away for not performing it), it's more acceptable. This is the *Star Wars Galaxies* approach.

Another solution is to abstract such activities out. Characters eat, perform their ablutions, and so on, only when the player is offline, in the same way that characters in movies go to the bathroom only when the camera is not on them (or when they're about to be murdered). This allows players to get on with the serious business of having fun, without having to concern themselves with minutiae yet while remaining within the virtual world's fiction.

If this abstraction is performed, the player can pay for it. In general, players are against their characters' being taxed, but they can be persuaded to put up with something equivalent if it fits the fiction; a support fee to cover the incidentals that they run up while the player is offline is one such pseudo-tax. Incentives to increase payments—for example, by granting characters more status if they do—will often work. Characters without the means to pay could either suffer attribute/skill penalties or be allowed to subsist by explicit foraging, depending on the fiction of the virtual world.

The abstraction must be strictly adhered to, though: If characters eat while the player is logged in (perhaps when visiting a restaurant or taking part in a banquet), then their support fee for that period must drop accordingly. Characters who do buy their own food should ideally get a better deal than ones who rely on the abstraction, but this may be hard to organize in a free market economy.

This technique of charging for abstractions can be used for similar tiresome activities such as reloading ammunition and recharging batteries. In general, any unnecessary detail[72] can be removed this way and its cost bundled into a support fee.

Non-Player Players

I did mention when I began this section that although the main virtual worlds were populated by characters, NPCs, and monsters, there was a fourth possibility: non-player players. These are the customer service representatives, techies, designers, and other members of the live team who need access to the virtual world but don't want to play it as regular players. They generally need supra-world powers in order to help people, to test the world, to fix problems, and so on. How should the game fiction account for this?

---

72. In *MUD1*, clothes were an unnecessary detail.

The simplest answer is "it shouldn't." If you can't ever hope to slip it unnoticed into the fiction why bother? Put non-player players in a uniform so that everyone else knows to expect odd goings-on when they're around, and leave it at that.

The second-simplest answer is also "it shouldn't." Hands-on event coordinators, as I mentioned earlier, can merge in to the player base and appear to be regular players while actually having irregular powers at their disposal. This is fine for them, but it doesn't work for programmers trying to track down bugs or for customer service representatives showing the human face of the live team.

The more traditional approach, at least in Fantasy worlds, is to have a formal hierarchy of gods/immortals/wizzes. In other words, find some in-context powerful beings and associate the non-player players with these. This may be unavoidable anyway in some virtual worlds—for example, it's hard to conceive that an Ancient Greece world would work without any gods. Your main problem here is likely to be that the non-player players believe the labels and start acting like deities instead of programmers or whatever. A superior character doesn't imply a superior human being.

There is also a danger that through their actions (or players' beliefs of their actions), non-player players may inadvertently extend a virtual world's fiction. If Thor shows up just as a character gets a lucky hit and kills a giant, that character may think Thor is responsible. Before you know it, web sites will be proclaiming that praying to Thor will help in battle, and unless this misconception is nipped in the bud it could become so widespread a belief that complaints from confused newbies occupy more community management time than the programmer time it would take to implement the idea.

Physics

The foundations of a virtual world are its geography and its population; they're like a board and its pieces. Whenever designers begin work on a new virtual world, among the first things they consider are the geography and the ecology/economy.

With *MUD1*, Roy Trubshaw began with the physics.

Designers today inherit so much from what has gone before that often they don't give thought to why things are the way they are. If they don't give thought, they don't have understanding; if they don't have understanding, they can't innovate. There are so many features of a virtual world that rely on its physics—geography and population included—that it's staggering how much is taken for granted.

Physics concerns the fundamental systems of change; it's the machinery of a virtual world. It's no accident that it was the first statement in the definition of virtual worlds I gave in Chapter 1. It implicitly defines all a virtual world's tangible possibilities; if the physics doesn't allow it, you can't have it.

Designers really should know *everything* about the physics of their virtual world. They should know what conventions have been adopted, they should know why they were adopted, and they should know their implications. Armed with this, they should consider ways and means to improve on them for the benefit of their virtual world and its players. If you do go with the flow, it ought only to be because the flow is going where you want to go.

Laws of Nature

The physics of virtual worlds is based on real-world physics. There is a reason for this.

If I push on a door, the door opens. If I push on a virtual door, the virtual door opens. I could just as easily make it that if I push on a virtual door, virtual birds fly out of a virtual mug. Unless the door was flagged as No Ordinary Door and the mug was flagged as No Ordinary Mug, this would confuse people. Why? Because human beings learn from an early age the cause-and-effect rules that govern the way reality works. In a virtual world, they are unable to stop themselves from applying these same rules except by an act of will. For virtual worlds therefore, anything that interferes with these rules acts as an out-of-context interrupt; anything that adheres to them implicitly supports the illusion that the virtual is real.

The real world operates under the laws of physics. The rules that people develop in their heads to model the laws of physics[73] are simpler, but they're good enough for almost all practical purposes. Virtual worlds wishing to be convincing to players must

---

[73] These rules are called naïve physics, and are an example of qualitative reasoning. Patrick J. Hayes, *The Naïve Physics Manifesto*. Donald Michie (ed.), Expert Systems in the Micro-Electronic Age. Edinburgh, Edinburgh University Press, 1978.

Johan de Kleer, *Qualitative and Quantitative Reasoning in Classical Mechanics*. Patrick H. Winston and Richard H. Brown (eds.), Artificial Intelligence: an MIT Perspective. Cambridge MA, MIT Press, 1978.

therefore implement at least these rules (and, paradoxically, perhaps no more; it's players we're trying to convince here, not reality).

Fundamentally, therefore, virtual world physics is concerned with implementing the obvious.

The key is transparency. Transparency means that players don't have to suspend any disbelief, because their senses pass the information right by without comment. The more successful a designer is at creating transparency, the less his or her work will be noticed: This is great for immersion, if not so great for the designer's ego.

The expectations that players have of a virtual world's physics don't *have* to map directly onto reality, if the context is right. The most conspicuous example is that of a genre boasting its own physics: cartoons. In cartoons, when you run off a cliff you don't fall until you realize you ran off a cliff. The laws of nature do apply, just not in the same way[74]. As long as people buy into the fiction, this can work. *Toontown* can be as immersive as *EverQuest*.

The central issue for virtual physics is the level of detail at which it operates.

If I let go of an object, it will fall. That's gravity in action. When it hits the ground, will it bounce? Will it become damaged, perhaps break? Maybe the ground will break? What if the ground is at an angle? Will the object roll down it? That depends on the object's shape, its mass, what it's made of, what the ground is made of, and so on. If there's a wind, what effect will that have?

If there's an object between the one I drop and the ground, what then? Will it trap the object; will it let it pass through; will the object bounce off or out? I could drop apples into a wicker basket, but how many would fit before it becomes full? Even if it were full, I could still add sand to it, if not apples. Then I could add water, which would be retained for a short while, but would eventually trickle out. Maybe if I'd added cement dust as well as sand it would have set instead.

---

74. See *Cartoon Laws of Physics*, which exists in several versions.
   http://funnies.paco.to/cartoon.html and
   http://www.bbc.co.uk/dna/h2g2/alabaster/A645095.

That's just the start of it. The physics of a virtual world must address all kinds of issues that the real world implements trivially. How long does a feather dropped out of a window take to land? Why does my compass point north? What happens when I shine my flashlight at a mirror? How long does ice last? Who will get wet if I throw a bucket of water at a crowd? Can I dismantle a bookcase and use the pieces to make a raft? What if I set fire to a wooden house?

The real world can answer all these questions because that's how it works. It has molecules and atoms and atomic particles and quarks and who knows what else, all working together under the influence of at least four forces[75]. Virtual worlds can't hope to compete with real physics. Unfortunately, as the above examples illustrate, virtual worlds can't cope with naïve physics yet, either.

That said, the virtual worlds of today have access to greater computational resources than those of yesterday, and it's not unreasonable to suppose they could have *better* physics as a result. At a time when modeling tools are available to perform real-time ray-tracing, fluid mechanics, fabric deformation, and surface friction effects, it's a little sad that virtual worlds rarely bother to implement concepts even as simple as "if you drop this in water it will sink."

There are practical limits to what can be done. As detail increases, the number of active components increases and the number of interactions between them goes up exponentially[76]. Throwing more computers at the problem will not even dent it. That said, if *MUD2* can let you drop an object down a well into an underground stream which carries it off until it reaches a grate that may or may not trap it, all the while accounting for object density, impact damage, water damage, and the possibility of hitting or being caught by someone, then there's no reason a large-scale graphical virtual world couldn't do better. The trick is not to implement all of physics, or even all of a naïve physics, but to implement *just enough* naïve physics to satisfy players' sense of detail.

That's still harder than it sounds.

---

75. Gravity, electromagnetic, strong nuclear, weak nuclear. There may be others yet to be discovered.

76. As does the number of potential exploits.

Virtual worlds operate at the level of commands. Players decide what they want to do in terms of effectively indivisible operations, and these make up the command set. They want to wear a pair of boots, they don't want (for each boot) to loosen the laces, pull it on, tighten the laces, and then tie them in a double knot. Simple goals that in real life most people could achieve without really thinking should be implemented in virtual worlds as such. Believe it or not, for *MUD1* Roy and I actually discussed these things before deciding exactly where to pitch actions. That's why we went for "unlock door" rather than "put key in door; turn key; remove key from door." It's also why we made "lock" and "door" be synonymous nouns.

To implement physics, you only *really* need to go one conceptual level beyond that of the deepest command. Anything deeper than that, the players won't see anyway. If a character can shoot an arrow, the virtual world engine should be able to show its flight and make its arrival be non-instantaneous; however, this doesn't have to be done by applying Newton's Laws to parabolic trajectories—it just has to look like it was done that way.

There is an argument that a deeper physics model can be used if it's less complex than a shallower model or if several complex shallower models can be built from it[77]. For example, if you have a good Newtonian simulator already built to implement your virtual tennis games, you may as well reuse it for arrows. This is reasonable, assuming you really did need the simulator for the tennis. In practice, it's programmers rather than designers who are more susceptible to going too deep: You may have specified that characters' breath should be visible in cold air, but it's not you who's spending 10 days implementing a brilliant new eddy-calculation routine.

So to summarize:

- ➤ Compiled into players' heads is a sense of how the real world works.

- ➤ If the virtual world mimics this, it helps immersion tremendously.

- ➤ Players need rarely think beyond the level at which they can "just do" something.

- ➤ This is the level at which commands should be written.

---

77. A virtual world's physics can itself be regarded as a model for implementing higher-level effects. Consistency benefits from this: If you can get the physics to handle some set piece event, it's usually better than if you hard-code it separately.

➤ The physics usually needs to be constructed only at the next level beyond this.

➤ The problems come from the fact that in many cases the physics is not written even close to this next level, if indeed they're written at all.

This being the case, designers have only limited ways to respond. In worst-first order, these are

➤ *Brazen it out.* The virtual world has ponds; players can walk on the surfaces of the ponds; big deal.

➤ *Knee-jerk reaction.* Players can't walk into ponds, for no in-context reason.

➤ *Remove the symptoms.* Players can't walk into ponds because the vicious fish that live there keep them out. This provides an in-context reason, but it's invariably feeble.

➤ *Paper over the cracks.* There are no ponds in this virtual world.

➤ *Implement the physics.* Characters who walk into the pond can stand there with water coming up over their knees and wetting their clothes as expected.

Players' commands imply the virtual world's physics. In deciding the level of physics to implement, designers should therefore look at commands.

The Big Six

Surprisingly, there are only six categories of commands for virtual worlds, only half of which are in-context. Implement these and you have the makings of a basic virtual world. The big six are

➤ Exit the virtual world ("quit").

➤ Get playing instructions ("help").

➤ Make a note ("bug")[78].

➤ Communication ("tell," "say," "shout," "pose," and so on).

---

78. You could lump this under communication if you wanted, but I consider it to be more fundamental than that.

➤ Create/destroy object ("chop wood").

➤ State change (movement, "get," "drop," everything else).

Of these, the last one is the most important from the point of view of the virtual world's physics.

Tangible objects in virtual worlds have properties, which in turn have values. Properties can take many forms: "Mass" might be an integer; "label" might be a string; "location" might be a set of coordinates; "contents" might be a list of objects; "components" might be a treelike data structure. Some of these values may be independent; others may be recomputed each use because they depend on many factors (for example, resistance to magic).

State-change commands alter properties. A simple "get," for example, entails changing the location of an object from the floor to the character; movement involves changing the character's location property from one point to another; "open door" means changing the door's "opened" property to true.

It's more complicated than this in practice, of course. There are all manner of preconditions that need to be satisfied (objects can be too heavy to pick up, or tied down, or on fire, or being stood on, or plenty of other irritating things); there is feedback to be generated (you see the door open, as do people on the other side of it); the properties themselves can take different forms (location as coordinates or as a contains/contained-by hierarchy). From the designer's point of view, though, the actual mechanics aren't particularly important; of more interest is what can be done with them. This is because everything tangible except object creation/destruction can be done with them.

This means that the properties you choose set the level of player commands, which in turn set the level of the physics. If the properties are fine-grained (as they might be if you kept a record of how many roses were growing in a bush, say), then the commands that change these properties must also be fine-grained—therefore, the physics that underlies the commands must be slightly finer-grained yet (because it's what gives the properties their meanings). It makes no difference whether people use the commands frequently or infrequently; once you have that level of detail, you have to support it.

Similarly, by going the other way and having coarse-grained properties, you get coarse-grained commands. If flowers are properties of a garden rather than objects in their own right, characters can't ever do so much with them (which means less detailed work for your physics).

As for what level of detail to go with, that depends on both the virtual world and the real one. It depends on the virtual world because some contexts need finer-grained properties that others can do without. A murder mystery detective game, for example, would need many detailed properties for each object, because meticulousness is a feature of detection; a space opera game would be able to gloss over most such properties because it concerns the grander scale. However, in all cases real physics is absolute. Players will have certain expectations, which they will proceed to act on. If you encourage them to look deeply, they may look deeper than you can manage; if you encourage them to look only superficially, it may be too superficial to satisfy their natural curiosity.

All that designers can really do here is to put themselves in the position of the player. Imagine what the completed virtual world would look like, then consider what players would want to do in it. Create objects to this level, set properties for objects at this level, and specify commands that operate at this level. From that, you'll get your physics level.

I'll discuss properties of objects in more detail shortly[79]. For the moment, though, we'll keep with the basic underlying physical system and ask the question: What happens when you want to model something that's impossible in the real world?

Beyond Real-World Physics

Reality can cope with more detail than virtual worlds ever can because it has more resources. However, there are two cases where the scope of virtual world physics extends beyond what reality can offer.

---

79. To save you from getting your hopes up, I'll warn you now that I'm not going to present a list of common object properties. The point of this section, after all, is to persuade designers to think about virtual world physics from first principles for themselves.

The first of these is that the virtual world interacts physically with a meta-world (reality), whereas reality does not[80]. Players in the real world can become personae in the virtual world, therefore a virtual world can influence the real one through its players (and vice versa). The commands that best illustrate this are those concerned with communication. There are four types:

➤ *Within the world, within the fiction.* Commands based on real-world physics are implemented within the context of the virtual world. Examples: "shout," "say," "whisper," "pose"/"act"/"emote."

➤ *Within the world, without the fiction.* Commands in the virtual world have functionality beyond what's possible in the real. Examples: "tell," "mail," group channels.

➤ *Without the world, within the fiction.* Material that concerns what goes on in the virtual world is created in the real and presented in-context. Examples: newspapers, criers.

➤ *Without the world, without the fiction.* Material that concerns events in the virtual world is presented apart from it. Examples: IRC, email, rant sites.

The second example of where virtual physics can go beyond real physics is in the area of *ultraphysics*. This concerns things that people are prepared to accept as extensions to mundane physics, whether or not they're actually compatible with it. Examples include faster-than-light travel, psychic powers, cybertechnology, prayer, time travel, and (everyone's favorite) magic. None of these phenomena can be demonstrated today with any reliability, and for some it's unlikely they ever could be. However, sufficient numbers of players have an understanding of the tropes that it's possible to accommodate these ideas into virtual worlds. It's sometimes necessary to produce a fiction to indicate which of several sub-tropes a virtual world is adopting (does this magic work using mana, spell memory, gesture programming, or what?), the decision having been made for gameplay reasons. As long as it's something that fits into the players' naïve ultraphysics, though, it's acceptable to them.

---

80. Anything reality interacts with physically is by definition part of reality. Theologians and philosophers may argue that there are worlds beyond reality that can coincide with it, but that's not quite the same relationship that virtual worlds have with the real one: We can prove that virtual worlds are part of reality.

Any ultraphysics needs to be implemented with the same rigor as regular physics. Players will not flinch while telling you that vortex-breathing dragons are unrealistic, whereas fire-breathing ones aren't. In the same way that your virtual physics must adhere to players' naïve physics, your virtual ultraphysics must adhere to players' naïve ultraphysics. Ultraphysics is not as supportive of immersion as real physics, but jarred ultraphysics is every much as unsupportive of it as jarred real physics.

The level at which ultraphysics is implemented is determined by the commands that use it (as spells, through skills, using artifacts), which in turn depend on the same kind of properties as real physics. There is great scope for experiment here. Just because every other virtual world implements magic in terms of one-off, powerful spells, that doesn't mean you have to. Why can't mages cast spells as often as archers shoot arrows? Why can't spells have continuous, streaming effects, so you can direct your healing stream towards whoever needs it? Why can't magic take time to work, so you have to guess who'll need the effect when it finally hits? There are many dimensions along which changes can be made, all of which can be adapted into the vague notions that players have of the ultraphysics that deliver it. You cast a spell, a fireball appears; how you cast the spell and how the fireball appears is for the virtual world to determine—players don't care, so long as they get the fireball.

An awkward consequence of ultraphysics is that it doesn't mesh well with genres that are based on real physics. Fantasy books may be able to ignore the consequences that winged horses have on castle construction, but they don't have to deal with airborne cavalry units landing troops behind fortified walls and wreaking havoc. Player characters may take advantage of the inexpensive healing and curing facilities of temples, but if NPCs did then the world would be a very different place.

A final point to mention about ultraphysics is that it allows for hyperdimensionality. Graphical worlds are less capable of handling this than textual ones, because they have to present a view of the virtual world that's rendered in the real one. Textual worlds can have objects inside themselves, objects bigger inside than outside, sounds you can pick up, and so on. Graphical worlds can have some hyperdimensionalities that textual worlds traditionally find difficult (such as portable holes), but on the whole they're not as flexible.

Objects

The rule with objects in virtual worlds is *integrate everything*.

When a virtual world is implemented, the entities of which it is constructed are its *objects*. The relationships between these entities are their *properties*. Together, objects and properties comprise the tangible part of the virtual world, which the physics brings to life. It doesn't have to be this way—you could in theory devise a system where objects are mere consequences of interactions between fundamental equations in the same way that numbers are. If you try that, good luck.

It is essential for designers to recognize that although many objects in their virtual worlds have wildly different characteristics from many others, fundamentally they're the same. They can be arranged into conceptually useful groups—player characters, mobiles, containers, rooms, portable objects, fixed features, and so on—but it's a big mistake to treat these as unrelated, partitioned sets. You'll get much better coherence (and a much better understanding of your own world) if you consider them to be specializations of a general abstract object rather than the roots of their own abstract hierarchy.

For example, suppose you decide that your player characters should have a "health" attribute. It would be an obvious step to use this same property to record the health of mobiles. You might also want to give ordinary objects a "wear" rating to track how close they are to falling to pieces. It should then occur to you that "wear" is measuring the same kind of thing as "health," therefore you should use "health" rather than "wear".[81]

This may seem rather obvious, but all too often it's not[82]. In the early days, all MUD designers were also programmers, and it wasn't until they picked up on object-oriented programming language ideas that some of them were prepared to accept that hey, maybe rooms and player characters are just objects after all? This is somewhat ironic because it turns out that the objects of virtual worlds don't correspond well to the objects of an object-oriented programming language like C++. To explain why, I'll have to digress for a while (but I'll try to keep it short).

---

81. Just be sure that people don't get their wounds healed at a blacksmith's or get their swords resharpened by a healer.

82. There are still plenty of virtual worlds that consider dropping an object on the floor to be a completely different action to putting an object into a backpack.

In an object-oriented programming language, there is a hierarchy of object classes. Individual objects are instances of a class. Thus, you might say that doubloons are a kind of coin, coins are a kind of treasure, treasure is a kind of portable object, and portable objects are a kind of (root) object. Although I've used the word "object" here, in programming terms these would be classes. Doubloon33 might be an instance of the class "doubloon," which would make it an object. The power of object-oriented programming lies in its removal of repetitions: I don't have to define "get doubloon1," "get doubloon2," and so forth, I only need to define "get doubloon."

If objects can be instances of more than one class, or classes can be subclasses of more than one superclass, you have a *multiple-inheritance* system. Otherwise, it's a *single-inheritance* system. For virtual world design, a multiple-inheritance system is *highly* convenient. If a room contains a doubloon, a penny, and a Ming vase, then when I issue the command "get coin" I want to pick up the doubloon and the penny; if I try "get antique" then I want the doubloon and the vase. The doubloon is both a coin and an antique, but not all coins are antiques and not all antiques are coins. It's a common situation: Not all mammals are carnivores and not all carnivores are mammals; not all pop stars are men and not all men are pop stars. Is the queen of diamonds primarily a diamond or primarily a queen?

Unfortunately, programmers are likely to want to use C++ or some derivative (for example, Java) that only uses single inheritance. They'll see that there are "objects" in the virtual word, they'll tie these to the "objects" in their object-oriented system, and then 95% of the way through coding they'll hit difficulties. It's possible to fake multiple inheritance in a single-inheritance system, just as it's possible to fake single inheritance in a flat system. It's a lot of work and it involves a lot of repetition; it's still doable, though.

What isn't so doable is inheritance of commands. Object-oriented programming involves the association of items of code (called *methods*) to object classes. These are not themselves objects; they don't exist in an inheritance tree. In other words, I can't say that the method "punch" is a subclass of the method "hit." If I want 30 different ways to hit something, I have to implement them separately. If I want the effects to differ depending on whether the objects I hit are soft or hard, I have to repeat for each. For large or complex worlds, this can rapidly get insanely tedious both to implement and to maintain. Object-oriented programming is about removing mindless repetition, not about enforcing it.

This situation arises because the virtual world "objects" were a bad choice for the programming language "objects." Instead, *commands* should be the objects. If "hit object" and "hit soft_object" are defined as (object-oriented) classes, then a command like "slap cushion" is an instance of a command (in this case the second one), from which the associated code can be located and run. It's essentially a programming issue rather than a design one, but because of the heritage of virtual worlds it has made it into the design paradigm. Designers often think in terms of objects and methods when they should be thinking of multiple inheritance hierarchies and commands.

Okay, end of digression.

So, object classes in virtual worlds are generally arranged in some kind of hierarchy. This allows the sharing of properties, which encourages integration, which in turn delivers coherence. The days when you had to "ring bell" because "hit" was already taken by "hit creature" are gone[83].

If asked, most designers would probably subscribe to the idea that integration is good. Sadly, though, they often don't give it much thought. Spells and skills have much in common, for example—they're the ability to perform a specialized task to a particular standard, which has to be learned. Few virtual worlds consider them at all related, though. Similarly, what player characters might have as skills or spells, artifacts could have as effects or enchantments. If I can learn to cast a lightning bolt spell, then why can't a magical staff be taught to do it, too? This approach has been used in single-player role-playing games (for example, Larian Studios' *Divine Divinity*), but it's uncommon in virtual worlds.

Although much of this discussion on objects has concerned textual worlds, it applies equally well to graphical worlds. Graphical worlds are generally nowhere near as functionally rich as textual ones, but the gap is closing; sooner or later, the limits of using single inheritance for virtual object classes will become an issue. You can get 95% of the way without multiple inheritance and the ability to quantify over actions, but then that last 5% becomes important.

---

83. You noticed the sarcasm there?

Common Problems with Objects

Given that virtual objects are, on the whole, intended to exhibit behaviors at the physics level that are consistent with reality, it might be expected that there are common problems that recur whenever some particular aspect or other of reality is considered. This is indeed the case: Some facets of reality are easy to implement and others are downright impossible. Many of these issues arise because what human beings think of as an "object" is actually just a conceptual entity. It works for naïve physics, but naïve physics doesn't have to implement it.

There are conventions to solve some of these issues, but, as usual, it's better if designers understand *why* a convention is in place rather than merely accept that it *is* in place. Who knows, you might well be able to provide a better solution if you understand the issues.

Let's look at them, then.

Solids: Assemblies

Assemblies are objects that are made of other objects. Is an iron key magnetic? Yes. Is a hatchet? Well, the head is. What about a pair of jeans? Not really, unless you include the zip and the rivets (if they're steel rather than copper).

People think of objects as unitary items most of the time, but they're quite happy to consider them as being made up of other objects should the need arise. In virtual worlds, this poses something of a problem. If objects are made out of other objects, those objects must also be made out of other objects, and so on until you reach a point where you just *have* to stop. Where does that point lie? Conversely, if objects aren't made of other objects, how do you refer to components of an object? Doors must have keyholes if they have keys, right?

By convention, virtual worlds do not have assemblies. You can't take objects to pieces. If you need to refer to a part of an object, the part is synonymous with the object as a whole. When I can look through a keyhole, I'm looking through a door.

The reason that assemblies don't exist is, quite simply, that the physics to support the functionality isn't up to it. Properties are associated with objects, not with configurations of objects; if you were to associate properties with configurations of objects, those configurations would themselves effectively be objects.

For example, suppose in real life I had a wooden ladder. I can climb up a ladder. I can't climb up a xylophone. Nevertheless, I could dismantle my ladder and use the components to make a xylophone. I can play music on a xylophone, but I can't on a ladder. The xylophone assembly uses the same objects as the ladder assembly, but the two have very distinct properties.

Now it's possible to hack a solution to this. You could say that "dismantle ladder" or "dismantle xylophone" destroyed the original object and created two new objects, "poles" and "nails." You could then allow "make ladder from poles and nails" and "make xylophone from poles and nails." Unfortunately, unless you've thought of it in advance, the player who tries to "make fence from poles and nails" is going to be disappointed.

In the real world, objects are only objects because people say they are. It's just a semantic ploy to describe certain manifestations within reality. Indeed, objects don't even have to be real: "If I had a sister, her name would be Moira;" "Nobody followed me." People routinely refer to objects that don't exist, and not only in terms of counterfactuals or uninstantiated variables. Whatever your view on religions, you have to admit that Zeus, Jehovah, and Vishnu are mutually incompatible beings, yet to some people they are (or were, in Zeus's case) as real as rocks.

In virtual world terms, all objects *are* as real as rocks (or at least as virtual as virtual rocks). They exist because that's how players understand their environment. However, whereas people in the real world can call upon new objects when the muse takes them, in virtual worlds this can't happen. Objects only get the properties they're given; assemblies can't be granted arbitrary emergent properties depending on their construction. You can't invent objects, just new uses for existing objects.

Virtual worlds don't have assemblies because it only pushes the problem one degree away. At some stage, you have to stop. If you're going to have to stop anyway, why even start? Players will try to disassemble objects, fail, have their immersion hurt, then give up trying. If the precedent of assemblies has been established, they'll keep on trying because sometimes it works and sometimes it won't. Each failure will hit their faith in the simulation of reality.

However, taking the same line of reasoning that I did earlier with NPCs (that is, even rudimentary AI is better than none), it can be argued that any consistent-depth implementation of assemblies is better than none at all. An axe is made of a shaft and an axehead; an axehead is made of six pounds of iron; six pounds of iron is made of two three-pound pieces of iron melted together, and so on. By defining all objects to be constructed from other objects and a limited number of recognizable resource "atoms" (which break down into ever-smaller versions of themselves), assemblies can be implemented. Although not a perfect system (every object type needs a "recipe," so new objects can't be constructed unless a recipe for them exists), this is a definite improvement over no assembly at all: It allows for additional gameplay, and is even better in terms of the immersion it delivers.

Nevertheless, players who try to build a glider from sails and broken barrels are probably wasting their time.

Solids: Collections

Some objects are sets or collections of other objects. You might have a bunch of flowers, a pack of cards, or a wad of notes. Using a principle of no-disassembly, these should be unitary items. They all have problems with this, though.

A bunch of flowers is fine as long as you have no individual flowers anywhere. Put in a single rose, and suddenly you're accepting the concept of unbunched flowers. Players will therefore want to take flowers out of the bunch.

A pack of cards only exists when no one is playing a game with it. Because cards are meant to be played with, you can hardly blame people for wanting to deal out the pack. When that happens, suddenly there are 52 individual cards (plus jokers) and no pack. You only get a pack again when someone collects all the cards.

A wad of notes has critical value. Although you might want to allow players to pick up pebbles from a beach arbitrarily, you can't let them peel notes from a wad in that way or they'll be rich in no time. However, if you make each note in the wad an individual object, how do you refer to the wad? Can you split it in two and get two wads?

These problems arise because although players will think of objects at a particular level a lot of the time, for similar objects (in particular) they like to stack them together and treat them as an abstract whole. Designers must decide whether to allow non-functional assemblies like this, and, if so, how to handle them.

There are two ways, alluded to in the preceding paragraphs. The first is to enumerate all the objects that make up a collection, but report them as a collection based on the number held. If you have three playing cards in your inventory, they're shown separately; if you hold seven, they're shown as a "hand;" if you hold 52 (plus jokers) they're shown as a "pack." Similarly, if you have a rose and a tulip, you have a rose and a tulip; if you have a rose, a tulip, and a daffodil, you have a "bunch of flowers." The designer lays down the criteria for when individuals become (or cease to become) a collection.

The second way is to use a generator. There are so many flowers in the garden or nuts on the tree or locusts in the swarm that it's pointless enumerating them. If a player wants one, they can have one. There is effectively an infinite number. For these collections, a dispenser function creates a new instance each time the collection is taken from; when an instance returns (or collections merge) the incoming items are deleted and the collection remains as it was[84]. If a graphical world has a beach texture-mapped with pebbles, characters can pick them up this way. The texture map doesn't change, but the characters get an object they didn't have before.

Collections are used as shorthand for quantities of objects. It's possible (but not essential) to give them properties beyond what the individual objects have—for example, giving a set of collectible bubble gum cards a greater value than sum of the values of each individual card. Oh, and yes, every other designer in the world *has* thought of making collections of too many uranium chips invoke an atomic explosion.

Solids: Containers

Objects in virtual worlds can be in various hierarchies. The main one is the class hierarchy (*X* is a kind of *Y*), but other possibilities include an assembly hierarchy (*X* is a component of *Y*), a spatial hierarchy (*X* is on top of *Y*), and a container hierarchy (*X* is contained by *Y*). The latter two are related, as we're about to see.

Container hierarchies are useful because they give players physical means by which to move around groups of objects in a virtual world. They're not essential: In the same way that early computer operating systems didn't have the equivalent of subdirectories or folders, so some early virtual worlds (most notably *Shades*) didn't have containers.

---

84. Note that one false move by the programmers here and you get the duping bugs that are the bane of so many virtual worlds.

However, they're very useful. In a nodal implementation of a virtual world, the work is already done anyway: Rooms can contain characters, characters can carry (that is, "contain") objects, therefore, it's not a huge leap of the imagination to allow objects to contain other objects too.

Virtual worlds that use a coordinate system to handle location typically have to switch to a nodal system for containership. Although it's possible to extend the coordinate approach to allow objects to be carried around in backpacks and pockets and on belts and so on, in practice it's too inconvenient for the players. It's no fun for the programmers, either, having to lock arbitrary objects onto the coordinate frame of a character so that wherever the character moves, so do the objects. For this reason, most graphical virtual worlds maintain a separate inventory for containership, using a coordinate system only for the top level (which can more easily be displayed graphically).

Graphical worlds don't have a problem illustrating the spatial relationship between objects. You can see that the bottle is on the table, the chair is next to the table, the boots are under the table, and so on. This is because of the rigid spatial structure imposed by the coordinate system. Nodal systems do not have this underlying structure: If two objects are inside a room, that says nothing about the spatial relationship between the two. Even the connectional relationships between two adjacent rooms are not implied; they have to be stated explicitly. Some nodal virtual worlds—for example, those developed by Skotos—do have a relationship network between objects. However, without absolute coordinates it's hard to make deductions: If X is next to Y and Y is next to Z, is X next to Z? Coordinate systems have this problem too, of course, when it comes to modeling the contents of containers. Fortunately, most players don't care to think beyond "X is in the bag"—they're not really worried about *where* in the bag, so long as it doesn't move around and they can get at it when they want it.

Containers are usually limited in what they can contain. They'll hold only a certain volume (or number) of objects. Sometimes only objects below certain dimensions will go in (you can't put a table spoon inside a beer bottle) and sometimes only objects above certain dimensions will stay in (you can't store pencils in a net bag). The containers may be rigid or soft, opaque or transparent, closable or always open—the same kind of properties you get for many other objects. There are some particular issues that containers have which don't affect other objects, however.

Most containers are *endocontainers*, in that they contain things inside them. Chests, bags, bowls, baskets—they all enclose what they contain. There is also, however, a smaller class of *exocontainers*; these contain other things outside them. Music stands, hat racks, and Christmas trees are examples of exocontainers. Exocontainers "wear" what they hold.

Some virtual worlds treat exocontainers and endocontainers as totally distinct, on the grounds that holding by enclosure is fundamentally different to holding by hooking or tying or anything else. The concepts are indeed disjoint, of course, but there is enough commonality that it's generally better to treat them as the same thing. "Take music from stand" and "take stand from case" are essentially the same action and can be implemented using much the same functionality.

The key differences are in two areas.

Firstly, although the contents of an opaque endocontainer can be concealed from prying eyes, you always see what an exocontainer is holding. This isn't too bad for textual worlds, but graphical worlds need to be able to construct animated images to match the almost arbitrary clothing permutations that players will try, which can be very tricky[85].

Secondly, for endocontainers, the containers protect their contents. If you hit an endo-container, the amount of damage suffered by what's inside may be reduced. For exo-containers, the reverse applies: The damage suffered by the container may be reduced because it's absorbed by what the exocontainer is holding. This is how armor works.

This brings up the subject of a very special endocontainer: the player's own character. In Fantasy worlds in particular, things the character carries or wears are position-sensitive. You don't put helmets on your arms, you don't put boots on your chest. Graphical and textual virtual worlds both have problems with this.

Graphical worlds have adopted a standard from single-player computer role-playing games, whereby an image of the character is displayed with the "slots" (usually) indi-cated, and players dress it up paper doll style[86]. Although not exactly immersive, it's in keeping with the way that the inventory in general works. Textual worlds have more to

---

85. Even in two dimensions it's tricky. KiSS dolls (Kisekae Set System—digital dress-up-dolls for your computer) regularly have problems with things like flouncy shirts that stick out through jackets worn over them.

86. This is KiSS dolls again. Check out `http://otakuworld.com/kiss/` to learn more about KiSS. Warning: Kids love these things.

worry about because players want to refer to body parts. It's okay to have "wear socks," "wear cravat," and so on, but players want "wear ring on left index finger." This implies that bodies should be treated as assemblies. They're not assemblies that players will typically want to dismember in a controlled fashion, and, except for in Horror genres, people aren't going to care to reassemble new bodies from parts, either. Nevertheless, if players want to reference parts of an assembly then the assembly has to be constructed or faked up; either way, it's very tiresome to implement and clues players in to the fact that assemblies are possible. First it's bodies, then suits of armor, then horses, then carts—before you know it, you've gone way further than you ever wanted and it's starting to have an impact on response times. If you do decide to implement bodies, make the decision then and there whether or not it's a one-off, and stick to it. You won't be swayed, you have a will of iron....

What about books, then? Books contain pages, but those pages are fixed in a certain order, so they're basically assemblies. If someone wants to "read page 24" are you going to let them? Or are you going to keep your books really short, so they only ever have one page?

It can be very tempting to turn a container into an assembly. Be careful.

Turning containers into generators is also tempting, but much less dangerous. A bag of nuts that always has nuts in it no matter how many you take out is fine, as long as you don't let anyone turn it inside out. A coat rack in a shop can have a fixed number of coats hanging from it, each of which is created using a lazy evaluation approach (that is, only when someone tries to access a coat is one created).

The final thing to mention about containers is the notion of *encumbrance.* This is an old (some would say dated) idea from table-top role-playing games. In general, the weight of objects that a container[87] can contain depends on its strength; the number it will hold depends on the dimensions of the container and of the objects concerned (although for exocontainers it also will involve some measure of viable contact points—that is, the container's dexterity). However, objects are often so awkward that they slow you down much more than others of a similar weight or shape would. An open umbrella is harder to handle than a closed one; a helium balloon gets in the way more than a soccer ball (both of which are easier to keep a hold of if they're deflated).

---

87. Because they're exocontainers, this includes characters. It's object-oriented programming in action.

The idea behind encumbrance is to quantify how much something affects the attributes of its container by virtue of its own attributes. It's an imperfect abstraction, but at times it can be a useful one. Even a virtual world that stored the exact dimensions of objects would still have to approximate some computationally expensive calculations—for example, knapsack-packing problems (emptying a full knapsack, then getting all that was in it back inside is non-trivial—it's like doing a 3D jigsaw puzzle).

Fluids: Divisibility

Most objects in virtual worlds are solids, and that's how they're implemented. However, when modeling the real world it's a little hard to avoid the presence of fluids, especially water[88]. I use the term "fluids" rather than "liquids" in order not to exclude those solids that (in naïve physics) act like liquids, such as sand, ash, and flour; I also mean it to discount substances like glass that are formally liquids but on human timescales act mainly like solids.

The central problem with fluids is that they're indefinitely divisible. You can split them apart and combine them arbitrarily[89]. If someone has a bottle of water and a glass, they should be able to fill the glass with water and have the excess remain in the bottle. This can be faked by giving all fluid-tight containers a pair of properties to indicate what fluid they have in them and how much, or it can be implemented "properly" by creating separate objects for each chunk of fluid that have their volume as a property tied to them. The latter is generally preferable because it means that fluids can be referenced and that they can exist independently of containers (for example, if you tip them out onto the ground). Tiresome players may create thousands of fluid objects by decanting from a large container into a tiny one many times, but so long as you're aware of this possibility it shouldn't be hard to prevent it from causing problems.

Beyond a certain size, large bodies of fluid can be regarded as generators. You can take as much saltwater as you want from the ocean, there'll always be plenty left. In practice, the amounts of fluid that can be used as generators can be much smaller; a beach has an inexhaustible supply of sand, and even ponds and private swimming pools can

---

88. Potions and ale are commonplace, too.

89. Assembly "atoms" can be split apart, too, but combining them takes more effort.

be considered effectively always full. Because virtual worlds aren't real, it's even possible to have small containers generate infinite amounts of a fluid[90].

There are potential difficulties when fluid is tipped out of a container into the environment. It's not a problem if there's already a fluid on the surface, as a large body of any fluid can safely be assumed to absorb (or otherwise disperse) any chunk of fluid added to it. Emptying oil into a (virtual) freshwater lake just destroys the oil no matter how often a player does it.

When the surface does not already have a fluid on it, that's another matter. On a smooth surface the fluid may flow away downhill, whereas on a rough one it could form pools or puddles; for a rocky surface or a boardwalk it could disappear immediately between cracks; for dry earth it could simply be absorbed. What actually happens depends on the surface and the fluid. At the very least, it implies that all surface types need to be classified so that the physics can determine what to do.

The final divisibility issue concerns leaks. Leaks can be regarded as loss to volume that occurs over time. Although in real life a fluid that seeps from a leaky container can leave a trail, this is quite hard to implement in practice. In general, if a bucket has a hole in it then all this means is that the amount of fluid it contains will lessen at a constant rate until there's none left. It doesn't mean you can fill the bucket with sand and try to write your name on a field.

Miscibility

Immiscible fluids pose few problems. If you have a pint jug containing half a pint of sand, you can top it up with water. Although in real life you'd be able to get more than half a pint of water in (because sand is a fluid, but not a liquid), in practice you're not going to upset many players if you keep it to exactly half a pint. The same applies to adding fluids to containers that already hold solids: You may as well compute volumes assuming that none of the solid objects float, because even if you account for partial displacement you'll never get it sufficiently accurate to satisfy anyone pedantic enough to check anyway. Immiscible fluids are implementation-friendly. Miscible fluids are implementation-unfriendly.

---

90. As in the joke where a man gets three wishes from a genie. On his first wish he asks for a neverending bottle of beer. The genie obliges, and the man drinks enough from it to satisfy himself that it works. The genie asks him what his other wishes are. "I'll have another two of these please," he replies.

If you have half a pint of alcohol and add half a pint of water to it, what you get is a pint[91] of weaker alcohol. If you added water to poison, you'd get a larger amount of weaker poison. If you added poison to alcohol you'd get something that was half toxic and half intoxicating. Mixing fluids involves mixing properties of fluids. This wouldn't be so bad if it weren't for chemistry[92].

By default, all solids are immiscible with liquids. However, some solids are affected by fluids in a major way. You might be able to package sugar in a paper container, but water would rapidly disintegrate it. The result of the exercise would be water and sludge, neither of which has the properties that a paper bag has. With fluids, you can add an acid to an alkali and get salt and water; neither the salt nor the water has any of the corrosive properties of acids or alkalis. Thus, mixing fluids can involve not only the creation and destruction of objects, but also the creation and destruction of properties of objects.

The keener designers among you might at this point be envisaging a nice chemistry system with a wide range of properties that fluids can have and a series of rules that govern how two or more properties combine to create other properties from the list. This could actually work quite well, and explorers would certainly thank you for it. Whether it's worth the effort involved when you could be doing something else is another issue, of course, and the fact that the recipes for anything that can be brewed will be on player web sites within days might take some of the fun out of it. If you have the time, though, hey, go for it!

One final point about liquids is that viscosity can be a pain. Apples and honey are immiscible, but if you dunk an apple in honey and take it out you'll end up with a lot of honey stuck to the apple. Whether or not you want to make the apple a leaky exo-container for the honey is up to you, but either way be sure you cover the inevitable player experiments that will result ("How come honey drips off kittens at the same rate that it drips off apples? Surely the fur would retain…").

---

91. Well, 98% of a pint if you want to be finicky about it.

92. Chemistry is part of real-world physics; alchemy is the ultraphysics equivalent.

Gases

Virtual worlds rarely implement gases, and when they do it's often as consequent properties of a location or some other object, rather than as objects in their own right.

The reasons for this are to do with the physical properties of gases (and of gas-borne particles, such as pollen and smoke). Gases are everywhere, they have miscibility and divisibility issues even worse than those of liquids, and they're hard to contain. Characters can do simple things like breathe them and smell them, but anything much more sophisticated entails capturing the gases, which then renders them inaccessible without the right apparatus. Some virtual worlds have gases dropped by certain monsters on death, but the result is rather clunky.

Air (or atmosphere) can conveniently be regarded as a generator object that's available to all locations and containers. Sometimes, though, it's useful to represent chunks of gases with unusual properties as separate objects. This allows for gusts of winds, clouds of dust, explosions, temperature gradients, swarms of tiny insects, foul stenches, and so on.

On the whole, though, the only gas that virtual worlds really need to consider is air, and then only for completion. Graphical worlds don't need even air[93]—it's "what there is when there's nothing else there"—but textual worlds should account for it because players in that context reference objects by name, rather than by pointing device.

Plasmas

In most virtual worlds, the only significant plasma is fire. Fires are usually treated as individual objects, but not always entirely realistically. It's easy enough to model them to emit virtual heat and light, but the problem is that in real life fires spread. In virtual worlds, they don't. You can set fire to combustible materials and they'll burn; they may even ignite nearby objects. However, they won't usually spread to the environment.

There are two reasons for this. The defining one is that it's very hard to do! Fires are transforming events: If you drop a lit match in dry grasslands, you transform it into a charred landscape; trees are replaced by blackened stumps, buildings are empty shells, and everywhere is bereft of life. Predicting the collapse of structures when arbitrary parts of them burn away is very difficult.

---

93. Fog and distance haze, on the other hand....

The second reason is that even if out-of-control fires could be modeled, it would be unwise to have them. Half of all real-world property fires are due to arson, and the temptation to destroy a virtual world that way would be irresistible. Even players who weren't crazed vandals might try it out just the once. "Gee, do you think I'd get experience points for killing 200 bears if I set fire to the woods?"

State Changes

When you heat up water, it turns into a gas (steam); when you freeze it, it turns into a solid (ice). Similarly, gases can condense and solids can melt. These are state changes. Do you want them in your virtual world?

A virtual world can be satisfyingly convincing without state changes. If you don't have any way to heat up things or cool them down, explorers might figure out why and get uppity but most of the population will take it in their stride.

On the other hand, state changes aren't all that hard to implement and can impress the players. It can be done quite easily as a destruction/creation pair: Destroy the steam, create the water; destroy the lava, create the rock. In real life, state transitions take energy to effect (it's how refrigerators work), but in virtual worlds where people don't have accurate thermometers there's no need to worry about it.

Properties

Properties are abstractions of objects' physical characteristics. In virtual worlds, this regularly extends to non-physical properties as we shall shortly see, but it's the physical ones (mass, density, shape, color, and so on) that dominate.

Properties are often implemented as functions, so that rarely used ones can be computed on a when-needed basis. However, although properties don't change any values when they are called, functions in general do: Checking the "diameter" property of a balloon won't change its diameter[94], yet calling the "inflate" function on the balloon might. In terms of implementation, though, they can look the same.

Properties have an uneasy relationship with object classes. Does a dropped bottle shatter because as a bottle it's a subclass of "fragile objects"? Or does it shatter because it inherits a high-value "fragile" property? How much encapsulation do you need?

---

94. Naïve physics doesn't have an uncertainty principle.

Perhaps it shatters because it has a "made of" property with value "glass," and glass has a high-value "fragile" property?

Creating a taxonomy that allows the physics to be implemented but doesn't turn designers into programmers is a tricky area (made all the worse because many designers started out as programmers). Strictly speaking, it isn't a naïve physics problem, but an issue of representation.

Unfortunately, there aren't really any conventions at work here (yet). You just do what you have to for your physics to work. All I would recommend is that you allow for properties to be objects (in the object-oriented sense) too, so you can quantify over them. If you can get the virtual world engine to answer the question "give me a list of all the properties of this object and their associated values," then that should be flexibility enough.

As an aside, lists of existing properties are very useful to have around when you're looking for new ways to discriminate between objects. "What should this magic shield do apart from add the usual protection bonus? Hmm, characters have properties for height, mass, speed, hmm…eye color, hirsuteness—hey, I could make them hairy if they used the shield! That could really freak people out. I'll make it a dwarfen shield because dwarfs value beards, females included, and…."

In an ideal world, could all functionality of objects be derived from their properties? Yes—in an ideal world. You could see that an object has a hard, thin, flat, robust, semi-sharp surface attached to a long, strong, lightweight but not brittle second component topped by a horizontal bar, and from that deduce that the object was suitable for digging a hole in a lawn. Virtual worlds are non-ideal, because this degree of functionality deduction would overwhelm them. Being non-ideal worlds, you can dig a hole with a spade because the "dig" action knows about spades (and maybe shovels and pickaxes). Beyond that, you can't make a spade out of a busted shield and a fence post.

So sorry fans of assemblies: You're unlikely to get them this way soon, either.

Ownership

It may seem odd to include a subsection on ownership when discussing physics, but (as pointed out in Chapter 3) ownership can be considered a physical quality for virtual worlds. Note that this is virtual ownership—that is, ownership within the context of the virtual world; real-world ownership of virtual objects is all about data and intellectual property (as is much else about virtual worlds).

There are two ways to implement ownership. The first is to give all objects an "owned by" property, which can be either empty (for example, no one owns characters) or point to some ownership-capable object (for example, a character, a guild). The second is to make it implicit: You own whatever you carry. The latter works for virtual worlds with low degrees of persistence. The former would be preferred for ones with higher persistence, except that it gets horribly complicated; they therefore extend the "possession is nine tenths of the law" concept to stuff stored on player-owned property, but don't track who owns individual objects in general.

At this point, you may be wondering why not. Computers are very good at bookkeeping tasks, and this is just bookkeeping, right?

Right, but the problem lies with formulating the rules.

Suppose character *A* owns a bottle of champagne and character *B* owns a bottle of orange juice. They both put their bottles on the ground; they still own them. I pick up the bottles; they still own them, and I'm a thief. I empty the contents of the bottles into a bowl and mix them up; who owns what now? I probably don't own it, but does character *A* or character *B*? Most of it may be character *B*'s by volume, but character *A*'s by value.

This same sort of tracking problem arises for components of assemblies and collections. If I steal five units of currency from each of five players, then lose 18 UOC in a bet, who can lay claim to the 7 UOC that I have left?

The simple "if I hold it, I own it" rule doesn't work universally, either. When your character picks up an object, it usually goes into a container; this will typically be some kind of backpack[95]. However, it could be a hand or a sack or…well, let's see what it could be.

Solid objects in virtual worlds will usually fit into one of the following abstract categories:

95. In most graphical virtual worlds, the invisible kind.

➤ Things that can be worn (for example, a hat)

➤ Things that can be carried by an individual (for example, a book)

➤ Things that can be carried by several people (for example, a bench)

➤ Things that can be moved but not picked up (for example, a cart)

➤ Things that can move of their own accord (for example, a horse)

➤ Things that are immobile (for example, land)

➤ Things that can appear to be carried without actually being carried (for example, coins)

I can wear a hat or carry a book and be certain that it is mine. If I buy a bench and want to move it, though, how can I be sure it'll remain mine? What about a horse or cart? As with land, some things *do* need to have their ownership tracked, like it or not.

Even tracking isn't always the answer, though. If I steal a sword and sell it for gold, does the new owner have to hand it back to the original owner? If not, great: I'll have my mule do the stealing and my main character do the buying. If so, also great: I'll have my mule steal the sword and sell it to someone else, then give the newly laundered coin to my main character. In either case, the location of the original sword is known, but the person who stole it is likely to get away with the theft (at least as far as the virtual world is concerned—the players may have other ideas).

Here come the virtual lawyers....

Time

Time is the one dimension that players and characters both share, and therefore it is completely beholden to reality. This does not mean that it has to be identical to real time, but it does mean that it must directly map to it.

Most actions that take place in virtual worlds are pretty well instant (lag permitting). Because of the way that people often routinely regard complex series of actions as unitary commands, there may occasionally be commands that take time to execute (cooking a meal, for example). Also, naïve physics can sometimes call for the effects of a command to take place after the action has been executed (such as the explosion that follows from lighting a fuse). As we saw with fire, some commands can have potentially chaotic effects that last potentially indefinitely. Most commands, though, give an immediate response and do not propagate except in strictly prescribed ways (typically, by giving feedback to characters who can detect the effects of the command).

One consequence of this, which is felt particularly hard in nodal implementations of virtual worlds, is that travel is much faster than it "ought" to be. The time it takes to climb a staircase can be the time it takes to pass through a forest. Speed is measured in nodes per second, which, as nodes don't necessarily conform to a fixed ground scale, makes a mockery of Newton's laws of motion. Fortunately, players aren't spooked by this; as long as travel between two locations that are conceptually "distant" takes longer than travel between two that are "near," they'll let it ride. It will be noticed, though.

In graphical virtual worlds, where speed can be measured using the traditional units of ground covered per second, travel can't be so fast or it would look ridiculous. However, this degree of realism can brutally shrink a world. In the time it takes a character to jog across a "continent" in *EverQuest*, a real-world marathon runner could perhaps traverse Singapore. Think of the map of Norrath transposed onto the tip of Malaysia and suddenly it doesn't seem all that huge.

Virtual worlds may be tied to real time, but they don't have to use it. In some (particularly low-persistence ones), it's always effectively the same time—the clocks may change, but there's no night and day. Others take an accelerated, linear approach: DikuMUDs usually map 30 minutes of real time to 24 hours in the game world. A more player-friendly strategy is to do it non-linearly, so that time at night (when NPCs are asleep) passes quicker than time during the day (when there's more content at large). The number of hours in a virtual day and the number of virtual days in a virtual week, month, or year may vary, but usually there'll be 60 minutes in an hour and 60 seconds in a minute (if time divisions go that low). Whether or not years increment depends on the context: If a virtual world set in the 1920s ran at DikuMUD time, the whole decade wouldn't last 11 real-world weeks. Seasons can have a gameplay use, but years rarely do (what, you want characters to get older?!). Virtual worlds with story arcs are a principled exception.

Some virtual worlds add seasonal content related to real-world time. *MUD1* had a supply of festive mobiles and objects for Christmas, for example, and *MUD2* added more for Easter, Halloween, April Fool's Day, Bonfire Night (November 5th—it's a U.K. thing), and March (there's a mad hare). *Ultima Online* introduced the idea into graphical worlds. Although in theory (and occasionally in practice) these are immersion-breaking, on the whole they're popular with players as they give a sense of permanence; the very fact that a virtual world *has* seasonal content shows that it's there for the long haul. Some meager fiction, such as having a "night of the dead" coinciding with real-world October 31st, can provide any necessary cover. It only works for worlds that don't have their own internal time, though. Celebrating Christmas in a world where it's officially Spring is going to seem bizarre; similarly, if virtual Christmas trees appear fully decorated in real July there won't be many players in the mood. There are other issues of concern, to do with the religious nature of some of these ceremonies; these are discussed in Chapter 8.

Night and day: What's the difference? High-permanence virtual worlds need to take a position on the subject; in any outdoor setting based on the real world, night and day are hard to ignore, but in general, one is going to be more fun for the players than the other. A strict implementation would have most NPCs asleep at night and a different set of monsters awake. This provides gameplay differences between the two that can make life more interesting for the players (but of course involves the creation of more content—expensive). As for the more physical differences, well the most obvious one is that it's darker at night[96]. There are two ways to handle this: by plunging the virtual world into gameplay-changing darkness; by making the virtual world suggest darkness without actually being dark (for example, use a blue wash). Full darkness is probably going to be implemented anyway for expeditions underground, so there are no real practical incentives not to make night as dimly lit as in reality. The reason many virtual worlds go for a cosmetic night that looks more like dusk is because it's less unfriendly for newbies that way (it's either that or give them a soon-to-be-mislaid lantern). Graphical worlds also have issues concerning the ability of various video cards to display images with low light levels—what might easily be visible to some players could remain totally unseen by others.

---

96. The second most obvious, that it's colder, is rarely considered. Night in virtual worlds is primarily about darkness.

The final point to make about time in virtual worlds concerns traveling through it. All characters do travel through it, of course, in the same direction and at a rate related to real time. They could, if content were available, all travel backward in time or forward at a faster rate (relative to real time). However, time travel for an individual character is not possible: One character can't go back to yesterday because for the other characters it's today[97]. Sealed time discontinuities are possible—you can put a character in a mock-up of yesterday and tell them it's yesterday—but interaction is limited. If a character "goes back in time" and shuts a door, this can only have consequences for a player in "today" under exact, predefined conditions. Time travel on a global scale—that is, everyone in the virtual world together—is possible[98]; on a local scale, though, it's no more possible in the virtual world than it is the real one.

Proactive Physics

People who play in a virtual world are bound by that world's physics, as implemented in computer code. Whatever tangible action they undertake in the virtual world, the consequences of that action are defined by the program. Players must accept this as part of the world, just as they must accept real-world physics in the real world. They may object to certain aspects of it, and they may even be able to persuade the live team to make changes, but they can't opt out of particular rules they don't like. If they get annoyed by the fact that their magic sword will eventually wear out, they can either continue under protest or quit.

Proactive physics uses this aggressively. Let's say you didn't want players to sell virtual objects to each other in the real world. You could give all objects a "sold on eBay" flag that was set (either manually or automatically) whenever an object was exchanged in this manner. Objects so flagged would wear out faster than unsold objects. Players who complain can be told that objects wear out anyway depending on how they're used, and that being sold in a different world (the real one) puts interdimensional stresses on them that reduce their integrity. There would still be lawsuits from people who felt this

---

97. Actually, some virtual worlds do let individual characters roll back to some earlier state without affecting anyone else. I'm sure the designers of these worlds believe they have a perfectly good reason for sanctioning such acts of desperation.

98. It can be fun, too. If you tell players in advance that there will be a time slip (save the database, let people play for an hour, then restore the saved version) they will show up in droves to take advantage of the temporary freedom from consequences offered.

unfair, and they may be able to make some argument about the intent (which is essentially the difference between normal and proactive physics); a consistent fiction is a strong defense, though.

Personally, I'm against using virtual-world physics to achieve real-world ends in this way except when it enhances individual freedom. That said, I'm very much of the opinion that all code and data belongs exclusively to the developers to do with as they wish. Virtual worlds are not tools like word processors, which folk use to create data that they own; virtual worlds are places that people visit. If you come to my house and use my paints on my paper to create an artwork, I'm sorry but you don't own that artwork and you don't get to sell it to someone else unless I say so.

Whatever deals players strike between themselves about rights of access to virtual entities, they don't concern virtual ownership unless the developers say so. If players don't like that, they can either quit and play in a virtual world where the developers cede data ownership to players (and hope that the real-world laws governing the changing of that virtual data are cast-iron) or they can set up and run their own virtual world.

The discussion in Chapter 3 about the rights of players and characters assumes good faith on the part of developers. Proactive physics can be an extension of this, but designers must be very careful not to set the wrong precedent. If a player uses the virtual world's physics to make life tough for other players, the exploit can be fixed and the perpetrator banned; if the live team does it, only revolt or emigration can ensue.

Reset Strategy

Players consume content quicker than it can be produced[99]. To prevent a virtual world from becoming "played out," therefore, some mechanism for reintroducing content must be installed—the *reset strategy* of the virtual world. There are two basic approaches: *sudden* and *rolling*.

In a sudden reset, the region to be reset (usually the entire virtual world) is closed down and its content reinitialized. This is a fairly quick procedure, but it can be very

---

99. This is not necessarily true of the virtual worlds of the future, in which content may arise from player actions rather than being introduced by designers, but it's true for virtual worlds of the present.

inconvenient for players who enter the virtual world at the wrong time or for players who are in the middle of doing something when the reset occurs. The sudden reset strategy is sometimes referred to as the *Groundhog Day* approach, because players relive the same day repeatedly, as in the movie *Groundhog Day*[100].

In a rolling reset, content is returned piecemeal at a rate roughly equivalent to that at which it is consumed. There is no need for the virtual world to be closed down. Rolling resets as a concept emerged in the second age of virtual worlds, the original idea being to use a "watched pot never boils" system whereby content was slipped in where players weren't looking (so as to conserve the fiction). This is rarely practiced today, however; indeed, in many virtual worlds players rely on being able to show up at the appointed place and time so they can have a crack at a monster[101]. Besides, in a large-scale virtual world, the high probability that individual griefers would stake out a reset site just to stop it from resetting rules the idea out. When rolling-reset content resets, it usually involves only a simple adjustment such as the introduction of monsters or objects; in this context, it's usually referred to as *spawning* (or *respawning*).

Sudden resets allow for much more complex content than rolling resets. Multi-stage puzzles in particular are notoriously difficult to reset in isolation. If a dam has burst and flooded a valley, putting back the water is a problem (more so if people are sailing on it) and so is restoring everything that was destroyed (except for what would have been destroyed but someone moved it first). Sometimes, events have such all-conquering effects that they impinge on all aspects of a virtual world and simply cannot be reset unless the whole world is reset. Thus, a rolling reset strategy is not going to be of any use in this situation. That said, rolling resets are more accessible—players can "drop in, drop out" better—and they are able to support[102] much higher degrees of persistence.

Sudden resets interfere with playing patterns more than rolling resets. Players who are present at the start of a reset will often stay for the whole period as they'll have been able to kit themselves up; players who arrive later may decide that the best content is

---

100. Danny Rubin (writer) and Harold Ramis (writer and director), *Groundhog Day*. USA, Columbia Pictures, 1993.

101. Although these players consider camping for monster appearances to be "adventuring," actually it's more like "farming."

102. If the code is robust enough not to crash every few hours; it's as well that some sudden-reset virtual worlds do shut down periodically or they'd do it of their own accord anyway.

accounted for and leave; late-comers will consider sitting around chatting until the reset occurs, whereupon they'll start playing in earnest. For rolling resets, session stickiness doesn't depend on time of arrival anywhere near as much.

Both sudden and rolling resets are anti-immersion. With a sudden reset, you get a huge dose of reality, but it doesn't last long; with rolling resets, you get smaller reminders of reality, but they drip, drip, drip the whole time.

Within the context of a sudden or rolling reset there are four main strategies in use to determine when and what resets:

➤ Fixed

➤ Contextual

➤ Requested

➤ Geographical

A *fixed reset* occurs after a set time period has elapsed. This is popular for virtual worlds using a sudden-reset approach, as it gives players fair warning of when they'll be kicked off. It's also popular for rolling-reset worlds, because spawn-on-timer is very easy to implement and achievers[103] like it.

A *contextual reset* is more sophisticated in that it has metrics to indicate when content is played out; these can then be used to trigger a reset. In practice, though, even with quite large differences in player flow a fixed reset is usually quite sufficient for most situations; virtual worlds using a wholly contextual reset strategy are therefore uncommon, although the occasional spawn-on-completion or spawn-on-character-properties isn't so unusual.

The *requested reset* approach passes control of resets over to players. It's commonly used in conjunction with other reset strategies, although *MUD1* used it basically standalone. In a sudden-reset environment, resetting is mainly the preserve of administrators; where regular players are allowed to do it, there's a vote first. In rolling-reset worlds it's less of an issue: Players wanting to recycle content (especially bespoke content) for their own characters' use will often have a quest system at their disposal for

---

103. Especially ones who have no desire to become further immersed.

this purpose. Although communication with NPCs is the preferred method, spawn-on-character-action is by no means limited to it; there's good scope for creativity here.

Geographical resets are mini sudden resets. Rather than a particular piece of content being identified as needing a reset, all content associated with a location is reset instead. This allows for slightly more complex content in a rolling-reset world, but in sudden reset worlds merely delays the inevitable. The location that is reset can be as small as a point, although it's more common to do it by area or region (faking an ecosystem—that is, spawn-by-world-properties). Smaller geographical resets are often spawn-on-proximity, a character's presence close to an area triggering the content introduction.

Chapter 5

Life in the Virtual World

Players are real people who enter virtual worlds through the instrument of their characters. Chapter 3, "Players," looked at players and Chapter 4, "World Design," looked at the world. This chapter looks at where they meet: characters.

Advancement

Players advance in intangible ways, through the knowledge they gain and the friends they make. Characters also can develop intangibly to some degree, in that they exist partially in the minds of the players who encounter them. However, characters are primarily a tangible phenomenon: They are defined by code and data. The virtual world determines what they can and cannot do and how mobiles react to them. When a character "improves," the improvement is measured in terms of tangible factors rather than intangible ones.

Characters don't *have* to advance, of course; for non-game worlds, the aim is often for players to gain or hone skills, therefore the success or otherwise of a character is entirely dependent on what players learn and how they apply this knowledge. Still, though, it's often the case that players will respond better if there is a reward in the form of some tangible improvement to their character, even if it's of only metaphorical significance.

For those that do offer advancement, there are basically two approaches: single or multiple. In a *single advancement* system, one process completely dominates; in a *multiple advancement* system, characters can improve along several dimensions. At first glance, it looks like no contest: Why would you want single advancement when multiple advancement offers so much choice?

There are two reasons why. Firstly, single advancement is focused and unambiguous. Players know what they have to do, and can therefore set about doing it. In a multiple advancement system, players might have to make choices before being fully informed; they may therefore make mistakes. The second reason is that multiple advancement suggests multiple content, which is more expensive to produce and harder to balance.

As an example, consider a hypothetical virtual world set in *Three Musketeers*[1] France. In a multiple advancement system, characters can acquire "military points," "romance points," "politics points," and "fame points." Thus, they can concentrate on acquiring points of a particular kind to advance their careers. If more people want to pursue one career than there is content to support, new content must be added for it (and the content that already exists for other careers will be relatively underused). Players who start their characters off collecting military points only to find that the romance approach suits them better will feel that their time has been wasted. A single advancement system, where characters collect "social points" that are an abstraction of the other four, would allow characters to switch focus without suffering, and if content of one type was running low they could overflow into another until the first recovered.

Multiple advancement wins out when advancement involves different mechanisms. If military rank depended on campaign experience and political rank depended on electoral influence, the two could not be reconciled so easily.

Virtual worlds measure advancement in terms of advantageous changes to tangible data. In considering advancement, it therefore makes sense to begin by looking at what can be advanced.

---

1. Alexandre Dumas, *Les Trois Mousquetaires*. Paris, *Le Siècle*, March–July 1844. Full text available online (in English) at `ftp://sailor.gutenberg.org/pub/gutenberg/etext98/1musk10.txt`.

Attributes

Attributes are the fundamental properties that define a character. Because they are tangible, they should properly only rate physical qualities, such as the character's strength and manual dexterity. However, under the influence of table-top role-playing games they often include non-physical concepts, such as intelligence and wisdom. This just about makes sense to a hard role-player, who can work with "My character is stupid," but it has its limits: "My character is a genius" would for most players entail pretending to be *cleverer* than they really are, which is not quite so simple. For most virtual worlds, though, these "mental attributes" are merely convenient labels: Intelligence is used primarily as a fiction to determine how much magic a character can use, and wisdom serves the same function for priestly types.

Attributes also are meant to be relatively fixed: If you have a poor constitution, tough luck, you just have to live with it. Aging effects could perhaps make a difference (older characters might gain wisdom, but lose strength), but on the whole attributes aren't supposed to change much, thereby preserving basic differences between characters. There has been increasing slippage in this over the years, however, with the old notion that attributes should indicate intrinsic abilities increasingly falling out of favor. Instead, attributes can be improved on by action or training, which makes them more like skills (discussed shortly). There are several reasons for this, having to do with fairness, motivation, and choice.

The result is that after a while character attributes[2] become fairly homogenized: In the real world, people can be any combination of good-looking/ugly and strong/weak, but in virtual worlds they usually have to start off more one than the other (for *balance*). They won't end up being high in both. It may take considerably more effort to raise an originally low attribute to a high value than it does to raise an originally high attribute to it, but that doesn't present a total barrier. Normally, one stat is raised relentlessly as far as possible first, with the lower ones being neglected until it's their turn; this leads to a world packed with puny geniuses and muscle-bound simpletons.

The problem with attributes is that they do make sense in real terms, but this isn't a sense that many players are willing to accept. Some people are simply never, ever going to be as strong or as fast or as tall or as fit or as good-looking as others no matter what

---

2. They're often referred to as statistics, or *stats*, in this context.

they do, but part of the attraction of virtual worlds is that these physical limitations don't apply. In design terms, fixed or ever-rising attributes are also undesirable: If you decide after some time that you want your character to become a ballet dancer but you built her like an ox so she could become a boxer, well, ballet dancing is out of the question.

For this reason, the trend is to treat attributes as little more than symbols during character creation, so that players have to think about their characters as they individualize them. This gives characters direction, but only in the minds of their creators; in practice, the relative differences between a character's attributes are not usually all that important in the great scheme of things, especially if values are regularly boosted as a reward for achievement[3].

The idea of attributes as important, player-defining properties is probably here to stay. However, whether they remain relatively fixed (as they do for most other objects) or they rise[4] over time (as do skills) remains to be seen.

Levels

In the development of virtual worlds, *levels* came first (as they also did in table-top gaming). Levels are the classic advancement system—easy to implement and to manage—and are based on the concept of goals and rewards. Characters undertake actions, for which they receive a payment in *experience points*; because the notion of experience is general enough to be associated with pretty well any activity, this approach has wide applicability. When a character's experience points reach a certain threshold, the player rises in (ability) level. This will typically involve things such as attribute boosts, skill boosts, resistance boosts, greater choices, and higher status (among NPCs and, often, PCs).

Looking at this analytically, boosting is implemented at times dictated by a step function. Why not use a more continuous approach? Instead of levels, raw experience points could be used. By using a finer grain for things such as attributes and NPC attitudes, a character who is one experience point below the threshold for level X

---

3. Not that players will consider them unimportant. "If you say the value doesn't really matter, you've no objection to adding another 3% to it, then, have you?"

4. Or fall, although this is a somewhat rare proposition.

wouldn't have exactly the same stats as a character exactly on the threshold for level *X*-1. In pencil-and-paper games, where humans do (or used to do) the bookkeeping, this is reasonable—keeping separate track of these things is just too tedious. Computers, though, excel at tedious, so why the need for levels?

The answer is that levels provide goals. They give players something to shoot for, so that their actions have more purpose. They give players a sense that their achievements do have effects. Levels use a step function because players like to feel they have taken a step.

The time taken to reach a new goal[5] must be appropriate, of course. If characters advance too quickly, levels effectively merge into a stream and offer no more bang than experience points. If levels are too far apart, players become disenchanted that their efforts rarely seem to get them anywhere. Note that although the experience points separating two fixed levels are invariant (at least within character classes), the time taken to acquire the necessary points will depend on two things—what the character does, and luck. Thus, characters do not level[6] with monotonous regularity, but with some unpredictability. This leads to what is known as a *variable ratio reinforcement schedule*, which behavioral psychologists have shown to be the most effective there is for maintaining a high, constant rate of play[7]—Las Vegas slot machines are designed this way to keep people pumping them full of money. The morality of using such an addictive system for virtual worlds is discussed in Chapter 8, "Coda: Ethical Considerations."

Another reason for grouping together several rewards is that this enhances the overall experience; the bulk adds value. Damming a stream and then releasing it has more of an impact than would letting it run freely, whether the stream is of water or of presents.

The relationship between levels and experience points varies, depending on the virtual world. However, it's almost always exponential rather than linear. *MUD1* used a doubling scheme, whereby the points needed to rise from level *X* to level *X*+1 totaled the same as the points needed to get from level zero to level *X*[8]. Most modern virtual

5. That is, the *pacing*.

6. Yes, the noun gets verbed.

7. John Hopson, *Behavioral Game Design*. Gamasutra, April 2001. http://www.gamasutra.com/features/20010427/hopson_01.htm.

8. So as not to annoy the mathematically minded reader, level 1 was set at 300 points from level 0 (it was later changed to 400).

worlds start off approximating a doubling regime, but gradually tend toward a more linear scale. Compare the examples[9] from *Asheron's Call* shown in Table 5.1.

Table 5.1   *Asheron's Call* Level System

Level	Points	Points$_{level}$/Points$_{level-1}$
3	2,777	2.769
4	5,697	2.051
5	10,247	1.799
…	…	…
33	8,803,044	1.143
34	10,024,047	1.139
35	11,376,914	1.135

A slowing curve enables more levels to be packed into the same range of points, which increases the rate of reinforcement for players of experienced characters. Even so, some virtual worlds allow characters to have so many points that they record scores using a floating-point representation. This kind of level inflation can get out of hand (in worlds without permanent character death, anyway), so there's often a maximum level beyond which characters cannot proceed. Some virtual worlds allow *remorting* at this level, which means a character gets to keep its abilities but must start back at level zero as a different (sometimes more powerful) class[10]. Other approaches are relative levels and ranking systems ("you are 386th out of 4,034 characters").

One of the problems with levels (for virtual worlds which make use of them) is that content has to be available for characters of whatever experience. If one character needs a million points to go up a level, they'll be doing different things to the other character who only needs a thousand[11]. This means that characters which are of markedly different levels can rarely play together—the lower character will find high-end content too difficult and the higher character will find low-end content insignificant.

---

9. Use of bizarrely precise numbers is industry standard. I'd have thought that players would have preferred rounded values, but no one seems to complain about it so what do I know?

10. For a longer description, see Natalia, *What is Remort? Imaginary Realities* Vol. 2 (5), May 1999.

11. They certainly *ought* to be; if they're not, they're going to need a lot of stamina to get anywhere.

Another issue concerns where points come from. Some of the most intense experiences of players result in low overall gains—or even losses—of their characters' points. If some monster beats you up, but you get healed then go back again and again until you beat the sucker, your character may be worse for it but you, as a player, may be better. Likewise, running around mindlessly collecting easy quest points is going to make your character improve, but it'll do nothing but bore you as a person. Ideally, points should be awarded for things you find exciting, rather than as some kind of compensation for being fed up.

I've been describing levels here as a single-advancement abstraction of other progression measures. It's possible to formalize this, with level changes being determined using a formula that accounts for a range of multiple-advancement schemes. Thus, a player may suspect from experience that they're close to going up a level, but don't know how much they need to improve their swimming skill or their dart-throwing skill to do so. This uncertainty makes a variable ratio reinforcement schedule even more powerful, and the morality of using it consequently even less clear.

Hybrid schemes are also being developed. *Neocron* [12], for example, has typed experience points: When your character is awarded experience points for doing something, the points go to a pool associated with one of five stats. When the pool fills, you go up a level in that stat only, and gain skill points that can be spent on skills related to that stat only. It's a cross between a level system and a class system.

Designers are thus increasingly becoming aware that the benefits of levels can be used in non-traditional areas. In particular, applying a level system to individual skills can be very fruitful, assuming some provision is made for achiever-type characters to compare themselves against others (and even that may prove unnecessary). Skill systems are present even in many single-advancement, experience-based virtual worlds, and could eventually take over from them as the predominant measure of a character.

However, skill systems are not without their problems.

---

12. `http://www.neocron.com`

Skills

In virtual worlds, skills are tangible representations of the abilities that characters have (supposedly) learned.

In real life, a skill is a related series of actions that a person has internalized to the extent that they can apply it "without thinking;" skills are either innate or learned through practice. In virtual worlds, the notion of what a skill *is* remains the same, but skill acquisition is often only tenuously linked to "practice makes perfect." In particular, some virtual worlds allow characters to improve skills when they go up a level, irrespective of whether the skills they choose to improve are ones they've actually used.

Why do virtual worlds need to make skills tangible? Actually, they don't: Character skills are very useful as a means for players to individualize their characters, and they provide a good delivery mechanism for achievement, but they aren't strictly necessary. The most important skills (like it or not) are those of the player, not of the character, and the virtual world can't hope to rate these[13].

Skills are interpreted by the virtual world in a number of ways, depending on the nature of the skill, of any tools required, and of the virtual world. The main four are

> *Binary skills* (*feats*[14]). Either you can swim or you can't.

> *Discrete skills* (*skill levels*). People can swim to an ability described by one of a fixed number (greater than two) of predefined levels.

> *Continuous skills.* People can swim with widely varying degrees of ability, from not at all to completely competent.

> *Binary-continuous skills.* Either you can't swim, or you can swim with widely varying degrees of ability.

The idea behind a binary skill is simple command guarding. If you have the skill, you get to use the command, and if you don't, then you don't. Discrete skills take this a step further, with increasing levels opening up new commands (swimming underwater, swimming in stronger currents).

---

13. Well, it can *hope* to, but it is unlikely to succeed unless there is a change of attitude among the playing public.

14. The term comes from table-top role-playing games.

Continuous skills work slightly different in that everyone has a shot at performing any command. Sometimes, the effects are also continuous (the higher your swimming skill, the faster you can swim), but often it's used as a form of binary skill based on the difficulty of the task at hand. For example, if swimming across a moat is rated at difficulty 30, then someone with a swimming skill of 30 or more will always succeed; someone with a swimming skill of 25 will fail some of the time, but not as often as would someone with a swimming skill of 10[15]. Binary-continuous skills work the same way, but with the proviso that if your skill rating in the area is zero then you can't even attempt it (this is in addition to any other applicable preconditions—for example, armless characters don't get to swim no matter how much they practice).

Skills can be *active* or *passive*. Passive skills are switched on the entire time, whereas active ones must be called into play explicitly. For example, if a character has a "deflect arrows" feat then that would be passive—the character automatically attempts to deflect any arrows fired at them. A feat such as "berserk fury," on the other hand, might be active: Players have to decide when to sacrifice defense for offense, it won't happen on its own. Most skills are passive, but only come into use as the result of an active decision: Your swimming skill is effectively dormant until you enter a body of water, but while there it'll be taken into account passively. Because putting active and passive skills in the same list can be confusing for players, there is a growing tendency to refer to active skills as *powers* rather than skills.

Skill Organizations

The "skill levels" approach is an example of a *linear skill progression*. To acquire a specialized skill, you have to learn its parent (or *prerequisite*) skill first. Thus, you can't learn, say, "diving," unless you already know "swimming."

A skill hierarchy takes this idea one step further and allows several specialized skills to be learned following the acquisition of a general skill. For example, having learned a "single-handed weapon" skill, a character may then learn "sword," "axe," or "club," and from there further specialize into particular weapons (longsword, shortsword, rapier, cutlass, and so on).

---

15. These numbers are usually modified for circumstances. For example, a character with a swimming skill of 90 might have an effective skill of only 10 if they were wearing full plate armor.

A skill network is like a skill hierarchy except that it allows for skills to have two or more other skills as preconditions. You can't learn the skill of "horse archery" unless you already have "horse riding" and "archery" skills; you can't learn "espionage" unless you have at least three from "stealth," "disguise," "bluff," and "hand-to-hand combat."

Looking at skills this way, it's easy to see how attributes came to be regarded as the same thing. "You can't be a blacksmith unless you're strong" is just like "You can't be a pearl diver unless you can swim." A concept such as "strength" becomes the concept of "being able to use strength;" although this is ultimately dependent on a character's physical prowess, it nevertheless offers enough leeway to allow for increasing the "attribute" as a device for character improvement.

Doing this has certain implications for skill systems, though. Ideally, all skills should be implemented using the same basic mechanism, so as not to distract the players. If two or more skill systems run in parallel, they must be disambiguated somehow (this is why feats get a separate name). When attributes are handled just like skills, this means that skills and attributes should "look" the same. In other words, if attributes are on an integer scale then they should all be on the same scale and it should be shared by skills.

In practice, this actually works quite well. There are some awkward intrinsic properties of characters that don't fit naturally into the scheme (the number of genders is fixed, for example) but they can usually be shoehorned in without too much bother. This isn't to say that there aren't better ways to do it, of course; however, it does mean there isn't too much incentive at the moment to do it some other way. As usual, as long as designers understand why things are the way they are, they can make informed judgments as to whether to keep them that way.

It's worth considering whether skills should be applicable to objects other than player characters. They can quite obviously be extended to NPCs and even some monsters, but what about objects in general? Could not a shield's ability to deflect arrows be implemented using the same skill that a character might use to deflect them? Or more frequently, shouldn't a fireball wand simply cast the spell? Skill transference like this is particularly useful for virtual worlds that use magic, where a wand could be given the same spell-casting skill as a player or a player given the same petrifying gaze skills as a basilisk. Could a sword improve, through use, to become better? Could it be trained (that is, enchanted) to learn new skills? If object qualities are implemented using the same system as player character qualities, at least these are options (albeit not necessarily ones every designer will want to pursue!).

Skill Sets

The biggest problem with skills lies in deciding which ones your virtual world should have. How many should there be in total? Is 100 skills too many? Too few? From whose point of view—newbies or oldbies?

We should begin by determining what is meant by a "skill." Most virtual worlds would admit derivatives of crafting—making or repairing things in the virtual world—as qualifying as skills. Some would include weapon skills, and others would also add spells. The disparity is in part due to the different mechanisms by which acquisition works: If you get crafting skills by collecting "skill points" for going up levels but you get weapons skills by buying "training," the two are distinct. It would be confusing to call them both "skills," so commonly some other term is used instead (for example, "weapon specializations").

Ideally, all forms of skills would use the same mechanism. Why should the system by which you learn to make a barrel be any different from the one by which you learn to swing an axe, to brew a potion, or to let rip a fireball? If they are fundamentally different even at abstract levels, that's fair enough; I wouldn't necessarily advocate implementing equipment as skills, for example. However, if they're the same but are implemented differently, perhaps the reasons for that different implementation should be examined.

Spells, for example, are often linked to a character's level. When you reach level 43, suddenly you gain the ability to cast sidewinder fireballs in addition to regular ones. The spells you could cast at level 42 you can still cast, but with slightly more efficacy. If this approach is good enough for spells, why not use it for crafts? When you reach level 43, suddenly you gain the ability to make mithril horseshoes in addition to regular ones. Alternatively, if you're using a "skill points" system for gaining new craft and/or weapon skills, why not apply it to spells?

Using the same skill system for crafting, weapon use, spells, and everything else (acrobatics, horse-riding, speaking Elvish) doesn't mean they can't be radically different in effect, of course. However, it also doesn't mean that the problems of deciding what skills to have go away.

Typically, however many different crafting skills, weapon skills, spells, and general-purpose skills a virtual world offers, a handful will be so essential that everyone has them, most will be secondary skills that people have because they had to choose *something* and another handful will be utterly useless. In a Wild West world, for example, only people who actively like building unusual characters are going to pass on the horse-riding skill.

If a skill is considered by all players to be essential, all characters should be given it anyway. Characters don't usually have a "walk" skill, because it's a skill everyone can be assumed to have. As a rule of thumb, if any one skill is adopted by more than 90% of characters[16], they all ought to get it. Similarly, if a skill is unused it should also be given to everyone (or derived from attributes)—it costs nothing to do so, and it means the remaining skills should be of roughly equal value to players. Of course, it may be that having done all this you find that a new handful of must-have skills emerges. If this happens, either repeat the exercise or split the skills into disjoint sub-skills.

It's not too difficult to hardwire a universal skill once it's been identified (assuming you do so before the virtual world leaves beta test). It's quite tricky to decide what should be skills in the first place, though. Should "horse training" be a skill? Is it different from "dog training," or are they both examples of "animal training?" Should there be a skill for tree-climbing, or are so few people going to want to do this that it'll be a waste of time implementing it? Should there be some weighting scheme so that unpopular skills cost less to learn than popular ones[17]? Should some skills be more difficult than others anyway—isn't learning a foreign language comparatively harder than learning to ride a bicycle?

---

16. *Qualifying* characters, that is, as some skills may be restricted because of character class, attributes, gender, or whatever.

17. And, if so, how are you going to break the news to the players when you find out you got the balance wrong?

There are, unfortunately, no clear-cut answers. My advice when deciding what skill set to have is to consider what message it sends to players. I've seen designs for virtual worlds that have a weapons skill tree five levels deep, yet which had a single "mining" skill that worked as well for iron as it did for diamonds. The message they were sending was, "This virtual world is all about combat." Similarly, I've seen designs that covered the minutiae of everyday life, with skills covering everything from corn-planting to calligraphy to bee-keeping to *savoir-faire*[18]. The message here was, "Nothing is all that important."

If you want crafting to be a viable career, the skill tree for crafting should be deep enough for people to take it seriously. If you want people to travel a lot, include several skills that make traveling easier. If you think players will want to play bardic characters, include bardic skills. If you don't want to attract sneaky-thievy characters, don't have sneaky-thievy skills. Rate each skill for its attractiveness to various player types; if any types are over- or under-represented, adjust accordingly. If you fear spreadsheet abusers, make key skills mutually exclusive (but be aware that this will create a *de facto* character class system).

Although the number of skills of a particular kind available to characters is one way to send players a message, it's not alone. In general, skills should be of roughly the same level of abstraction as one other. If in one area they are represented in greater detail than in others, this also can point to an increased sense of importance. Were the "swordplay" skill to be described in terms of how much it increases the damage done, critical hit percentages, weapon recovery time, parrying capability, and resistance to being disarmed, this would give it more significance than a "lumberjack" skill defined solely in terms of how quickly you can fell a tree. Crediting skills with a false sense of importance this way is a particular example of *selective depth*, a trap that often ensnares the designers of virtual worlds.

As with objects, skills don't *have* to have a tangible purpose. If characters need an "interior decoration" skill to change the wallpaper in their houses, then if they want to change the way their house looks they can either acquire this skill themselves or go to someone who has already acquired it. Either way, the result is a matter of aesthetics: The virtual world doesn't necessarily ascribe any meaning to how the inside of your

---

18. This one was ripped straight out of *GURPS*.

house looks. Of course, also as with objects, it doesn't necessarily *not* ascribe any meaning to it either. Unless you want to make some kind of "we have some skills just for the fun of it" point, if you can find a way to give tangible value to skills, you should do so. Having your house redecorated to a higher standard could win you the envy of NPCs, say, or reduce the chances of its being infested with termites.

Skills that can be used for more than one thing are generally good to have but difficult to contrive. If you can use an axe in combat, does that qualify you to use one as a lumberjack? Or is that a different kind of axe skill? If they're different, how many people are going to bother with a lumberjack axe skill? If they're the same, characters will become lumberjacks so they can increase their axe skills while making money. Multipurpose skills have more justification for existing than do single-purpose skills, but they also can have annoying consequences.

Caps

Levels and (in most implementations) skills operate on a linear scale. A character starts at 0 and improves incrementally. A level 22 necromancer isn't as powerful as a level 55 necromancer, but would be roughly on a par with a level 22 monk or assassin or whatever and much better than a level 11 necromancer[19]. So what's the highest value that a level or skill can have?

If you have no limit, characters will improve relentlessly, getting more and more powerful until newbies are little more than insects by comparison. Once-daunting content will appear trivial; players will demand more to satisfy their appetites.

For this reason, many virtual worlds have *caps*—absolute limits on how high a level or skill can go. For level caps, this stops characters from getting too far ahead of what the virtual world can offer as content; however, it can lead to frustration as there's nothing to do except wait for other people to catch up in sufficient numbers that new content will be added. For skill caps, players will max out their characters in all the important skills so they still end up ultra-powerful.

---

19. On the face of it, a level 22 anything should be twice as powerful as a level 11 anything. However, without an absolute measure for "powerful" it's impossible to define such a mathematical relationship. For many virtual worlds, levels become closer in power equivalence as characters advance through them.

The only solution that is truly guaranteed to stop this from happening is permanent death (PD), but this is often taboo—especially in commercial virtual worlds. Some designers have mooted the idea of having PD as the price for cap-busting (if you want to go off the scale you can do, but your character can then die permanently), a solution that has been implemented many times already in non-commercial worlds. The uproar from paying players who want the skills but don't want their characters to die would likely be considerable, however. Players offered Achilles' choice between a short life of glory or a long life of obscurity will want a long life of glory.

Without PD, either characters are going to become all-powerful or (achiever) players are going to become frustrated. That really is the bottom line. It's possible to relieve these symptoms without resorting to PD, though. One way is to have an advancement curve that makes it increasingly difficult to progress to new levels, but not actually impossible. As long as the powers at level N are tangibly better than those at level $N-1$, players will want to have them. Eventually, though, an effective cap will emerge beyond which few characters will ever rise. Taking the caps off might mean someone can increase their archery skill to 134 instead of being stuck at 100, but they're never going to reach 1,000. It's a bit like world records for athletics: They're always falling, but there has to be a limit. No one is going to run the 100 meters in 7 seconds unless the authorities change the rules currently disallowing the use of motor bikes. Steep advancement curves like this can work, but they really only ever delay the inevitable: Sooner or later, players decide that the treadmill is simply no longer fun.

An approach pioneered by *Ultima Online* was to make skills *atrophy*. Characters can learn several skills, but the more they learn then the less attention they give to other skills, which lose their values. This allows for characters to excel in only a few skills at once, while retaining some scope for changing what those skills are. Players can remain powerful, but can use different skills as ways to express their power. It sounds good, but unfortunately players don't like it: If they learn a skill, they believe that they should always have that skill. They do have a point: It's not like an English-speaker who learns French will forget the French if they then learn Spanish; indeed, a knowledge of French could *help* you learn Spanish. It's true that if you become unpracticed at something, then it'll take you a short while to get back up to speed, but this will be nowhere near as long as the first time you learned it. Being rusty at something is different from completely forgetting all about it.

The first-century Greek philosopher Plutarch said, "The mind is not a vessel to be filled but a fire to be kindled.[20]" Atrophy systems embody the "vessel to be filled" approach: You can only learn so much; if you're all learned out, you have to unlearn something to make room for new stuff. Although *UO* players weren't exactly happy about skill atrophy as a principle, what *really* annoyed them was the fact that they couldn't state which skill they wanted to atrophy next. *Star Wars Galaxies* uses basically the same idea, except that atrophy doesn't occur automatically: If you want to recover points from one skill to spend on a different one, you have to do it explicitly. Skills you already know cost less to advance in than others, so the temptation is to specialize rather than take the jack-of-all-trades route.

"Vessel to be filled" approaches cap the totality of skills a character can have while leaving the distribution of individual skills relatively free. A more "fire to be kindled" way of doing it is to cap earlier in the process—that is, limit the amount of time that players can (or are willing to) spend in a virtual world (but not so much that they don't feel it's worth their investment). Ultima Online also pioneered this method[21], although not until 2000. The idea behind *UO's* *power hour* is that advancement happens faster during a character's first hour of play each day, but drops off thereafter. Interestingly, the advancement rate to which it falls is the same as it was before power hour was introduced, but players are reluctant to rack up points in it because they're "paid" less for their efforts than in power hour. Consequently, whereas the average time players spent in *UO* before power hour was introduced was three to four hours a day, afterward it dropped to around one hour a day. The result was that although characters advanced faster per *game* hour, they advanced slower per *real* hour and therefore took much longer in real terms to rise than they had done previously.

This approach worked for *UO*, but it can only be taken so far: If a character that was played four times as much as another character could only ever be 110% as good as it, for example, that would certainly lead to the loss of many long-term players. It has other disadvantages, too, in particular it discourages players from adventuring in groups and it isn't easy to make remotely realistic within the virtual world's fiction.

---

20. Plutarch, *Parallel Lives of Famous Greeks and Romans*. 75.

21. The fact that it significantly reduced bandwidth demand (and therefore overhead costs) may have been a contributing factor here. Certainly, the explanation bandied about that *UO* did it out of concern for the health of their players rang rather hollow.

Skill Improvement

How do characters improve their skills? To preserve the notion of what a skill is, there ought to be some relationship between what you do and how your skills improve; but what?

If skills are rated using a points system (as most are), the question becomes one of deciding when to increment a skill by a point. There are basically two ways to do it:

> ➤ *Random chance*. Each time a skill-enhancement opportunity arises, there is a small chance of causing a skill point increment. This chance may increase over time.

> ➤ *Cumulative chance*. Each time a skill-enhancement opportunity arises, a random number of pebbles is thrown into a bin. When the bin is full, the skill point is incremented.

The advantage of the random approach is that you can gain a second skill point shortly after having gained a first, if your luck is in. The disadvantage is that you may never gain a skill point while your luck is out, and you will complain loudly about this. The cumulative chance approach does have some randomness, so you can't ever be sure when you'll gain a skill point (unless you can see the numbers); however, you can be absolutely certain that it won't be immediately after having gained one.

Where skill nets exist, it may be possible to arrange for some skills to support others. It's not a precondition of veterinary science that you know human anatomy; however, if you do know human anatomy, then you could expect to pick up veterinary skills a little faster. This can be managed by increasing the random chance of success or by preloading the bin with pebbles so that fewer new ones are required to fill it[22].

It's in deciding what qualifies as a "skill enhancement opportunity" that things start to get interesting. There are several ways to do it, none of which are entirely satisfactory.

The traditional method is *improve from success*. Each task requiring skill use has a difficulty rating; when a character attempts the task, their skill rating is compared against the difficulty rating to see if they succeed. If they do, it counts as a skill enhancement opportunity; otherwise, well, they should maybe try something less difficult next time.

---

22. Warning: Don't have skills or attributes that affect how quickly characters learn skills. If you do, players will max them out at the first opportunity. Regard a learning skill as "essential," and give it to everyone.

A variant of this is *improve from failure*. The theory here is that people learn from their mistakes, not from their successes, therefore characters should get a skill enhancement opportunity for coming close to success but not actually succeeding. If they do succeed, well, they're happy anyway because they performed the task; this way, they're rewarded for nearly succeeding too. If they try something so hard that they don't even come close, well, maybe they should have attempted something easier. This is my own favorite method, by the way, but it's not for everyone. It can produce inappropriate messages, too: You don't really want to know that your character's shield-use skill has gone up if the blow it only just failed to stop was fatal.

Many virtual worlds use *improve from leveling*. Although some increase in a skill may occur through use, the idea here is that experience points are a sufficiently good reflection of player activity that skill acquisition can be linked directly to character level. When you go up a level, you (may) get skill points to spend on improving yourself (also known by its fiction name, *training*). This approach has three advantages: Players look forward to going up levels more; it's much easier to balance for skills that are used with wildly different frequencies (fighters swing swords more often than tailors make robes); characters don't have to waste their time repeatedly shooting arrows at static targets, trying to learn from being bored. The disadvantage is that the skills that players decide to invest their skill points in may have no bearing on what they did to get the skill points in the first place—that is, it's unrealistic. Some games try to limit you to only spend points on something you did in the last level (that is, you had to make a piece of clothing at least once to advance tailoring). Players will find and jump through these hoops very quickly.

Star Wars Galaxies uses a very novel approach that impressed designers because of the way it manages to kill several birds with one stone. The idea is that for craft skill points, the measure of success is whether anyone wants to buy your goods or not. Therefore, the more people use the products of your skill, the more skill points you get. This gives crafters a reason to produce the items that PCs want rather than the items NPCs will pay for. It helps stake-holding, it helps community, and it integrates crafters more fully into the economy. Players are as excited over the potential use of their skill as over the actual use of it. Presumably, there could be an *improve by failure* equivalent, whereby characters gained skill points by making items nobody wanted, but this has none of the advantages of the *SWG* original. Unfortunately, improve by failure does have one very important advantage that the *improve by success* version doesn't: It makes sense. In real life, people buy a crafter's goods because the crafter is good at making them, not the other way round.

There is a final skill advancement mechanism that isn't used much at the moment but may become more important in the future: *improvement from purchase*[23]. If the virtual world's business model and player base are right for it, characters could gain skills by simply paying for them. This was first done implicitly in the early 1990s by *Avalon*, which allocated skill improvement points to characters depending on how long their players stayed logged in (at a time when it charged by the hour). *Achaea* is more upfront about it: You pay real money for credits, which you can then turn into skill improvement points.

When skills can rise inexorably along a linear scale, it's worth asking what the values *mean*. Is a character with a strength of 100 five times stronger than someone with a strength of 20? Unlike the case with character levels, it could well be possible to measure this directly—for example, by considering the maximum weight that the virtual world lets a character carry. If something approximating a proportional relationship is established, this raises a number of issues:

- ➤ If the principle is established for one skill, should it not apply to all skills?

- ➤ Is it realistic to have skill disparities as large as this?

- ➤ Are players agonizing at character-creation over whether to give their character a strength of 15, 16, 17, or 18 simply wasting their time thinking about what's basically just noise?

That mention of character design brings us conveniently to our next topic.

Character Generation

Player characters do not come from nowhere. They have to be created. If players themselves do the creation, they will identify more with their characters right from the beginning. However, if they don't know what they are doing, then this could easily backfire as they make arbitrary decisions that they shortly come to regret.

---

23. In virtual worlds where this is not official policy, the equivalent is *improvement from bribery*.

Although it's not part of the virtual world *per se*, character generation is the first thing players have to do when they start to play a virtual world. It's therefore very important, as the impression it leaves will shape how players view the virtual world proper when they enter it.

In *MUD1*, players were asked for their character's name and gender, and that was all. Nowadays, characters will typically need to have their class, race, skills, and appearance set before they can set foot in the virtual world—a far more complicated exercise. Let's take a look at what's involved.

Appearance

The first two questions that need to be answered for any virtual world are still character name and gender, but increasingly character *appearance* is becoming important. In graphical virtual worlds, obviously it's paramount (although even there it's not mandatory—*lineage* succeeds despite having thousands of characters that all look the same). In textual worlds, a character description is usually optional and can be added or changed at any time; a non-default description can often be thought of as a badge of non-newbiehood. Even some graphical virtual worlds allow players to create textual vignettes for their characters, to enhance role-playing.

Almost always, a character's appearance is intangible: The virtual world itself makes no reference to it, so gameplay effects are non-existent. Although gender and racial[24] characteristics will affect the image, other attributes won't: You can be short and skinny yet still have more strength than someone twice your size. Unrealistic though this may be, players like to customize the look of their characters more than they like realism; at this stage, identification with a new character is more critical than its future effect on immersion.

An idea yet to be taken up by any major commercial virtual world[25] is that of hyperlinks. It's a simple matter to associate a hyperlink with any object in a virtual world, characters included, such that activating it opens a browser window to the character's home page. This gives players even more of an opportunity to flesh out their characters, and can include other useful information, such as objects the character has for

---

24. Remember that the term "race" here is in the sense of elves, dwarfs, and humans rather than human ethnicity.

25. *Meridian 59* excepted.

sale or is looking to buy. It's convenient, and it's extra content that costs the live team nothing to create. However, it's also 100% immersion-breaking and very open to abuse. Some players will create links to inappropriate web sites, and other players will complain about it; the live team's workload will increase accordingly. Linking to pages hosted on the developer's own servers and limiting content to that auto-generated from predefined forms would help enormously, but would lead to increased bandwidth requirements (that is, expense).

Graphical virtual worlds use a *paper doll* approach to character image design. A basic, randomly featured model of the character is presented, which the player can tweak within certain parameters (the client is going to have to animate this, so changes can't be too esoteric). Some adjustments concern the underlying wire frame (for example, height), some concern the palette (for example, skin tone), and some concern texture maps (for example, facial features). There are so many variables involved (some of which are interdependent) that most characters will look distinct from one another, except when someone is deliberately trying to create a doppelganger of someone else. Players generally like their characters to be unique[26].

When players create their character's appearance, it's the first opportunity they have to engage with their character. It therefore represents a powerful iconic representation of their identity goals. Unfortunately, these goals can change: You might start off as a dark, brooding, menacing figure, but in the course of interacting with the virtual world and its players discover a lighter side to yourself. However, the first impression you're giving when you meet someone new is "I am a dark, brooding, menacing person." Changes to apparel can have some impact on this, and there may be hairstylists, beauty therapists, and magic/plastic surgeons able to take it further. Your decision to change has to be conscious, though, which can present a barrier to identity exploration. Short of making characters change physical appearance based on their emotional behavior (which, were it implemented, would lead to a world full of characters looking like their own Dorian Gray portraits[27]), this is something that graphical virtual worlds simply have to live with.

---

26. They'll even pay for it if the uniqueness is sufficiently guaranteed. If yours is the only character in the game with a facial scar, that's worth more than if other people also have facial scars but theirs are different shapes. Actually, this suits developers: Downloading a "facial scar" texture map onto a quarter of a million PCs for the benefit of one player isn't something they really want to do all that often.

27. Oscar Wilde, *The Picture of Dorian Gray*. London, *Lippincott's Monthly Magazine*, 1890. Full text available at http://www.bibliomania.com/0/0/57/103/frameset.html.

Appearance is a two-way cipher. It encodes what you want other people to think of you, but it also encodes what you want to think about yourself. When a non-newbie male player creates a female character, that character encapsulates idealized values that the player is aiming both to project and to experience—only very experienced role-players can keep the two separate. The same applies to all other aspects of character appearance—race, hair, eyes, skin tone, height, and so on. These are lexical tokens that combine to create impressionistic symbols meaningful in an emergent, cultural language of identity. Although rooted in the tangible (and, in the case of gender, in reality), it's the abstractions that players make, and the common vocabulary they adopt for communicating these through appearance, that are important.

This semiotic view of appearance comes with two caveats. Firstly, not all players will invest time creating characters—they'll take the random image with which they were first presented (unless perhaps it's outstandingly hideous). The players most likely to do this are

- ➤ Newbies who are super-keen to enter the virtual world for the first time.
- ➤ Potential newbies checking out the virtual world before committing themselves.
- ➤ Players creating secondary characters for some specific purpose.
- ➤ Oldbies who are already as one with their online selves.

The other semiotic caveat is that some players use a more concrete real-world symbolism of direct identification. As noted in Chapter 3, Tolkien's Gandalf character is one favorite role model, but there are plenty more from other works of fiction. Thus, in a Fantasy virtual world you may find a female character with dark, wavy hair, dressed in tight-fitting, purple clothes and calling herself "Deanna[28]." However, although this phenomenon is widespread across virtual worlds, each individual world usually has only a small number of people determined to role-play against the world fiction to this degree.

---

28. This would be Deanna Troi, from *Star Trek: The Next Generation*.

Character Generation Methods

It seems a simple task: Set the initial values for a fixed number of genders, races, classes, attributes, and skills. What is the best way to do it, though, so that it provides enough dilemmas to make players think about what they're creating, yet can be completed quickly for those who just want to play?

There are many different ways to go about it, a surprising number of which can be offered simultaneously. Let's go through the main ones.

Random

The easiest method to create a character is at random. The server[29] rolls digital dice to determine all values.

This is fast, and it may produce interesting character ideas that the player had not considered, but some characters will be measurably better than others (depending on how the dice fell). A modified version uses a balancing scheme, whereby each attribute, skill, or whatever is allocated a points rating. Random values can then be adjusted upwards and downwards so that the sum total of points is the same for all new characters but their distribution won't be. This modified system has the advantage that it can be done on the client, with the server merely sanity-checking the results.

Pick Points

Starting from the modified random position, pick points allow players to tinker with the results. This saves players from re-rolling continuously until they get the result they want. They can reduce some values to gain pick points (equivalent to their rating) and spend them on raising other values. Sometimes, not all the pick points initially available will have been spent by the randomizing process, leaving a pool for players to draw from. This is better, because players don't feel as if they have to harm their character before they improve it; however, it does mean that a "randomly flesh out" option should be available for players who don't want to waste time messing around.

---

29. Because if the client did it, it would be like printing a "please hack me" label on the box.

The cost of attributes and skills will normally increase (and sometimes decrease) disproportionately beyond a mid-range, to stop players from minimaxing. For example, if a character's default tracking ability is 40, then it may cost one point to rise to 50, another point to rise to 60, but then two points to rise to 70 and a further three to rise to 80.

One of the ways by which classes and races can be made more distinct is to provide different base (and, sometimes, ceiling) values for skills and attributes. A stereotypical elf, for example, may begin with higher defaults for dexterity and archery than a stereotypical dwarf; the dwarf may have higher strength and axe-wielding abilities to compensate. In these cases, pick point costs may be relative to the defaults rather than to some absolute scale: If the elf's default archery skill is 60 then it would only cost one point to raise it to 70 instead of the two it would cost the dwarf with default 40.

The total number of pick points available to a character may in some systems be increased by taking a *flaw* (or *quirk*). The idea here is that the character has some flaw that the player is willing to accept in return for more pick points. For example, if a player is designing a "desert warrior" character, then it might be worthwhile accepting a flaw of "fear of heights" (on the grounds that the character will never encounter any). Were a giant eagle to pick up the character and drop it at the top of a minaret, however, the flaw would kick in; at the very least, the character could expect a catastrophic loss of attribute points while the situation prevailed.

In addition to flaws, some systems have one-off improvements that can be bought for pick points (for example, "language aptitude"). In this case, the improvements are known as *advantages* and the flaws *disadvantages*[30]. Because most advantages fit (or can be fitted) into a skills/feats/attributes scheme, though, they are popular.

Kits

Character kits are predefined pick point spends optimized by the designers for particular playing styles. For many newbies, going through extensive skills lists without having a clue as to what's useful and what's not is very daunting. It's easier to look down a (shorter?) list of character kits and make just one major decision, and then maybe fine-tune the result.

---

30. Or, colloquially, *perks* and *quirks*.

Character kits have a special significance for classless virtual worlds, because they allow players to create a character that is a "sorcerer," "ranger," "merchant," or whatever, but don't lock them into it. You can start off as a mendicant priest and end up as chief of the assassins' guild; the character kit you begin with points you in a direction of your choosing, but you don't have to follow it.

A nice feature of character kits is that they can be saved and loaded. Because all the action in character creation happens at the client, this means players can customize their own character kits and give them to their friends, post them on web sites, and so on. This makes for a more involved community, although the temptation always exists to create a crock kit and label it "arch-wizard" to trick newbies.

Questionnaires

Questionnaires offer a different approach to character creation. Players answer a series of (usually) multiple-choice questions, from which a piece of software constructs a customized character. Questions may or may not be focused—that is, later questions may or may not depend on your answers to earlier questions. This can be done independently or tied into a kit system; it's easy to see how a player-written web-based tool could construct characters from forms even if the developers decided against doing it officially.

There are basically two ways that questionnaires can be used: Ask players about the character they're creating; ask players about themselves. Examples:

- ➤ Your character prefers to deal with enemies
    - ➤ Face to face
    - ➤ At a distance
    - ➤ Behind their backs
    - ➤ By giving them what they want
- ➤ You view your fellow players as
    - ➤ Potential victims
    - ➤ Part of the world
    - ➤ The reason you play
    - ➤ Competition

The first approach constructs a profile of the character that the player wants to play, then attempts to spend pick points in a way that best reflects this. In the example given: The first answer might suggest a confrontational role such as fighter or lawyer; the second answer might suggest archer or magic-user; the third answer might suggest thief or politician; the fourth answer might suggest crafter or merchant[31].

The second approach tries to create a character that is right for the player; this may be radically different from what the player would have chosen otherwise. In the (somewhat unsubtle) example given, the answers basically point at player types—killer, explorer, socializer, achiever. Although players can enjoy the surprise results that this technique can deliver (if only to scoff at them) and can have fun wrestling with off-the-wall questions ("If you were a color, what would it be?"), nevertheless it's a form of psychometric testing; many players find the idea of this uncomfortable[32].

Tabula Rasa

This method creates characters by constructing a backstory for them. Starting as a callow youth with no skills, no quirks, and no unusual attributes (that is, an empty slate, or *tabula rasa*[33]), the player chooses a profession from a list. This adds some skills and perhaps changes a few attributes. The player is then presented with a second list that omits many of the original choices but offers new ones instead (depending on what the character decided). The process iterates, with new opportunities and specializations presenting themselves. When it stops, not only can a character be created, but a short history, too.

For example:

> "Zayre spent much of her formative years helping her carpenter father. The call to adventure was too strong, however, and so she joined a merchant train as a traveling cooper. Soon, she turned her talents to fletching, and became adept with the bow. Her reputation grew as she defended the caravan from bandits and raiders,

---

31. Developers would do well to hire a professional psychologist to help put together such a test.

32. As a general rule, anything that the developer's marketing manager would want, players will find uncomfortable.

33. This has nothing to do with the virtual world called *Tabula Rasa*.

until eventually she left to join the army as an archery instructor. Finding the discipline too stifling, she volunteered to become a scout, patrolling the barbarian wilderness with only her horse, her bow, and her thoughts for company."

I first encountered this idea in the single-player role-playing game *Darklands*[34], where it was very effective. It doesn't seem to have made much of an inroad into virtual worlds, though, perhaps because it implies that characters age. This is a shame, as it remains my personal favorite.

Essay

High-powered role-playing virtual worlds turn character creation into an art. Players of games such as *EverQuest* and *Anarchy Online* who regard themselves as "role-players" would do well to consider whether they could have written an essay on their character and its background before ever playing, to be submitted for approval to the world's staff members. That's what's required of some MUSHers.

Role-playing virtual worlds work consensually. People who do not buy into the fiction or who are disruptive of it have no place. This makes all players simultaneously guardians and perpetuators of the fiction. To gain admittance, newbies must therefore demonstrate that they both honor the fiction and have an aptitude for role-playing. An essay forces a player to create a fully rounded character, in the process satisfying both these goals. As mentioned in Chapter 1, "Introduction to Virtual Worlds," some virtual worlds will conduct interviews, too.

This kind of freeform character creation only works for small-scale, intimate virtual worlds with very dedicated players. Given that most players regard essay writing as a form of torture that should be outlawed by international convention, this is perhaps not surprising. Nevertheless, in its place it can bring character creation to the highest planes. It's not by chance that some of the best role-playing MUSHes have waiting lists[35].

---

34. Arnold Hendrick and Sandy Petersen, *Darklands*. Hunt Valley, MA, MicroProse Software, 1992.

35. The first commercial graphical virtual world to enforce role-playing was *Underlight*, a contemporary of *Meridian 59* that is still going strong. Instead of an essay, it uses a low-options (name, gender, class) approach to character creation, presumably so as not to scare off newbies (or create a huge workload for its administrators). `http://www.underlight.com/`.

Physical Differences

Elves are taller than dwarfs, but not at tall as humans. Dwarfs are stronger than elves, but elves are more dexterous. Elves and dwarfs can see in the dark, but humans can't. There are physical differences between character races, which are reflected in their default attribute settings.

Okay, so what about character gender?

Ah. In virtual worlds, the differences are usually purely cosmetic. Male and female characters look different, but apart from that gender X is every bit as good as gender Y and vice versa. There are three main reasons for this:

- ➤ If characters of one gender were more able than characters of another gender, it would greatly annoy real-life representatives of that gender because it would seem to be saying things about them.

- ➤ On the whole, ability differences between genders really are negligible. In day-to-day situations (as opposed to extreme ones), tasks are usually gender-independent.

- ➤ Virtual world designers are a liberal lot who don't want real-life prejudices either seeping into their virtual world or being reinforced by it.

It may surprise many students of gender studies to learn that the third of these is perhaps the strongest. It certainly applied to *MUD1*[36], which made no tangible distinction between character genders except in three instances that I'll discuss shortly. Such gender-blindness is all very noble, of course, and it promotes attitudes that can only be good if carried out to the real world. Unfortunately, there *are* some real-life physical differences between men and women that really *can't* be dismissed in virtual worlds.

In real life, genetic females can have babies, but genetic males can't. Few real-life women can grow a beard, most real-life men can. Any virtual world that suggested that either of these statements were untrue would have a hard time maintaining immersion.

---

36. In fact it more than applied: Roy was so proactive that he wrote the documentation using female personal pronouns rather than male (which was the default in those days) or gender-neutral (which is what I used).

What about differences in height? That's a little fuzzier. The average adult male is taller than the average adult female, but some women are taller than some men. I'm taller than my wife, but her brother is shorter than his wife (who is also taller than me). Nevertheless, I'm noticeably taller than most of the women I know. In a virtual world, would I have to be the same height so as not to disadvantage female characters?

Well, perhaps not, because in a virtual world height can easily be regarded as cosmetic. Humans won't bang their heads in dwarf houses, and dwarfs can reach things from the top shelf of a bookcase. Graphical worlds might have a more practical problem in that super-tall races simply won't fit in small places, but if they do it's a problem of their own making[37]. Nevertheless, in general female characters can be made to look smaller than male ones while having collision-detection boxes the same size.

However, what about strength? Men have significantly greater upper body strength than women. I may be shorter than my sister-in-law, but I can easily beat her at arm-wrestling. Should male characters have a higher base strength than female characters? If so, should female characters be compensated with a higher dexterity and/or stamina? This is precisely what *MUD1* did: Initial attributes for characters were set using a random-number generator, then female characters had 10 subtracted from their strength and 5 added to each of their dexterity and stamina. It was possible to get strong female characters, but strong males were more likely.

In reality, though, the differences between male and female dexterity and stamina are marginal compared to the male advantage in strength (dexterity may be more related to size than gender). I was balancing genders in *MUD1*, but not in a realistic fashion. How far should virtual worlds reflect reality as it is, as opposed to reality as people wish it were?

There were two other ways that *MUD1* made a distinction between male and female characters. One of these was to have a matched pair of puzzles that you had to be a certain gender to complete, namely kissing a sleeping beauty (for males) and kissing a frog prince (for females). I was never happy with these, though, because they were

---

37. *Horizons* has a dragon race that suffers in this respect. The designers' preferred solution is to give dragons an ability to shape-shift into humanoid form (rather than simply an ability to shrink), so they can interact with other PCs. Sadly, the ability to shape-shift back into dragon form while inside someone's shack is unlikely to be available.

unfair on gay players: Both the sleeping beauty and the frog prince were heterosexual, and didn't take kindly to advances from members of their own sex[38]. I did not migrate either of these puzzles to *MUD2*.

The other tangible way that *MUD1* used gender was that it had magic to flip it: Male characters could become female, and female characters could become male. This was non-consensual—other characters could cast the necessary spell on you whether or not you wanted them to. It wasn't something that people did very often: It had a high chance of failure, the penalty for which was the caster's falling asleep; besides, most people didn't actually care if it happened to them[39]. Having their character's gender changed commonly angered only two groups of players:

➤ Newbies and recently ex-newbies, who hadn't yet grasped the fact that virtual worlds can have a different culture than the real one.

➤ Players deliberately playing characters of the opposite gender who viewed it as an interruption of their experiment.

It's possible to have tangible but neutral differences between genders that (in theory at least) hurt neither. For example, plate armor breastplates could reasonably be restricted so only characters of the gender they were made for could use them. This might lead to economic imbalances, though: If supply and demand differed by much, one gender could end up paying more for their breastplates than another. Should a designer strive to eliminate such unfairness, or accept it as an inevitable consequence of increasing the virtual world's depth?

To conclude: There are significant physical differences between men and women in the real world. For the short-term periods that characters exist in virtual worlds, these can be embraced fully, embraced cosmetically, or conveniently ignored. Unless they're

---

38. Interestingly, gay players liked the "he's a prince, not a queen" line that accompanied an attempt by a male to kiss the frog prince. The complaints I did receive were from non-gay players who took it on themselves to speak out on behalf of the gay community.

39. Players of high-level personae would frequently lose track of their character's gender; they'd know which gender they were "supposed" to be and would act according to that, but wouldn't necessarily know what gender they were physically presenting at the time.

making a deliberate point about gender, most virtual worlds will stop short of adding tangible gender differences between characters. There are too many real-world consequences otherwise.

Yet character gender isn't really all that different to character race. Why is it fine to suggest that one race might be stronger or smarter or more pain-resistant than another, but it isn't fine to say the same thing about gender? These may be made-up "races," but it's easy to see how such casual references to "racial differences" can perpetuate false notions of racial differences in the real world. Chapter 8 considers this issue in greater detail.

Long-Term Characters

Should player characters age? There are some characters in text MUDs that have been played for so long that, were they alive in the real world, they'd be entitled to vote.

For virtual worlds with moderately low persistence, it's perhaps not an issue. If the world periodically resets, it never ages; it's not inconsistent to suppose that the characters entering such a timeless world shouldn't change either.

For greatly persistent worlds, it's not this easy. *EverQuest*'s night/day cycle is 90 real minutes in length. That means 3 years of real time is nearly 50 years of virtual time. As the virtual world never formally resets, shouldn't 3-year-old characters be in late middle age by now? Everyone must sup regularly from a fountain of youth.

Aging, like gender differences, is one of those inconvenient facts of real life that designers often omit from virtual worlds. They don't even address it cosmetically: Beautiful characters are forever beautiful.

The reason for this, of course, is that aging implies decay and, ultimately, death. The decay part might be acceptable to players if it's balanced by something else—for example, dexterity might drop but intelligence might rise. What they are unlikely to accept without a great deal of persuasion is that they themselves are responsible for supplying the main gain that comes with aging: experience. Their character will be better when it is older because of what it experienced when it was younger—that is, how they played it.

Character death is not something that sits easy with players, even when it's "natural" through aging. Would people buy a music CD if it was guaranteed to stop playing after five years? Why would a player want to start in a virtual world knowing that their character would be taken from them when at the height of its powers? What about the players of elf-types, whose characters are practically immortal? Would female characters get an extra two or three years, as they do in the real world? It's almost inevitable that in such a climate, some fiction would have to be created to assuage the concerns of long-term players. Characters don't age because, er, there's something in the air.

Okay, so they don't age. Time still passes, though. Characters get married all the time in virtual worlds—it's a common ceremony (and one I've performed many times myself). Do they get to have virtual children?

Virtual children pose so many problems for virtual world designers that most will avoid the topic at all costs. Unfortunately for me, as author of this book I can't do that. Here, therefore, are the main issues:

➤ Children have to be conceived. We all know how this happens in the real world, but....

➤ Women bear children and men don't. Is this unfair on male characters, unfair on female characters, or unfair on both?

➤ It takes nine months from conception for a human baby to be born. Even at accelerated time, this is plenty long enough for the player to have second thoughts. Are virtual abortions allowed?

➤ After a few months, pregnant women look different to non-pregnant women. Do their character models change?

➤ The final few weeks of pregnancy can be quite disabling. Should pregnant characters still be able to hack dragons with the best of them, or would suggesting this be irresponsible?

➤ Labor and the birth: These are going to be faked up to happen when the player is logged off, right?

➤ Naturally all babies are born in perfect condition without any complications. So, who looks after them, and how?

➤ Are children shown in the virtual world? If so, they grow, they change shape—all that needs to be modeled.

➤ How are children's looks and attributes computed? Are "designer babies" possible? What about something basic, such as choosing a child's sex?

➤ Parents don't age, but their children do?

➤ Can you sell your children into slavery? Every real-world parent has thought about it....

➤ Have you any idea how *expensive* it is to bring up kids?!

➤ Are children educated automatically? Do parents have any say in the matter? What if they disagree?

➤ Can children die before they reach adulthood? Can they be killed?

➤ Who gets custody of the children when the parents split?

➤ Can parents abandon their children? In worlds with permanent death, what happens to orphans?

➤ Who gets to play a child once it reaches adulthood?

➤ What tangible reasons are there for having children anyway?

There are serious moral, practical, and implementational issues concerning virtual children. They can all be addressed, but never to the satisfaction of everyone. In most virtual worlds, the cost of implementing virtual children so outweighs the benefits that it makes sense to put the idea in the "forget about it" pile. The main exceptions are

➤ Virtual worlds with a strong, realistic theme (particularly ones in an historical context). Children may be necessary for gameplay reasons, and the prevailing morals of the modeled reality can be used to answer some of the more awkward questions.

➤ Virtual worlds actually about children—for example, educational ones.

➤ Virtual worlds with permanent death, where children are used in an inheritance fiction to replace dead characters[40].

And that, thank goodness, is quite enough of that.

---

40. This means that the death isn't actually permanent, of course, as characters are reincarnated as their offspring. There's more on this subject later in this chapter.

The Virtual Body

Players enter virtual worlds through the medium of their characters. Although in general the player determines the appearance of a character, characters are not merely ghostly projections of the spirit: They are tangible entities within the virtual world, as real (to it) as any other object. As representations of sentient beings, they have attributes and skills; however, they have other functionality merely by virtue of their being objects. From this point of view, the virtual body is a machine that the character lives in. What should this machine do? And what happens when it stops doing it?

Maintenance

You wake up, you visit the bathroom, you wash, you brush your teeth, you have breakfast.

You wake up because you went to sleep. You have to go to sleep because human (and most other animal) brains won't work if you don't.

You visit the bathroom because your body is powered by chemical reactions that generate waste products.

You wash and brush your teeth for cultural reasons. You don't *have* to, although the chances are it'll prolong your life considerably if you do. People used to die if they got an abscess on a tooth.

You have breakfast because you need fuel. You noticed you were breathing too?

This is an example of a maintenance schedule. It varies from person to person. Some people might include a bit of exercise, others might count their morning prayers as "maintenance for the soul." The point is, it's a routine. Except in special circumstances (for example, illness or vacation), it's something you do daily; it's not for fun, nor for gain, but to avoid the consequences of not doing it.

Should virtual bodies have maintenance routines like real ones? Characters have no need to sleep or eat or anything else unless designers say so. Why lock them into the same tyranny of routine that players must observe?

The only strong argument in favor is that of realism (that is, it helps immersion). Unfortunately, in this particular case it's very powerful. Players don't actually *want* to undertake a routine for their character, but they do need to know that their character *has* a routine, and that it's being followed. It's a general principle of virtual world design that if every player has to do exactly the same boring thing, none of them should have to do it. Thus, the solution suggested in Chapter 4, "World Design," of abstracting the maintenance routine is a good one; furthermore, the fact that characters are charged for it means that players will notice, thereby reassuring them that these strongly ingrained but wholly irrelevant activities are taking place[41].

There is a difference between abstracting and removing, though. A character who puts on make-up might want to wash it off right there and then; in this case, it's not an act of general maintenance, but a normal action to achieve a specific purpose. Similarly, just because characters by default empty their bladders when their player is logged off, that doesn't mean they shouldn't be able to do it at other times: Urinating on a small campfire is as easy a way of putting it out as any other (at least for men)[42]. If characters want to eat, drink, and sleep explicitly rather than behind the scenes, they shouldn't necessarily be prohibited from doing so.

To summarize, then: Routine maintenance should always be abstracted, but the actions that it abstracts should also be available independently (cultural circumstances permitting).

Survival

Don't go to sleep on the ground if it's covered in snow; if you do, you'll get hypothermia and die. The same thing will happen if you swim in icy water. In a desert, if you don't freeze to death at night you may bake to death during the day.

That's in the real world. In virtual worlds, you will either suffer some minor, temporary skill or attribute degradation or you won't notice any ill effects at all. Characters are generally immune to the environment.

---

41. It can be removed at higher levels of experience; we can assume that demi-gods don't need to bother with this kind of thing, for example.

42. For fairly obvious reasons, this particular action is more acceptable to textual worlds than to graphical ones.

So? Why be unpleasant to players just for the sake of it?

Why indeed....

Well, it's because there are subtle side effects to this kind of automatic survival. For example, people live in houses primarily for shelter. If they don't have anything from which to shelter, they don't have to live in houses. Sure, they might want them as warehouses, but that's hardly the stuff of which communities are made.

There are other survival reasons that cause people to want to live close to one another. If characters are going to forever anyway, though, these don't apply. Easy access to food and water is only an issue if players have maintenance schedules that need them; healthcare is only important if people can fall ill; mutual defense is unnecessary if attackers can't hurt you.

In other words, some of the more primitive and tedious aspects of the real world that players don't want to experience act, unfortunately, to set up some of the more advanced and enjoyable aspects that they do want to experience. This conflict between what players want and what they are prepared to put up with to get it is a constant that runs throughout virtual world design[43].

Sensing the Virtual World

Traditionally, human beings have five senses: sight, hearing, taste, smell, and touch. These are the means by which individuals can detect the world about them. Virtual worlds that have human or humanoid characters will usually want to account for these senses, with perhaps some additional ones for special cases (bat-like sonar, insect-like infravision, and so on).

Most virtual worlds, whether graphical or textual, emphasize vision. When a character enters a location, the player experiences what the character can see. They may also experience what their character can hear. Textual worlds also will make occasional reference to smells and tactile sensations (for example, heat from a fire), but taste only really comes into it when something is eaten or drunk.

---

43. For a brief, but cogent, overview of other aspects of virtual world design that dampen the formation of societies, see Darien Kane's essay *Sins of the Empire*. http://www.stratics.com/content/editorials/articles/sins.shtml.

In graphical worlds, the players' senses double up as the characters': Players actually see what their characters see[44] and actually hear what their characters hear (plus the annoying soundtrack). In textual worlds, players are told what their characters see, hear, smell, and feel (through the skin—not emotionally). The scene is constructed in the imagination of the players, which paradoxically can lead to a more vivid experience. Although most players of textual worlds will of course use their own sight to read what is sent to them, this does not have to be the case: There are numerous examples of blind players using speech synthesizers or non-blind friends to read the text aloud; graphical worlds are not conducive to this.

Although textual worlds can utilize more senses and deliver a more compelling experience, graphical worlds have three main advantages over them:

➤ The graphical experience is more immediate: You don't have to interpret what you see, you just see it.

➤ Graphical images can display more information of a certain kind than can textual images. Scanning 50 faces for a friend is easier (for most people) than scanning a list of names[45].

➤ Graphical worlds use multiple channels. You can hear while you see. Textual worlds are essentially linear: You're told what you see before or after you're told what you hear.

For newbies in particular, text is unappealing. The fact that you can take photographs of smells in textual worlds is less relevant than the fact that you can see where you're going in graphical ones.

Sometimes, senses are impaired or ineffective. In real life, for example, you can't see in total darkness. What happens in virtual worlds?

Well, there are a number of solutions. Here are the most common:

➤ Suggest the impairment, but don't enforce it. A graphical world may darken the screen, but not actually black it out.

---

44. Or, if they don't have a first-person viewpoint, the same scene that their characters can see.

45. Even though in graphical worlds people will often scan above-head names rather than faces, this is still easier than in textual worlds as the names aren't scrolling.

➤ Provide a trivially easy remedy. Give everyone a portable light source.

➤ Make it temporary. If you enter a dark room from a light one, your eyes need to adjust to the dark before you can see; when you return, your eyes need to adjust to the light first. The process only takes a few seconds, but the wait can be scary. Popular in textual worlds.

➤ Play it straight. Actually black out the screen. Don't send update packets, either, so players can't hack the client to make it think it's full daylight. Only relent if they're under attack.

Impairment is one thing, but what happens when one or more of your character's senses isn't working at all? What if, as a result of accident or magic, your character loses the ability to see or hear?

In graphical worlds, the answer is simply "It Does Not Happen." It would be possible to continue playing without sound, but without vision there simply isn't enough other sensory information available to compensate.

In textual worlds, it's a different story. You can try things and get feedback. If you walk into a wall, you can be told there's a wall in the way (rather than a tree or a door or a dragon). Things that make noises or have smells or give off heat can still be described. You can pick up things and know what they are by their shape. Losing a sense could even be essential for solving a puzzle—for example, if you're blind, then the snake-hair ugly woman can't turn you to stone.

The way to do this is to use *dynamic descriptions*. Most textual virtual worlds, it should be noted, use *static descriptions* and therefore also have problems implementing lost senses (generally they take out too much information—blind characters can't hear either). Here's an example to illustrate what I mean.

A description of an object might be "Ticking in a corner is an antique grandfather clock." If a deaf character (or one wearing ear defenders) came into the room, they wouldn't know it was ticking. Should they see the description of the clock or not? Well, strictly speaking, not. If it were a static description, though, either the whole description stays or the whole description goes, neither of which is satisfactory. Dynamic descriptions individualize the text depending on the character's sensory abilities. Thus, a deaf character would see "Standing in a corner is an antique grandfather clock;" a blind character (or one wearing a blindfold) would hear "Ticking nearby is a grandfather clock." If the designer doesn't consider ticking to be enough to identify an object, it might just be "Something ticks nearby."

Dynamic descriptions allow for changes due to a character's skills or knowledge, too. In the preceding example, the use of the adjective "antique" may depend on whether a character is an historian or not, for example. If a character is running, they may notice less than if they're walking; if they're concentrating or searching, they may notice more. A virtual world can incorporate this information into a dynamic description appropriate to each character.

Although senses can work below their normal levels, they also can be implemented to work beyond them. Characters can be given the ability to see like they were looking through a telescope, or to hear heartbeats at a hundred paces, or to taste the recipe that was used to create a dish. Superhuman senses in a world that contains superhumans do make, er, sense. Although there is no problem with this for active senses (ones you have to decide to invoke—for example, touching something to discover how it feels), passive senses can be more problematic. If you can hear heartbeats at a hundred paces and there are fifty people within a hundred paces, that's a lot of heartbeats. For this reason, even passive senses will usually be considered active beyond a certain threshold. Switch on your bionic ear when you want to hear how many guards there are at the other side of the door, then switch it off afterward.

Body Composition

When a character picks up something, strangely this does not mean that the object teleports into their backpack. To make sense, they need to use their hand. Similarly, when they walk, their legs and arms move, when they look to one side their head moves, and when they're fleeing in mindless panic every part of their body moves. The issues involved here extend beyond mere animation: If characters can move their hands, that implies they have hands to move.

It doesn't take long following this line of argument to conclude that bodies must be regarded as assemblies, as discussed in Chapter 4. Following on from our look at senses, though, it's natural to ask the question: What happens if a body part works above or below normal levels?

As with senses, the default is that every body component works to its full potential. Because of the way that they interact, it's more difficult to make individual body parts superhuman than it is for senses; there may be comic potential in giving a character a hugely muscled ring finger, but it wouldn't be a lot of use unless the rest of the hand and arm was muscle-bound too. For this reason, most of the consequences of having improved body parts in virtual worlds are abstracted as character attributes instead.

When body parts don't work for whatever reason, it's a different matter. Tedious though it may be from a programming perspective, it is nevertheless possible to put a guard on all commands to restrict their individual use if a body part (or assembly of parts) is out of action[46]. For example, if your hands are tied behind your back and you want to pick something up, you can't. You might be able to "get key with teeth," but then you wouldn't be able to use your mouth assembly until you'd let go of it. Note that some body parts are connected to senses. Most importantly, if a character's eyes are shielded or missing, then they can't see anything.

It's tempting to use this idea to build an abstract anatomical model of a human body so that the effects of various events can be worked out. "Ah, when the nose and mouth are both blocked that means no air can reach the lungs, therefore no blood can be oxygenated, therefore no muscles can work, therefore death results." In practice, though, this can be handled explicitly without the need for deduction. A spear through the chest means your character is dead—that's really all you need to know.

Body parts can cease to function for three main reasons:

> *Restraints.* You can't run because you're wearing diving boots.

> *Damage.* You can't run because a tiger ate your leg.

> *Flaws.* You can't run because you have a club foot.

Damage can arise in some combat systems that allow for "critical hits" or "targeted damage." Although ostensibly permanent, there will almost invariably be some means by which a lost limb can be recovered.

Flaws are the quirks that some virtual worlds allow players to assign to their characters in return for more pick points. Again, although these are supposed to be inherent

---

46. I know this is possible because in the past I've designed it and seen it implemented.

aspects of a character's identity, they can frequently be cured. The fact that quirks can (literally) "add character" is only of long-term interest to hard role-players; soft role-players may regret an early decision to take a flaw, and in a virtual world without permanent death they will complain rather than start anew.

Note that a character lacking one or more organs, limbs, or senses can be considered disabled[47]. There are ethical issues arising from this, discussed in Chapter 8.

Groups

In virtual worlds, being the social beasts they are, it is imperative that players be able to form groups. The more populous the world, the more important it is that there is hard-coded support for this activity.

Chapter 3 introduced the idea of groups as the foundations of community. The point was made that people should be able to join multiple groups, so they can participate in multiple communities that are not hermetically sealed from one another; this gives players a greater sense of belonging to a virtual world (translation: They'll find it harder to leave if they can't take all their friends with them). When players can join only one group, that group will develop to maturity quicker but can leave as a unit; also, individuals who leave their group will often find hooking up with another group difficult, which could mean a crisis for them.

Single or multiple group membership is just one of the dimensions that can be used to describe groups. Other important ones are

- ➤ Formal or informal?
- ➤ Temporary or permanent?
- ➤ Flat or hierarchical?
- ➤ Hardwired or softwired?

Let's take a closer look at these distinctions.

---

47. I'm using this word in the technical sense: An ability the character had has been turned off. If you prefer a euphemism, use that instead.

Formal or Informal?

In small-population virtual worlds, everyone knows everyone else and there is no need for formal grouping commands. If you want to create a group for whatever purpose, you chat to prospective members and there you have it, a group.

This is an *informal* group. The main problem is finding someone willing to do the organizing, rather than the virtual world's lack of support for it. Informal groups arise in all virtual worlds. In small-scale ones, they're all you need; when more players are involved, some notion of a group as a tangible entity usually surfaces.

If members of a group are to communicate on a special group channel, or are to accept mutual concessions (such as seeing one another's basic stats or pooling experience points gained), or if the group as an entity is to possess anything (money, property), the virtual world needs to be able to reference that group. There must therefore be a formal process by which the group is created, which gives us the concept of *formal* groups. It is quite common for formal groups to be created from informal groups.

Note that it's conceivable in either case for a group to have NPCs as members, although for informal groups the AI necessary to support it would be considerable.

Temporary or Permanent?

Sometimes, people want to group together for only a short period—a single session. A group of characters are hanging out at a bar, someone comes in and announces that there are wolves attacking the village, so everyone bands together to beat off the wolves. This would be a *temporary* group.

Groups that persist (in particular, that would continue to exist when all their members were logged off) are classified as being *permanent*. Even if the group has a definite aim and will cease to exist after a certain point (for example, a consortium to sell virtual pumpkins on Halloween), it counts as being permanent if it would survive as an entity were all its members to log off.

Temporary groups tend to be (but aren't always) informal; permanent groups tend to be (but aren't always) formal. For formal groups, there may be differences in facilities depending on whether they are temporary or permanent: It doesn't really make sense for a temporary group to own property, for example. Although it's possible to implement a temporary group as a permanent one, there are two principal reasons why a designer might decide not to do this:

> ➤ People are often more willing to sign up to a group on the understanding that it's a one-off commitment than they would be if it were permanent. They might want to join a lynch mob, but not the police.

> ➤ Players may be limited to one permanent group (to help it develop quicker) but allowed to join any number of temporary groups (to assist the development of a wider sense of community).

It is important that temporary groups be quick to form and quick to disband. Players regard them as a superficial convenience, therefore anything that makes them inconvenient (even having a hard-to-remember command name) will reduce usage.

Flat or Hierarchical?

When all members of a group have the same powers as one another, that group has a *flat* organization; if some members have more powers than others, it is *hierarchical*.

Most formal groups are at least nominally hierarchical, as they usually have a designated leader who (minimally) can expel individual members but can't be expelled by them. In practice, though, there is a big gulf between this shallow tree structure and a full-blooded hierarchy with multiple levels, promotion and demotion between levels, and increased powers the higher up the hierarchy you go. This degree of structure is almost always only present in formal groups, and aspects of it may be supported by the underlying code. For example, if the group has money and can own things, there may be provision for "treasury powers," allowing a designated individual to determine who is allowed to spend the money and within what limits (that is, give a budget).

There have been many experiments in virtual worlds with customizable hierarchies, with textual worlds (as usual) at the forefront. These have the benefit, however, of relatively small and innovation-friendly populations compared with those of graphical worlds, so even poorly thought-out ideas can work well enough in practice.

For the big, graphical worlds, it's more hit and miss. *Meridian 59* had a system whereby ranks could be created within a guild, allowing extra hierarchical levels that enabled groups to restructure themselves as they grew. This was a step in the right direction, although the powers associated with the new ranks weren't easy to fine-tune.

The bravest early attempt at building a hierarchy was made by *Asheron's Call* with its *allegiance system*. In this, a *vassal* character swears allegiance to a *patron* character. The patron may already have other vassals (up to a dozen), and may have their own patron (hence the hierarchy). The primary tangible benefits of the relationship are that a proportion of the experience points earned by all a patron's vassals is also passed to the patron. There is additionally a ranking system, whereby titles are conferred on characters the more vassals they have beneath them[48]; there are tangible benefits to a high rank, in that some magical artifacts won't work below a certain threshold.

Asheron's Call only allowed characters one patron (that is, they could only be in one hierarchy). It did permit them to join temporary formal groups, although in practice these were usually composed of members of the same near branch of a hierarchy. Although it's easy to criticize *AC* for limiting characters to a single social group in this way, actually that wasn't the reason its allegiance system fell short of fulfilling early hopes. The problem was, although there were tangible reasons for a character to have vassals, there were only intangible reasons for a character to *be* a vassal. Although intangibles can hold together vast clans in (and sometimes across) virtual worlds, *AC* had an unbalanced system. By trickling up experience points, it asserted that allegiance was a part of gameplay; by trickling nothing back down, it denied it.

Most people need no incentive to be the boss of other people, but they do need incentive to be bossed by them. Critical to this is the belief that they themselves may be able to rise in a hierarchy, where "rise" means "getting nearer to the top" rather than "getting further from the bottom." *AC* got it the wrong way round. It was close, but no cigar.

Hardwired or Softwired?

A *hardwired* group is one that is programmed directly into the virtual world. A *softwired* group is one that is created by the players. All hardwired groups are permanent, and therefore they can be thought of as a subset of permanent groups. Similarly,

---

48. It's actually more complex than this, as it accounts for how well the vassal tree is balanced.

although it's possible to conceive of hardwired informal groups (built around prede-fined, labeled communication channels in the style of CB radio), in most virtual worlds that have them all hardwired groups are also formal; they can therefore be thought of as a subset of formal groups, too.

It used to be that all formal groups were hardwired into virtual worlds. Nowadays, players can set up groups themselves, of course, and virtual worlds are much the better for it. That doesn't mean there's no room for hardwired groups, though. What softwired groups gain in flexibility, they lose in specialization. It would, for example, be unwise to allow softwired groups to impose taxes on the inhabitants of a town; it would per-haps be acceptable, however, to allow the town council to do so. The town council is an example of a hardwired group.

Hardwired groups exist mainly for functional purposes; although social networks can benefit from having features that are coded in (for example, you can't join the local bandits unless your horse-riding skills are sufficiently high[49]), the more practical groups tend to dominate. They're particularly useful for newbies, because they guaran-tee there's an immediate place for them in the virtual society.

Note that there is a difference between hardwired *features* for groups and hardwired groups. All formal groups have hardwired features (it's what makes them formal), but these are configurable. Even if new groups can choose arbitrary values for arbitrary properties to use as entrance criteria, that would still make them softwired as the play-ers can do something about it. Hardwired groups are fundamentally inviolate: They're as much a part of the virtual world as the landscape and the mobiles.

One of the main advantages of hardwired groups is that it's much easier to arrange for NPCs to join them. Few players will care to stand around bored for hours on guard duty, but (presumably) someone has to do it; NPCs fit the bill perfectly. In this respect, NPC members of a group can be thought of as resources that the player characters can control—an option not really open to other kinds of groups.

---

49. Informal groups have to police this themselves, but formal groups can do it automatically from entrance criteria specifications if the virtual world is sophisticated enough to have these.

Typical hardwired hierarchies (yes, they do tend to be hierarchies) are

- ➤ *Ruling/legislative.* The people that make the laws. Monarchs, councilors, presidents....

- ➤ *Military.* The defense (or offense) forces. There may be different branches for land, sea, air, space, or whatever. Captains, sergeants, wing commanders....

- ➤ *Religious.* Those who concern themselves with the spiritual well-being (as they see it) of the virtual world. There may be competing religions, with different temples offering different services and worshiping different gods. Priests, mullahs, bishops....

- ➤ *Judicial.* My gimp takes *A*'s gold and *B*'s silver and passes it to my smith, who makes it into an electrum brooch. The judiciary sorts it out[50]. Judges, magistrates, lawyers....

- ➤ *Guild.* Craft- or service-oriented groups of people pooling resources, determining prices, offering employment. Whether these are hardwired or softwired depends largely on how the economy is run[51]. Guild masters/mistresses, branch secretaries, shop stewards....

- ➤ *Educational.* People who teach and train. Some of these may be part of other hierarchies. Professors, drill instructors, gurus....

- ➤ *Law enforcement.* Those who prevent crime and apprehend criminals. This hierarchy could be part of the military in some cases. Strictly speaking, law enforcement only has to enforce the laws made by the legislator; some hierarchies may have their own law enforcers with a very specific remit (for example, the religious police). Inspectors, inquisitors, speed cops....

All formal groups have powers. The extent of these powers is mainly over the members of the group, but in the case of hardwired groups this can extend significantly to non-members. Furthermore, although players can take their characters out of softwired groups and set up with someone else, this is not an option with hardwired groups.

---

50. Aside: Is the fact that the gimp and the smith are both played by me admissible as evidence? If so, what fiction would explain this?

51. *DikuMUDs* often use guilds as an alternative to character classes.

Although some of these powers can be limited by the code, they remain highly susceptible to abuse. Judges, for example, are always working with intangibles; otherwise,
the virtual world could sort out the problems itself and judges wouldn't be needed.
Low turn-out elections can be hijacked by special interest groups (for example, griefer
clans), guards can be made to abandon their posts, training can be withheld or offered
only to friends; the list goes on.

Because there are significant issues concerning the control of hardwired groups, community management staff should be consulted about their design. Players who have an
important position in such a group are often assumed by other players to be acting
with the live team's blessing, whether or not this is indeed the case. Even if the players
who hold high office are vetted for suitability first, there could still be problems: Just
how long can you make a character's jail sentence be before it amounts to permanent
death? With power comes responsibility; sadly, those on the receiving end of power
rarely have the same notion of "responsibility" that those wielding it do.

Common Configurations

Although there are many different ways that softwired groups can be set up, some tend
to be more useful than others. Designers may therefore want to have easy-to-use templates for these in place, so that players don't have to worry about setting flags that
don't interest them. As long as the basic models are all configurable, this is fine.

Common configurations are

- > *Fellowships*. Temporary groups of characters that get together for a single session
  then go their separate ways.

- > *Parties*. Permanent or (more usually) casual adventuring bands. People who play
  together regularly.

- > *Clans*. Large, disparate groups of characters. Although mainly a social network,
  individual members may come together occasionally for activities that require
  numbers. They're generally too unwieldy to organize for extended periods.

- > *Guilds*. These are like clans, but with a supporting game fiction. Some virtual
  worlds pursue this vision more than others: *Dark Age of Camelot*, for example,
  allows players to design their own guild crests, with the result that guilds feel
  more integrated into the virtual world than they otherwise might.

➤ *Alliances.* Groups of guilds or clans acting as if they were one. A single, huge alliance that completely and aggressively dominates its virtual world is known as a *überguild.*

Many mid-sized groups are run by politician-type players, who chivvy people into doing things and generally keep the group together. Such groups can rapidly fall apart if their leader quits or moves on. Some designers regard this as a good thing, because it allows for players to join other groups with a better chance of survival (an evolutionary argument); other designers don't like it because any failure of community could cause players to leave (the "other groups" that players join could be in another virtual world). The latter designers will institute automated rules of succession so that groups always have leaders, and votes of confidence so that inert leaders can be replaced; the former designers won't.

Combat

Combat is an important feature of most game-oriented virtual worlds. It embodies conflict, drama, risk, bravery, friendship, honor, glory—it has everything! Indeed, in some virtual worlds it *is* everything; there's very little to do *apart* from move from one battle to the next. As explained in Chapter 3, by no means all virtual worlds are like this, of course: Merely having combat[52] doesn't inevitably mean that the virtual world will end up being "all about" it. Nevertheless, many virtual worlds are indeed "all about" combat; this causes an ideological conflict with worlds that are "all about" something else (for example, role-playing), and annoys the balanced worlds who are lumped in with them even though they may be anti-conflict[53].

The subject of combat in virtual worlds brings out some of the most passionate arguments in the whole field. Let's take a look at it in detail.

---

52. Or some equivalent. I've worked on an adult-themed virtual world where sex was implemented using the same routines that other virtual worlds use for swordfights.

53. It's an established principle of *MUD2* that attacking other players is a losing strategy; players discover that committing unjust acts of aggression simply won't get them anywhere, until eventually only those with a constant need to reinforce their self-worth (or who have already "won") undertake it.

How Combat Works

Taking a wide perspective, combat involves many activities: Magic-users cast spells, archers shoot arrows, clerics patch up the injured. Important and battle-winning that these may be, they are nevertheless mere adjuncts to the central conflict: Two individuals standing toe to toe, slugging it out with close-up weapons. The reason for this is simple: Hand-to-hand combat is more thrilling than ranged combat. The monsters are in your face. Yes, the wizard cranking up the spell that will nuke the bad guys is excited, but it's an excitement borne by what's going on at the front line: If the tanks aren't excited by the fight, the wizard won't be either.

For this reason[54], most virtual worlds that have combat put hand-to-hand at the forefront. This defines the basic mechanism and the measures for success or failure. Ranged combat conforms to the same system, as does magic (whether the offensive or defensive kind). In discussing combat, therefore, it makes sense to focus on the hand-to-hand variety.

Here's how *MUD1* did hand-to-hand combat:

> ➤ One character attacks another player in the same location.

> ➤ An automatic fight sequence begins, in which characters take turns hitting each other.

> ➤ The chance of hitting is based on the character's dexterity attribute.

> ➤ The damage done is based on the character's strength attribute.

> ➤ Damage is deducted from the character's stamina[55] property.

> ➤ When one character's stamina falls below 1, that character dies and the fight ends.

This is still pretty much the paradigm. Damage can be increased by weapons and reduced by armor and shields; spells can buff attributes, repair injuries, and do the opposite (to opponents); some combatants may have multiple attacks (dragons can breathe fire while clawing at you); skills may allow for additional special actions. In all these, the underlying mechanism remains basically the same.

---

54. Actually, many designers use a different reason: "It's how the virtual world I grew up on worked."

55. Nowadays, "stamina" typically refers to how much exhaustive activity a character can undertake; *MUD1*'s stamina is called "health."

Why did *MUD1* do it this way? It looks suspiciously like the way that *Dungeons & Dragons* combat works—so similar that many virtual worlds openly refer to characters' health as "hit points," in the *D&D* tradition.

MUD1 did it this way because it delivered the gameplay. Roy wanted combat to proceed as exchanges of blows—I swing, you swing, I swing, you swing—because that was the most appropriate level of abstraction. He wanted it automated because otherwise it would have been tedious for players continually to type "hit them[56]." When one character swings at another character, there has to be some chance of hitting: This was encapsulated by the dexterity attribute. As for what to do when a hit got through, well, obviously there had to be some damage.

Roy and I discussed how to handle this. Although I knew the *D&D* combat system well, I also knew other ways to do this kind of thing (I didn't only play *D&D*, after all). Come to that, I'd already designed board games and a computer game[57] that used different mechanisms. Overall, though, the classic approach won on the basis of simplicity. When you're in a fight, you want an instant readout on how well you're doing. Anything too complicated wouldn't give players enough time to absorb it; anything much simpler and combat wouldn't have been any fun.

We decided, therefore, to give characters a number of "lives." Whenever a character was hit successfully, one life would be removed. To make this less predictable than it sounds, we scaled up everything by a factor of ten and added some randomness. Thus, although your character could usually survive ten blows, sometimes they'd hold out for longer and sometimes they'd capitulate sooner. We did some tuning to make sure that battles neither ground on too slowly nor ended too quickly to be fun, and that was that. Everything else—spells, weapons, artifacts—followed.

As a game mechanic, this worked well. As a representation of reality, it was somewhat off the mark. Real-life combat with hand weapons is not a gradual wearing down, a cut here, a nick there, until eventually someone dies of attrition. Instead, most blows are blocked, dodged, or parried, and when one does finally land it either has little effect or

---

56. Note that clicking a mouse is much easier than typing, which is why graphical virtual worlds can get away with non-automatic hand-to-hand combat.

57. A two-player tank warfare game in BASIC which is now lost to the world (not that the world should be bothered about this!). It used a target location approach, whereby each hit could knock out a system or crew member, reducing the options that the player had for their subsequent commands.

it pretty well incapacitates the recipient. In real-world medieval warfare, once someone suffered a telling wound they could take no further part in the battle and were fairly certain to die even if no one finished them off (medical science couldn't deal with infection). Virtual worlds set in different periods or having some kind of magic available in them don't have to stick with these facts, of course, but they still need a fiction to rationalize it.

So what other combat systems are available that retain the gameplay but make more rational sense?

Enhanced Combat Systems

Actually, the *MUD1*-style approach does make some sense if, instead of stamina/health/hit points, armor/shield is used. You bash at people until their armor comes to pieces, then the next blow hits their body and they've lost. Where characters' injuries would heal with rest after a fight, "wounded" armor is repaired. Of course, to be "realistic" some hits should possibly get through despite the armor, but even so they might not do fatal damage, yet fatigue can set in and…blah blah blah.

Combat systems can rapidly get very complex. However, the same approaches crop up time and time again, not only in virtual worlds but also in single-player and tabletop games. Here's a run-down:

➤ *Reaction and recovery times*. Traditional combat is *round-based*, in that characters trade blows either in turn or simultaneously. This is unrealistic, because some weapons take longer to recover from than others. In the time it takes you to raise your two-handed sword, I might have been able to run you through twice with my rapier. Defense also can have reaction and recovery times: Your heavy shield may take more damage, but if I switch the point of my attack you might not be able to bring it into play before I strike.

➤ *One-off attacks*. Instead of having fights proceed automatically after the first blow has been struck, each one must be performed manually. If I throw my axe at you, I can hardly do so round after round anyway—it's a one-off attack. Special boosted attacks (such as stunning punches or called shots) are usually treated as one-offs.

➤ *Stances*. These are a crude mechanism for trading offense against defense. If you want to hold out until your allies come, you increase your defense but pay for it with a reduced offense. If you want a fight to be over quickly and can take excess punishment, you raise your offense[58] but your defense suffers as a result.

➤ *Hit location*. The damage you do depends on what you hit. A blow to the leg is not as bad as one to the head. This brings in the possibility of having hit points for individual body parts instead of one value for the whole character. Where a blow lands depends on the weapon, the characters' skills, the relative sizes of the characters, the relative sizes of the body parts, and (the strategy bit) where the player aimed.

➤ *Damage types*. The theory here is that different weapons do different kinds of damage, to which different armors (or, combined with a hit location system, different parts of the body) are differently susceptible. Heads can take less crushing damage (for example, from a mace) than they can slashing damage (for example, from a longsword). If you're armed with a mace, you should therefore target the head rather than, say, the midriff. Characters may have special quirks that make particular blow type/location combinations unusually effective (for example, a "glass jaw").

➤ *Wound levels*. This approach gets away from the hit points idea entirely. Wounds are instead rated by category—for example, light, medium, heavy, disabling, destructive. They compound, so several light wounds make a medium wound, and so on. Heavy wounds may lead to some loss of functionality, and disabling wounds will lead to an entire loss of it. Destructive wounds disable permanently. Thus at light level your hand may be cut, at medium it may be gashed, at heavy it may be fractured (you couldn't write with it, but you can still hold a sword), at disabling it may be smashed (you can't do anything with it), and at destructive level it might be severed. Different weapons have different wound profiles for different body parts. A mace may have a greater chance of disabling a head than does a sword, but a sword has a (small) chance to decapitate.

➤ *Critical hits*. Critical hits incorporate hit location and wound levels into a hit points system. Combat proceeds in the traditional "death of a thousand cuts' style," but if a character hits well enough (maybe one time in 20, depending on the location),

---

58. This is frequently known as *berserk mode*.

they do special damage (usually equivalent to a disabling or destructive wound). Opponents who weren't even breaking into a sweat can suddenly be knocked unconscious by a well-aimed blow. Thus, players who are losing a fight might stay rather than flee, in the hope that they can pull out a critical hit and win.

➤ *Afflictions.* These are temporary side effects from blows/spells that impact on a character's ability to conduct combat. If combatants accumulate enough of these, it makes taking them down a lot easier. A few knocks on the head won't necessarily do much damage in themselves, but if they make you dizzy then that could reduce your ability to parry something more serious.

➤ *Combat scripts.* This approach owes much to pencil-and-paper role-playing games such as *En Garde!*[59]. Combat commands are entered into a queue, and executed in order simultaneously for each combatant. Combinations of commands can be prewritten and hot-keyed, so that players can have time to think rather than relying on first-person shooter twitch skills. If you have a script effective against a particular kind of opponent, you can call it up instead of your default one. Of course, if you don't but they have one effective against you, it could be problematical. This "program your battle" approach was adopted by *Star Wars Galaxies*, so it's likely to become more popular as clones of this game appear[60].

All these ideas can be (and often are) incorporated into gloriously complex wholes. The level of detail can become so great that the rest of the virtual world pales by comparison. Few virtual worlds with an immensely complicated combat system avoid being completely dominated by it—*Achaea* is the best-known exception.

Although these combat systems are intended for melee, they can be used for other forms of combat, too. In particular, if characters control or are crewmembers of fighting vessels (spacecraft, pirate ships, mechs, and so on) then similar mechanisms can apply. "Number One: Take out their hyperdrive."

As I mentioned earlier, whatever combat system is adopted for hand-to-hand combat underpins all other forms of combat. If you're using a hit points system for sword fighting, then arrows will also cause characters hit point loss; if you're using a wound level system, then damage-causing combat spells will have to use it too. These

59. Darryl Hany and Frank Chadwick, *En Garde!*. Bloomington IL, Games Designers Workshop, 1975.

60. Yes, I am aware of the name of Episode II of the *Star Wars* saga....

secondary combat activities come with their own issues, of course (arguments over the range and accuracy of crossbows versus longbows being particularly prone to starting flame wars). Weapon statistics aside, though, combat systems face in general a common set of difficulties of which designers should be aware.

Problems with Combat

There are many social problems with combat, which I shall come to shortly. First, though, I'll briefly address some purely practical concerns.

➤ *Equalizer weapons.* Anyone who can flip off a safety catch and pull a trigger can kill someone else. Highly trained individuals have a better chance of success, but even complete novices—children playing with daddy's pistol—are in with a good chance. Equalizer weapons brook no defense except a physical barrier (a good shot is no better at avoiding bullets than is a poor shot) and the damage they do tends heavily towards the disabling and destructive levels. Unless a convincing fiction for why this isn't so can be produced[61], equalizer weapons take a lot of the fun out of (combat-oriented) virtual worlds.

➤ *Multiple weapon types.* You might find that swords work best with a hit points system, but muskets work best using a wounds-based approach. Which do you use? What do you do when someone using a sword attacks someone who is using a musket?

➤ *Over-robust defense.* How long does it take for a newbie to kill an old-timer who isn't putting up a defense? Typically, it will take much longer than it ought to. The unarmed veteran stands yawning while the newbie repeatedly swings their sword; when they hit, the damage done is merely a fraction of that necessary for victory. It would be like chopping down a tree if it weren't for the fact that you frequently miss the target completely.

➤ *Concurrent combat.* How many creatures can you fight at once? Do you get the same number of attacks against each one, or do you have to share them out. Do you defend equally against all of them, or against some more than others? How do you stop people from ganging up in large numbers and beating the stuffing out of their foes?

---

61. In a Science Fiction context, this is usually quite easy; in a U.S. Civil War one it isn't.

➤ *Targeting.* Do I aim at an individual or at a point in space? As pointed out in Chapter 2, "How to Make Virtual Worlds," there are implementational considerations here. There's also the issue of consistency: If I aim an arrow at a point rather than at a character, then the same solution should be used for hand-to-hand combat. What about semi-autonomous weapons, though—for example, heat-seeking missiles? Are both relative and absolute targeting systems needed? Who is hit if someone fires a bullet into a crowd?

➤ *Area effects.* If I throw a grenade or cast a fireball spell, the result affects everyone in an area. The whole point of such an attack is to avoid the targeting issue. What happens, then, if there is someone in the area who is on your side? Can you be blown up by your own bomb? This is mainly a problem for graphical worlds, because textual ones don't commit to *exactly* where anyone is standing.

➤ *Twitch.* First-person shooter games rely on the skill of the players. There are two components to this: experience and twitch. Experience comes from having done something often enough that you know what to expect. Twitch comes from having fast reactions, good manual dexterity, and reasonable vision. Both experience and twitch transfer to virtual worlds, but neither ought strictly to be there: The knowledge and speed of a character shouldn't be that of the player. Twitch is the more annoying[62], especially when coupled with client hacks or go-faster macros that can make someone almost unbeatable. Where should you put the threshold, though? How many seconds is it reasonable to make people wait before you process their next combat command? What effect will lag have on this?

➤ *Combat skills.* My character can do things I can't. What are these things, and how do they affect combat? If there are too many or too few, it could send players the wrong message. What can I do while I'm waiting for the next combat round? Will it occur instead of or in addition to my attempt to hit my enemy?

➤ *Disengaging.* When fights are handled automatically, under what conditions do they end? Can I simply run away? Do you get to hack at me while I do? Can I surrender or be captured? If so, how could I escape and why wouldn't you just kill me anyway? What happens if I'm stunned, but not actually dead? Does the fight end there or does it carry on until you strike the killing blow?

---

62. Only, it should be said, when player characters fight other player characters. No one but the most die-hard achiever really cares when people use triggered macros against mobiles or NPCs.

There are, of course, many other tedious-but-important decisions that designers have to make about combat. If the planned system is deep and complicated, these can take up disproportionate amounts of time to resolve—not because of complex interactions between components of the system, but because designers can become so involved that they try to treat what are essentially subjective choices objectively.

The main thing is to be able to step back, look at a combat system, and ask three things:

> ➤ Will it work?

> ➤ Will it keep players immersed?

> ➤ Will it be fun?

If the answer to all these questions is "yes," go with it.

There is a fourth question we could ask, which on the face of it looks like it follows from the preceding three. It has deeper implications of its own, however.

Will players accept it?

To find out why this is important, we need to consider two notions: opposition and consequences.

Opposition

Conflict concerns opposition. Combat is the most obvious manifestation of this, but it occurs throughout virtual worlds. Two people wanting to get through the same turnstile at once are in conflict; two people aiming for the same job are in conflict; two merchants pitching to the same potential customers are in conflict. Combat may be one way to resolve this conflict, but others tend to work better.

In virtual worlds, conflict is typically categorized in terms of opposition: Who is in conflict with whom? There are three main possibilities:

> ➤ *Player versus Environment* (PvE). Players are opposed by the environment—that is, the virtual world. In a combat situation, this means player characters (PCs) fight monsters.

➤ *Player versus Player* (PvP). Players are opposed by other players. In a combat situation, this means PCs can fight each other.

➤ *Group versus Group* (GvG). Players are members of groups that are in conflict with other groups. In a combat situation, this means PCs can fight any PCs who are members of enemy groups but not those who are members of their own (or a neutral) group[63].

PvP and GvG both assume PvE. GvG is a restricted version of PvP that will usually operate within other limits too, for reasons that we shall come to shortly.

The difference between PvE and PvP is central to virtual worlds. In a strictly PvE environment, PCs can do nothing to other PCs. In a strictly PvP environment, PCs can do to other PCs whatever they could do to NPCs or monsters—and potentially a lot more.

Why the distinction? The answer is, fundamentally, *consensuality*: Players don't want other players doing things to their character without permission. It's one thing for a trident-wielding NPC mermaid to attack you, but another thing entirely for a PC to do it. Hard role-playing virtual worlds solve this almost trivially: If a player wants to do something to another player's character, they ask permission on an out-of-character channel first. Other virtual worlds don't have this luxury.

In a pure PvP world, there is no consensuality: People can try to mess you about, whether or not you like it; they may run the risk of being attacked by you, your friends, and perhaps the local police force too as a result, but they can still try. In a PvE world, the world itself prevents anyone from messing you about in the first place (and you from messing them about).

In practice, absolute PvE is untenable. If I want to pick up some treasure lying on the ground and you get to it first, you have interfered with my enjoyment of the virtual world and I am entitled to feel peeved as a result (even more so if you did it deliberately just to annoy me). Weak forms of PvP such as this (looting) are always present in multi-player environments, otherwise there would be no way of knowing they were multi-player. The question is not whether to have PvP at all, but how *much* PvP to have?

---

63. This is often known as *Realm versus Realm* (RvR), as it was popularized under this name in *Dark Age of Camelot*.

The issue of consent becomes blurred here. Plainly, players have to put up with some degree of interference from other players merely by virtue of sharing the virtual world with them; in this sense, entering the virtual world can be regarded as offering implicit consent that a player is willing to accept the PvP it supports. Unfortunately for designers, players will still complain if they are the victims of what they see as a violation of their character, even if they knew it was a possibility when they signed up.

The problems are compounded by the fact that different players have different ideas of what's okay and what's not okay. Some players may think it's fine that characters can't walk through each other, because that's how reality works; others may dislike it because it means access to locations through pinch-points (for example, doors) can be blocked. Then again, some of these people may relax their point of view in cases where 50 characters have just killed a monster then some non-combatant with maxed-out running skills races through the mob and steals whatever reward was dropped. Is a reasonable compromise solution to allow characters to move through other characters but at a greatly reduced speed? A gang could still totally surround someone and continually move around them so that wherever they were headed there would always be people in the way.

Some abuses of PvP can be stopped by giving people switches they can toggle. Generally, players are fine with allowing strangers to speak to them, but not if this is used as an offensive weapon (for example, spamming). Thus, some ability to squelch or gag incoming messages from other characters is often incorporated into virtual worlds. This works, but it's not always realistic (if your character is asleep, then why would one person's voice wake them up but not someone else's?). Stopping people from spamming in the first place is a better answer, but one harder to implement.

This idea can be extended to a system of permission levels. Every character has a disposition to every other character, ranging from "they don't exist as far as I'm concerned" to "they can mind-control me into doing anything they want." The default for meeting a complete stranger might perhaps be to allow communication but no physical contact. Permissions can be changed either explicitly (using a "change permission" command) or implicitly (if I offer you my hand to shake, I am implicitly giving you permission to make formal physical contact with me). If someone tries to act beyond the permission level you have set for them, you get the option to turn them down ("Gilead declines to shake your hand"), to allow the individual action, or to raise the permission level ("You shake hands with Gilead").

The "they don't exist" permission level raises an interesting question: If virtual hearing can be selectively filtered, what about other virtual senses? One very good way to annoy a player is to follow their character around. In a strongly PvE world, there's no way to stop it except by running faster; it feels like an invasion of privacy (which of course it is), but the virtual world engine can't distinguish between friends, stalkers, and strangers who just happen to be heading the same direction. Giving players the ability to squelch the images of other characters would sort the problem out, but again it stresses the fiction.

Fiction is the main enemy of PvE. If you can do something to NPCs, why (in the context of the virtual world) can't you do it to PCs too? If I create a rogue-class character with high thieving skills, why can I apply them to any NPC from the lowest to the highest, but not to a single PC? The real answer is that NPCs won't complain but PCs will, but in the virtual world NPCs and PCs are supposed to be the same thing (characters). Although it's possible to make a formal, fictional distinction between them (for example, NPCs are "normal people" and PCs are somehow "gifted by the gods"), most virtual worlds that impose this kind of restraint don't bother; it's justified by its existence. If players moan that this is unrealistic, well, okay, so do they want to hold a vote on whether to allow PvP?

The extent to which PvP is permitted in virtual worlds is historically defined by three factors:

➤ How much freedom to be pains in the asses the prevailing culture of the majority of players allows.

➤ What the players say they want.

➤ What the community management staff can handle.

These are in increasing order of refinement. The real-world culture of players gives them notions of personal liberty in some kind of balance with the rights of other people; players are prepared, in principle, to accept these as the default for the virtual world. Virtual world culture is unlike real world culture, though, because of the anonymity that virtual worlds afford. Some behaviors that would be unwise in the real world because of the repercussions are "who cares?" issues in virtual worlds.

Therefore, the players will suggest changes. If this is the first virtual world they've played, they'll immediately think of the most obvious (but not necessarily the best) solutions; if it's everyone's first virtual world, everyone will think of these same solutions and it will become a tidal wave of opinion that the live team will find hard to resist. The changes will be added—some for better, some for worse—and tinkering will take place until some kind of consensus is reached.

The tinkering will stop when the noise from players is down to sufficient levels that the live team can cope with it (hopefully before the end of the open beta). Players will occasionally get into conflict, but not so frequently that the community managers can't sort them out. This degree of PvP becomes the standard for the virtual world; designers of later virtual worlds will consider it as a prototype (or even a paradigm) for the "prevailing culture" of PvP/PvE with which they begin.

This would all be fine except for one thing: Virtual worlds with more PvP are manifestly more exciting than virtual worlds without it. There are two reasons for this: Players are more intelligent than mobiles; players have feelings and mobiles don't. If you're in conflict with an intelligent opponent, it makes success and failure more meaningful; if you win or lose to an opponent with emotions, your own emotions are affected.

PvP is "me against you;" PvE is "me against random number generator." Which is the more thrilling?

Recognizing this, strongly PvE virtual worlds have tried to developed ways to have the good bits of PvP (the excitement) without the bad bits (lack of consensuality). There are basically two ways to do it: arenas and character flags[64]. With arenas, different locations of the virtual world have different PvP rules. To enter a location where the rules are different from the norm, you must give your consent. This will either be explicit (you won't get into the gladiator pits unless you confirm you understand what could happen) or implicit (you should expect to be robbed if you walk into the thieves' guildhouse). Arenas don't have to be small: Huge swathes of *Dark Age of Camelot* and *Shadowbane* are effectively arenas, for example. With character flags, players elect to be PvP-able, and can therefore interact in PvP ways with any other players who have flagged their characters thus.

---

64. There are several ways to implement both of these. I won't list them here, however, because they match pretty well the options for implementing permanent death that I outline later in this chapter.

Neither of these solutions really works. One problem is that there's no tangible reason to do it: Why accept full-blown PvP when you're no better off than those who don't? Sure, you get the extra intangible content that PvP delivers, but while PvPers are taking kit from each other PvEers are getting new kit from monsters with less effort. If everyone else has it easy, why not have it easy yourself?

The big virtual worlds tried to counter this attitude by devoting whole incarnations (shards) to PvP, so every character you met could be PvPed. This didn't help, though, because players still advanced faster in the strongly PvE incarnations. PvPers felt they were taking on more opponents and being penalized for it. They might have been happier if they were compensated somehow—for example, by a higher level cap (even if it was only *one* level higher than a PvEer could get); the PvEers wouldn't have accepted this, though. Besides, a virtual world designed for PvP has different requirements to one designed for PvE; they're similar, but by no means identical[65].

This is where GvG comes in. The idea here is that the virtual world is divided into sections (the "realms" of RvR), within which "normal" PvE rules apply. There is a further section to which these are connected, however, in which PvP rules are in force (except between characters hailing from the same realm). There is typically a reward for combat success in this area, which means that characters who enter it do get an advantage over those who don't. Entry into the PvP arena isn't mandatory—you don't *have* to do it—but you'll benefit in terms of increased stats or whatever if you do. The fact that you can enter with a bunch of guaranteed-trustworthy friends and stay there for only as long as you want makes it far more palatable.

The term RvR comes from *Dark Age of Camelot*, but it's not the only virtual world to use this approach; indeed, it's not the only big, graphical world to do so. *Anarchy Online* has characters divided into three groups, with people meeting in PvP areas for combat. *Lineage* has clan-like groups called *bloodpledges*[66], which can conquer castles from one another in (scheduled) sieges; success here has material results, in that owners of castles get tax income they can invest in preparing for the next siege. *Shadowbane* is trying something similar for western audiences with its guild versus guild mechanic: PCs can build cities, rule countries, lead armies against other countries, and so on.

---

65. The fact that PvP was basically added as an afterthought didn't help.

66. Uniquely, lineage allows only characters of a special class—"prince"—to lead a bloodpledge.

GvG does add some of the features that PvP has but PvE lacks. It still misses out on an overall point, though, in that in most GvG virtual worlds it's impossible for any side actually to be wiped out. In *DAoC*, for example, Midgard is never going to conquer Albion or Hibernia. This is for various reasons, the main two being content and balance.

Preventing defeat to keep content is understandable. If a virtual world has been advertising itself as having three realms, if strategy guides are out in the shops describing the three realms, if each realm has distinct styles of architecture and dress that took months to create, then yes, one realm's annihilation of another would be a mite inconvenient.

Balance is a less good reason to keep realms from beating on one another too much. Strictly speaking, it doesn't matter if one side completely conquers another as long as the resulting empire can split through civil war[67]. If for content reasons you don't want realms to be obliterated, though, the aim should still be equilibrium rather than balance. It doesn't matter if one side can win *some* of another side's home territory, so long as it becomes increasingly harder to do so the more they advance. It's like two fencers dueling with bungee ropes tied to their waists: There comes a point when the elastic pulling on the better fencer is so strong that the worse fencer can win and push them back. They don't even have to have the same strength elastic—equilibrium will eventually be reached.

A problem with GvG combat is what to do if one or more sides give up and don't get involved in it. Does the virtual world save them, by not allowing enemies to pass a frontier? Does the live team save them, stepping in to avoid putting all that beautiful elf artwork to waste? Or does the opposition sweep through in an orgy of destruction and pillage?

The main problem with all these PvE solutions to PvP is that there are two levels of consensuality at work here: Consensuality in principle, and consensuality in fact. The former is when you accept that something *may* happen to you, but you're not necessarily going to like it when it does happen and it had better not happen too often; the latter says that you expect something *will* happen to you and therefore won't be too bothered when it does. Part of PvP's appeal comes from the assumption that a foe has

---

67. If there's no chance of a fight-back, players on the losing side may find the temptation to quit irresistible. Indeed, even if there *is* they may still leave in a huff.

accepted the principle but won't easily accept the fact unless they win; this is equally true for attackers and defenders—neither will be pleased if they lose, but both will be over the moon if they win. In PvE-based PvP solutions, consensuality is by fact; in full-blown PvP, it's by principle. Unless players are prepared to accept the principle, they'll have to make do with the fact.

Unfortunately, they may accept the principle but still have a justifiable grievance. This is best illustrated by what has come to be known as *Marian's tailor problem*[68]. If a rich virtual world offers characters careers in both non-adventuring and adventuring, how are the non-adventurers protected from the adventurers? Marian's character is a tailor because Marian likes creating clothes for other characters and the opportunities for interaction that this affords. She understands that there are other players who prefer hacking monsters (and each other) to pieces with sharp weapons. She understands *and accepts* that other players may on occasion attack her. What she doesn't accept is that they can do so indiscriminately, on a whim. She is completely unable to defend herself, so will always lose. Is her only recourse to take up arms? If so, what's the point of putting in tailoring as a career if everyone is eventually forced to become a fighter anyway?

The issue of opposition (PvE, PvP, GvG) is wider than combat, but combat nevertheless is the litmus test that decides whether a virtual world "is" PvE or PvP. If you can attack other player characters, it's PvP; if you can't, it's PvE. There may be other PvP elements—for example, casting nasty spells on characters, or nice ones on the mobiles they're fighting—but combat is the issue that tips the scales. Who you fight, however, is only part of the issue. The arguments *really* begin in considering what happens if you lose.

Consequences

Different locations have different risks associated with them. A PvP arena, for example, has a greater risk associated with it than a marketplace; a dragon's lair comes with a greater risk than a raccoon's.

Players like to know their risks in advance. They like to be able to tell by looking whether or not they can beat a potential foe in combat. Some virtual worlds helpfully color-code PCs and mobiles to make it easier to check them out. Although in real life

---

68. Named for the person who first identified it, Marian Griffith. See http://www.kanga.nu/FAQs/ MUD-Dev-L/30.html.

you might not be able to tell a martial arts expert from anyone else merely by looking, in virtual worlds you often can. If there's no fiction explaining why you might be able to do so, well, you still probably can.

Risk makes things exciting, but it's only part of the equation. Equally important are the stake (what you stand to lose) and the prize (what you stand to win).

In virtual world combat, what you stand to win can be anything the designer chooses. There are constraints imposed by other areas of the design (for example, the economy) and by the combat system itself (high-risk or high-stake fights should have high-stake rewards), but this still leaves a lot of leeway.

So, what do you stand to lose?

This is harder, because it must be something that you already have. It should also be commensurate with the risk and what you stand to win. It's okay to favor the player statistically, because otherwise characters will not advance. In real life, if you stand to win $10 on the toss of a coin, then $5 is a fair stake. In virtual world combat, it's like you get four tosses of the coin to win $10 for a $5 stake—the odds are stacked so you're generally going to win. However, (in this example) one time in 16 you're going to lose. If it's only $5, who cares? The problem with virtual world combat is the size of the stake.

Fights can have three outcomes: victory, inconclusiveness, defeat. Most fights with mobiles end in victory; most fights with characters (where PvP is allowed) end inconclusively; a very small number of fights against whatever opponent end in defeat. Defeat can mean many things—capture, injury, loss of possessions, loss of prestige, loss of time, and so on. For mobiles it means death. Does it mean death for PCs?

As with PvP, character death is not entirely a combat issue: It can occur in other ways, too. In the real world, most people die through disease, old age, or in accidents. The number one cause of peacetime death among British men under the age of 35 is suicide[69]. Death happens to everyone in the real world, combat or no combat.

---

69. http://www.doh.gov.uk/newsdesk/inside/sept2002/

Virtual worlds, however, are not real ones. Characters *don't* "have to die."

Old age in virtual worlds can traditionally be eliminated without the need for any explanation because only very long-term characters would ever qualify for it. Disease and illness, while okay as a temporary inconvenience[70], also don't have to be anything more than that; this is just as well, because players would seethe with rage if their characters were merely confined to bed with influenza, let alone if they were dying of something incurable.

This leaves death by accident (deliberate or otherwise) and death by being killed.

In virtual worlds, characters are in theory physically capable of doing acts that would, in the real world, result in their death. They can jump off cliffs, stand in bonfires, swallow plutonium, throw a grenade short of its blast radius…. The virtual world can of course be crafted so as to prevent such events from ever occurring, albeit at a cost in realism. If someone in full armor is paddling a coracle across a wide river and they decide to light a fire, they really should expect to drown. Nevertheless, this can be prevented—for example, by not making coracles ignite while people are in them. It can be programmed round.

Death by being killed can't be programmed round. You stick a mobile full of holes and it dies; a mobile sticks your character full of holes and it also dies—it wouldn't make sense otherwise. Is it the same kind of death, though?

When a mobile dies, it ceases to exist. It is permanently *gone*. Some reinitialized version may appear at its spawning site after a period, or when the virtual world resets; it's not the same mobile, though—it has none of the experience or possessions it had when it died. At best, it's a clone.

Never-to-return death is called *permanent death*, or PD[71]. It's the single most controversial subject in virtual worlds.

---

70. Characters can catch colds in some virtual worlds, passing them on to one another and to mobiles.

71. Some old-timers prefer the expansion *persona death*. Exceedingly old-timers might even use *player death*, but at least we're trying to break the habit.

Permanent Death

PD is not the same as PvP. PvP means that one PC can do things to another PC that the latter didn't agree to; PD means that if a PC suffers death, it is consigned to oblivion. When PvP and PD are combined the result is *player killing* (PKing): One PC can directly cause the PD of another PC[72]. Players often use PD and PvP as euphemisms for PKing, but the distinction is there and is very important. Many of the benefits that advocates of PKing cite are primarily due to PD; some of the strongest objections to PKing are due to its PvP element, rather than to PD.

Like PvP, PD has consent issues. These are not, however, with other players; rather, they are with the virtual world itself. As our Chapter 4 analysis of virtual world physics showed, players are normally quite happy for the virtual world to model the real one, because it reinforces their immersive experience. In the real world, though, none of a virtual world's players have had the experience of dying.

Because the whole aim of virtual worlds is to bring the character and the player together as a persona, players will routinely consider their character to be themselves. On the face of it, then, their character's PD would thus be like their own death in reality. In practice, players at the persona level of immersion don't feel anywhere near as bad as players who are approaching it, because they have the duality of player/character sorted out. The character has died, but the player *is* the character, and the player (clearly) hasn't died, therefore the character hasn't either. The character can be reborn in a new manifestation, much as a PD mobile respawns from scratch. It's not a pleasant experience—it's like losing three months' work while trying to back up your computer's hard drive[73]; frustrating, but not the end of the world. Players who are near to total immersion but aren't quite there will suffer the most, because not only do they lose the work, but they also feel they've lost a dear friend. The word "gutted" is frequently used to describe the experience, but even that doesn't come close to how bad it can feel. Unlike the death of a real person, though, virtual PD grief can be overcome relatively quickly. Players usually can rationalize what has happened and come to terms with it after giving it some thought; the emotional impact is

---

72. Given that so few large-scale virtual worlds have PD in them nowadays, it's becoming common practice to use "PKing" to refer to unjustified PvP combat. I, however, shall be using it in its traditional context, because otherwise there isn't a handy term to describe the action of committing PvP with PD.

73. Speaking as someone who has experienced both.

strong, but at an intellectual level all that's gone is a chunk of over-anthropomorphized computer data. If they can cope with the emotional hit, the intellectual gain can more than make up for the loss. *If* they can cope with the emotional hit....

There is a quantitative difference between the emotion felt at losing a character to the virtual world and that of losing it to another PC. In the former case, players will be incredibly annoyed but will rapidly conclude that it was either their own fault or the result of incredible bad luck[74]. In the latter case, though, they'll be angry, too[75]. For long-term PKers (as opposed to newbies), if they started the fight and got killed then their self-image will fall even lower than it was before. For the victim of a PKer (or, worse, a pack of PKers), there is the sense of unfairness that the heavily armed attacker will have selected a target on the basis of their likelihood of winning, and therefore the odds were stacked from the beginning. Unprovoked attacks cause enough indignation to blow an industrial indignationometer.

Consent is an issue. Emotional attachment is an issue. Wasted effort is an issue. None, however, are *the* issue. *The* issue is that people don't like losing. PD amounts to a statement of total, that's-all-folks loss. There's no wheedling out of it; it's final. That's what people dislike about it. Whether this is merely a passing phase due to virtual worlds' comparative immaturity or a permanent situation rooted deep in the human psyche we shall examine presently.

For the moment, the important thing to come out with from all this is the sense that PD is not popular. People who fear it are as much—if not more—against it than people to whose characters it has actually happened. Returning to the gambling metaphor, if PD is the potential result of losing a fight, players are wagering a very, very high stake.

Such a stake is constant across all combat, because in a PD world it's the only thing a player can bet. Because of this, the risks of losing must be small or the rewards for winning must be high (or both). Unfortunately, this can make matters even worse because it means PD actually occurs only very infrequently. Players aren't expecting it to happen, therefore when it does there's the shock to contend with, too.

---

74. There may be allegations that members of the live team rigged the random-number generator, too. This is mundane conspiracy-theory claptrap, leavened only by the fact that sometimes the live teams of some virtual worlds with PD really *do* tinker with the code to harm (or, more likely, protect) particular PCs.

75. Jessica Mulligan likens PD at the hands of another player to rape, which isn't quite as over-the-top as it sounds. You'll find out why if you stay awake in Chapter 6, "It's Not a Game, It's a ...."

In real-life gambling, if a risk looks too great you can usually pull out of the bet and lose only a fraction of your stake. In virtual worlds, it should always be possible to cut your losses and flee from a fight. There may be tangible consequences for the partial defeat, but the main loss will probably be your pride. Only if you decided to stay (for example, because your opponent looks like they're going to die sooner than you are) would you risk losing your whole stake.

PD is not appropriate for all virtual worlds. It would be ridiculous in most non-game contexts, and doesn't add greatly to games without combat, either. For virtual worlds where non-PCs can (and regularly do) suffer PD, though, it has serious contributions to make.

Approaches to Permanent Death

Let's assume for the moment that a designer has decided they want permanent death to feature in their virtual world. The reasons why they might (or might not) make such a decision we'll go into shortly, but for the moment we'll suppose they've done it. What are the various ways it can be incorporated into a design?

It all depends on how you intend to ensure that a death is "fair." Here are the classic ways to do it (most of which also can be applied to PvP):

➤ *Unmoderated.* If your character dies, that's it. There's no comeback: It's gone. PK versions of such worlds will frequently descend into barbaric slashfests, although this is not inevitable: If fleeing is not unlikely to succeed and the player base is too small to support gang warfare, an unmoderated world can thrive (and with a vibrancy it's hard to match elsewhere).

➤ *Post-moderated.* PCs can appeal to administrators to be resurrected if they feel they were harshly treated. The classic reason is because of communications difficulties (lag, line noise, cosmic rays, whatever) that prevented a character from fleeing at a critical moment. The administrators will look at logs to determine whether the player has a case. In worlds with PKing, there may be a *justification system* in place to ensure that high-level characters don't wipe out low-level ones indiscriminately, but they can nevertheless avenge intolerable acts (for example, you stole my stuff). Again, administrators would normally enforce this on appeal. This approach also works, but is only sound in small-scale virtual worlds that can log absolutely everything (that is, textual ones).

➤ *World-moderated.* The idea here is to implement a justification system by tracking player actions. Unfortunately, it can only ever track *tangible* actions: If someone insults your ancestry and you hit them, the virtual world will flag you as the aggressor. There are several ways to have a virtual world moderate PvP and PKing, none of which ever really work: Karma systems and NPC justice systems are the most popular. Grudge systems are the most interesting, because they allow slights to be traded: If I hit you, you get a grudge against me that you might sell to someone else who can beat five kinds of Hades out of me. This makes people think twice about performing unprovoked attacks, but has the disadvantage that it's blatantly unrealistic.

➤ *Player-moderated.* These approaches don't work either, at least not yet. Here, the decision as to whether a character has done wrong is made by players, not by the virtual world (although the world will act on what the players have said—for example, by making NPC shopkeepers charge more to people with low reputations). In player justice systems, there may or may not be NPC enforcers available to make sure that justice is done. The problem with player-moderated systems is that they are too easily undermined by groups of players acting in concert. If 100 players say that some random other player is a thief, that player is going to have a problem clearing their name. There are experiments under way to circumscribe this problem. Sure, it works for eBay, but eBay doesn't have 10% of its user base trying to screw it over for fun.

➤ *Opt-in.* This is the classic response of designers who disabled PD or PvP and then came to regret it. They re-enable it, but only in certain arenas or between consenting duelists. It fails to deliver any of the major benefits of either PD or PvP. If your virtual world has no PvP or PD, you've already handed it over to people who don't want it; adding it is not going to make them happy, nor will it attract people who do want it.

➤ *Opt-out.* This is an approach that *ought* to work but which has yet to find favor. The idea is that by default PD and/or PvP applies (moderated using one of the other approaches) but characters can flick a "pacifist switch" to opt out—some kind of "holy person" fiction covers for it. They pay for this security by having a lower level cap than characters for whom the gloves are off. While this seems fair to non-pacifists, it's deeply unpopular among pacifists: They want the benefits of not getting killed but don't agree that they should give up anything to do so. If higher level content is available, they should have access to it.

➤ *Inevitable, but distant.* Characters have a shelf-life, after which they die of old age, retire, or otherwise cease to exist except as a memory. This form of PD serves only one purpose: To force people to start afresh instead of staying on with the same, stale character indefinitely. Unfortunately, as mentioned earlier, even at accelerated timescales it would probably take several real years for a character to "die," and guaranteed impending death would dishearten everyone—even newbies.

The preceding list gives the main approaches to PD. They all treat dead PCs as "gone forever," resurrection being limited to external factors such as bugs, rule violations, and the occasional act of gross favoritism by members of the live team.

Most virtual worlds don't go for PD, however; this is fairly clear from the fact that it's PD that has the acronym, not "NPD" (which is just "death"). In non-PD virtual worlds, PCs do die in combat (and perhaps in other ways) but it's not the same kind of death that the cookie-cutter NPCs suffer. What exactly it is instead, however, varies.

Alternatives to Permanent Death

Let's assume now that a designer[76] has decided they don't want permanent death to feature in their virtual world. If there's no NPC death either (because of world's genre or application), that's it, end of story, skip to the next section.

If there is NPC or (in most cases) monster death, the designer has to find some non-PD equivalent for PCs. If your character fights a monster and loses in the worst possible way, what happens to it?

Okay, well the *big* mistake is to say the character *dies*. It doesn't die. If it did die, that would be PD[77]. One of the absolute, defining features of death is that the dead don't recover from it[78]. Whatever it is that happens to the character, if it can continue its existence afterward then it hasn't died.

---

76. Or, more likely, a designer's boss.

77. At least in the context of the virtual world it would. Strictly speaking, characters can never "die" because they can never "live;" nevertheless, in the same way that real-world people mapped into the virtual world are characters, the real-world concept of death mapped into the virtual world is PD.

78. At least they don't in the physical universe. People with religious views may differ on this point in the absolute sense.

The words "kill" and "death" have all kinds of powerful emotional connotations that often in no way resemble how the concept is handled in a non-PD world. This isn't necessarily a problem, but it becomes one when designers transfer too many of those connotations to something that doesn't merit them. Sadly, this is something they are wont to do when discussing alternatives to PD.

Merely labeling something as "death" doesn't make it a serious matter. In many cases (particularly in large-scale graphical worlds), the penalties for losing a fight are so lax that even the word "hurt" would overstate them. When I act as a consultant to in-development virtual worlds that don't have PD, I insist that the designers don't use the words "death" or "kill" in relation to PCs. This concentrates the mind on the mechanics and not the ideal. If someone says "when a mobile kills a PC," I'll correct them based on how they plan on handling it; unhappily, more often than not this means "when a mobile wuss-slaps a PC." It may be sarcastic, but it leaves them in no doubt as to what they're actually talking about, rather than what they thought they were talking about.

Okay, so let's look at the usual ways that non-PD virtual worlds handle what they call "death" but isn't:

➤ *Resurrection.* PCs that die come back to life, perhaps in a worse condition than they were in at the point of death, perhaps not. As with most forms of death eva-sion, in PvP worlds the exact penalties may vary depending on whether the PC was the aggressor.

➤ *Insurance.* This is a form of resurrection that PCs pay for in advance. It's popular among Science Fiction worlds such as *Federation II*, but can work in Fantasy ones too. In *DragonsGate*, for example, players can accumulate "favors" by doing quests "for the gods," which can be translated into resurrections. Sometimes, insurance works on a "save game" principle, whereby resurrection is only to the state the character was at when it was last insured; this means characters will reg-ularly pay for new insurance, thus giving the economy a healthy cash sink.

➤ *Ghosts and spirits.* The fiction here is that PCs' bodies die, but their spirit lives on. The spirit is usually separated from the body (appearing at some local last-save point or generic shrine) and has to find it to affect a resurrection. In the mean-time, other PCs or mobiles can loot the body and steal the "dead" PC's gear. Losing a fight therefore means a time penalty (you have to find the body) and possible tangible loss (if people loot it).

➤ *Realm of the dead.* This is a variation on the ghosts and spirits approach. "Dead" characters appear in some other dimension (that is, they're teleported to a set of locations disconnected from the main part of the virtual world). They have to find/fight their way out, whereupon their soul returns to their body and they're back to life again. Their body has taken the opportunity to recover from its massive system failure, too. Again, it's mainly a time penalty to stop people who have just been "killed" in a battle from immediately wading back into the fray.

➤ *Left for dead.* Although PCs are clever enough to know when a mobile is faking death, mobiles are universally stupid. They think that the moment a PC hits the deck it's Game Over. However, the PC is only stunned or unconscious or winded or otherwise wuss-slapped, and will be right as rain in no time!

➤ *It wasn't a fight to the death.* This is absolutely fine in PvP situations, where it doesn't really stretch the imagination too much to envisage duelers or gladiators who honorably fail to deliver the final death blow of a fight. It makes no sense against mobiles though unless the mobiles also accrue the benefits of it.

➤ *Inheritance.* Lefty gets killed. He really is PD gone. However, he happened to have a relative to whom ownership of all his kit passes. The relative is very close in looks, skills, and experience to the character who just died. Welcome, Lefty II! This works best in materialistic virtual worlds that define characters by their possessions more than by their attributes. The character may be nominally dead, but the player is no worse off for it. This is perhaps the best of these alternatives to PD because it offers some opportunity for players to start new characters when their old ones are wuss-slapped. Instead of Lefty III, you might go for Leftina instead (not that many players do—they treat it basically as resurrection). The fiction is basically sound, too, although it's invariably stretched so thin as to be transparent.

➤ *No believable fictional explanation.* Characters who "die" bounce back with whatever time, movement, kit, experience points, and skills that the designers decide. There's no sound rationalization, they just *do*. *Asheron's Call 2* with its progressive attitude that penalties for death in virtual worlds are "outdated" is the jaw-dropping epitome of this approach.

All these are alternatives to PD. However, the concept of actual PD is surprisingly incomprehensible to many players, who can't quite bring themselves to believe that there are virtual worlds in which death really does mean death; occasionally, therefore, some of the preceding will be described as being PD even though they're not. I've read reviews that described an insurance system as being PD, presumably on the grounds that your character is actually *not there* for a short period before rematerializing.

There also seems to be a good deal of denial among designers of virtual worlds. I've sat in on meetings where designers agreed among themselves to go with a PD system, then started to think of ways they could get around it ("Maybe we could have like a soul ring, that stores a character's essence and…").

As a designer, either you want or you don't want PD in your virtual world. If you do, bite the bullet and have it. Don't argue that what you have instead is "as good as" PD, or that it "hurts just as much as" PD; it isn't and it doesn't unless it *is* PD. If you don't want PD, that's your call; don't refer to the effects of a wuss-slap as "death," though, or you'll be perceiving consequences that aren't there.

It may seem from the preceding that I'm a die-hard PD fan unable to move with the times. Actually, it's not so much that I'm a fan of PD as that I'm an unfan of the alternatives as they are often used—that is, with complete ignorance. In many cases, PD should indeed rightly be off the agenda; I have no problem with that[79]. What infuriates me is when people put up ill-considered alternatives to PD without addressing the consequences, setting unwise precedents that the equally badly informed designers who follow slavishly copy.

If you want PD, you *must* understand what it buys you, and what you have to pay for it. Likewise, if you don't want PD then you also *must* understand what *that* buys you, and what you have to pay for it. If the consequences of PD are too hideous to contemplate, fair enough, go for non-PD; however, if you do so you should make sure you can address the consequences of not having PD, too, or you may end up with something equally hideous.

So, let's take a look at these consequences.

---

79. At the time of writing, my last two consultancy outings involved virtual worlds where PD—or any D, come to that—would be wildly inappropriate.

The Unfortunate Consequences of Permanent Death

People really do not like it when their character dies. That's *really* do not like it. Not only will they say they'll leave if it happens, some of them actually *will* leave. There's ample evidence of this from virtual worlds that launched with PD but toned it down in the face of player opposition. You can take steps to minimize this—keep the incidence of PD low but the awareness of its possibility high—but it'll still happen. Even non-PD PvP was softened in early flagship graphical worlds. People don't like to lose, they don't like to suffer, and they especially don't like other people making them suffer.

It's easy to dismiss this as a short-term thing, and that once players "mature enough" to see the benefits that PD brings they will be willing to tolerate it; there's informal evidence to support this position from long-term textual worlds with PD. However, even supposing that it's correct, this still doesn't help. Virtual worlds rely on newbies for their survival. Newbies are, by definition, immature (in their appreciation of virtual worlds). Given the choice between a virtual world that they can explore in complete safety and one where it seems a moment's lapse of concentration could undo weeks of play, well, they'll take the safe one, thank you very much.

Ah, the argument continues, but in time people will come to realize that such virtual worlds are unsatisfying, and, although they may be newbies to my virtual world, they won't be newbies to virtual worlds in general. They will be mature enough to give PD a chance. Well, perhaps, yes, but remember that people view all virtual worlds in the context of the virtual world with which they started. If they began with a virtual world that had no PD, they'll judge your virtual world from that standpoint[80]. It had better be a damned good one if they're to give it a try.

Even if they are "mature enough" for PD, their attitude is analogous to the way that people in the real world view public transport. I like the idea of public transport, so do you, so does everyone else. I like it because the more that other people travel by bus, the roads will be less congested for me to travel by car. So do you, so does everyone else. We're all in favor of it, but only for other people. So it is with PD: It's fine when it happens to *you*, but not so fine when it happens to *me*.

---

80. This is why precedents are so important.

Another issue is that PD is regularly confused with PvP. Players of *Ultima Online* didn't like it when their characters were attacked by large numbers of PCs operating in well coordinated gangs. It was unfair: These PKers were ruining the game. That's true, it was unfair and they were ruining the game; but it's a PvP issue, not a PD issue—those "PKers" weren't actually PKing. Nevertheless, because PvP and PD are so often combined to such disastrous effect, in many players' minds they're two sides of the same coin. Most players today haven't even experienced PD but are categorically opposed to it.

So, PD has an (not entirely unjustified) image problem which means players will probably stay away. Furthermore, if it occurs too often or too unexpectedly, so that players feel it's either arbitrary or unavoidable, even those players who came may decide to go. This is why developers of virtual worlds are rarely keen on PD.

There is, however, another reason why PD (in combination with PvP) is off-putting: The need for a *very* strong elder game. Players who manage to survive to "the end" need something to occupy them fully. If the designers don't provide it, they'll make their own entertainment. This may well take the form of employing their finely honed combat skills (possibly using a secondary character) to attack other PCs. A single, highly skilled killer can literally *empty* a small virtual world of other players, and it's very hard for administrators to stop them. After all, they're not exactly cheating. The fact that they want to protect the integrity of their rank by ensuring no "undeserving" characters reach it is, to them, incidental. For larger virtual worlds, these people would probably lead mobs rather than work alone, but the effect is the same: Other players quit to avoid the intimidation. As Chapter 3 pointed out, there is often a place in virtual worlds for small numbers of players of this type. Beyond a certain threshold, though, they can rapidly bring a virtual world to its knees. If you let fun PKing become your virtual world's elder game, prepare for the worst.

Despite all this, PD nevertheless has a lot going for it. Quite how much is best shown by considering what happens when it's taken away.

The Unfortunate Consequences of Non-Permanent Death

Let's imagine what the real world would be like if the philosophers of ancient Greece had discovered the secret of eternal life. If you take your daily dose of elixir, you won't age and will live forever. How would today's society be different?

Well, it's almost impossible to say, but one thing is for sure: Alexander the Great would still be in charge.

In virtual worlds, this is called *sandboxing*—the people who are first to positions of power get to keep them. There is no opportunity for change. Ensigns on the *Star Trek* spaceship *Voyager* (which was transported millions of light years from home) did not have a great career path no matter how able they were.

With no permanent death, virtual worlds consist of relentless progress toward either "the end" or some point of equilibrium (where the losses from whatever replaces permanent death balance the gains accrued in between such pseudo-deaths). When players feel they aren't advancing, they can become very frustrated; most virtual worlds without permanent death therefore endeavor to keep losses lower than gains. This keeps players' sense of achievement intact until they reach "the end," although a side effect is that it devalues what that achievement means: If anyone can plod to success, no one successful gets bragging rights.

What happens at "the end" is also problematical. "The end" is when highly experienced (or highly plodding) players run out of content. Ideally, these characters should be retired and new ones started. That, however, is too much like PD for many players to stomach. Remorting is a way of restarting with an existing character (as a different class), but it's a cop-out that really only delays the inevitable.

This irresistible rise problem is endemic in DikuMUDs. Eventually, high-level players will either join their virtual world's administrators or find something else to do with their lives. Interestingly, this may involve starting a new DikuMUD of their own. Thus, although it may be bad for an individual DikuMUD that players leave when they run out of content, it could be good for the species of DikuMUDs as a whole.

This isn't possible for players of large-scale graphical virtual worlds; it would be like a big-shot movie director telling a complaining member of an audience that if they don't like what they see on the screen they should go away and make their own movie instead. That said, there are many graphical worlds being developed by people who cut their teeth playing *EverQuest*, so in a sense the same well-worn path is being taken.

Of course, if you're a business that makes its money running an individual virtual world, you may not want your players to leave and set up ones in competition. Therefore, you need to encourage them to stay. The only solution not involving PD is to create new content, which is (as ever) expensive.

There is theory behind this, which anecdotal evidence from *EverQuest* suggests has some basis. The idea is that when new high-level content is added, it benefits not only the players for whom it was created, but also those that follow. It's called the *trickle-down effect*, although it's perhaps a misnomer in that content doesn't trickle down so much as characters trickle up to meet it. Nevertheless, the point is that although it may seem that content is being added only for the benefit of a few very powerful players, eventually all players will benefit from it as they reach that level. It's like building a road as people walk along it: The ones at the back of the line eventually get to use what was created for the people at the front of the line.

It sounds all well and good, but it's not without flaws:

➤ To newbies, the finishing post looks very, very distant. It may indeed look so distant to some that they decide not to bother embarking on the journey.

➤ Newbies (and not-so-newbies) feel they can never catch up. The people in front will always be in front, and there's no way to overtake them.

➤ The horizon advances at the speed you approach it. You're a donkey following a carrot on a stick.

It's like running a city marathon. You know from the start that it's a very long way, and not for the unfit or faint-hearted. You won't beat any of the people who started two hours before you, so you can only judge your performance at a personal level. Oh, and the course keeps lengthening, so you're not actually ever going to finish anyway.

In a virtual world with no PD, you only get to experience a body of content once. After you've consumed it, you rise in power such that the old content is no longer a challenge, so you go on to the next content. Aside from the fact that this is a huge waste of resources (players will repeat content many more times if they can come at it from different angles, for example with different characters or different strategies), it's not necessarily even the content as it was originally formulated. When greater monsters are created, greater treasure must also be created as a reward. Any weapons, armor, or other kit that's better than what a character has will be retained, and their old equipment sold on to characters at a lower level. These, in turn, will sell their old stuff to yet lower-level characters, and so on.

The result of this is that characters often have better gear than they ought to have for their level of experience. They can better tackle the adversities they face, and when victorious the rewards they obtain may be less useful than what they have already. Thus, they'll sell those on, too. It's a form of inflation that devalues objects at lower content levels.

The situation is not as bad as it sounds, in that there are more characters at lower levels than at higher ones and therefore they can't *all* have overpowered equipment. However, it's also worse because of deliberate *twinking*. Formally, twinked characters[81] are ones that have acquired equipment that they couldn't ever have obtained through the normal channels; in *EQ*'s case, this means killing monsters and trading with other characters. Although strictly speaking even trading to buy a better sword than you "should" have is a form of twinking, most people use the term to mean using your own high-level character to obtain goods for your low-level character.

Twinking isn't necessarily bad for a virtual world's economy (especially if objects can wear out), but it throws a dark shadow over content. Newbies who are twinked by a high-level stranger are often very impressed; they'll like the virtual world much more as a result. However, newbies who don't have a higher-level benefactor are resentful of people who do—especially when those people don't seem to see anything wrong with it. It's like a Hollywood actor researching a role as a homeless person, who turns up at a soup kitchen, takes a bowl of soup, then produces a freshly baked baguette and some croutons to eat with it. That soup was meant for a homeless person, not a Hollywood actor; similarly, newbies who see experienced players consuming their content aided by luxuries no one else has will feel resentful. No amount of "I worked hard for this" is going to mollify them. It exposes the newbie experience as worthless.

Even at higher levels, it's an issue. If you experience content with a twink (or otherwise overpowered character), you have an easier time of it than the designers planned. It's like taking a calculator into a mental arithmetic test: You'll finish sooner and get all

---

81. Or *twinks*.

the answers right, but you won't learn as much. Players with twinks won't necessarily see anything wrong with this, of course, because in their eyes they already sat the test once without a calculator, their main character. However, that assumes that only the answers are important; in terms of immersion, *how* you answer can be more telling than *what* you answer.

Twinking happens in virtual worlds with PD, but not to the same extent. This is because PD usually involves the total loss of all the kit you had with you when you died. If you get eaten by a dragon, the dragon gets whatever of your stuff survived; if your new character wants it, they'll have to take it off the dragon. It's not inherent to PD that object loss on death is implemented, but it usually is because it makes more sense. Virtual worlds without PD have moved slowly in the opposite direction, ensuring that even if you do "die" you won't lose certain bound items to looters, lessening the impact of "death" even more. In some virtual worlds, you don't lose anything tangible at all if a monster "kills" you.

The trickle-down effect requires that new content be added. The highest-level characters, for whom it is intended after all, will invariably want input on this. It's very tempting to listen to them. Power gamers[82] are an excellent resource for regular computer games, and their opinions on possible changes will regularly be sought. Discussions on web sites devoted to *Sid Meier's Civilization III*[83] have led directly to several code modifications released in the official patches. Unfortunately, however, in a virtual world where people can plod to the top without exhibiting the slightest sign of imagination, it is not guaranteed that the players of highest-level characters are power gamers; they could just be people with a lot of time on their hands. If you do listen to your highest-level players in determining content issues, make sure you can distinguish between the ones who have good ideas and the ones who merely think they do.

Note that these aren't reasons why your virtual world should have PD; rather, they're the situations you must tackle if you decide not to have it.

One of the biggest things you'll need to decide is what to do with the fiction. I listed earlier the more popular ways of explaining how come PCs recover from mortal blows, but the problem doesn't stop there. In particular, if you want a rational fiction then

---

82. This term hails from the board games community, hence players are "gamers."

83. Mainly `http://www.civfanatics.com/` and `http://apolyton.net/civ3`.

you'll need to produce some reason why the mobiles that the characters kill don't recover when they die and why they themselves don't go up levels when they "kill" characters[84]. Note that saying nothing may be better than saying something unconvincing, as at least it leaves open the possibility that a plausible fiction exists; if you pass off some cock-and-bull nonsense instead, you're stuck with it[85].

It is particularly hard to reconcile non-death with historical or licensed worlds. When authenticity is a selling point, the inauthentic can be jarring. For example, setting a virtual world in war-torn France with PCs as members of the resistance could work, but it would rather lose something if the PCs weren't ever in any danger of being killed. If the real-life French guerillas had been indestructible, the Nazis wouldn't even have invaded. Non-PD isn't the only authenticity issue with historical scenarios, of course (the fact that Paris was occupied for only 50 months somewhat limits the lifespan of a resistance scenario); it is, however, the biggest one.

Even in original fictional worlds, effective immortality has major implications. Society would develop in entirely different ways if everyone knew they weren't going to die. What careers would people have? How would laws be made and enforced? Would science advance faster or slower? Would there be war? If not, how would groups resolve their differences? Would there be religions? Jesus' resurrection would be no big deal if the same thing routinely happened to everyone. Where would everybody live? What would children do when they grew up?

Most designers take the point of view that these are not questions that need to be answered. The loss of immersion delivered from saying nothing on the subject is minuscule compared to the loss that would be incurred by dumping players into a virtual world that followed through the implications of immortality—it would be seriously alien to players' real-world experiences. Under the circumstances, this is therefore the most sensible approach.

Pro-PD people may still urge caution, in that systems which work fine in the real world may behave less well when applied in a virtual world with no PD. Example: If no one died it would play havoc with the housing market. It's often the case that churn

---

84. Actually, in some virtual worlds they do. It's uncommon, though.

85. This is especially bad for virtual worlds with a story arc, because they don't have the option of leaving it unsaid, either. If you're promoting story, you can't be selective about it and expect people not to notice.

will take on the role that death does in the real world, though: Characters *do* die when their players quit, therefore a house will go back on the market if its owner cancels his or her account. There are some exceptions (for example, no PC would take out life insurance, therefore insurance companies would not be as rich as in the real world, therefore investment in stocks and shares would be lower) but these are invariably swamped by other factors anyway.

A virtual world without PD can be created to address all these issues, some of which are, frankly, of the "clutching at straws" variety anyway. Most virtual worlds do, in fact—worlds without PD greatly outnumber those with it. You *can* have a successful non-PD world.

So why is it, then, that time after time designers and long-term players will sense there is something missing from their virtual world, take a good, hard look at it, and conclude that, you know, maybe PD really isn't all that bad?

Why Permanent Death?

Players are against PD because they don't want to die. Although some socializers wishing to flaunt their loving and caring credentials might disagree, players in general don't care if someone *else* dies—they just don't want it to happen to *them*. Because no one wants it to happen to them, it doesn't happen to anyone. So everyone is happy, right?

For a time, yes. Then, the fact that the whole experience is vacuous begins to nag at them.

Achievement—and with it a sense of personal advancement—can come in two ways in virtual worlds, neither of which occurs without PD or some equivalent. Characters can either advance gradually via a series of small actions done well, or heroically through single, life-changing events. Without PD, "small actions" are steps on a treadmill and "done well" means you move slightly faster than people who have "done badly." Heroism is no such thing—it's just another example of a "small action." This is the root cause of the dissatisfaction that many players of non-PD virtual worlds develop.

Players play virtual worlds to explore and celebrate their identity. The undertaking of courageous acts, whether for gain or to help others, can make highly significant contributions to personal development. It's the uneasy realization that actually these acts weren't as courageous as you thought they were that can cause the problems.

Note that it's not the immediate thrill that's important. Fights in *EverQuest* wouldn't necessarily be any more exciting if death really meant death. It's in the rationalization where it differs. When failure at an action means oblivion, you can say more about someone who attempts it than you can when all they'll suffer is a wuss-slap. The difference is of immense importance, because they're not only putting their tangible character on the line, they're putting their nascent identity on the line too.

People may not want to undertake such risks. This is fair enough—bravery doesn't have to mean stupidity. In a PD world, players assess the chance they'll escape with their lives: If it's too low[86], they'll pass. In a non-PD world, players don't want the risk but still want to perform the action. The penalty for failure is therefore lowered to acceptable levels. Even stupid players won't lose their characters. Failure may be annoying, but it takes more than that to make success heroic.

Acts are only heroic when there is a significant, perceived chance of real loss *and* no easier alternative. The following acts are not heroic:

➤ Standing in the way of a runaway cat. (No chance of real loss.)

➤ Walking across a minefield you didn't know was there. (No perceived danger.)

➤ Swimming across a crocodile-infested river next to a bridge. (Brave, but unnecessary.)

Putting PD into a virtual world does not make people heroic. It does, however, ensure that those who talk heroic *are* heroic. The designers of virtual worlds can make all their players immortal, but they can't make any of them heroes. Only players can make themselves heroes. If they later come to realize they're not the heroes they thought they were, disenchantment sets in.

The most compelling reason for having PD is that it makes a virtual world meaningful in its own terms. Players can always construct meanings for activities in their virtual world, but these are not intrinsic to it or (crucially) to the real world. Without PD, a virtual world can still be real-world meaningful, but in external contexts only (for example, it's a dating agency).

---

86. To enhance excitement and reduce the incidence of death, the actual risk of PD is generally lower than players estimate it to be—that is, favorably "unrealistic." For example, although a dragon will always beat a newbie, higher-level characters might be able to survive more often than they would against a "real" fire-breathing lizard the size of an apartment block.

Virtual worlds are about identity; if you can't lose something, you don't value it; therefore, you can never value your identity in a non-PD world as much as you can in a PD world. This is less fierce than it sounds, in that immersion to persona level can provide the external context that makes a virtual world meaningful (to the immersed player); it's just harder to reach that level of immersion in a virtual world that doesn't have PD.

Meaningfulness is the fuel that powers the engine of identity development. It helps you get where you're going. Without it, you either have to freewheel (non-PD) or get out and push (role-play).

Pleasure only works if there is pain against which to compare it. For many players, the virtual world is the pleasure and the real world is the pain; these players don't want to experience pain in the virtual world too, hence the issue of consent is important. However, withdrawing consent also withdraws meaning—not just from the withdrawer, but *from everyone else, too*. It violates the "no easier alternative" requirement of heroism. Mechanisms to prevent this aren't hard to propose—a simple level cap for immortal characters would do it—but the problem is that many players won't stand for it: They want meaning *without* consenting to what's required to give it to them. If the virtual world can't provide it, they have to provide it for themselves. Is it surprising that they often end up dissatisfied?

You can see their point of view, of course. As far as they are concerned, they are role-playing a hero in a virtual world built for heroes[87]. Heroes are special people who don't get killed, *ergo* their character shouldn't get killed either. Players may be nobodies in real life, but in virtual worlds they're *somebody*.

In the Gilbert and Sullivan musical *The Gondoliers*[88], there is a celebrated song, "There Lived a King." It tells the tale of a monarch who, determining it to be unfair that he can drink Rhenish wine while other people have to drink toddy, promotes all his subjects to the highest ranks. The kingdom swarms with lord chancellors, bishops, ambassadors, prime ministers, dukes, field marshals, lord lieutenants, admirals, and party leaders.

---

87. This isn't true for all virtual worlds, of course, but it is for most game-oriented ones.

88. William S. Gilbert and Arthur Sullivan, *The Gondoliers or The King of Barataria*. London, Savoy Theatre, 1889.

The result isn't hard to predict:

> *In short, whoever you may be,*
>
> *To this conclusion you'll agree,*
>
> *When every one is somebodee,*
>
> *Then no one's anybody!*

If everyone is a hero, no one is.

This argument is very pessimistic. It suggests that everyone can't be a hero even if they do heroic things: Everyone does heroic things, everyone becomes a hero, heroism is commonplace, therefore no one is truly a hero. The meaning has been stripped by its ubiquity.

Heroism does have a saving throw, though. It's true that if everyone were a hero then no one would be. The thing is, everyone *can* be a hero, just *not at the same time.*

The Hero's Journey

In his influential book, *The Hero with a Thousand Faces*[89], academic Joseph Campbell asserted that the various heroic myths of all cultures follow the same, basic storyline. His theory was that myths are tied to the human psyche; they are cultural expressions of a universal need to explain the same, fundamental concepts of social, worldly, and other-worldly realities. Not all narratives follow the basic pattern (which is called *the hero's journey*[90]), but all myths and epics do. Famously, the movie *Star Wars* follows the hero's journey almost to the letter.

Many of the steps in the hero's journey are symbolic or metaphoric, so it may take a student of myth to recognize some of the more subtle ones. Once they have been iden-tified, however, the basic sequence will usually be standard. Occasionally, steps may be omitted or reversed in order, but on the whole the overall structure of the myth will be the same. Heroes are heroes because they complete the hero's journey.

---

89. Joseph Campbell, *The Hero with a Thousand Faces*. Princeton, *Bolllingen Series 17*, Princeton University Press, 1949.

90. It works for heroines too, but this is 1949 speaking.

This is a different perspective on heroism to that understood by players of virtual worlds. The hero's journey includes heroic acts, but these alone don't make someone a hero. If you risk life and limb—even in a PD world—to save an innocent, that's an heroic act. People may regard you as a hero, but it's a simile: They're holding you in the same esteem they would hold a hero of ancient myth. If you want to *be* a hero, though, you have to complete the hero's journey.

This, you can do. Let's examine how.

The hero's journey consists of a number of steps. Some of these are more significant than others, some take longer to occur than others, some have more symbolic connotations than others. They are grouped into three phases: departure, initiation, and return. Here's a brief description of the steps.

Departure

- *The call to adventure.* The hero is given an indication that everything is going to change. The call may be symbolic, and the hero doesn't have to realize what it means.

- *Refusal of the call.* The hero is required to act, but initially refuses. This can be through fear, duty, or a whole bunch of other things. If the hero holds out, they may be subjected to assault until they take the hint.

- *Supernatural aid.* Once the hero accepts the call, a supernatural guide is revealed to help them. Now they can enter the world of their quest.

- *The crossing of the first threshold.* The hero leaves their own world and enters that of their adventure. This is a dangerous place, with unknown rules and unknown limits. The new realm may have a guardian that the hero has to defeat or befriend to get past the threshold.

- *The belly of the whale.* This is symbolic, representing the final separation of the hero's old world, old self, and a developing new world, new self. By entering the belly of the whale (or anything womb-like), the hero is committing to rebirth and transformation.

Initiation

- ➤ *The road of trials.* These are a series of (often three) ordeals that the hero must undergo to begin their metamorphosis. They could well fail at least one.

- ➤ *The meeting with the goddess.* This is another highly symbolic step. The goddess represents the totality of knowledge; if the hero is not consumed by exposure to it, they are liberated by it. This is usually described in terms of the hero's experiencing absolute, unconditional love. The understanding the hero gains leads to a "union of opposites;" the hero's self-image begins coalesce as the hero gains awareness of the forces of life and death, of mortal and spiritual.

- ➤ *Woman as the temptress.* Woman here is a metaphor for the temptations that may cause the hero to stray from their journey. The hero's old-world origins are at odds with the new world, but the hero overcomes the urge to return to them.

- ➤ *Atonement with the father.* This is the key point of the journey, in which the hero faces whatever entity has the supreme power in their life. The hero recognizes the darkness in his or herself and discovers the light. The hero's old self is killed (literally or metaphorically) and the new self steps forth.

- ➤ *Apotheosis.* A period of peace, rest, and bliss that the hero experiences before commencing the return home. Old cultural assumptions are finally broken, and old prejudices forgotten.

- ➤ *The ultimate boon.* Although the hero has already achieved the real aim of their quest, this is where they pick up the object they set out to acquire. The boon is often a token for which the hero is now sufficiently pure to obtain. They must bring it back for the benefit of all.

Return

- ➤ *Refusal of the return.* Life in the new world is so pleasant and carefree that the hero doesn't see any reason to go home.

- ➤ *The magic flight.* The hero can't stay *and* have the boon. This is the exciting escape with it.

- ➤ *Rescue from without.* The hero still doesn't want to return, is prevented from returning, or is too weak to return. Powerful friends or allies help it happen.

> ➤ *The crossing of the return threshold.* The hero returns to their old world and old life. How will they reconcile the old and the new? How will they apply their new-found wisdom?

> ➤ *Master of the two worlds.* The hero achieves a serene or transcendental balance between the old, material world and the new, spiritual one. They accept their destiny.

> ➤ *Freedom to live.* Due to their mastery, the hero no longer fears death; they can live for the moment, unconcerned with whatever the past has held and whatever the future holds. It's the journey that's important, not the destination.

In the context of virtual worlds, the hero's journey is normally discussed in terms of its relevance (or lack thereof) to story arcs. That's not how I shall be applying it here.

The hero's adventurous journey betokens a journey to find the self. It's the same journey that players of virtual worlds undertake. They play to have fun, but they gain much more than that: They develop as people.

Let's take a look at the steps as they apply to virtual worlds.

Departure

In this discussion, the "old world" is the real world and the "new world" is the virtual world. The departure action therefore takes place in real world.

> ➤ *The call to adventure.* Something triggers the would-be player's attention. It may be a specific advertisement, testimonial, shelf unit, cover disk, magazine article, or pushy friend—it doesn't really matter. The point is that the player now finds the idea of virtual worlds appealing when previously either they didn't or they hadn't thought about it.

> ➤ *Refusal of the call.* There are lots of reasons not to enter a virtual world: expense, time, fears of inadequacy, a social life. However, the appeal of the virtual world grows. The player really wants to try one.

> ➤ *Supernatural aid.* This step may be skipped if the player concedes to their desire. Where it isn't, it's likely that the player will know someone else who already plays and is able to help, or is a member of a group of friends who decide to try the virtual world together.

➤ *The crossing of the first threshold.* The player installs the software on their computer and powers up. They enter the virtual world, which is a dangerous place with unknown rules and unknown limits. The quality of the interface determines whether or not it counts as a guardian.

➤ *The belly of the whale.* The character generation system. The player creates a new self for the new world. It's a formal rebirth; the player is undertaking to become someone else.

Initiation

This stage takes place in the virtual world, and is therefore the one that is most important to virtual world designers (more important than they may realize!). You may want to look back at the player development tracks shown in Figure 3.5 before you read this. You also might like to refer to the review of Hedron's Six Circles, because this (at last!) is why I mentioned it[91].

➤ *The road of trials.* The player finds their feet. This is the opportunist/griefer step, where players meet and respond to small challenges to determine the extent of their abilities. Their success or failure at these will establish their course of future action.

➤ *The meeting with the goddess.* The player seeks knowledge, either through experimentation (as a scientist) or from others (as a networker). The more that players learn about the virtual world and its inhabitants, the more they learn about themselves. If they can handle what they learn, they are stronger for it. They begin the process of immersion—that is, of coalescing their real-life self with their virtual self.

➤ *Woman as the temptress.* Once players have learned enough to become accomplished, they are at last informed enough to judge whether they want to attempt to complete it. Are they in it for the long haul, or is their academic curiosity sufficiently satisfied that they don't feel they need to continue? This step covers the transition from discovery to application, from learning to doing.

➤ *Atonement with the father.* This is the step that players spend most of their time taking, putting the skills they have acquired into practice. It's where the planner-type achievers and politician-type socializers strive to improve and impress. The

---

91. See if you can match the circles up to the steps—it's not all that difficult.

virtual world's achievement metric (for example, character level) charts the players' progress to their goal. When they reach the end as the virtual world defines it, they "win." It is the key moment in their virtual existence. The "father" who they are confronting is the virtual world's (lead) designer, whose will is expressed by the virtual world and who wields its ultimate power. When the designer (through the implementation of the virtual world) accepts them, then they have the closure they need to move on to the final, serene state of total immersion.

➤ *Apotheosis*. Players wind up here as friend-type socializers or hacker-type explorers. They understand the virtual world, its people, and themselves; they are at peace with all. Challenges from the virtual world, when they arise, are no longer important.

➤ *The ultimate boon*. Oh dear. Virtual worlds don't have an ultimate boon. Players have no token of their achievement. They have skills and wisdom that they can bring back with them into the real world, but nothing formal to symbolize it.

Return

This final stage accounts for players' return from the virtual world to reality (or, perhaps more tellingly, the acceptance of players that the virtual world is part of reality).

➤ *Refusal of the return*. The player has power, respect, friends, and peace. Why would they want to return to the real world?

➤ *The magic flight*. The live team will usually not want a player to leave, and may provide a compelling elder game to try to ensnare them. They don't, however, want their boon back (or wouldn't, if they had one in the first place) and the barriers they erect are of the temptation variety rather than the physical or emotional of common myth.

➤ *Rescue from without*. Your parents, your workmates, your significant other—"Stop spending so much time on that computer!"

➤ *The crossing of the return threshold*. The player finally separates from the virtual world. Contrary to what many players think, this rarely involves a "burn all your bridges" deletion of characters (that will typically happen in the atonement step). If it involves an account cancellation, it's for practical rather than symbolic reasons. The player stops playing simply because they don't *need* to play any more.

➤ *Master of the two worlds.* The player's virtual and real self are the same. The player can return to the virtual world, but it's a place like any other. It has lost its mythical significance (to that player).

➤ *Freedom to live.* Players can finally be themselves.

Apart from the problem with the boon, this all looks very neat and tidy. The very general nature of the hero's journey, however, with its mythical and symbolic components, means that with a little imagination it can be applied to stylized sequences of action where perhaps it isn't really appropriate[92]. To what extent is this true for its use concerning player development tracks?

Analysis

Conjecture: Playing virtual worlds is a kind of hill-climbing activity through identity space; the hero's journey is an algorithm for finding a very good local maximum, if not necessarily a global one.

I believe that the hero's journey does directly apply to player development in virtual worlds. However, the fit is not exact. Given that the hero's journey has evolved independently in all cultures through the millennia, should some effort be made to try and make the fit better? Or is the fit not exact because in truth it isn't a fit at all?

I'll go through what I perceive to be the main issues. This is all speculative; see what you think:

➤ *The belly of the whale.* Although it's fine to identify the character creation screen as "womb-like" in its effect, normally a myth would have something that was suggestive of a womb in appearance, too. A cave, a pit, a log cabin, a belly of a whale…. Would making character creation take place in such an environment speak more deeply to players' subconsciousnesses? Or does the fact it's called "character creation" do away with the need for such symbolism as it's pretty obvious what's happening anyway?

---

92. The breakfast's journey: The story of one cereal's transformation through the other-worldly human digestive tract. "When I first saw the flash of a silver spoon, little did I realize that through its purity I would embark on a journey that would take me, literally, to the world's end and beyond…."

➤ *The meeting with the goddess*. It's very tempting to equate the addiction that many players feel about virtual worlds with the "unconditional love" metaphor here, but sadly it doesn't work. Not only does addiction share none of the qualities that unconditional love is meant to symbolize, but it doesn't really bite until the next stage anyway, where the player gets to use their new-found powers. That said, then, what is the virtual world's equivalent of "unconditional love?" The goddess could be a player's guide or a web site or some other fount of knowledge, but where does love come in? It's a very common metaphor in myth.

➤ *Woman as temptress*. This is a stage that all players go through, but it's not really any more special than the transition from griefer/opportunist to networker/scientist. If we lost lots of players here who decided that now they know the rules they don't want to play, fair enough; but we don't. Why is this step important for the hero's journey but less important (although still present) in player development terms?

➤ *Atonement with the father (I)*. The mere existence of this step suggests that the player's presence in the virtual world must come to an end; players need the closure, they can't go on forever. This is not something with which the developers of virtual worlds would necessarily concur. They don't want players to leave[93], so they continually add new content—thereby denying atonement and initiation. In such circumstances, players have huge difficulties satisfactorily completing their hero's journey: They can only do so by rejecting the father (who has rejected them), which is not pleasant.

➤ *Atonement with the father (II)*. Atonement implies that acceptance isn't automatic: The player must "deserve" it. This is where a PD world delivers and a non-PD one doesn't. If success is guaranteed with time, acceptance isn't in question.

➤ *Atonement with the father (III)*. Virtual worlds can only measure tangible things. For planner-type achievers this is easy enough (experience levels, skill levels, possessions, and so on), but for politician-type socializers, how do *they* gain final acceptance by the designer?

---

93. Commercial virtual worlds are particularly keen on keeping players.

➤ *Atonement with the father (IV).* What happens when control of the virtual world is wrested from the design team and handed to, say, the marketing or the community service group? An individual can act as a foster-father figure, but they didn't actually create the virtual world. Has the father abandoned the hero?

➤ *The ultimate boon.* The reason that most virtual worlds don't have this is because developers don't want people to leave. Although some players may accept the inevitability of their departure, most developers don't. It wouldn't be hard to give players recognition either within the virtual world or without it; indeed, some virtual worlds do this[94]. It doesn't have to be the player's ticket home, but it should be something special that players can only ever obtain once.

➤ *The magic flight (I).* Without a boon, this still sort of goes to plan: Players try to leave against the wishes of the guardians of the virtual world. With a boon, the magic flight would perhaps work counter to this. It's easy to see how forcing a player to retire would lead to attempts by that player to continue to play. Secondary accounts would be opened then closed, attempts to masquerade as a new player would be made then detected, and so on until eventually the player would get the message and stay away. This is *not* how magical flights normally work! Heroes will usually have to break out of the new world to reach the old, rather than be stuck in the old because they fail to break back into the new.

➤ *The magic flight (II).* If players don't leave, does not their continuing presence interfere with the progress of other players? Can heaven become full? Doesn't the sheer number of heroes still wandering around debase the currency of heroism[95]? Perhaps trying to keep players involved indefinitely is actually bad for a virtual world in the long term?

➤ *Master of the two worlds.* The keepers of the virtual world can't give anything to the player that is of material use or value in the real world because people will cheat to get it (imagine what would happen if there were a substantial cash prize for reaching the level cap, for example). Unlike the new world of myth, people really *can* enter virtual worlds; what's more, they can visit it with their buddies

---

94. *MUD1* listed the names of its wizzes on tombs in a graveyard. *MUD2* also does this, and gives out wiz manuals and other goodies to people who get this far, too.

95. This is the "when every one is somebodee" argument again.

and bring out boons by the truckload. Players take from the virtual world the confidence, self-esteem, friendships, and life skills they picked up there, but that's all that's of any use. It's up to them what they do with these.

> *General*. Players can achieve immersion without following all these steps. If there is no formal end-point, for example, that doesn't stop people from reaching full immersion; it might be harder or more frustrating for them, but they can still do it. This may be a template for a hero's journey, but you can become a hero by following your own path, too.

You don't have to leave a virtual world if you don't want to (they're just places, after all), but for some people it's a necessary closure. Is denying an exit—through the design of the world—therefore immoral? As you've probably come to expect now, this is discussed later in Chapter 8.

Not everyone can complete the hero's journey; not everyone can be—or wants to be—a hero. People can and do stop beforehand; some may even be heroes before they start. Everyone can *try* to be a hero, though, and a well-designed virtual world gives them a better chance of succeeding than almost anything else available to ordinary people.

The critical thing is, although you can do heroic deeds in the virtual world, you have to leave for them to count. You visit the virtual world to become a hero, but you can only *be* a hero in the real one. The virtual world is a part of the real world.

Warriors are only heroes when the battle is over. While the battle is raging, they're just trying to stay alive.

Attitudes to Permanent Death

Will attitudes to permanent death change?

If some way could be found to retain the desirable consequences of PD while losing the undesirable ones, attitudes wouldn't need to change. With our current knowledge of PD, however, this seems unlikely.

Change *will* have to occur, however, if virtual worlds are to remain faithful to their essence, at least in combat-oriented worlds. Dilution of the virtual world "product" will leave people unsatisfied. Will they stop playing all virtual worlds, or continually drift from one to the next, forever unable to find something that satisfies their long-term aims without violating their short-term criteria?

Existing virtual world culture is anti-PD. Upcoming virtual worlds are therefore also likely to be anti-PD. This is primarily due to imperfect early implementations[96] and bad customer service decisions; nevertheless, the legacy is there. Trying to stop it is like trying to prevent a herd of cattle stampeding toward an oasis in the desert: You know they're going to drink it dry and then they won't be able to make it to the distant but flowing river you want them to go to. But if you stand in their way you're only going to get trampled.

Players, fortunately, are not cattle. Those who think about the subject—what they want and what they don't want—may change their views and (reluctantly) support PD. Then again, they may become even stronger in their opposition to it. Change would amount to a paradigm shift, however, which is very hard to effect. That said, we've already had one the other way (early MUDs had PD) so it's not impossible.

Many designers feel that the reason PD fails is because it isn't "done right," at least on the large scale. They could be correct. However, they also believe that the way they plan on implementing it *is* right. When it turns out to be wrong, they set back the cause of PD even more. The more that designers know about PD and non-PD, the more they can base their decisions on experience rather than hope. With any luck, this section has gone some way toward helping inform such decisions, whichever way they eventually go.

I have one last thing to say before I leave the subject, which I present here without comment. It's a statistical observation from a well-known, large-scale graphical virtual world:

> *A change from PD to non-PD has no effect on the number of customer service complaints.*

Draw your own conclusions.

---

96. Note that this does not imply that there must necessarily be a perfect one. It may be that PD will always be flawed beyond redemption and therefore it's just as well that emerging virtual worlds reject it—even if this is for the wrong reasons.

Crafting

When characters are not fighting one another, what *are* they doing? Socializing, exploring, and being pains, yes, but in gameplay terms what do they have to occupy them? Except in the elder game (which I'll come to later), they'll typically be creating something (for example, digging iron, making arrows) or providing a service (transporting iron, selling arrows). Because in most virtual worlds the service side is either trivial or automated, it's normally lumped together with manufacturing under the general heading of *crafting*.

Much of this was covered earlier in the Chapter 4 section on economics, but there are a few more points that can be raised in the light of what has been discussed since.

Manufacture

Here's how a simple real-world manufacturing process works:

➤ Raw materials are grown, dug from the ground, or captured. Examples: wheat, ore, cows.

➤ The raw materials are refined to get rid of the useless bits. Examples: grain, copper, milk.

➤ The refined materials are made into components or finished goods. Examples: bread, wire, cheese.

➤ Components are combined with other components to make new components or finished goods. Examples: sandwiches, circuit boards, pizzas.

➤ Finished goods are sold to consumers, who use them to destruction.

➤ Destroyed goods are recycled into refined materials.

In virtual worlds, it's usually even simpler. Except for animals, raw materials typically emerge in refined form. Components don't exist: Raw/refined materials are combined (using an abstract formula known as a *recipe*) to make finished goods. Recycling does not occur, except perhaps when encapsulated in some grand closed-economy scheme.

Needless to say, the excitement derived from crafting approaches 0% in intensity.

There are exceptions. The virtual world *A Tale in the Desert*[97], which is set in ancient Egypt, has a full-blown crafting system at its core. Players can collect slate from riverbeds, that can be used to pay for tuition in stone blade fabrication; they can then make a stone blade from slate, which will pay for tuition in the carpentry skill; using wood obtained from trees, they can manufacture a wood plane and create boards; also using wood from trees, they can pay for the tuition necessary to make a brick rack; they can then make a brick rack; grass can be harvested and dried to make straw; they can obtain sand from the desert and mud from riverbeds; using their brick rack, they can finally manufacture bricks.

Needless to say, the excitement from crafting using this far more sophisticated system still approaches 0% in intensity. Fortunately, because it's so tedious players will manufacture components that they sell to each other; this introduces an element of interaction that makes for some fun (at least it does if people will sell you what you need). There are some gameplay bugs to be ironed out, but designers have high hopes for *A Tale in the Desert* as a proof of concept if nothing else.

If a virtual world has a craft system of any substance, there are three golden rules to obey:

➤ All crafts should have gameplay value.

➤ The range of craftable objects should be great.

➤ The depth of crafting skills should be deep.

I've covered these elsewhere already, but I'll quickly reprise the reasons for them here.

Crafts should have gameplay value because this adds to immersion and interaction. This applies even to basically intangible objects such as "pretty" jewelry: Anything that impresses PCs should also impress NPCs, even if only crudely so by comparison.

The range of craftable objects should be great or people will end up making the same things and flooding the economy with more goods of one type than it needs.

---

97. http://www.egenesis.com/

The depth of craftable skills should be great or players will not consider crafting as a career. If crafting is something that adventurers do in their spare time, this is enough; if you want to cater to people who would rather create objects than destroy mobiles, however, they'll need skill sets potentially as deep as adventurers'.

There may still be a problem when player expectations come up against virtual world economics. The "I'm role-playing a hero and I don't see why I should be killed" adventurer has an equivalent in the "I'm role-playing a swordsmith and I don't see why I shouldn't sell my swords" crafter. Sorry, guys, but no one is buying the identical swords that NPC swordsmiths are making, and they're not going to buy yours either unless you drop the price.

Recipes

My house is within five miles of four large supermarkets. The bread in the first one is too doughy; the bread in the second is too crusty; the bread in the third is too soft; the bread in the fourth is perfect (a shame the rest of the stuff they sell is so rubbish). Bread has been manufactured for thousands of years, but even today bakers use different recipes.

To make crafting more palatable to non-socializers, some virtual worlds have introduced explorative or competitive elements to it. One favored technique is to have multiple recipes for the same basic object (or, commonly, spell—this can be applied to more than just manufacture), some of which will endow the resulting creation with different properties than others. A recipe typically consists of a set of ingredients; these will often have to be explicitly arranged in some (usually linear) sequence, but in some implementations the "use recipe" action will do it implicitly.

This is one of those suggestions that sounds reasonable until you think about it. Unfortunately, it is frequently implemented without being thought about.

The idea is that players should be rewarded for experimentation. If you sit around mixing reagents and come up with a recipe for a steel that is more hard-wearing than regular steel without being any more brittle, you should be able to profit from your experiment. This is fair enough: If people discover through use that your swords are better than Joe NPC's, they'll come to you next time they need a new one. This is, of course, until some helpful soul puts a ton of sword recipes on their web site with a description of the precise effect of each one.

To counter this possibility, designers will usually try one of two approaches. The first of these is to allow characters to patent a recipe if they discover it first; subsequent use of this recipe by any other crafter will result in a royalty for the patent holder. This is fine for those who start playing the virtual world early, but it's no use to those who come along six months later.

The second solution is to individualize recipes, so that the proportions of ingredients that you need to make the perfect sword are different to the ones that I need. This is unrealistic when applied to mundane object creation, but works for things like magical artifacts. *Asheron's Call* allowed for spell experimentation through different ordered combinations of "spell components," and incorporated a *random taper* to make these unique to every character. These yielded easily to brute-force cracking methods, though. *AC* did have a back-up mechanism to discourage spell recipes from becoming commonly known, in that the more often a spell was used the weaker it grew. Mages who knew the recipe were thus disinclined to tell others what it was. Unfortunately, it only takes one recipe-holder to break ranks (for example, an explorer who doesn't care if a spell loses its potency) and anyone who wants to find out can.

The root of the problem is that players don't *like* having personal recipes. They *want* recipes to be global, so they don't have to figure them out in advance. Designers may want to convince them otherwise, but it's not going to happen. Like any other discovery in virtual worlds, once a recipe is unearthed it rapidly becomes common knowledge.

Ironically, although recipes are typically conceived to help crafters, it's adventurers who are most likely to end up using them. There is some scope for using recipes in directly competitive situations—that is, as combat scripts. There, the efficacy of your recipe is directly dependent on the recipe your opponent is using. Cooperative recipes, where I do this while you do that, are also possible; however, they're not going to make manufacture any more fun.

Beyond the Virtual World

So, I want to bake a loaf of bread. I get the ingredients, I mix them up, I stick them in the oven, then—I wait? What if I'm not baking bread but am manufacturing swords? I get the metal together, heat it, beat it, rapidly cool it, heat it, beat it, rapidly cool it, heat it—for how long? Do I actually have to *do* this? My character has the skills, not me—why should I have to be present while it happens?

The sheer monotony of repeatedly clicking on the same icon (or, for really advanced systems, the same three icons) for long, long periods has led designers to look at ways to alleviate the boredom. The most promising one opens up other possibilities, too: offline action.

Although many players may find this hard to believe, they cannot spend 24 hours a day playing in their virtual world. There are real-world demands that have to be met, most notably sleep. Some of the time, players are disconnected from their characters. What do the characters do during this offline period?

Well, the answer is that they can do the stuff that the player didn't want them to do while being played. Thus, the character can sleep, eat, visit the bathroom, and so on. For reasons of safety[98] and confusion[99], they will usually not be visibly present in the virtual world while they do this (that is, they're not temporarily NPCs); however, they are there in the abstract[100].

It seems obvious, therefore, that if players want their characters to do something mindlessly boring, this would be the time to do it. You set your character digging, you log off, go to school, come back half a day later, log back on and your character has deposited six truckloads of ore in your depot.

Virtual worlds always took some account of characters' continued existence while their players are offline. *MUD1*, for example, would gradually heal characters' wounds while no one was playing them. These weren't actually offline activities, though; you didn't really have a choice about what your character did while you weren't there.

The first steps in that direction concerned trade. You hired an NPC to buy and sell stuff for you (usually the latter rather than the former) while you went away adventuring. The NPC remained in place when you finished your session, therefore when you next returned you might have found that someone had bought something from you or

---

98. In PvP or PD worlds.

99. People trying to interact with them.

100. How they reappear when the player starts a new session without shattering immersion is an issue that concerns all virtual worlds. For some genres, a fictional (but rarely convincing) explanation may be possible, but for most you just have to accept that it's out of context. Characters blink into and out of existence and that's all there is to it; tough luck if you weren't expecting it.

sold you the materials you wanted. There are some issues as to how price changes function in this situation, but in general it works well. Offline manufacture extends the same principle to the PC, rather than some NPC hireling, and simulates what the PC was doing rather than actually doing it (as it does with the NPC).

Skill learning fits this system well. Learning how to make a pot isn't something that occurs the instant you hand over your training fee; to make sense, it ought to take time. By making it an offline occurrence, this passage of time can be suggested without drying the brains of the players. Furthermore, it makes them eager to come back next session to try out their new skills, and hey, it benefits adventurers, too!

There are other applications for offline action of which travel is perhaps the most interesting. Virtual worlds are large, but players don't really get a feel for how large because of the (economy-wrecking) instant travel solutions that are available to them. No one wants to make players march their characters across a desert, but how can you convey a sense of remoteness if you let them press the magic button and materialize instantly? Well, offline action lets you do it. You set off walking, riding, flying, or whatever, then disconnect. When you reconnect the next day, there you are. If you were to reconnect prematurely, you would appear in the desert or whatever, your exact location interpolated from your starting position, destination, the elapsed time, and your mode of transport.

There are two ways to handle offline activities, whatever you use them for.

The first way is to give orders in advance. Just before you log off, you instruct the virtual world as to what your character will be doing while you're away. Some of these tasks will take longer than others, but you can create a queue of orders so it doesn't really matter. When you next log in, the character will have worked through some or all of the queue, and you can pick up from there. The advantages of this approach are that you can be informed (for example, by email or phone message) when a task is complete, and that you can set orders without using the virtual world's client software (for example, via a standard web browser from work).

The second way is a more quantum mechanics approach. Your character accumulates activity time while you are offline, but you don't have to decide how it's spent until you log in and collapse the quantum wave. This means you can take into account events that have occurred while you were offline—for example, if gold has been discovered in them thar hills in the direction opposite to where you were intending to travel. This retroactive approach doesn't allow for interrupts when actions are complete, but it's handy for meeting up with friends who have wandered off since you last played.

There's no reason why a virtual world couldn't use both of these approaches, of course: When the action queue is empty, subsequent offline time is banked for when the player next logs in.

Offline actions aren't a panacea for boring activities. In practice, there will usually be some limit to the amount of offline time that can be spent, if only to stop players from setting up programmed mules to act as craft factory cash cows. Some people object to it in principle, as it can break the bond between player and character ("How can I be in the virtual world and at work in the office at the same time?"). Nevertheless, this idea does have potential and the advantages seem to outweigh the disadvantages.

The Elder Game

There comes a point when players have advanced so far that they feel they have achieved everything that they set out to achieve. They are no longer interested in the activities that used to occupy their time: They feel they have "made it." The question then arises: What can they do instead?

Who Plays the Elder Game?

The content that occupies players in advanced states of immersion is known as the *elder game*[101]. It deals with four types of player, each with differing needs. In hero's journey terms, these are those who are in the following states:

> ➤ *Pre-apotheosis.* Players whose characters have advanced quicker than they themselves have. This may be because the players have had too much help on the way, or they didn't recognize/understand the atonement (that is, final achievement) process. These players will want more of the content that they were consuming before they reached the elder game, but which they have now exhausted.

---

101. The term was first coined by Raph Koster. Although he applied it to game-type virtual worlds (hence the name), it extends to non-game virtual worlds, too.

➤ *Apotheosis.* The players for whom the elder game is primarily intended. They have succeeded in their goal, and are enjoying resting on their laurels prior to returning to the real world.

➤ *Refusal of return.* They don't want to stop playing, and the live team usually doesn't want them to go either. However, they've either used all the elder game content or are *self-generating* it.

➤ *Post-crossing of the return threshold.* These players can return happily to the virtual world at any level. They have nothing to prove, and can therefore play how and when they want for the sheer joy of it.

Let's take these in order.

Looking back to Figure 3.5's player development tracks, the main types of player in a pre-apotheosis state will be politicians and planners. Politics has long been promoted as one of the two great elder games for large-scale virtual worlds[102], because it self-generates content: Players do things that impact one another, which leads to new courses of action with different impacts, indefinitely. Self-generated content is inexpensive and long-lasting. Evidence from textual worlds suggests that politics[103] is indeed a good elder game for players with conveyor-belt characters that traveled at the wrong speed; it's also a useful delaying pursuit for players at the refusal to return step. It doesn't really help those in apotheosis, though.

The other pre-apotheosis player type likely to have characters in advance of their degree of immersion are planners. These are the achiever types who went at it too mechanistically and matured their characters before they matured themselves. They're still looking to achieve. For these players, remorting is probably the best solution, as it at least holds out the prospect that they'll reach a sense of fulfillment at some point; however, the existence of remorting as a possibility may lead other players not to feel they have "finished" when perhaps before they might, therefore they'll head off on another dispiriting achievement ladder that will do them no favors at all.

---

102. The other, which we'll look at in detail shortly, is player-created content.

103. Note that this does *not* have to be democratic politics, no matter how much players bang on about "living in a democracy." It can be different at different tiers, too—for example, local democracy, national theocracy.

For some virtual worlds, the reason that planner-type achievers reach the elder game is because the virtual world itself has no formal indication that they have reached "the end." In this situation, the human thing to do would be to add a recognition that the player has undergone a rite of initiation. The inhuman thing to do would be to add more content to keep the players achieving. Sadly, the latter is not uncommon, particularly in commercial virtual worlds.

Players who are in a state of apotheosis will be either hacker-type explorers or friends-type socializers. The former can usually be catered for by allowing building privileges (assuming that they didn't have them already; if they did, building is part of "the game" rather than "the elder game," so won't be of much use here). Building may be only a limited option in a commercial virtual world, where real-world copyright laws could be enforced to devastating effect. Legal solutions are likely to be found, however, which will remedy this situation.

Friends-type socializers will want to sit around chatting to one another, and are therefore easy to deal with as long as they have something in-context to chat *about*. Historically, chat content has been generated by the *snoop* command, which allows one player to see what another player sees without that player's knowledge. Again, although this works for hobbyist virtual worlds, there may be legal problems if it were tried in commercial ones; people value their privacy, even if they've signed an end-user agreement that says they don't.

As mentioned earlier, politics works well for players who are refusing to return. It gives them something vaguely meaningful to do, which they can practice almost indefinitely (even when, as a party leader, they lose an election and are rejected by their party—at least it gives them a goal to reclaim what they've lost). Unlike the situation for politician-type socializers, it is unlikely that post-apotheosis players will actually enjoy what they are doing, however, and resentment could well build up. The end, when it comes, could be acrimonious.

Players who have crossed the threshold are the easiest to deal with as they require no new content; their elder game, if it can be called that, is to do whatever they like doing the most. Responses vary. At one extreme, they may never feel the need to enter the virtual world ever again; at the other, they might take up residence and spend their whole time exploring or helping newbies or politicking or whatever (but hopefully not slaughtering newbies). Some may become members of the live team.

Player Interest and the Elder Game

I mentioned in Chapter 3, while deriving a third dimension for the player interest graph, that *MUD2*'s wizzes are griefers, politicians, networkers, or friends: They are not the world-oriented types of planners, opportunists, hackers, and scientists. Why is this? Shouldn't they be hacker-type explorers or friends-type socializers?

MUD2 has rules about what wizzes can and cannot do. To prevent abuses of their (considerable) powers, they are not allowed to use them to play "normally" as a non-wiz (that is, a *mortal*). In other words, if a wiz wants to play in the mortal world as a mortal, they can't use their special wiz abilities; they have to use a different, non-wiz character. In the discussion from which the original player types graph was derived, wizzes therefore considered what they did as a wiz to be separate from what they did as a mortal. Some of them spent most of their time as a wiz; some spent most of it as a mortal. The rules forbade them from doing achiever or explorer things as wizzes, which is why they didn't show up in the analysis of what wizzes did. In fact, these players did all these activities, just not using their wiz personae[104].

The reason that wizzes weren't exclusively hackers or friends was because many of them had crossed the threshold and were no longer in apotheosis; they were playing merely because they enjoyed playing. Some things they could do using wiz powers; others they couldn't, so they did them as mortals. This is why Figure 3.3 doesn't include any world-oriented player types—it only lists what wiz-level players were allowed to do using their wiz-level characters.

MUD2's wizzes were automatically co-opted to the live team, a duty they could dispatch to whatever degree they cared. They could only use their wiz characters, because wiz-owned mortals had to remain incognito so as not to compromise them[105]. Thus, there were only four ways to behave as wizzes. Here they are

---

104. Actually, that's not quite true. As we shall see shortly, they did do explorer things using their wizzes, but they were lumped in with socializers because their activities looked superficially the same.

105. I was chatting to a man on the platform for the train from London Paddington to Heathrow Airport, telling him I thought it was a great line even though it was getting bad publicity because of the ticket prices, when he revealed that he was the chief engineer who had planned the project. Everything I said to him thereafter was informed by this knowledge, and therefore useless to him. If you know that the person you're speaking to has power, you treat them differently whether or not they want you to.

➤ *Griefers*. Griefers with power will either use it responsibly[106] or abuse it and be banned. In a well-designed virtual world, griefers who are unable to move on will rarely reach the elder game anyway; those griefers-at-heart that do will understand that they *can* act explicitly on other players in a benevolent fashion, even if the delights of malevolence ultimately prove too tempting. In *MUD2*, for example, griefer wizzes would try to make the lives of mortals more interesting by tinkering with the virtual world itself in subtle, undetectable ways. Done well, it was like being guided through trials by your own, personal angel; done badly, it was like being tormented in perpetuity by your own, personal devil.

➤ *Politicians*. These people see themselves as good guys, organizing fun activities like leaders at a children's holiday camp. These activities can be invaluable as bonding exercises, but they also can be immersion-busting and incredibly irritating to those who don't want to take part. Politicians tend not to get on with other politicians, whose events (and even presence) clash with their own endeavors.

➤ *Networkers*. These are oracle-like players, who are happy to help others by sharing what they have learned, yet rarely in a boastful kind of way. Unlike explorer types, for whom the acquisition of knowledge is itself intrinsically fun, these people give it away for free. Although their help and advice is limited to low-level activities that help people get involved with a virtual world, it's generally fine. If they spout less well-known information, this will annoy achiever types (who see people getting an easy ride) and some explorers (who see the dissemination of information as taking away the potential fun of other explorers).

➤ *Friends*. They snoop on mortals, they chat, they laugh, they complain about how things aren't the same as they were when they were a mortal. They like each other's company, and don't like it when other wizzes fall out.

To this list, we should add hackers and scientists. Hackers use their knowledge to create things, but aren't all that bothered in exploiting it. Whereas politicians will build a whole new area and dump players in it to have fun, hackers do it because the creativity itself is the interesting part—they don't care if players actually use it, except maybe so they can test its functionality.

---

106. No, that's not a contradiction in terms.

Scientists are like friends-type socializers, in that they snoop a lot. However, this is because they can find out more about the virtual world, rather than finding out about the players. Scientists use snooping like it was a documentary; friends use it like it was a soap opera.

So the wizzes did, in fact, spend their time doing more than four things. If players have mastery of both worlds, they can live how they see fit. That means they have passed *beyond* the confines of player development tracks (which stop after apotheosis), and can be themselves. They can be any of the eight player types—it's just that these didn't show up in the analysis. When playing as achievers, they looked just like any other achiever; when playing as hackers, they were mistaken for politicians; when playing as scientists they were mixed in with socializer-type friends. So the analysis that led to the inclusion of a third player types dimension was, while not exactly flawed, a little incomplete.

Well, it's complete (for) now.

Player-Created Content

Most content in virtual worlds is created by the development team (to the specifications of the designers). Some is created by the live team[107]. Some is created as a community statement because the players will it[108]. Some is created by the players themselves.

Players "add content" whenever they play by their in-context actions. Anything they do that affects the virtual world or its inhabitants is adding content. There's always a positive effect to this, even if the action as a whole is detrimental to the virtual world: In the same way that any publicity is good publicity, it can be said that any content is good content (because it's better than no content).

Content that arises from the natural actions of players within the design framework is said to be *emergent* or *self-generating*. Although designers recognize its importance, normally when they talk about *player-created content* they mean content explicitly created by players; players as designers and developers, in other words.

---

107. Reminder: For small-scale virtual worlds, the designers, development team, and live team may be the same people (or even the same person).

108. These will typically commemorate virtual events (for example, *A Story About a Tree*) or real-world ones (for example, 11th September 2001).

Player-created content is extremely sticky, at least for those who do the creating[109]. This makes it prime elder game material. Some virtual worlds have player-created content from the very beginning, of course; these can't really use content creation as an elder game, unless it's a different kind of creation.

From a designer's perspective (especially one working on a commercial virtual world), allowing only experienced players to create content lessens the chances of its consisting of the low-quality, inconsistent, illiterate, out-of-context, gratuitously profane, sporadic, incomplete, atmosphere-snapping, unimaginative nonsense that experience has shown is inevitable if people can (effectively) self-publish their creations. In practice, using only experienced players does indeed raise the overall quality of what's created; at least they're not going to try to subvert, mock, or otherwise deliberately undermine the source material. Nevertheless, their creations are still very hit and miss; some are bad, some are good, but without training[110] even the excellent ones are prone to making the same errors that professional designers spend all their time trying to avoid (particularly selective depth).

In one sense, it doesn't matter. If people *like* doing this, why stop them? A single virtual world could act as a content aggregator for thousands of individual demi-worlds in various states of permanency. Then again, experience with TinyMUDs has shown that virtual worlds that couple unrestricted building with unrestricted access have tended to have short (albeit occasionally glorious) lives. Restricting building to only the most experienced players will remove a lot of the in-fighting that dogs content addition, but it won't guarantee quality.

It's the quality issue that bites hardest. Players are harsh judges. It doesn't matter to them that a fellow player spent eight weeks creating a castle in the air: If they think it sucks they'll either say so or keep away[111]. In virtual worlds where players have been cosseted up until this point, such a reaction can be something of a shock. There's no point in complaining, either: "I'm not playing if a character I spent two months building up can die!" may galvanize a live team, but "I'm not playing if an area I spent two months building isn't played" won't.

---

109. Commercial virtual worlds love the fact that it effectively makes artists pay a standing charge if they want to see their own works of art.

110. Or recourse to books such as this one.

111. Developers are harsh judges too, but they lose their judgment rights the moment they consent to players adding unrestricted permanent content to their virtual worlds.

The answer might be to have all content vetted for quality before it is accepted into a virtual world. Most books have one author, but some have two, three, or more. When there are several authors, there will usually be an editor involved to ensure that the writing is consistent, complete, and correct. Even books with just one author will have a publisher-appointed editor to make sure everything fits the house style. Even *this* book has such an editor (hi, Stephanie!). If content for virtual worlds were subjected to the rigors of an editorial process, the result would be much higher-quality material.

Unfortunately, the central reason why developers like player-created content is not because it's sticky, or because it works as an elder game; they like it because it's free. If it stops being free (for example, because an editor is spending time looking at it), it becomes less attractive. Why employ someone to look for diamonds in the rough when you could employ someone else to make those diamonds for you[112]?

Power to the Player

Chapter 1 stated that players can create content in a number of ways, which can usefully be categorized as being either in-context (you put a minotaur on retainer and hire a bunch of NPC peasants to construct your labyrinth) or out-of-context (you manifest a minotaur and a labyrinth from nothing). People with the ability to make out-of-context changes are "builders." An analysis of who can build and how long their creations last determines who "owns" a virtual world.

Although the switch between in-context and out-of-context creation is a step change, on either side of the discontinuity the power to change is more continuous. Again, although designers do consider content creation using in-context methods to be important—especially for the elder game—they don't mean that when they talk about player-created content. Player-created content means building, and there is an escalating scale of what can and can't be done using it. In describing this, the important concepts are

- ➤ *Objects*. Tangible virtual world entities, including mobiles and geography.

- ➤ *Functionality*. Code that changes the properties of objects.

---

112. A possible answer might be to charge people a fee to have someone look at their proposed content, although this would only work for virtual worlds with the right business model and player base. In the real world, vanity publishing is a legitimate industry.

> *Building blocks*. Prefabricated components that are combined to make a whole.

> *Free-form*. New components can be constructed from nothing.

In increasing power of expression, these can be combined as follows:

> *Objects from predefined components*. A musket is a heavy, antique, two-handed firearm. Its default weight, value, and accuracy have these new default values: mass=8000, value=125, ammo=ball, and so on.

> *Functionality from predefined components*. To load a musket, you must put in the gunpowder, the wadding, and the ball, in that order. Only then can you fire it.

> *Free-form functionality*. When you fire a musket, there's a chance it could explode and cause a new kind of damage to your hands, arms, torso, and face. The noise could deafen people close by.

> *Free-form objects*. There's this entirely new object, a grenade. When you release the trigger, you have 10 seconds before it explodes. It has entirely new properties for blast radius and the distance it can be thrown, with these default values: mass=250, delay=10, blastradius=50, and so on.

The latter two can perhaps be combined, because for functionality to be truly free-form it would include the ability to create objects anyway. Free-form object creation appears last because it cannot occur without free-form functionality.

In-context object creation occurs by combining components within the (possibly loose) constraints of a recipe, therefore it's not hard to extend to out-of-context creation. You may get some fairly bizarre constructions, but they're not going to cause the virtual world to crash.

Functionality additions are more problematical. If they're from components, again your virtual world should be fairly safe. So long as you ensure that there's no danger of recursion (for example, your new "load musket" function contains a call to "load musket"[113]), all should be well.

---

113. Mutual recursion, while more tiresome to detect, can nevertheless be checked for when a function is being created.

Free-form functionality is dangerous. People can do things that cause crashes (for example, dividing by zero) or hangs (for example, non-terminating loops). Crashes can be trapped, but the state of the virtual world after a function has aborted mid-way through will not necessarily be consistent. Loops can't be detected, only assumed: The virtual world's engine can stop a player-created loop after a million iterations only to screw up everything because the critical million-and-oneth iteration never got to execute. Resource hogging also can be a problem: Players really will create 99 red balloons[114] without a moment's thought, and if that works they'll go for 1,001 Arabian Knights (that's humor for you).

TinyMUDs and their ilk have evolved mechanisms to prevent these issues from becoming too problematical, using approaches similar to those adopted in the old days of mainframe computer timesharing systems. Crashes are handled by the operating system's interrupt mechanism. Hangs and processor-hogging are handled by interrupting functions after they have exceeded some guaranteed minimum amount of processor time. Disk and memory usage is limited by the number of objects (and, optionally, properties and functions) that an individual can create in total—you have to delete old stuff to make room for new stuff once your quota is reached. Some virtual worlds have allocation committees to decide who gets what resources.

The more powerful player-created content forms are prevalent only in textual worlds. This is for practical reasons more than anything: Everyone who plays the virtual world can by definition type, therefore they can all create word-based content. For graphical virtual worlds, few of the players can draw (and, unlike the situation with writing, it's usually apparent even to them[115] that they can't). This isn't to say that their ideas are no good; it merely means that they are unable to put them into practice. Given that most people can't even take professional-quality photographs, this situation would likely prevail even were the best graphics-creation tools to be made available to players.

For the time being, graphical worlds that want to allow some degree of building are therefore pretty well stuck with using predefined components or restricting creation to artistically blessed players. That's for object creation; new functionality would need to be hugely controlled if it were to escape being employed as a tool for abuse—so much so that it hardly seems worth bothering implementing.

---

114. Or, as happened in *MUD2*, 99 red "baloons."

115. I guess I should say "even to us" here, given the limitations of my own illustrative capabilities.

The first 3D graphical virtual world to take player-created content seriously is World Fusion's *Atriarch*[116]. This Science Fiction world has modifiable terrain and allows characters to purchase components for the construction of buildings. Construction is open to all who can obtain the components[117], therefore it's neither an end-game thing nor even out-of-context. Still, it's a start[118].

Another approach is to push the problem one level back. This is the tactic adopted by Bioware with *Neverwinter Nights*[119]. The idea is to make the necessary development tools for virtual worlds available to players so they can create their own independent (in this case) games. Bioware makes its money from selling the boxed sets and from hosting secure servers for characters (so they can move from one mini-world to another[120]). It's a business model that has potential, but each virtual world is limited to 64 simultaneous players, so it's hardly going to challenge the likes of *EverQuest* on that basis[121].

Also, as I said, it pushes the problem one level back. Bioware are the developers of the game engine and they maintain network operations for players, but that's all. The same design and customer service issues that apply to virtual worlds still apply, just to the (from Bioware's perspective) players. It's like the way that *Dungeons & Dragons* defines a gaming system but the players themselves design and (within the confines of that system) develop the individual game worlds; this is perhaps not surprising, given that *NWN* is a *D&D* license and implements the *3rd Edition D&D* rule set.

This tool-oriented attitude is set to become increasingly important in the development of virtual worlds. If cheap engines are available to run the virtual worlds and enough customizable predefined artwork exists to satisfy most needs, at a stroke the two most expensive development costs are removed. Hobbyist designers will be able to create their own graphical virtual worlds in the same way that for years they have been

---

116. http://www.atriarch.com

117. Characters with higher-level skills have a greater variety of building blocks available to them.

118. Some 2½D graphical worlds have been doing it for years, most notably *Furcadia*.

119. This 2002 game is *not* the *Neverwinter Nights* that was on AOL in the 1990s. The name is the same because it has the same license, but they're different products.

120. This was the plan; it has yet to come to fruition.

121. It may be possible using a zoning technique, but a better solution would be to allow more than 64 players per virtual world in the first place. To be fair, Bioware wasn't aiming for a "build your own virtual world" product—that was the players' idea.

creating textual ones. A start has been made with the use of virtual reality VR viewing software (*Active Worlds*[122], for example, allows people to create custom, shared virtual spaces, albeit not ones you can do much in except look around). If actual game engines are made open source, we'll see the same codebase branching occurring that drives much textual world development, too. There is some movement in that direction, most notably with Nevrax's[123] decision to make its NeL (Nevrax Library) development toolkit available under the GNU General Public License[124] (GPL). They stop short of giving their server source code away, however.

A way to introduce some element of freeform player creation while maintaining the integrity of the virtual world is to allow link-outs to the general Internet. Depending on the degree to which developers are willing to sacrifice design control and immersiveness, there are many possible scenarios. Some examples:

➤ Clicking on a character extracts data from a file on the player's own web site and presents it as a biographical description of that character.

➤ Clicking on a character's shop opens a browser window showing the prices of the goods available for sale.

➤ Clicking on a player's castle reads the definition of its interior layout from files on its web site.

➤ Clicking on a magic portal teleports your character to another virtual world entirely.

➤ Clicking on a web site queries the virtual world and produces data that can be incorporated into the web site (for example, prices, character name lists, remote views).

There is, obviously, great scope for abuse here. Instead of prices, that browser window might contain pornography, for example. In small, tight, role-playing virtual worlds, misbehavior can be controlled relatively easily because players know that there is a line of people waiting who would be only too happy to replace someone who was spoiling things for others. In large-scale commercial worlds, this measure of restraint is simply not going to happen except perhaps when players have a lot to lose (for example, in the elder game).

---

122. http://www.activeworlds.com

123. http://www.nevrax.org

124. http://www.fsf.org/licenses/gpl.html

The Content Conundrum

Player-generated content is popular with those who design it, aspirational for those who see it being designed, inexpensive for developers, and it satisfies a perceived need (that is, a constant flow on new content to prevent a virtual world from becoming stale). Arrayed against it are concerns about quality, which, although legitimate, can to some extent be alleviated by the provision of design tools, documentation, testing facilities, and a person to act as content editor. Given the advantages, why aren't more virtual worlds looking at this as an option?

It's because of intellectual property (IP). People who create content can claim certain rights over it. For in-context creations (for example, planting differently-colored virtual flowers in such a way that they grow to show a picture) this isn't a problem[125] because all works can be considered to be transient; you can no more complain that someone dug up your virtual flowers than a pavement artist can complain that the rain washed away their chalk masterpiece. If the context of the virtual world allows it, then by creating within that context you have no redress.

It gets much, much trickier when out-of-context creation is considered. Different laws apply in different countries and different states, but basically:

➤ If work is done honestly and for hire (that is, they were contracted to do it) then you get the most rights. They can ask that their name be taken off the credits, but that's about it. The downside is that individuals must be paid whatever minimum wages apply for work to be considered for hire, and "a free account" is below this level.

➤ If work is bought when complete (as you might buy a painting from a gallery), the artist retains more rights. They could, for example, object if you used it in such a way as to affect their reputation adversely. A photographer might have grounds for complaint were you to display his or her amusing images of clothed farm animals in an exhibition about bestiality.

➤ Paid-for licensed content (for example, a *Star Wars* franchise) will typically state the boundaries within which content must operate. It may also give the license-holder a veto over aspects of the virtual world's design (for example, no one gets

---

125. Warning: I am not a lawyer. I am only giving you my interpretation of the law as it stands here, and therefore from a legal standpoint you should believe none of it. If you want advice about the law, seek a qualified lawyer. This has been a public service please-don't-sue-me announcement.

to kill Luke Skywalker), but as long as it operates within these formal constraints the developer still has a reasonably high degree of freedom.

➤ If work is donated for free, the artists may have even more rights. You might have to ask their permission before you make any changes affecting it; in extreme cases, this could mean all patches to the virtual world, on the grounds that they alter the context of the work and therefore its meaning. Also, just because they gave it to you for free, that doesn't mean it's not an asset—you can still be taxed on it.

➤ Content with sufficient creative input from the developer can be considered to have joint copyright. This means you ought to be able to do whatever you like with it, whether the other copyright holder objects or not. However, so can they. Disrespect them and you could come heavily to regret it.

➤ Content created without any formal signing over of ownership gives you very few rights. You can throw it out if you don't like it, but provided that you invited its creation there's little else you can do. If I put up a sign saying that passers-by can create sculptures in my garden, I don't get to alter—or even necessarily move—them. All I can do is demand that the sculptor take their work away. A sledge-hammer is not a legal option.

➤ Virtual worlds that are paid to show content have least control over it; this is effectively sponsorship. If the Brown Fizzy Drink Company pays you to put cans of virtual Brown Fizzy Drink in your virtual world, it can claim copyright abuse when the players buy those cans and arrange them to look like cartoons of suggestive parts of the human anatomy.

For non-commercial virtual worlds, none of this is normally much of an issue (basically because they have no money and are therefore not worth beating on[126]). For commercial virtual worlds, many of whose players could well be lawyers themselves, it's frightening. The legal situation is by no means clear, and nobody wants to be the one who has to empty the bank paying lawyers' fees to determine the precedents. Consequently, developers are very keen *not* to dilute their IP with anyone else's[127].

---

126. The "normally" there is because occasionally some license-holders do let loose the dogs of law on tribute virtual worlds, no matter how insignificant they may be.

127. They are, of course, happy to dilute license-holders' IP with their own.

Chapter 6 has more on the new legal issues that virtual worlds are raising. Chapter 7 looks at some of the effects of player-created content on storytelling within virtual worlds.

The Whole Picture

So as to make it easier to describe, I've partitioned the virtual world design process—however, it's actually holistic. You can't treat the individual aspects of design in isolation: They impact on one another in ways that may not be immediately obvious.

Example: Crafters complain that their towns are lifeless. You determine that this is because crafting (unlike combat) is a solo activity. You introduce manufacturing processes that entail several characters' working together. Players build houses in close proximity to one another so they can get to and from the crafting centers quickly. Towns become more vibrant as a result. However, now that people spend more time in the towns than in the wilderness, adventurers complain that the wilderness is lifeless.

If you spot the problems in advance, you can tackle them as a whole. Taking them one at a time may merely push them about. It's like trying to put out a burning hoop by dousing it a section at a time—as soon as you move from one bit to the next it catches fire again. You have to extinguish it all in one go: You can't solve the problem by partitioning it. Unfortunately, you'll *always* get some partitioning if the design team consists of more than one person; balancing the various issues in this situation is therefore even harder.

Problems due to the interaction of subsystems tend mainly to be of the consistency, compatibility, and depth varieties; these are, fortunately, tractable. Hard decisions have to be made, however, when a design calls for two elements that are in direct opposition to one another: You can have permanent death or some form of resurrection, but you can't have both. Indirect contradictions can be almost as difficult to resolve while being less easy to spot. Players want to be able to sell the goods they manufacture at fixed prices to guarantee an income, but that will cause lots of people to manufacture those goods, which will raise the price of raw materials, which will reduce the income players get from their goods.

Solutions are hard to come by. The difficulties that arise by partitioning can be addressed by sound development practices—communication, regular design meetings, internal web sites, lead designer sign-off, and so on. For problems with the design itself, the team must strive for robustness: They can tackle whatever they notice before-hand, but once the virtual world goes live they have to rely on the checks and balances they build in to ensure that nothing goes horribly wrong[128]. Any new design for the economy in particular is almost certain not to work straight away, so damage-limitation code will have to be in place ready for the inevitable tribulations.

Under- and Over-Design

Under-design is a frequent problem with virtual worlds that have been written from scratch. Developers spend so long creating and building the world that they forget to add any gameplay. There's not a lot for players to do, but lots of things for them not to do it to. Alternatively, there is a lot to do but only to the same things, over and over again. Either way, there simply isn't *enough*. The virtual world may be immense, beauti-ful, and finely crafted, but just a shell. What players want, there's no way they can have: It's like going on a shopping expedition and finding that all the shops are closed[129].

Over-design is also a problem. In this scenario, designers go into such detail that it overwhelms all activity. What players want to do is lost in the noise of what they have to do to facilitate doing it. There is a place in virtual worlds for a modicum of annoy-ing detail, and some players will find particular details more irritating than do others; when they feel it's irrelevant, though, they'll rebel. I don't want to have to specify the barb style, shaft length, and flight composition/configuration of the arrows that I buy, I just want something I can shoot in my bow!

Both over-design and under-design are the result of the same thing: misdirected focus. The designers look at something in too much detail: For under-design, it's the infra-structure of the virtual world; for over-design it's the structure built on this foundation.

---

128. Given that checks and balances are themselves one of the most fruitful sources of exploits for players, care must be taken in their design too. Personally, I find that the best way to reduce exploits and design bugs is to play devil's advocate: How would I break the system if this or that rule were in place? Perhaps the fact that many successful virtual world designers are ex-hackers (in the traditional sense of the word) is not some mere accident of history?

129. Apparent under-design can arise from unrealistic deadlines or insufficient development staff. The designers might have done their job properly, but if there isn't time to implement their design fully, then what the players *see* could be the same as if the designers had under-designed.

They both illustrate another aspect of selective depth: Too much detail in one place gives an impression of shallowness elsewhere—even if looked at objectively the detail elsewhere is just right.

Participatory Design

When a bunch of musicians get together and start jamming, they're engaging in a form of *participatory design*. Everyone has ideas, which they offer up for approval to everyone else. Some ideas work, some don't work, and others suggest better ideas. Computer programmers hacking together work the same way: Someone types, other people make suggestions, changes are made in the light of these suggestions, new suggestions are made. It's an editing process undertaken (ideally) by members of a spiritual community[130].

Participatory design is good because everyone gets involved, everyone can contribute, and everyone's contribution is acknowledged. It helps build a sense of community, and gives all participants an investment in the final product. It's ideal for virtual worlds, then?

At the design team level, yes. Final approval must formally be made by one (lead) designer, but this is essentially a rubber-stamping of the consensus opinion[131]. Brainstorming works.

Extending participatory design beyond the design team, however, is another matter entirely. Designers have always been open to ideas from players once their virtual world has entered beta testing, but what about before then? It can be very difficult to manage; in particular, inviting prospective players of a virtual world to participate in design increases the number of contributors by several orders of magnitude. The design team itself can either act in concert as a single unit, or split along individual lines. It'll usually be the former, because otherwise players will try to play off designers against one another. However, that's not the only reason they may do it. I'll explain....

---

130. As described in Chapter 3.

131. Nevertheless, if there weren't one participant who had the ultimate veto (that is, the lead designer), a consensus might be less easy to obtain.

Why would designers want to get players involved in design? There are several laudable grounds for doing so:

- ➤ It allows players to feel they have an investment in the virtual world.
- ➤ Ten thousand minds are better than ten.
- ➤ Designers can act as culture seeds.
- ➤ Players feel influential—they really can make a difference.
- ➤ If players understand the design process more, they won't make knee-jerk objections to things that superficially annoy them.
- ➤ It draws players into a community.

There also are some less laudable reasons:

- ➤ Players can be manipulated into accepting suggestions that they may otherwise have found unpalatable.
- ➤ Designers can accept "new" suggestions they had already thought of, tricking players into thinking they're participating when they're not.
- ➤ Designers get to pick the choicest fruits of players' unpaid endeavors.

The cynical view (and players can be very cynical) is that the whole effort is primarily a public relations exercise. Nothing important is ever discussed, unless it's to get players to suggest a preferred solution in order that criticism will be deflected when it proves unpopular once implemented. After all, although some players' ideas will be excellent, most will be unusable (jaded, inconsistent, off-the-wall, dull, unimplementable, copyright someone else, and so on); it's a simple matter when posting a question to wait for the "correct" response to appear and then seize on it as a great, original idea. Players participating in design are at best sounding boards and at worst betrayers of the players yet to come. In this context, it's easier for designers to stage-manage participatory design if they work as a unit than if they don't.

This scornful view of participatory design has, fortunately, yet to gain a strong hold of the player population. Participatory design does work, and can bring substantial benefits. It was used extensively for *Star Wars Galaxies*, where in time it will probably prove to have been a success. On one great test—players' coming to understand that newbies can't be allowed to start with a Jedi character—its advantages are particularly clear[132].

Its long-term future is cloudier, however. As with player content creation, there are legal issues concerning the "rights" to aspects of a design. If a scriptwriter pitched a movie concept to a director, they would be calling in the lawyers were that concept to appear as a movie five years later without even a credit (let alone payment)[133]. Why should a player of a virtual world who pitches a design concept receive no recognition (professional or monetary) when it's used?

The response that it's "advice freely given" only goes so far. It may, for example, be material that already exists in some other virtual world to which the designers of that world hold copyright. Besides, even though the assumption that the inclusion of your idea in a design is reward enough holds sway at the moment, this will not necessarily always be the case. Were a new, high-profile virtual world to *pay* for any player-suggested ideas it used, the situation could well change. Under such circumstances, full participatory design could be hard to apply effectively.

Testing a Design

Large-scale virtual worlds are designed before they are implemented[134]. After implementation, play-testing can be used to pick up the many design bugs (as well as programming bugs) that will have crept in. However, fixing them at this stage is expensive as it involves code changes (potentially quite large ones). The more flaws in a design that can be fixed before implementation, the better.

---

132. See Kurt D. Squire, *Star Wars Galaxies: A Case Study in Participatory Design.* Joystick101.org, July 2001. http://www.joystick101.org/story/2001/7/14/18208/3248.

133. This is why screenplay authors register their scripts with the Writers Guild of America.

134. Small-scale ones are usually designed *while* they're being implemented, which is a much more organic way of doing it. This can mean the overall systems are better balanced and more stable, but it also can cause numerous rewrites as the consequences of early bad decisions finally make their appearance.

How, though, do you test a design when there's no world to test it in?

Some facets can be tested by writing quick-and-dirty programs or macros. An economy becomes a spreadsheet; combat becomes a few screens of C. This helps get the numbers right, but doesn't say anything about the gameplay. You could end up with a well-balanced virtual world that is an absolute chore to play.

Surprising progress can be made by simulating the virtual world, tabletop style. You draw out a rough map of an area, put some tokens on it to represent PCs and monsters, then move them around and do things like you might expect the finished product to work. This does, however, require a discipline that is beyond most designers; although you should really take notes and discuss what happened after the session, most designers are unable to prevent themselves from launching into a debate the instant the first opportunity arises; the result is that such pencil-and-paper simulations are not usually as productive as they might be.

Two things I normally recommend to design teams on new virtual worlds address these problems: *dummy logs* and *mock diaries*. Both start from the premise of imagining that it's some time in the future when the virtual world has been implemented and people are actually playing it. What will those players be doing?

Dummy logs work better for textual worlds than graphical ones. The idea is to write an imaginary transcript of a session as it might be recorded by a stereotypical player. It forces the designer to face up to concrete consequences of their decisions: the interface, room descriptions, movement, communication, the general atmosphere, and (crucially) what the player will be *doing*. This exercise will typically expose the greatest strengths and weaknesses of a design: The designers can then play up to the strengths and root out the weaknesses.

For graphical worlds, dummy logs are more like dummy storyboards, and they don't work so well[135]. That said, there is still a lot of mileage in asking the enthusiastic, wannabe designers of new virtual worlds what they think their players will actually be doing once the doors are open.

---

135. They can look better in a design document, though, if your aim is to impress publishers into giving you their money.

Mock diaries[136] are like dummy logs, but they address longer-term issues. The idea is that you write a series of pretend diary entries for a player covering several imaginary sessions, outlining how the player's character(s) got on and what they did. If the entries often lack excitement or fun, or they start to look the same, you may have discovered a potential problem.

Dummy logs and mock diaries can be constructed for a variety of player demographics at different stages in their career. Your first session will be different to your sessions after a week (or it should be!), which in turn will be different to your sessions after a month, six months, two years, and so on. By writing dummy logs or mock diaries for these periods, you can reassure yourself that there will be sufficient gameplay to sustain long-term play, and that this applies to all the main player groups you're targeting.

Dummy logs and mock diaries have their variations. Jessica Mulligan recommends using mock letters rather than diaries, for example; these help the designer consider *why* things are fun, instead of merely assuming that they *are* fun.

Whatever, designs *must* be tested. In the same way that every time a programmer finishes a new section of code they test it, so a designer should consider the effects of every new addition to the virtual world. You don't have to write out 20 new mock diary entries every time, I hasten to add, but you should at least consider whether it will work in the context of the rest of the design. Although occasionally you really do have to say, "Oh, let's just put it in and see how it goes," most of the time you don't. Think what the players, good and bad, will make of it, and you'll have your answer. If an idea is so original that you can't do this, okay, *then* you can put it into the design document and hope—but be sure that if it does fail there's nothing important relying on its working.

---

136. These are also known as *user stories*

Chapter 6

It's Not a Game, It's a...

Simulation. Or a service. Or a medium.

Actually, it's none of these: It's a place.

(What's he talking about?)

I'll explain.

Points of View

Virtual worlds began as games. However, right from the beginning—*MUD1*—it was clear there was more to them than being mere games. Trying to convince people to take what they considered to be a "game" seriously was problematical, though. In academic circles, the only intellectually acceptable games were traditional ones, such as chess and checkers. A new game was not a worthwhile object of study. Playing games was a waste of computer resources.

Thus, virtual worlds became "simulations"—and far more respectable!

When commercial virtual worlds made an appearance, they became "games" again. People will pay to play games, but not simulations. However, what computer games developers understand by "game" is some distance from what virtual world designers do. In particular, many games portals didn't recognize that these were products you had to remain involved with indefinitely—seeds to be nurtured rather than cut flowers to be left in a vase and forgotten. MUDs are not *Quake*. Industry experts (led by Jessica Mulligan), horrified at seeing so many people making the same mistakes again and again, rebranded virtual worlds as "services." The sooner developers realized that their business primarily concerned providing a service for players, the better.

Thankfully, the message got through. The portals (and, later, independent developers) who maintained their virtual worlds adequately succeeded where their predecessors had struggled.

Virtual worlds became games again—"massively multiplayer online role-playing games." They attracted players in increasingly large numbers. *EverQuest's* population exceeded 10% of Norway's. The people were coming, but virtual world design stumbled: So-so bandwagon products were announced that were little more than riffs on an ossified *EverQuest* theme. Senior designers, with Raph Koster at the forefront, contested this decline: Virtual worlds were a medium through which many services (games included) might be delivered. Like any medium, they could—and should—be used creatively. Virtual world design was promoted as an art form, and the ripping-off of old designs instead of pursuing innovation was decried as a travesty. This ought to be the most exciting period in all virtual world design history, yet the best that people can come up with are feeble clones? Augh!

All these definitions of what virtual worlds are were created for different purposes to make different points. Knowledgeable players may quote them in response to the don't-get-it ridicule of the "it's just a game" crowd, but they're not accurately describing what virtual worlds really *are*.

Virtual worlds are *places*. Remember that, and many design issues cease to be issues at all. People go to places, do things there, and then they go home.

Virtual worlds are not simulations, because they don't simulate anything. They approximate aspects of reality—enough for the purposes of immersion—but that's all.

Virtual worlds are not services. Yes, providing access to them is a service of critical importance—they can't exist otherwise. However, that doesn't mean the virtual worlds themselves are services. Restaurants provide a service, but the food they serve isn't a

---

1. This doesn't mean that the continued *provision* of a virtual world is not a service, of course.

service[1].

Virtual worlds are not a medium. Well, let's put it this way: If they are, so is the real world. A medium is a channel open for communication with a (large) number of individuals. Although most virtual worlds do have such channels within them, they are not intrinsically channels themselves. You can play in a virtual world without communicating with any of the other players[2].

Most certainly of all, virtual worlds are not games. Even the ones written to *be* games aren't games. People can play games *in* them, sure, and they can be set up to that end, but this merely makes them venues. The Pasadena Rose Bowl is a stadium, not a game.

Virtual worlds are *places*. They may simulate abstractions of reality; they may be operated as a service; creating them may be an art; people may visit them to play games. Ultimately, though, they're just a set of locations. Places.

So, why say this now, at the beginning of Chapter 6? Wouldn't it have been better in Chapter 1?

Actually, I did sneak it into Chapter 1, "Introduction to Virtual Worlds," right at the beginning[3]. The reason I've restated it now is only as a consequence of showing the other ways virtual worlds can at times profitably be visualized (that is, simulation, service, medium, goal—there are others, these are just the best-known). I wanted to demonstrate there are different, yet gainful, ways to look at virtual worlds from within the field itself; yet there are many more from without it.

Part of my original aim in writing this book was to stake out the study (as opposed to the playing) of virtual worlds as a worthwhile human endeavor *for its own sake*. Most academic work on the subject has been undertaken by researchers from other disci-

---

2. It could be argued that designers are communicating with the players, in the same sense that the author of a book is communicating with its readers. This can indeed occur, even without the players' knowledge that they're being given a message. However, being able to use a virtual world as a medium doesn't mean it *is* a medium. Crops may be a medium when crop circles appear in them, but most of the time they're just crops.

3. To save your looking: "Virtual worlds are places where the imaginary meets the real."

plines, who (naturally enough) have tended to concentrate on only those particular features of virtual worlds important to them. Nevertheless, there is a great deal of work here, and the question must be asked: Is there anything about virtual worlds that makes them sufficiently different from other objects of study that they merit examination from within? Or is the whole subject catered for well enough already from without[4]?

Even assuming there is a niche for virtual worlds, that doesn't mean research in the area is necessarily worthwhile. A measure of the value of a discipline is its relationship to other disciplines; it's an indirect form of peer review. Homeopathy, for example, has nothing to articulate about conventional science except that it's missing something very important, and of mainstream scientists only psychologists have an academic interest in homeopathy (and that's for reasons that won't please homeopaths). At the very least, this makes university courses on homeopathy and grants to homeopaths from government agencies rather thin on the ground. Do other disciplines view virtual worlds as credible entities? Or are they laughing stocks, of only passing interest to anyone except those who study laughing stocks?

Let's find out.

Making Sense of Virtual Worlds

Science is concerned primarily with observing, recording, and interpreting data. The information gleaned is used to support, modify, or deny existing theories, and occasionally to propose new theories. In "hard" sciences, such as physics and chemistry, hypotheses can be tested through experimentation. It is rare the same experiment performed under the same conditions will produce different results; in a sense, for hard science there is a "right" answer which experimentation leads toward discovering.

Contrastingly, "soft" science deals with facts that can and do change depending on conditions; this is because at heart they defer to the ever-transforming marvel that is human nature. Quantum physics aside, in hard science there is a fixed relationship

---

4. I am not the only person to ask these questions. In particular, see Lawrie Brown, *MUDs: Serious Research Tools or Just Another Game*. Technical Report CS14/93, Department of Computer Science, University of New South Wales, 1993. http://www.unsw.adfa.edu.au/~lpb/papers/mud93.txt.
Alan Schwartz, *Mud Research and Methods*. 1996. http://www.legendmud.org/Community/lectures/mudres.html.

between theory and experiment: Your opinion on how rocks are formed may change in the light of new evidence, but the behavior of the rocks themselves will stay the same. With soft science, this is not the case: An anthropologist can, merely by collecting data, change the very behavior being observed. Similarly, although with most hard science the experiments can be intrusive, with soft science they can't be. "Let's break up this crystal to see how new crystals form from the remains" is fine; "let's break up this community to see how new communities form from the remains" isn't.

Hard science is concerned with what is real. When it comes to virtual worlds, therefore, they don't have a lot to say about them. Virtual worlds may be useful as sources of inspiration, perhaps, or as applications for physics simulations, but they don't raise any new issues.

Soft science, on the other hand, has a lot to say about virtual worlds. People follow the lines established by the "great thinkers"[5], but there is nevertheless ample opportunity for original work. There are three basic attitudes:

➤ Virtual worlds are just one of many areas of interest to the particular scientific discipline. The job of the researcher is to make sense of virtual worlds and to address any questions peculiar to virtual worlds that arise. Whether virtual world designers make use of the results of any analysis isn't as important as how much it advances knowledge in the subject field

➤ Virtual worlds are subsumed by the discipline. They are merely exemplars of some greater area of study, and can only really be understood in that context. Virtual worlds are claimed as a subfield, which may or may not have something new to say about the discipline in general.

➤ Virtual worlds are tools for the discipline. They can be used to some greater purpose in their application than in themselves. Researchers are more interested in what they can do with them than what goes on in them.

---

5. For virtual worlds, the book that established many of these lines is Michael Benedikt (editor), *Cyberspace: First Steps*. Cambridge MA, MIT Press, 1991. Although some of the essays within its covers are excellent, many are infuriatingly but influentially wide of the mark. This is therefore the only time I shall be mentioning it here.

Insofar as discussing the acceptance of virtual worlds is concerned, the third of these is not particularly useful. This isn't to say there is not a lot of valuable work in the area that might be of direct relevance to designers; indeed, the chances are that some of it will be very helpful indeed, its being applied in nature. However, from the point of view of assessing the status of virtual worlds in the wider scientific community, this is not hugely important.

Similarly, the second attitude (virtual worlds are subsumed) also downgrades virtual worlds. They are regarded as a subdiscipline, rather than a discipline unto themselves. Again, therefore, virtual worlds don't come out of any analysis in this context as being a particularly plausible independent field of research.

Thus, although I'll spend some time going over the highlights of the second and third of these attitudes, I'll concentrate on the first one.

I do mean "concentrate," too.

Geography

It might surprise many designers to discover that geographers have an interest in virtual worlds. They do. They are interested in spaces, they regard cyberspace as a space, and virtual worlds are an exceptionally good example of the concept in use.

Note, there is a distinction[6] between *space* and *place*. A *space* is an abstraction that groups objects of a particular type under a set of fixed rules; a *place* is a region (under adjacency rules) of some space. For example, matter operating under the laws of physics gives us the 3D space we call reality; Athens is a place in this space. Historical events operating under the laws of causality give us an "event space;" the French Revolution is a place in this space. Mathematicians are particularly fond of spaces, and will readily refer to name spaces, function spaces, and object spaces.

Spaces are distinguished from *sets* by the imposition of their governing axioms. Although it is true to say a place is a subset of its space, these axioms mean there is far more to the relationship than that: Things can be inferred about one place relative to another place in

---

6. One that is surprisingly lost on many of the theorists who dived into the subject the moment it became trendy.

the same space. This is because places are connected to other places under adjacency rules, through which they can influence the character of these other places. Whether the spaces are real or imaginary, discrete or continuous, finite or infinite, it is with the study of the rules that underlie them that geographers are ultimately concerned.

In terms of virtual worlds, this means they are interested in

- ➤ Virtual worlds as places (what they comprise).
- ➤ Virtual worlds as instantiated spaces (what comprises them).
- ➤ The (hopefully new) forms and relationships underlying virtual worlds.

As places, virtual worlds constitute one small part of the data space known as the Internet[7]; other parts include the World Wide Web, email, instant messaging, bulletin boards, and Internet relay chat (IRC). Formally, "cyberspace" covers anything implemented using information and communication technologies, and therefore includes non-Internet forms of interactive digital data transfer such as television and telephones. However, in practice it is with the conceptualization of these technologies known as the Internet that most of the research in this area concerns.

Geography begins with *maps*. Maps formalize the space to be mapped, and determine the nature of the adjacency relationships. Maps, like spaces, can be multidimensional; they are only, however, abstractions of the space[8], illustrating solely what is important from the point of view of the cartographer or the person using the map. By making a map of a new place, a geographer can begin to understand the nature of that place and of the space in which it is located.

How easy the Internet is to map depends, therefore, on the viewpoint of the cartographer. Most places on the Internet have a real-world geographical association, in that they are located on servers or operate through routers that have a physical presence in the real world. Thus, one obvious way to map the Internet is to overlay a map of the real world with the locations of major nodes, using data traffic flows to show their connections.

---

7. William Mitchell characterizes them as "neighborhoods." William J. Mitchell, *City of Bits: Space, Place, and the Infobahn*. Cambridge MA, MIT Press, 1995.

8. If they are as fully detailed as the space, you may as well use the space itself; this situation is known as *conflation*.

This wouldn't be a map of the Internet, though; it would be a map of the real-world network that supports it. The Internet itself is a construct in the mind; to map it is to determine those constructs common to the individuals who experience it. Fortunately, most people have sufficient experience of real space to conceptualize cyberspace in similar ways, guided by the underlying structure of the data being presented. Thus, for example, they will regard a web site as a location; a hyperlink to another web site indicates adjacency (a browser's Back button making it bidirectional, at least temporarily). Distance is identical between nodes, therefore the map will be topological rather than spatial.

On any map of the Internet, virtual worlds are only going to show up as different from other nodes if the cartographer captures and reflects details that are prominent for them—number of simultaneous connections, or period of continuous connection. Even then, they may not have a signature any different from an Internet radio station. A map of the Internet in general only makes statements about the relationships between nodes and about the variables that these relationships consider. It can only respect variables that are meaningful across all nodes (for example, bandwidth, uptime, router connections); the place of virtual worlds in cyberspace can therefore be located, but only in those terms. Unfortunately, interesting though this information may be to geographers and network managers, it's not something virtual world designers are going to regret not knowing.

Homing in on virtual worlds, though, and looking at how they are constructed, is a different story.

In their two hugely impressive 2001 books[9], Martin Dodge and Rob Kitchin lay out the foundations of Cyberspace Geography as a discipline. They map everything: infrastructure, traffic, web sites, email, bulletin boards—even some individual Usenet threads. In so doing, they offer different ways of looking at cyberspace for different purposes. Because virtual worlds use richer, more intricate spatial metaphors than any other Internet social space (IRC, chat rooms, email, and so on), one of these purposes is virtual world design.

---

9. Martin Dodge and Rob Kitchin, *Mapping Cyberspace*. New York, Routledge, 2001.
   Martin Dodge and Rob Kitchin, *Atlas of Cyberspace*. London, Addison-Wesley, 2001.
   The former has more theory, the latter more pretty maps.

Beginning with *MUD1*[10], Dodge and Kitchin examine a number of virtual worlds, both textual and graphical. They reproduce player-drawn maps[11] of varying quality and scale, commenting on the ability of each to convey in a clear manner the salient points that would be of interest to users[12]. They conclude that there are four main categories of space in a virtual world:

➤ A core public space, accessible to all characters.

➤ Private spaces, accessible only to individual characters, but directly connected to the core space.

➤ Private spaces that are disconnected from the core space—that is, only accessible using teleportation.

➤ Multi-scale spaces that break the rules of realism—for example, a house inside a grandfather clock.

The prevalence of private spaces will, of course, be related to the number of people able to build them[13]; there will be more in a MOO than in a DikuMUD, for example[14]. In builder-heavy worlds, spaces more distant from the core in spatial terms will be more distant in thematic terms, too.

Dodge and Kitchin examine other ways to map virtual worlds, apart from this "physical" approach. They reproduce maps created from data gathered by a *LambdaMOO* bot[15] concerning the social interactions of virtual worlds; these enable the trained eye to pick out cliques and other social groupings among players.

---

10. The *Atlas of Cyberspace* reproduces a nodal map of *MUD1* that I drew in 1983.

11. Some clients (*zMUD* is the best-known) constructed for use with generic textual worlds can *automap* arbitrary room connections, exploring a virtual world exhaustively to produce an accurate map. http://www.zuggsoft.com/zmud/zmudinfo.htm.

12. Note that for players, constructing a map can be a worthwhile exercise unto itself. If you make your own map of a virtual world, you will end up with a greater understanding of that world than if you use someone else's.

13. And also on what they plan on getting up to in those private spaces.

14. Graphical worlds are coming to realize the importance of customized private spaces, too. *EverQuest 2*, for example, has *pocket zones* to serve this purpose.

15. Michael Kearns and Charles Lee Isbell Jr.'s *Cabot*.

An important consideration for any kind of space is *navigation*: How do you get from one location to another (whether this "location" is a point, a person, or a web page)? This is, after all, one of the primary reasons people use maps. The classic work on navigation by individuals is Kevin Lynch's *The Image of the City*[16], which describes how people build up a cognitive map of their environment and use it (among other things) to get from place to place. Lynch demonstrated that this "environmental image" is constructed in terms of five features:

➤ *Nodes* are distinct locations people can enter

➤ *Paths* are channels connecting nodes, along which people travel.

➤ *Edges* are borders that are difficult or impossible to cross.

➤ *Districts* are parts of the environment that share a common theme, look, or character. "The old town" or "the docks" would count as districts.

➤ *Landmarks* are strong reference points. The more important an object is, the more likely it is to be a point of reference. Being visible from far away is, in this context, considerably important.

Note these vary from person to person and from context to context. A path for a motorist may be an edge for a pedestrian; a junction may be a landmark for one, but not the other.

Although Lynch's work concerned real-world cities, its principles can often be extended to environments in general. This was demonstrated categorically for textual virtual worlds in Andreas Dieberger's 1994 Ph.D. thesis[17], using results from two questionnaire surveys undertaken by Jolanda Tromp[18]. Players of textual worlds have particular problems in that

➤ There are holes in the virtual world, where there "ought to be" rooms but there aren't.

16. Kevin Lynch, *The Image of the City*. Cambridge MA, MIT Press, 1960.

17. Andreas Dieberger, *Navigation in Textual Virtual Environments using a City Metaphor*. Faculty of Technology and Sciences, Vienna University of Technology, 1994.
http://www.lcc.gatech.edu/~dieberger/Thesis/Thesis.html.

18. Jolanda G. Tromp, *Results of Two Surveys About Spatial Perception and Navigation of a Text-Based Spatial Interface*. University of Amsterdam, 1993.
http://www.cms.dmu.ac.uk/~cph/VR/JolaPaper/jola.html.

➤ Rooms are of different sizes, which players perceive only through their descriptions. A room that would take up several squares on a grid layout can still seem "small" to players.

➤ Exits are limited to eight compass points, plus: non-standard contextual exits such as "out;" hidden exits you have to work to discover; teleport exits that look like normal ones.

➤ There are unconnected rooms accessible only by teleport. Some exist for special purposes (for example, the virtual world's mailing system), but this doesn't have to be the case.

➤ Mazes that are fiendishly difficult to solve are not fiendishly difficult to construct.

➤ Z-axis movement (steps, ladders, cliffs, gradients, and so on) are hard to realize effectively.

➤ Distance is perceived in terms of time taken to traverse between rooms. Although this is related to the number of rooms passed through, inconveniences like doors and monsters can make a journey seem longer.

Nevertheless, even given these problems, Lynch's model applies. Nodes are rooms. Major landmarks are rooms containing some special functionality or (very interestingly) ones where there tend to be other players. Minor landmarks are often where people find unidirectional movement ends—for example, the place where if you keep going east you suddenly find a wall that stops further travel in that direction. Paths are room exits or chains of rooms that get you from one landmark to another. Districts are used, but with theme being more important than look. Edges are only implied through room descriptions and the lack of exits at the "edge," but rooms that have them will usually be on paths or act as landmarks.

Bearing this in mind, therefore, designers of virtual worlds should be able to construct their virtual worlds in such a way as to make them easier for players to navigate. Obvious nodes, paths, edges, districts, and (especially) landmarks should be provided to give players a sense of where they are and how to get to where they want to go; a sense of place, in other words.

Although this work was undertaken for textual worlds, Dieberger noted that graphical worlds (which have few of the "unrealistic" spatial problems that textual worlds do) were even more amenable to this kind of analysis. Designers should not simply assume people will find things to use as landmarks: They should follow the lead of urban planners and actually *provide* them. Furthermore, they should provide them in a structured manner, rather than as an accident of geography[19]. In textual virtual worlds, they can go one step further and provide landmark-seeking commands[20].

Unrestricted teleportation is perhaps the greatest threat to the geographical integrity of a virtual world, as it breaks all the adjacency rules that make a space anything other than a set of points. Designers should therefore be careful to ensure it isn't overdone. The other major problem (which affects textual worlds more than graphical ones) is the virtual world's geography should be relatively stable. Experienced players don't want to have to check all their maps every time there's an update "just in case" the designers added a few new rooms somewhere off the beaten track, and inexperienced players will think you're playing with their heads.

Geographers look at how space appears and how people (through their maps) visualize it; although they can offer up general principles relating to what makes a geography understandable and useful, they are not immediately concerned with designing spaces themselves. This may change if geographers seize on virtual worlds as test-beds for their theories of geography; geographers are already being called on to advise in the construction of geographically correct virtual worlds[21].

There is, however, a group of people for whom the design of space is precisely their main interest: architects.

---

19. To discover more about the application of architectural design principles for the benefit of virtual worlds and other Internet spaces, see Judith S. Donath, *Inhabiting the Virtual City: The Design of Social Environments for Electronic Communities*. School of Architecture and Planning, MIT, 1997. `http://smg.media.mit.edu/people/Judith/Thesis/`.

20. *MUD1* had a "swamp" command, which moved players one room in the direction of the swamp from (almost) anywhere. The swamp was a major landmark because it's where players had to go to cash treasure in for experience points.

21. Christian Carazo-Chandler, *Comceptualising Geography in a Virtual World Environment*. `http://cybergeography.hypermart.net/Conceptualising Geography in a Virtual World Environment.doc`.

Architecture

Architects think about spaces for reasons that differ from those of geographers. They are interested in the physical construction of objects within a space, yes, but also in the functional and aesthetic values they can project through such a construction.

In the real world, buildings are designed to fulfill some purpose. This purpose (and the proposed budget) provides the hard parameters within which architects operate. What about cyberspace, though? It's clearly a space, but then so is the space of possible solutions to a crossword puzzle; architects would not be concerned with the latter, so why should they be concerned with the former?

The answer is that cyberspace in general, and virtual worlds in particular, share with the physical world features important to architects that more abstract spaces do not. In a good introduction[22] to these issues, Anna Cicognani derives five interrelated characteristics that describe what makes a space interesting to architects:

➤ *Possibility of action*. It must be possible to effect changes of state within the space.

➤ *Livability*. It must be possible to dwell in the space. This implies that the space can be organized into structures.

➤ *Construction of communities*. The space must be social, in that communities should be able to develop by acting on the space while existing external to it.

➤ *Time organization*. Only through alterations to space can changes in time be detected, therefore the space must be organized such that these changes can be perceived in a manner that allows them to be mapped onto some consistent ("actual") time organization.

➤ *Spatial organization*. It must be possible to orchestrate the space into structures to allow it to be worked with and studied.

Architecture is about organizing space (or, more specifically, about arranging things into space), therefore of these conditions the fifth is the most important. Virtual worlds satisfy all the criteria.

---

22. Anna Cicognani, *On the Linguistic Nature of Cyberspace and Virtual Communities*. *Virtual Reality Society Journal* Vol. 3(1) 25-33, Springer-Verlag, 1998. `http://www.arch.usyd.edu.au/~anna/papers/language.pdf`.

Some of the same observations about the nature of virtual spaces that were made by geographers Dodge and Kitchin also show up in architect Peter Anders's book *Envisioning Cyberspace*[23]; this also has large tracts devoted to virtual worlds, and should be on the bookshelf of anyone who takes the design of virtual worlds seriously. Anders advances a thesis that certain types of space are bad for the well being of the virtual world as a whole (at least if it's a textual world). Textual worlds use episodic movement rather than dynamic movement—that is, you move a room at a time[24]. This contradicts any illusion of conventional "real" space, but is nevertheless so compelling that it forms the basis for all the features that make the virtual world a "world." The reason it can do this is because players are willing to discard their disbelief, and buy into it. This means they trust the designer to maintain their faith; if the designer pops them out of their immersion, it amounts to nothing less than a betrayal.

Virtual worlds where players can build, transfer this trust to the builders. Unfortunately, many builders *do* betray it (largely through ignorance or incompetence). As Dieberger also noticed, there will be rooms with non-intuitive connections, "black hole" rooms you can enter but can't leave, and areas unlinked from the "orientation space" where players enter the virtual world. Unsuccessful rooms that people never visit will be abandoned; anyone who does enter them will find nothing of interest—not even other characters—thereby contributing to an overall sense that the virtual world is "empty." Although the central space is generally occupied, the further away from it you are the less likely you are to meet anyone by chance. This robs the virtual world of the spontaneous interaction that gives it much of its immediacy. Everything seems static.

Anders notes one of the problems is that people will usually teleport to locations if they can, rather than walk there. This means they are unlikely to bump into people on the way, of course, but it also suggests they won't explore. In graphical worlds, you can "see" into adjacent locations, and go over to look at anything that seems interesting; in textual ones, rooms act as their own boundaries, so players are blind with respect

---

23. Peter Anders, *Envisioning Cyberspace: Designing 3D Electronic Spaces*. New York, McGraw-Hill, 1998.

24. Graphical worlds with a *zone of resolution* also do this—that is, ones that only render objects that are present within a certain range. *Island of Kesmai* and *AlphaWorld* (the name of the main *Active Worlds* environment) are examples of such worlds.

to the contents of adjacent rooms[25]. If people don't explore, they have less chance of coming across anything (or anyone) new. Exploration can help socialization.

To give players more opportunity to meet people, Anders therefore makes the following recommendations:

➤ Restrict teleporting.

➤ Make all private rooms link into the general space.

➤ Have multiple entrance points, for multiple local hangouts.

Although these only officially work for textual worlds with a lot of building, they're sound advice for all other virtual worlds, too. The fewer anomalies that players must suffer to experience a virtual world, the better; the more opportunities to meet one another the better, too[26].

Anders makes a distinction between textual and graphical virtual world design because he sees the former as using cognition rather than perception; information is conveyed in symbols rather than in senses, and space is inferred rather than experienced. One way to interpret this is that for graphical worlds you feel that you are part of the environment, whereas for textual worlds you feel that the environment is part of you. This may partly explain the difference in attraction of the two systems.

Although real-life architecture and virtual world architecture are not the same[27], the desire of virtual world designers to mimic aspects of reality (for reasons of immersion) means that many of the processes involved *are* the same, particularly where there are social concerns. Architects are interested in virtual worlds, and virtual world designers should be interested in architecture.

---

25. To be fair, some textual worlds do allow you to look into adjacent rooms (assuming line-of-sight). This uses almost the same room/room links as movement, but will have exceptions. For example, you can't look through fog even though you can walk through it, and you can't walk across a raging river even though you can look across it. Of course, this is still an active thing—you deliberately have to look to see, it doesn't "catch your eye" in the background like it might in a graphical world.

26. This isn't a call for the removal of all barriers to communication, otherwise what would result would be a simple IRC-like channel. As Tom Erikson points out, the spatial constraints that virtual worlds impose can be the dynamos that generate activity.
Thomas Erikson, *From Interface to Interplace: The Spatial Environment as a Medium for Interaction*. Elba Italy, *Proceedings of Conference on Spatial Information Theory*, 1993.
`http://www.pliant.org/personal/Tom_Erikson/Interplace.html`.

27. For a useful overview, see Anna Cicognani, *Architectural Design for Online Environments*.
`http://www.arch.usyd.edu.au/~anna/papers/kolko.pdf`.

Social concerns, of course, arise from the presence of large numbers of people in virtual worlds. Where there are people, there will always be other people willing to study those people. When the people share a space—or perceive that they do[28]—it's time to call in the anthropologists.

Anthropology

The discipline of science concerned with the study of other cultures is anthropology. With ever-dwindling numbers of unstudied cultures, it is unsurprising that anthropologists should take an interest whenever new cultures develop on their doorstep (as they have in virtual worlds). That virtual worlds have not been flooded with anthropologists, however, can perhaps be ascribed to three factors:

> The traditional view that virtual worlds are games and therefore not worthy of serious study[29].

> The fieldwork for virtual worlds isn't as exotic and exciting as that promised by the real world.

> These cultures are so new, they could well be considered to be a subculture of that of the anthropologist, which makes their study sociology rather than anthropology.

Nevertheless, formal anthropological work has been undertaken for virtual worlds, some of it producing results of interest to virtual world designers.

There are several subfields of anthropology, not all of which are applicable to virtual worlds. In his excellent modern anthropology textbook[30], Daniel Bates lists these as

> *Biological anthropology*. Also known as physical anthropology, this concerns the study of biological variations among populations. It has virtually no applicability in the context of virtual worlds[31].

28. Jennifer A. Clodius, *Concepts of Space and Place in a Virtual Community*. 1994.

29. Scrupulous open-mindedness about other cultures relative to their own is practically institutional among anthropologists, therefore they are far less susceptible to this kind of prejudgment than most other researchers. However, an overabundance of hastily written undergraduate papers on the subject in the 1990s may have made professors more wary about virtual worlds than they might otherwise have been.

30. Daniel G. Bates, *Cultural Anthropology*. Needham Heights MA, Allyn & Bacon, 1996.

31. It could be used to inform the design of the cultural set-up for newly invented character races, but no one seems yet to have done this in earnest.

➤ *Archaeology*. Archaeologists investigate the relationship between the artifacts people create and their behavior. This is unlikely to be applied to virtual worlds for many years, as the people who created the artifacts still live and their behavior can be assessed directly rather than deduced from what survives them.

➤ *Linguistic anthropology*. Linguistic anthropologists study the way language is constructed and used, and from this come to understand the nature of the culture it supports[32].

➤ *Cultural anthropology*. This is what everyone generally thinks of by "anthropology": going out and living among a population for months on end, observing and recording aspects of their everyday life.

There are, furthermore, two different results of anthropological study. The first is the *ethnography*: This is a detailed examination of an individual culture that is purely descriptive; it paints a detailed picture of a culture, but offers no interpretation of the results. An *ethnology*, on the other hand, attempts to discern cultural patterns of behavior from the ethnographical data. Ethnographies describe the way things are; ethnologies explain *why* things are the way things are.

Ethnographic data usually begins with a demographic study of a population to determine where the cultural boundaries lie. In 1996, for example, Gamespot undertook an influential survey[33] of players of multi-player online games of all kinds; it uncovered different patterns of play for players of different types of games. Although useful for identifying possible areas that may be worthwhile as subjects for individual study, this kind of data snapshot has only a limited shelf life if the rate of change of player behavior is unsettled[34].

Virtual worlds, as (in this context) a subfield of multi-player computer games, do have a long enough history to have achieved some measure of stability. The earliest serious attempt by a non-player to collect ethnographic data about virtual worlds *only* was

---

32. The study of the way individuals adapt their language to different social circumstances and needs is called *sociolinguistics*. It's a specialist subfield of linguistic anthropology which, as we shall see, finds virtual worlds particularly appealing.

33. http://www.gamespot.com/features/olsurvey/index.htm

34. Many of the industry-leading companies named in the Gamespot study were to fold in the five years that followed it.

Herbert Emert's 1993 survey[35], which was formally an investigation into the social effects that playing in virtual worlds had on the players themselves. It succeeded in discerning the different attitudes players had, particularly in why they played (that is, the presence of different player types).

Unfortunately, early surveys (and there were several that followed—Usenet requests for people to respond to questionnaires were a seasonal event at term paper time for several years) regarded the players of virtual worlds as a single community—something that hadn't been true since the days of *MUD1* (and even that had a distinction between its "internal" and "external" players, who played at different times of the day and rarely overlapped). Later studies[36] by non-players made a distinction between "adventure" and "social" virtual worlds, but still treated them as if they were communities as a whole.

Some aspects of virtual world culture are universal, of course, and others aren't but are prevalent in many related worlds. This degree of homogeneity is caused by inheritance from parent worlds and the occasional arrival of immigrant players bringing ideas from more distantly related worlds. Nevertheless, individual virtual worlds must be regarded as the entities in which values are passed from one generation of players to the next, and it is therefore individual virtual worlds that anthropologists must study if they are to learn about these cultures.

Anthropologists studying virtual worlds will stay in a single one over time in the same way that in the real world they would stay in a single village. Expeditions to neighboring "villages" to examine differences and similarities of behavior are possible, but on the whole the research is based in one place.

It is interesting to consider whether large-scale virtual worlds that exist in multiple simultaneous incarnations have different cultures across those incarnations. The evidence seems to suggest that although there may be differences when particular servers have been set up to attract a particular playing style (for example, PvP is allowed or

---

35. http://www.tao.ca/~peter/athesis/MUDs/emert93.txt

36. I have hard copies of two such surveys, one from the University of Vienna and one from the Friedrich Schiller University of Jena, both of which show interesting results but neither of which bears their author's name. They've disappeared from the web, too, so I can't really say much about them here. Sorry!

not), in general the culture seems to be fairly uniform. In *The Norrathian Scrolls* (Nick Yee's exhaustive demographic study of *EverQuest*), no strange age/gender combinations were discerned for individual shards; the composition of player populations was pretty much the same from one to the next. This doesn't mean that their players would necessarily *behave* the same way, of course, but it suggests that if they don't conform, then their behavior is not sufficiently *outré* to affect overall population balance.

Data gathering for individual virtual worlds has generally been conducted either for administrative use only or as a means to some non-anthropological end. Indeed, researchers who want to look at virtual worlds for one main purpose will often pick a particular one and study it in great depth. This can be viewed as a form of anthropological study. Dieberger's work on navigation was focused entirely on *Igor MUD*[37], for example, and Pargman's examination of community management arose from a study of *SvenskMud*[38]. There have, however, been anthropological studies by anthropologists, for anthropologists, of virtual worlds.

The first of these was Michael Rosenberg's 1992 ethnography[39] of *WolfMOO*. Rosenberg joined this virtual world as a participant observer, and spent several weeks of regular evening play getting to know and understand it. Although his report only scratches the surface of what is possible, it nevertheless sets a high standard. Reading it, you get a good sense of what *WolfMOO* was about and how its players behaved; it's like a first-person travel guide to a distant city that gets the facts over without the hyperbole. The value of this kind of work is perhaps made all the more clear by the fact *WolfMOO* is no more; Rosenberg's ethnography is all that remains to reflect the culture that once was.

John Masterson's 1994 ethnography[40] of *Ancient Anguish*[41] draws directly on Rosenberg's work, although it's less formal and more speculative in places. He played *Ancient Anguish* for two years before writing his (unpublished, but widely read) paper.

---

37. http://www.igormud.org:1703/

38. http://svmud.lysator.liu.se

39. Michael S. Rosenberg, *Virtual Reality: Reflections of Life, Dreams, and Technology. An Ethnography of a Computer Society.* 1992. http://www.eff.org/Net_culture/MOO_MUD_IRC/rosenberg_vr_reflections.paper.

40. John T. Masterson III, *Ethnography of a Virtual Society, or How a Gangling, Wiry Half-Elf Found a Way to Fit In.* 1994. ftp://ftp.game.org/pub/mud/text/research/ethno.txt.

41. http://ancient.anguish.org

Many of his observations would be regarded as unexceptional in today's virtual worlds, but of course part of the reason for this is because pioneers like he and Rosenberg made those observations in the first place.

Masterson put his field experience of *Ancient Anguish* to further good use, writing a 1996 master's thesis[42] on the sociolinguistics of virtual worlds. In addition to *Ancient Anguish*, he also spent extended periods in two other adventure-oriented virtual worlds[43] for comparison: *Paradox II* and *TrekMUSE*[44]. For linguistic anthropologists, virtual worlds (especially textual ones) are unusual because people write in them as if they were speaking. Formally, linguistic anthropology concerns language that isn't written down, so on the face of it textual communication via a keyboard ought to be disqualified. It's the fact the players consider themselves to be speaking that validates it; their words are as ephemeral as spoken words are in real life[45]. Logging these communications is more like recording conversations than it is reading a book.

Linguistic anthropologists have looked at non-verbal communication in some detail. In real life, people use many physical gestures other than mere speech while communicating. Bowing is so ingrained in Japanese culture, for example, that people will often do so to individuals with whom they are communicating by telephone. Picking up on the nuances of this kind can be very difficult for anthropologists, therefore it's very useful for them to be able to look at virtual worlds where all communication is by text only—there's only one channel to examine. The first person to examine this in detail was Lynn Cherny, who in an 11-month study[46] of *ElseMOO*[47] categorized five different kinds of emote command as mechanisms for conveying non-verbal communication:

> ➤ *Conventional action.* These are actions that have a practical effect, much like any regular action. Example: "*Name* waves."

---

42. John T. Masterson III, *Nonverbal Communication in Text Based Virtual Realities*. University of Montana, 1996. `http://www.johnmasterson.com/thesis/`.

43. Around 2,000 hours in total over the three.

44. `http://www.trekmuse.org/`

45. Jennifer A. Clodius, *Orality in a Text-Based Community*. 1996. `http://dragonmud.org/people/jen/oral.html`.

46. Lynn Cherny, *The Modal Complexity of Speech Events in a Social MUD*. Stanford University, 1995. `http://bhasha.stanford.edu/~cherny/ejc.txt`.

47. This is not its real name; Cherny uses pseudonyms to protect the integrity of the MOOs she studies.

➤ *Back channels*. These occur during conversations, indicating continued attention/ understanding. Example: "*Name* nods."

➤ *Byplay*. Jocular meta-comments on conversation. Example: "*Name* dusts off some adjectives."

➤ *Narration*. Comments usually related to real-life events, often indicating boredom. Example: "*Name* munches on a ketchup sandwich."

➤ *Exposition*. Statements describing internal or factual background. Unlike the other four categories, these can be in any tense. Example: "*Name* hated the movie."

Influential though this was, Cherny was later to surpass herself with a full-blown linguistic ethnography[48] of *ElseMOO*, exhibiting the same kind of depth and scholarship seen in any other major sociolinguistic work. It's very impressive; the discussion of the ethics of studying virtual communities is worth the cover price alone[49].

More pragmatic virtual world designers than I may wonder what there is in all this for them. Clearly, the more you know about virtual worlds, the better informed you are when designing one; however, why should sociolinguistic studies of particular virtual worlds be compelling reading? The potential of virtual worlds for sociolinguists has been apparent since Eva-Lise Carlstrom's 1992 linguistic ethnography[50] of *LambdaMOO*; is there any traffic of useful information the other way, though?

There is, yes; or rather, there would be if designers were to take the time to look. Anthropologists offer a unique opportunity for designers to see themselves through the trained eyes of others; it is foolhardy to ignore the objective portrait of themselves that results. Anthropologists may not like it (they try to avoid altering any culture they are studying, so for members of that culture to act on an ethnography is anathema), but that's their problem.

There are practical advantages, too. Take sociolinguistics: By looking at why people use the emotes they do, it is possible for anthropologists to draw up structured lists of

---

48. Lynn Cherny, *Conversation and Community: Chat in a Virtual World.* Stanford, CSLI, 1999.

49. As is the chapter on communities, which I referred to in Chapter 3, "PLayers."

50. Eva-Lise Carlstrom, *Better Living Through Languages: The Communicative Implications of a Text-Only Virtual Environment, or Welcome to LambdaMOO!.* Grinnell College, 1992.
   `ftp://ftp.game.org/pub/mud/text/research/communicative.txt`.

commands that address these needs; virtual world designers have previously had to evolve such lists through requests from players (plus hours of thumbing through a thesaurus). Such emote lists are only of marginal use in textual worlds, where exhaustive sets of emotes have accrued over the years sufficient to cover all situations. For designers of graphical virtual worlds, though, these sets are unusable. It may only take seconds to add a new emote to a textual world, but for graphical worlds it's a non-trivial exercise—it could mean a trip to the motion capture studio in some circumstances (expensive enough in itself, but ruinously so when it must be modified for all valid skeleton types). It's important that players of graphical virtual worlds have available to them the same non-verbal forms of communication they can use in real life, but graphical worlds aren't as expressive as textual ones in this regard. Players of graphical worlds can't use free-form emotes like players of textual worlds do (except textually), and neither they can they expect every fixed-form emote to exist—it's too expensive. Only *some* emotes can be implemented: The question is, which ones?

Sociolinguistics provides some of the answers. Rather than picking what players *say* they want, or what the designers *think* the players want, it's possible to look at what players actually use and what they need to know is available (whether or not they use it). This means players can get on with the business of communicating, instead of having to attribute new meaning to bizarre combinations of whatever emotes the designers have actually provided.

This is just one example of where linguistic anthropology can be of possible use to virtual world designers; if you read Cherny's or Masterson's work, others will present themselves, too.

As for cultural anthropology, that also has things to say about virtual world design. Jen Clodius is a cultural anthropologist who immersed herself in *DragonMUD*[51] (the oldest continuously running TinyMUD) so extensively it could almost be said she "went native." In a series of short papers, some of which have already been cited here, she made a number of penetrating insights about why people in virtual worlds do what they do; in this sense, her work is ethnology rather than ethnography. For example, in a 1996 paper[52] she describes how the players of *DragonMUD* developed and maintained a community of interest, touching on issues of identity construction to suggest

---

51. http://www.dragonmud.org

52. Jennifer A. Clodius, *Creating a Community of Interest: "Self" and "Other" on DragonMUD.* 1996.

why this may be. Developers of large-scale virtual worlds who rake in several million dollars in subscriptions monthly would do well to engage people such as Clodius to tell them how their community works, instead of operating in the dark (or worse, over-reacting to the unrepresentative minorities who often dominate the public forums).

Ethnologies teach us about other cultures. By comparing behavioral similarities across many cultures, it is possible to discern universal patterns that can then be sought in more diverse cultures, including our own. This is, for example, how Joseph Campbell formalized the hero's journey and why George Lucas was then able to use it for *Star Wars* (of which the virtual world *Star Wars Galaxies* is a direct result).

The first major thesis[53] about virtual worlds, written by Liz Reid in 1994, was an attempt to identify patterns of cultural formation common to virtual worlds. She traced behavioral tropes back to the mechanisms that underlie virtual worlds, rather than the culture of the people who played them. For example: The reason people are more open in virtual worlds than they are in the real one is because of the anonymity virtual worlds afford them; it's not because they come from a real-world society that empha-sizes openness. Players have needs that virtual worlds can fulfill; however, if they are to satisfy those needs then they must live alongside other players. This implies they must develop a set of mutual understandings that support both their goals and their rela-tionships; these feed back to provide a context to give meaning to their actions (and themselves). These are the cultures of virtual worlds.

Reid is right: Virtual world cultures are formed by the needs of the players, acting under environmental conditions both inherent to the access medium and provided by the virtual world's designers. I would add, however, that these cultures rarely form spontaneously any more: It is possible to shape a culture in advance of its creation, because much of what new players learn about a virtual world they pick up from exist-ing players. The original, seeding players therefore have a strong influence on the direction a culture takes; since most of these players will have played other virtual worlds beforehand, so some aspects of culture are passed from virtual world to virtual world to virtual world. As an illustration, consider whether the attitude to cross-gender

---

53. Elizabeth Reid, *Cultural Formations in Text-Based Virtual Realities*. Department of English, University of Melbourne, 1994. ftp://ftp.ee.mu.oz.au/papers/emr/cult-form.ps.

play in virtual worlds would be the same today had they been invented in a right-wing, reactionary college in the Deep South rather than a British university notorious for its left-wing politics[54].

Were virtual worlds to be created from nothing, quite different cultures could develop as per Reid; nowadays, though, much culture is passed on and therefore evolves, rather than forms. Furthermore, as increasing numbers of people become involved with the Internet, virtual communities are starting to have an impact on real-world ones. Given that (as always) the virtual is governed by the real, it therefore makes sense to suppose that to some degree at least, virtual society can be regarded as a subclass of society as a whole.

This brings us to our next topic: sociology.

Sociology

Sociology is the study of the organization, functioning, and development of human societies. It is very closely related to anthropology; basically, sociologists and anthropologists got to pretty well the same place but came from different starting points. Indeed, an excellent way to annoy a sociologist or anthropologist is to ask what the difference is between the two disciplines. It essentially boils down to three things:

➤ Sociologists study only industrial societies, whereas anthropologists concentrate on (but don't restrict themselves to) pre-industrial societies.

➤ Anthropologists are big on qualitative methods, particularly participant observation (that is, immersing oneself in a society to learn about its ways). Sociologists are big on quantitative methods, especially making deductions from statistics.

➤ They have different traditions, and follow the theories of different individuals.

More and more, however, the distinction is becoming blurred. For example, Reed Riner and Jen Clodius[55] explored the idea of using a virtual world predictively, to see how people might behave in a future Mars settlement; whether this qualifies as sociology or

---

54. Cross-gender play would still have occurred, because it happens in table-top role-playing games. Whether it would have been as commonplace as it is now is a cultural issue.

55. Reed D. Riner and Jennifer A. Clodius, *Simulating Future Histories: The NAU Solar System Simulation & Mars Settlement. Anthropology & Education Quarterly* Vol. 26(I):95-104, Spring 1995. `http://dragonmud.com/people/jen/solsys.html`.

anthropology is anyone's guess! My own personal definition of the difference is that anthropologists study other peoples, whereas sociologists study their own. I'm neither an anthropologist nor a sociologist, though, so feel free to ignore this.

So what do sociologists have to say about virtual worlds?

Well, it's actually quite hard to pin down. There seem to be four areas of activity[56], as follows:

- Cyberculture
- Computer-Mediated Communication (CMC)
- Gender Studies
- General Sociology

Cyberculture is an interdisciplinary area concerning the study of online culture. Unfortunately (from the point of view of this book), it makes little distinction between virtual worlds and other sources of online culture. It's basically a catchall for people who want to write about stuff with an Internet connection but are unable to do so within the traditional limits of their chosen field. Although some of the best books on virtual worlds I've found were stocked under "cyberculture" at the bookstore, most of what's there typically concerns something else.

Cyberculture also suffers from an overly hip and trendy image, attracting a disproportionate number of authors who want to be seen to be at the cutting edge of the social sciences and are willing to pull out every polysyllabic word in their vocabulary to do so. Some of the best (and, from the perspective just described, worst) early papers on cyberculture were collected in *The Cybercultures Reader*[57]; if you are interested in learning about the subject, this is as good a place as any to start. Although I refer to some of these papers later under more specific subheadings, I shall not, however, be examining cyberculture itself in further detail; it's simply too amorphous.

56. Five, if you include undergraduates who write essays on the subject because they were playing games when they should have been working.

57. David Bell and Barbara M. Kennedy (editors), *The Cybercultures Reader*. New York, Routledge, 2000.

CMC and gender studies I do look at, as they have much to say about virtual worlds; so much, in fact, that they get their own sections (although CMC doesn't get as much as gender studies).

This leaves us with general sociology. Despite the presence of virtual worlds on the syllabus of many university sociology courses, in terms of actual substance this isn't actually a lot[58].

Nevertheless, the paper that introduced sociologists to virtual worlds is (by virtue of this fact) one of the most important ever written on the subject: Pavel Curtis's *Mudding: Social Phenomena in Text-Based Virtual Realities*[59]. In this, Curtis described observations made as a result of his experience as maintainer of *LambdaMOO* at Xerox PARC. After describing virtual worlds[60], he noted the following:

➤ Around 90% of *LambdaMOO*'s players connected from colleges and universities.

➤ At most 50% of the players had a computer science background.

➤ Around 70% of the players were male.

➤ A common phenomenon is that some males play female characters.

➤ Female characters are subject both to harassment and special (favorable) treatment.

➤ Although player names are varied, their descriptions are not. Characters who are "mysterious, but unmistakably powerful" are relatively common.

➤ Player anonymity is the most significant social factor in virtual worlds. Players do not feel at risk and are consequently less inhibited than in real life. Some of this disinhibition is manifested by irresponsibility, rudeness, pestering, and so on.

---

58. Alternatively, and perhaps more likely, it's my ability to track down papers from alien disciplines that is at fault.

59. Pavel Curtis, *Mudding: Social Phenomena in Text-Based Virtual Realities*. Berkeley, Proceedings of Conference on Directions and Implications of Advanced Computing, 1992. This, along with several other classic papers I mention in this chapter, also appears in Peter Ludlow (editor), *High Noon on the Electronic Frontier: Conceptual Issues in Cyberspace*. Cambridge MA, MIT Press, 1996. http://www.ics.uci.edu/~jpd/moo/curtis92mudding.pdf.

60. He called them MUDs, but this was at a time before people got uppity about the term.

- ➤ To cope with offensive behavior, virtual worlds have a special class of players (the wizards) who have a policing role (among others). These players are treated differently by the other players; typically either with complete respect or with complete disrespect.

- ➤ When more than two people are in the same location, anyone passing through will tarry awhile on the grounds that something interesting may be happening.

- ➤ Gagging is available, but rarely used on *LambdaMOO*.

- ➤ Conversations in virtual worlds use emotes and smileys to supplement pure text.

- ➤ Partly due to the time it takes to type speech, it is common for several conversational threads to be extant simultaneously in a location, even when there are only two people involved.

- ➤ The disjoint nature of virtual world conversations makes it much easier to join in on one without appearing to be rudely interrupting.

- ➤ Large-scale gatherings of players can occur for specific events, of which virtual weddings are a particularly impressive example.

- ➤ Popular board games are often implemented and played in virtual worlds.

- ➤ The overall size of a virtual community is larger than the number of people actually playing at any one time. *LambdaMOO* had 700–800 different players connecting per week, but rarely more than 40 of them at once[61].

- ➤ Some players play so much that it's a form of addiction.

- ➤ Players can achieve a social consensus about how they ought to behave. This differs from virtual world to virtual world, and from virtual world to the real world.

Most of this will seem obvious to players of virtual worlds now, and indeed it seemed so at the time, too. However, for those individuals who hadn't encountered the concept before it was dazzling stuff. Almost all the sociology work on virtual worlds that followed took points raised by Curtis and ran with them; this may explain why gender studies in particular attracted more attention than might otherwise have been expected.

---

61. This was before people read Curtis's paper and descended on *LambdaMOO* in droves, of course.

In his paper, Curtis also gives a definition of what constitutes a MUD (that is, a virtual world), or at least what distinguishes it from an *Adventure*-style game. He lists three major factors:

➤ MUDs are not goal-oriented; they have no concept of winning/losing, and record no scores.

➤ MUDs can be extended from within by the players.

➤ They generally have more than one player connected simultaneously; these players can communicate with each other in real time.

Although only the third item of these applies universally to virtual worlds (the first two work for *LambdaMOO* and other TinyMUD derivatives, but they don't for even the AberMUDs and LPMUDs that were around when Curtis wrote this), nevertheless this definition has gained considerable currency. It is still seen occasionally in cyberculture articles by people who want to make points about virtual worlds without actually ever touching one.

Being a computer scientist rather than a sociologist, Curtis's later work concerned practical uses of virtual worlds[62]; in a social sciences context, it is therefore usually only referred to when there is a requirement to illustrate that virtual worlds have uses beyond mere entertainment.

Mudding: Social Phenomena in Text-Based Virtual Realities gave social science researchers a lot to think about, but it was by no means exhaustive in its enumeration of behaviors. Although Curtis never claimed it was, few sociologists have looked beyond it. Graduate students surveying the literature for term reports[63] will discover the big issues are identity, pseudonimity, gender difference, and pretty much nothing else. The first two of these are related, and I discuss them in the next section; the third, I discuss in the section after that.

---

62. Pavel Curtis and David A. Nichols, *MUDs Grow Up: Social Virtual Reality in the Real World*. Xerox PARC, 1993. `http://www.eff.org/Net_culture/MOO_MUD_IRC/muds_grow_up.paper`.

63. A good representative example that focuses on virtual worlds in particular is Vickie Edwards, *The New Societies: Issues within MUDs and Other Virtual Communities*. Department of Sociology and Anthropology, University of South Alabama, 2000. `http://www.nacave.com/vickie/cyberculture/newsocieties.html`.

Because of this reduction of the sociology of virtual communities to a few key issues, it has been left to non-sociologists to explore new areas of social research in virtual worlds. This particularly has been the case in community management, where community service representatives have found themselves having to invent the theory that matches their practice as they go along. Amy Jo Kim, for example, who presented an influential paper[64] at the 1997 Computer Game Developers' Conference on how to design sociability into online games, has a background in behavioral neuroscience.

The most outstanding piece of original research of direct interest to both sociologists and the designers of virtual worlds is Christian Carazo-Chandler's study[65] of population mobility in a virtual world (*Ultima Online*, to be precise, with a nod to *EverQuest*). Carazo-Chandler found that movement within a shard and between shards did occur, following theories of migration that apply in the real world; they could therefore be reasonably well predicted. Players had many reasons for and against leaving one shard, and for and against joining a new one (following a *push/pull model*). They would want to leave (push) because of

- ➤ Housing shortages

- ➤ Lack of local services (such as vendors selling the wares you need)

- ➤ Change of character preference

- ➤ Harassment

- ➤ Their poor reputation

They would be thwarted in their desire to move (barriers) by

- ➤ Housing shortages where they wanted to go

- ➤ Distance from starting point (where no instant transport is available)

- ➤ Lack of funds

- ➤ Too high or low concentrations of other players in target location

---

64. Amy Jo Kim, *Ritual Reality: Social Design for Online Gaming Environments*. Santa Clara, *Proceedings of Computer Game Developers' Conference*, 1997.

65. Christian Carazo-Chandler, *Online Migration and Population Mobility in a Virtual Gaming Setting—Ultima Online*. `http://cybergeography.hypermart.net/Copy of Online Migration in a virtual gaming setting - Ultima Online.zip`.

They would want to be somewhere else (pull) because of

- ➤ Greater opportunity for adventure
- ➤ Different or more local services
- ➤ Higher levels of conflict
- ➤ Greater or less popularity of the area
- ➤ More social activities
- ➤ Proximity of friends
- ➤ Profit maximization

Virtual world designers who are of the opinion that players should be given everything they want might use these results as evidence to support their conjecture; players will move to some other virtual world if they find their needs are not being met. This is true, but the barriers for cross-world movement are stronger than for in-world or cross-shard movement; it also assumes that giving players what they want is something they want.

Carazo-Chandler applies other models of population migration apart from push/pull. One of these, concerning circulatory movement, shows how individuals move location within a virtual world as their characters' experience and abilities grow. This is again of use to the thoughtful virtual world designer, because it allows the connection of physical[66] movement with the personal movement of the hero's journey (not that the players would necessarily notice).

Carazo-Chandler is a geographer, not a sociologist, and was investigating population migration from the perspective of how players' decisions to migrate are affected by the structure of their virtual environment. It would be nice if his work sparked sufficient interest among sociologists for them to investigate virtual world populations as populations, rather than as cultures or jumping-on points for ideological bandwagons, but I don't expect it'll happen.

---

66. "Physical" in the context of the virtual world's physics, not the real world's.

Talking of geographers and sociology, it was Rob Kitchin who wrote the first comprehensive introduction to the social science of cyberspace[67]. Chapter 4 of his book summarizes the options of sociologists and other cultural scientists concerning cyberspace in general, and virtual worlds in particular. He describes two main points of view:

➤ Cyberspace engenders disembodiment, allowing the construction of new self-identity.

➤ Cyberspace is where nature and technology merge, allowing the reconstruction of the body.

There's no reason why anyone can't experience some degree of each of these, of course; completely shedding the one (body or identity) completely frees the other, but there can be movement in both directions. That this occurs at the level of the individual indirectly highlights why perhaps sociologists haven't taken to virtual worlds as much as they might have been expected to do.

Except in the case of the large, graphical virtual worlds that weren't around when Pavel Curtis wrote his beacon paper, maybe virtual world societies simply aren't big enough to permit sociologists to make general statements about them? Individuals are just too important. There is scope for looking at large-scale virtual worlds with player bases numbered in the hundreds of thousands; there is scope for looking at virtual worlds as a part of wider society—that is, from without instead of from within. At the moment, though, when it comes to looking at virtual worlds from a sociological perspective, researchers very soon find themselves discussing psychology rather than sociology.

Psychology

Anyone with the remotest interest in the psychology of players of virtual worlds must—that's *must*—look at John Suler's hypertext book[68], *The Psychology of Cyberspace*. Much of it is 100% relevant to virtual worlds (he talks about them directly), and some sections are classics in their own right. Others are merely short monographs, but almost no subfield of Internet-related psychology goes untouched. Suler has something

---

67. Rob Kitchin, *Cyberspace*. Chichester England, John Wiley & Sons, 1998.

68. John Suler, *The Psychology of Cyberspace*. 1996 (orig.) http://www.rider.edu/users/suler/psycyber/psycyber.html.

to say about everything I mention in the remainder of this review, and more besides. There are other, more cohesive and directed introductions to the subject[69], but none that I have encountered are as comprehensive as Suler's.

Psychologists have found many things to interest them in virtual worlds, but two topics dominate: identity construction and addiction. I'll take these in the order in which they were first written about; perhaps surprisingly for many people, this means I'll be starting with addiction.

In 1989, the year Jim Aspnes wrote *TinyMUD*, Margaret Shotton of Nottingham University in England published a book[70] about computer addiction. It reported a formal study she had undertaken in the mid-1980s, comprising data from a number of questionnaires and psychometric tests, coupled with interviews. Shotton explicitly included players of *MUD1* in her survey, and referred to that world during the discussion of the results; indeed, one of the people with whom she conducted extensive interviews was a *MUD1* player.

Shotton confirmed some people were indeed computer-dependent, and they could be divided into three types:

➤ *Networkers* used the computer as a means for communication.

➤ *Workers* used the computer for programming and other work activities.

➤ *Explorers* used the computer to program in an investigative manner for self-education.

Networkers was the category into which the majority of *MUD1* players fitted. Shotton discovered that they were less likely to suffer (from their dependency) in their real-life relationships than workers or explorers; that said, neither of these other categories were particularly bad either. There was no evidence to suggest that people who spent a lot of free time on their computers pained their family any more (or any less) than people who spent a lot of time playing golf or star-gazing through telescopes. Computer addiction is like an addiction to stamp collecting or photography, rather than like drug or gambling addiction.

---

69. I quite like: Patricia Wallace, *The Psychology of the Internet*. Cambridge. Cambridge University Press, 1999. That isn't just because she discusses my player types model, either.

70. Margaret Shotton, *Computer Addiction? A Study of Computer Dependency*. London, Taylor & Francis, 1989.

Shotton actually goes further than this. Not only did she demonstrate that the intense use of computers doesn't turn outgoing extroverts into pale, reclusive hermits, but she also suggested that for some people the experience was very positive. Given that the print media at the time were publishing scare stories about "computer junkies"[71], this was great news for the developers of computer games[72].

Most of what Shotton wrote about computer dependency continues to apply, even though computers and the Internet have now become mainstream. This has not, however, prevented people from talking about "Internet addiction" as if it were a worse social evil than gun warfare. It is only to be expected that when an individual indulges for long periods in an activity that their close friends and family don't understand, it will be cause for concern; that doesn't mean that the people who are concerned are necessarily right, though. Concern is best addressed (one way or the other) through information: Either an activity is basically harmless, or it's dangerous enough to warrant intervention.

Sadly, some psychologists and psychiatrists side with the friends and relatives without even listening to the other side of the argument. Kimberley Young, founder of the Center for On-Line Addiction[73], conducted a three-year study[74] of Internet addiction and pronounced it generally a bad thing. People sit around in chat rooms when they should be saying goodnight to their children! Well yes, that is a bad thing, but then people sit around in bars or watch TV when they should be saying goodnight to their children; the Internet provides the opportunity to become obsessive about more things, but it doesn't actually *make* people obsessive—they're like that already.

Although I don't doubt there are some things on the Internet that can cause real social problems (pornography, for example), lumping together everything Internet-based as if it were the same thing is, in my opinion, a mistake. I'm particularly unimpressed by Young's profile of an "on-lineaholic" called Steve who is addicted to *LambdaMOO* (she follows this up with helpful advice for a recovery strategy he could use).

---

71. It was in response to media interest that Shotton published her work, which was originally her doctoral thesis.

72. Computer games for adults, that is. Shotton treated children differently, recognizing that computer dependency among youngsters is often the result of family or social problems, rather than personality type.

73. http://www.netaddiction.com/

74. Kimberley S. Young, *Caught in the Net: How to Recognize the Signs of Internet Addiction—and a Winning Strategy for Recovery*. New York, John Wiley & Sons, 1998.

LambdaMOO? Excuse me? *LambdaMOO* is a place—how can you be addicted to a place? You can be addicted to what you *do* in a place, which in Steve's case seems to concern increasing his low self-esteem, but you can't be addicted to the place itself[75].

Besides, who is to say that the addiction isn't a positive thing? Virtual worlds are places where social interaction occurs, which is more than can be said for many of the alternatives (for example, watching TV). People can be addicted to things for good reasons, not just bad ones; personal development is, I believe, one of the former. In this kind of situation, the dependency will disappear on its own after the individual has achieved their goal (assuming they're allowed to); any "addiction" here is psychological, not physical.

David Greenfield takes a more open view of Internet addiction[76], recognizing that in many cases all that people need to do is cut back, rather than give up; in this sense, the "addiction" is really "intense interest." His attitude is that the Internet can offer unique and stimulating experiences, and only becomes a problem when it truly interferes with daily life[77]. This is good sense: Just because you have a virtual life, you can't ignore the maintenance of your real life that is required to support it.

Dinty Moore summarizes[78] the different points of view about why people can't leave virtual worlds alone as follows:

➤ The players are addicted. Computer games are addictive, and gamelike virtual worlds are even more so because they blur into reality and players don't realize they're playing a game[79].

➤ The players are learning valuable lessons. They get to meet interesting people, and can socialize better than in the real world. Some learn to code, too.

➤ The players are college students who will do just about anything to avoid doing academic work.

---

75. Marketing virtual worlds as "utterly addictive" doesn't help get this message across, of course....

76. David N. Greenfield, *Virtual Addiction: Help for Netheads, Cyberfreaks, and Those Who Love Them*. Oakland CA, New Harbinger Publications, 1999.

77. He says this explicitly with respect to children playing MUDs (although he calls them MUDDs).

78. Dinty W. Moore, *The Emperor's Virtual Clothes: The Naked Truth about Internet Culture*. Chapel Hill NC, Algonquin Books of Chapel Hill, 1995.

79. Which, of course, they aren't.

The third of these has probably more truth in it than the other two put together....

So, what does all this mean for the designers of virtual worlds?

Well, it means that although virtual worlds may be highly conducive to activities that cause addiction, playing them is not itself inherently addictive. It means that when people do become addicted, whether it's a good or a bad thing depends on what exactly they're addicted to. It means that people who satisfy every field test for addiction may actually be pursuing an important personal goal with great determination. It means that you could be doing people a favor if you allow them to complete their goal.

Oh, and it also means you shouldn't go out of your way to make the activities in your virtual world addictive; that way lies lawsuits. Popular is one thing, but real addiction is something else.

The possibility of deliberately addicting players to activities in virtual worlds has been investigated in a series of articles[80] by experimental psychologist John Hopson. His work confirms that goal-oriented virtual worlds already have powerful addictive features of conditioned reinforcement, which explains why some players will run on a leveling treadmill[81] for months on end and still want more. A morally unscrupulous or unthinkingly irresponsible virtual world designer could tune what has evolved anyway to intensify the experience even more; if they did, however, they'd be advised to seek premium legal counsel about what to put on their product's box about it.

Incidentally, Hopson's work shows it's possible to look at the reasons people play virtual worlds purely in terms of this casino-style addiction; in such situations, there's no requirement that players are undergoing the kind of potentially life-changing personal journey I have described in this book.

---

80. John Hopson, *Basic Principles of Reinforcement for Muds*. MUD-DEV, 2000.
    `http://www.kanga.nu/archives/MUD-Dev-L/2000Q3/msg00364.php`.
    John Hopson, *Matching and Maximizing: How Players Choose Between Activities*. MUD-DEV, 2000.
    `http://www.kanga.nu/archives/MUD-Dev-L/2000Q3/msg00725.php`.
    John Hopson, *Conditioned Reinforcers: Getting Players to Do Things for Free*. MUD-DEV, 2000.
    `http://www.kanga.nu/archives/MUD-Dev-L/2000Q3/msg01101.php`.
    See also: John Hopson, *Behavioral Game Design*. Gamasutra, 2001.
    `http://www.gamasutra.com/features/20010427/hopson_01.htm`.

81. This is a technical term, believe it or not, used to describe the process of going up levels in a boring, never-ending but strangely irresistible way, as experienced by hundreds of thousands of virtual world players daily.

Which segues neatly to the topic of identity construction....

Addiction and identity issues are actually related; for many people, the chance to escape from the physical body is greatly attractive, and therefore the search for identity could be the addictive quality that keeps many people playing in virtual worlds. This was a point suggested by the first paper[82] to recognize the importance of identity experiment in virtual worlds, written in 1992 by Amy Bruckman.

Bruckman began her research as an investigation into what the cyberspace envisaged by Cyberpunk writers might be like when it arrived; when she discovered virtual worlds, she realized that it already *had* arrived, and switched the focus of her inquiry. Over the course of a month, she studied a number of virtual worlds, but concluded that she'd have to concentrate on a single one if she was ever to understand the phenomenon fully. She selected *TrekMUSE*.

Following Pavel Curtis, she noted that male-as-female cross-gender play occurred fairly frequently, commonly as a psychological exploration, but occasionally as a practical joke; as usual with practical jokes, they're only amusing for the perpetrator, not the victim[83]. She did some investigation into female-as-male play, too, but discovered evidence only of the "psychological exploration" style of cross-gender play[84]. She also found that although men treated female-presenting characters with excessive courtesy, they often did the same to male-presenting newbies, too.

In examining addiction, Bruckman came to the conclusion that although playing virtual worlds was habit-forming, most players were able to stop if they wanted to and few long-term players were truly "stuck" in them. This makes any decision as to the goodness or badness of spending lots of time in virtual worlds essentially a value judgment (that is, the point unhappily missed by many of the "Internet addiction" brigade).

---

82. Amy Bruckman, *Identity Workshop: Emergent Social and Psychological Phenomena in Text-Based Virtual Reality.* MIT Media Laboratory, 1992. `ftp://ftp.cc.gatech.edu/pub/people/asb/papers/identity-workshop.rtf`.

83. They often reveal deep insecurities in the perpetrator, so it's interesting to consider why someone would think getting other people of the same sex to fall in love with them was funny.

84. This may be because the number of real-life women playing in virtual worlds was so low that she simply didn't encounter anyone who masqueraded as male for kicks, or it could be something more psychologically fundamental.

Although Bruckman linked addiction and identity issues, they were soon to become separated. This is perhaps due in part to the tremendous influence of Donna Haraway's *A Cyborg Manifesto*[85]. This is a utopian thought-experiment that envisages human beings as cyborgs in order to make a number of stinging points about the direction that feminism should go. It starts by stating three areas in which age-old boundaries have become blurred:

➤ Human and animal

➤ Organism and machine

➤ Physical and non-physical

Haraway argues that the lowering of these boundaries admits the possibility of the future existence of cyborg life-forms, then tokenizes such an entity so as to explore the consequences of its existence on feminist thinking.

It's due to the second and (because it's related) third of Haraway's blurred boundaries that researchers became interested in virtual worlds. Traditionally, psychologists have separated mind, fantasy, and information from body, reality, and materiality, but virtual worlds don't fit into this scheme at all well. By examining virtual worlds, perhaps some new ways of looking at issues of identity could be raised?

Lynn Cherny, taking Haraway's point that cyberspace makes the position of "the body" problematical, looked at[86] different ways by which the player is split between being a physical entity at a keyboard and a virtual entity encoded in a computer. As Cherny is a sociolinguist, much of her paper concerns describing some idiosyncratic (from the point of view of other virtual worlds) communication constructs used by players of her pseudonymous *ElseMOO*. She noted that although most of these activities were for fun, sometimes they were used in ways that are most definitely not fun: She was distressingly spoofed[87] at one point during her investigation, and recommended that for ethical reasons players should not be able to manipulate other players as if they were puppets.

---

85. Donna Haraway, *A Cyborg Manifesto: Science, Technology, and Socialist-Feminism in the Late Twentieth Century*. Written in 1985, this appeared in numerous forms, finally crystallizing in Donna Haraway, *Simians, Cyborgs, and Women*. New York, Roytledge, 1991. It's this version that is extracted in *The Cybercultures Reader*.

86. Lynn Cherny, *"Objectifying" the Body in the Discourse of an Object-Oriented MUD*. Stanford University, 1995. http://fragment.nl/mirror/Cherny/Objectifying_the_body.txt.

87. Spoofing occurs only in textual virtual worlds, and involves creating a free-form message that gives the impression something has "happened" which hasn't.

As I myself have argued in this book, I concur that there is a split between the physical and the virtual self. Furthermore, I believe that it is a purpose—no, a *duty*—of virtual worlds to facilitate the reconciliation of these selves, for the benefit of the real-life[88] individual.

As for the manipulation of other characters, well that's an expectation issue. If you know it's going to happen, and the degree to which it's going to happen, there's not a problem. If there were, then stage hypnotists couldn't manipulate willing subjects for a living. What Cherny objected to when she was spoofed was basically that she did not have an expectation that this would happen; even if she knew it was possible, it was still a betrayal of trust. When people go into virtual worlds that look and behave in ways consistent with a particular kind of environment (real or imaginary) such that they can expect to have a reasonable understanding of what it will be like, then if something happens within that understood context it's (morally, if not emotionally) fine. For example, a player in a fantasy world who goes up to a snake-eyed necromancer NPC famed for his mesmeric powers can hardly complain if their character is made to run amok while clucking like a chicken; they may not *like* it, but they can't say it was unfair. If, however, the same thing happened in the same virtual world while the player's character was buying provisions at a mundane downtown store, there'd better be a very good explanation (or an easy defense against the assault), otherwise it *would* be unfair.

Unfairness occurs when it's your understanding that nothing awful is, in the current circumstances, permitted to happen by the virtual world's rules (physics or terms of service), then it happens anyway. This is whether the consequences of the unfairness are (in virtual world terms) tangible or intangible. Most problems with unfairness come when groups of people (especially newbies) have a false view of cultural norms and do one of the following:

➤ React to what they perceive as unfairness, but most people think is fine.

➤ Perpetrate something most people think is an unfairness that they don't perceive as such.

---

88. Real-life, because reality always wins. Wherever you may think you are, your mind's hardware is always in reality, and you can only leave by dying.

Allowing players to spoof other players' actions is an absolutely classic and obvious way to cause this kind of trouble. In *MUD1*, I didn't even consider giving spoofing capabilities to anyone but the virtual world's administrators; it beggars belief that regular players were ever allowed to use it in MOOs except perhaps in the most rigorous of role-playing situations[89].

Charles Stivale analyzed[90] the different opportunities virtual worlds present for players to harass one another to various degrees; he found identity assault to be the strongest form of harassment. The most interesting part of his paper is his discussion of how players of *LambdaMOO* reacted following an incident of "virtual rape" (the specifics of which I discuss in the next section[91]). They spent a great deal of time debating ways and means to define what forms of action could be construed as serious harassment, and although the discussion eventually floundered on arguments about what constitutes free speech in a world where everything is typed (and therefore covered by the First Amendment), it's interesting to note that one obvious solution—remove the ability to spoof—was never on the agenda. In adventure-oriented virtual worlds, these commands are usually far too immersion-busting even to contemplate for everyday use, yet in early 1990s *LambdaMOO* they were apparently regarded as indispensable despite their obvious potential for misuse.

The major work on identity discovery in virtual worlds is Sherry Turkle's superb *Life on the Screen*[92]. This is a wonderful book by a very influential author. In it, she makes a number of central points in a clear, easy-to-follow style[93], charting her own personal experiences, but including such a rich seam of anecdotal excerpts from interviews with subjects that other researchers will be quoting her for years. What I particularly like about this book is that I agree with pretty well all her conclusions, despite having come from inside virtual worlds, whereas she comes from outside.

---

89. That said, most pre-client textual worlds didn't do a great job of stopping other spoofs anyway, especially from line-wrapping (separate two messages with enough spaces that the second one wraps to a new line so it looks like it's independent output from the virtual world itself).

90. Charles J. Stivale, *Spam: Heteroglossia and Harassment in Cyberspace.* David Porter (editor), *Internet Culture.* New York, Routledge, 1997.

91. Interestingly, the coda of Amy Bruckman's *Identity Workshop* paper includes a transcript that refers to these events, which were ongoing at the time.

92. Sherry Turkle, *Life on the Screen.* New York, Simon & Schuster, 1995.

93. Contrast this with Donna Haraway's prose, which in places resembles that of a program I wrote in 1978 to generate random social science essays: full of so many meaning-loaded, context-heavy words as to be almost impenetrable.

As I already mentioned in my Chapter 3, her Chapter 7 is the big one insofar as virtual world theorists are concerned; it's there she gets to the heart of the identity issue. Is identity unitary or multiple? Is it a structure of mind or an illusion? She observes that on the Internet people "build a self by cycling through many selves," which previously in real life this was very hard to accomplish. Virtual worlds, because they provide reality-presenting environments, are where this happens most intensely[94]; she characterizes them as "laboratories for the construction of identity," and looks at them in considerable detail.

Turkle poses a series of important questions, most of which are yet to be answered (although I make an attempt to address some of them in this book). Those of most interest to virtual world designers are

- ➤ What kind of virtual selves do people make?

- ➤ Do real-world selves learn lessons from virtual selves?

- ➤ How do the different selves communicate with each other?

- ➤ Why do people do this?

Using a number of case studies to support her theory, Turkle argues that virtual worlds allow individuals to express unexplored facets of themselves, or facets that they are unable to manifest in real life. She concludes experience in virtual worlds can greatly encourage personal growth and self-awareness, but cautions they can also be places where people lose their way and become trapped. The mechanism for this is identity drift (she calls the changes *slippages*), where character and player merge, where multiple selves join to form what the individual believes is their true self.

As a clinical psychologist, Turkle is keen to identify explicit ways by which people can work through issues in virtual worlds in therapeutic[95] fashion—for example, by role-playing their real-life situation (or an analogy of it) in different ways. However, she

---

94. This has been noted by several observers, and has support from a sociolinguistic study that compared the communicative structure of *LambdaMOO*, Internet Relay Chat, and VaxNotes (a BBS system). See: Jill Serpentelli, *Conversational Structure and Personality Correlates of Electronic Communication*. Haverford College, 1992. http://www.zacha.net/articles/serpentelli.html.

95. For a review of the therapeutic uses of virtual worlds, see: James Sempsey III, *The Therapeutic Potentials of Text-Based Virtual Reality*. Journal of MUD Research Vol. 3(2), 1998. http://www.brandeis.edu/pubs/jove/HTML/v3/sempsey.html.

notes that some people can repeatedly replay the same mistakes, learning nothing from them; this only serves to harden their attitudes and they hate themselves all the more for it, like ghosts doomed forever to echo the reality of their former-life's deeds. This is reenacting, not reworking; it's much less common than reworking, but it's a serious problem for those who fall into it. Virtual worlds allow people to find *who* they want to be, but it's up to the individuals themselves to *become* those people. Maybe for some, the distance between existing self and ideal self is just too great to travel.

On the other hand, it may be the design of the virtual world itself gets in the way. As John Hopson noted, there are ways to keep people playing in virtual worlds that have nothing to do with personal development. This is a point also made by Jonathan Baron, who describes[96] a dialectic between game worlds that emphasize development over achievement and those that emphasize achievement over development. His assessment is basically that the former are the goal, and that people who aim for the latter are asking for trouble in the long term. For hero's journey reasons, I totally agree with him on that point.

Although, as Sherry Turkle describes, some people do deliberately create characters with different personalities to see how they work, I contend that most people don't. When they experiment with an archetype (for example, a new character class[97]), it's usually because they're bored with their first one, curious about the new one, or think they'll have some in-world advantage as a result; they don't make a conscious decision about which direction their personality should go in next (or if they do, it's because they're psychology majors or have experienced psychotherapy). To be fair, Turkle does-n't say that everyone thinks explicitly about what identity they want either, but it could be easy for people unfamiliar with virtual worlds to come away from her book believing that identity drift is something that happens to only a few players; in my experience, it happens to pretty well all of them.

---

96. Jonathan Baron, *Glory and Shame: Powerful Psychology in Multiplayer Online Games.* San Jose, *Proceedings of Computer Game Developers Conference,* 1999.
   http://www.gamasutra.com/features/19991110/Baron_01.htm.

97. I would be very interested to discover what psychologists make of the identification with anthropomorphic animals that define virtual worlds like *FurryMUCK* (http://www.furry.com). Studies to date seem to consider only what people do in these worlds (see the following section on gender issues) rather than why they do it.

I suppose this is as good a place as any to describe my own views on identity. Personally, I view an individual as having a core self (or agglomeration of selves, it doesn't really matter), which projects itself through the filters of action and word to present images to other individuals. The filter can be changed according to circumstances, but in the real world it's difficult to do this because of the anchors of family, community, and society. People can find themselves projecting through filters they don't like, or with which they don't feel comfortable. Virtual worlds allow the filters to be changed experimentally and (as a consequence) experientially. Through playing them you can find the filter closest to clarity: The one for the person you feel yourself truly to be.

Identity exploration is generally seen as a good thing. Sherry Turkle noted that it can be problematical for individuals who discover their ideal self but resist moving toward it; Mark Slouka warns[98] that there are further difficulties when an individual wants to change but their identity issues are irreconcilable. He describes a male friend who, while masquerading as female, fell in love with another female character; she reciprocated his feelings without knowing he was male in real life[99]. In this example, the virtual person and the real person can be reconciled intellectually and emotionally, but never physically; the female character's personality can influence the male player's (and vice versa), but they can never become one in the physical world. They can in the virtual one, therefore the male player is committed to spending as much time as possible there, but this is a relationship that can never be consummated. The fate of Slouka's friend reminds me of that of Rilian, Prince of Narnia, enchanted so that he was only ever himself for one hour every night while bound in a silver chair[100].

Slouka is right, too: There can be problems when the virtual world acts as a bridge between different parts of the real world. In general, players treat virtual worlds as if they were separate from the real world; this is an incredibly useful approximation to the truth, but (as I keep pointing out) virtual worlds exist courtesy of reality. Newton's laws of motion work for everyday situations, but they break down when objects are traveling at close to the speed of light[101]; similarly, rules of virtual behavior work for everyday situations, but they break down when they travel close to reality[102].

---

98. Mark Slouka, *War of the Worlds: The Assault on Reality*. New York, Basic Books, 1995.

99. Of course, she could have been male in real life, too. These things are rarely simple….

100. C. S. Lewis, *The Silver Chair*. London, Geoffrey Bles, 1953.

101. Relative to the observer.

102. Also relative to the observer.

Every occurrence in a virtual world has a real-world effect: If nothing else, it is presented to the minds of those who observe its occurrence or who observe its effects. In most cases, this effect can be regarded as negligible compared even with the mere noise of existence surrounding the player. However, over time the accretion of these mental effects can be life-changing. People will develop as people, of course, but even in so doing there can be very unpleasant real-life physical effects. It's quite conceivable, for example, that for the wrong person at the wrong time the permanent death of a character could cause the permanent death of the player[103]. Less drastically, falling in love can and does occur regularly in virtual worlds.

Virtual worlds may offer respite from reality, but reality is always, always in charge. You *always* have to come back. Of course, this could be used as a reason for not leaving it in the first place. Fortunately, my reality at the moment is in describing the psychological research I have discovered that addresses issues of identity exploration, so I'll spare you my further speculations and return to that.

As with any science where the collection of data is expensive and time-consuming, psychologists have a tendency to talk about other people's experiments rather than conduct their own. This means that eloquent or forceful essayists can pile interpretation on interpretation until they reach a collective explanation of an idealized state that may not equate with the truth. In looking at identity issues, MOOs, and other *TinyMUD* derivatives are the standard; much of what psychologists know about virtual worlds comes from MOOs (*LambdaMOO* in particular), even though they are hardly representative of virtual worlds in general.

Rather than relying on second-hand observations and idealistic interpretations, Elaine Raybourn conducted her own study[104] of MOOs in 1998. She found that several of the tropes that had become current were actually quite wrong.

Raybourn started from the standpoint that players construct identities in virtual worlds. Her aim was to discover how they did it. Through interviews and participant observation, she discovered three themes that reflected the processes at work:

---

103. Note to compensation lawyers: The same applies to sports matches, TV news, share price readouts, and surprise birthday parties, so don't get your hopes up.

104. Elaine M. Raybourn: *The Quest for Power, Popularity, and Privilege in Cyberspace: Identity Construction in a Text-Based Multi-User Virtual Reality.* Denver, *Proceedings of Western Speech Communication Association Conference,* 1998. http://www.cs.unm.edu/~raybourn/moo5d~1.htm.

➤ Developing the programming skills that lead to privilege and status and to being a contributor to the community.

➤ Using creative communication skills to become more popular.

➤ Treating newbies to displays of active engagement, indifference, or abuse, so as to present an image of powerfulness.

These are not the kind of touchy-feely counterculture ideals normally described as being embedded in MOOs.

There are two main assumption failures:

➤ Although social virtual worlds do not have an explicit gain-points-for-doing-things hierarchy in place, that doesn't mean there is no goal-oriented behavior. It's not tangible (that is, programmed in), sure, but it exists. Players have, through their interactions, created a goal-oriented pecking-order system themselves.

➤ Community building is no more democratic than in real life. The earlier consensus among researchers was that more egalitarian communities formed in virtual reality because, freed from their bodies, people could project aspects of themselves which were received more positively, thereby creating stronger and more meaningful relationships. Raybourn discovered that community formation is actually heavily influenced by people's efforts to gain respect, privileges, and popularity.

However much that players of adventure virtual worlds may welcome any research demonstrating that players of social virtual worlds are not their ideological superiors, the argument about goal-oriented behavior doesn't actually say much. The "games" that people play in MOOs are the same ones "played" in any other social environment that has a power elite, such as an office, school, or factory (or, indeed, a too-easy adventure world that ceases character development before personal development has taken place; Michael Lawrie's discussion[105] of how he made *MIST* work as a game is very enlightening in this regard). It's politics, and game-type virtual worlds have politics, too.

---

105. Michael Lawrie, *Confessions of an Arch-Wizard*. 1991.
    http://lorry.org/arch-wizard/confessions.html.
    Michael Lawrie, *A Footnote to Confessions*. 2003.
    http://lorry.org/arch-wizard/footnote. html.

So people in a MOO may use political success to validate their identity constructions, but it's the identity constructions that are at the heart of it because they're the only material (real-world) change that can emerge from playing them (educational MOOs are an honorable exception).

One of the points that Raybourn makes most forcefully is that in virtual worlds "communication *is* identity"—with disembodiment, it's all there is by which to judge anyone. This may be basically true in MOOs, but in adventure-style virtual worlds there are other ways to get a message across, too. All actions have a communication component: If I go off and fetch you something you need, I'm communicating an aspect of my personality even if I don't say a word. Similarly, all communications have an action component: If I want to get through a locked door, then threatening you to give me the key could be considered an action undertaken by me to cause the door to open[106]. Actions speak louder than words, the pen is mightier than the sword; they're different ends of a continuum. Raybourn is right, communication *is* identity, but communication isn't only speech.

Raybourn's paper has its flaws, but it goes some way to debunking the more idealistic views of virtual worlds that were becoming orthodoxy. Perhaps had she invested more than the 50 hours she did as a participant observer, she could have provided some insight into the way her three themes relate to one another among a community of players.

As for disembodiment, I offer the following summary: Actions can be physical or communicative, their effects real or virtual, to various degrees[107]. The same applies to people.

Although MOOs have a special place in the hearts of social science researchers, some do look at other codebases. Mizuko Ito's object of study[108] was the (now defunct) LPMUD *Farside*.

---

106. This is a central tenet of *speech act* theory, although I've taken it further here than is usual.

107. You can plot them on a graph if you're really keen.

108. Mizuko Ito, *Virtually Embodied: The Reality of Fantasy in a Multi-User Dungeon.* David Porter (editor), *Internet Culture.* New York, Routledge, 1997.

While, in general, toeing the Haraway disembodiment line and therefore saying pretty much the same as everyone else about virtual worlds' capacity to blur the boundaries of mind and machine (reporting that it happens, rather than how or why it happens or what the consequences are for individuals), Ito also touches on something most other researchers missed by virtue of concentrating on MOOs and MUSEs: PKing (player-killing). Here, she does look at consequences and (because of the contested nature of these) accountability. She identifies several different reasons that players PK:

➤ Vigilantism, defending the innocent from PKs[109].

➤ In response to extreme provocation.

➤ They consider it to be part of the game.

➤ They are thrill-seekers, who enjoy the hunt.

➤ They are sociopaths.

Ito operates under the not unreasonable implicit assumption that everyone in a virtual world knows what the consensus attitude to PKing is (which, in general, is that the first two reasons are acceptable, as is the third between consenting adults). She notes that there is a qualitative difference between killing PCs and killing NPCs and mobiles, in that people are real. It's interesting to consider whether this will change as NPCs get increasingly better artificial intelligence; Haraway's analogy cuts both ways.

The best article[110] I have found about the reasons people PK was written by Lexley Vaughan, a *MUD2* player rather than a psychologist (and a case study in identity exploration herself). In addition to Ito's list, she adds

➤ *Wannabes*. People who think PKs are cool, and hang around in gangs talking up themselves into occasional acts of violence.

➤ *Achievers*. The classic player type, testing the viability of PKing as a means of scoring points.

➤ *Explorers*. Another classic player type, exploring this aspect of the virtual world just like they would any other.

---

109. The killing of PKers is known as *PKKing*.

110. Lexley Vaughan, *Player Killers Exposed. Imaginary Realities* Vol. 2 (10), October 1999. http://imaginaryrealities.imaginary.com:8080/volume2/issue10/pks_print.html.

➤ *Broken achievers*. Achievers who have been attacked once too often and snapped. They PK as a form of protest.

➤ *Broken explorers*. Like broken achievers, but deadlier. They don't even care if they lose.

➤ *Provers*. These form the main body of PKs, characterized by their identity issues. They are people with low self-esteem, who choose to beat up other players (usually ones completely unable to defend themselves) to prove their self-worth. Unfortunately, more often than not this only reinforces their (and everyone else's) belief that they're losers.

➤ *Big whackers*. Alpha males strutting their stuff.

Lexley also identifies different types of PK run by administration-level players; she doesn't, however, address the issues of marauding bandit gangs that plague large-scale virtual worlds where PKing is allowed.

Another player who has eloquently expressed how the identity issues of some people can spoil the fun of others is Arios Truthseeker. His 2000 *Essay on D00dism*[111] describes the phenomenon of the *d00d*, a class of individuals prevalent in game-oriented virtual worlds (especially graphical ones) characterized by their stylistic spelling, their uniformity of self-perceived coolness[112], and their complete disregard for the sensibilities of everyone else. They exploit virtual worlds as places to gain the acceptance and gratification that they lack in the real world, little realizing that their almost total objectification of other players means they are achieving nothing of the sort except perhaps among fellow d00ds. Truthseeker[113] offers a number of strategies for dealing with d00ds as a player and, more importantly from the point of view of this book, as a designer.

---

111. Arios Truthseeker, *An Essay on D00dism and the MMORPG.* http://www.kanga.nu/archives/MUD-Dev-L/2000Q4/msg00166.php.

112. Or kewlness, in d00d-speak.

113. One of the consequences of writing as a character rather than as a player is that you make people who quote you in formal texts like this one look slightly ridiculous. It's worse when you write on a web site that subsequently disappears such that no one can get in touch with you ever again. At least I could ask Hedron (quoted in Chapter 3) if he preferred whether I used his real name or his character name (he chose the latter). Unfortunately, Arios Truthseeker disappeared off the web before I could afford him this courtesy.

The only major solution Truthseeker doesn't appear to consider is that of letting d00ds complete their hero's journey. Over the years, I've encountered several players who, had they been around today, would have qualified as d00ds. Some of them turned into the best wizards (even arch-wizards) I ever had. The d00d of today could be the responsible leader of tomorrow, if someone hasn't tracked them down in real life and used physical threats to stop their playing ever again.

This almost brings me to the end of my discussion of the psychology of identity with regards to virtual worlds. There's a lot more out there on the subject, especially in the cyberculture literature, some of which I'll be coming to shortly from a different angle.

Firstly, as an aside, I confess that I was both surprised and elated when I discovered that psychologists had so quickly latched onto the fact that virtual worlds are catalysts for identity exploration. My only disappointment was that they didn't realize that this was in part because virtual worlds had been *designed* as such. The best functional designs are supposed to be those that work while remaining invisible to the user, so I guess virtual world designers should take this as a compliment. On the other hand, it reinforces the common prejudice that we're unrounded, geeky, emotionally adolescent individuals who couldn't tell a Renaissance from a Reformation if one came up and bit us. Oh well, such is our lot.

Now the remaining points about identity construction.

For some people, an important component of their identity is their race. This is particularly true of individuals who find themselves in an environment where their own race is not dominant. Although for some people race is a physical notation of (their or others') difference, this is not always the case: Other people may regard it as a cultural marker (genetic difference correlating with, rather than defining, cultural difference); others ignore race entirely. This latter approach ("color blindness") is the liberal point of view, but it diminishes people for whom their race is a part of who they are.

This is a point made by Lisa Nakamura, who examined[114] issues of race in the context of (you guessed it) *LambdaMOO*. Nakamura asserts that by not giving players the option of defining their characters' race, *LambdaMOO* is in fact defining it for them:

---

114. Lisa Nakamura, *Race In/For Cyberspace: Identity Tourism and Racial Passing on the Internet.* 1996. David Bell and Barbara M. Kennedy (editors), *The Cybercultures Reader.* New York, Routledge, 2000. http://www.humanities.uci.edu/mposter/syllabi/readings/nakamura.html.

All players are assumed to be white[115]. Unfortunately for her, even if they *were* able to define their characters' race, there's still a strong chance that all players would be assumed to be white, in the same way that female characters in a male-heavy virtual world are assumed by default to be real-life male. *LambdaMOO* characters are not *LambdaMOO* players.

Nakamura discovered that race does make an appearance in *LambdaMOO*, however, through the recreational appropriation of stereotypes. She encountered many Asian-presenting characters in the form of replications of TV, movie, and book characters. She portrays the (presumed white) players behind these characters as identity tourists, staying awhile in another race before moving on somewhere else; naturally, as with all stereotyping, they were only ever going to reinforce their stereotypes this way, rather than actually learning something about the race they were pretending to be.

Nakamura characterizes this racial tourism as "passing," but I don't believe it is. The stereotypes chosen are almost universally obvious as being stereotypes: No one is going to believe that someone claiming to be a samurai warrior really *is* a samurai warrior, therefore the whole point of passing—getting away with pretending to be something you're not—is undone. Were a non-Asian to pretend to be a Japanese student of English, *that* would be passing; pretending to be Sulu from *Star Trek* is no more passing than pretending to be Spock.

Many virtual worlds do have "races," of course, it's just that these just don't correspond to real ones: You can be an elf, a dwarf, a halfling, and so on. In virtual worlds for virtual characters, these are as meaningful as any other race—more so in tangible terms, because whereas with real-world races it would be improper to give members of one race superior characteristics to those of another, for imaginary races it is acceptable (although see Chapter 8, "Coda: Ethical Considerations," for a discussion of why perhaps it shouldn't be).

These "races" are actually more like subspecies than races, of course, which blurs the issue even further. If I can be an elf, can I be a Jewish elf[116] or a Zulu elf? Can I be an Inuit leprechaun, or are all leprechauns Irish?

---

115. Nakamura doesn't say whether she, as a player of *LambdaMOO*, found herself making the same assumptions.

116. In some games, I could be. See http://my.homeip.net/hack/torg/rachel_kairo.html for a beautiful example.

To experiment with issues of race in virtual worlds, Beth Kolko has established a virtual world (*MOOScape*) specifically for this purpose[117]. Sensing that an important element of real-world identity is missing from virtual identity, her aim is to ask how the global marking of a character's race affects the social environment of virtual worlds. It's a reasonable thing to do; after all, if *LambdaMOO* lets you define your character's age, why shouldn't you define its race[118]?

In setting up *MOOScape*, Kolko had to decide how to put in the racial specifier. She had basically three choices:

➤ Very intrusively, like gender. Reflect it in every third-person message concerning the player.

➤ Moderately intrusively, like mood. Reflect it in every reference to the player's actions—for example, their movement.

➤ Moderately unintrusively. Reflect it only in the descriptions of players that people get when they look at them.

She eventually decided on the latter; you know what race other characters are, but it doesn't intervene overtly in interactions between players.

A trickier issue was what races people were allowed. The problem with a closed data set (that is, a list of races from which people should select one) is that not everyone finds a description with which they feel comfortable. On the basis that *MOOScape* was introducing race into virtual worlds, rather than defining it, Kolko went with an open data set: Despite reservations that races like elves and lizardfolk would make an appearance, players are allowed to describe their race in whatever terms they wish.

The results of the *MOOScape* experiment should be interesting. Race only makes sense in the real world; by asking about race, *MOOScape* is asking players to reveal something about themselves, rather than about their characters. If your character *is* you, there's not an issue here, of course: In situations where the virtual world is being used

---

117. Beth E. Kolko, *Erasing @race: Going White in the (Inter)Face*. Beth E. Kolko, Lisa Nakamura, and Gilbert B. Rodman (editors), *Race in Cyberspace*. New York, Routledge, 2000.

118. I'd rather ask the reverse question: If *LambdaMOO* doesn't let you define your character's race, why should you define its age?

as an adjunct to reality—hosting a business meeting, for example—your character is merely an avatar and people will always relate to you rather than to it.

However, in most virtual worlds your character is *not* you[119].

In an absolute sense, race is a purely physical property. It does not transfer to virtual worlds except when referencing a physical entity (that is, the player—something to be avoided in virtual worlds if they are to maintain their immersive integrity). Put bluntly, if you say you want your character to be a certain (real-world) race in a virtual world, you are arguing *only* for a cosmetic change to your character's appearance. That cosmetic change may be associated (by you or other players) with certain real-world cultural baggage, but the nature of this baggage is dependent on the real-world culture of the players that participate in or witness it.

For example, let's suppose that race is a choice. People cross-gender play out of curiosity, so we'll assume that some will cross-race play, too. Let's further assume that some non-Asians play as Asians and truly (rather than in the Nakamura sense) try to pass. Would they learn about what it is like to be an Asian that way? No: They would only learn what it is like to be viewed as an Asian character by the players of that particular virtual world. They get insights into mind-sets, but not into genetics.

You can't learn about the physical aspects of a race by role-playing a member of it; all you can learn about is the culture with which that race is associated (by its representatives, by other cultures, and by you). You might learn about any of these, but they *only* tell you about states of mind. In reality, race (like gender) is a badge that people are forced to wear wherever they go. In virtual worlds, like it or not, that badge is removed. You can put it back on your virtual self, but so can anyone. In real life, people who wear the same badge may feel disposed to interact differently with other people depending on the badges they wear, and cultural differences will arise because of this. In virtual worlds, badge-wearing is arbitrary; race is therefore expressed only through the culture of individuals of that race (if that race has a race-specific culture).

Players of virtual worlds for whom their race is an important part of their identity have a dilemma here. To be true to themselves, they want their characters to exhibit the same indelible mark that they use to define themselves; however, in virtual worlds

---

119. Unless you're totally immersed, of course, in which case you are also your character.

these marks are not indelible. Do these people therefore campaign to bind the cosmetic features of characters to those of their players (knowing it would be unpoliceable)? Or do they discard that part of their identity that is coupled to the nature of their physical body and align with the portable aspects of their culture instead?

Another important component of identity for people in the real world is their sexuality. Unlike the situation for race and gender, people in the real world do not have to wear irremovable badges that proclaim their sexuality (although they may choose to present indicators, overt or otherwise). This means that there's not much call to implement sexuality as a physical characteristic in a virtual world[120]; sexuality-defined subcultures are not tied to physical markers (although in real life obviously they are tied to physical activity), and therefore they transfer reasonably easily to virtual worlds.

Most virtual worlds take no line on sexuality, which (apropos Nakamura's argument about race) perhaps means they actually do take a line—that is, heterosexuality[121] is the norm. Actually, for a fair number of them sexuality really *isn't* an issue, because sex itself isn't; the subject simply wouldn't arise in a virtual world written for children, for example, and the same is true of many other (particularly gamelike) virtual worlds.

That said, even in gamelike virtual worlds, people do meet and fall in love. Both heterosexuals and homosexuals can operate in this kind of environment; it's pro-heterosexual, but usually more tolerant than real life (you can play characters of the opposite gender, after all) and therefore not a major barrier for homosexuals who (like it or not) are obliged to operate under these conditions in reality anyway.

The real world has its homosexual subcultures, however, and it's natural that people may want to bring theirs with them into virtual worlds. There are essentially three ways to do it:

➤ Set up a virtual world for which this is the dominant culture.

➤ Join a virtual world that has similar or related subcultures.

➤ Incorporate the culture in a ghetto within a regular virtual world.

---

120. An exception would perhaps be a sex-oriented virtual world, where a tangible, examinable "sexuality" property for characters might save players considerable small-talk time.

121. Standard disclaimer: Whatever word I use to describe opposite-sex or same-sex attraction is going to bother someone, if not today then tomorrow. I apologize if you're one of those someones whom this particular word or its same-sex counterpart annoys.

Virtual worlds of the first kind do exist, although they are not in general advertised outside their target player base (probably so as to avoid attracting homophobes[122]). They are split by gender, because the subcultures for men and women are different. The two most interesting experiments are both aimed at women, *Shoujo-Ai MUSH*[123] and *Isle of Lesbos*[124].

General sex-oriented virtual worlds, which are usually friendly to people whatever their sexual orientations and preferences, have been around since *Void*. Despite what people may think, players do not spend their whole time in these worlds engaging in imaginative acts of virtual sex. They are as likely to sit around chatting about nothing as players in any other virtual world (although their very nature makes their cliques and communities quite tightly knit). *HavenMUSH*[125] is probably the best-known example of this kind of "responsibly adult" world.

Randal Woodland describes[126] the third of these approaches (all of which, incidentally, he calls *queer spaces*). In examining how four different online systems (the other three are BBS/forum-oriented) cater to homosexual identity, he describes a part of *LambdaMOO* called *Weaveworld*. This subworld is[127] both accessible and distinct from the rest of the virtual world, using a series of very subtle symbols to indicate to those passers-by attuned to such things as the nature of its contents. The reasons for this tactfulness are so as not to appear in-your-face to other players of *LambdaMOO* (as both a courtesy to the general population and a defense against potential hate-players), and to impart a sense of sophistication (that is, to tell visitors that it's not a place built for devotees of narcissistic sex).

In terms of the effect of these different queer spaces on identity, Woodland is reticent. He describes, for example, a case where the creation of a psychologically safe haven for

---

122. I guess, to be fair, I also ought to apologize to those homophobes who prefer to use some other word to describe themselves.

123. http://www.shoujoai.com/mush/

124. telnet://muds.crodo.com:6667

125. http://www.geocities.com/HavenMUSH/

126. Randal Woodland, *Queer Spaces, Modem Boys, and Pagan Statues: Gay/Lesbian Identity and the Construction of Cyberspace*. 1998. David Bell and Barbara M. Kennedy (editors), *The Cybercultures Reader*. New York, Routledge, 2000.

127. Or rather *was*, because it was removed by its author in 1995.

gay men fell through because of freedom of speech objections. He doesn't say whether in a virtual environment where no one knows who you are, the issues of psychological safety are different from those of real life. Can cultural tropes that have evolved in response to real-life hostility be shed? Are people who follow the same rituals in virtual worlds that they do in the real one passing up on liberation, or merely being pragmatic? What are the implications of a virtual world where every character (if not player) is the same sex?

To speculate further, for many people gender, race, and sexuality are part of their real-life identity. They are not of equal status, however, because of their visibility. Gender is visible in the real world (through physical characteristics) and in the virtual world (through pronouns in textual worlds and avatars in graphical ones). Sexuality is invisible in the real world and invisible in the virtual world; people who want to display it have to use signs, which may be understood by everyone (you walk around with a notice hanging round your neck saying "I am gay") or only by those in sync with such matters (*Weaveworld*'s references to paganism, sensuality, ancient Greek warriors, and so on).

Race, however, is visible in the real world but (in the textual case at least) invisible in virtual worlds. Is race only ultimately important because it is visible in the real world (in which case, wouldn't a virtual world undermine real-life identity?), or is it legitimately important for cultural or biologically imperative reasons too (in which case, will people for whom race is important have to develop their own codified signals for recognizing one another?).

There are many questions here to which it would be interesting to know the answer; unfortunately, the research on virtual worlds concerned with race and/or sexuality is relatively thin on the ground[128].

This is in stark contrast to our next topic: gender studies.

---

128. Alternatively, I haven't looked in the right places.

Gender Studies

I learned through experience as an undergraduate at Essex University that as a male I have been irredeemably socialized to hold oppressive, androcentric views about all things gender and that therefore my opinions on the subject are worth less than nothing. Even seemingly neutral actions on my part are inherently tainted by my early conditioning and testosterone-charged world-view, so can therefore only be regarded as manifestations of my poisoned, male psyche. Consequently, if you don't want the purity of your beliefs about gender issues adulterated, you should skip this section.

For those of you who know sarcasm when you see it, read on....

The general point here is correct: Anything people say about gender is inevitably moderated by their own experiences. Whatever I write on the subject—even my selection of research paper references—really is influenced by my upbringing and physiology. However, the same applies to every individual on the planet, so I'm not alone in that; furthermore, it isn't only true for gender studies, but pretty well "anything else," too.

Much work in gender studies is from a feminist perspective[129], which makes my position slightly more dubious. There isn't a lot I can do about this, though. I shall strive to be impartial (although not necessarily unopinionated where virtual worlds are concerned); if I slip up you can blame me, not my gender.

So here we go....

Gender Studies is not Sex Studies; there is a difference between sex, and gender, essentially anthropological. Sex is a biological condition; gender refers to the behaviors associated with the sexes. Sex is uniform across all cultures; gender varies across cultures.

Gender influences people in two main ways: Through their *gender identity* (that is, their feeling of being male or female) and through their *gender roles* (that is, what their society establishes as appropriate behavior for females and males). Although there are only two sexes, some societies have more than two genders (usually to account for individuals whose biological sex does not match their gender identity). Gender roles may have a biological origin (the "boys will be boys" argument) or a cultural evolutionary one (tribes whose womenfolk fought and died alongside their menfolk had

---

129. Not as much as the casual observer might think, however.

fewer babies than ones where only the menfolk fought, so the former were eventually outnumbered and defeated by the latter). Alternatively, gender roles may arise as the result of pressures from other cultural activities.

Although this is the classic, anthropological view of gender, it is not one that is universally held among gender theorists. They regard sex as an essentialist concept (that is, something that has intrinsic meaning beyond what perception reveals), whereas their preference is for a more constructivist[130] approach (that is, that things only have the meanings that individuals construct for them based on the sensory data). This would suggest that sex/gender were part of the same system, but as Tomasz Mazur describes in an early review[131] of how gender studies theory applies to virtual worlds, this doesn't work either—it flounders on the concept of identity. Mazur argues that virtual worlds themselves have a similar problem, with "real" being essentialist and "virtual" being constructivist, and identity existing in both and neither at the same time. He adopts a post-modernist[132] stance to address these issues.

Problematical though the fundamentals may be at a philosophical level, this is not something that normally concerns students of gender with regard to virtual worlds. Rather, they are primarily interested in two specific aspects of player behavior that introduce new variables into their own equations: *cross-gender play* and *virtual sex*. I'll take these in that order.

If there were a pill that changed your real-life sex for one day only, would you take it? The science isn't important—a mass of nanotechnology DNA-tampering machines could perhaps do it—but would you take it? Why would you want to? Why wouldn't you want to? What would the effect be on gender issues in a world where anyone could take such a pill?

In virtual worlds, that pill is already available, without prescription.

---

130. The tendency to look at things in absolutist ways is regarded as typically a male trait, whereas taking a more discursive approach is considered a mainly female quality.

131. Tomasz Mazur, *Working Out the Cyberbody: Sex and Gender Constructions in Text-Based Virtual Space*. Department of English, University of Florida, 1994.
http://www.well.com/user/tmazur/ research/sexgen.html.

132. Postmodernism is discussed in a later section of this chapter.

The paper that brought the practice of cross-gender play to the attention of non-players was Amy Bruckman's *Gender Swapping on the Internet*[133]. This followed up on some of the activity she had noted in her earlier *Identity Workshop* paper, and includes interviews and other set pieces that have been heavily quoted by later researchers. She observed two behavioral patterns in particular that were to resonate with many people: That female characters are subjected to unwanted sexual advances; that female characters are assumed to be in need of help.

Bruckman indirectly suggests that the two may be related. Offers of help can be viewed as tokens of interest; by accepting the token, the recipient is signifying their acceptance of the other person's interest; they are then obligated to respond favorably. Although some may see this as buying favor—and it may well be just that in some cases—it isn't always. Sometimes, it's just social interaction. Similarly, whether an offer of help is an esteem-damaging, patronizing assumption of vulnerability or the first move in a mating game depends largely on the attitudes of the players involved.

Unusually, Bruckman views gender as just one aspect of identity, on a par with (say) nationality. I share this view, but it's not one that cuts much ice with those who politicize gender; Bruckman has been criticized for taking this position. I personally find it difficult to see why gender should be preeminent; race and sexuality are perhaps as much a part of a person's identity as their gender, but these don't get anywhere near the coverage that gender does. Perhaps it's more to do with the way that most languages (through pronouns) force gender to be an issue; race and sexuality are not denoted in this way, and therefore have a much lower profile[134].

Bruckman characterizes gender as being malleable in virtual worlds. She means in the self, not in the character, but other researchers don't always realize this and have occasionally questioned it. Bruckman, as (by then) a player of virtual worlds, could understand the difference between real and virtual self from an experiential point of view; researchers who have only an intellectual understanding are more prone to miss the point.

---

133. Amy S. Bruckman, *Gender Swapping on the Internet*. San Francisco, Proceedings of the International Networking Conference, 1993. `http://www.cc.gatech.edu/elc/papers/bruckman/gender-swapping-bruckman.pdf`.

134. The other obvious explanation is that gender identity really is of preeminent importance for most people, and I'm some kind of an exception who can't ever hope to understand it at an emotional level.

Sherry Turkle also writes about cross-gender play in *Life on the Screen* (in her Chapter 8); she even interviews some of the same people as Bruckman. She sees cross-gender play as challenging and psychologically complicated; characters that are neither male nor female she finds disturbing, yet evocative. As a result of her studies, she puts forward the hypothesis that gender exploration is a valid part of identity exploration in general; it can lead to the development of a person as an individual, due (at least) to the extension of their emotional range that it stimulates.

The existence of genders other than male and female in some virtual worlds is discussed[135] by Brenda Danet. Danet regards gender as a tyranny, and is therefore interested in the opportunities presented by the Internet—where all conventional gender cues are absent—for gender-free existence. She looked at Internet Relay Chat (IRC) and MOOs, and found that in both, individuals can successfully camouflage their identities for very long periods. Cross-gender play in MOOs, though, was much more elaborate than in IRC[136].

MOOs typically have more than the usual two genders available to them[137], some of which may be considered a third gender, others a non-commitment to gender, and others completely genderless. Examples include

- *Neutral* ("Sam puts its cards on the table")

- *Either* ("Sam puts his/her cards on the table")

- *Plural* ("Sam puts their cards on the table")

- *Spivak*[138] ("Sam puts eir cards on the table")

- *Person* ("Sam puts per cards on the table")

---

135. Brenda Danet, *Text as Mask: Gender and Identity on the Internet*. Venice, Proceedings of the conference on Masquerade and Gendered Identity, 1996.
`http://atar.mscc.huji.ac.il/~msdanet/ mask.html`.

136. This is perhaps ironic, given that nowadays people with an interest in gender studies (including Danet herself) will typically look at the far more researcher-friendly IRC than at *MOOs*.

137. The same is not in general true of adventure-style games except those for which a fiction for other sexes exists—it's too hard on immersion otherwise. Perhaps in time this may change as reality changes.

138. Named after mathematician Michael Spivak, who uses this system in his books (most notably Michael Spivak, *The Joy of TeX*. Providence RI, The American Mathematical Society, 1990).

From my point of view, this is interesting because in *MUD1* I didn't want gender to be a tangible property of characters. My own dialect of English—Yorkshire—uses near-plural by default for people whose gender is unknown or unspecified (as you will doubtless have noticed in this book, where I habitually refer to singular but generic players as "they" or "them"). As a student, I was once told off for using the word "themself" in a report, which up until then I hadn't even considered not to be an English word[139]. For me, if I were informed that a new teacher had joined a school, it would be perfectly natural to ask "what's their name?" rather than "what's his or her name?"[140]. This approach was not suitable for *MUD1*, though, because for non-dialect speakers it looked bizarre (although it has since gained much wider acceptance, at least in England) and because sustaining it when gender *is* known is untenable.

My preferred alternative to implementing gender was to use a pronoun-free denotational approach instead ("Sam puts Sam's cards on the table"), but I abandoned this on the grounds that it was too intrusive—I wanted to draw people into the virtual world, and the erection of constant billboards that said they were reading text was too much of an interference[141]. It's amusing to note that neither of the ways I considered for the linguistic avoidance of gender (near-plural[142] or denotational) have found any currency in MOOs.

Danet looked at gender choices for two large MOOs: *LambdaMOO* and (Amy Bruckman's) *MediaMOO*[143]. Both have non-binary gender classifications in place, and Danet examined the proportion of players who chose to take advantage of the alternatives to male/female that were available. She found that on *LambdaMOO*, roughly 50% of the characters were male, 30% were female and 20% were neither; on *MediaMOO*, 50% were male, 20% were female and 30% were neither.

---

139. The spell-checker built into the word processor I am using to type this doesn't believe it to be a word either; it kept helpfully converting it to "themselves" when I wrote it just now, until I insisted.

140. In some heavily gendered languages, it's impossible to refer to a teacher without revealing the teacher's gender because the word for "teacher" has a different ending depending on whether the individual is male or female. This must be tricky in situations where you don't *want* to convey the gender of the teacher, so as not to inflame a jealous spouse, for example.

141. It also meant awkward constructions like "Sam did it Sam's self."

142. That is, "themself" rather than "themselves"—we may not know their gender, but we know there's only one of them. This is also known as the *singular they*; see Henry Churchyard's anti-pedantry work for details. http://www.crossmyt.com/hc/linghebr/austheir.html.
For an in-depth look at gender-neutral pronouns in general, see John Williams's *The Gender-Neutral Pronoun FAQ*. http://www.aetherlumina.com/gnp/.

143. http://www.cc.gatech.edu/fac/Amy.Bruckman/MediaMOO/

There may be any number of reasons for this difference. Perhaps the media professionals of *MediaMOO* have a more progressive attitude to gender, or the balance of players' real-life genders in the two games is significantly different. Danet's observation that the real-life identity (and therefore gender) of *MediaMOO*'s players is known, whereas that of *LambdaMOO*'s isn't, muddies the waters still further. Are MediaMOO players more likely to make gender-political statements, knowing that they may be called to account afterward if they don't? Or is the fact that no one can accuse them of attempting to be deceitful by playing with their gender a liberating factor?

Danet's paper ends with 11 questions for future research into cross-gender play, all of which have yet to be fully answered.

I should point out at this stage that there are two opposing views concerning whether cross-gender play is a good thing or a bad thing. They can be summarized as

> ➤ Cross-gender play is good, because it emancipates the individual.

> ➤ Cross-gender play is bad, because it subjugates the group.

At one level, its researchers' views are inconsequential: Cross-gender play happens, and it will continue to happen no matter what people believe should happen and no matter what ideology they want it to fit. They can't stop it, police it or exploit it, so incorporating it into their theories is purely an academic exercise. Virtual designers know implicitly, however, that things can be done to promote one side of the argument over the other, thereby encouraging or discouraging the practice. Creating mechanisms for characters' gender to flip periodically through the use of magic or magiclike effects, for example, would encourage cross-gender play[144]; making graphical avatars physically plain (if not ugly) would discourage it.

So, let's look at some of the objections in more detail.

One of the hopes that feminists had about cross-gender play was that it would lead to a fluidity of gender. Lori Kendall points out[145] that in practice it does the opposite:

---

144. Given that I did this in *MUD1* (for reasons explained in Chapter 3's *Polly's Tale*), I guess my own views on the subject are fairly unequivocal.

145. Lori Kendall, *MUDder? I Hardly Know 'Er! Adventures of a Feminist MUDder*. Lynn Cherny and Elizabeth Reba Weise (editors), *Wired_Women*. Seattle, Seal Press, 1996.
   http://www.rochester.edu/College/FS/Publications/KendallMUD.html.

People come to entertain a more rigid understanding of gender identities than they had before. They focus on the "true" identity behind the mask, rather than the one that is presented[146]. Women came to virtual worlds later than men, therefore the cultures they had to join were already in place when they arrived, and thus the likelihood of changing this situation is not going to increase by much even if more women do participate in these virtual worlds—at least, not unless everyone makes a conscious effort.

This argument looks fine on the face of it, but it relies on regarding virtual worlds as extensions of reality. In an absolute sense, they are part of reality and therefore can indeed be considered physical extensions of it. They are not, however, extensions of the models of reality that players have in their heads. Even social MOOs are separate from reality, as many players understand immediately and those that don't will come to realize in the long-term. The hardware that supports each virtual world, and therefore the implementation of the virtual worlds, is in reality; however, the virtual worlds themselves only exist in the imaginations of their players. They're not worlds because they *are* worlds; they're worlds because people *think* they're worlds. What's more, players think these worlds are *not* the real world.

The only things that exist in both the virtual world and the real world are the players' identities. Kendall is correct in her observation that gender types in virtual worlds can be very stereotypical, tending to crystallize around some falsely perceived "essence" for each gender. Where I believe her to be mistaken is in concluding that these only serve to reinforce existing notions of gender and therefore add to the general woes of women (in particular) when they are acted on in real life. For players who can't yet separate the real from the virtual, this may be true; for the rest, it isn't[147].

Characters and players both move. The formal role that a character takes on may be some stylization of a false perception of reality, but experience in playing that role will change both the character and the player. The character will change when behavioral expectations meet the reality of other players' attitudes; the player will change when these expectations meet the player's own attitudes. There *is* a fluidity of gender identity, and the stereotype drives it; in other words, where the stereotype exists it's to show that it's wrong.

---

146. In this sense, they're taking an essentialist point of view.

147. As Mizuko Ito perceptively notes in her *Virtually Embodied* paper, virtual worlds are not a commentary on or reflection of real life; they aren't even about real life. They're spaces in their own right.

Over time, the relevance of both Kendall's and my positions may diminish. As players' experience with virtual worlds grows, it could be that gender moves on and that stereotypes become irrelevant. While newbies still arrive with real-world gender issues to address, however, the likelihood of any such paradigm shift's occurring is doubtful.

A second objection is raised by Jocelyne Voisin. She points out[148] that in radical feminist theories, separatism sometimes plays a central role: The creation of a woman-only environment is seen the only way to escape patriarchal oppression. In the real world, such safe haven environments do exist—spaces from which men are banned—but they are relatively small in number. A separatist virtual world would be easier for many women to reach, and more conducive than real life to discovering whether the assumed benefits of such an environment (a supportive, egalitarian, nurturing community) would in fact arise and be sustainable over the long term. Gender masquerading, however, rules this out as a possibility: If there's no way to tell that a female-presenting character has a biologically female player running it, the extent to which these spaces can be considered exclusively feminine is limited.

Voisin is right: Cross-gender play does undermine such feminist virtual utopias (as transsexuals pose problems for real-life "female-only" spaces). Deliberate infiltration of a female space is not likely to happen often, but even so that may be more often than is acceptable. Unfortunately for the radicals, there's very little that can be done about this; even proof of real-life identity when an account was created doesn't guarantee that the person later *using* the account is the one whose identity was proven[149]. Creating a virtual world with all-female characters doesn't mean you'll get all-female players; the only way to guarantee all-female players is to have them under constant real-world surveillance as they play—hardly a situation that could be described as supportive or egalitarian. So although cross-gender play validates feminist conspiracy theorists' worst fears, it's unstoppable and unavoidable; taking an uncompromising view of it isn't going to change a thing.

Countering that view is the suggestion made by Michèle White that perhaps virtual worlds are intrinsically not female-friendly places anyway, at least as they are currently

---

148. Jocelyne Voisin, *Women's Virtual Communities: Utopia or Dystopia?* Department of Mass Communications, Carleton University, 1995.

149. A common excuse for regretted misbehavior in commercial virtual worlds is that "someone else was using my character." Sometimes, it's actually true.

designed. White's complaint[150] is that the commands used in MOOs to obtain information about other players suggest a surveillant attitude and use voyeuristic terminology ("watch," "scope," "glance," "peep," "gawk," "examine," and so on). The "look" command itself, with the third-person messages it triggers, is worst of all; frequently, new players are distressed when they are continually looked at by other players. The concept of "gaze" is important in feminist theories, because implicit in it is a communication between the gazer and the gazee. MOOs unequivocally empower the gazer: Gazing is active; self-image is passive. In other words, you describe yourself for the benefit of the person who looks, not for the benefit of yourself. This limits the identity constructs that people can create, which is bad for everyone no matter what gender they are playing.

I have some sympathy with White's position. In my own virtual worlds, players don't get to describe their characters—I believe that allowing it anchors character development too much. On the other hand, looking at a character *is* permitted (it concocts a brief description based on their tangible properties), along with large numbers of other commands that have characters as their objects (including "hit"). Although White herself doesn't argue this, anyone willing to construe such commands as empowering those who issue them at the expense of those against whom they are issued would surmise that virtual worlds (even graphical ones) were less than ideal. Quite how to implement these kinds of commands some other way is non-obvious, too. That said, virtual worlds are still much better than the real one in this respect, because at least the "empowering" actions are open to anyone.

Returning to the issue of how cross-gender play undermines attempts to set up female-only virtual communities, it could be that the problem might be worse in theory than in practice; it depends on the actual incidence of cross-gender play. If far fewer men play as female characters than anecdotal evidence suggests, the effects of their presence might amount to mere background noise. It would therefore be very useful if empirical evidence existed to show how widespread cross-gender playing really is. At a more general level, it would also be very nice to know if the predictions as to *why* people play across gender are in fact accurate.

I know of two studies that have attempted to answer these questions[151].

---

150. Michèle White, *Visual Pleasure in Textual Places: Gazing in Multi-User Object-Oriented Worlds*. Eileen Green and Alison Adam, *Virtual Gender: Terminology, Consumption and Identity*. New York, Routledge, 2001.

151. This means there are probably two dozen more that I don't know about.

The first study is by Kathryn Wright, who is the resident consulting psychologist at womengamers.com[152]. Her perspective is that of female computer game players (among whom she numbers), rather than of gender studies; nevertheless, the results of her study[153] are relevant in this context.

Wright surveyed men who played female characters across a variety of game types, but mainly those of first-person shooters and (gamelike) graphical virtual worlds. 57% of her respondents (all of whom claimed to be male in real life) played as female characters for over half the time. Respondents were asked to describe in their own words why they played as female characters; when Wright analyzed the results, she found they fell into the following categories[154]:

➤ 25% said it added to the role-playing experience (of which 19% cited gender exploration as a motivation).

➤ 23% did it for the visual stimulation (that is, sexual aesthetics[155]).

➤ 19% did it because the avatars were smaller and harder to see/hit.

➤ 16% did it to be given gifts.

➤ 14% did it because female characters had better skills.

➤ 14% said they preferred the modeling (that is, non-sexual aesthetics).

➤ 13% did it for variety.

➤ 11% did it to get a psychological edge over the other players.

➤ 6% preferred the sounds that female avatars made.

➤ 6% did it to amuse themselves at the reactions of male players.

➤ 6% did it from habit: They started, and hadn't found a reason to stop.

---

152. `http://www.womengamers.com`. Hey, consistency is consistency!

153. Kathryn Wright, *Gender Bending in Games*. Womengamers.com, 2000.
   `http://www.womengamers.com/articles/gender.html`.
   `http://www.womengamers.com/articles/gender2.htm`.

154. Some respondents gave several reasons, and answers are rounded to the nearest percent; this is why they add up to more than 100%.

155. If you have to stare at a character's backside the whole time you play, you may as well enjoy the view.

Although role-playing comes out as the top reason, many others are for gameplay purposes, that is, female characters have an edge for whatever reason, and so they are played as a means to an end. Wright anticipated this and asked a series of follow-up questions; read her papers if you want to know what she found (it's interesting, but not relevant to the current discussion).

As a final question, Wright asked whether cross-gender players thought there was a correlation between men who played as women and men who were homosexual or confused about their gender; this was in response to something that happened when she advertised for respondents to her survey (she was accused of doing the survey in order to meet homosexual *EverQuest* players). She found that among the respondents themselves

- ➤ 60% said there was no correlation.

- ➤ 15% said there may be for some people, but not for everyone.

- ➤ 12% said there was for them personally, but not for everyone.

- ➤ 12% didn't answer.

Wright notes that no cross-gender players reported a belief that men who play as female characters are homosexual by default.

Wright's survey was limited, in that she had 64 respondents of which only 33 actually completed her survey (the rest gave their opinions via email). She concluded that lumping together role-playing, fighting and action gamers was inadvisable, because too many answers were dependent on the type of game that the players played. Nevertheless, her results do suggest that some cross-gender players really do perform it for reasons of exploring their identity.

A much more formal and detailed survey[156] was undertaken by Lynne Roberts and Malcolm Parks in 2000. Their methods were very thorough: They selected the largest two social MOOs plus five others chosen at random, and from these selected (also at random) 1,200 candidate characters[157] that had been played during the previous

---

156. Lynne D. Roberts and Malcolm R. Parks, *The Social Geography of Gender-Switching in Virtual Environments on the Internet*. Eileen Green and Alison Adam, *Virtual Gender: Terminology, Consumption and Identity*. New York, Routledge, 2001.

157. Not players, because it was possible for multiple characters belonging to the same player to be selected.

14 days. A second study included players of role-playing MOOs. The candidates were contacted individually, and around 30% agreed to take part.

Unlike Wright's survey, which looked only at the cross-gender players themselves, Roberts's and Parks's examined the views of all players on the subjects. Their findings make very interesting reading. For example, they discovered that the male/female player breakdown[158] in the MOOs they surveyed approached parity (48.1% female in study 1, 47.0% in study 2); this is a much higher ratio than is common for regular computer games[159].

Roberts and Parks discovered that around 60% of the players of social MOOs had never played cross-gender, but that around 20% were engaged in it at some time during the 14 days the survey covered. In role-playing MOOs, 43.3% had never tried it but 40.0% were currently cross-gender playing. Including all the personality and sexuality tests that the studies incorporated, playing in a role-playing MOO was found to be the greatest predictor that an individual selected at random from the respondents was or had tried cross-gender playing. Perhaps surprisingly, real-life gender was *not* found to be a predictor of cross-gender play: Female players were as likely to play another gender as were male players.

I said "another gender" there, because of course MOOs have multiple genders. 78.7% of cross-gender play was found to be to the opposite gender (that is, male or female) of the real-life player, whereas the remaining cross-gender[160] players opted for something else; this is in line with Danet's figures from *LambdaMOO* four years earlier.

As for why they played across genders, the reasons players gave were consistent but the proportions varied between those who were currently doing it and those who had tried it but stopped. Among current cross-gender players, 31.3% said it was part of role-playing or a challenge to their role-playing skills, whereas 13.4% of former cross-gender players did. Conversely, 13.5% of current cross-gender players said they had started cross-gender playing to experiment with gender, whereas 34.3% of former cross-gender players did. Why there should be this reversal clearly merits further investigation.

---

158. Assuming that the respondents weren't lying about their real-life gender, of course.

159. It's rumored to be way higher—90%+ real-life females—in some PernMUSHes.

160. Roberts and Parks call it *gender switching*, which is a more accurate term in non-binary circumstances.

The surveys produced many other results about who cross-gender plays and why; read the paper itself for the full details. From the point of the discussion here, there are two issues the results raise that are of particular importance.

Firstly, the studies do seem to show that cross-gender play is a widespread activity. Roberts and Parks themselves do not conclude that it is prevalent, pointing out that although many players had played cross-gender in the two-week period the study covered, only 22.6% of those Study 1 respondents who had done so had spent more than 60% of their playing time pursuing the activity. For Study 2, the figures were better: 31.5% of cross-gender players spent more than 70% of their time doing it, of which 20% said they played the whole time during the previous two weeks as a gender other than their real-life one. Roberts and Parks are correct that cross-gender play isn't prevalent (if "prevalent" means "more than 50%," which from a strictly statistical point of view it must); their results would seem to indicate that it's quite a common activity, though, even in purely social (as opposed to role-playing) MOOs. I suspect that the figures for goal-oriented virtual worlds would be higher, since players of these are more formally embarked on an exercise of identity exploration[161]; my only caveat is that some people object to cross-gender play in principle, and these may be more common in such gamelike worlds.

This brings me to the second point of special significance in Roberts's and Parks's results: Why people *don't* play cross-gender. The studies found that many of those players who had never played cross-gender believed that the activity was manipulative, was used to lure people into having virtual sex, and was a way to cause trouble for people who didn't do it. They were upset and uncomfortable when confronted by someone not playing as their biological sex. Personally, I'm very disappointed by this; the cited activities are ones that cross-gender play should weaken, not strengthen! I can only hope that the people who hold these points of view do so out of ignorance, and that as they come to understand the difference between the real and the virtual (that is, that there is one) they may revise their opinions[162].

As I mentioned earlier, Roberts's and Parks's survey showed that cross-gender playing by female players was far more common than is usually supposed; their studies showed

---

161. This isn't to say that they're necessarily aware they're undertaking the hero's journey, just that they know (at least implicitly) that there *is* a journey involved.

162. I'm sure they feel the same way about me, too.

that it happened as often as it did for male players. The reasons that women play cross-gender are different, however. A short article[163] by (female) player Natalia, who plays as a male character 90% of the time, explains that she does it mainly to avoid the nuisance of unwanted attention that female characters get (gifts and pickup lines). This treatment of female characters has been noted many times before, however a point that Natalia makes which is often not reported is that it's only a very small minority of players who make playing as a female character unpleasant—sometimes only *one* in the whole virtual world. After all, when she plays as a male character and doesn't hit on female characters, no one comments at all—it isn't regarded as unusual. This would seem to suggest that intervention by the community management team could eliminate the problem, at least in relatively small virtual worlds.

Daphne Desser undertook a small study[164] of women who mask their gender in virtual worlds, to judge the effectiveness of female rhetorical practices in an environment where gender was not a factor. The theory is that in real life, women use social connections through language, gestures (nodding, smiling, and so on) and linguistic tags that show agreement; this is because they have diminished power in patriarchal real-life societies. In virtual worlds, where no one need know a player's real-life gender, such defensive insertions should not be necessary; women have the same social and physical presence as men. Previous studies of chat groups had suggested that even when women are gender-masked by pseudonyms, they are still more vulnerable than gender-masked men to harassment. This would mean that somehow people were picking up on the fact that they were "harassable" (if not that they were female); if women did not change their discursive style of interaction even when playing cross-gender, that could perhaps explain it.

Desser analyzed transcripts of gender-masked chat sessions from *LinguaMOO*[165], and discovered that real-life females do indeed still use social connections much more than real-life males; their behavior in virtual worlds in this respect was not substantially

---

163. It was on the popular but now defunct Game Commandos web site, lost even to www.archive.org. Unfortunately, this means you'll have to trust me as to the content of the article (written February 1999).

164. Daphne Desser, *Gender Morphing in Cyberspace*. University of Michigan, *Journal of Electronic Publishing*, Vol. 6 (1), September 2000.

165. http://lingua.utdallas.edu/

different to their behavior in the real world. Desser sees this as an indictment of the power that real-life expectation wields to cause people to conform to gender roles[166].

She also, however, looked at the behavior of male characters playing as female characters, to see whether their behavior was equally unchanged. Perhaps surprisingly, she found that it wasn't: The vocabulary of males playing as females alters in a way that the vocabulary of females playing as males doesn't. This may well be because men have a stronger stereotype to work to than women; on the other hand, it could be that men are more willing to behave differently than women. It would take a much wider study to determine whether men were, in practice, any better at cross-gender play than women, however[167].

The differences between male and female characters has been the subject of speculation for many years. Back in 1994, Lynn Cherny examined[168] behavioral differences in *JaysHouseMOO*, a small virtual world where many of the players knew each other in real life and didn't switch gender. She discovered that in this context, men and women treat their virtual bodies differently: Women engage in hugs and other cuddlesome contacts with one another, but otherwise don't interact "physically" much beyond that; men, conversely, have a much wider range of emotes, some of which evoke quite violent imagery. When women use such emotes, it's almost invariably when in the presence of men who are using them; Cherny suggests they're adapting to male behavior so as to fit in.

Cherny's work pointed to differences between male and female behavior in non-anonymous virtual worlds. Whether these differences could be used as "gender fingerprints" to spot cross-gender playing in a virtual world with anonymity is another matter, of course. Spotting cross-gender playing isn't easy even when you're looking (which, most of the time, people aren't).

---

166. Alternatively, of course, it may be that the different sexes are wired up differently. As Mindy McAdams succinctly puts it, "if my body is female, is my mind also female?"
Mindy J. McAdams, *Gender Without Bodies*. CMC Magazine, March 1996.
`http://www.december.com/cmc/mag/1996/mar/mcadams.html`.

167. An interesting project that may provide the answer is *The Turing Game*. See Joshua Berman and Amy S. Bruckman, *The Turing Game: Exploring Identity in an Online Environment*. Convergence Vol. 7 (3), 2001.
`http://www.cc.gatech.edu/~asb/papers/convergence-tg-01.pdf`.

168. Lynn Cherny, *Gender Differences in Text-Based Virtual Reality*. Berkeley, Proceedings of the Berkeley Conference on Women and Language, 1994.
`ftp://ftp.lambda.moo.mud.org/pub/MOO/papers/GenderMOO.tex`.

In Kathryn Wright's survey, players were asked whether they felt they could tell the real-life gender of characters accurately. She found

- ➤ 50% believed they couldn't.

- ➤ 31% believed they could most of the time.

- ➤ 19% believed they could sometimes, but couldn't at other times, depending on the skills of the person doing it.

As I indicated in Chapter 3, it's actually not all that hard to pass as someone you are not (irrespective of their gender) if you know what you're doing. I've played characters incognito for years at a time. Two of those that lasted for over 24 months of pretty well daily play were female, and neither was detected. I even had people asking me if I were female in real life when my female *alter ego* was playing a male character, their having "seen through" her charade. My experiences are not uncommon. Someone who made a real study of it and read all the literature could perhaps keep something like this up indefinitely (although quite why they'd want to do so isn't clear).

For instance, it's often observed that no men play unsexy female characters[169]. Whether this is any different from what women do is immaterial—it's the perception that counts. So, knowing that people commonly believe that men don't play unsexy females, the crafty male cross-gender player will reduce his chance of being outed by masquerading as an unsexy female. The same applies to all other metrics for detecting differences between the genders, once the diligent role-player has read up on them.

Gender is an important part of the identity of many individuals in the real world. Crossing gender therefore raises important questions: Does it give people a wider appreciation of the opposite sex? Or does it give them a dangerously false impression?

In real life, gender has a biological basis. Male and female exist because that's how human beings reproduce. Virtual worlds enable people to escape their bodies, and be whatever gender they wish.

Well, that's the conceit. Unfortunately, although you can take the person out of the body, you can't take the body out of the person. If the virtual person is told a joke,

---

169. For an arbitrary example of this, see Jonny Nexus, *Men in Dresses. Critical Miss* 2, 1999. "No bloke ever plays an ugly, unsexy woman." http://www.criticalmiss.com/issue2/mid1.html.

their real-world body may laugh; if something very upsetting happens, their real-world body may cry; if they get excited, their real-world heart will definitely beat faster and they may get an adrenaline rush. Real-world bodies can react to virtual-world events, because the player's mind is in both places at once.

This brings us to the second activity of players of virtual worlds that interests gender theorists: virtual sex.

The practice goes by many names, including *netsex*, *cybersex*, *tinysex*, and worse. I'll be following Sherry Turkle's line and calling it *virtual sex*, because that's its most accurate designation. It occurs only in textual worlds and the text channels of graphical worlds[170].

Virtual sex was not common in early, adventure-style virtual worlds, only really taking off with *TinyMUD* and its immediate descendents[171]. Whether this was because the worlds or the players were more social, or because there wasn't a great deal else to do in them, is a matter for conjecture.

As for what virtual sex *is*, well in practical terms it's a series of emoted actions that simulate a sexual encounter. The command

```
:bats the ball to Jill.
```

when issued by a player called Jack will create the message

```
Jack bats the ball to Jill.
```

Jill can then enter the command

```
:returns with a sliced backhand.
```

to generate the message

```
Jill returns with a sliced backhand.
```

---

170. Attempts to produce graphical forms of virtual sex (for example, with *SeduCity*, http://www. seducity.com) have met with limited success. Players don't have the exquisite level of control they require, and in many countries the law is stricter about explicit images than explicit words.

171. Hence, the term "tinysex."

Okay, so I'm showing how you'd use emotes to play virtual tennis here, but virtual sex is the same except that it entails much ritual removal of virtual clothes and inserting virtual objects into virtual containers. If the characters involved are not binary-gendered, they make up their own ways to exchange virtual bodily fluids, usually involving intermingling super-sensitive tentacle organs.

Transcripts of virtual sex taking place are presented in Laurel Gilber's early investigation[172] into the phenomenon. As is usual with logs, these appear dead on the page; it looks like you really had to be there to appreciate the emotion of the moment.

Gilber's analysis takes a post-modern approach that manages (as is almost inevitable with post-modernism[173]) to explain absolutely everything without actually telling you any more than you knew anyway. However, she does make some interesting points, most notably that because seduction[174] is involved in these encounters they are not pornography. She also points out that in a world where AIDS is a dangerous reality, virtual sex is a much safer prospect.

But why engage in virtual sex? It's perfectly possible to fall in love with someone remotely without having to enact a romp in the hay. In the days before email, people occasionally fell in love by exchanging correspondence with individuals whom they had never met. Even in virtual worlds, it happens through mere conversation: At one stage in *British Legends* I was able to trace a chain of 14 people who had fallen in love with someone who professed to love someone else. What does emoting the sex act give that whispering sweet nothings doesn't?

In her *Life on the Screen* examination of the issues, Sherry Turkle focuses on the effect of virtual sex on real-life relationships. She asks whether to have virtual sex is to be unfaithful, and whether the violation of trust amounts to infidelity. Again, though, the same could be said about explicit email exchanges; it's not something that virtual sex delivers which is unavailable by other means, and neither is it of practical use in real life[175].

---

172. Laurel Gilber, *Virtual Sex: The Final Frontier*. 1995. http://www.usyd.edu.au/su/social/papers/gilber2.txt.

173. As I mentioned earlier, Post-modernism—the science of fitting facts to post-modernist theories—is discussed later in this chapter.

174. She uses this word in a more stylized fashion than usual, but the sentiment is the same.

175. Although it's possible to learn new sexual techniques this way, you'd probably get much more out of a respectable sex manual.

Jennifer Mulcahy examines[176] virtual sex as an aspect of virtual romance. When people form relationships, either the relationship is real (in the minds of the participants) or it is simply role-play. In the former context, virtual sex can be used as a means to seek out potential partners for relationships, or to consummate/strengthen an existing relationship; in the latter context, it can be a personal exploration of sexual identity or a way to have some relaxing fun. Clearly, there are problems if one virtual lover thinks they're in a relationship and the other doesn't.

Mulcahy also looks at FurryMUCKs, some of which have a very sexually liberal culture[177]. In these, players take on the role of humanoid animals, reacting as animals to various degrees. Citing a player who genuinely[178] believes he's a porcupine trapped in a human's body, Mulcahy hypothesizes that players often don't want to meet their partners in real life because it would collapse the images that they have built in their heads concerning their virtual lovers. In this situation, virtual sex takes place because real sex can't. She makes the important point that the actuality of physical attraction can stop a virtual relationship—no matter how intense—in its tracks. Players enjoying the experience of a virtual relationship implicitly understand this, and may therefore be apprehensive about meeting their partners in real life.

So, is it that virtual sex is the lust that accompanies virtual love?

Shannon McRae also looks at the use of anthropomorphic characters in her discussion[179] of virtual sex, in particular the symbolism involved. Players' choice of what animal to play reflects their attitudes to sex: A wolf, for example, is likely to be very dominant and predatory, whereas a rabbit would be timid and submissive. Virtual sex in this context allows players to explore aspects of their own sexuality; it's practical role-playing.

---

176. Jennifer K. Mulcahy, *Romance—Online: A Study of the Internet's Effect on Romance in America.* 1996. `http://www.intercom.publinet.it/ic11/romance.htm`. Warning: This version of the article is in Italian, the original English incarnation having seemingly disappeared from the web except in search engine caches.

177. Contrary to the belief of a certain class of newbie, however, the letters "urryM" in "FurryMUCK" are not spurious.

178. This is Mulcahy's word; I don't believe such superficial nonsense for a moment.

179. Shannon McRae, *Flesh Made Word: Sex, Text and the Virtual Body.* David Porter (editor), *Internet Culture.* New York, Routledge, 1997. It's also in *Wired_Women.* `http://www.usyd.edu.au/su/social/papers/mcrae.html`.

The bulk of McRae's article examines the attraction of virtual sex. She finally pins it down to eroticism, in which regard I think she's correct. She also tries to ascertain why players find the experience so intense, but is less successful there: She applies three theories, none of which convince her (and none of which convince me, either). Personally, I see it as a consequence of immersion; then again, given my arguments earlier in this book, I would, wouldn't I? (Virtual sex Zen moment: What is the sound of one hand typing?)

For some people, the attraction of virtual sex is pure hedonism. You can emphasize features of your sexuality without fear, you won't catch any sexually transmitted diseases, and no one will become pregnant as a result. This view of virtual sex was popularized by Claire Benedikt in an up-beat, influential 1995 article[180] on the subject. With virtual sex, you get all the emotional pleasure and none of the dangers of real sex. If people try to mess you around by emoting an event you don't like, you can quit, ignore them, or emote the inverse of the event just as easily. If someone tears off your shirt, you can snap your fingers and the shirt reappears; your virtual power is equal to that of any abuser. Role-playing is consensual; actions are only validated by the consent of all individuals concerned. If you don't want to play along, all they can do is to go look for someone else who will.

Benedikt makes her point forcefully and with examples. Virtual sex is (in an implementational sense) intangible; anything that "happens" only happens if your mind accepts it or its consequences as real. Investing words with emotion doesn't make them true; even if you *feel* violated, you haven't been. If someone is harassing you, speak to a wizard and they'll punish your tormentor. The only real threats are the ones that involve real life, and for those you can call on the real police.

But if you can't prevent or undo the virtual abuse? If there are no administrators you can call on to stop it while it's taking place? If it's witnessed by passers-by who think you're a willing participant?

Thus, we come to the most famous of all articles about virtual worlds: Julian Dibbell's *A Rape in Cyberspace*[181]. Oft-reprinted not just because of its subject matter but also for

---

180. Claire Benedikt, *Tinysex is Safe Sex. Infobahn*, June 1995.
    http://www.cwrl.utexas.edu/~claire/texts/thoughts.html.

181. Julian Dibbell, *A Rape in Cyberspace: How an Evil Clown, a Haitian Trickster Spirit, Two Wizards, and a Cast of Dozens Turned a Database Into a Society. The Village Voice* Vol. 38(51), December 1993.
    http://www.juliandibbell.com/texts/bungle_vv.html.

the quality of its writing, its main concern is not the incident of virtual rape to which its title refers; rather it describes the way the community of *LambdaMOO*, where the event took place, reacted. Nevertheless, the virtual rape itself is a potent totem for gender theorists; a reagent rather than a catalyst.

Warning: If you thought cross-gender play was controversial, you're almost guaranteed to be offended by some of the discussion that follows.

Virtual sex was quite prevalent on *LambdaMOO* at the time of the incident Dibbell reports, to the extent that he suggests that it was in their first act of virtual sex that many newbies experienced what would now be termed as immersion. There is a difference, however, between virtual sex in private between consenting players and that conducted in public against the will of at least one of the participants. This is nevertheless precisely what one of the *LambdaMOO* players did. His character's name was Mr. Bungle.

Mr. Bungle used a virtual object called a *voodoo doll* to force other characters to behave in ways that their players had not instructed. He caused his victims to perform a number of debased acts, all to the accompaniment of his maniacal laughter. Because he had an audience in the form of the other players who were in the room when his assault began, his victim's logging off would have made no difference—enough witnesses could see what was going on. For the same reason, the victim's gagging of him would have had no effect[182]. Simply ignoring someone who is controlling your character is not an option, either. Mr. Bungle was only making intangible changes to the virtual world, but was doing so using a device with tangible functionality such that no one could prevent him. It wasn't until a player called in an experienced old-timer who had some kind of virtual stasis gun at his disposal that the orgy of violence stopped.

Dibbell goes on to describe what happened afterward as the community struggled to come to terms with the events. Most players wanted Mr. Bungle expunged from the database (that is, the character would cease to exist), but unfortunately none of them had the power to do it. The administrators had handed over *LambdaMOO* to its players some four months earlier, and would only act on social issues when requested by the community as a whole. Unfortunately, the players had not formed a body to represent

---

182. Gagging had a dubious status on *LambdaMOO* anyway, on account of how it empowers victims of abuse only at the price of making them responsible for their own suffering when they don't use it.

their views, so before they could get Mr. Bungle removed they had to create one. They disagreed over how to effect this, and in the end the wizards had to implement/impose a voting system themselves.

Many interesting points are raised here. The first is that the violation of a character was referred to almost universally as its "rape." Although this word can technically be used in a non-sexual context ("the rape of the country"), that's not how it was meant here: The players—those who experienced it and even those who merely had it described to them second-hand—all saw it as the non-consensual sexual desecration of an individual, for which the word "rape" was entirely appropriate. This is not to say that they felt it was the same as real-life rape, because there was no physical side to what had happened. It was a rape of a mind, but not of a body.

The community debated the possibility of responding to the virtual crime in reality. The player behind Mr. Bungle was a student at a university with a strong antiharassment policy, and it was conceivable that had its authorities been presented with evidence of his actions (committed while using their computer) they might have removed him from his course. The players determined that a *LambdaMOO* crime best warranted a *LambdaMOO* response, but that's not to say that players of other virtual worlds would necessarily feel the same way if something similar happened there. Indeed, as we shall see shortly, there is good reason to suppose that the crime was more real-world than virtual world.

Also, the proposed punishment amounted to character death at worst and permanent exile at best; in a social virtual world like *LambdaMOO*, this is about the most drastic thing that can happen to anyone. Heinous though rape is, it is second to murder in seriousness. By ordering the death of the alleged rapist, wouldn't that mean the punishment was more severe than the crime? And what purpose was the punishment to serve—was it a warning to others, a step toward rehabilitation or merely an act of revenge?

As a developer, I can only shake my head that this situation ever arose. Non-admin players have a prevailing attitude that anything the virtual world lets them do, they're allowed to do. The only exceptions they will countenance are those that involve freeform input (for example, speech) that the programmers can't reasonably be expected to prevent. Over time, they come to appreciate other rules of behavior that exist, too, but the default is that if the world lets you do it, it's allowed. If it weren't allowed, the programmers would just stop it, right?

Consequently, it came as no surprise to me at all to learn that a virtual world in which players could control other players' characters would, lo and behold, lead to a situation where one player did exactly that. Why would they do it? In the Mr. Bungle case, Dibbell suggests it was because the perpetrator was a sociopath: He looked on the virtual world as a laboratory for experimenting with other people's emotions, a viewpoint that is only perhaps excusable when held by total newbies.

A Rape in Cyberspace succeeded in drawing the attention of researchers and journalists to virtual worlds (Dibbell himself is a journalist), its ultimately positive spin doing much to help people take virtual worlds seriously. Virtual sex was not presented as a sordid activity undertaken by emotionally crippled adolescent males; players were depicted as responsible individuals genuinely shocked by the actions of a madman. The critical differences between the real and the virtual were thrown into relief.

Players are real, characters are virtual. Immersed players are their characters—they're personae—and therefore any assault on a persona is an assault on the player. The assault can only be emotional or intellectual, because those are the only aspects of the real that can be affected by the virtual. A player who doesn't understand the difference between a character and a persona (for example, someone who thinks "it's just a game") may assault other characters—and therefore players—without fully realizing the consequences. A player who does know the difference can perform an assault without censure if the context of the virtual world reasonably permits it (for example, it's clear from the genre[183] that characters can be raped). A player who knows the difference and isn't in a virtual world with a culture that allows such assaults, yet who still goes ahead and does it without provocation anyway, is indeed a sociopath[184].

As to whether these assaults violate real-world law, that's a matter for the lawyers. In a real world where people can be successfully sued for inflicting emotional distress by failing to deliver on a promise to meet Jesus Christ in the flesh[185], who knows what a gullible player might come to believe? Personally, I feel that anyone who enters a

---

183. I'd still advise developers to make any such context explicit in a warning, though, at least in the current climate of public opinion. People may routinely expect characters to be killed in games, but even in a post-apocalyptic, dark future world they might not expect they can be raped.

184. If they're acting under the influence of personality-changing chemicals, this may be only a temporary situation. Many players do things while drunk that they later regret. However, if it was their decision to get drunk in the first place, they still have to accept the consequences as being their responsibility.

185. http://www.ananova.com/news/story/sm_508436.html

virtual world takes a certain emotional risk in doing so, and that they've no more right to sue than has a member of the crowd at a golf match who is hit by a stray ball. By the same token, though, any golfer who deliberately or irresponsibly hits a ball at someone knowing it would cause them physical damage could expect to be sued; anyone in a virtual world who deliberately or irresponsibly causes real-life emotional distress beyond that which a reasonable individual could expect to endure in the context of that world deserves all they get.

For those who think that freedom of speech rules would act as a defense, consider a different incident of virtual rape reported by Elizabeth Reid in her 1994 *Cultural Formations* thesis. This occasion did not involve emote commands: Rather, the "rapist" depicted the violations he[186] was committing through use of the "shout" command. The effect on the other players was actually worse than in Dibbell's example, because of the nature of the virtual world in which it took place. *JennyMUSH*[187] was set up to help the victims of real-life sexual assault or abuse overcome their trauma, and developed into a strong, supportive community where people could talk through their problems openly with others who had suffered similar violations. Consequently, when the rogue player waited until there were no administrators playing before changing gender to male, name to Daddy, and then screaming graphical and violent messages of virtual assault, it was calculated to cause maximum psychological damage. If someone had used a public address system at a psychiatric hospital to manifest the worst fears of everyone attending a recovery group, they could expect to be punished; the same should be said when people choose to conduct similar real-life violence through actions undertaken in virtual worlds. New prospective players of *JennyMUSH* now have to be recommended by two other players and give their real-life contact details to the system administrator before they are admitted. They remain anonymous from the other players, but can be called to account if they violate trust.

Simply the best discussion I have read about virtual rape is by Richard MacKinnon[188]. He takes the view that the concept of "rape" is a social construct that varies from

---

186. As the real-life gender of the character who did this is not certain, Reid points out that actually "he" could have been a "she."

187. This is not its real name. Reid changed it, for reasons that will become apparent when you stop reading this footnote and get back to the main text.

188. Richard C. MacKinnon, *The Social Construction of Rape in Virtual Reality*. Fay Sudweeks, Margaret McLaughlin and Sheizaf Rafaeli (editors), *Network & Netplay: Virtual Groups on the Internet*. Cambridge MA, MIT Press, 1998.

culture to culture; in plain English, what members of a society understand by "rape" defines what rape is in that society. The *LambdaMOO* players who witnessed Mr. Bungle's actions or heard them described almost universally viewed it as rape, therefore in that community it *was* rape.

Virtual communities differ importantly from real-life ones, however, in that their members don't have bodies. The wholesale importing of real-life concepts of rape into virtual worlds is therefore a bad idea: Instead, players should reconstruct the notion of rape within the context of the virtual world. Furthermore, because there are theories of rape, this can be done in a guided fashion—learning from real life, rather than repeating its mistakes.

MacKinnon describes the main prevailing theories that explain the causes of rape in real life. These are

- ➤ *Feminist.* Rape is the result of deep-seated social traditions dominated almost totally by men.

- ➤ *Social learning.* Aggressive sexual behavior is acquired through repeated exposure to it.

- ➤ *Evolutionary.* Rape is a manifestation of the different reproductive priorities of the sexes.

Whichever of these is used in the context of virtual worlds, it must be broad; virtual worlds involve no body, therefore any definition of rape that requires one is inapplicable. In this regard, some of the wider feminist viewpoints are most appropriate, defining rape to be any "damage to the self" inflicted by physical, emotional, psychological, or material means. This being the case, rape (of the mind) is indeed possible in virtual worlds. The question is, therefore, how to prevent it?

In considering his solution, MacKinnon notes that Mr. Bungle's actions were automatically accepted as events in the real world by the observing players. Had Mr. Bungle used his voodoo doll to make his victim appear to burst into flames, the players would not have accepted this as a possibility and would have mocked him for it. Putting this in terms I have used elsewhere in this book, the players would have thought spontaneous human combustion to be "unrealistic;" why, therefore, did they not look on the virtual rape this way? MacKinnon's answer is that they were using a definition for rape taken from the real world that didn't fit; it would have been better were they to create a new definition appropriate to their virtual world. Claire Benedikt's seemingly *blasé* suggestion of deflecting the attacker's weapon by deferring to the consensual nature of the virtual world's reality is actually the solution. Rather than accepting rape to be an assault on the mind even when there is no body, players should merely point out the obvious: You can't sexually assault someone when neither you nor they have a body. The act of attempting to do so is ridiculous, and therefore so is anyone making such an attempt.

MacKinnon accepts that during any period where new definitions of rape are coming into acceptance there will be problems, but the eventual reconstruction of the concept for virtual worlds will be far more helpful in the long term. I'm not convinced that it's this simple: Immersion means that character and player are, in a sense, one persona, so an assault on such a character *is* an assault on a player. Unless they consented to it, it really could be damage to their self that amounts to rape under this broad definition[189]. To respond as MacKinnon suggests would mean unimmersing, but this could be problematical for some players if they didn't realize what was happening in time.

MacKinnon makes another interesting point concerning Mr. Bungle's punishment. He is of the opinion that punishing a character is no punishment at all unless the player has a stake in that character. Mr. Bungle's player didn't care about the Mr. Bungle character, therefore any sanctions imposed on him were worthless. As Mr. Bungle's player deliberately hurt his victim's player[190], the offense was in real life, not in *LambdaMOO*. Perhaps it would have been better if the *LambdaMOO* denizens had asked for the offending player to suffer the consequences of his actions in real life? I subscribe to this same view, while also noting that deleting Mr. Bungle might nevertheless have served some small purpose in serving as a deterrent for other players contemplating similar rapes.

---

189. This is the thrust of Jessica Mulligan's opinion that PD amounts to rape, and is why I inserted the "unless they consented to it" clause in there. If you know that your self could be "damaged" in advance in a context that you willingly enter, then should this happen it's ultimately your responsibility alone. Someone else may have been the instrument of the damage, but you can't call it rape; sure, you didn't "ask for it," but you did make the person who gave you it unaccountable. If you step into a boxing ring, you expect to get hit; if you step into a dark alley at night, you might also expect to get hit. The difference is that in the former case you give your attacker implicit permission to hit you, whereas in the latter you don't.

190. Although the victim is usually referred to by character name, legba, the identity of the player behind it is less well known. It was Shannon McRae, whose *Flesh Made Word* article I discussed earlier.

I also ought to state that personally I don't feel that the violations delivered by Mr. Bungle amounted to rape. They were certainly cruel and certainly unpleasant, but to label this incident as an example of perhaps the second-worst[191] crime a person can commit in reality tends, in my opinion, to trivialize the latter rather than raise the former's significance.

I mention all this for two reasons. Firstly, it's the brief of this chapter to report on what researchers in other fields think about virtual worlds, and this is one of the areas in which there is particularly constructive activity. Secondly, it raises a general point concerning the responsibility of virtual world designers for what goes on in their worlds. Consider the "rape" command in a text-based virtual world.

Yes, you heard me.

Look, someone in your virtual world—probably a newbie, but it could be a more experienced player—is going to try the command "rape." They can "kill Xyzzy" and get away with it, murder is a greater crime than rape, and so it should be okay to try "rape Xyzzy," shouldn't it? Or maybe they're doing it in an educational virtual world because, hey, their watching friends in the real world will think they're big. However they reason, someone is eventually going to do it. You, as the virtual world's designer, have to decide how to respond.

Here are some typical solutions:

➤ Do nothing. The response to the command "rape" is the same as would be generated by any other non-command. This is the solution most designers take. They do so either because they didn't consider rape to be an issue, or they did but it was too hard so they ducked it, or they have some rationale along the lines of "I won't dignify it with a response." None of these are acceptable. It *is* important, it *shouldn't* be avoided, and you *are* giving it a response (specifically, that you don't mind having in your world people who think rape is okay).

➤ Issue a response telling the player off. This has the advantage of showing that you don't approve of this kind of behavior, but the disadvantage of being toothless. The would-be rapist can simply laugh it off.

---

191. In addition to murder, physical maiming could be regarded as more serious than rape, given that the threat of it is often used successfully by rapists to prevent their victims from attempting to escape. If being raped were the worse fate, this strategy wouldn't work.

➤ Issue a warning, and also alert the customer service staff. A 20-minute lecture by an unamused admin undertaken in a disconnected sin bin room is enough to persuade most of the "I just wanted to see what would happen" brigade that no, actually, you didn't. This works, but administrators don't like doing it, especially if they end up being hated for "not being able to take a joke" as a result. It also runs the risk that people will try it simply to gain attention.

➤ Give the warning tangible force. Don't just say you think that this is inappropriate for your virtual world, but (temporarily) damage any character that tries it. Now they know you're serious.

➤ Give the command tangible meaning. They want to assault another character, okay, so invoke whatever combat routines the virtual world uses. Couple it with one of the preceding responses (it works particularly well with an automatic hit point loss). Hey, if you attack someone while your pants are round your ankles, you're bound to be at a disadvantage....

➤ Mete out instant PD on any character that issues the command. If the player wants it back, they can come cap in hand to the administrators and beg. Only after a suitable display of contrition will their character be resurrected. This zero-tolerance approach makes its point, but can be overkill. Furthermore, experienced players will persuade naïve newbies to try the command, then laugh their socks off at the result. The newly dead newbie, however, will suffer all the usual effects of PD and may be hurt as a result. Their punishment is beyond their crime.

➤ Do any of the above, and warn the intended victim. They can then take action to avoid the odious individual concerned in future. This sounds a good idea, but in practice it isn't; it can be highly disturbing if, during the course of normal play, you suddenly receive a message telling you that your character has just successfully resisted an attempted rape by some other character. There is a strong possibility that a player would eventually exploit such a rape command solely to hurt their victim—even if it meant they'd eventually lose their own character as a result.

I've had numerous debates[192] on this subject over the years concerning *MUD2's* approach to the command, and have tried various different solutions. The one I have

---

192. For one that took place in 1990/91 in the pages of the newsletter of the short-lived *Organisation Against Sexism in Software*, see: http://www.mud.co.uk/richard/oadec90.htm
http://www.mud.co.uk/richard/oafeb91a.htm
http://www.mud.co.uk/richard/oafeb91b.htm

settled on is "tangible meaning," without informing the intended victim that the attack came from a "rape" command. This means that the perpetrator suffers the consequences of their action, but they're the only person who does. On the whole, people prefer not to see the word "rape" coming from their virtual world, even if this is at the expense of not being informed when someone tries it[193].

Returning at last from the fringes of Gender Studies back to the mainstream, how can attitudes to virtual sex (and virtual rape) best be summed up? As with cross-gender play, there are basically two points of view:

➤ The radical view is that virtual sex victimizes women. There is a continuum of harassment, with virtual rape at the end-point.

➤ The liberal view is that virtual sex liberates women. Sex can be as frequent and different as you want, and is often better than in real life.

Neither of these is satisfactory, as Nicola Döring points out in her excellent critique[194]. Victimization sees women as always having the status of objects, and does not admit the possibility that virtual sexual experiences can exist and be enjoyed; liberalization idealizes women's choice and control, and does not admit the possibility that there may be a power imbalance between the genders. Döring proposes a third, empowerment model that addresses the concerns of the other two. Central to this is the notion that sexual empowerment is an individual learning process, as well as a process of political emancipation. Women should question their needs, and explore them critically; in other words, through their actions in the virtual world, they should develop a better understanding of themselves.

Yes, that does sound strangely familiar. Isn't it nice when all these theories come together?

---

193. When players implement events by play-acting them (as happens in those virtual worlds that enforce role-playing), out-of-character communication can have this same effect. This can be doubly disconcerting, because the consensual nature of such role-playing means that not only might players ask OOC if their character can rape your character, but they also might ask if your character can rape theirs. Indeed, anecdotal evidence seems to suggest that more people want to play out being the victim of rape than want to play out being the perpetrator.
Karrin Dailey, *The Dreaded "R" Word*. Skotos, 2003. http://www.skotos.net/articles/medium11.shtml.

194. Nicola Döring, *Feminist Views of Cybersex: Victimization, Liberation, and Empowerment*. CyberPsychology and Behavior Vol. 3 (5), 2000. http://www.nicola-doering.de/publications/cybersex-doering-2000.pdf.

Back in Chapter 4, "World Design," I referred to J. C. Herz's 1994 *zeitgeist*-capturing book, *Surfing on the Internet*. Her experiences with virtual worlds cover several chapters, as she moves from newbie to seasoned veteran[195]. When she begins, she has experience of IRC but not much idea of what's possible in a virtual world. She starts with a look at the education-oriented *MicroMUSE*[196], then moves on to the more socially oriented *LambdaMOO*. There, she meets a character called Thorin who gives her a tour of the place.

Herz leaves *LambdaMOO* and explores many other virtual worlds over the coming weeks, playing several quite extensively. Finally, she returns to *LambdaMOO* no longer a newbie, and seeks out the friendly Thorin. At first he doesn't recall her, having showed around many guests in his time, but when she jogs his memory he remembers. He then furthers her education by demonstrating how to create her own virtual space within *LambdaMOO*. Then he hits on her.

As a guest, Herz was an "it." Now she is experienced and has created her own character, she's a "her." When Thorin helped her as a guest, he didn't know she was female (although he suspected it). Now she's confirmed her real-life gender and accepted his further help, he thinks she's obligated to him.

Well yes, maybe she is, but she's not obligated *that* much. When she turns down his advances, Thorin's mood changes drastically. He subjects her to a torrent of power-trip emotes, describing the mean things his character is doing to hers and how her character is reacting. Herz subverts this in exactly the manner described by Benedikt, undoing his every virtual act with an emote that returns to the *status quo*, all the while pointing out his foolishness with smiles and laughter. She ends with the comment, "Ooh. MUD harassment. Think I'll have to see a shrink about this. Not."

Now *that's* the attitude.

---

195. You can read the book as an example of a hero's journey if you're exceptionally keen.

196. She calls it *Cyberion City*, which is the name of the main region in the *MicroMUSE* world.
    http://www.musenet.org/.

Lexicography

After so many pages of dense theorizing concerning nigh-inaccessible ideological positions using elitist vocabulary, I thought I'd go on to something a little less stressful next: lexicography—the compilation of dictionaries.

Lexicography is one small part of lexicology (the study of the structure and history of a particular language), which itself falls under the scientific umbrella of linguistics. We've already met sociolinguistics in the context of anthropology; other major subfields include phonetics, syntax, semantics, and translation, none of which touch on virtual worlds very much (which isn't to say that they shouldn't). Three other subfields of linguistics do have something to say about virtual worlds, however: cognitive science and computational linguistics (which I file with artificial intelligence), and language acquisition (which comes under education). This leaves lexicography, with a dash of lexicology as a context.

Virtual worlds are great for learning foreign languages. They're great for learning your mother tongue, come to that. They're also great for the development of new terms. This is why lexicographers are interested in them.

There are two opposing stances on the purpose of dictionaries. One, the *prescriptive* view, is that dictionaries tell you what words actually mean, as opposed to what certain individuals might think they mean. By ensuring that everyone uses the same words in the same way, clarity is maintained and the subtle interrelationships between words are upheld. The contrary, *descriptive* view, is that dictionaries are for recording words as they are used, its not being the business of the lexicographer to make judgments about the "correctness" of usage.

As an example, a prescriptive dictionary will tell you that the word "enormity" means "extreme wickedness" (as in "when the enormity of his murderous deeds sank in"), whereas a descriptive dictionary will add that it means "huge scale" (as in "when the enormity of her tennis victory sank in"). Initially, as they struggled to formalize spellings and dialect terms, dictionaries were prescriptive. There were even "dictionary wars," in which rival lexicographers vied to have their version accepted as definitive—sometimes for very political reasons[197].

---

197. This is why I had to install an American English spell-checker into my word processor for this book, rather than stay with the British English one I normally use.

Nowadays, though, dictionaries are mainly descriptive. They do give the "correct" meaning of a word, but report it as "archaic" if it is; upstart new meanings come in as "informal." Pedants may lament the passing of prescriptive dictionaries, but languages do change. The word "enormous" meant "extremely wicked" back in the 1500s.

So, how do modern dictionaries define virtual worlds?

Basically, they don't. This is not surprising for two reasons:

➤ Players disagree over what virtual worlds are called (which is why I began this book by defining the terms I'd be using).

➤ Virtual worlds are an online phenomenon that lexicographers don't necessarily know exists.

There are many hundreds of dictionaries around, of course, and some undoubtedly do have references to virtual world terms if not virtual worlds themselves. I'm certain that the mighty *Oxford English Dictionary*[198] does, because one of their lexicographers phoned me to ask me where the acronym "MUD" first appeared in print[199]. In general, though, definitions have been limited to specialist lexicographies. The first time I saw "MUD" was in a 1991 dictionary of personal computing[200], which referred only to *MUD1* and not MUDs in general; it did, however, have a definition of MUG as an abbreviation for "multiuser game" (although apart from directing the reader to the definition for MUD, that was the sum of it).

Doubtless this situation will change as lexicographers latch on to the fact that virtual worlds are played by more people than read their dictionaries, and are therefore worthy of consideration. If they do, they may be tempted not only to define concepts such as "virtual world," "avatar," and "permanent death," but also to look at the words that players use in everyday communication.

This is where, finally, it gets interesting.

---

198. John Simpson (chief editor), *Oxford English Dictionary*. Oxford, Oxford University Press. Updated quarterly. `http://www.oed.com/`.

199. Answer: Richard Bartle, *A Voice from the Dungeon. Practical Computing*, December 1983. `http://www.mud.co.uk/richard/avftd.htm`.

200. Ian R. Sinclair, *Collins Dictionary of Personal Computing*. Glasgow, HarperCollins, 1991.

Players of virtual worlds often develop new words (or, as with "avatar," new meanings for old words) to label things that they find important. The same applies for any subculture, of course; indeed, one of the signifiers of a subculture is the development of its own jargon. Knowledge of jargon terms can be used to erect barriers between a subculture and its mainstream culture; if someone doesn't know what a term means, or misapplies it, that flags them as an outsider. Academics, for example, will frequently drop the names of other academics in conversation to sum up viewpoints or ideals in a single word; this isn't deliberately to be exclusive, but if you don't know the work to which they're referring then it can have that effect. For example, if I were talking to someone I believed was an expert on identity issues in virtual worlds, I might in the course of the conversation refer to Sherry Turkle's work expecting them to know what I meant; if they replied "Sherry who?," I'd maybe wonder if they were indeed the expert they professed to be.

The use of jargon terms can define membership of a community. This can go two ways:

➤ The community excludes people who don't use its jargon.

➤ The community includes people who learn its jargon.

For virtual worlds, we want the second of these: Newbies arrive, they don't understand many of the terms, but in being taught them by members of the community they feel they are being accepted into the community (which is true—they are). It's therefore in the interests of virtual world developers to ensure that there is a certain amount of jargon in their worlds, to help act as community glue.

For example, newbies to worlds like *EverQuest* will hear people referring to "mobs." In the real world, the word "mob" means a large, unruly crowd; in virtual worlds, a "mob" is a computer-controlled monster. When players learn what a "mob" is, it draws them one step further into the community.

Some virtual world jargon comes from related subcultures. "Rooms" get their name because that's what people called them in adventure games such as *Zork*. A good many words hail from the general computer hacker subculture, the jargon of which is maintained as the *Jargon File*[201] (published in book form as *The New Hacker's Dictionary*[202]).

---

201. http://www.tuxedo.org/~esr/jargon/jargon.html

202. Eric Raymond (editor), *The New Hacker's Dictionary*. Cambridge MA, MIT Press, 1991.

This work not only defines many commonly used words and phrases, but it is packed with interesting background notes and information; in places, it almost amounts to an historical record, rather than a mere noting of usage.

There are two comparatively large[203] dictionaries of terms that are used by players of virtual worlds. One of these, the *Encyclopedia of MUDs Dictionary*[204], covers textual virtual worlds in general; the other, the *MUDspeke Dictionary*[205], collates only those terms that have found favor in *MUD2*. There is some overlap between these, partly because of their common heritage and partly because of external factors. Some terms are more exportable than others, and are therefore more inclusive or exclusive.

Looking at the various terms that have found favor in virtual worlds, they can be classified along their lines of general utility as follows:

➤ Those exported into mainstream culture. "Wtf" (what the f*ck?) has appeared in mainstream U.K. newspapers and magazines, as has "bot" (an intelligent conversational agent). Both began in virtual worlds.

➤ Those exported into a wider subculture. IRC users use "afk" ("away from keyboard"), "brb" ("be right back") and "bbl" ("be back later") because players of virtual worlds did (not that many IRC users know this).

➤ Those exported into other virtual worlds. "Rehi" ("hello again"), "mobile," and "rl" ("real life") are endemic across virtual worlds, but began in *MUD1*.

➤ Those not exportable to other virtual worlds. *MUD2* players know who "the twins" are, but players of other virtual worlds wouldn't because they don't contain the objects to which the term refers.

➤ Those not exportable to the same virtual world at a different time in its history. Terms that mention characters by name are particularly prone to lose resonance over time. Others, however, inexplicably cling on. *MUD2* players will say they "fetched" when their modem chokes on them, solely because a long-deceased specialist piece of client software that one incarnation of the world used would display the unhelpful message "fetch error" when this happened.

---

203. They each have more than 500 entries in them.

204. http://www.iowa-mug.net/muddic/dic/academic.html

205. http://www.mud.co.uk/muse/muse/speke.htm

➤ Those that look exported but were probably reinvented independently. Mobile phone users don't key in "b4" ("before") or "thx" ("thanks") because virtual world players did; they do it because it takes less time (which is precisely why virtual world players did it).

➤ Those that were exported but were reinventions in virtual worlds. People today use the word "newbie" because *MUD1* players invented it, however unbeknown to those players they were merely reinventing a word that had been used in select British fee-paying schools for years.

As I noted in Chapter 3, from a game designer's point of view a certain amount of jargon is a good thing. Too much can act as a barrier to newbies, of course, but too little can weaken a community's hold on its members. Although I don't recommend the out-and-out inventing of terms for the players to use, there's no harm in ensuring that any idiosyncratic vocabulary that has arisen to fill a need during development of the game is passed on. Players use words like "shard" and "zone" because that's what the designers and programmers called them. Members of the live team can, by frequently using a term (especially one invented by the players), make that term "official"—thereby greatly increasing its acceptability. Understanding any new term adds to a player's stake in a virtual world. Jargon is your friend: Treat it well.

In her analysis[206] of the use of jargon in virtual worlds, Diane Shortt suggests that as more and more people play these worlds, specialist terms will seep more and more into the mainstream—just as hippie terms from the 1960s are now part of everyday speech. She sees this as an inevitable consequence of the increasing popularity of virtual worlds, but notes that players do express regret that "their" language is becoming less "theirs."

Whether this seepage is a good thing or a bad thing, I'm not sure. On the face of it, it looks like it should be bad because jargon makes for community. However, if there are so many people playing these virtual worlds that their terminology has become mainstream, why worry?

A final note: As the "fetch" example illustrated, words can preserve history. For some virtual worlds, this may indeed be the only way that their history is preserved. Historians have yet to show any interest in virtual worlds at all—there's no History

---

206. http://www.mala.bc.ca/~soules/CMC290/hackslay.htm

section in this chapter—and yet some of these worlds have the potential to last almost indefinitely[207]. When culture is only maintained by word of mouth, the words in those mouths are important. Dictionaries can be the gatekeepers of history; would your virtual world benefit from one?

Economics

Virtual worlds (the more persistent ones, anyway) have economies. Economists study economies. Virtual-world economies are therefore legitimate objects of study for economists.

This doesn't mean that many economists do study virtual worlds, however. Those who are involved in the area are more often than not players of virtual worlds who happen to be economists in real life, rather than economists coming to virtual worlds from the outside. That said, academic economists are becoming increasingly aware of virtual worlds, and we can expect more of them to become interested in the topic as time goes on.

I said "the topic" there, but there are actually three main areas of importance:

> ➤ Using virtual worlds to simulate a real-world economy for experimental purposes.

> ➤ Figuring out how the in-world economies of virtual worlds work (or fail to work).

> ➤ Examining the interaction between virtual-world economies and the real-world economy.

The first of these is not perhaps as widespread as might be expected. I have only one paper in my collection that addresses it, by Thomas Grimm and Johann Mitlöhner[208]. Their approach was to take a regular textual world and add commands specific to performing monetary transactions. The first of these, "deal," proposed a contract between two individuals (the buyer and the seller), concerning

---

207. Specialist archivists in related fields do make occasional note of virtual worlds in an historical context, but only peripherally (because their main interests lie elsewhere). For example, *MUD1* (as *MUD*) gets a one-sentence mention (out of 1,370 pages) under "Games and Toys" in John Clute and Peter Nicholls (editors), *The Encyclopedia of Science Fiction* (2nd edition). London, Orbit, 1993.

208. Thomas Grimm and Johann Mitlöhner, *Developing a Virtual Reality for the Simulation of Agent Based Economic Models*. Departments of Applied Economics and Applied Computer Science, Vienna University of Economics and Business Administration, 1995.

one object. Negotiation could then follow, using an "offer" command to change the terms of the proposed contract (price, quantity, delivery date, and so on), plus "accept" and "widthdraw" commands to terminate the deal one way or the other. The system (that is, the virtual world engine) would then either execute or delete the contract, as appropriate. None of the contract commands accrued any cost in themselves (it was a lawyer-free environment).

Grimm and Mitlöhner's purpose was to create artificial agents that exhibited different "lifelike" behaviors, and see just how well these worked in practice in an environment shared with each other and with real people. They were using a virtual world to simulate theories that are hard to test in the real one. Economic modeling by computer is not a new idea, of course; virtual worlds offer the additional presence of humans, which makes the model they present more plausible[209].

The problem is, virtual world economies don't seem to work the same way as the real one. When they're constructed to work like the real world works, they don't. Money quickly becomes either worthless or (less often) impossible to acquire; yet trade still happens. This is fascinating stuff, made all the more interesting because although it's not too hard to see why the design for a particular virtual-world economy might fail, it's much harder to come up with a design for one that wouldn't.

It should be noted that there are several different types of economy available in virtual worlds. Some, such as *TinyMUD*'s tokens, are little more than permissions to interact with the virtual world: They limit the amount of building that can be done, but there's not a lot else for which they can be used. The designers of the early graphical world *Habitat* characterized this as a "socialist economy"[210], based as it was on the equitable distribution of limited real-world computer resources. Their own solution (which was, almost inevitably, inflationary) involved having in-world money that could be spent on in-world goods; again, though, it was still basically one-on-one between character and database—a point well made in a 1995 talk[211] to economists by Julian Dibbell. Economies only *really* get going when players trade between each other, so as to obtain

---

209. Most importantly in providing a solid basis for the concept of "demand."

210. F. Randall Farmer, Chip Morningstar and Douglas Crockford, *From Habitat to Global Cyberspace*.
     http://ftp.game.org/pub/mud/text/research/hab2cybr.txt.

211. Julian Dibbell, *MUD Money: A Talk on Virtual Value and, Incidentally, the Value of the Virtual*. Rutgers University, Proceedings of Stages of the Virtual, April 1995.
     http://www.juliandibbell.com/texts/mudmoney.html.

things on which they place different values. This brings us to the second topic of interest to economists: the internal economics of virtual worlds.

The first report on the economics of an individual world remains the archetype: Zachary Booth Simpson's *The In-game Economics of Ultima Online*[212]. This seminal work describes the similarities and differences between *Ultima Online*'s economy and real-world economies, the thought that went into its design, and the places where the expectation did not match the eventuality.

There were five reasons that the designers of *UO* wanted their world to have an economy, universal across all large-scale virtual worlds:

➤ To ration power, so that not everyone can have every piece of desirable kit.

➤ To support specialization (and therefore diversity), so that players concentrate on finding their own individual niche because of the limits on what they can own.

➤ To encourage interaction, for trade and work.

➤ To provide goals.

➤ To support economic role-playing, for people who like to be artisans, merchants, and so on.

These were the aims. Simpson identified the following areas where the designers had to make unconventional[213] decisions because of *UO*'s virtual nature:

➤ Balancing fun and realism. The real world's way of doing it may not be fun.

➤ What to do with characters when players log off.

➤ How to handle muling by players with more than one character.

➤ Hoarding of objects by players creates database load and must be discouraged.

➤ Newbies need to be given help so they can advance quickly, but this must not be exploitable by experienced players through their mules.

➤ What to do when bugs allow people to cheat.

---

212. Zachary Booth Simpson, *The In-game Economics of Ultima Online*. Origin Systems Inc., 1999.
    `http://www.kanga.nu/mirrors/www.totempole.net/uoecon/uoecon.html`.

213. Unconventional with respect to real-world economies.

The original solution to all these criteria was a closed economy where resources, money, raw materials, goods, and character inventory were all interlinked through player and system actions to create a single economic flow. Within a year of launch, it had switched to faucet/drain. Why was this?

Simpson argues that it was a failure of the original design to consider microeconomic aspects of the world, concentrating as it did on the macro economy. There was severe over-production of goods, because players created many items solely so that their creation skills would rise. This led to a fall in prices that players were not willing to accept. If a player makes a ton of identical shirts and takes them to some NPC vendor that already has a ton of these shirts and has been unable to sell them, the player *should* expect that the vendor refuses to buy any more; unfortunately, the player instead regards it as a bug—the virtual world encouraged them to create clothes, so it ought to obey its obligations and buy them.

A second problem was that the NPC shopkeeper economy didn't work. NPC shopkeepers set their prices using a hugely complicated formula based on many different factors. The problem was, players wanted to sell things to NPC vendors but didn't want to buy anything from them. This meant that vendors operating to a positive cash flow paradigm would cease buying when they ran out of money. Those objects they sold that players could not get elsewhere were subject to a pricing scheme that groups of players could combine to exploit once they figured it out (which of course they did—buying low in one place then teleporting to where they could sell high, for example).

A third problem was hoarding. In a closed economy where the number of resources is constant, new resources are only added to the system when old resources are expended. For example, if a sword breaks, then the metal it is made up of is returned to the resource pool and a miner somewhere will dig up some ore that replaces it. This keeps down inflation (which is its intention), but unfortunately it means that whenever people hold on to objects, rather than using them, there is a resource shortage. Scarcity then encourages players to hold onto the resource even more (because who knows when they may next find some?). The solution of increasing the pool didn't work—people kept on hoarding and resources kept on drying up. Only by switching to a faucet (constant input of resources, irrespective of use) did that problem go away, but at the expense of server load (because people still hoarded objects they couldn't or wouldn't sell). The faucet needed sufficient drains to match it, but these weren't present. Had these been there at the start, people would have accepted them; because they weren't, though, players regarded attempts to impose new drains (for example, taxes) as taking things away from them, which was deeply unpopular.

The final reason that the *UO* economy failed was because of counterfeiting. Loopholes existed that enabled players to clone money, and because of this, they could create as much as they liked until the programmers could fix the bug. This took much longer to tackle than it should have.

Simpson finishes his report with some suggestions as to how future virtual worlds might be able to address these issues, while noting that actually the failure of *UO*'s economy was not as bad as it would have been for a real world economy—players still had fun. I won't list all his conclusions here, because there are too many of them; besides, if you're at all interested in any of this, you would do better to read the original report. I'll list his most important recommendations, however, for comparison with what other people propose:

➤ Create enforceable contracts. If people agree to pay for work, or to perform work for pay, then neither should be able to rip off the other without serious consequences.

➤ Create auctions. These define price very efficiently, and are fun social events.

➤ Allow player-controlled vendors to buy as well as sell.

➤ Deepen production paths. If there are transitional steps to producing goods, newbies can have an apprenticelike intermediate role to play in production instead of creating finished goods themselves.

➤ Make characters purchase skill improvements, rather than improve them through use.

As a result of Simpson's paper, later large-scale virtual worlds have invariably gone for an open model rather than a closed one. However, that isn't to say that a closed one can never work. Although in Chapter 4 I suggested that no one has yet created a successful closed model economy for virtual worlds, that's actually only true for the big, graphical worlds. In smaller-scale worlds, with fewer player management issues, a closed economy can be implemented and run successfully. Geoff Wong describes[214] how by adhering to a strict monetarist *Loans Standard* policy, the designers of *Shattered World*[215] have created an economy in which prices have remained relatively stable since the early 1990s. The key to this is ensuring that all manufacturers, shops, and banks in the world are owned by PCs, rather than by NPCs. Players specify the prices for absolutely everything—nothing is set by the system itself except the amount of money that the individual banks can loan.

The success of the *Scattered World* economic system is evidenced by its stable prices. It does have periods of boom and bust (related to changes in the size of the player base), but has never suffered the kind of collapse that befell *UO*. Its main problem is that to keep the money supply under control, newbies can't be given a grubstake when they enter—they have either to persuade a banker to loan them the money or perform menial tasks for other players who don't want to do the tasks themselves. Only when a newbie has demonstrated that they're likely to become a regular player will bankers deign to lend them any money. This is fine for a small-scale virtual world, but it's easy to see how one with thousands of newbies couldn't expect to keep them for long.

There are other problems, too. In a comparison[216] of open and closed virtual-world economies, Dan Hastings notes the following difficulties:

➤ There is a huge amount of work involved in tracking the creation and destruction of economically significant items. Pretty well everything must be audited so as to ensure that the overall money supply remains under control. This can lead to very serious overheads in implementation[217].

➤ Virtual worlds where not all characters are PCs must simulate the behavior of their implied NPCs. The virtual world must somehow attempt to model the fact that PCs are "really" only a small fraction of the total population, even though they drive its economy. This is very hard to get right for a closed economy.

214. Geoff Wong, *A Working Mud Economy. Imaginary Realities* Vol. 3 (5), May 2000.

215. http://www.shattered.org

216. Dan Hastings ("Scatter"), *The Model Economy. Imaginary Realities* Vol. 2 (9), September 1999. http://home.clara.net/stormbringer/mudos/economy.html.

217. This is something you'd probably want to do anyway, though, so customer service staff can discover where reportedly "lost" items and money have gone.

➤ Closed economies remove some of the designer's freedom. If you create a city with a "poor" area, under a closed economy it's very difficult to prevent this from becoming a "rich" area if players decide to make it such. This means any premade quests or whatever that assume it's a poor area will become out of date. Deliberate, artistic placement of economic entities is also hard to sustain.

It may be possible to combine the best of open and closed systems by maintaining a fixed pool of total wealth and using taxation as a mechanism for managing it. This is the approach that has been taken by *Star Wars Galaxies*, for which excellent documents[218] exist describing the virtual world's economy itself and the rationale behind its creation. It features a central bank, to control and monitor the cash flow into and out of the virtual economy, ensuring that the amount provided by the faucet is the same as that recovered by taxation. The plan is to keep taxation[219] constant and vary the incoming wealth (amortized across all distribution mechanisms) to match it; this avoids the tax-level changes that players so hate. There is some leeway in the system, in that calculations are performed weekly rather than continually; these calculations also account for net increases in the number of players joining the virtual world since they were last run. The hope is that this economy will

➤ Discourage hoarding, because objects decay.

➤ Increase immediate spending, because money devalues quicker than goods.

➤ Create equal opportunities, because newbies don't have to play catch-up with players who have been around for months.

In general, as long as a taxation system is imposed from the beginning, the players will accept it; they would not feel that anything was being taken from them as a punishment for their collective success. Personally, I believe that this is probably the right way to go in the long term, but of course it greatly depends on its actual implementation; it may have unforeseen consequences on gameplay. Nevertheless, having taxation as a weapon right from the start should make solving most of the unexpected problems that do arise a great deal easier.

---

218. Py Rathedan, *A Real Player Economy*. Stratics, May 2001.
   http://swg.stratics.com/content/feature/editorials/editorial051501.shtml.
   Gil Breau, *Online World Economy*. May 2002. http://swg-de.emr.net/a29.php.

219. In this context, I'm including object decay and other ways that wealth is effectively returned to the bank as different mechanisms of taxation.

Part of the issue with virtual-world economies is that they touch on so many aspects of design. Certain things have to be in place for the economy to function, and some of these are directly at odds with what would otherwise be preferred for gameplay reasons. For example, if there's a severe recession in the real world, then there's not a lot you can do about it; in a virtual world, you can go play some other world instead where there isn't a recession. Periodic recessions may be required to cool down overheated economies, but they're no fun for the players caught up in them.

This is particularly problematical for players who enjoy the economic side of virtual life. Primarily, this means gatherers and crafters rather than traders (although it will mean traders too in any world where people can't teleport about at will, buying stuff at source). In a celebrated attack on the hack-and-slay disposition of many virtual world designers, Sie Ming wrote an article[220]—*I Want to Bake Bread*[221]—pointing out some of the things that gatherers/crafters liked to do that weren't being addressed by existing virtual worlds. This was followed up a few months later by a second article[222]—*I Want to Forge Swords*—describing mechanisms by which designers might tackle these issues. It's essentially an argument for an integrated economy, whereby there is a symbiotic relationship between those who create objects and those who consume them (that is, supply and demand). Although some of the suggestions are too specialized for many virtual worlds[223], most are eminently sensible and should not be difficult to incorporate to some degree in any reasonably open-ended new design. That the sentiments the articles express have not become widespread is due mainly to three main factors: A lack of understanding by well-meaning designers who *want* to be nice to crafters, but somehow just can't get "it's all about combat" ideas out of their heads; designers who subscribe to the overall sentiments, but lack the time and budget to do them justice; designers who perfectly understand the issues, but are creating a virtual world that really *isn't* about crafting.

---

220. Sie Ming, *I Want to Bake Bread*. Stratics, December 2000. http://www.stratics.com/content/editorials/articles/bread.shtml.

221. A dig at *Shadowbane*'s "We don't play games to bake bread, we play them to crush!"

222. Sie Ming, *I Want to Forge Swords*. Stratics, May 2001. http://www.stratics.com/content/editorials/articles/swords.shtml.

223. Conversely, some virtual worlds (such as *A Tale in the Desert*) really take them to heart.

Crafting is an area where virtual-world economic activity doesn't match the real-world version it hopes to model. Real-world economies can grow through extension of manufacturing, improved production methods, and better distribution. In virtual worlds, all these have to be programmed in and are therefore inviolate. In the real world, I can figure out a new way to make toothbrushes that takes less time or creates better toothbrushes; in a virtual world, I can only do this if the designers have anticipated me.

So far, I've described how those players of virtual worlds who have an interest in the subject have undertaken economics research concerning virtual worlds. There are, however, economists who come to virtual worlds as economists rather than as players. Their starting point is almost invariably the economic set-up of the real world, in which light they look at the economies of virtual worlds.

This isn't a bad way to go about things, as long as you realize that there are differences between real-world and virtual-world economies. Although virtual worlds strive for realism when this helps immersion, nevertheless there are situations where the virtual cannot work the same as the real. Given that economies touch on so many aspects of virtual worlds, it would be surprising if they weren't affected by some of these.

In an underrated introduction[224] to the topic, John Beezer sets about assessing the differences between real-world and virtual-world economies. He lists the conditions that must be satisfied in order to create a virtual economy recognizably close enough to a real (mercantile) economy that it could be studied as such. The conditions are categorized under three headings:

- ➤ *Technical.* To do with the hardware and software.

- ➤ *Natural.* Facts of real life, which are so fundamental to real-world economies that they must be transferred to virtual worlds.

- ➤ *Cultural.* Related to the way that people interact within the virtual world.

Of these, the most interesting ones are the natural ones. Beezer makes some very uncomfortable points here. For example, a major economic motivator in real life is fear of dying. Indeed, an "economic good" can be legitimately defined as "any product or

---

224. John Beezer, *Virtual Currencies and Virtual Worlds.* 1996.
    http://adhostnt.adhost.com/beezer/resume/virtec.doc.

service that prolongs or protects life"—it's that fundamental. Death must be permanent, and also sufficiently unpleasant that players will take it seriously[225]. Characters must be able to kill one another, so that those characters with economic power can be prevented from abusing it (by armed insurrection). Virtual worlds without permanent death are therefore not going to work like the real world, right from the start.

Similarly, a lot of real world economic activity is concerned with the provision of food and shelter. People need to eat a range of foods, too, not just a certain number of calories worth. Virtual worlds where the necessities aren't necessary will also not work like the real world.

Thirdly, the way the real world's economy works is moderated by transaction costs. Resources are not spread out evenly: Some crops grow better in one place than they do elsewhere; some minerals occur in one type of rock but not another; some animals prefer a particular climate. The further away you are from where something is produced, the more it costs to get it. Teleporting should therefore require effort, and teleporting lots of things should be proportionately harder than teleporting just a few of them. Virtual worlds with instant teleportation in them also aren't going to have an economy like the real world's.

Beezer's points are all attainable: You could create a virtual world economy as he describes, and it would indeed work like the real one[226]. The thing is, most virtual worlds do *not* adhere to these principles, and therefore their economies are not going to make sense if designed along real-world lines. The reason they don't adhere to the principles is because if they did then their players would migrate to some other virtual world where "life" was easier—ironically, this is basically an economic argument.

The problem thus becomes one of creating a virtual world economy that looks to the players like a real economy but that behind the scenes is not. To this end, some of the ways in which virtual worlds differ from the real one can be used to their advantage. In the real world, for example, central banks aim to keep the money supply in equilibrium with the supply of goods; they do this by tweaking interest rates and by printing

---

225. Beezer suggests that one way of doing this would be to make players put down a deposit in real money that is lost when their character dies.

226. Beezer's aim was to get a close enough match that the economic variables of the virtual world could be altered experimentally, and the results used to draw conclusions about what would happen if the same were done in the real world.

banknotes. The virtual world *There.com*, on the other hand, plans on doing something that the real world can't—increasing the number of goods created so as to be in equilibrium with the money supply[227]. A second weapon they have is to maintain an exchange rate between their internal currency and the real-world dollar, so that the value of the newbie grubstake (and potentially other fixed-amount items) can be kept reasonably constant even if there is rampant inflation. It should be interesting to see how all this pans out.

There.com is a commercial virtual world that explicitly acknowledges the fact that its internal economy is linked to that of the real world. This has been something that has been evident for some time, ever since *Ultima Online* characters and equipment started being offered for sale on eBay[228]. Some virtual worlds encourage it as part of their business model; others condone it; most condemn it. Basically, though, it's going to happen with any large-scale commercial virtual world. It's just a case of whether this is a black-market, gray-market or white-market economy[229].

And so we come to perhaps the second most famous[230] of all writings about virtual worlds: Edward Castronova's *Virtual Worlds: A First-Hand Account of Market and Society on the Cyberian Frontier*[231]. From its somewhat dry title, you might guess that the paper itself hasn't been read by millions of people. Its conclusions, however, made national newspapers across the globe.

Castronova looks at Norrath (the name of *EverQuest*'s world) as if it were a real country. He does it absolutely straight, discarding objections that it's "just a game": If it's important to people, it's important to study it. Choosing Norrath on the grounds that it

---

227. Matthew Maier, *Can a Metaverse Have Inflation?* Business 2.0, March 2003. `http://www.business2.com/articles/mag/print/0,1643,47159,00.html`.

228. It went on before then, of course, albeit on a much smaller scale. Even in *MUD1*, a player tried to pay more experienced players to gain his character some levels when he went off on vacation (although I don't think anyone took him up on the offer). In *Shades*, people charged £100 to play your character up to wizard level for you. Still in the 1980s, someone on *MUD2* actually sold his wizard character to another player; the character was terminated when we found out.

229. Hi again, readers from 2053. How are phrases like "black market" viewed now?

230. After *A Rape in Cyberspace*.

231. Edward Castronova, *Virtual Worlds: A First-Hand Account of Market and Society on the Cyberian Frontier*. 2001. `http://papers.ssrn.com/sol3/papers.cfm?abstract_id=294828`.

was the biggest virtual world in terms of subscriptions and revenues[232], he spent four months playing and collecting data. This was supplemented by a survey that attracted 3,619 respondents over a two-day period; the results of this survey (weighted so as to account for the activities of less involved players who didn't hear about it) form the basis of Castronova's analysis.

Although this study is all very absorbing, particularly the sections concerning the different markets for commerce within Norrath, it's what Castronova further did with his data that hit the headlines. He noted that there was considerable trade between Norrath and the real world, and decided to collect further information concerning currency auctions so as to estimate its volume. He found that in May 2001 one Norrathian platinum piece sold for $0.0133 (that is, about one and a third cents), although by September it had dropped somewhat to $0.0098. He then looked at auctions of characters, to see if they were over- or under-valued according to this exchange rate. He found that a $1,000 character typically had more than $1,000 of wealth (in terms of platinum piece prices), so they were undervalued. It then occurred to him to figure out how much a character was typically worth per level, and use data from his user survey about the rate at which characters gain levels to calculate how much wealth Norrath generates as a whole.

He discovered that each level of a character is worth about $13 at auction. Across the whole of Norrath, players were adding around $15,000 of levels per hour. This leads to a gross national product (GNP) of about $135,000,000. Dividing this by the number of players to get the *per capita* GNP gives a figure of $2,266—roughly the same as that of Russia, and the 77th richest in the world. *This* is what attracted the attention of journalists. Virtual worlds may be inhabited by people you wouldn't want your daughter to marry (not that she'd ever meet one), but ye gods! They comprise the 77th richest country in the world! Maybe there's something important going on here that merits significant attention?

As pleased as I am whenever virtual worlds are being taken seriously, I nevertheless feel slightly uneasy here. GNP *per capita* is used as an indicator for the social and economic well being of a country; it's more to do with standards of living than absolute wealth. Although it is indeed frequently used to measure the relative wealth of countries, it's very sensitive to population figures; low-population countries that are faring

---

232. The biggest English-language one, this is; otherwise, he'd have had to learn Korean.

well will rate better than high-population counties that aren't, even though the higher-population countries have *as countries* far more wealth than the lower-population ones. Norrath may equate with Russia in GNP *per capita*, but I don't see Norrath financing a space program.

Castronova followed up his findings with a second paper[233] six months later that considered whether virtual economies might grow to the extent that they have an impact on real economies. From a virtual world designer's point of view, this is the more interesting paper, mainly because of the many philosophical points it raises. I personally believe that most of these can be addressed by an understanding that virtual world developers rule by divine right, but I appreciate how this may not be to many players' liking.

Castronova ends this second paper with a list of areas where virtual-world economies don't fit the standard models of real-world economies:

➤ In the real world, governments shouldn't fix prices. In virtual worlds, developers can create and destroy goods effortlessly, therefore they don't care about excess supply or demand. Some price-fixing could work in them.

➤ People in the real world would rather not work. People in virtual worlds would rather *not* not work—they get bored with nothing to do.

➤ In the real world, economic growth is good. In virtual worlds, increases in *per capita* wealth make it easier to accomplish tasks and therefore lower the challenge that they present. This means the world is less interesting, so growth can be bad.

➤ Real-world economics treats populations as fixed and assumes that their members' tastes and (initial) abilities are fixed. In virtual worlds, people can choose (through player class selection) to exhibit a subset of their abilities. They also can choose (in the context of the world) to be more than one person, and when to be alive.

Virtual world developers who employ real-world economists to design their virtual economies would do well to ensure these individuals have read *On Virtual Economies* first.

---

233. Edward Castronova, *On Virtual Economies*.2002. `http://papers.ssrn.com/sol3/papers.cfm?abstract_id=338500`.

Castronova's work suggests that people can make a living from virtual worlds. This is borne out by the facts, too: In an April 2001 discussion[234] among *Ultima Online* eBay sellers, it transpired that some of them were taking in nearly $20,000 a month. On the whole, it was much less than this, of course: High sellers are often resellers, who (to use a real estate analogy) invest hard cash in acquiring run-down "properties" that they then spend considerable time and effort "refurbishing" to sell at a profit.

As it happens, many big deals in *UO* involve what would be called real estate if it weren't actually virtual estate. People buy and sell houses the whole time. For an article[235] he was writing, Julian Dibbell tracked the sale of a three-story tower from seller to middle-man to buyer—just one such transaction of the thousands that are undertaken daily in the real world for imaginary items.

When you can sell the virtual, how real does that make it?

Well, it makes it real enough for real companies to want a presence in virtual worlds. After all, when you've run out of real-world territories to reach, where else can you go? *The Sims Online* started the trend by integrating McDonald's kiosks into their virtual world; although intended mainly as a marketing ploy (it certainly garnered a lot of publicity), this also had the interesting effect of making the virtual seem more real (and, perhaps in time, the real seem more virtual). It may be that the most important thing that economists have brought to virtual worlds is the realization that they are part of reality.

Whether this is a good thing or a bad thing remains to be seen, of course. If you bring the real into the virtual, you can't pick and choose what you get. Virtual McDonald's means virtual anti-McDonald's protesters[236].

This links rather nicely (although, as will immediately become apparent, not exactly convincingly) to our next topic: politics.

---

234. http://www.kanga.nu/archives/MUD-Dev-L/2001Q2/msg00242.php

235. Julian Dibbell, *The Unreal Estate Boom. Wired*, January 2003.
http://www.wired.com/wired/archive/11.01/gaming.html.

236. Tony Walsh, *Big Mac Attacked. Shift*, November 2002.
http://www.shift.com/print/web/425/1.html.

Politics

When players of virtual worlds refer to "politics," they're really talking about systems of government. Politics will be involved in any process by which people gain office, whether that office is head of a country or head of the local chapter of Hell's Angels. It can happen in any virtual world where players have the ability to gain power through the support of others. On the whole, though, players use the term in the context of offices that grant tangible, law-making powers to their holder, enforced by the virtual world itself. There are other forms of politics that are important for virtual worlds, especially so-called "issue" politics such as feminism; these, I cover where the particular issue is discussed. Thus, with one exception that I'll give at the end, this section examines the research that people have undertaken concerning the government of and in virtual worlds.

As with economics, most of the work done with politics in virtual worlds has come from players and designers who happen to have a background in that area. The best explanation[237] as to how and why political systems as a gameplay mechanic make good sense in virtual worlds is by Matthew Mihaly, who has experience of just such a system in his virtual world *Achaea* (plus a degree in Political Science from Cornell University). He characterizes political situations in general as lying along a spectrum from *static* to *dynamic*. Static systems, such as monarchies, have no competition for power at the top but may have some lower down. Dynamic systems, such as democracies, have competition for even the very highest offices. Clearly, dynamic is more fun, but it does need a static element or it becomes incapable of doing its job. If governments changed daily, they wouldn't get a lot done.

For designers of virtual worlds, implementing a formal political system is good for four[238] reasons:

> ➤ It provides a non-violent way for players to gain a sense of achievement and involvement in the world.

---

237. Matthew Mihaly, *Constructive Politics in a Massively Multiplayer Online Roleplaying Game*. Gamasutra, March 2000. http://www.gamasutra.com/features/20000309/mihaly_01.htm.

238. Matt's paper only gives the first three, but because he's a reviewer of this book he gets to add another one that he missed.

➤ It creates a class of opinion leaders. When the live team wants to make a major change, it only has to win over the opinion leaders, not the whole player base. Opinion leaders take much of the flak that would otherwise be directed at the live team.

➤ It provides an incentive for experienced players to help newbies.

➤ It can provide another dimension to gameplay, as there are many interesting social dynamics that arise in situations where characters have formal control over aspects of other characters' lives. This also increases the possibility that "storyline" content can emerge from player actions.

As for why *players* would want a political system, that's not so clear. Many of the reasons that people care about who governs them in real life don't apply in virtual worlds. They don't, for example, react the same way to despots: In the real world, citizens may fear for their lives, but in virtual worlds they simply leave if someone is taking the fun out of playing. Matt narrows down the reasons that players might genuinely want a system of in-world government to the following (none of which are particularly strong):

➤ *Comradeship.* Players connect with other players in their community, and care what happens to them. Comradeship is good for a virtual world, but its presence isn't dependent on the existence of an in-world government.

➤ *Public services.* Players get access to facilities they wouldn't get access to if there wasn't a government. This is only the case because it is forced by the virtual world design, of course, so it's really an artificial reason.

➤ *Glory by association.* Your faction does well, so you feel good about it.

This all assumes, of course, that some players will actually *want* to be leaders. Matt concludes that there are four basic motivators involved (yet another set of bullet points—sorry folks!):

➤ The desire for power (over other players)

➤ The desire for glory (that is, recognition by your peers)

➤ The challenge

➤ The desire to help

Checkpoint: Let's see how the player types I described in Chapter 3 fit into this. Power is clearly the domain of politicians and glory is that of griefers. The other player types are more general: Challenge is a motivator for both opportunists and planners (that is, achievers); the desire to help is present in both networkers and friends (that is, socializers). Because of what politicking involves, I'd guess that more opportunists than planners would be interested in the challenge aspect, as it's quite a long-term activity. I also suspect that fewer friends than networkers will want to get involved, as the former tend to interact mainly with the people they know, rather than the population in general. This means that potential leaders would be in the front, top-left corner of the 3D player interest graph shown in Figure 3.4.

Okay, back to Matt's analysis....

The critical thing about creating a system of offices is that they must have meaning. Power doesn't itself imply meaning: There should be perceived benefits for letting people have the powers in the first place. This is best done through the provision of public services, but there are other ways that can work well, too. Comradeship comes from the collective fear of, and responses to, threats to the organization concerned; glory by association follows from this (assuming that the organization does occasionally triumph).

As for the type of government, Matt advocates a republic or democracy with a hierarchy of offices (rather than standalone "mayor" posts or whatever). Democracy is best, if only because players who live in real-world democracies won't accept anything else[239]; hierarchies are desirable so that people can get a taste of power without having to challenge influential players for the top job, and because it's another ladder to climb. The nature of the hierarchy doesn't have to be the same as in real life governments, because there is no need to build in "checks and balances"—real-live governments can abolish elections, but virtual ones can't if the programming enforces them. This means that the system of government can be designed to address directly the reasons for having it, making it more fun for the players.

The hardest part of government design is deciding what powers the player holders of offices have. With too little, the offices are little more than sinecures; with too much, life for governed players can become unbearable to the extent that they leave for some

---

239. This isn't to say that there can't be some organizations within the virtual world that work to a different system—for example, a religious hierarchy that works like a monarchy.

other virtual world[240]. There's also the problem of law enforcement: Should the government only make laws that the virtual world itself can enforce (for example, to ban stealing it throws a switch that stops the "steal" command from working) or can it add other laws ("spying," "treason") that would need police and a judicial system to enforce? Even then, what could the punishments be? Imprisonment in a virtual world isn't quite as big a deal as in the real one. What alternative justice systems are there[241]?

Matthew Mihaly aside, most of the other articles about politics in virtual worlds concern how particular virtual worlds implement the concept. This is one field where large-scale graphical worlds are breaking new ground, because their textual predecessors didn't often have the kind of player numbers that made such a system viable. There are exceptions, of course: *Achaea* itself, and (as mentioned in the Mr. Bungle case) *LambdaMOO*.

The fact that *LambdaMOO* had politics might suggest that there would be dozens of academic papers describing the goings-on. That there isn't is something of a surprise; *A Rape in Cyberspace* pretty much says all that has been said. There is a good paper[242] about the legal system that emerged from *LambdaMOO*, but nothing[243] about its politics.

Freed from any legacy of the past, designers have come up with some very interesting approaches to politics. Nexon's *Dark Ages*[244], for example, uses a notion of "political clout," Clout is a tangible measure of political ability attached to a character and granted by the formal support of other characters; it must be spent to attain office and to execute the political control that comes with it. Roy Wilson, Jr. gives a good explanation[245] of how this works, at the same time illustrating the refreshing absence of serious grief play that it engenders. The theory that underpins it is described in a rather more

---

240. Or, less problematically, for another country/guild/whatever in the same virtual world that has a more palatable government.

241. For some suggestions, see *Derek Sanderson, Online Justice Systems.* Gamasutra, 2000. http://www.gamasutra.com/features/20000321/sanderson_pfv.htm.

242. Jennifer L. Mnookin, *Virtual(ly) Law: The Emergence of Law in LambdaMOO. Journal of Computer-Mediated Communication* Vol. 2 (1). 1996. http://www.ascusc.org/jcmc/vol2/issue1/lambda.html.

243. Nothing I have found, this is. As usual, it's quite possible that there is an entire series of books on *LambdaMOO* politics that I have blithely failed to notice.

244. http://www.darkages.com

245. http://www.darkages.com/2002/community/lore/Paladine_Politica/toc.html

difficult article[246] by *Dark Ages's* designer Dave Kennerly, which is hard to follow without knowing what the virtual world is all about beforehand.

Another virtual world planned to have a strong political element is *Star Wars Galaxies*. Here, drawing on ideas from *Lineage*, politics is regarded as a profession; it has a skill tree associated with it, and characters must have the right skill before they can take political office. *SWG's* design incorporates a very flexible "player associations" system that allows players to form large groups to focus on some aspect of the virtual world; politics is one such aspect. There is some concern[247] as to how griefer-resistant this all is, however, especially as some of the powers that players can obtain could make virtual life quite unpleasant for other players.

Atriarch follows the general trend by allowing players to build their own cities, install their own governments for those cities, set taxes and laws, instigate trade routes, and so on. *Shadowbane*, on the other hand, goes for a purely guild-based system, allowing guilds to swear fealty to other guilds like *Asheron's Call* players do to other individuals. Guilds can build cities, choose which government type to have (monarchy, oligarchy, republic, democracy), and set tax rates for shops.

So, the ideas are there, if it's not yet clear what kind of consensus solution will emerge. It's important to note that with the exception of *LambdaMOO*, all the examples I've described so far have concerned in-context government of virtual worlds. Overall control of virtual worlds does not, in general, use the same systems. You may be able to elect a town mayor, but that mayor can't change patch release dates, subscription rates, or the extinctness of a virtual volcano. That said, not all virtual worlds are run by individual megalomaniacs, and some do involve players in real-world policy decisions (*A Tale in the Desert*, for example).

I've found two reasonably good studies that (as part of wider investigations into the subject) look at how virtual worlds are governed. Both were written by groups of students in 1998/99.

The report[248] from Stanford University compares the approaches of virtual worlds, chat systems, email mailing lists, and newsgroups. Different types of government are

246. Dave Kennerly, *Dark Ages Politics in Theory and Practice.* Imaginary Realities Vol. 3 (9), September 2000.

247. Py Rathedan, *Py's Politics.* http://swg-de.emr.net/e3.php.

248. Jed Burgess, Michael Jahr, Jonathan Keljo, Josh Schroeder and Wilson Sweitzer, *Controlling the Virtual World: Governance of On-Line Communities.* Stanford University, 1999. http://www-cse.stanford.edu/classes/cs201/projects-98-99/controlling-the-virtual-world/index.html.

described, along with their strengths and weaknesses concerning the online services under discussion. Virtual worlds[249] are usually feudal by nature, with a monarch having overlord powers over an oligarchy that has powers over the rest of the player base. Some virtual worlds are anarchies, which allow only for ostracism and flaming to influence deviant behavior. *LambdaMOO* was highly unusual in that not only was it a democracy, but it was a direct-participation democracy rather than a representative democracy.

The joint report[250] from MIT and Harvard Law School mentions the same monarchy-like hierarchical power structure that is typical of most virtual world administrations, but notes that there *is* a form of democracy at work because players can choose which world to play. If they don't like what the government is doing, they are at liberty to leave and find somewhere more appealing. In other words, they can vote with their feet. This makes virtual world developers accountable in a way that real-life autocrats are not. The report also looks at *LambdaMOO*, and concludes that the ultimate failure of its democracy was evidence that this is not a viable form of government for virtual communities. The LambdaMOO developers had power but didn't want the responsibility that went with it, so they passed power to the players. Unfortunately, the one power they couldn't pass—control of the physical hardware—overrode all the other powers. Attempting to separate social from technical issues does not work when the social is rooted in the technical.

The control of virtual worlds only involves player politics if it involves players. So far, the experiments in that direction have had mixed results[251], and the paradigm is for a developer hegemony to rule. It's conceivable that players could set up cooperatives to develop and run virtual worlds on democratic or shared-ownership principles, but it's not going to happen until the cost of creating and operating commercial virtual worlds has dropped substantially.

---

249. The report only considers textual ones, which isn't entirely surprising given the date.

250. Jennifer Chung, Jason Linder, Ian Liu, Wendy Seltzer and May Tse, *Democratic Structures in Cyberspace*. MIT, 1998. `http://www.swiss.ai.mit.edu/6095/student-papers/fall98-papers/democracy/whitepaper.html`.
There were some other interesting papers that year, too.
`http://www.swiss.ai.mit.edu/6095/student-papers/fall98-papers/student-papers.html`.

251. For a review, see Charles J. Stivale, *"Help Manners": Cyber-Democracy and its Vicissitudes*. Department of Romance Languages and Literatures, Wayne State University, 1995.
`http://www.utdallas.edu/~cynthiah/lingua_archive/help_manners.html`.

Something that is rarely mentioned is the possibility of using virtual worlds to make political statements about the real world. The reason, of course, is that designers are wary of making overtly political points for fear of putting off prospective players. Nevertheless, as we shall see in Chapter 7, "Towards a Critical Aesthetic," it's quite possible to use virtual worlds to make artistic statements; politics drives some people's art.

Another point that is not made very often[252] is that if virtual worlds are places with populations and governments and a currency with a real-world exchange rate, at what point should they be considered to be countries in their own right? *EverQuest*'s population is bigger than that of Iceland, Qatar, Luxembourg, Equatorial Guinea.... If Malta can send a representative to the United Nations and accept ambassadors from other countries, why can't Norrath?

And now we reach the final piece I'd like to mention about politics in virtual worlds. This one really *is* about politics—genuine, polemical, oh-my-gawd-get-me-out-of-here ideological theory applied to virtual worlds.

Brace yourself....

Using a Marxism *versus* capitalism line of reasoning, Annalee Newitz argues[253] that the freedom to be a different person online is only illusory. The Marxist perspective is that people work to get beyond their material needs, thereby acquiring an intellectual freedom; work is therefore the fundamental that gives life meaning. In a capitalist system, this is not the case: You sell your labor to other people and must therefore behave as *they* require. This means adopting a work persona different from your real self (smiling at customers when you're not happy, working on despite being tired, and so on).

Newitz's argument is that people in capitalist societies are so used to believing that different social environments require them to manifest different personalities that they create one automatically when they enter a virtual world. This virtual personality has no direct link to the material world, and therefore it is surplus, worn only for pleasure.

---

252. The first place I saw it mentioned was in a 2002 series of three speculative articles by a player who used the handle Moron (it must have seemed a good idea at the time).
http://www.joystick101.org/story/2002/2/12/14207/1757
http://www.joystick101.org/story/2002/2/13/124943/302
http://www.joystick101.org/story/2002/7/11/142124/517

253. Annalee Newitz, *Surplus Identity On-Line. Bad Subjects*. 18, January 1995.
http://eserver.org/bs/18/newitz.html.

Surplus is capitalism's promise, and people are seduced by it. Individuals in a capitalist society don't consider that they work to survive; instead, they feel that they work so as to produce a surplus of free time. They believe that free time liberates them from their material needs, whereas really it strips their lives of meaning (because meaning comes from labor). From this perspective, adding an extra, unnecessary self merely increases the number of partial selves that an individual has but that can never (except by adopting the Marxist approach) be reconciled. People would be better off if they stayed with the real instead of flirting with the virtual.

In other words, your virtual self is meaningless because you can't do what makes your life meaningful in virtual worlds.

This is a very powerful point, whether or not you accept the Marxist reasoning by which it was derived. Personally, I don't know enough about the ideology to be able to comment on it[254]; I do know about virtual worlds, though, and (as I've argued in this book) I believe strongly that they bring multiple selves together rather than keep them apart. You may not be able to change your work self, but you *can* blend your virtual self and your real self together into one. Thus, although it may from a Marxist standpoint be possible to level all manner of charges against virtual worlds, I don't think that the installation of contradictory identities is one that necessarily holds.

Autobiography

Virtual worlds have such an effect on people that often they want to write about their experiences. Although most of this takes the form of what might be called "fan fiction," a little is more personal. Some players keep logs, some keep diaries; some write essays, some write poetry. A very small few write full-blown autobiographies that cover the period of their life that they spent in (and out) of virtual worlds. As the ethnography of an individual, these are remarkable resources; as a recounting of their author's own, private hero's journey, they're invaluable.

I am aware of only two[255] such autobiographies: those of Julian Dibbell and Indra Sinha.

---

254. This is rarely a barrier for more politicized people, of course.

255. As usual, this doesn't mean there aren't scores more out there.

My Tiny Life[256] concerns the three intense months that Julian Dibbell spent in *LamdbaMOO*. It begins with a retelling of *A Rape in Cyberspace*, then launches into Dibbell's experiences as a player in this post-Mr. Bungle world. Although the book chronicles these goings-on very well, actually it isn't *really* about them at all: Instead, what it charts is how by playing *LambdaMOO*, Dibbell overcame the insecurities he was experiencing about his love for his then girlfriend (now wife). The virtual world gave him an outlook on the real world that he didn't have previously, enabling him to look at himself in new ways. From this, he developed a stronger sense of self-worth, through which he was able to overcome any lingering doubts about commitment that he still had. Dibbell doesn't say this directly in his book, but it is hinted at throughout; it's clear he feels genuine gratitude to *LambdaMOO* for what it taught him. Basically, *LambdaMOO* was where he finally grew up.

The picture of *LambdaMOO* itself that emerges is vaguely disturbing, like some ghastly reality TV experiment gone hideously awry. All you can do in *LambdaMOO* is create objects and talk to people. There are some elements of gameplay within individual creations, but these do not connect with one another cohesively. All activity therefore revolves around creating (for which a strict quota system exists) or talking and emoting. This doesn't leave great scope for people to have fun: They're pretty well limited to acquiring quota (which acts not so much as a currency as *Dark Ages*-like clout) or performing acts of virtual sex—both of which involve tiresome interpersonal politics. Some of what Dibbell describes should give designers pause for thought, in particular the *schmoo wars* (where players rose up against the "power elite" that they felt governed *LambdaMOO*); most of it seems incredibly shallow and petty, however. This, of course, is part of Dibbell's point.

The book has some nice stylistic touches that help blur the lines between the real and the virtual; in particular, events that occur in real life are written like transcripts of a *LambdaMOO* session whereas events in *LambdaMOO* appear in conventional narrative form. Its main strength, however, is its content: It is the perfect riposte to anyone who tells players of virtual worlds that they should "get a life!" For this, we should all be grateful.

The second autobiographical work I'm going to mention is a much harder read, not least because it consists of over a hundred very small, choppy chapters. *The*

---

256. Julian Dibbell, *My Tiny Life: Crime and Passion in a Virtual World.* London, Fourth Estate, 1999.

Cybergypsies[257] is Indra Sinha's account of his time in *Shades* and *Void*[258] (which he switched to once British Telecom closed down *Shades*).

Yes, *Shades* and *Void*—his experiences predate Julian Dibbell's by several years.

Again, what the book purports to be about isn't what it's *actually* about. Its subtext is the author's relationship with the love of his life (his wife, whom he greatly neglected while playing in virtual worlds). This time, though, the view expressed seems somewhat harsher: Ultimately, Sinha stopped playing because he realized that events he thought important in the virtual world were trifling and inconsequential when compared with events of the real world[259].

The book consists of three main threads—a device to highlight the way that the real and the virtual are interwoven. The first of these threads concerns virtual worlds; the second concerns reality; the third concerns computer viruses. This last one does not sit at all well with the other two: Although *Shades* and reality overlap (Sinha met *Shades* players in real life), the viruses thread could be unpicked without affecting the integrity of the whole work one jot. Its presence serves mainly to propose an analogy: Playing virtual worlds introduces an addiction into the lives of players that can be as disruptive for them as the arrival of a virus is on a personal computer. This works if the payload that is delivered by playing virtual worlds is not considered benign, but (as someone who believes that in general it *is* benign) I'm not convinced by it myself.

From the preceding it may appear that Sinha is contemptuous of virtual worlds, but this is not the case. His fondness for *Void*, if not *Shades*, is apparent and sincere. Rather his attitude seems to be that virtual worlds are places you visit to find out what your problems are and where you can grow as you address these problems, but that once this is done you will inevitably come back to reality. I wouldn't disagree with this, except to note that you can be "master of the two worlds"; later return is possible.

---

257. Indra Sinha, *The Cybergypsies: A Frank Account of Love, Life and Travels on the Electronic Frontier*. London, Scribner, 1999.

258. He calls it *Vortex*, but it's *Void*.

259. There's no indication as to whether his wife got any more attention once he directed his energies toward Amnesty International than she did when he was playing *Shades* though.

Sinha does, however, have one particularly serious concern about virtual worlds that he expresses as "what we imagine, we make." In *Void*, one of his friends described an incident where she and others ate another character at a feast; she further explained that far "worse" things often happened. It was okay, though, because the virtual world was imaginary, and anything done in the imagination is "safe." Sinha's reaction was that no, it is not safe: People use the same emotional faculties in the real world that they use in virtual worlds, and by tolerating a sickening virtual action they are also modifying what they would tolerate in reality; they are becoming desensitized. If imaginary cruelty is considered to be acceptable, real cruelty inevitably becomes more acceptable than it was previously.

Although this is a powerful observation[260], it is quite selective. I agree that such things do indeed occur in virtual worlds, but would counter that in the majority of cases the virtual world is formulated such that positive changes in attitude greatly outweigh negative ones. Designers bear the primary responsibility of ensuring that this should be so, although the players themselves are also culpable: The cannibalistic feast in *Void* was enacted entirely through emotes, not some bizarre "eat person" command. Any virtual world set up (deliberately or otherwise) to change players' attitudes in ways that society finds unacceptable is for society to deal with. As far as I know, there are no such virtual worlds in existence; that's not to say that this will always be the case, however.

In Sinha's book, his father-in-law gets interested in Scientology. The way that this eminently sensible man is gradually drawn in as he strives to gain different "levels" of awareness is contrasted with the way that players of virtual worlds find themselves on leveling treadmills that they somehow can't leave. It's an amusing analogy: virtual world designers as theocrats.

It also provides a handy link to the next topic....

---

260. And one regularly used as ammunition against the portrayal of violence in computer games, movies, comics, rap music, and cartoons (but less so against the real violence shown in TV news and documentaries).

Theology

Theology? Why would a theologist…?

Then it hits you: As the real is to the virtual, so the spiritual is to the real. Theologists should be more interested in virtual worlds than perhaps anyone else except the designers of such worlds themselves.

I have two points to make before I begin this discussion.

Firstly, I'm an atheist. I'm going to be talking about religions here, and try as I might to be objective it's inevitable that my views are going to show through in places. If this is likely to offend you, please skip the remainder of this section.

Secondly, I'm an atheist. I regard ethics and morality as important issues, but I don't associate them with particular religious doctrines. Therefore, some of the things I'll be talking about might not seem to be theology-related at all. If this apparent belittling of faith is likely to offend you, you too should skip the remainder of this section.

Okay, so let's get started….

A July 1999 poll[261] in *The Mud Journal* asked "What kind of Mud would you like more of?" Of the 362 people who responded 10.3% indicated that they would like to see more religious-themed virtual worlds. This was lower than any of the other genres (horror 24.2%, futuristic 21.8%, old western 19.8%, sci-fi 13.3%, real world events 10.6%) but nevertheless 10.3% is not insignificant.

Even so, many players and designers would be surprised to learn that there are virtual worlds in existence right now that were built as places of worship for real-life religions. I don't just mean techno-paganism, either, although this was among the first to be studied[262]; there are virtual worlds created as places for people to participate in main-stream religious services, too. The E-church[263], for example, was set up by a group of

---

261. Tony Allen, *MUD Stats. The Mud Journal*, July 1999.
    `http://mudworld.inetsolve.com/TMJ/editorials/jul99/allen2.php3`.

262. Stephen D. O'Leary, *Cyberspace as Sacred Space: Communicating Religion on Computer Networks. Journal of the American Academy of Religion* Vol. 64 (4), 1996.

263. So as to protect it, this is not its real name. Interestingly, it's a graphical world, rather than the textual kind that might be expected.

Christians in the charismatic tradition, and has met with some success at reproducing some of the essential features of a conventional church service[264], if not the experience.

Technopagans attempt to create a virtual space that can be sanctified as a place in which spirit is manifested. The E-church's congregation, on the other hand, tries to replicate the real in the virtual; it only partially succeeds, because the technology gets in the way of some aspects of the service. Nevertheless, the E-church is adapting to account for these, and also to exploit some of the advantages that virtuality brings.

Whether these experiments will lead to more or less real-world religious activity in virtual worlds depends on the specific religions involved, of course. It would take something of a debate before conventional Christian churches allowed baptisms or weddings in virtual worlds, for example; the Roman Catholic Eucharist presents particularly thorny problems.

In an examination[265] of religions and cyberspace (including virtual worlds), Lorne L. Dawson noted the following additional traps awaiting anyone intending to move any religion from the real to the virtual—or, indeed, to create a new religion for virtual spaces only:

➤ The propagation of misinformation and misunderstandings

➤ Loss of control over religious materials

➤ Loss of group identity among practitioners of religions

➤ Negative effects of the interface

➤ Blurring the frames of reality

For the most part, virtual worlds are not regarded by their inhabitants as places where religion is important. Morality is important, but the basis of this—religious or otherwise—is rarely mentioned. Not only would it often be non-immersive to bring real-world religion into a virtual world, but (along with discussions about politics) it offers

---

264. Ralph Schroeder, Noel Heather and Raymond M. Lee, *The Sacred and the Virtual: Religion in Multi-User Virtual Reality. Journal of Computer Mediated Communication* Vol. 4 (2), December 1998. http://jcmc.huji.ac.il/vol4/issue2/schroeder.html.

265. Lorne. L. Dawson, *Doing Religion in Cyberspace: The Promise and the Perils. The Council of Societies for the Study of Religion Bulletin* Vol. 30 (1), 2001. http://www.arts.uwaterloo,ca/SOC/relcybercsssr.htm.

a good opportunity to fall out with your friends. That said, many virtual worlds do have a formal or informal system of etiquette in place for the bulk of their players, along with a stronger system of ethics for their administrators. Some of the latter go back years: The MUSH favorite *Amberyl's Wizard Ethics*[266] has remained unchanged since 1994, and *MUD2*'s *Good Wiz Guide*[267] dates back to *MUD1*.

In an early analysis[268] of the problem of determining an ethical system for virtual worlds, Chuck Haeberle poses the question: Should the moral values and ethics which we consider to be valid in real life be applied to the virtual world, or should we look at the virtual world as existing with a separate set of ethics? Ethical standards exist wherever humans exist, so virtual worlds—even anarchic ones—must have them.

Haeberle notes that a virtual world operates over a potentially unending period, and that its players define how it is played by how they play it. They must always abide by the rules of the virtual world in which they play, but if they don't like those rules they can play elsewhere. For this reason, some real-world values *must* be carried over—they're part of the value judgment.

Virtual worlds are an extension of real life; the interaction between players gives rise to a real-life morality that makes virtual worlds more than the mere games they would otherwise be. In other words, it's because *we're* real that virtual worlds must be treated in moral terms as if they were equally real.

That said, there are big differences between virtual worlds and reality. An ethical system that has evolved for real life may need to be adapted if it is to hold in virtual worlds, too. This is the position of Michael Cranford, who identifies[269] the desire to be more greatly immersed as the great allure of virtual worlds. Virtual worlds offer the prospect of existence without limits; yet without limits, whence comes meaning? If everything is possible, if risk and consequence are not factors, why would anybody treat other people in a dignified or sensitive manner? Haeberle is right in that people

266. Lydia Leong, *Amberyl's Wizard Ethics.* http://www.godlike.com/mushman/wiz-ethics.html.

267. Not available to non-wizzes—sorry!

268. Chuck Haeberle, *An Essay on Ethics and Virtual Reality.* http://www.legendmud.org/Bibliography/texts/essay.html.

269. Michael Cranford, *The Social Trajectory of Virtual Reality: Substantive Ethics in a World Without Constraints. Technology and Society* Vol. 18, 1996. http://sundoulos.com/articles.aspx?in=18.

should bring real-world morality into virtual worlds, but that doesn't mean they *do*. Furthermore, if other people treat you badly in this virtual world, there's no guarantee they won't follow you to whichever other virtual world you go to instead. Cranford is ultimately pessimistic, seeing the ethical systems of virtual worlds as potentially eroding those of reality. Because virtual worlds have fewer constraints than reality, some degree of retrogressive behavior is inevitable.

Cranford's argument is basically anthropological. It's interesting, therefore, to see what *bona fide* students of anthropology have to say on the subject of religion in virtual worlds. Many anthropologists take the view that a culture without religion is no culture at all; however, they have quite inclusive views as to what "religion" may be. Any system of beliefs in supernatural forces—with accompanying symbols and rituals—that serve to help people make sense of the world is a religion; deities are not a necessary component. From this perspective, do virtual worlds have anything in them that would qualify as "religion"? If so, it strengthens their claim to separate culture status; if not, it weakens it.

There is an argument[270] that although virtual world cultures don't usually have an explicit religion, nevertheless they do have so many components that are analogous to what religions have that they could be treated as if they did have religions[271]. For example, logging in is an acceptance of the "truth" of virtual worlds, signifying a belief in the non-real—a very ritualistic process.

That there is, for certain people, a religious aspect to virtual worlds is the conclusion of Jen Clodius in her discussion[272] of religion in *DragonMUD*. She noted that there were many traditional religious symbols in *DragonMUD*, but that these were present entirely for their evocative effects; if *DragonMUD* did indeed have a religious aspect, it would need to have symbols of its own. It did have some ceremony (particularly concerning the raising of players to the rank of wizard, that is, junior administrator). Could it be argued that this was basically a religious act at root?

---

270. I first encountered this in a 1998 anthropology paper by a student at the University of Twente in The Netherlands. Unfortunately, although I have a hard copy of the original, it does not bear the name of the author, nor is it any longer available on the Internet.

271. In other words, they "virtually" have a religion.

272. Jennifer A. Clodius, *Ritual and Religion in DragonMUD*.
    `http://dragonmud.com/people/jen/ritual.html`.

Starting with a very well-known anthropological definition[273] of religion from Clifford Geertz, she invited members of the *DragonMUD* community to debate the suggestion that there was a religious aspect to that virtual world. Twenty-five participated in the resulting discussion. Taking a check-list approach to each element of Geertz's definition in turn, the players decided

➤ *DragonMUD* has symbols. Some objects have a permanent place in the virtual world and have real-life significance to players, therefore they act as symbols.

➤ These symbols can act to establish long-lasting moods and motivations. Furthermore, they do so *in themselves*; however, these motivations are primarily social. On the whole, the consensus was that the virtual world's symbols did satisfy this clause of Geertz's criteria, but not everyone agreed.

➤ There are conceptions of a general order of existence in *DragonMUD*, assuming the context is *DragonMUD* itself and not the real world.

➤ DragonMUD's symbols clothe the conceptions of order with an aura of factuality because of their permanence and their meaning to the players.

➤ DragonMUD has a unique realism. It's less clear whether the clothing of conceptions of an order of existence in factuality caused this, though.

Clodius concludes that for some players there is a religious aspect to DragonMUD, but she is hesitant to go beyond that due to what she perceives as her own possible cynicism concerning their motivations. Personally, I believe her cynicism to be more than justified.

The *DragonMUD* players involved in the discussion criticized Geertz's definition for its omission of any reference to a sense of "awe" or of the "sacred." I think perhaps they missed the point: These are implicit in Geertz's definition, which the players did not realize in their haste to show that *DragonMUD* did indeed have a religious aspect to it. If more of them had understood what Geertz was actually saying with his definition, they might have been less quick to assert that it applied to their virtual world. This

---

273. "A religion is a system of symbols, which acts to establish powerful, pervasive and long-lasting moods and motivations by formulating conceptions of a general order of existence and clothing these conceptions with such an aura of factuality that the moods and motivations seem uniquely realistic."
Clifford Geertz, *Religion as a Cultural System*. Chapter 4 of Clifford Geertz, *The Interpretation of Cultures*. New York, Basic Books, 1973.

isn't to say that it doesn't apply, of course—some players expressed that they did have a sense of awe concerning *DragonMUD*—but rather that the debate was incomplete[274].

So far, I've described what religion has to say about virtual worlds, but not what virtual worlds have to say about religion. This is no different to what I've done in discussing other disciplines, of course: Virtual world designers may be interested in what geographers have to say about virtual worlds, but they're not concerned with the problems that virtual worlds give geographers—that's for geographers to worry about. In the case of religion, however, the creator/created analogy is too strong: The questions that virtual world designers pose for theologians are questions that PCs and NPCs pose for designers.

In her book *The Pearly Gates of Cyberspace*[275], Margaret Wertheim argues that what cyberspace offers (in both its virtual-world present and its cyberpunk promise) is akin to the world-view of medieval Christians. Back then, people had the notion that they were simultaneously embedded in both a physical world and a spiritual world. Wertheim charts this view through various scientific and mathematical spaces until she arrives at cyberspace, which has a physical/virtual split that mirrors the physical/spiritual split of the medieval age.

This book is a great starting place if you want to look into the spiritual and the virtual more fully. It's not specific to virtual worlds, but they are mentioned, and what she says certainly applies to them. Her contention is that human beings have always had "other worlds," whether Aboriginal Dreamtime or Greek Olympus, and that Western cultures in particular have always associated immateriality with spirituality[276]. Virtual worlds' offer of death that isn't death is precisely what is promised by many religions. The level system of virtual worlds is like Dante's description of the nine circles of Hell, the nine cornices of Purgatory and the nine spheres of Heaven: Players advance in experience and understanding until their ultimate ascendance to wizardhood. Cyberspace is being claimed as a realm for the self; this book explores how it could be a realm for the soul.

---

274. *DragonMUD*'s creator, Caern, was present at the debate and admitted to no feeling of awe at all. His reason, which every designer of virtual worlds will immediately understand, was, "it's hard to be awed by the wires one's pulled oneself."

275. Margaret Wertheim, *The Pearly Gates of Cyberspace: A History of Space from Dante to the Internet*. London, Virago, 1999.

276. She doesn't mean this in the atheistic sense, that is, "spirituality is immaterial to me, mate." On the other hand, she doesn't take the truth or otherwise of spiritual existence as a given; she talks about the beliefs of others, but does not push her own beliefs (whatever they may be). Her book is very objective in this regard.

Although the analogy between virtual and spiritual spaces is easy to draw, the consequences of it are not. Wertheim identifies the morality and ethics present in virtual spaces as much harder to explain than is the case for spiritual spaces. Although she takes some tentative steps, she never really comes close to answering her question. The moral underpinnings of virtual worlds cannot be explained in a self-contained fashion by the same appeal to the word of some deity that is available for spiritual worlds.

Kevin Kelly's *Out of Control*[277] makes a very interesting point about the recursive nature of creation. In a wide-ranging eclectic mix of cyberholism, Kelly invests a few pages talking about virtual worlds. At first, this is the usual stuff about MUDs, MOOs, and quotes from Turkle. Then, however, he makes his killer observation.

The ultimate "god game" would be a vast world, set into motion with a few well-chosen rules and populated by PCs and autonomous, AI-driven NPCs. Time would pass, relationships and interrelationships would form and tangle. All entities—PCs and NPCs—would alter their world, physically and socially, until it evolved into something quite different from how it started. At that point, the god who created it *descends into it*.

Kelly's is not a religious book, let alone a Christian one, but he uses a Christian analogy to pursue his argument. He describes the Biblical story of the Creation in terms of a designer creating a world. At the end, the designer (that is, God) creates a simulacrum of himself that he instantiates as Adam. He makes Adam just like he himself is, with free will and creativity. He turns Adam loose in the world.

Mankind is now repeating the exercise; we are creating our own worlds. Is this the final act that completes God's genesis—makes us truly the copies of him that we were always intended to be—or is it a foolish audacity?

Put another way, is it a sacrament or a blasphemy? If you accept God as the creator of the universe, it *must* be one or the other—there's no partial solution. By creating a virtual world, either you are completing God's plan that humanity be in his image (sacrament, but does this mean God's work is now done?), or you are mocking him through your arrogance and false pride (blasphemy, but does this mean humanity can never consider itself truly to be in God's image?).

---

277. Kevin Kelly, *Out of Control*. New York, Addison Wesley, 1994.

Either way, just like God's creation of mankind, any free-willed virtual creatures the designer creates will not be under the designer's control: The creator has to pass control to the created. The designer—whether you or God—must "let go to win"[278].

A third book, *TechGnosis*[279] by Erik Davis, reverses the argument: By creating virtual worlds, we become the gods that we weren't before. Like Wertheim, Davis takes the point of view that the technical merely hides the same mystical that humanity has always sought (although his approach is less anthropological and more evangelical). Virtual worlds are just one example of where this happens—the scope of the book is much wider. Nevertheless, in the few pages that he dedicates to the virtual worlds, Davis raises a number of interesting points.

Firstly, he notes that virtual worlds of all kinds use magic as a metaphor to explain the kinds of things that you can do in them that you can't do in reality. They present a mystical fiction to account for the technological fact.

Secondly, he observes that permanent death crystallizes a philosophical question concerning immersion. Do we identify with our online selves because they are as liberated as we want to be, or because they are as constrained as we really are[280]?

Finally, he makes a connection with Hinduism. The word *avatar*, used in (mainly graphical) virtual worlds to denote the virtual object under the player's control, has Hindu roots. It came to virtual worlds through *Habitat,* although it was also used in the (single-player) *Ultima* series (of which many virtual world designers were aware) so it didn't need any explaining to them[281]. In Hindu belief, avatars have two identities: As

---

278. An idea that I don't explore here but which might nevertheless give people food for thought is: Under what circumstances would you, as a designer, let your AI-controlled NPCs know that you exist? Why wouldn't you do it immediately? Why not periodically? Why not once they've reached the ability to create virtual worlds within their virtual world? And how do your answers to these questions compare with the choices apparently made by (the Christian) God?

279. Erik Davis, *TechGnosis*. New York, Harmony Books, 1998.

280. He doesn't ask whether the identification could be due to the fact that ultimately they *are* us, which is my own point of view.

281. It was also, you may recall, the name of a very early virtual world on PLATO.

separate from the gods; as indivisible from the gods. Virtual world avatars have the same duality of separation (two worlds) and identity (same person), but they apply the concept in reverse: People become gods; gods don't become people. Davis remains undecided as to whether this is an ascent or a descent of the spirit.

The similarity between virtual world existence and Hindu mysticism has been noted many times[282]. A remarkable 1992 paper[283] by Thyagi NagaSiva goes one step further, and proposes the use of virtual worlds as a foundation metaphor for a new, Western mysticism.

NagaSiva takes the view that virtual worlds are places where different aspects of the individual can exist—different selves, in other words. The existence of different selves is not restricted to virtual worlds, however—reality has many situations where individuals can be regarded as having a self different to that present in other situations. NagaSiva suggests that it is insightful to regard these different selves as existing in their own, private "virtual world." Whether this virtual world is an actual virtual world running on an actual computer or a metaphorical virtual world is immaterial; the two may be considered as equally "real." What we normally mean by reality is therefore simply an agglomeration of multiple virtual worlds; true reality would be the superset of all virtual worlds[284], a subject/object unity akin to the Buddhist Nirvana or Christian Heaven. Individual virtual worlds are merely the worlds inhabited by particular instantiations of the self. People can find NagaSiva's notion of Reality in any of their virtual worlds, although they will not usually perceive it in normal states of consciousness. You find Reality by unifying with the divine, thereby both transcending and subsuming the virtual world experience.

NagaSiva's paper seems a good place to end this discussion of theology and virtual worlds, but I shall nevertheless carry on (not least because ending here would imply I was for NagaSiva's proposal, which I'm not[285]).

---

282. Most unexpectedly in Edward Castronova's *On Virtual Economies* paper.

283. Thyagi NagaSiva, *The MUD as a Basis for Western Mysticism*. 1992.
    `http://www.luckymojo.com/avidyana/gnostik/mudpsyc.html`.

284. Remember here that from NagaSiva's point of view, "virtual world" means the world inhabited by a single virtual self; he doesn't mean an enumeration of every descendent of *MUD1*.

285. If you insist on knowing why, it's because I find his concept of reality distinctly unappealing and never wish to find any of my selves there.

Instead, I'm going to take a brief look at the design of in-context religions (or, strictly speaking, deities) for virtual worlds. There isn't a lot of work in this area; the main paper, Dan Hastings's *Designing God*[286], is very short. It does, however, cover most of the basics[287]:

➤ Are gods necessary?

➤ If so, do the gods exist in the virtual world or are they merely fictional?

➤ Who are the gods?

➤ What do they want?

➤ Where did they come from?

➤ Why are they here?

There's great scope for designer creativity in this area; pantheons in particular offer fine opportunities for combining philosophical and artistic points with gameplay elements. Do the gods represent: emotional concepts (love, hate, trust); aspects of life (time, fate, chance); aspects of nature (air, sea, forest); natural forces (fire, storms, earthquakes); aspects of balance (law, chaos, good, evil)? Or do they represent something else entirely?

There are some interesting consequences of having gods[288] in virtual worlds, all of which need to be determined by the designer. What, for example, is the effect of worshiping a god (or of not doing so)? What are the myths, and do they conflict? How did these give rise to the symbols and rituals of faith that turn it into a religion? How much of the religion should be programmed in as laws of nature (which wouldn't be tangibly different to laws of the land?) and how much should be left to enforcement by players or NPCs?

A very interesting mechanism for implementing religion is described in an article by Paul Schwanz[289]. His idea is to codify morality as tangible properties along four dimensions: health, wealth, power, and information. Players choose their characters to be

286. Dan Hastings, *Designing God. Imaginary Realities* Vol. 3 (1), January 2000. http://home.clara.net/ stormbringer/mudos/designing_god.html.

287. The main omission is how characters interact with deities (if indeed they can at all).

288. Or a single god; the designs for monotheistic, dualistic, and polytheistic worlds have their own distinct issues.

289. Paul E. Schwanz II, *Morality in Massively Multi-Player Online Role-Playing Games.* April 2000.

givers or takers along each dimension, and the degree to which they are so. When players undertake an action, any reward they gain is split along those dimensions. Thus, for example, a character who kills a king would gain points if they were an assassin (rating high for taking health and power) but the king's physician would lose points (because they are life-giving and loyal, that is, power-giving). Conversely, an assassin who healed a king would lose points, whereas a healer would gain them. By this ruse, players get to decide on the morality of their characters and can role-play them appropriately.

As a system of morality, which could be used to give value to any virtual religion, this is an excellent approach. For identity exploration, though, it presents a barrier. This, perhaps, is the great irony of all virtual-world religious experience: It changes the player, but it can't itself change in response. For such adaptability, people must rely on either themselves or on other people. Whether these other people are real, virtual, or imaginary depends entirely on the religion.

Virtual Worlds as Subfields

At the start of this chapter, I said that I would not be going into great detail concerning the disciplines that regard virtual worlds as a subfield. Hopefully, this will be something of a relief, given how long I spent looking at disciplines that regard virtual worlds as (on the whole) independent phenomena.

Some of the points I'll be making here do have wider application in the context of this book, and I'll describe these in more detail. Others don't, and for them I'll limit myself to an overview and some pointers as to where interested readers can look if they don't feel their academic energies have yet been exhausted.

Oh, I should mention that the brevity of my discussions here means that I am perforce required to make sweeping generalizations that could well cause anyone who actually works in the areas concerned to splutter with rage. Don't say you weren't warned.

Literary Theory

Virtual worlds fall awkwardly between literary theory and dramatic theory, and are claimed by both.

> ➤ *Literature.* Authors tell stories. Some stories have multiple authors. Some stories are made by the telling. Some stories are modified as they are told. Some stories are improvised as the author proceeds. Some stories are interactive with the reader. Some stories allow the reader to become the author.

> ➤ *Drama.* Actors perform plays. Some plays have multiple dramatists. Some plays are scripted. Some plays are frameworks. Some plays are improvised by the actors. Some plays are interactive with the audience. Some plays allow the audience to become actors.

The view of literary theorists is that ultimately action in virtual worlds is textual[290], therefore literature. The view of drama theorists is that ultimately action is performance, therefore drama. Researchers from both fields realize that the other has a point, however, and that with virtual worlds they share common ground. Occupying that ground already is the role-playing community, who have basically had to develop their own theories from scratch and now find that these are attracting more widespread attention.

So, literature first.

From the point of view of virtual world designers, the most interesting thing that students of Literature have to say about virtual worlds is that they do not have story in the conventional sense. Virtual worlds are open storytelling environments—that's precisely what literary theorists find exciting about them. It's almost taken as a given that conventional storytelling ideas do not apply to virtual worlds. There are plenty of reasons why virtual world designers might *want* them to apply[291], but there doesn't appear to be any interest in this from people whose job it is to study story. Indeed, some come

---

290. Although most of the work that has been undertaken in this area concerns textual worlds, that does not preclude graphical worlds from the equation. In the same way that writing can be regarded as performative, images can be scriptualized. This is a general point made in Mike Sandbothe, *Digital Entanglements: A Media-Philosophical analysis of Images, Language and Writing on the Internet.* 1998. `http://www2.uni-jena.de/ms/digi/digi.html`.

291. Chris Klug, *Implementing Stories in Massively Multiplayer Games.* Gamasutra, September 2002. `http://www.gamasutra.com/resource_guide/20020916/klug_01.htm`.

right out and say as much: Jesper Juul, looking at[292] narrative as it occurs in computer games in general[293], concludes that the two are in conflict and that "it is the *strength* of the computer game that it doesn't tell stories."

The major work on literary theory as applied to virtual worlds is Espen Aarseth's *Cybertext*[294]. Although his book covers a wide range of what Aarseth calls *ergodic literature*[295], the author is himself a former player of *TinyMUD* (the original, rather than the codebase class) and he devotes a chapter to the subject of virtual worlds. Ergodic literature is not so much text as a machine that generates expressions of text, and therefore virtual worlds are extreme examples of the concept in action. Although cautioning against romanticizing the reading and writing processes of virtual worlds, Aarseth is upbeat about their prospects as a meaningful mode of literary communication.

Aarseth's and others' views are taken to task[296] by Julian Kücklich, who sees a number of problems with the application of literary terminology to virtual worlds (and, from the examples he gives, he has a point, too). His solution is to view virtual worlds as a deconstructive process, where people discover meaning only by taking it apart. It's possible that both he and Aarseth are right, however, and that it depends on the players as to which applies[297].

Some other papers concerning literature and virtual worlds:

> ➤ *Jeffery Young, 1994*[298]. Young evangelizes on behalf of virtual worlds as places where human beings can express themselves. He wants virtual worlds to be studied for their speech and for their writing, and with controlled enthusiasm

---

292. Jesper Juul, *A Clash between Game and Narrative: A Thesis on Computer Games and Interactive Fiction*. Institute of Nordic Language and Literature, University of Copenhagen, 1999. `http://www.jesperjuul.dk/thesis/AClashBetweenGameAndNarrative.pdf`.

293. Virtual worlds get a short mention because their persistence makes for further problems with narrative.

294. Espen J. Aarseth, *Cybertext: Perspectives on Ergodic Literature*. Baltimore and London, The John Hopkins University Press, 1997.

295. This is a term borrowed from Physics, which in this context means that non-trivial effort is required by the reader to traverse the text, unlike the situation with normal "reading."

296. Julian Kücklich, *In Search of the Lost Text: Literary Theory and Computer Games*. Game Culture, March 2001. `http://www.game-culture.com/articles/insearch.html`.

297. No, I'm not proposing a player types model for "reading" virtual worlds, here....

298. Jeffery R. Young, *Textuality in Cyberspace: MUDs and Written Experience*. 1994. `ftp://sunsite.unc.edu/pub/academic/communications/papers/muds/Textuality-in-Cyberspace`.

explains exactly why. That this paper seems a little dated now is perhaps because Young succeeded in his aims.

➤ *Mikael Cardell, 1994*[299]. In this early attempt to look at virtual worlds from the point of view of literary theory, Cardell compares the processes involved in the construction of virtual worlds with those of a literary world (that of *Lord of the Rings*) and concludes that they are fundamentally the same. Nevertheless, although virtual worlds are used as locations for storytelling—quests in particular—he sees little evidence of contextual role-playing in most of them except for social experimentation (for example, cross-gender play).

➤ *Phil Goetz, 1994*[300]. This is a classic article that shows how virtual worlds can be used for highly literate role-play. Although the sample transcripts it presents suffer from dead-on-the-page syndrome, nevertheless Goetz makes his point. If you want to know what literary role-play is like in practice, this is where to find out.

➤ *Catherine Wylie, 1999*[301]. In this paper, Wylie argues that virtual worlds are the natural successors of the ancient "memory theatre" approach to storytelling, where stories were told aloud rather than being written down. Such stories evolved in the telling, as the storyteller and listeners engaged in a dialogue. She sees virtual worlds as offering the same opportunity for their communities to direct the moral tide, which are unavailable in other common examples of post-modernism in action.

➤ *Torill Mortensen, 2002*[302]. Mortensen's concern is that literary theorists have difficulty understanding virtual worlds because they are removed from them; they speak with experience of literature, but not of virtual worlds. She suggests that instead of looking at virtual worlds remotely, researchers should roll up their sleeves and actually play them[303]. Only through such ethnography-like fieldwork

299. Mikael Cardell, *Computers, Storytelling and World Creation: The Reader as Writer in Multi-Participant Interactive Fiction*. Department of Language and Literature, Linköping University, 1994. `http://www.hack.org/~mc/writings/world2.txt`.

300. Phil Goetz, *Literary Role-Play in Cyberspace*. Andrew Rilstone (editor), *Interactive Fantasy 4*. London, Hogshead Publishing, 1995. `http://www.mud.co.uk/richard/ifan295.htm`.

301. Catherine Wylie, *MUDs, Memories and Morals: A Revisioning of Primary Orality and Late Literacy*. Denver University, 1999.

302. Torill Mortensen, *Playing with Players: Potential Methodologies for MUDs*. Game Studies Vol. 2 (1), July 2002. `http://www.gamestudies.org/0102/mortensen/`.

303. A tiny minority of literary theorists do have meaningful experience of virtual worlds, of course, Aarseth being the most notable example.

can anyone hope to understand what it really means to be a "manipulating reader." Interestingly, her own experience of this results in an explanation that reads very much like the hero's journey.

Role-Playing Game Theory

Role-playing gamers have theories of role-play. Actors have theories of role-play too, of course, but players of role-playing games (RPGs) do not consider these to be appropriate to their particular circumstances. Instead, they've developed their own theories, the origins of which lie in the discussions of role-playing that occur on the Usenet group rec.games.frp.advocacy. Most of this work was done in the context of human-moderated games, whether face-to-face or live action; nevertheless, much of it can be applied to virtual worlds (and to single-player computer role-playing games, come to that).

There are two key aspects to the theories: *mode* and *stance*.

Mode is the style of play that players adopt, and concerns the reason that they participate in role-playing games. The usual answer they give—"to have fun"—is the same that players of virtual worlds reply. The RPG categorization of the answers, however, is different to the one I derived for virtual world player types. In fact, there are two main approaches: The *GDS* and *GNS* models, named after the initial letters of their categories (Gamist, Dramatist, Simulationist, and Gamism, Narrativism, Simulationism). GDS came first, and is described in the rec.games.frp.advocacy FAQ[304]. *GNS* is a refinement by Ron Edwards[305].

I'll outline GNS here:

➤ *Game mode.* This concerns competition between players, rather than their characters. Players create victory/loss conditions for themselves that are reflected in their playing strategies.

➤ *Narrative mode.* Here, the idea is the creation of a story with a recognizable theme. Characters are protagonists, and the referee provides the narrative cloth from which the players cut the story. The GDS model has drama mode here instead.

---

304. John H. Kim, *The rec.games.frp.advocacy FAQ.* http://www.darkshire.org/~jhkim/rpg/styles/faq_v1/faq1.art.

305. Ron Edwards, *GNS and Other Matters of Role-Playing Theory.* Adept Press, 2001. http://www.indie-rpgs.com/articles/1/.

> *Simulation mode*. This style of play focuses on exploration—of the character, setting, situation, atmosphere, and/or game mechanics. Internal logic and consistency of experience are regarded as paramount.

These playing styles are specific to individuals. The same game may have players in different modes, and conflicts will therefore occasionally arise (for example, game mode players might hire a half-orc tracker when their characters are all elves, whereas simulation mode players might object that their characters "wouldn't do that").

From a virtual world designer's point of view, it's interesting to compare these modes to the player types model (RPG theorists have done the reverse, too). There are some definite similarities: Game mode means achievers; simulation mode means explorers. Narrative mode could fit either socializers or killers, but serves neither very well. Why is this?

The root of the disparity is that in a virtual world, different characters do different things at the same time; in a human-moderated role-playing set-up, they don't. Human beings can't listen to instructions in parallel and react to each instantly; computers can, so they facilitate the person-to-person action and interaction that killers and socializers seek. Conversely, computers cannot adapt to unexpected actions to keep a series of planned events on track; humans can, therefore they can sustain a narrative.

In terms of mode, RPG theory has some relevance to virtual worlds; where it doesn't apply, its limitations are clearly defined.

The second characteristic of role-playing theory, stance, concerns how individuals decide what to do in response to a role-playing event. There are four basic stances, although only the first three typically apply:

> *Actor stance*. Players decide what their characters do based solely on the knowledge that their characters have. *I* know there's a dragon behind the door because I saw the referee's notes, but my *character* doesn't: My character goes through the door.

> *Author stance*. Players use their own priorities to determine what their character does, then retroactively[306] provide a rationale for their character to act that way. If we found the dragon this early, the gaming session would end too soon; the fact

---

306. If this second step is not taken, the result is called *Pawn stance*.

that my character is greedy enables me to send him back to look at some other doors he walked past, "before I get too far away."

> ➤ *Director stance.* The player determines their character's actions with no reference to that character's knowledge or abilities. My character pulls out their secret, dragon-slaying sword and goes through the door.

> ➤ *Audience stance.* Events unfold, my character merely watches. This doesn't apply in a role-playing situation: If I'm called on by the referee to act, my character must act—even if that means explicitly "doing nothing." It can apply in virtual worlds in certain stylized situations (one of which is described in the section on drama theory that follows).

The director stance is rare among players of RPGs. It may be more common in virtual worlds where players have build privileges, but it's impossible in those where they don't. The important stances are the first two, which equate to in-character (IC) and out-of-character (OOC) action. Edwards suggests that stances may be linked to the concept of immersion, too, which seems reasonable.

I've mentioned GDS and GNS here, but they aren't the only models in RPG Theory. Ever since the appearance of GDS, people have been creating their own player type models, almost invariably working to a threefold template. Brian Gleichman argues[307] that this archetype has become so ingrained that people don't consider there may be better ways of doing things. It occurs to me that there may be a similar problem in virtual worlds following on from my own fourfold player types model.

Drama Theory

There are two standard works that look at virtual worlds from the perspective of drama theory: Brenda Laurel's *Computers as Theatre*[308] and Janet Murray's *Hamlet on the Holodeck*[309].

---

307. Brian Gleichman, *ThreeFold Debates.* 2001. `http://home.attbi.com/~b.gleichman/Theory/Threefold/Main.htm`.

308. Brenda Laurel, *Computers as Theatre.* Menlo Park CA, Addison-Wesley, 1991.

309. Janet H. Murray, *Hamlet on the Holodeck: The Future of Narrative in Cyberspace.* New York, Free Press, 1997.

Laurel's big idea is that computers are a medium, rather than a tool. She sees drama as a conceptualizing theory that should be applied for designing engaging human/ computer activities, its advantages over narrative being its emphasis on enactment— people *perform*. She argues that by arranging the action (in any software engineering project) about the interface, the rest of the design falls into place. When the interface is the human imagination, the possibilities are limitless.

This interest in interface leads Laurel naturally to virtual reality, which she regards with great enthusiasm. It is primarily for this reason that her work is often quoted with reference to virtual worlds, although it's something of a distraction in today's post-hype VR climate. More relevant is her general belief that the relationship between human and computer should be about creating imaginary worlds that have a special relationship to the real one[310].

Laurel's approach focuses on the players, as both performers and (when the computer acts) audience. Murray, on the other hand, focuses on the work; for her, this is the performance that results from interaction between the players. She does mean players (rather than characters), too: Characters are like the masks of classical Greek drama, a device that by delimiting actor and role liberates the actor to become their role. Although it's tempting to think of the virtual world itself as the theatre in which the roles are played out, this is not Murray's approach[311]; rather, she sees it as a narrator, telling the story that unfolds as the players perform. Her vision is essentially constructivist: Players gain by building the context through their actions—they define the world.

Thus, she conceives of virtual worlds as being the collaborations of virtuosi, rather than the works of single geniuses: *commedia dell'arte* as opposed to Shakespeare. They follow a folk-story model, where the story form is passed down through succeeding generations and repurposed by each for their own needs; the high culture model, by comparison, fixes the work and passes it down verbatim. This means that although the resulting stories may look derivative to the outsider, they can be intensely meaningful to the performers. Hopefully, as narrative formulae are developed, understanding the stories and creating more advanced ones will become easier.

---

310. Laurel's direct references to virtual worlds mainly concern *Habitat*, which given when she was writing is not entirely surprising. She is mainly addressing software engineers, not virtual world designers; virtual worlds are an illustrative example for her.

311. Neither is it Laurel's, of course, as for her the computer is a medium, not a stage.

Murray's approach is far more story-oriented than Laurel's, but she still basically regards computers as a medium. She identifies three important properties of this medium, which by now should be familiar to virtual world designers:

> ➤ *Immersion*. How it helps people construct, rather than merely suspend, belief.

> ➤ *Agency*. How it allows users to do things that affect what is being represented.

> ➤ *Transformation*. How the medium can change to enhance immersion and agency.

Although much of what Murray says is relevant to the design of virtual worlds, its applicability is limited by the fact that (from our point of view) she's looking in the wrong place. In virtual worlds, players don't *perform* the work, they *are* the work. The closure that effectively ends a performance occurs when its structure is understood; for players, that's the key part of their hero's journey.

Also, purely from a designer's perspective, much of what goes on in virtual worlds occurs because of the way the world is structured. The virtual world itself *may* be created by a presiding genius who provides a context that allows the players to excel beyond what they would have done otherwise. Virtual world designers can certainly count such geniuses among their number; Raph Koster is the most obvious example.

Virtual worlds are not narrative components, they're places. As places, they can be venues for genuine performance without reference to the art of their creation—"art within art," in other words. There are genuine virtual theatre companies who act out pieces of interactive drama within virtual worlds to audiences. The most famous of these, the Plaintext Players[312], have been performing regularly since 1994. They don't work to a formal script: They are provided by the director with a basic scenario[313], and improvise to fulfill it.

Although the Plaintext Players often record (that is, log) their performances, it takes an experienced reader of transcripts to get any sense of the power and inventiveness of the piece. It is unlikely that someone who is not accustomed to reading log files would find them inspiring, even if they were replayed in real time. Basically, you have to be

---

312. `http://yin.arts.uci.edu/~players/`

313. The scenario is the same for every actor; it is interesting to speculate what would happen if actors were each given different scenarios for the same performance.

there, live, witnessing the performance taking place in the context of your own ability to influence it, in order to appreciate it[314]. This is despite the fact that there is some heavyweight drama theory behind them[315].

Part of the reason for this is that the Plaintext Players work exclusively in textual worlds. Graphical worlds are more accessible in this regard, and unsurprisingly many players do record activities in these worlds for later consumption[316]. Most of these recordings are of a "home video" nature, with subject matter concerning things like weddings, fights, and bloopers. Others, though, are parodies; some are actual scripted dramas.

At the moment, these graphical pieces are limited by the fact that the audience cannot enter the drama either actively (by moving the camera wherever they want) or passively (having a director choose the camera angles). They are recordings of events from a single perspective; they only show what is on the recording player's screen at the time. In theory, since the data exists anyway, it should be possible for members of the audience to change the camera angle themselves, switching points of view between participants, and getting in among the action. It should also be possible for a director to edit a cohesive and compelling narrative from the unlimited camera recordings that could be made available to them. All it would take would be for the graphical client to be able to record the incoming data stream and play it back. As a bonus, the amount of data needed to store a performance would be low compared with what is needed to store it frame-by-frame; feature-length events would be possible, instead of the five-minute shorts we have today. In practice, though, this is much harder than it sounds due to synchronization and cross-patch compatibility issues.

Some other papers concerning drama theory and virtual worlds are

➤ *Howard Rheingold, 1991*[317]. Chapter 13 of this well-known book describes drama in virtual worlds as envisaged in the VR-optimistic days of the early 1990s. Although many of the predictions related may in time come true, if they do it will be because of the worlds, not the interface.

---

314. I should mention here that I haven't seen the Plaintext Players in action myself, but having read thousands of logs in my time I can look at their transcripts and gain some sense of what they're about.

315. Antoinette LaFarge, *A World Exhilarating and Wrong: Theatrical Improvisation on the Internet. Leonardo* Vol 28 (5), 1995. http://yin.arts.uci.edu/~players/leo/leo95.html.

316. For examples, see http://camelotvault.ign.com/videos/.

317. Howard Rheingold, *Virtual Reality*. London, Secker & Warburg, 1991.

➤ *Jen Clodius, 1996*[318]. Here, Clodius describes the use of dramatic performance to give in-world context to a meta-world event (the return of a former player to an administrative position). She characterizes performance in virtual worlds as a form of spontaneous communication, people playing off each other to express and convey ideas. The actual event she describes used a framework script (which is presented), enhanced by improvisation during its execution to account for the reactions of the audience.

➤ *Susan Warshauer, 1994*[319]. Warshauer has the refreshing idea of examining (through interviews) the aesthetic approaches of two different virtual designers, to ascertain what they believed was important to virtual world design (simulation of reality, quality of room descriptions, and so on). Focusing on their attitudes to role-playing, she constructs a "dialectic of interacting"[320] that describes the motion that players experience between IC and OOC states. This is strongly related to the stances of RPG theory and the concept of immersion.

➤ *Shannon Appelcline, 2001*[321]. In this experiment, Appelcline wrote his regular Skotos column in screenplay format to demonstrate the problems that arise when material created for one medium is presented using another. Things work in different ways in different media, and not all transfer; some aesthetics intersect, but some don't. You always need to adapt a work of art for a different medium, and therefore you always have to adapt your understanding of works of art for different media. In particular, models of narrative and performance appropriate for the silver screen are not necessarily appropriate for virtual worlds.

This depiction of virtual worlds as a medium links suspiciously neatly to the next topic.

---

318. Jennifer A. Clodius, *Shar's Return: Performance as Gift.* `http://dragonmud.org/people/jen/shar.html`.

319. Susan Warshauer, *Aesthetic Approaches to the Design and Study of MUDs (Multi-User Domains) in English and Performance Studies: Interface, Realism and the Dialectic of Interacting. Computer Writing, Rhetoric and Literature* Vol. 1 (1), Spring 1994. `http://www.cwrl.utexas.edu/cwrl/v1n1/article3/mudmain.html`.

320. Given that it has three points—self, character, actor—perhaps "trialectic" would be a better word.

321. Shannon Appelcline, *Why Marrach Isn't the Movies.* Skotos, 2001.
`http://www.skotos.net/articles/TTnT_31.html`
`http://www.skotos.net/articles/TTnT_36.html`
`http://www.skotos.net/articles/TTnT_40.html`
`http://www.skotos.net/articles/TTnT_41.html`

Computer-Mediated Communication

Communications studies is a broad field, concerning the ways by which human beings convey information and emotion to one another. Inter-disciplinary almost by definition, it attracts mainly sociologists, sociolinguists and psychologists. Computer-mediated communication (CMC) is a subfield that addresses human communication through the medium of the computer. It specializes in email, Instant Messenger, Usenet, IRC, and virtual worlds (particularly textual ones, and very particularly MOOs). To CMC specialists, virtual worlds are simply one of many forms of CMC: They are important because they are media, not because they are places.

The main concerns researchers have about CMC are[322]

> ➤ The absence of social context cues (for example, body language, facial expressions)

> ➤ The recordability of conversation

> ➤ The rate of information exchange

> ➤ The level of formality

> ➤ The effects of anonymity

This means that CMC has lots to say about virtual worlds, but usually in the context of some wider theory, rarely addressing what virtual world researchers might like to think of as the unique circumstances that pertain in their subject matter[323]. For this reason, it's actually quite hard to track down CMC writings specific to virtual worlds that aren't using them to make some more general point[324]. That said, CMC researchers are often interested in the same things as virtual world researchers (albeit for different reasons), and much CMC work touches on topics I have already mentioned in this chapter; indeed, some of the works I've cited were published under the CMC banner.

---

322. This list comes from Rick Dietrich, Jill Grear, and Amber Ruth, *How Real Is Communication in the Virtual World of Cyberspace?* http://www.units.muohio.edu/psybersite/cyberspace/cmcreal/.

323. Particularly disappointing is the way that textual worlds are routinely mentioned in the same breath as IRC.

324. It's even harder when you do find a paper but it's one of a dozen collected in a single volume and you have to buy the lot to get it.

I have, however, refrained from redirecting all CMC papers in this way, for two reasons: Firstly, to bring home to virtual world designers that CMC is an area they should be looking at; secondly, because some of the points of interest concern CMC itself.

So here are some CMC papers that might interest you:

➤ *Elizabeth Reid, 1995*[325]. Reid looks at the different forms of communication available in virtual worlds, and the social experiences that result from them. She asserts that virtual worlds are new realities that exist in the shared imaginations of the players. The CMC spin is that this is made possible by the way the server actualizes players' commands into forms that can be communicated; it enables language to substitute for nonverbal cues, and the specialized meanings it employs to do so bind players into a common culture[326].

➤ *Don Langham, 1994*[327]. CMC has been criticized for causing people to speak before they have had time to reflect, encouraging them to think less deeply. Langham defends CMC from this by likening it to Plato's description of Socrates objecting to writing because it disrupts oral society. In the same way that Socrates felt writing corrupted the individual's relationship to society, CMC objectors feel that it destroys the individual's relationship to their self. Langham, however, sees virtual worlds as coming round full circle, re-introducing orality to society through the written word. Michael Docherty, 1994[328], criticizes Langham's approach (if not his conclusions) on the grounds that the supposedly anti-CMC camp are actually merely speculating about what might happen, rather than predicting what will. Writing began as a tool, but literature made it a realm; CMC is currently a tool, but only future generations will know what realm it becomes.

---

325. Elizabeth Reid, *Virtual Worlds: Culture and Imagination.* Stephen G. Jones (editor), *Cybersociety: Computer-Mediated Communication and Community.* Thousand Oaks CA, SAGE Publications Inc., 1995.

326. Although this is a common hypothesis among CMC researchers, it's interesting to note that it doesn't apply to the same extent in graphical worlds. This occurs time and time again in CMC research: The explanations proposed concerning phenomena in textual worlds do not account for why the same phenomena apparently arise in far less textually oriented graphical worlds.

327. Don Langham, *The Common Place MOO: Orality and Literacy in Virtual Reality. Computer-Mediated Communication Magazine* Vol. 1 (3), July 1994. http://www.december.com/cmc/mag/1994/jul/moo.html.

328. Michael E. Docherty Jr., *MOO as Tool, MOO as Realm: A Response to Don Langham. Computer-Mediated Communication Magazine*, Vol. 1 (7), November 1994. http://www.december.com/cmc/mag/1994/nov/moo.html.

➤ *Nancy Deuel, 1996*[329]. This paper discusses virtual sex, mainly in context of writings by other people on the subject; it is therefore a good starting point for further investigation into how CMC regards virtual sex. Deuel depicts it as a phenomenon of social interaction; while not tangibly productive, participants insist it contributes to their personal development and exploration. To this extent, it is a form of personal expression that is inevitable no matter what wider society may prefer.

➤ *John Ryan, 1995*[330]. Ryan looks at why people choose to communicate via virtual worlds, rather than through some other medium. He employs a *uses and gratifications* model; these are popular in CMC, and involve using statistics to find categories of common behaviors. He proceeded by interviewing 222 old-time *LambdaMOO* players using a fixed set of questions, then analyzing the results. He successfully identifies several reasons why people choose to continue playing *LambdaMOO* when they could easily have been doing something else. An interesting conclusion (from the point of view of this book) is that these long-term players seemed to have become more "themselves" as a result of their *LambdaMOO* experiences.

➤ *Sonja Utz, 2000*[331]. Utz examines how friendships develop in virtual worlds, which she sees as a highly developed form of CMC. She sets out to verify a number of commonly held hypotheses concerning: Virtual-world players; the way they develop friendships; the role that the communication forms available to them play in this. She produced a questionnaire that was answered by 103 players of German textual worlds. Although she does reach some interesting conclusions concerning her primary goals, of particular interest to readers of this book is how a cluster analysis of respondents' answers found four different player types that bear some similarity to...well, read it yourself.

---

329. Nancy R. Deuel, *Our Passionate Response to Virtual Reality*. Susan C. Herring (editor) *Computer-Mediated Communication: Linguistic, Social and Cross-Cultural Perspectives*. Philadelphia, John Benjamins North America, 1996.

330. John Ryan, *A Uses and Gratifications Study on the Internet Social Interaction Site LambdaMOO: Talking with "Dinos."* Ball State University, 1995. `http://www.zacha.net/articles/ryan.html`.

331. Sonja Utz, *Social Information Processing in MUDs: The Development of Friendships in Virtual Worlds. Journal of Online Behavior* Vol. 1 (1), 2000. `http://www.behavior.net/JOB/v1n1/utz.html`.

➤ *Tari Fanderclai, 1995*[332]. This is only a short paper, but it is notable for alerting the possibilities of educational virtual worlds to a wider audience. Because CMC is interdisciplinary, people from other disciplines get to hear about things they might otherwise not.

Post-Modernism

Post-modernists view virtual worlds as examples of post-modernism in action. Then again, they view everything like that, so virtual worlds aren't necessarily particularly special in this regard. What makes them interesting to post-modernists (in the sense that anything at all is interesting to them) is that they illustrate certain post-modernist concepts more clearly than usual, and thus make good examples when explaining post-modernism to people who don't get it.

Post-modernism[333] only really arrived in the mid-1980s. As an intellectual movement, it has things to say about a very wide range of topics. Fundamentally, though, it's about the meaning of meaning (or, rather, the lack of meaning of meaning). Human beings are entirely subjective; all objectivity is therefore illusory. Meaning is constructed from individually meaningless signs and symbols; the truth is hidden behind the image, but the truth itself is an image. Ultimately, human beings are constructs created by themselves; deconstruct them, and at best all you find is another layer to deconstruct.

As I've just explained it (which is *very* much only a brief summary), post-modernism is basically a "so what?" subject. It's full of theory, the theory seems to apply, but it also undermines itself in a recursive fashion. In the end, you may understand it but so what? This is what: It enables people to look at things in a non-traditional manner, giving greater insight into what things mean and why they mean it. It's incredibly easy to overdo, though.

Insofar as virtual worlds are concerned, their importance to post-modernism is that they clearly demonstrate two of its tenets (both due to Jean Baudrillard[334]). The first of

---

332. Tari Lin Fanderclai, *MUDs in Education: New Environments, New Pedagogies. Computer-Mediated Communication Magazine* Vol. 2 (1), January 1995.

333. Many people prefer "postmodern" to "post-modern," but who gives a damn?

334. Jean Baudrillard, *Simulacra and Simulations.*
`http://www.stanford.edu/dept/HPS/Baudrillard/Baudrillard_Simulacra.html`.
Baudrillard developed both concepts over time in several essays. This one has the advantage (from the point of view of this book) of being short and available online in English.

these is the individual as a simulacrum of the self: In virtual worlds, with their lack of physicality, how could the individual be anything else? The second is the concept of the *hyperreal*, where representation becomes simulation (reality as a simulation of itself); virtual worlds, being simulations of reality as people both understand and desire it to be, can seem to them to be more real than reality[335].

It's unsurprising, therefore, that there is a virtual world set up specifically to exemplify these theories in action: *PMC2*[336], sponsored by the journal *Postmodern Culture*[337]. Perhaps even less unsurprising is that many of the post-modern writings about virtual worlds concern this particular virtual world. Well, it makes a change from *LambdaMOO*.

Some papers (with great titles) that refer to virtual worlds as post-modernist icons are

> ➤ *Mark Nunes, 1995*[338]. This is a good statement of the post-modern line regarding virtual worlds, making useful reference to the "modern" that post-modern is "post." Nunes sees virtual worlds as places that defy the unavoidability of modernist futures, allowing people to play with the assumptions that modernity bequeathed us concerning community, information, liberation, and self. They offer the chance to thwart inevitability by allowing us to redefine and rewrite whatever we choose.

> ➤ *Jeffrey Fisher, 1997*[339]. Fisher takes viewpoint that cyberspace is not the equivalent of medieval paradise that many people seemed to think it was (and he wrote this before *The Pearly Gates of Cyberspace* was published). Virtual worlds allow individuals to re-create themselves and to archive that re-creation[340]; thus, they

---

335. A philosopher's view of whether virtual worlds are themselves real or illusory is presented in Wesley E. Cooper, *Virtual Reality and the Metaphysics of Self, Community and Nature. International Journal of Applied Philosophy* Vol. 9 (2), 1995.

336. *PMC2* is the second iteration of the original *PMC-MOO.* http://www.iath.virginia.edu/pmc/pmc-moo.html.

337. http://www.iath.virginia.edu/pmc/

338. Mark Nunes, Baudrillard in Cyberspace: *Internet, Virtuality and Postmodernity.* Style Vol. 29, 1995. http://www.dc.peachnet.edu/~mnunes/jbnet.html.

339. Jeffrey Fisher, *The Postmodern Paradiso: Dante, Cyberpunk and the Technosophy of Cyberspace.* David Porter (editor), *Internet Culture.* New York, Routledge, 1997

340. I personally feel that that this is more like a test/edit cycle that brings the archived self closer to the "real" self, at least to the degree where the two are isomorphic.

can transform people. Virtual worlds are not universally available to everyone, though, nor can they ever be: Although they can transform people, they can't transform everyone because not everyone has (nor ever will have) access to them. There are thus real social costs to a virtual world existence.

➤ *Troy Whitlock, 1994*[341]. A concerted and deliberate example of post-modernism disappearing up its own backside. Whitlock set up a player class, "terrorist," in the dying days of *PMC-MOO*. Every worst post-modernist nightmare ensued as the consequences of post-modernist theories came back to bite the theorists—as a legitimate example of their theories in action. Deconstructivists were deconstructed; self-reference was used as a weapon against self-reference. Amusing though this is, it makes many serious points in the detail. A splendid illustration of how reality always wins, even against hyperreality.

➤ *Chip Morningstar, 1993*[342]. This is one of my favorite papers related to virtual worlds, written by a pioneer of the subject. It's a wonderful cutting-through of academic weed to find the ideas that flower at the center of post-modernism. Chip takes a marvelous, pragmatic approach, pointing out what's bogus about post-modernism as it is applied to virtual worlds (and everything else), and what's valuable (which isn't a lot, but neither is it nothing). It's a magnificent dose of *real* reality to counter the hyperreal reality of post-modernist thought. After reading this, you need never feel daunted by anyone who renormalizes the phenomenology of narrative space through intersubjective cognitive strategy again.

Virtual Worlds as Tools

The third way that virtual worlds are viewed by researchers is as tools. In this situation, virtual worlds are interesting purely because of what they can be used for, rather than for any intellectual merit of their own. This isn't to say that researchers in these areas disparage virtual worlds, it's just that their focus is different. If such an attitude were a crime, it's one that virtual world designers would themselves be guilty of. They

---

341. Troy Whitlock, *Fuck Art, Let's Kill: Towards a Post Modern Community.* 1994. http://www. evolutionzone.com/kulturezone/futurec/articles/Moo.Terrorism.

342. Chip Morningstar, *How to Deconstruct Almost Anything: My Postmodern Adventure.* 1993. http://www.ibiblio.org/pub/academic/communications/papers/habitat/ deconstr.rtf.

rely on computer scientists for the hardware and software expertise they need, but are only really interested in what this allows them to do design-wise (or, more likely, prohibits them from doing); computer science provides the tools they need, but is only a curiosity beyond that.

Some of the fields that use virtual worlds as tools do so because they can derive new techniques in their own fields that way. Virtual worlds can therefore expect to be the immediate beneficiaries of such techniques. Incredibly tempting though it is to look at what these fields promise for virtual worlds, this is not the book where it's going to happen. My mission here is to promote virtual world design as a subject worthy of serious attention; although the general development of virtual worlds may benefit from an examination of worlds-as-tools research (I certainly hope it does), these don't actually validate virtual worlds as a worthy pursuit in themselves. Thus, I shall restrict myself to giving a very limited overview of the fields concerned as they impact on virtual world design; designers who are sufficiently enthused can hit a few search engines if they want to find out more.

Computer Science

I re-read the previous paragraph immediately after having written four pages about computer science and virtual world design. I bit the bullet and cut them.

Many virtual world designers[343] have a soft spot for computer science because their own backgrounds are in this area. However, the fact is that computer scientists in general are not tremendously interested in virtual worlds except when they're working on them[344], in which case they have a direct relationship with the designers anyway. Designers who are former programmers can call on their own experience, of course: Program design methodologies can certainly help in the process of virtual-world design, and systems analysis techniques are invaluable, too. The greatest benefit of computer science training to designers, however, is perhaps the understanding it gives of what can be programmed (and how long it will—or might—take).

---

343. Myself included.

344. Or when they're playing in them, in which case they may well want to work on one of their own.

When it comes to using virtual worlds as a research application, though, computer science's interest is very limited. There are some programming languages that have been designed to support virtual worlds (most notably *LogiMOO*[345]), but other than that, virtual worlds are used either to show off some object-modeling system's capabilities or to explore distributed processing/programming ideas. Both of these are likely to have an eventual impact on virtual world design, but only through the additional weaponry they provide for the programmers who implement virtual worlds.

So, although there are many computer science papers I'd like to tell you about here, I have to concede that basically I only want to do so because that's my background, not because there's anything hugely relevant to virtual world design there.

Artificial Intelligence

I also have a background in artificial intelligence (AI). I did my BSc in computer science but my Ph.D. was in AI. Why? Because AI is highly relevant to virtual worlds.

The reason AI is relevant is because of mobiles. Okay, well there are other reasons, too—object representation, pattern recognition, route-finding, parsing, and so on—but mobiles were why I went for it. Virtual worlds are places, but (except for heavy role-playing or educational worlds) they're places that are better for having denizens. The virtual world designer has to create not only the environment, but also the occupants of that environment. This is where AI comes in.

Next to me as I write this is a stack of 26 AI research papers, every one of which I'd love to write about here. These represent perhaps 40% of the AI-and-virtual-worlds papers in my collection—the ones I pared it down to. Unfortunately for me, but perhaps fortunately for you, I'm only giving an overview here. So, here it is.

As far as virtual worlds are concerned, AI is all about *agents*. Agents are what AI people call independent entities capable of action (they also call them *actors*). In virtual worlds, we call them mobiles, NPCs, and, if they're not integrated into the virtual world itself, bots.

---

345. Paul Tarau, Koen De Bosschere, Veronica Dahl and Stephen Rochefort, *LogiMOO: An Extensible Multi-User Virtual World with Natural Language Control. Journal of Logic Programming* Vol. 38, 1999.

Mobiles don't have to be clever. You can implement wind as a mobile. Bots don't have to be clever either, but there's not a lot of point to writing them if they're not. AI researchers like virtual worlds because they're shared, complex environments that human beings and AI programs can interact with on equal terms; they therefore use them for bots (although they might actually implement them as mobiles; go figure).

Bot research integrates many aspects of AI. Bots need (among other things) natural language understanding, planning, knowledge representation, learning, plan recognition, and the ability to model their own thought processes. Some of them are created with particular applications in mind (interactive drama or storytelling, for example), and there is an emphasis on making them "believable" (for the benefit of humans), but the great thing about AI is that bots are interesting purely for their own sake. They don't have to show off any theory: They're AI in action.

From the point of view of virtual world design, AI promises great things. If virtual worlds could be populated by intelligent NPCs, all manner of doors would open. Examples: Quest generation becomes contextual; reputation becomes intangible but works better; the economy behaves like it should; PC clans can't dominate politics. Worlds will seem—will *be*—so much more alive.

I could go on and on about this, but restraint has prevailed. To find out more

> ➤ Read Andrew Leonard's book. *Bots*[346].

> ➤ See Leonard Foner's paper[347] about the famous bot *Julia*.

> ➤ Consider the Skotos[348] approach, which comes at bots from a different angle.

> ➤ The American Association for Artificial Intelligence[349] has been sponsoring yearly symposia on the subject of AI and Interactive Entertainment.

Oh, I would like to add one more thing....

---

346. Andrew Leonard, *Bots: The Origin of New Species*. San Francisco, HardWired, 1997.

347. Leonard N. Foner, *Entertaining Agents: A Sociological Case Study*. Montreal, Proceedings International Joint Conference on Artificial Intelligence 1995.
http://foner.www.media.mit.edu/people/foner/Reports/IJCAI-95/Julia.txt.

348. Christopher Allen, *The Skotos Cellular Automata Simulation System: A Tech Summary*.
http://www.kanga.nu/archives/MUD-Dev-L/2002Q2/msg00521.php.

349. http://www.aaai.org

Don't try to make your virtual world *itself* be intelligent. Don't make it spawn creatures that are appropriate to the skills of the players who are about to try kill them; don't make mobiles in combat act clever against clever opponents and stupid against stupid ones; don't make the treasure that people find adapt to whoever finds it. This will not only be perceived by the players as unfair and frustrating, but it will seem to mock them. A constant challenge is constantly beatable and constantly patronizing.

Education

I had 26 AI papers I would, given a free rein, have liked to have discussed here. I have 37 such education papers. Yes, I have a background in teaching, too.

Computer games and education have an uneasy relationship. Computer games are fun, education isn't. Educationalists figure that by marrying the two, education can be made fun; unfortunately, all too often computer games are made unfun instead. It is this precedent that puts off many game-style virtual world designers from looking at educationalist virtual worlds. This is something of a shame, because there is a *lot* of very interesting work going on in the area. Books could be written about virtual worlds in education; indeed, books *have* been written about them[350].

Virtual worlds offer educators the following features:

- ➤ They are collaborative.
- ➤ They are motivational.
- ➤ They involve language use.
- ➤ Children find it easier to express themselves in them.
- ➤ They are a change from classroom learning.
- ➤ They can be used remotely.
- ➤ The interface is easy to learn.
- ➤ Disruptive behavior is easier to deal with.

---

350. Try this one, a collection of papers edited by the founders of *LinguaMOO*. Cynthia Haynes and Jan Rune Holmevik (editors), *High Wired: On the Design, Use and Theory of Educational MOOs*. Ann Arbor, University of Michigan Press, 1998.

Almost all educational virtual worlds are textual, using mainly *TinyMUD*-heritage codebases. MUSHes and MOOs are favored because of their flexibility; text is favored because it is inexpensive. That said, there may also be educational reasons for using text over graphics, the first 3D graphical educational worlds having performed less well pedagogically than hoped[351].

The use of virtual worlds for educational purposes has a long history. The first such world, Stan Lim and Barry Kort's *MicroMUSE*[352], was founded in 1990; Julie Falsetti and Eric Schweitzer's *schMOOze University*[353] and Jeanne Butler McWhorter's *Diversity University*[354] have been running classes since 1994; Amy Bruckman's *MOOSE Crossing*[355] began in 1995. Educational virtual worlds are used primarily to teach

- ➤ Second/foreign language use
- ➤ Simple programming skills
- ➤ Composition (that is, writing)
- ➤ Team skills

This is all very interesting, but as I've been at pains to point out throughout this book educational virtual worlds share many characteristics with social- and game-oriented ones. Why give their use by educationalists any kind of special mention?

Well, it's because all virtual world traditions have the same aim: learning. With social- and game-oriented worlds, players learn about themselves; with educational worlds, players learn whatever they're taught *but also* about themselves. Educationalists know about teaching and learning; does it not make sense, therefore, to look at how they design virtual worlds and in-world courses for teaching purposes, to see if these ideas can be applied to what virtual worlds are, at heart, all about—the search for the self?

---

351. Jason Elliott, Lori Adams and Amy Bruckman, *No Magic Bullet: 3D Video Games in Education*. Seattle, *Proceedings of International Conference on the Learning Sciences*, 2002. http://www.cc.gatech.edu/~asb/papers/aquamoose-icls02.pdf.

352. http://www.musenet.org/

353. http://schmooze.hunter.cuny.edu:8888/

354. http://www.du.org/. You can tell something on the Net is old when it has a URL like that.

355. http://www.cc.gatech.edu/elc/moose-crossing/

Two papers, two perspectives, one aim:

➤ *Marina Bers, 2001*[356]. The creation of a 3D virtual world with the specific intention that it be used for identity construction.

➤ *Dianne Butler, 1999*[357]. What players of a regular adventure-style virtual world consider that they learn from it.

Law

Lawyers are almost all concerned only with real-life laws as they apply to virtual worlds. They are overwhelmingly not interested in the design of in-context legal systems for virtual worlds. Even so, for this reason alone virtual world designers should listen to what they have to say; there are also other reasons, however, that we shall come to shortly.

Virtual worlds raise several issues for real-world law with which legislators have yet to get to grips. These include

➤ *Ownership of data.* Can players sell characters and property? Can the virtual world owner[358]? What are the liabilities that the virtual world developer has in either case? What would PD mean in such a world? Do players of loss-making virtual worlds have any grounds for complaint if the developer shuts it down?

➤ *Ownership of intellectual property.* Do players have rights concerning anything they create in the virtual world? Does it make a difference whether it's in-context (they made a picture from colored stones) or out-of-context (they created a complex of rooms)? Can they claim usage royalties? Can they insist their creation is removed? Is joint ownership between player and developer a solution? What if the virtual world uses a licensed franchise?

---

356. Marina Umaschi Bers, *Identity Construction Environments: Developing Personal and Moral Values through the Design of a Virtual City. Journal of the Learning Sciences* Vol. 10 (4), 2001. `http://www.tufts.edu/~mbers01/JLS-Bers.pdf`.

357. Dianne P. Butler, *MUDs as Social Learning Environments.* 1999. `http://www.medievia.com/mudslinger/solpaper.html`.

358. *Ultima Online* jumped the shark in September 2002 when the announcement was made that players could buy advanced characters at source instead of having to work their way up.

> *Employment law.* When does what people do for fun become work? Should volunteers be able to claim the minimum wage?

> *Governing law.* If I as an Englishman interact improperly with an American in a virtual world that has its server in Canada, under which country's laws can I be sued? How are disputes in virtual worlds resolved[359]?

> *Responsibility and liability.* Are virtual world designers responsible if their players become addicted? Can they be held to account for real-world violence meted out for virtual-world reasons? Are they liable for repetitive strain injuries incurred by players performing activities that the designer has encouraged?

The country where virtual worlds are taken most seriously by the legal establishment is Korea. In 2002, the Ministry of Culture and Tourism announced changes to its online game rating system that effectively meant virtual worlds featuring PKing could only be played by people aged 18 and over. NCSoft's shares fell dramatically with this news, as the realization that *Lineage* could lose half its players sank into the minds of investors.

The Korean government acted because of incidents of real-life unrest that were apparently resulting from activities undertaken in virtual worlds. Virtual worlds were associated with reports of suicide, violence[360], and prostitution (selling real-life sex for in-world reward[361]). That their response was something of a knee-jerk reaction is clear from the way that it linked PKing to the intention of the PKer to steal virtual goods from their victim (presumably as a means of disambiguating the *Counterstrike*-like PKing of non-persistent characters with the *Lineage*-like PKing of persistent ones). Nevertheless, as virtual worlds become more and more mainstream, it's a sign of things to come.

I did say that there were other reasons that virtual world designers should look at what lawyers have to say apart from the obvious one of being possibly bankrupted if they get things wrong. These are those few (and they are *very* few) occasions where case studies of happenings in virtual worlds are looked at from a lawyer's standpoint; they constitute the beginnings of a jurisprudence for virtual worlds, and should be

---

359. For a discussion of this particular gray area, see Todd H. Flaming, *The Rules of Cyberspace: Informal Law in a New Jurisdiction. Illinois Bar Journal*, April 1997. http://www.sw.com/rulescyb.htm.

360. Note that people have been stabbed to death after chess matches before, so this is not something unique to virtual worlds.

361. This, on the other hand, does look new.

welcomed. My only concern here is that laws may be drawn up prematurely, without proper consultation with those who "get" virtual worlds[362], and we could be stuck with something unsuitable or unworkable as a consequence.

I'd like to finish this section on law by mentioning a book[363] by Tim Jordan that isn't about law at all: It's about government. Ultimately, laws are made by people with political power, not by lawyers. Jordan looks at who has this power in cyberspace, and who wants it. If you know who's going to make the rules, you can get a good idea of the rules they are going to make.

Virtual Worlds as...Virtual Worlds

I set out in this chapter to examine how researchers in various fields view virtual worlds. I feel I ought to end, however, with a reminder for virtual world designers that there is very relevant work going on much closer to home.

Community Management

Sooner or later, community management[364] is going to become a social science in its own right if it isn't one already. Virtual world designers create virtual worlds, but it's the live team that keeps them going. Designers should therefore take this into account when they create worlds in the first place. Of course, as I've been mentioning throughout this book, designers *do* pay serious attention to the way that the virtual world will be run; unless they have live-team experience (which the best of them do, of course), their views may, however, be somewhat idealized. As a designer, ask yourself if you would know what to do if

➤ A confused player asked for help.

➤ A player whose character was stuck in a pit asked to be extracted.

---

362. Or, worse, those who think they get them but don't. Not every virtual world is *LambdaMOO*.

363. Tim Jordan, *Cyberpower: The Culture and Politics of Cyberspace and the Internet.* New York, Routledge, 1999.

364. I'm using the term here to cover all community management, that is, in-world and out-of-world. There is a tendency for the big commercial virtual worlds to apply "community management" only to out-of-world activities such as running the web site; in-world management is usually "customer support" or "customer relations." Smaller virtual worlds don't generally make this distinction.

➤ Either of the preceding occurred involving the same player for the third time in 30 minutes.

➤ Two players were arguing about ownership of loot.

➤ A grief player who doesn't think they are a grief player used earlier anti-grief pronouncements of yours to cause grief.

➤ A concerned relative of a player got in touch asking about addiction.

These are just some of the kinds of things that customer relations staff have to handle routinely.

When a virtual world goes live it becomes part of the real world. In the real world, things happen that the designer can't control:

➤ Players multi-line—that is, play more than one character simultaneously. This can be a big problem for small-scale virtual worlds.

➤ Players divert risk. They will do anything dangerous with a character they don't care about, then hand the benefits (treasure, and so on) over to one they do care about.

➤ Players collude. They form large gangs, and create their own agendas that may be at odds with those of other players.

➤ Players play the system. If they know you have an attitude of "the customer is always right," they will milk it dry.

➤ Players communicate outside of the virtual world. This puts them at an advantage over ones that have to communicate within the virtual world where they can be overheard. Carefully synchronized diversionary tactics to occupy administrative staff while a bug is exploited are not unprecedented.

➤ Players use bots and macros to automate functionality to the detriment of other players.

Community management staff need out-of-context tools so they can spot these problems and implement any decisions they make as a result. If the design can help, so much the better.

There's a governmental issue here. If the community management team wants something in the virtual world, does the designer *have* to put it in or can they say no? There are dangers in both approaches: Big-budget commercial virtual worlds have failed to materialize because designers wouldn't compromise their designs to account for community management concerns, and others have collapsed in a heap because their designers did. It's my belief[365] that in the end, the designer must be in overall charge—but that only a foolish designer would ignore the community management team's input.

Without community management experience to draw on, the following writings are the next-best thing:

> ► *Daniel Pargman, 2000*[366]. This is Pargman's Ph.D. thesis, which examines the administration of the textual world *SvenskMUD* over a period of three and a half years. It is amazingly detailed and full of insight; every professional virtual world designer should have a copy, even though it is somewhat obscure.

> ► *John Suler, ongoing*[367]. Psychologist Suler explains who misbehaves in virtual worlds, why they misbehave, and (most incredibly usefully) how to manage their misbehavior. It's as simple as that.

> ► *Jonas Heide Smith, 2002*[368]. This MA thesis describes the design features that virtual worlds should incorporate if they are to promote co-operation among their players, rather than conflict. It has some very good explanations of well-known[369] viewpoints about behavior, as they apply to virtual worlds.

---

365. As a designer.

366. Daniel Pargman, *Code Begets Community: On Social and Technical Aspects of Managing a Virtual Community*. Department of Communication Studies, Linköping University, 2000. `http://esplanaden.lysator.liu.se/svmud/pargman/` (extracts only).

367. John Suler, *The Bad Boys of Cyberspace: Deviant Behavior in Online Multimedia Communities and Strategies for Managing It*. This is part of his ongoing hypertext book, *The Psychology of Cyberspace*. `http://www.rider.edu/~suler/psycyber/badboys.html`.

368. Jonas Heide Smith, *The Architectures of Trust: Supporting Cooperation in the Computer-Supported Community*. Department of Film and Media Studies, University of Copenhagen, 2002. `http://autofire.dk/jonas/the_architectures_of_trust.pdf`.

369. Among students of psychology and sociology, if not among virtual world designers.

Conclusion

This has been a long and difficult chapter. It took me longer to write it than it did the rest of the book put together. However, I hope it has served its purpose, which is to show

- ➤ Virtual worlds are a meaningful object of study.

- ➤ Most of those research fields that look at virtual worlds do so with respect.

- ➤ Virtual world designers can learn much from researchers in other fields and vice versa.

- ➤ No existing field of research entirely subsumes virtual worlds.

- ➤ Virtual world design in particular is not covered elsewhere.

The study of virtual worlds is a valid academic objective for its own sake, in the same way that the study of literature, film, theatre, or any other art form is valid. People who look at virtual worlds professionally need feel no shame for doing so; they can hold their heads up high. The stigmatization of virtual worlds as "just games" or "just simulations" or "just services" or "just a medium" is over. Virtual worlds are—virtual worlds! Rejoice in it!

Yes, I did assert back there that virtual world design is an art form. In the next chapter, I explain why I believe this to be so.

Chapter 7

Towards a Critical Aesthetic

Virtual worlds are works of art. I refer to their creators as "designers," but that's a misnomer; really they're artists[1]. Although there is some debate over the distinction between art and design, it's generally true that "design" has to convey a given package of information or utility whereas "art" is an end in itself. You tell a designer what you want; you ask an artist what they've got. What virtual world designers do is more Art than Design.

It's like the difference between Science and Engineering: Scientists seek truth, whereas engineers seek solutions. If you ask an engineer to change a construct because you don't like it, they'll do so; if you ask a scientist to change a theory because you don't like it, they'll stare at you blankly. Similarly, if you ask a designer to change a decoration because you don't like it, they'll do so; if you ask an artist to change a picture because you don't like it, they'll attack you with a hammer.

Virtual world designers must work within many constraints, and they *do* have to deliver a certain amount of utility. This is something they consider an intrinsic part of their art, though. If you want a formal portrait, you go to an artist who specializes in portraiture and considers that as part of their art; you don't pick an artist at random from the Internet who might spend two weeks making preliminary sketches then present you with a wooden sculpture of a ship that is supposed somehow to capture your personality. Top virtual

---

1. The term "artist" is claimed by the people who draw the pictures in computer games (and thence in virtual worlds), so I'm not proposing a name change here.

world designers create worlds because that's how they express themselves artistically; utility is intrinsic what they design, in the same way that likeness is intrinsic to what a portrait artist paints. Designers who create worlds because they've been told to may still be able to put some self-expression or meaning into the product, but at the end they're creating for you. Artists create for themselves.

I have a namesake who is a fully fledged professional artist[2]. His medium is acrylic and collage. His work involves cutting images from magazines, which he then laser-copies multiple times and incorporates into an artistic whole. The uniform reproduction of what are themselves mass-market images allows him to comment on things like commercialism, politics, stereotypes and many other things that interest him. He likens his process of creation to alchemy: He takes a base copy and turns it into art. As with any alchemy, this can only be achieved through a proper understanding of the materials involved and a meticulous approach to experimentation, hence all the painstaking cutting-out. The fastidious and craft-intense *process* of creation gives him an understanding of the work he is creating, which enables him to embody it in the final artifact.

Virtual world designers might not have quite this degree of internalization about their work, but nevertheless if you plan to tell one of them mid-way through a project that you want them to drop something for marketing reasons, hide all the hammers first.

Some of what virtual world designers do really is design rather than art. Design is often used to create tools that can be used for making art, or to construct building-block objects that can be assembled in an artistic way. There are even theories for this[3]. It can be regarded as part of the designer's craft. It's not why they do what they do, though; it isn't itself Art.

Of course, virtual worlds are often such large-scale projects that many people have artistic input. The same also applies to movies; and in the same way that a movie's director[4] ultimately holds artistic responsibility for that movie, the lead designer holds artistic responsibility for their virtual world. Actors and cinematographers, programmers and 3D modelers, they can all be artists; directors and designers, however, are "the" artist.

2. He's http://www.richardbartle.co.uk; I'm http://www.richardbartle.com.

3. Anna Cicognani, *A Linguistic Characterisation of Design in Text-Based Virtual Worlds*. Department of Architectural and Design Science, University of Sydney, 1998. http://www.arch.usyd.edu.au/~anna/phd/final.html.

4. Directors aren't called artists either, because in their case actors bagged the term first.

A Theory of Virtual Worlds

It's all very well for me to make these pompous assertions that serve to glorify my own position. Unfortunately for me, it takes more than slapping a pretentious label on something to make it art[5]. Art may be expression, but it's worthless unless it can be recognized as such. People don't have to know what a piece of art "means," but they do need to know how its meaning is conveyed. This requires the development of a *critical aesthetic*[6].

Motivation

A critical aesthetic is a system of ascribing meaning to individual examples of an art form. When formalized, it amounts to a theory for that art.

The "aesthetic" here isn't in the general sense: It's not a branch of philosophy concerned with matters such as "beauty" and "taste." Rather, it's to do with the rules and principles that underlie an art (in this case, virtual world creation). A virtual world may look beautiful and have a great visual aesthetic, yet suck as a world. The art director controls the look, but the designer controls the world. Designers who want a particular look hire art directors whose work exhibits that look. The look is part of the overall aesthetic. Introducing the notion of criticism allows for rationalization of the communicative aspects of this aesthetic.

A legitimate question to ask is whether virtual worlds need such a theory. The number of professional practitioners of virtual world design is low, and they don't have trouble interpreting each other's work. Wouldn't it be better to wait until the field has developed more before attempting to nail it down? It probably would, yes. I have three reasons for going ahead and trying to do it anyway:

> ➤ The virtual world community has a sense of inferiority in comparison to more established art forms. My Sunday newspaper is happy to spend two full pages discussing the merits of *avant-garde* glassware lamp stands, but what non-geek takes virtual worlds seriously? A critical aesthetic would demonstrate that there is more to virtual worlds than killing virtual monsters and learning written French.

---

5. Exception: If an established artist slaps the label on, then it *is* art.

6. I apologize unreservedly for the pretentiousness of this term. Regrettably, the alternatives are even worse, so we're stuck with it.

➤ I want to get straight in my own mind how I judge a virtual world.

➤ If I don't write all this down, someone else is only going to do it anyway.

The first of these mirrors the main reason that film theory was developed in the 1970s, but the other two are purely selfish. Fortunately, the first reason is good enough that I can indulge the other two.

The pro-art position is actually worse than I've made out in that there is some debate within the virtual world development community over whether treating virtual world design as art is counter-productive. In 2001, as major virtual world designers (particularly Raph Koster) made increasing pronouncements that took for granted the artistic nature of what they did, players began to express concern. Jessica Mulligan, the most long-standing and forthright proponent of players' rights, voiced these opinions in her well-read Skotos column, *Biting the Hand*[7]. Her remarks caused a firestorm.

Jess's argument was that players were becoming incidental to virtual world design. They signed up to play a game[8], but they were being misled; the grandiose ideas of designers were making players unwilling participants in experimental performance art. By treating players as mere objects to be controlled through the brilliance of their creativity, designers were showing staggering arrogance and contempt. This elitist attitude could ultimately be sourced in designers' belief that they were creating art. It would be better if they were disabused of this belief.

Jess did accept that art was involved in the design of virtual worlds, because it's fundamentally a creative exercise. What she objected to was the view that players were a *part* of the work. Players want to be entertained; if, while playing, some art form were to entertain them, fine, no problem. When they're considered a component of the art form, or to be paying in order to experience the art form, that's not so good. Designers shouldn't try to impose their vision on players at the expense of what players actually *want*.

Skotos published two responses to this article.

---

7. Jessica Mulligan, *Just Give Me a Game, Please*. Skotos, *Biting The Hand*, August 2001.
   `http://www.skotos. net/articles/BTH_07.html`.

8. This debate was in the context of gamelike virtual worlds.

The first, by Travis Casey[9], defended the pro-art point of view by considering whom virtual world designers ought to try to entertain. He concluded that of all the possibilities, the only one that guaranteed anyone at all would find the world entertaining was if designers designed to entertain themselves. Travis sees this as essentially an artistic stand: If you don't like what's being produced, you're not one of the people for whom it was being produced. I'm more ambivalent; most design teams do design for themselves, but a top-notch designer doesn't get any enduring pleasure from *playing* a virtual world, just from *creating* it.

The second response was by Raph Koster, in Jess's own column at her invitation[10]. Raph agreed that it was the first duty of a virtual world to be fun[11], but argued that art subsumes entertainment. Art can do many things, of which "entertain" is but one. Just because you do art, doesn't mean you can't do entertainment. Raph further argued that art brings an emphasis on craft, perfectionism, and ethics—things that the virtual world design community desperately needs. At a time when virtual worlds are struggling for legitimacy, attacking articulations of artistic purpose is not helpful.

Raph didn't directly address Jess's point that the objectifying of players leads to bad art, but from the passion of his argument it's fairly clear that he doesn't feel he himself is guilty of it. I personally don't believe it is *necessarily* always a bad thing: Different problems can need different paradigms, and sometimes you do need sociology rather than psychology. It becomes inexcusable when it's used inappropriately. Players are players first, components of an elaborate, orchestrated simulation only occasionally; however, "occasionally" is not "never."

Designers that are the caliber of Raph Koster shouldn't have to defend what they do. Players should be thinking, "this is a Raph Koster game—I really want to play it!"; they shouldn't be looking to prick what appears to be (but isn't) a bubble of pomposity. Their concerns arise because although they have been immersed in virtual worlds,

---

9. Travis S. Casey, *What's Entertainment?* Skotos, *Building Stories, Telling Games,* August 2001. http://www.skotos.net/articles/BSTG_15.html.

10. Raph Koster, *The Case for Art.* Skotos, *Biting The Hand,* September 2001. http://www.skotos.net/articles/BTH_09.shtml.

I ought to point out here that Raph has a Master's degree in Fine Arts and Jess's background includes a stint as a professional actor, so they both know what they're talking about.

11. Remember, he was talking in the context of gamelike virtual worlds. The first duty of other virtual worlds—educational or conferencing systems, for example—is usually different.

they have not been involved in the design process; the more they were to know about virtual world design, the more they would be able to appreciate the special qualities that individual designers bring to their creations. A critical aesthetic would help qualify what they should look for, if not dictate what they think when they see it.

There is a danger in having a critical aesthetic for an art in that it can take the edge off it, making it self-conscious. As a corollary, the more an art form is deconstructed, the less it means as a whole. As I noted in Chapter 2, "How to Make Virtual Worlds," designers can't play virtual worlds for fun (at least in the same sense that players do) because they can see too much of the machinery. They may be impressed by the way the virtual world is put together, by the nice touches and subtle nuances they perceive, but they aren't going to get excited by mounting an expedition to rescue a villager from a bunch of hobgobbledygooks. They don't get caught up in their world's fiction. This is not a situation that it would be wise to imbue in players; it's good if they can appreciate aspects of a design when they reflect on them, but bad if they're into the aesthetic so deeply that they can't appreciate the whole point of playing—that is, to have fun.

So if self-consciousness, leading to pretentiousness and humorlessness, is the disadvantage of having a critical aesthetic, what are the disadvantages of *not* having one?

Well, designers will make the same mistakes that other designers have made before; they'll do things without knowing why, advance in directions that are doomed to disappoint—all the failings that I have been ranting on about throughout this book[12]. Designers like to think of themselves as creative people, who instinctively know what's right and don't need any "rules." Without rules, though, how can you be a rule-breaker?

Virtual worlds *need* a critical aesthetic. Indeed, they may need more than one: I'm considering them as an art form in their entirety, but, as I pointed out, there is plenty of scope for creativity in their component parts. A player who designs their own area to fit into the greater design may work to some more specific aesthetic peculiar to that task. What is right for designers doesn't have to be right for everyone else. It does, however, have to be right for designers.

---

12. I'm not the only person to rail against it, either. Howard Collins calls it "The Grandfather Clause of Stupidity" in his excellent manifesto for holistic game design, *Mu's Unbelievably Long and Disjointed Ramblings about RPG Design*. 2001. http://mu.ranter.net/theory/printversion.html.

This book is about the design of virtual worlds, and therefore the critical aesthetic I shall attempt to develop is for virtual worlds as a whole.

Some Questions

In developing a critical aesthetic for virtual worlds, we need to answer some difficult questions. I won't pretend I answer any of them, but here they are anyway:

- ➤ How is the "value" of the virtual world experience determined?

- ➤ What do you need to understand when you have fun, and how do people with different understandings interact?

- ➤ What rules apply to all virtual worlds, and what are their limitations?

- ➤ What symbolism exists within the virtual world itself and within the way it is presented?

Earlier in this book, I advanced the theory that the value of the virtual world experience is that individuals come to understand more about themselves through the virtual world. This is only one interpretation, though: Players will rarely cite identity issues as the reason they play a virtual world. Then again, when players are asked what they *do* find fun, they come up with the same answers that gave rise to my player types model in the first place. When developers and publishers are asked to determine the value of the virtual world experience, they point to the length of time people keep active accounts; although this may be a metric, it's not a value. I don't want to know what people are prepared to lose in terms of time or money; I want to know what they gain.

The player development model I presented in Chapter 3, "Players," describes what players need to understand when they have fun. It also showed the way that players at different stages of development interact with one another[13]. The result is as much of a formal Theory of Virtual Worlds that we have at the moment—that is, about half of a framework.

---

13. Only for the four "original" types, though; the eight "new" types map onto the original four, but I didn't do the type/type comparisons for them as there are 36 combinations.

The third question has a facetious answer: The rules that apply to virtual worlds are those imposed by *reality*. Reality always wins. Although this is true, when it comes to playing virtual worlds a number of "rules" are nevertheless in place. Designers don't *have* to create a virtual world with a physics that looks kind of like real-life physics, but they *do*. They do it because these are part of the paradigm. I discussed the way virtual worlds hang together and the rationale behind it in Chapter 4, "World Design" and Chapter 5, "Life in the Virtual World;" this isn't to say that new paradigms won't arise, but for the moment we're still exploring what we have.

So that's three questions out of the way.

I shall attempt to address the final question in the remainder of this chapter. Because it involves practice that has evolved over time in the design of virtual worlds, it doesn't link directly into the rest of the theory, although it does touch on it. Nevertheless, its subject matter is as much a part of the theory as words are of language.

That doesn't mean finding an answer is going to be easy, though.

Template Theories

It's easier to create something new by beginning with something old than it is to start from nothing. In developing a critical aesthetic for virtual worlds, it makes sense to look at existing theories for related art forms and see what light they can shed. It's unlikely that they'll fit very closely, but nevertheless they could provide a framework on which to build. Perhaps the symbolism used in virtual worlds is gifted to us already through that of its nearest relatives?

I assert that the two closest art forms to virtual worlds are computer games and film[14]. Computer games don't yet have a theoretical underpinning; everything is still too transient because technology is always ahead. The reason your mobile phone has more computational power than the 1970s mainframe on which *MUD1* was written is entirely due to computer games. Business users didn't push for faster CPUs, better sound, better graphics, higher-capacity portable media; computer gamers did. I bought my first CD-ROM drive after installing a game that came on nine floppies; because enough people like me did the same thing, the price of CD-ROM drives fell and new

---

14. Sorry, theatre fans, but virtual worlds aren't performance. Sorry, literature fans, but virtual worlds aren't story. Sorry, urban planning fans, but virtual worlds aren't community.

PCs started appearing with them fitted as standard. I didn't buy a 19-inch monitor so I could keep more spreadsheet windows open at once; I bought it because it allowed me to see more of the *Civilization II* map. Early adopters—who will pay a premium for the latest technology if it means they can play the latest games—play games. Unfortunately, this implies the level of innovation is currently too high for a critical aesthetic to be viable.

The alternative view is that innovation is actually low because publishers too often play it safe, and a critical aesthetic doesn't exist because no self-respecting academic would sacrifice their career to develop one.

Computer games do have critics, in the form of reviewers who describe the latest games in professional magazines. In comparing the various merits of games, clearly some aesthetic is in action (even if it's moderated by the fact that many magazines are heavily reliant on income from advertising taken out by the publishers of the very games reviewed). Reviewers will in general comment on a game's genre, its graphics and sound quality, its gameplay, any special features, any technical issues, and its relationship to similar games; mainly, though, they're interested in whether it is fun to play. If it doesn't engage them, they will criticize it; if it does, they'll give it a high rating. Some magazines attempt to break down ratings into their contributing parts (graphics, sound, gameplay, and so on), but that's as far as it goes.

Given that the form of reviews has now stabilized (you could take a review from five years ago, bring its references up to date, and it would read like a review from today), there may well be the makings of a Theory of Computer Games here. Unfortunately, we don't have one yet. Thus, although I can draw parallels between virtual worlds and computer games, clearly I can't use any Theory of Computer Games as a foundation for looking at virtual worlds because there isn't one.

For film, on the other hand, there does exist a mature critical aesthetic[15]. Because of this, movies can entertain *and* have meaning beyond entertainment. Although there's nothing to stop computer games from having meaning beyond entertainment, their lack of a critical aesthetic makes this a rare occurrence; this is why when something entertaining does arrive that gives players cause to introspect, it's regarded as something special[16].

---

15. Rooted, incidentally, in those of film's closest relatives, photography and theatre.

16. Example: the *Ultima* series.

I shall therefore base my analysis of virtual world aesthetics primarily on that of film theory. Those readers about to panic in fear that I'm justifying subjecting them to yet another dose of reference-heavy academic prose will doubtless be pleased to learn that no knowledge of film studies is assumed. You may need to know *where* I'm coming from, but you don't need to know *what* I'm coming from....

Signs and Symbols

So, let's start with symbols.

When movies were first made, directors had to develop a language and their audience had to learn it: Real life doesn't have jump cuts. When something happens in the way information is presented on a movie screen which runs counter to the way that human senses accept information in the real world, this signals an interrupt that the mind needs to interpret consciously. By codifying the interrupts so they are always used under the same circumstances, the brain can learn what they "mean." This done, subsequent occurrences of the interrupt don't register unless they subvert the code in some way.

I recall as a child seeing a film on TV where the action started going on in several small mini-screens at once. I figured this meant the story had branched and I had a choice about which mini-screen to watch. Not knowing which story was going to turn out best, I asked my father for his advice. He explained that it was all part of the same story, and the activities shown were meant to be going on simultaneously; therefore I should try to pay attention to all of them at once. Nowadays when I see a split-screen effect, it doesn't even record in my consciousness, I just "know" it means that several things are happening at once. It's a symbol for which I have a reliable meaning. However, if early directors had gone a different way, a split-screen could have signified something entirely different.

The field of semiotics is concerned with the associating of meaning to signs. When the signs are structured according to a grammar, the result is a language; when they are merely systematized, the result is a vocabulary. For movies—and, as we shall see, virtual worlds—they aren't organized even to that degree. Nevertheless, the codes do exist, and they do have meanings that have been implicitly agreed on by those who create and experience them.

Determining the meaning of the signs (that arise because of the difference between virtual world technology and the way reality works) is therefore important. You didn't think virtual worlds *had* signs? When you watch a TV drama, you don't think you're actually a character participating in it, yet when you play a virtual world you do. Why? Is it merely because you control a character? No: It's because you accept that the character you control is a token that represents you. Accept it enough, and it *becomes* you (and you become it). Immersion is accepting the signifier as the signified. Those pixels on the screen are just pixels; *you* associate meaning with them.

For a critical aesthetic to be useful, it has to aim for universality. Everyone should understand the signs and their denotations in the same way. If I visit a textual world for the first time, I expect new conversational messages to appear below those I have already read[17]; I could play some other world that puts them above, but it would feel (to me) seriously weird. For textual worlds, there are reasons (ultimately to do with the way people read books) which explain why "above" connotes "before" and "below" connotes "after." For graphical worlds, though, conversational messages don't have to appear in a single window at all—they can (and do) appear in multiple embedded windows—for example, as speech bubbles[18]. These are still signs, though: Even though I can see words above some character's head, I don't assume I can pick them up like I could fruit hanging from a tree.

The coming of graphics to virtual worlds is like the coming of sound to movies. The same old rules apply, but the emphasis is different; there are also some new rules. These are rules, however, that are learned very early in a player's career, if indeed they didn't already know them from other art forms. It is possible (albeit tedious) to list them all, but doing so would only be of academic interest—a chart showing every color and its emotional impact doesn't make everyone a landscape artist. Where signs are important to designers is in their use, and I shall therefore refer to them in this context rather than enumerating the major ones here and continually referring back to the resulting table.

Symbols in virtual worlds have two roles. One is to make statements valid in the real world, and the other is to make statements valid in the virtual world. A virtual world that imposes a character class regime is "about" order and conformity; one that doesn't

---

17. I'm assuming the language used is English, here.

18. Co-opted from comics, therefore already understood by most players.

is "about" choice and independence. Both of these are political statements, irrespective of designers' bleatings to the contrary; they're statements that the virtual world makes in the real world through its design. A room complex that has increasingly lower light levels, on the other hand, is a statement within the context of the virtual world itself: It says that these rooms are successively more dangerous, because darkness is a metaphor for danger.

I'll address the external symbolism first, then move on to the internal symbolism.

Dimensions

External symbolism in virtual worlds can be explicit. You can create a virtual world where everyone is a dolphin trying to save the ocean from the evil oil companies that pollute the water[19]. This is not the kind of symbolism that I mean here, however. Rather, I'm concerned with the implicit kind, which are manifestations of the different views that designers hold regarding what is important about virtual worlds.

Debate—both verbally and through the action of design—takes place along several dimensions at once. Formally, these are known as *dialectics*—opposing viewpoints, the eventual resolution of which leads (hopefully) to the development of new viewpoints and, consequently, new dialectics. Movements may spring up that oppose the consensus or propose new ways of looking at things; sometimes, these extend across several art forms (as did impressionism, for example).

So what are the dialectics for virtual worlds? Let's look at our antecedents.

In film theory, the main historical dialectics[20] are/were

> ➤ *Life versus drama.* Should film be used to record life or to create fiction?

> ➤ *Realism versus expressionism.* Can more be said by showing the real or the artificial?

---

19. Of course, those same oil companies provide electricity companies with the fuel they need to generate the power used to run the computers that implement the virtual world itself, but politics doesn't have to be consistent.

20. These are taken from James Monaco, *How to Read a Film: Movies, Media, Multimedia* (3rd edition). New York, Oxford University Press, 2000.

➤ *Genre versus auteur.* How is the demand for predefined, stylized story forms reconciled with the artistic feelings of film makers?

➤ *Reality versus fantasy.* What is the role and power of authenticity?

➤ *Entertainment versus communication.* Is it the purpose of film to entertain the audience or to change it?

➤ *Innovation versus derivation.* Should audiences be given what we think they want or what they think they want?

Computer games don't have a formal theory, but two obvious themes that probably qualify as dialectics are

➤ *Hard core versus mass market.* Are games for games-players or for everybody?

➤ *Graphics versus gameplay.* How much substance should be sacrificed to form?

Scanning through these lists, some dialectics seem more appropriate to virtual worlds than others. Taking them in turn:

➤ *Life versus drama.* This is either a non-issue or an all-embracing meta-issue that highlights what makes virtual worlds different from all other art forms. From the point of view of the player, virtual worlds are clearly not real—they're virtual!—therefore it's a non-argument. Designers, while in the main also subscribe to this view, bear a responsibility for the consequences of their designs that players don't. This means they must accept that virtual worlds and their players are part of reality, and that the fiction is part of the fact: What happens in the virtual can affect the real. It's ridiculous to suggest that virtual worlds should record reality, yet in some sense reality can record the consequences of virtual worlds. That said, although this may be an important point, it's not a dialectic. Designers are able to apply both paradigms as the context dictates.

➤ *Realism versus expressionism.* This is perhaps a dialectic-to-be. Currently, designers regard realism as a tool for immersion, and any attempt to express emotion through artificial devices would break this immersion. It may be that as virtual worlds develop, the bond between realism and immersion can be made more supple, in which case an expressionistic approach could be attempted. We shall have to wait and see.

➤ *Genre versus auteur.* This is an emerging dialectic. Most designers are happy to work within a predefined genre, or even a particular licensed franchise. What makes them less happy is when bumbling, opinionated, know-nothing manager types demand changes without appreciating the effects it would have on game-play, let alone the implications for the work as a whole[21]. As designers gain reputations for their work, their power will increase. At that point, this dialectic will become an issue. When they're strong enough to form their own development companies, it will cease to be one. You will have noted that this chapter comes down firmly on the side of auteur; whatever virtual world development companies may wish, ultimately the designers are going to win this argument.

➤ *Reality versus fantasy.* The main question here is that of *authenticity*. It concerns the degree to which the situations and issues depicted in the art form reflect those of reality. It doesn't mean the same thing as *life versus drama*; it doesn't present a record of reality, but it does say things about reality. For example, a virtual world in which players take on the role of members of a contemporary oppressed people struggling under a dictatorship might have powerful resonance with whatever real-life situation it is based on, giving players a deeper insight into the plight of the individuals who have to suffer that fate from day to day. Although there is a place for such virtual worlds, they are clearly unlikely to have any great artistic affect on the majority; they're just too bleak to keep players in them for extended periods. Thus, any dialectic that does arise from looking at virtual worlds as social or political commentary is probably going to be of only minor importance.

➤ *Entertainment versus communication.* This is an ongoing dialectic in virtual worlds[22], as the exchanges between Jessica Mulligan and Raph Koster demonstrate. The crux of the matter is that what the players want syntactically (a virtual world that looks good, plays well, and is fun) is not what they want semantically (a virtual world that helps them define who they are). In fact, it's probably a lot worse than this in that many players will reject outright the suggestion that they could be playing for any reason other than to have fun[23]. Players and designers

---

21. Hopefully, those manager types reading this book hoping to gain an insight into virtual world design will, by now, have realized that the best thing to do is leave the design to the designer. If the designer steps outside the agreed remit, fair enough, jump on them. If their work looks iffy and they are unable satisfactorily to articulate why, again, haul them over the coals. If you have an idea that might help, tell them, it can't hurt. If you order them to make a change, though, that's a mistake. They're the designer, not you.

22. This is true even when the virtual world is not intended to be used primarily for entertainment.

23. I've presented in this book my arguments to the contrary, but people are entitled to believe whatever they like.

alike agree that it is axiomatic that virtual worlds should be entertaining. However, although designers might understand that there is no communication without entertainment, many players and publishers don't accept that there is no entertainment without communication.

➤ *Innovation versus derivation.* The most spectacularly successful virtual worlds have been those significantly different from their predecessors. The same applies to the most spectacularly unsuccessful ones. Those who lack the time, money, or creativity to innovate prefer derivation, but players who prefer the comfort of the old to the uncertainty of the new also drive it. Codebases and middleware solutions can help deliver a virtual world that wouldn't have existed otherwise, but if it means designers are forced to work within a moribund paradigm, then ultimately it's a bad thing. This is one debate that is never, ever, going to be resolved.

➤ *Hard core versus mass market.* In the early days of online services, 10% of users provided 90% of revenues[24]. Computer games manufacturers noticed the same thing: A small number of dedicated, hard-core players bought far more games than did casual gamers. When games-only online services went for the hard core, they almost always failed; when computer games publishers went for the mass market, they almost always failed. Where does this leave virtual worlds? Should they target a well-served existing hard core of players, or spread their net further to tap the possibly ambivalent mass market? As with entertainment versus communication, this is an ongoing dialectic with an end that is not in doubt: Virtual worlds must become more mass-market, because luring players away from other virtual worlds is simply too hard[25]. However, in so doing they will develop their own hard core of players, which cannot then be ignored.

➤ *Graphics versus gameplay.* How much of the available investment in a virtual world should be spent on making it look good as opposed to making it play well? In the computer games industry, graphics rule: Unless a product looks bang up to date, reviewers won't review it and players won't buy it. The same applies to virtual worlds that compete in the same marketplace, but with a sting: Regular

---

24. Or 20% of users provided 80% of revenues. The true figure is probably somewhere in between.

25. Bruce Woodcock's analysis of virtual world subscription base growth shows that *DAoC* may have got up to 75% of its players from *UO* and *EQ*. But Nick Yee's *Daedalus Project* suggests that these are loyalty-free, floating players who will switch to a newer virtual world from whatever one they are currently playing. In other words, you may be able to get them, but will you be able to keep them?
    http://pw1.netcom.com/~sirbruce/Subscriptions.html,
    http://www.nickyee.com/daedalus/archives/000195.php.

computer games are fire-and-forget, in that once you (as a developer) have sold them you don't care how great the long-term gameplay is—you already have the customer's money. Virtual worlds, however, make their profits from subscriptions, which depend on good long-term gameplay for their success. So, do you go for graphics or gameplay? Or do you spend double and go for both? The text/graphics split of virtual worlds makes this apposite, but it's not really a dialectic as such. Players want both looks *and* gameplay; the only question is whether the look is on the computer screen or in the player's mind. Textual worlds may have the stronger intellectual claim on a *construction versus reconstruction* basis, but graphical ones have the players. So for this dialectic, graphical worlds win; end of argument.

Besides these dimensions of debate, virtual worlds have some of their own. The ones that attract the most tension are

➤ *Direction versus non-direction.* Should the designers and/or live team guide player activity explicitly?

➤ *Responsibility versus liability.* What do players agree to when they sign up to play a virtual world?

➤ *Story versus history.* To what extent are players part of the work or part of the production?

➤ *Individual versus community.* Is this a world for individuals or for groups of individuals?

Again, taking these one at a time:

➤ *Direction versus non-direction.* There is always some directedness in virtual worlds—even the most open-ended of them—because designers cannot create them neutrally even if they want to. Reality is neutral; anything else is mere interpretation. The degree of direction is in question, however. Players often find their choice of character type restricted, or their goals, or even their narrative. How much should designers hold players' hands and how much should players be left to roam free[26]?

---

26. This can be related to other factors, too. For example, hard-core players may want their hand held less than do mass-market players.

➤ *Responsibility versus liability.* This is this issue of players' perceived rights to do stuff, opposed by their rights not to have stuff done to them. It's the dialectic that underlies PvP and PD. What risks to their characters and to themselves do players accept when they join a virtual world, and what happens when those risks bite? Are such risks necessary? Or are the consequences of not having them ultimately worse?

➤ *Story versus history.* Although this is sometimes linked with *direction versus non-direction*, the two are different. The question is whether virtual worlds are works of art that are handed over to players to do with as they will, or whether the players are themselves part of the work. Does the designer ever let go? Or is the virtual world designed so that whatever players do conforms to some greater vision?

➤ *Individual versus community.* What's good for the individual is not necessarily good for the community, and *vice versa.* For example, selling characters on eBay may be good for the two people involved, but it can hurt the virtual world as a whole. Similarly, players who band together can rip through content quicker than can the same number of individuals playing independently. At the moment, this is a fairly dormant argument, but its issues have not yet been resolved and it could reawaken any time (especially if real-life court cases make enough noise).

So, having looked at all of these various dimensions along which opinion is (or may become) divided, which are the most important? Any answer can only be subjective, but my own opinion is that these are currently the top five:

➤ Genre versus auteur

➤ Entertainment versus communication

➤ Direction versus non-direction

➤ Responsibility versus liability

➤ Hard core versus mass market

This book advances an opinion on every one of these; you might want to bear that in mind when reading the rest of this chapter, because it is in the context of these dialectics that the discussion takes place.

I should also point out that even if people do agree on a position, their interpretation of it can differ radically. *Asheron's Call 2*, for example, aims for the mainstream (good), but does so by imposing a cosseted blandness on everything. People don't like it when their arrows run out during combat? Here, have an infinite supply! Is running to the shop to sell your loot too onerous? You can convert it to cash in your backpack! Turbine may believe that dumbing down is the way to make its world more appealing to a mass market, but it's not apparent why it should be. Why *do* people play virtual worlds? No, really, *why*? What's the *fundamental* reason? Clue: It's not "to have fun," and even if it were, removing any challenge by wrapping characters in virtual cotton wool wouldn't deliver it.

Virtual world designers can have contrasting views on what virtual worlds are about, and contrasting views on how best to address those issues. They express their opinions in designs; the differences in philosophy lead to differences in design. By reading the differences in design, the differences in philosophy can be divined. If, when you look at a virtual world, you can associate a feature to a particular dialectic, you have the crucial insight you need to have a critical aesthetic. If not, you need to think about it until you do.

I could at this point produce a list of things to look out for (symbols) and link them to particular viewpoints (dialectics), thereby creating a system for interpreting what virtual world designers are saying with their worlds. Tempting though this is, I shall nevertheless refrain. This is a book for the designers of virtual worlds, not for their players. If designers were to create virtual worlds deliberately to convey a particular message, it would make sense to explain the symbols through which this communication takes place. However, designers don't do this. The message arises from their internal artistic conflicts along the various dialectic dimensions, and is merely revealed through their designs. Designers don't think what to say and then figure a way to say it; they say it, and leave it to others to figure out what it means.

This isn't to say that such an analysis isn't worth undertaking; it would be a powerful aid to people looking at virtual worlds seriously for the first time and struggling to understand the competing philosophies. It's just that this book is not the place to embark on such an exercise.

Whence the Symbols Come

An analysis of internal symbolism *is* justifiable here. Virtual world designers have many options available to them about what they put into a virtual world, what they leave out, how they put it in, and so on. In selecting between all the possibilities available to them, designers are employing their artistic faculties; furthermore, they are doing so deliberately. They want (for design/artistic reasons) to achieve an effect, therefore they arrange the virtual world to create it.

So what weapons do designers have in their armory? And how do they employ these to tell players things?

Well, first let's look at what they don't have in their armory. They don't have the ability to cut, fade, or do anything else that shatters the basic "you are here" conceit. They have no pausing, saving, replaying, scene breaks, or acts. These limitations make them different from both film and computer games in fundamental ways.

Players get to pan, track, and zoom; players get to decide where they point the camera; players decide whether they see themselves in first, second, or third person. Designers give them this control, and don't get it back. Although *players* can in theory record and edit their own content for public consumption, this facility is not available to designers; the nearest they get to it is the patch cycle, which is something of a blunt instrument (but nevertheless usable, as we shall see shortly).

So although film directors are concerned with what to shoot and how to shoot it[27], virtual world designers are not because the players make those decisions. Instead, designers are concerned with what to cause to exist and how to cause it to exist[28]. Composition is of static objects and the starting locations of non-static objects (or restarting locations, for static spawns)[29].

---

27. Students of film call this *mise-en-scène*, which is French for "setting in scene" or "staging."

28. Not so much *mise-en-scène* as *mise-en-forme*.

29. It's easy for designers to underestimate the power of context—that is, the statement they make by the juxtaposition of objects. For an excellent essay on this subject (albeit in the context of single-player worlds), see: Roger Giner-Sorolla, *Crimes Against Mimesis*. April, 1996.
http://bang.dhs.org/if/library/design/mimesis.html.

It is important to distinguish between the art that the designer creates within the virtual world and the art created by others in the same context. If a designer lays out boulders in a certain way to imbue a location with a particular feel, that's not the same as if a player takes those boulders and builds a statue out of them. They're both works of art, but they're not works of the same art; the former enables the latter. It's not like sampling or collage, which reuses art in different ways; it's art-within-art. Chapter 6, "It's Not a Game, It's a …," mentioned virtual theater companies whose players[30] perform on the stage that virtual worlds provide. Again, this is art in its own right, but again it differs from the art of the world's designer. Why? Because the *symbolism* is different. The same objects mean different things to the different artistic traditions. There's also the issue of ownership.

Developers can and do claim legal ownership of the entire database that defines their virtual world and all images generated from it. To reproduce so much as a screenshot, you need their permission. This has implications on art-within-art, in that an artist can't claim ownership of their work even if it's of higher quality than the art it is within. If Leonardo Da Vinci had painted *The Last Supper* on the sidewalk, he couldn't have dug it up and taken it home. Why? Because *it wasn't his sidewalk*. Similarly, any art created in virtual worlds is fundamentally transient, with the sole exception of that intrinsic to the virtual world itself. Sea level stays where it is until the designer says otherwise.

As a bit of an aside, although ownership of the bytes is not (or should not be) in dispute, ownership of the photons they generate is perhaps less defensible. Virtual worlds are places. If I visited New York and took a photograph of a street scene, I would not be violating anyone's copyright. Sure, if I were doing something disruptive such as a movie shoot, then I'd need permission from the authorities first. For a snapshot, though, forget it! Furthermore, any artistic statement made by this would be all mine. The cult 1960s TV show *The Prisoner* was made in the Welsh village of Portmeirion and owed much of its other-worldliness to this location's singular appearance. Its architect, Clough Williams-Ellis, did not "own" *The Prisoner* artistically, though; he made his statement through his architecture, and left its interpretation to individuals. Designers of virtual worlds need to let go; if they don't they're not creating virtual worlds, they're creating something else.

---

30. In two senses of the word.

Virtual world designers provide the tools and the toys. They covenant with the players that, within the virtual world, these

- ➤ Have value

- ➤ Have meaning

- ➤ Make sense

When the sense they make is two-fold (text and subtext), that's symbolism.

A Chemistry for Virtual Worlds

In screenplays, every action and every piece of dialogue must have a purpose. Movies are so expensive to make that anything that doesn't advance the plot or round out a character must be ruthlessly cut. This even applies to comedies: You may laugh at the joke, but if the joke weren't there, then at a purely structural level there would be a minor plot hole.

Virtual worlds don't have quite the same financial or narrative constraints. It's not the case that everything must have a purpose, but everything[31] ought to have a *potential* purpose[32]. The players may determine a different purpose entirely to the one intended, deliberately or otherwise, but so long as they find *some* purpose they're happy. It's very frustrating to look for an object's use when it doesn't actually have one, and even worse if your complaints bring only hoots of laughter from the live team.

In screenplays, the dialogue, action, characters, and locations are the "atoms" that are built up into the "molecules" of scenes. Each atom has a purpose; using a different atom will change the chemistry of the resulting molecule, making it react differently with the other molecules that make up the screenplay as a whole. Sometimes an atom can work at multiple levels, as in the example of a one-liner in a comedy: It might make you smile, it might move the plot forward a notch, it may say something about the character

---

31. Some designers would limit this to "the vast majority of objects." As I mentioned in Chapter 4, it's preferable to give even decorative objects some tangible meaning, if only for immersive reasons. However, if there are players who get excited specifically by intangible-only content, what harm does it do to indulge them (so long as it's clear that the content's meaning is intangible)?

32. Communicating this purpose to players can be something of a challenge. Not everyone wants to read page after page of lore, for example.

who utters it (or the character who is its butt), it could influence the pacing, it might even make a point out of context for the screenplay itself altogether. And this applies to every line out of 110 pages of lines? Therein lies the art of the screenwriter.

Virtual world design documents have similar atoms: objects, commands, characters, and locations. What molecules are these atoms built into? Quests?

At a tangible level, yes. Players want things to do, and by arranging design atoms such that in combination they enable the solving of quests (whether generated by the world itself of by its players), the whole can behave differently from its parts. Quests are valid design molecules, but they're not the ones I'm going to talk about here. This discussion concerns the symbols used in virtual worlds, and symbols need both a tangible and an intangible meaning[33]. Quests do have intangible meaning, but it's to the individual player at a hero's journey level[34].

Designers use tangible objects to construct intangible meaning by combining them to influence breadth, depth, and atmosphere.

Breadth means player choice. The size of the world, the number of objects within it, the variety of commands: Breadth is form. *Depth* means understanding. The effects of commands, the complexity of the physics, the ability to use things in unintended ways: Depth is function. Where breadth reflects the range of opportunities that players have to change to the world, depth reflects the extent of change that each individual opportunity can effect.

When a newbie joins a virtual world, it's the breadth that interests them. They want to know that there *is* depth but they don't want to be exposed to it (otherwise it will seem too daunting[35]). Depth is for more experienced players, for whom breadth is unsatisfying. The further along their development track a player is, the more they will favor depth over breadth.

---

33. If the symbols became abstract, the only tangible meaning they would really need is that of existence. However, as I just said, in virtual worlds (at least for the moment) all objects should have *some* purpose apparent to the players; this means they need a tangible meaning, even if over time it becomes increasingly nominal.

34. It's open to designers to associate other meanings to quests, thereby enabling their use as symbols. They don't seem to do this at the moment, though, probably because quest systems themselves are still in flux.

35. This is why the manuals for virtual worlds don't often go into detail; besides, detail can be sold separately as a players' guide.

In terms of symbolism, depth is easier to deal with than breadth. Breadth is by definition global to the virtual world, therefore any differences in breadth that might be picked up by players as symbolic have to be in global systems. If, for example, there were 50 different ways to combine fruit to make desserts but only five legal weapon/armor configurations, that would tell players that combat was not as important as cookery in this virtual world, or at least that cookery was more important than they might ordinarily think.

Depth effects can be more local. If the kobolds in one part of a virtual world have no names and are of indeterminate age and gender, yet the ones elsewhere have first names, surnames, families, and children, this says that the ones here are not as important as the ones elsewhere. If players notice this, they will act on the information (although whether they choose to emancipate or slay the unnamed kobolds is another matter, of course).

Unfortunately, too few players are attuned to virtual world design enough to realize that differences in breadth and depth may be deliberate. They'll see them as careless inconsistencies or bugs. Actually, they may well be right a lot of the time and they *are* bugs; this merely compounds the problem of using breadth or depth to say anything beyond the basics of what players are able to do and how doing these things affects the virtual world. Breadth and depth, while something that designers do build from the design atoms available to them, don't yet have the fidelity necessary to be used symbolically.

I did mention atmosphere....

With atmosphere, at last, we have a way of using virtual world mechanisms and objects as symbols that players actually interpret as symbols.

Atmosphere is the means by which designers influence players' moods. It can be active (for example, it tells the players they are in danger), passive (for example, it puts players at ease), or interactive (conducive to exploitation by players). Atmosphere is used to

- ➤ Signal the start or end of an action sequence.
- ➤ Signal a breathing space during an action sequence.
- ➤ Throw players off their guard, ready for a big surprise.
- ➤ Warn or encourage players.
- ➤ Reward or punish players.

- ➤ Hint at what is to come.

- ➤ Facilitate various social activities.

- ➤ Make a philosophical or ethical point. (This may or may not be in combination with any of the above.)

Some obvious ways to suggest atmosphere are

- ➤ *Open versus closed form.* Cramped areas restrict choice, wide areas open it up; dungeons are more oppressive than wilderness. When players enter a very narrow passage or descend underground stairs, they know their options are being limited; if they continue, it symbolizes their readiness to accept the danger. When players enter a vast plain, they know their options are maximized; if they continue, it symbolizes their readiness to accept responsibility.

- ➤ *Lightness versus darkness.* The less you know, the more easily you're spooked. The same applies to other sensory information that the virtual world supplies: Sudden silence is also spooky. When players find that the light levels are falling, they can interpret this as a warning. If they keep on going, they are accepting the challenge of whatever awaits them. If they see light at the end of the tunnel, it tells them their ordeals are nearing their end.

- ➤ *Vistas versus corners.* Corners hide information. You know the information is there, but you don't know what it is. The less you're told, the more you want to learn—but the more you fear you won't like what you discover. A passageway that has a number of short, sharp turns increases the sense of urgency; a long, straight passageway reduces it[36]. On the other hand, a vista can symbolize the distance of goals: You emerge from the trees to see a vast tract of open country, on the far horizon of which you can just make out the spires of the City of Bronze. The designer is showing you what you'll have to go through to get there: By proceeding, you're reaffirming your goal.

- ➤ *Familiarity versus alienness.* A sudden change of terrain or architecture can induce either relief or a sense of unease. The more sudden the change, the greater the impact. This may look like a regular Middle Eastern bazaar, but when it gives way

---

36. Textual worlds can use long and short descriptions to achieve this kind of pacing, too. If a room has a minimal description, it takes less time to read it; you therefore leave for the next room quicker, which ups the tempo even if you're actually only traveling in a straight line.

to a snowfield there's a jarring of expectations. This is not a normal bazaar. Do you investigate, or do you get out before anything dreadful happens? More gradual changes can serve to label areas: The more spiky the architecture, the more spiky the inhabitants[37]. The same technique can be used on a smaller scale. Your blacksmith's hammer breaks, you get a new one, it happens all the time; this time, though, the replacement hammer changes its appearance the first time you use it, and makes a noise different to that of regular hammers. It tokenizes the unknown: Do you explore it, or shy away?

➤ *Ease versus difficulty*. In the big city, you're asked to deliver bread; in the frontier town, you're asked to kill bandits. Can you stand the heat, or do you get out of the kitchen? By giving players harder quests in rougher areas, designers inform them that these *are* tougher areas. If some NPC asks you to wipe out a nest of vampires and you refuse, you've nevertheless been told that this is the kind of place where there are nests of vampires. If you go wandering off on your own, you can't say you weren't warned. The quests act as notices that players should heed.

➤ *Large versus small*. Big monsters are strong monsters; tall NPCs are authoritative NPCs. Smaller monsters can be dominated; smaller NPCs are servile. Tiny monsters may be fast, poisonous, or otherwise awkward; tiny NPCs have some hidden power. An impression of size can send potent, primal messages to players. It's why real-world animals such as cats will try to make themselves look bigger when facing off an opponent.

➤ *Beauty versus ugliness*. Breathtaking panoramas and glorious palaces can generate feelings of awe and wonder. Misshapen creatures and ruined buildings can make an otherwise normal situation seem unpleasant. Beauty represents success, ugliness failure; beauty goodness, ugliness evil. It operates at different levels (the superficially beautiful can be ugly deep down, and *vice versa*), but the symbolism remains the same. This is one area where the players call the shots: They'll assume beauty to be indicative of goodness, safety, aspiration, and so on even if the designer just wants to make their world look better than competing virtual worlds.

---

37. *MUD1* used time as a metaphor for danger. The more contemporary a scene (up to about the 1930s), the safer it was. The really dangerous places were flagged by their great age. This imbued areas with an atmosphere that players were immediately able to pick up on (even though most didn't recognize the symbolism explicitly).

There are many others, too. Intense colors mean warmth, vibrancy, and action, whereas washed-out colors mean coldness, placidity, and melancholy; changes over time can question the permanence of your knowledge and your willingness to adapt. Individual designers have their own styles of controlling the atmosphere of locations and situations; all are subtly different.

Symbols can be combined and contrasted to create new symbols: The alien can be beautiful; a corner can turn into the light; warmth and softness can make a cramped space seem secure. The priests of Gheen wear sumptuous gowns but disfigure their faces with hideous scars.

Designers place the symbols in context; players interpret them and divine the context. Thus, we have a basic chemistry for our critical aesthetic.

The Story of Story

Symbols of atmosphere react with "adjacent" symbols, but in a non-linear fashion. Linearity can be enforced (for example, by making characters "run a gauntlet"), but this is itself an expression of atmosphere. Non-linearity is good for making statements, but bad for advancing arguments. Is there some other way that symbolism can be introduced such that it can be structured in a linear (and therefore more contributory) fashion?

Narrative

The way that both film and computer games handle this is through *narrative*. Film is the more structured: The scenes in a screenplay link causally to tell a story (generally in a classic, three-act form). Syd Field's famous analysis[38] of script form puts act I at pages 1–30, act II at pages 30–90, and act III at pages 90–120. Around pages 10–15 will be an inciting incident that knocks the initially stable situation out of balance; around pages 25–27 will be a big event that gives the protagonist a goal; around page 60 will be a pinch point where the protagonist becomes fully committed; around pages 85–90 will be a crisis point where all seems lost; the resulting showdown lasts until about page 115, then the story wraps up with a realization section where the audience

---

38. Syd Field, *Screenplay: The Foundations of Screenwriting*. New York, Dell, 1979.

can see how events have grown the protagonist as a person. The position of the later events can slip a little, but many professional screenplay readers really *will* look at pages 25–27 and reject a script if it doesn't have a big event there.

Virtual worlds don't—*can't*—have this degree of narrative control, because players don't follow scripts. However, some causality can be introduced, and it can be done in such a way as to stimulate emotional or other involvement in players. It is important to realize that virtual worlds do *not* have, nor ever *can* they have, narrative in the conventional sense. They're places. Players can act out narratives of their own within them, but the virtual worlds can't impose a three-act structure or anything like it. Nevertheless, they can do some things. Here's their full narrative spectrum:

➤ *Non-fiction*. Changes are introduced without any explanation. One day a new area, spell, class, or weapon is available that wasn't available yesterday. There's no rationalization, it just happens. This may be in response to player suggestions or complaints, or it may have been planned from the beginning but omitted so that the virtual world could meet its launch date—whatever. The change is made with no supporting context, therefore any meaning that players read into it can only be intrinsic to it. "Oh, there's a new class of bards. They must want to give role-players more choice."

➤ *Backstory arcs*. These are narrative tricks intended to explain a virtual world's pre-history, and are the mainstay of regular computer games. The better worlds use them to add richness and depth, explaining why things are as they are; the worse ones retro-fit a backstory to make illogical gameplay features seem logical. If a virtual world's initial configuration is constructed to echo events of a fictional past, this can be a great aid to immersion. When it's to erect some façade to justify why characters don't die, or why magic-users can't wield swords, or why artifacts exist that no one can make, that's less satisfactory. The backstory should come first, not second. Unfortunately, so many virtual worlds now use the retro-fit approach that players are growing accustomed to it. This means that backstory is often merely a designer's commentary on their creation, rather than an inherent part of it.

➤ *Idea arcs*. With these, events occur that give players things to do, but they are not related to any central theme. Individual mini-dramas may be played out by the eruption of a volcano, an invasion by teeming hordes of monsters, a failure of the grain harvest, or whatever, but the events that trigger them are not part of any central narrative. Designers can make statements through these—for example, about the transience of all things or about their own ambivalent feelings concerning their powers—but these would be inserted as part of the wider work, rather than as threads in a narrative.

➤ *Story arcs.* These consist of interlinked series of events. The volcano erupts because the dwarfs dug too deep in their search for gold. The disaster awakens the ancient, half-remembered demi-god who once ruled all, but who was defeated in a cataclysmic battle and sealed beneath the sacred mountain. Through the causality of the events, the designer is making a point about the consequences of unmitigated greed. Unfortunately, the players have no say whatsoever in it: The drama unfolds whether they like it or not. They must react to the change in circumstances that the unfolding events dictate, but they can't affect even the timing of what follows: A monthly patch is a monthly patch.

➤ *Responsive arcs.* Here, the designer changes the narrative in response to players' reactions, much as a table-top referee might. For large-scale virtual worlds with multiple shards, this is very expensive as individual shards can have divergent narratives[39]. Nevertheless, it is the strongest narrative form available to virtual world designers: It allows them to enter into a dialog with the body of players, and if the trust is there, it allows for expression on both sides[40].

➤ *360 degree arcs.* There is a narrative path, but it's circular. Players are involved in a perpetual struggle, sometimes making gains and sometimes making losses, but never able to achieve final victory or defeat. They're locked into a story that never changes. Whatever the designer may be trying to say with this technique, the players will eventually conclude that the struggle is meaningless. If that's how newbies see it too, the virtual world could end up in trouble.

➤ *Player arcs.* The virtual world is richly featured enough that players themselves are empowered to create personal narratives through their own ongoing actions. Designers get to give them the tools and the space in which to do this, but they don't affect the narrative itself directly. Thus, although they can make statements by what they give the players to work with, they can't tie these into a story; that's for the players to do.

---

39. The problem is not as bad if arcs are kept short so there's little opportunity for them to diverge.

40. There is a good introduction to this topic in Jessica Mulligan's, *Show Me the Path.* Skotos, *Biting the Hand,* November 2002. http://www.skotos.net/articles/BTH_38.shtml.

From this we can see that it is possible for virtual world designers to construct a narrative, but there are a number of barriers. Players don't like being treated like ants whose nest is being stirred up for the amusement of some kid with a long stick. If a volcano is set to erupt every once in a while pseudo-randomly, that's one thing; if it's set to erupt because the live team say so, that's another thing altogether. The same event begs different interpretations based on the perceived intent of its creator. It's not enough for the designer to say that the event is what matters and it's for players to construct their own meaning from it: Players (through their characters) are directly affected by the event, and their understanding of it is heavily moderated by the notion of deliberateness.

Say I walked into an art gallery containing a paint gun installation. I know the paint gun will shoot at random intervals, and I can construct some statement about the nature of risk from that. If I walk in front of it and get hit, well, that's going to make me ponder on it some more. If, however, I walk in front of it and the artist presses a button that makes it shoot me, the conditions from which I construct my meaning are different. Yes, I get hit by the paint gun in both cases, and yes, the artist set up the paint gun the same way both times. However, being hit at random is not the same as being hit deliberately.

So it is with virtual worlds. Imposed storylines mean reduced freedom. Through narrative, designers can explore important issues; however, by forcing players to participate in those narratives the issues change.

Story elements *can* be added in reaction to what players do. For example, if a bunch of characters mine deep into a mountain they could encounter a colony of dwarfs or dark elves or crystalloids. It's hard to predict in advance when (if ever) players would dig deep into a particular mountain, and harder to list all the other possible things they may do that could reasonably lead to new content; for these reasons, it's therefore not usually worth hard-coding bespoke content into a virtual world. However, it may be worth building a pool of content that can be released when appropriate to advance players' stories. These also can be used by the live team to spice up a waning incarnation of a virtual world, for example when some überguild is enforcing a dreary *status quo*.

The main difficulty with this form of interactive content provision is that many players resent the fact that there's someone pulling the strings and will level accusations of favoritism or victimization. "Hey, I dug a hole in this mountain over here, how come you didn't give *me* any dwarfs?" Players like to think that the world is fair; interference by the live team in response to the reactions of individual players is unfair. Basically, they trust the code to be impartial but they don't trust the live team to be so (except in very refined worlds). The new content inevitably becomes symbolic of the management's disregard for players, regardless of whether it has some other, greater interpretation.

I've discussed narrative thus far on the global scale. Where narrative most often occurs is on the local scale, primarily through quests. In these, players as individuals are targeted by the narrative, rather than players as an amorphous group. Thus, although the designer is talking to fewer people with each narrative, what is said can be more finely tuned to those people. The different degrees at which independent narrative episodes can be sustained are

➤ *Puzzles.* These are fixed in their location and solution; a standard maze is the classic example. Puzzles provide a search-space framework for branching narratives. Their inflexible nature means they can cover predetermined narratives in greater depth, but at the expense of becoming uninteresting very rapidly. Once solved, they're solved.

➤ *Static quests.* These have standard locations and goals, but allow some open-endedness in their solution. They're generally mindless and repetitive because they're targeted at newbies rather than at more experienced players. Because newbies undertake them, though, designers will use the opportunity to promote shared cultural contexts. Although the narrative possibilities may therefore be reduced to making general statements about the nature of the virtual world, they nevertheless lay the groundwork for more sophisticated forms of expression that players may encounter later.

➤ *Dynamic quests.* These change every time in locations or goals or both. They serve gameplay purposes only, and rarely matter beyond their existence. Although the means by which they are generated may be symbolic, the quests themselves can't be so as they have no direct human input in their construction.

➤ *Chained quests.* These are a series of interlinked quests, each one leading to a new, usually greater one. They may be plotted manually by a designer or dynamically by an AI, or in combination. There is greater scope for narrative here with the potential to make an impact on individuals; even AI-generated chained quests can conform to a predefined concept, such as whether it matters more to rescue a friend or save a village of strangers. Chained quests can be used as part of an overall story arc, or to introduce new spells, resources or whatever that would otherwise appear without reason.

➤ *Player quests.* The virtual world is so broad and deep that players can find things to give each other to do. This is the *emergent gameplay* approach, which is good for the players (those with the desire to participate) but allows for no narrative content on the part of the designers other than in the form.

Narrative is frequently seen as an important artistic feature that is often lacking in computer games; by extension, virtual worlds are also often criticized for their lack of story (except those that have it, which are criticized for the quality of the story). Implicit in this is the elitist notion that players aren't all that good at storytelling, therefore anything that emerges from their actions is not going to be compelling; better to find the people who are best at storytelling and have them write the stories for everyone.

I don't dispute that some people are better at storytelling than others. The question is, what is storytelling's place in virtual world design? Are people participating to be part of someone else's story, or to be a part of their own? In the major part of this book, I have argued strongly in favor of the latter. Virtual world designers may use narrative as a way of joining related concepts into a coherent whole, but these can only ever be steps along the way of a player's personal narrative, which is what they make of *themselves*. Virtual worlds that impose narrative—even narrative written by a famous author—are overlooking what virtual worlds are *about*.

Why Story Arcs Don't Work

Most narrative art forms are passive, in that the audience doesn't participate directly in their creation. An author may be creating a novel to speak to a particular group of people, but can only estimate how they will respond, and thus how the novel should be changed as a result of this imagined response. In virtual worlds, the audience can in theory participate to the point of collaboration. Are they part of the work? Are they part of the production? Are they neither, or can they be both[41]?

In most virtual worlds, the dialogue between designer and player is indirect. Players can influence production from the beta test onward, but as individuals only in very

41. In which case, it is interesting to speculate how they might symbolize themselves.

minor ways. Some virtual worlds do go as far as to give the player body control over the actual programming, but most don't. The fact that *LambdaMOO* famously introduced this has created a false impression among researchers that the practice is widespread. It is not. Commercial virtual worlds in particular would consider this degree of player involvement in production insane. Players may be part of production within the context of the virtual world, but not of the virtual world itself.

It is the question of whether players are part of the work that is more contentious. As I mentioned earlier, I don't regard the objectification of players as by definition a bad thing; after all, I don't expect road construction engineers to look on me as anything other than a driving statistic, so if a designer looks on me as a bandwidth statistic at some point, fair enough. The objection comes when this is done inappropriately; in particular, players do not like being thought of as components of someone else's art installation. If a virtual world is advertised as being such, they can hardly complain, of course (any more than can an actor in a play); indeed, it may be that over time players gain a maturity and understanding that allows them to appreciate the skill of the storyteller more fully. They would then become more akin to an improvisational theater group rather than players of virtual worlds, though. Sure, there's a place for this kind of art, but it's not a place that appeals to the reasons players play.

Designers who want virtual worlds to have storylines usually cite from the following reasons:

- ➤ It keeps people playing, because they want to find out what happens next.
- ➤ The virtual world seems richer, more immersive, and more vibrant.
- ➤ New content can be introduced that would be fiction-breaking otherwise—for example, a new race of lizard people.
- ➤ Pre-planned, higher-level content can be released in a controlled manner.
- ➤ It provides cover for nerfs and bug-fixes.
- ➤ It lets players know they haven't been forgotten.
- ➤ It demonstrates the design team's creative credentials.
- ➤ It helps market the virtual world.

➤ There is increased opportunity for tie-in books and other merchandise, arising from having more intellectual properties.

➤ It's *de rigeur*.

These look reasonable enough, but there are some serious flaws:

➤ Either the player is impotent or the arc is derailable.

➤ You can follow the story without playing. I know a former *Asheron's Call* player who got wrapped up in the story but not the world; she now follows it from web sites.

➤ People don't like coming in on a narrative after it has started.

➤ Players like to create stuff of their own more than they like to see what other people have created—whatever its artistic merits.

➤ Explorers don't mind new content being added, but dislike having to check over changed old content. They much prefer to be told explicitly what changes have been made, rather than having to deduce them from some piece of story.

➤ Player actions are limited by future storyline considerations. You can't build here because there'll be a castle on this spot four months from now.

➤ The more story that designers add to a virtual world, the less world there is, because the world is constrained by the story[42].

➤ What happens when the story arc ends? Everyone quits and plays some other game? Or does the arc never end?

➤ Players' destinies are not under their control, *nor can they ever be*. A hero's journey in such circumstances is nonsensical.

Even without these objections, there are practical difficulties concerned with writing a narrative for virtual worlds. Stories in most cultures of the world traditionally follow the classical three-act structure of beginning, middle, and end. As noted previously, if you try this for a virtual world it means there's an end. This is fine if the story is one of many stories that make up a player's experience, but it's not good if the virtual world is itself the story. The three-act structure is replaced by a recursive structure instead:

---

42. I do mean story here, not fiction. A virtual world based on a book can be incredibly detailed, so long as it adheres only to the fiction and not the story.

➤ A single, beatable individual is identified as the enemy. It's not the police state that's trying to crush you, it's one particular member of the secret police.

➤ You identify the enemy, collect the plot tokens, and defeat them. But they were just a pawn, controlled by the *real* enemy!

➤ Variant: They aren't really dead! They come back bigger and stronger!

➤ Recurse.

This is the conspiracy theory approach: When in doubt, widen the conspiracy. Eventually, the whole world ends up as a conspiracy and then you have nowhere to go. It's a narrative trap.

Oh well, you can cross that bridge when you come to it.

Designer-level narrative has a place in virtual worlds, as a method of delivering content, information, and/or meaning. It is very good for presenting and identifying symbols. It is hopeless for presenting and identifying choice. Sparks, yes; arcs, no.

The fact is, any virtual world that places designer-driven story above players' personal stories is a prison. This is why story arcs don't work.

The Koster-Vogel Cube

At the 2001 Game Developers Conference, Raph Koster and Rich Vogel introduced[43] their well-received *storytelling cube* as a model for describing the various ways by which players can experience virtual world event sequences as narratives. The following year, they explored it in more detail[44]. Their model classifies the elements that make up narratives along three binary dimensions:

---

43. Raph Koster and Rich Vogel, *Online World Design Patterns*. San Jose, Proceedings of Game Developers Conference, 2001. http://www.legendmud.org/raph/gaming/despat_files/frame.htm.

44. Raph Koster and Rich Vogel, *Storytelling in the Online Medium*. San Jose, Proceedings of Game Developers Conference, 2002. http://www.legendmud.org/raph/gaming/gdc_2002_Storytelling_files/frame.htm.

➤ *Control.* Is the story told by the designer, or does it arise from player interactions?

➤ *Context.* Does the story arise more from real-world events or from the virtual world itself?

➤ *Impact.* Are the story's effects short-lived or lasting?

These dimensions give eight possible combinations:

➤ *Designer/in context/static.* All content exists at the beginning, and players uncover it. Example: *Majestic.*

➤ *Designer/in context/dynamic.* Designer-created content is delivered episodically, possibly making major changes. Example: *Asheron's Call.*

➤ *Designer/out of context/static.* This recognizes real-world events such as Christmas holidays as part of its fiction. Example: *Ultima Online.*

➤ *Designer/out of context/dynamic.* Designers attempt to weave any new features they add into a consistent narrative. Example: *Achaea.*

➤ *Players/in context/static.* Players role-play in the designers' world. Example: *EverQuest.*

➤ *Players/in context/dynamic.* Players role-play in the designers' world, and through their actions can change that world in major ways. The designers adjust the context to take account of the events. Example: *Castle Marrach.*

➤ *Players/out of context/static.* Players do things for their own reasons, irrespective of what the context says they should do. They tell each other stories that make myth of their adventures; they go on themed jungle crawls. This is the default player activity.

➤ *Players/out of context/dynamic.* Players act outside of any designer-driven plot, but through their own actions can cause important and permanent changes to the virtual world. Example: *Lineage.*

The idea behind the Koster-Vogel cube is that it helps virtual world designers conceptualize what kind of virtual world they want; it lays bare the narrative choices that are open to designers. The cube has certainly proven effective in this regard, but I have a few misgivings about it.

My main complaint is that the dimensions seem to change their meanings. Players can role-play in *Asheron's Call* as much as they can in *EverQuest*, so why is *EQ* classified as having player-driven narrative when *AC* isn't? The main difference between the two in storytelling terms is that *AC* gives (the designers') stories more impact than does *EQ*'s static "vision," so what's the justification for having differences in two dimensions instead of just one? Similarly, *Ultima Online*'s players role-play more than *EQ*'s and arguably have a stronger ability to determine their own destinies, so why is *UO* designer/out of context/static and not player/out of context/static? Perhaps *EQ* should be in the designer/in context/static sub-cube instead (or perhaps it should be acknowledged that virtual worlds can be in more than one sub-cube at the same time).

The context axis is especially tricky: I'd have thought the way *Achaea* strives to weave real-world events (such as the appointment of a new administrator) into its fiction would make it a more in-context world than one like *EQ* that presents the events with no in-context explanation at all. But if the "out of context" flag means "giving in-context meaning to real-world events," how does that agree with the default player activity sub-cube? There, players are not making any reference to real-world events, just to the in-context events that occur through their own determination of their story. Personally, I think the context axis is weaker than the other two; it's a distraction, and the model makes better sense if reduced to two dimensions (impact and control).

To illustrate my point, where would *MUD1* fit in this scheme? Well it had real-world events programmed in, so that means it's out-of-context (even though most of the time those events were dormant). It was reset-based, so any story impact was static. Control of narrative events was in the hands of the players, operating in the space of events made possible by the design. This suggests that *MUD1* should be placed in the default player activity cube. This may well be correct: *MUD1* had no backstory. What difference would it have made if it had have *had* one, though? Bear in mind that if I hadn't added the real-world holiday stuff to *MUD1*, it would appear in the same sub-cube as *EQ* (which does have a backstory of sorts—more than *MUD1* does, anyway).

Back in Chapter 1, "Introduction to Virtual Worlds," I discussed persistence versus change as a way to categorize virtual worlds. The Koster-Vogel cube's impact dimension is roughly the same as persistence, and its control dimension is roughly the same as change (or player impact[45]). There is a difference between in-context building and

---

45. I mention the alternative term here only so as to point out that "impact" can be used to refer to two different things: The long-term effect a story has on the world and the inclusivity of storytelling ability.

out-of-context building, but it's not orthogonal to the other two dimensions; in particular, the groups of players able to build in-context in a world may differ from those that can build out-of-context in the same world.

The Koster-Vogel cube looks at virtual worlds as a medium for storytelling, and as such succeeds. It is, however, neutral concerning the likely success or otherwise of a virtual world that follows any particular classification. Designers using the cube should bear this in mind; in particular, virtual worlds with overarching designed-in storylines (as opposed to opt-in, opt-out mini-narratives) face a long struggle.

The Place of Narrative

Virtual worlds are places, not stories. You can have a story about New York, or a story set in New York, and New York can have a history, but New York is not *itself* a story unless you stretch the definition of "story" so far that it loses all meaning[46]. The same applies to virtual worlds: Trying to impose a story on the inhabitants of a virtual world is as sensible as trying to impose a story on the inhabitants of New York. You can impose events, but not stories; people make their own stories.

The designers of virtual worlds write the history, either explicitly (as a piece of prose) or implicitly (in the design). This gives the initial context, at which point the designers cede narrative control to the players *whether they want to or not*. Through play, the players write their own stories, but only to the extent they do in real life; there's nothing intrinsic to virtual worlds that makes player actions any more "storytelling" than real-life actions. You do things, things happen, you recount these happenings to other people: story.

Virtual world designers can't add story, they only can add content. Content provides experiences that can be made by those who come through or observe them into story. If the content itself is story, players' own stories become worthless incidentals.

Narrative is linear. Virtual worlds are not linear. You can't control the order in which players do things without railroading them, removing significant freedoms. There is

---

46. The other extreme is to narrow the meaning of "story" so much that most of what players would describe to one another as a story wouldn't count. In *Hamlet on the Holodeck*, for example, Janet H. Murray looks at narratives in virtual worlds as fitting within traditional forms of narrative. This assumes that interactivity is entirely "in character" and players have goals determined by the world rather than by themselves. The result is a much tighter judgment of what constitutes "narrative" in virtual worlds.

only one path into the past, and thence comes story; there are infinite paths into the future. Virtual world designers build a bagatelle board and release the ball, but have no way of knowing where it is going to land. If they did, where would the fun be?

Episodic release of content is guaranteed its place in narrative theory, but the real reason for its existence is purely practical: Developers want to stop players from getting bored. Dressing it up as story is merely a handy conceit. Any developers who believe otherwise are deceiving themselves (and their players).

Some content needs to be added for other reasons: Virtual worlds continually need fine-tuning; real-world occurrences can have an impact on the virtual world that requires an in-context explanation. In these cases, content can be slipped in such that it disrupts the world's fiction less, but it does still disrupt it. It adds another peg to the bagatelle board, and no amount of hand waving or appealing to artistic imperatives can disguise the fact.

The Critical Aesthetic in Use

Let's return to the concept of a critical aesthetic. How is it used? How is it developed? Do different virtual world architectures give rise to different aesthetics? If so, is there any cross-fertilization between them or are they immiscible?

The Job of the Critic

Films have critics, computer games have reviewers, but what do virtual worlds have?

Virtual worlds have rant sites.

That's not entirely fair; the main listings sites for textual worlds do carry player-written reviews that are often thoughtful and insightful (and not necessarily written by people with a vested interest in making prospective players either play or fail to play the world in question). For graphical worlds, though, with their much bigger player bases, rant sites rule.

When it comes down to it, virtual worlds are places. In the real world, if you want to go on vacation somewhere you buy an up-to-date guidebook before you go. The guidebook tells you all you want to know, using language you can understand, in a reasonably unbiased manner. Virtual worlds do have guidebooks that you can buy, but as I mentioned earlier these are usually just extensions of the manual (and they're not necessarily up-to-date). If you have a real-world guidebook for Egypt, you may on the strength of reading it want to go there even more; if you have a guidebook for a virtual world, it's because you've already been there but couldn't get to grips with it. Unfortunately, if you scan through the articles on a rant site for either Egypt or for a virtual world, you're only ever going to come away with misgivings.

Rant sites are almost non-stop interpretation and criticism. Sometimes the criticism is constructive[47], often it is justified, but always it is biting. To paraphrase Mr. Burns in *The Simpsons*, rant sites "know what they hate."

Much of the criticism that rant sites direct at virtual worlds is non-comparative. You have to decide which virtual world you want to try on the basis of whichever attracts the fewest complaints on subjects that matter to you. Occasionally, they do describe virtual worlds in terms of one another, but this is normally to petition for the inclusion or removal of a feature on the grounds that some other virtual world has or doesn't have it. Usually, though, the comments are prescriptive and fairly self-centered: This is what the virtual world *should* be like so that people like *me* will enjoy it. Nevertheless, individual writers do have consistent opinions, and if you find one whose views agree with yours on something you know about, it makes eminent sense to consult them when it comes to something you don't know about.

The problem that a critic/reviewer of virtual worlds has is that these take a lot of time to get to know. Food critics only have to eat in a restaurant once to be able to fill half a page of newsprint with colorful invective; film critics can watch five movies a day. Even computer game reviewers diligent enough to play something all the way through will rarely have to spend more than a week at it[48]. Virtual world reviewers can only do

47. On occasion it can be positively euphoric if a new virtual world looks to be significantly different. This enthusiasm rarely lasts long, however, as design flaws become apparent. Rant sites *want* to like virtual worlds, and are predisposed to do so; their cynicism comes from the disappointment of being frustrated time and time again.

48. Many can't do this anyway, even if they want to, because to get their articles written so that publication coincides with the game's release, they're often provided with beta copies that may still suffer from a few, er, glitches.

a good job if they take *months*—and then, having invested so much of themselves in the world, they have the problem (common to ethnographers) of disconnecting from their subject matter enough to write about it objectively.

When reviewers manage to do this, they are capable of writing excellent critiques. It can be very difficult making these accessible to non-players, though. It's like reading the blurb of book six in a Fantasy series that you haven't read books one through five of: "After the fall of Khanex, Modorph's future looks secure. But now the Jeek-riders of Xethen threaten the southern borders and Wachel roam the Dillith Marches. Can Luth and his Darok blade, Shaash, ever…." So it is with virtual worlds: To explain what is truly wrong or right with one, it's often only possible to do so with reference to things that people may only understand having experienced them.

There are exceptions, of course. Back in Chapter 1, I described the ways by which virtual worlds are readily categorized from a newbie-friendly historical perspective; such information is often sufficient to put off people trying one or cause them to look at it in more detail. This hardly amounts to criticism, though. Another technique, favored mainly by researchers rather than reviewers, is to play a virtual world for a few evenings to get a sense of its look and feel, then interview players to form a picture of what life is like after six months. This can be useful, and the critic's ability to collate and summarize opinion comes to the fore. Unfortunately, it's not always easy obtaining a representative sample of players: A higher proportion of the ones you bump into or who respond to interview requests seem to have a chip on their shoulder than is statistically correct. Nevertheless, an experienced reviewer can account for this, knowing it will happen. This is one of many reasons why I am very excited by the (as I write this) impending re-launch of the print magazine *Massive Online Gaming*[49], the first issue of which (before it hit publisher problems) was hugely impressive.

The role of the rant-site critic in virtual worlds is large in terms of forming player opinion, but small in terms of relevance to prospective new players. If you've grown disenchanted with one world and want to try a different one, or if you're a total newbie looking for somewhere to start out, a rant site won't help[50]. Intelligent reviewers can be invaluable guides, but ultimately you need a means to assess virtual worlds *yourself*.

---

49. http://www.mogonline.com/

50. Indeed, because they concentrate more on what's wrong than what's right, a rant site is probably the last place anyone wanting to find a good virtual world should look.

This must be both accessible and supportive of a Theory of Virtual Worlds to which you give allegiance. The theory gives the ideal; the experience gives the reality; the critical aesthetic connects the two.

Perhaps one day virtual worlds will have travel guides, written by independent correspondents whose job it is to report on them. Until then, however, players are essentially on their own.

Content Created by Players

Back in Chapter 1, I described the two mechanisms by which players can add content: Within context and without context. In my discussion thus far, I've assumed that any content added by regular players will be within context, as with house building in *Ultima Online*. What are the implications of allowing them to add it without context, as with arbitrary room construction in *LambdaMOO*?

A first observation is that allowing players to build out of context passes control of the critical aesthetic to those who consume it. This implies accessibility, removing the pretentiousness and snobbishness that comes from artistic elitism (which I've undoubtedly been guilty of demonstrating in this chapter). One player's opinion is just as good as any other player's opinion.

A second observation is that this critical aesthetic is recursive. A player's creation when considered as a work of art is legitimate purely because it was created, not because it was created in line with some theory. Thus, any theory that tried to explain players' creations would contradict its own existence.

The existence of worlds where players can build has implications for virtual worlds where they can't (and for which the existence of a Theory of Virtual Worlds is less problematical). It ensures that the theory can't stray too distant from the player, because otherwise it would be exposed as distant. Players will create according to what they perceive as the critical norms, but if those norms become too esoteric, then they won't. This gives designers of worlds where players can't build a ground wire. Naïve art may be naïve, but it's still art—and it's art that informs designers' own art. Virtual world designers may be better at creating their art than the average player, but it's the average player who judges them. If the average player lacks the critical faculties to appreciate the work, it's the designer who is asking too much, not the player who has learned too little.

On the final day of the 2002 Game Developers Conference, there was a panel discussion about the next generation of virtual worlds. On the panel were Raph Koster, Rich Lawrence, Jessica Mulligan, Jake Song, and Gordon Walton. Raph's opinion was that the next generation of virtual worlds would see much more player-generated content. A question from the floor asked how designers should deal with this, given that 99% of it would be crap[51].

Gordon Walton summarized this as meaning that most people have the desire to be creative, but not the skill. Raph Koster turned it around, in a celebrated defense of the ability of players to create: Players don't care that 99% of everything is crap because they see their own creations as being in the 1% that isn't. Virtual worlds give the ability to create art to people who never had a platform for it before. People want to express themselves, and in virtual worlds they can. Film directors, writers, poets, and painters should get over themselves, because the rest of the world is coming.

This is a rousing sentiment. Raph's suggested first step to achieving such a goal was to permit in-context creation in virtual worlds, which allows for authorship within authorship; whether in a large-scale virtual world this could ever be extended to designer-level authorship is less clear, however[52].

Although I applaud the ideals involved here, I'm not convinced they'll work in practice (at least not as described). Players may like to think their creations are in the 1% that is excellent, but when they are disabused of the notion they will rarely be happy. My elder daughter has a web site with cartoons on it that she has created for her friends[53]. She likes it, her friends like it, she's happy. Someone else I know has a web site with cartoons on it that she hopes will attract the interest of animators[54]. The cartoons are crap. Animators make polite noises, but no way are they ever going to give her any money. She is frustrated, she is unhappy, and every push she makes to convince anyone that her work is good is met with yet more evidence to the contrary.

---

51. This is a misquotation of Theodore Sturgeon, who said that 90% of everything is crud. Some sources report that he also added that the remaining 10% is worth dying for.

52. There are worlds in development that attempt to address these problems. *Pirates of the Burning Sea* (http://www.burningsea.com), for example, envisages player-generated content being peer-reviewed for acceptance. I remain skeptical, but am open to persuasion.

53. http://www.jennybartle.com

54. URL not given, to protect me from her wrath.

So long as people don't set their sights too high when they create things in virtual worlds, it's fine. If they do—and this is perhaps the default—then it turns sour.

There is an interesting possibility that virtual worlds can be used as gateways to sub-worlds. This happens in some textual worlds already, where there is an overarching "context" world onto which players build their own public or private extensions; it's not yet the case for 3D graphical worlds, but that will surely come[55]. Consider, for example, allowing players major build powers within their own pocket zones in *EverQuest 2*: In this situation *EQ2* would act as a gateway, providing plenty of content for newbies, but players could build their own games within the game. Some would be bad, some would be good, and some would be good enough that people might even consider paying their creators to enter them. In time, the host world need not have any gameplay elements at all; it would merely act as a portal to the worlds it supported. What would result would be a kind of World Wide Web for streamed content, with players creating places rather than pages, hyperspaces[56] rather than hypertext. Were such a system to evolve, the applicability of this book would fall a level, because it assumes that virtual worlds are self-contained. If they could contain or can connect to other (arbitrary) virtual worlds, or if other worlds could connect uncontrollably to it, the artistic integrity of the world as a whole would be called into question (but not necessarily that of its sub-worlds).

It's also interesting to consider the impact on the hero's journey metaphor of making creation the primary activity in a virtual world. People play virtual worlds to discover themselves. They can do this through a hero's journey or through the self-expression that comes through art. Which of these does the inherent nature of virtual worlds best support? Can they exist side by side, or will one always dominate the other? Which is the more effective? Which would keep people playing for longer? Which can virtual worlds deliver in ways that other forums for artistic endeavor can't?

My Take on All This

Ideally, designers should create their world in such a way that they never need to add new content. In practice, this can never be. Nevertheless, new content should only be added to rectify problems in the way that the world works—that is, bug-fixing,

---

55. *Furcadia* already does it for 2½D worlds.

56. Unfortunately, because this word is used for a well-known Science Fiction trope, I doubt it's going to catch on here. "Hyperplace" would work, but place is not analogous to text.

balancing, and functional enhancing. Designers should not look to add or change content—even for artistic reasons—if it is not necessary[57]. All other content should be emergent from player activities. This means you need a virtual world with enough depth and breadth that players can, through the effects of their own actions, create content for themselves, and for others. The real world does it, so why can't we? Players should have no access to out-of-context content creation tools. Whether they have access to non-trivial in-context tools is open. This kind of "hands off" world is what I was trying to create right at the beginning with *MUD1*. Hopefully, some day someone will get close to achieving it.

Narrative: You can only tell a story when it has ended. Designers can create the obstacles, but the players themselves must overcome them. Players may come across self-contained, narratively driven sequences of events, but story arcs are out of the question.

In the end, all that designers can do is load, take aim, and fire. What happens after they pull the trigger depends on how good a shot they are. They provide an environment, they seed a starting culture (or multiple cultures), and then they yield control to the players. Of course the virtual world needs managing thereafter, because the nature does need nurture. Artistic expression by the designer stops with the launch, though.

This is my world. I created it. It's my gift to you. Take it. Live in it. Make of it what you will. It's your world now.

The central theme of Arthurian myth is whether the king is for the kingdom or whether the kingdom is for the king[58]. This has a hugely important spiritual dimension, as Arthur is a metaphor for the human soul. Merlin teaches Arthur with a view to his becoming a king for the kingdom, but Mordred exploits the relationship between Guinevere and Lancelot to cause Arthur to use his kingdom for his own ends.

Are designers for their virtual worlds, or are virtual worlds for their designers?

The answer is *both*. The king is for the kingdom; the kingdom is for the king. They're the same.

---

57. For an assessment of the consequences of over-tinkering, see Tenarius, *Welcome to the Player Wimping Guidebook! Or How to Dry Up your MUD in No Time.* 2000. http://www.memorableplaces.com/mudwimping.html.

58. Charles W. S. Williams, *The Crowning of Arthur. Taliessin through Logres*, London, Oxford University Press, London, 1938. He actually asks whether the king is *made* for the kingdom or *vice versa*.

Locate, learn, apply, internalize: As characters reflect players, so virtual worlds reflect their designers; as players learn from their characters, so designers learn from their worlds. The more of yourself that you, as a designer, put into a virtual world, the more you become it and it becomes you. Your experiences will develop the world's, and its will develop yours.

The virtual world is your (the designer's) exploration of yourself. It's your hero's journey.

The king *is* the kingdom. How could it be otherwise?

Chapter 8

Coda: Ethical Considerations

I'm writing this short chapter because, believe it or not, the designers of virtual worlds carry a responsibility for the consequences of their designs. Real people play these worlds, and the effects that a design has on them are real. Naturally, players themselves are in many ways accountable for their own actions: If you know that a virtual world has PD and you know that experiencing PD can be distressing, then when you play in that world and suffer PD and find it *is* distressing you can only blame yourself. Nevertheless, designers ought to be aware when some aspect of their design is likely to become an issue; its inclusion then becomes an artistic statement, rather than merely an element of gameplay.

This book is aimed at designers rather than players, so I'll primarily be exploring the moral and ethical considerations that arise concerning virtual world design[1]. All these are still open for debate: Where I express an opinion, that's all it is, opinion; your opinion is worth just as much as mine in such matters.

I don't claim to have any answers here, just questions. They're questions that every designer of virtual worlds should ponder, though. With power comes responsibility; designers have power, therefore they must accept the responsibility that goes with it.

---

1. This doesn't mean that designers should ignore what players (or anyone else) consider to be an unethical design; even if their point of view is highly misconceived, they can still sue.

A word of warning; this section only concerns virtual worlds that do not have young-sters playing them. Virtual worlds that are written for (or that can be expected to attract large numbers of) children have a whole extra layer of ethical issues to their design, about which I do not feel qualified to comment.

Censorship

The first topic I shall look at is that of censorship: The deliberate exclusion of material that would warrant inclusion on purely informative, artistic, or gameplay grounds. The libertarian viewpoint is that all censorship is bad; everyone has a right to free speech, whatever they want to say and to whomever they want to say it. The common-sense interpretation of this is that there are certain conditions where what is said can be pro-foundly damaging (thus the libel laws) or dangerous (shouting "fire!" in a crowded theater[2]), and in these situations free speech takes second place to some greater right. Otherwise, people can say what they want[3].

There are still exceptions, though. Elizabeth Reid argues in a paper[4] about the ethics she employed when undertaking her research into virtual worlds that she should per-haps have self-censored some of the details that were given to her, even though they were provided willingly by people in the knowledge and expectation that they would be published. Her reasons for this are that her discussion of *JennyMUSH* provoked such interest among social scientists that they descended on it *en masse* to study the community; needless to say, this put it under such pressure that it almost fell apart. Legally—and ethically, as far as the players were concerned—Reid had every right to publish the details she did. Nevertheless, in retrospect she wished she had made every quotation anonymous (even if that meant being unable to use some of them) because then people wouldn't have been able to find *JennyMUSH* so easily and their sheer num-ber wouldn't therefore have impacted upon it.

---

2. This assumes that there isn't a fire in the theater, of course, or that the shout doesn't come from an actor deliv-ering a line in character on the stage.

3. A third point of view is that free speech is not an issue: A virtual world is a place of business, and therefore its proprietors can legitimately refuse entry to people whose business they don't (or no longer) want. Players like to refer to this as the "fascist" approach.

4. Elizabeth Reid, *Informed Consent in the Study of Online Communities: A Reflection on the Effects of Computer-Mediated Social Research.* New York, *The Information Society* Vol. 12 (2), Taylor & Francis, 1996. http://venus.soci.niu.edu/~jthomas/ethics/tis/go.libby.

Currently, censorship in virtual worlds is performed almost entirely by the designers. The marketing group may insist on some changes, and licensed worlds have to remain true to the franchise, but beyond that there is only the law of the land (whatever "land" that may be). In the U.S., virtual worlds have been able to pitch themselves as examples of free speech in action, so they have been relatively free of legal interference. It may be just a matter of time before a major test case comes to court over violations of anti-hatred, libel/slander, or property laws, but for the moment this has not occurred. This is in part due to two factors:

➤ It's fairly clear that virtual world operators are no more responsible for what players say within them than telephone companies are for what people say on phones. They relay communication; they don't publish it[5].

➤ Virtual world designers self-censor their virtual worlds so that contentious or provocative content does not appear.

So, let's look at the kind of thing that might, at a glance, seem legitimate material for virtual worlds but that never seems to make it into them.

Unpleasantness

Some things are found unpleasant by enough of the population that even though they accurately reflect reality it would cause dissent were they to be included. Slavery, for example, was a fact of human existence for millennia; even now, some countries allow bonded labor that is slavery in practice if not in law.

So, you're designing a virtual world set in the swashbuckling Age of Piracy. Players take on the role of a buccaneer, sailing the Caribbean in search of treasure, glory, and infamy. Within a week of beginning your research, you (the designer) have come to the conclusion that slavery was such an important part of Caribbean trade and industry that were you to omit it your economic model would be missing a third of its goods. Do you put it in, or leave it out?

---

5. It could be argued that virtual worlds create an environment that encourages people to engage in hate language or whatever, but see the next point.

If your virtual world was for educational purposes, you'd probably leave it in. If it was primarily for entertainment, though...? The game *Europa 1400: The Guild*[6] lets women become Catholic archbishops, even though this somewhat undermines its historical accuracy[7]. Virtual world designers tend to do this kind of thing too.

Unpleasant history is one example where self-censorship comes in. Another is unpleasant present. In the 19th century, it was the general consensus in the western world that men were stronger and more clever than women. Now, it's the general consensus that men and women are of equal intelligence. What about their comparative physical strength? Studies have shown that past academic examinations and intelligence tests were invariably biased in favor of men. Er, strength? Women and men may emphasize different aspects of their intelligence, but neither one gender nor the other is fundamentally the more intelligent. So will you answer the question about strength? Women excel at linguistic tasks, whereas men are good at spatial, and so on.

Most virtual worlds give men and women equal physical strength, even though in reality women are palpably not as strong[8]. Some women are beefy enough to haul a truck, sure, but not ones that look like the female avatars in *EverQuest*. Those virtual worlds that don't give female characters the same strength as male characters will usually try to compensate by making female characters shine at something else instead. It's all for show, though. Real-life, non-cosmetic differences in gender and race are so charged with potential for problems that virtual world designers simply edit them out of their worlds rather than suffer the political problems that come with including them.

A third example of unpleasantness is that which is fine now but which may not be in the future. Movies in the 1950s were full of people smoking cigarettes, but today's certainly aren't. Virtual worlds can have very long lives; what should designers omit that might cause future offense?

---

6. Lars Martensen (lead designer), 4HEAD Studios, *Europa 1400: The Guild*. Rottenmann Austria, JoWood Productions, 2002.

7. It's not universally popular among Catholic players, either.

8. So powerful is the taboo against mentioning this that I'm actually wondering whether I should write half a paragraph of disclaimers here.

It may seem foolish to speculate on these possibilities: How can you know that something in your virtual world that is currently acceptable will cease to be so in a few years' time? In general, of course, you can't, but in some areas you can, particularly terminology. For example, in this book I have referred to people having same-sex orientation as "gay" and "homosexual." It is practically guaranteed that in 50 years' time even the phrase "same-sex orientation" will not meet with approval. The situation is yet worse for describing different races: Whatever currently prescribed term I use to describe a race or ethnic grouping, the historical evidence is that in 50 years' time I'm going to appear a racist[9]. It's very tempting therefore for virtual world designers to counter this by omitting anything that has a track record of being controversial. This, of course, has other consequences (that we shall come to later).

As a final remark on the subject of unpleasantness in virtual worlds, it should be noted that the definition of "unpleasantness" varies between real-world cultures. For example, computer games that concern the hunting of wild animals are big-sellers in the United States but aren't even released in the United Kingdom—there'd be a public outcry if they were. Many examples of such "localization issues" exist; designers must choose either to ignore them (and lose sales), to make their presence switchable (which is expensive), or not to put in any offending content in the first place (hey, there's an idea).

The Real as the Virtual (and Vice Versa)

Virtual worlds have their own communities and their own laws. Some things that are depicted in virtual worlds are legal in the context of that world, but would not be legal when practiced in the real world. For example, a virtual world set in the time of the British Raj may implement the Hindu custom of *suttee*, whereby widows threw themselves onto the funeral pyres of their recently deceased husbands. This would be allowed in the virtual world, but it's been all but stamped out in the real world[10].

Other examples abound. Virtual worlds routinely allow murder and the libeling of one character by another; some permit cruelty to animals, some promote the use of narcotics. It's one thing to portray real-world crime as a virtual crime, as would be the

9. Hi, readers in 2053. "African-American." Was I right?

10. Although different cultures have different ideas about whether suicide is right or wrong, few suggest that the enormous pressure sometimes put on widows to enact *suttee* (to the extent that many were thrown onto their husbands' pyres) was acceptable.

case in a virtual world set in prohibition-era Chicago. It's another thing, though, to make real-world crimes legal in their virtual-world implementation. Nevertheless, this is quite possible; in combat-oriented worlds, it's even quite probable.

On the one hand, this distinctness from reality can be seen as a freedom from oppressive real-world laws: You may need to have your identity papers with you at all times in the real world, but you don't in a virtual one. On the other hand, it could be seen as the dangerous encouragement of antisocial behavior: Whom does it harm when an adult PC has virtual sex with a child NPC?

Although virtual worlds are generally more freedom-oriented than the real world, there are a few occasions where the situation is reversed. This is mainly because of restrictions that the real world places on the virtual world. For example, what two adults do in the privacy of their own bedroom is generally no one's business but theirs, yet the graphical depiction of this behavior in a virtual world could well qualify as hard-core pornography. Virtual worlds that show things that would be illegal to broadcast to any television can rationally expect to be closed down. Nevertheless, people doing those things in real life are not breaking any laws[11].

Another issue is the manner in which real-life objects are shown. Basically, you have more freedom to mess about with a name-branded object in the real world than you do in a virtual one. It used to be that if you wanted to show a brand in a computer game, you had to pay the brand-owner; nowadays, it's more likely to be the other way around. These are mostly legal issues, of course, and therefore not of direct relevance here. Ethics become involved when things that can be recognized in real life make an appearance in a virtual world against the wishes of the people who own them.

For example, chase/combat game *The Getaway* incorporates a 3D model of central London built up from tens of thousands of photographs. People who own the properties shown have no right to object to this, under the same laws that apply to movie

---

11. For an extensive guide to the way that role-playing games handle (or can be made to handle) the sex act, see: Various authors, *The Complete Guide to Unlawful Carnal Knowledge for Fantasy Role-Playing Games*. http://www.kanga.nu/mirrors/www.lysator.liu.se/%257Ejohol/netbooks/ CarnalGuide/carnal.txt.
For those who find it useful, the equivalent for alcohol use is: Various authors, *The Complete Guide to Alcohol for Fantasy Role-Playing Games*. http://www.kanga.nu/mirrors/www.lysator.liu.se/%257Ejohol/netbooks/ AlcoholGuide/AlcoholTCGTA.txt.

shoots in streets. A virtual world could use similar real-world data to produce an accurate visual model of some identifiable portion of the real world. Property owners can't complain (well, they can, but the developers don't have to listen). So what would happen if a player took over a virtual building that in the real world was a fast food franchise, then turned it into a brothel or a drug den? Could the owners object after that? To whom? What if shop-fronts displayed advertising logos for major corporations that players then defaced. Would that be right (because players are making a political statement in a virtual world) or wrong (because logos are free speech even in virtual worlds and defacing them is censorship)? Can designers deface these, as they might if they were creating a post-apocalyptic virtual world?

Supposing brands do appear with permission, players may still use them immorally. If you buy enough cups of virtual cola, you can lay them out in a pattern to look like any part of the human anatomy you like. You can write words with them. You can put them in demeaning contexts, such as public lavatories. Is it ethical to do so? It's ethical enough in the real world, as long as you send the cans for recycling after you've made your point. In a virtual world, though, you may be paying a smaller subscription than you would be if the cola company hadn't paid for product placement. Doesn't accepting the reduction in price impose on you an obligation not to interfere with the message?

Virtual world designers handle these issues by self-censorship. Except in certain key areas where public expectation is on their side (for example, killing monsters), they avoid anything that could raise major ethical issues. It's understandable why they would do this, of course, but it stifles debate. It's left to the designers of small-scale worlds to push the boundaries, but all too often they use off-the-shelf codebases that have already made the decisions for them.

If you're a virtual world designer looking for an area in which to make your artistic mark, this could therefore be quite a fruitful area.

Passive Censorship

Censorship is generally active: You have a design that includes an element that you want, but you decide to take it out. If you did nothing, there would be no censorship. However, on occasion it can be passive: Information comes to light that is not in the public domain, and by doing nothing you are keeping it there. This amounts to censorship by inaction.

Here's an example of what I mean.

Many virtual worlds have the concept of "guild ownership" of property. Characters pay money or give objects to a guild, and this can be used to obtain items collectively that individuals could not own themselves; the guild is like a company in real life—a legal entity that can be treated as a person in many respects. Real companies have directors, guilds have leaders. So what happens if the leaders decide to asset-strip the guild, then close it down?

Most virtual worlds don't account for this kind of activity. On the face of it, why should they? If players sign up for a guild and are ripped off by the leadership, well, that's just the way of things. Guilds are for groups of like-minded people; choose your friends more wisely next time.

If it were only that guild leaders gave guild property to their other characters, well, okay, a "dog-eat-dog" argument is perhaps tenable. What happens when they sell the stuff on eBay, though? They could be a team working to a long-term plan, inveigling themselves into other players' confidences to maneuver themselves into positions of power. Think this sounds improbable? It's happened; it's probably happening right now.

So, what does the developer do if they spot players ripping off one another? If they do nothing, this would be a form of censorship. So do they stop it? If it doesn't break their terms of service, on what grounds could they do that? They would be breaking a trust. One solution would be to make a change to the virtual world design so that there was always an audit trail available and players can see where their stuff came from. That's somewhat unrealistic, though; it's not going to please characters who play as thieves in a PvP world, for example.

This is just one example of many. Censorship is the deliberate exclusion of material, but that material does not have to be tangible, and the decision *not* to act can be as censorious as the decision *to* act.

Players as People

"It's just a game."

When you play a game and you know the rules and something happens within those rules, you just have to accept it. You may not like it that the other team scored the touchdown, but you knew it was a possibility. All you can do is try harder.

This would be a fine analogy if virtual worlds were games. They're not, though: They're places. Some activities may be game-like, but not everything is. When players treat non-game behavior like it was a game, this can have a nasty impact on other people in real life.

In normal computer games, you can do anything that the code allows you to. This is not an attitude that extends to virtual worlds, though. Most of the time it's a good rule of thumb, but sometimes the virtual world lets you do things that you shouldn't. As a trivial example, they aren't coded to prevent your saying things that in real life would constitute verbal abuse.

Persona Issues

When people sign up to virtual worlds, they will have a number of preconceptions as to what they can expect to happen to their characters and what they can expect not to happen to them. This may come from publicity, from what friends have told them, or from a general sense of what "this kind" of product is like. If they know the virtual world is "about" combat, they can expect their character to kill things in it. If they don't know initially, but in the character creation system discover that there is a wide range of combat options available, then they should read this as a warning that nevertheless there is combat in this world. If they don't like the idea, they don't have to play[12].

If something happens that could not be reasonably expected, that's of course a different matter. In many cases, it will be a surprise—possibly even a pleasant one—but not an issue. You didn't know this Victorian Science Fiction game incorporated a race of

---

12. It may be that they already paid before finding this out, though.

troglodytes, but hurray, you do now. In other cases, it will be less pleasant but not emotionally damaging (for example, forcing players to make their characters use the lavatory). In some instances, though, it could be hurtful. The classic example of this is rape.

As I explained in Chapter 6, there are occasions when players are immersed to the extent that an assault on their character feels like an assault on them personally. If they knew this was a possibility before it happened, then no matter how bad it feels when it does happen they can blame only themselves. If I sit in the front row at the sea lion pool, I shouldn't be surprised if I get wet; if I play a virtual world with PD, I shouldn't be surprised if my persona gets killed. In either case, I should be surprised—and possibly deeply injured—if I were raped. It doesn't fit the context; it's not something I signed up for. Even if it did fit the context (plenty of wars in the past involved rape and pillage, so a brutally realistic historical world could perhaps justify including it), an explicit warning would be a good idea: So few worlds implement the concept of rape that it would come as a shock to find that one did even if it made perfect sense in the milieu.

Other real-world effects can also be disturbing. If you were to chop off some character's leg in combat, a reasonable result might be that they couldn't walk. Similarly, if you threw boiling water in their eyes, you might blind them. Some people are disabled in real life, and they could well play in your world. Is it right to show their disability in a negative light like this? What if their character suffers the same disability as the player? It's tiresome being deaf in real life[13]; why should anyone have to put up with it in the virtual world, too? It's not like virtual deafness gives any great insight into the condition, so education is no grounds for inclusion.

What about illnesses and diseases? If your virtual world includes cigarettes, it might seem fun to give characters that over-indulge lung cancer. Hey, it's responsible, too, encouraging people not to smoke. That's not going to cut much ice with a player whose grandmother just died of lung cancer, though. Poisons also have to be handled thoughtfully: The sensibilities of people whose relatives went to Nazi death camps must be respected. I should point out that it's by no means impossible to incorporate these themes into virtual worlds; the difficult part is doing so responsibly.

---

13. I speak from personal experience, having gone almost totally deaf at age 5. Fortunately, surgeons were able to restore my hearing, the only lasting effect being that I have difficulty determining what direction sounds come from.

There are further examples of seemingly innocuous things in virtual worlds that can have real-world effects on people. In *MUD2*, there is (among other things) a piece of ham that characters can eat to restore lost stamina. Should a real-life vegetarian allow their character to eat the ham? Am I, having put the ham there, hurting the feelings of vegetarians? Should I remove it? Was I wrong ever to create it, knowing that it might offend vegetarians[14]?

The problem with looking at the effects on players of virtual events is, of course, that people can be affronted by practically anything. Plenty of people in the real world are frightened of spiders, so should there be no spiders in virtual worlds so as not to alarm them? What about those people in the real world unlucky enough to be afraid of oranges? They do exist: Should their concerns not be given equal weight?

Personally, I take the view that the only morally consistent approach is for designers to be true to their own beliefs. Do what you want to do: If players don't like it, they can stop playing. General content warnings, like film classifications, can be used to fore-warn people of what range of material they can expect. Beyond that, though, it's up to players to decide whether they want to visit your world. Developers should not have to take out product liability insurance for content any more than publishers should have to for books. It's for players to weigh the odds of participation, not for designers to second-guess them.

Morality: Another candidate for inclusion in a critical aesthetic?

Privacy

Anything you do in a virtual world can be logged or snooped. In commercial textual worlds, it probably will be; in graphical worlds, cover is rarely 100% at the moment but will become so eventually.

So, is this an invasion of privacy? No more than is a closed-circuit television system (CCTV) monitoring a shopping mall. Indeed, it's probably less so, given that log files are only usually looked at when there's been a complaint whereas CCTV cameras are watched the whole time (in theory, at least).

---

14. I did know, too: I put it in deliberately, just to give vegetarians an interesting dilemma.

Well, that's one point of view.

Here's another. If I (as a player) issue a string of profanities at someone, impugning their real-life person, will they sue the developer or me? They'll sue me, because the developer will argue[15] that they are merely a common carrier with no control over what their players say. That being the case, they should need a wiretap warrant before they can record any of my communications. If they log me otherwise, they're accepting responsibility for controlling what I say. They can't claim I consented to be monitored when I signed their terms of service agreement: That would mean I was consenting to a form of self-incrimination, which is counter to human rights legislation.

Before this drifts too far away from morality toward legality, here's something else to think about. Suppose in a virtual world you stand around in a reasonably private space chatting to a friend. Both of you are adults, and both of you are okay with using strong language. The moment anyone else appears in the room, you tone down your vocabulary, but when they go you start inserting profanities again. Is this ethical behavior or not? Would it (still) be ethical if you knew that you were being logged, and that an administrator might therefore come across your gynecological language and be profoundly shocked? What if it wasn't the presence of rude words that was offensive but your unorthodox political views?

Can you ever consider yourself to be in private in a virtual world, or must you always act as if someone is watching?

Addiction

Virtual world designers are creating something that they know is addictive. Addiction is a bad thing, because of its personal and social costs. At a moral level, are designers of virtual worlds little better than drug pushers?

The first person to question me on the ethics of making an intensely addictive experience available to unsuspecting members of the public was computer journalist Guy Kewney in the mid-1980s. His point was that even if I didn't know *MUD1* would be addictive when I started on it, I knew now and should therefore give some thought as to whether I should continue running it. This I did, and I concluded that although

---

15. Note that this has yet to be tested in court, as far as I know.

players might at times exhibit behaviors that could be considered symptomatic of addiction, it wasn't that simple. Virtual worlds are places: You can't be addicted to a virtual world any more than you can be addicted to Las Vegas. You can be addicted to the things you do in a virtual world, as you can be addicted to the things you do in Las Vegas. Unlike Las Vegas, however, in *MUD1* it wasn't me who made the experience addictive, it was the players themselves through their imaginations and interactions.

No, it didn't convince me then, either.

I certainly didn't set out to make *MUD1* addictive. I wanted it to be a place where people could be and become themselves. It just happened that for many people this turned out to be a very intense experience that they wanted to repeat again and again. The question I should have been asking was not whether playing in virtual worlds was addictive (if "addictive" is the right word, which in this context it almost certainly isn't), but whether this addictiveness was a bad thing given the potential rewards. In this respect, I see it morally defensible on three counts:

➤ People come out of the experience as better individuals than they were when they went in.

➤ Most players would not develop as much if they did something else instead of playing in the virtual world.

➤ The process has a definite end. When your hero's journey finishes, all signs of addiction/dependency/habit are gone.

Players of virtual worlds don't all have periods of what could be called addiction to the experience, but even those who do will on the whole come out the better for it[16]. Virtual worlds are a force for good.

The problem is, not all virtual worlds satisfy the preceding criteria. Some, for example, use gambling-psychology feedback systems to drive their addictiveness, rather than the sheer freedom to *be*. The player is addicted but isn't developing; they play to feed their addiction, not to end it. It's all the worse when the virtual world is especially designed this way; accidental incompetence is a lesser crime than deliberate incompetence. As I

---

16. This assumes they are allowed to come out of it. Taking away someone's computer to stop them from playing in a virtual world could be worse for them than letting them reach closure.

mentioned in Chapters 5 and 6, most game-oriented virtual worlds have a certain inherent amount of addiction-promoting activity as a part of their gameplay; it helps their players have fun. Plenty of regular computer games also have it, however these don't attract anywhere near the degree of dedication that virtual worlds are able to rely upon. It's the player's development that is the critical "addiction;" that being the case, virtual worlds that deliberately implement in tandem with this a variable feedback system of rewards have something of an ethical case to answer.

The other common violation is in closure. If players are on some version of a hero's journey and the virtual world designer, knowing this, interferes with their progress, they will have to play for longer to reach the end (if indeed they ever reach it at all). The virtual world itself may never "end," but individual journeys must; the never-ending journey is an eternity of frustration. Give people an out and they'll come back; force them to stay and they'll go. Virtual worlds that move the winning post as players approach it are meting out an unnecessary cruelty.

Mental Illness

This is more of a game management thing, but I thought I should mention it here because it does impact on designers.

Some players really are crazy. If you accept that the word "crazy" can be applied to an individual, then statistically some crazy people will play virtual worlds. A user base the size of *EverQuest*'s will include several *bona fide* psychopaths. That's assuming that virtual worlds mirror the general population: It could be, for example, that the nature of these worlds is such that fewer crazy people play them. Alternatively, they could act as magnets. I suspect the latter

I'm aware that the word "crazy" is emotive; I used it here to make a point. Most of the people who suffer from various forms of mental illness are not crazy by any definition of the word. Some, however, are—dangerously so. What does your virtual world say to them? Are you responsible if they take what it says to heart?

The "crazy people" quandary is not unique to virtual worlds. Film, television, and computer games all suffer from the same problem. If you dramatize a killing spree, there is a possibility that it could inspire a seriously disturbed person to go on an actual killing spree. Where virtual worlds are unique is that they blur the boundaries between fantasy and reality until the two become one and the same. For someone who may have difficulty separating reality from fantasy at the best of times, this could prove too much. In such circumstances, can virtual world designers still hide behind the "you can't legislate for crazy people" argument? If not, how could virtual worlds as an industry ever be viable?

Most mentally ill people who play virtual worlds are not, fortunately, crazy. They may have serious issues, and could even be a danger to themselves[17], but they will listen to reason. System administrators accept a duty of care for players while they are in their virtual world, and if it is apparent that someone is behaving worryingly oddly then it could be best for them to be barred entry. Of course, this could well make the individual's problems worse, so it's always wise to seek external advice first if possible. I've only ever had to do this twice (once with *MUD1*, once with *MUD2*), but for large-scale games it's going to happen more often.

Designers of small-scale virtual worlds who are panicking at having just read this can probably calm down. I can't comment on the legal issues, but from an ethical point of view you're on solid ground as long as you act in good faith. If you see that someone needs help, and you give what you (or any reasonable person in your position would) believe to be help, then you can't be expected to do more. The alternative is to do nothing, which may be the legally sensible position, but it'll feel worse if something awful does happen.

There is ample anecdotal evidence that virtual worlds can help with certain kinds of psychological problems. Sometimes, they merely make life easier—an agoraphobic may not be cured of their fear by playing a virtual world, but at least they "get out" a little. It's the same as with many physical disorders: You can play a virtual world with both legs in plaster. More interestingly, though, are situations where people use virtual worlds to work through personality problems and come out "cured." I know of no formal medical studies of this phenomenon, but I'm convinced it happens. Whether designers can claim any responsibility for effecting such changes is another matter, of course; I suspect it's more to do with the fundamental nature of virtual worlds, rather than anything value-added by designers. That said, it's perfectly feasible for designers

---

17. Over the years, even *MUD2* (which isn't exactly large) has seen two suicides and at least one attempted suicide among its player base.

to remove this therapeutic value by interfering with the way players progress; it's obvious, for example, that any self-realization that comes from completing a hero's journey is not going to happen if the designer never lets anyone finish.

Tempting though it is to feel all warm inside about how virtual worlds can help people with mental illness, there is another side to the coin. If we accept that virtual worlds can have tangible positive effects on the minds of players, then shouldn't we also accept that they can have tangible negative effects, too? Could they make someone's condition worse? Or could they give someone a problem who wouldn't have had it otherwise?

The answer to the first question is yes; we saw this in the Chapter 6 discussion concerning psychology and virtual worlds. People can relive the same issues the same way time and time again, hardening their views rather than changing them. In most cases this is unfortunate, and it means they're not going to get anything out of the virtual world; for the mentally ill, it could be beyond unfortunate and make their situation worse. If this happens, then it's time for the player to seek professional help. Normally it would be the player's friends who raised the alarm, but it could be the live team who has to deal with making the real-life phone calls to find out what the best response is.

On the whole, I believe that many more people benefit from playing virtual worlds than suffer, but then I'm a virtual world designer so it's not like I'm going to say otherwise.

The second question—whether virtual worlds can cause mental problems—is very disquieting. It is almost certain that the intense experiences that virtual worlds are capable of delivering will push some people over the edge. They may develop anxiety attacks, delusions, fears of persecution—pretty well anything. The virtual world acts as a trigger. The crucial point is whether this is something that would probably have happened anyway, or whether it was induced by the virtual world?

The standard defense, used in many industries, is that some people are predisposed to this kind of thing and you can't blame the author, composer, artist, director, or news editor whose work tipped the balance. Virtual world designers could argue this too. However, it's not quite that simple. Virtual worlds have a strong psychological element to their design. Could it be that with their huge capacity to promote introspection they might cause some people to become neurotic or worse when no other everyday experience would? I'm not suggesting that designers would attempt such a thing deliberately, but that's not to say it couldn't happen by accident.

If it did, this would be cause for concern. There would be a danger to playing virtual worlds that was not associated with *any* other leisure-time activity.

It's impossible to gauge the possible extent of the problem without a formal study. However, given that anecdotally it's difficult to say whether it happens at all, the incidence is likely to be low. It's also quite likely that obsessive behavior will be picked up by friends or the live team before things come to a head, and that any potential catastrophe can thereby be averted. Designers of small-scale worlds where everyone knows everyone else can therefore probably rest easy. Designers of large-scale worlds can also probably do so if the mechanisms are in place for detection and prevention.

Virtual worlds with mental healthcare schemes? It could happen.

Religion

As I mentioned in Chapter 6, I'm an atheist. All religion looks like an aspect of anthropology to me. I see where religions come from, I see why they succeed and fail, I see why people follow them, and I see how they propagate. I also see why my making any observations about religions is likely to be highly contentious no matter how impartial I aim to be, therefore I shall keep this short.

The necessity of my having to make the preceding disclaimer in this book transfers directly to virtual worlds. If you want to know what the phrase "treading on eggshells" means, this is a great way to learn. In real life, it's almost impossible to mention religion without offending someone; the same is true of religion in virtual worlds. Yet for many people, their religion is the absolute focus of their life. So what does the designer do?

There are basically four options:

➤ Discreetly ignore religion. Simply never mention anything about it.

➤ Make up a religion (or use a dead one). Here, the virtual world conveys the sense that religion or spirituality is important, but it doesn't use anything that anyone actually believes.

➤ Include references to real-world religions, but only passively. You might have a cathedral, but it has no tangible effects in the virtual world beyond its physical properties.

➤ Embrace one or more real-world religions. This can be explicit (rituals and cere-monies that have tangible effects) or implicit (the virtual world conveys a system of values and beliefs without directly referencing the source). When implicit, it can be combined with one of the other options mentioned previously.

Discreetly ignoring religion is the safest approach, especially if it makes sense in the context. This is the way most movies do it: If a character in a screenplay is a priest, he's a priest for a reason. Science Fiction virtual worlds work this way.

When the genre demands a religion, the usual solution is to make up one[18]. Fantasy religions in Fantasy worlds are generally accepted; those who don't accept them usually don't accept the basic Fantasy premise either. Interestingly, the "need" for religion in Fantasy worlds stems mainly from the assumption that cleric-class characters must obtain their healing-type spells as gifts of their deity. Although this is a common fiction, it's not one that is a necessity; despite its religion-influenced creation myths there are no priestly types in *Lord of the Rings*, for example (and few wizards).

The third option is to put in real-world religious paraphernalia, but not imbue it with any special functionality. Players may choose to conduct weddings in temples or churches or wherever, but to the virtual world engine none of this has any signifi-cance. The designer treats a religious building like anything else—a castle, a cave, a boatyard—and religious objects as no different from other expensive or coveted items. This is the safest approach for an historical genre where religion plays a part without being the central theme[19]. For example, clergymen and churches have a place in Wild West mythology, but they are stylized to the extent that they can be used sensibly with-out offense. In later settings this also can work, although you'd probably need a reason to use it rather than simply ignore religion altogether[20].

---

18. This also applies when you want to lampoon or otherwise say something about a religion, although it's still something of a risky undertaking.

19. But beware of gaffes such as this message that I saw in *Civilization III: Play The World*: "We have information that the Arab city of Mecca has completed a great project, JS Bach's Cathedral."

20. This is what I do in *MUD2*, my reason being essentially artistic. For an excellent (although in places misin-formed) critique of this approach, see: Lexley Vaughan, *Playing Religiously. Muddled Times*, February 2003. http://www.muddled-times.com/article.fod?IssueId=19&ArticleId=1382.

Finally, designers will often work threads of their own philosophy into a virtual world, and this could include their religious beliefs. A deliberately allegorical work would be more difficult to construct, but it's by no means impossible. Overtly religious virtual worlds that give tangible virtual world effects to implementations of real-world religious practices are making themselves targets for all kinds of troublemakers, whether from their own faith or some other.

Even seemingly innocuous things can be hurtful: Making Santa Claus appear every Christmas and give out presents is "only a bit of fun," but to a non-Christian it could appear evangelical. Not having Christmas in the virtual world when it's in full swing in the real world is also saying something, though. Should characters have a "religion" flag that turns on the effects of a religion? Or is it then unfair when Christian characters are given presents (that is, tangible advantages) by Santa Claus but no one else is?

The religious sensibilities of players can cause design issues elsewhere. Earlier, I mentioned that I put ham into *MUD2* to challenge vegetarians to look at their beliefs, but it also challenges Jews and Moslems too. Even if it were some other foodstuff, that could still give Moslems a problem during Ramadan. If your virtual self eats virtual food in a virtual world during daylight hours, are you breaking your fast or not? Is it the principle or the actuality that matters? What if the virtual world had its own clock or calendar that was out of step with the real one? Would that make a difference?

Virtual worlds can depict or allow activities that are legal in the real world but that are disapproved of by established religions. Homosexuality, alcohol use, usury, and non-pacifism are all frowned on by one religion or another. Some religions look on the depiction of their symbols, buildings, or teachers as blasphemy, whereas for others it's good publicity. Some think that showing "evils" such as black magic or devilry is corrupting, but others think it's a case of "know thine enemy."

Of particular difficulty is when there is a schism within a religion. Virtual worlds are very good at giving male and female characters equal opportunities, but some creeds are divided over whether such equality transfers to them. Some versions of Christianity allow female priests, but others don't. Not only does the designer have to choose which religion to depict, but which sect of that religion.

Another problem with using real-life religions is omission. A cyberpunk world might have references to fundamentalist Christian churches, high-tech Buddhist and Hindu temples, but have nothing about Islam at all. This definitely insults either Islam or the other religions mentioned, but it's not obvious which!

Then there are the non-standard religions. Some years ago I wrote a series of children's stories that I put on my web site. One of those stories concerned vampires[21]. People would look up vampires using search engines and, finding 18 references in my story, would read it. They would then send me emails criticizing me for mocking their religion and publishing blasphemous untruths; about half would include dark threats about what they were going to do to me[22]. I now have a link on the page explaining the context, which has cut the number of complaints to practically zero; these people may have unconventional views, but that doesn't mean they're stupid. The point is that they had beliefs every bit as strong as those held by adherents of conformist religions. A designer hoping to avoid confrontation with zealots can reduce the possibility of its happening, but can't eliminate it.

There are really two sets of morals involved here. The first is the system of morality that comes with a religion; there is a practical aspect to this, in that if your virtual world promotes a morality that runs counter to a particular religion's views, you shouldn't expect to get many players from that congregation. If you go really overboard, there could be real-world protests or worse.

The second set of morals involved is your own. I've assumed throughout this chapter that you will do what you think is "right," of course, but religion raises the tricky point of how to treat views you think are "wrong" (but that other people think are "right"). I used to know someone who refused to believe Gödel's Incompleteness Theorem; he accepted the proof, just not the theorem. Whatever your own system of morality, someone else's could well seem as absurd as that. If a player asked you to remove references to Gödel's Incompleteness Theorem because it was wrong, would you do it? What if they asked you to remove references to Easter? Or Ramadan? Or the Festival of Lights?

Real-life laws make some boundaries clear, but the others you must set yourself.

---

21. `http://www.mud.co.ul/richard/sbos10.htm`

22. The "I will sup your blood" ones were the best.

Groups of Players as Groups of People

If someone makes a statement with which you disagree, you might want to take issue with them. There are social norms that dictate how far you can go with your riposte—verbal abuse warrants in the first instance only a verbal defense, for example. Although this can get out of hand, on the whole it works. If an individual says something, then other people can challenge them about it.

What if it's not the individual who makes the statement but an organization of which the individual is a member? If a political party issues a general pronouncement, then that announcement is on behalf of the party's members. If you disagreed, you could reasonably expect to bring it up with any members of that party you knew, to take them to task. Sure, they might not agree either, but what to do about it then becomes their problem.

It gets fuzzier for groups that people are members of non-voluntarily. If two countries are at war, should they round up each other's nationals and intern them? It happened in the 1940s. The innocent suffer, but the argument is that far fewer innocents suffer overall than would if enemy agents were free to wage a campaign of sabotage behind the lines.

Terrorism is another area where this logic can be applied. If you know that all terrorists are members of a particular religious group, can you intern members of that group that haven't committed any crime but that are acting like they might were they given the chance? Membership of a religion is voluntary—plenty of people convert to other religions—so why not? This happened in Northern Ireland in the 1970s.

I'm sure you can see the slippery slope here. By taking a series of seemingly short but justifiable steps, pretty soon you reach the stage where individuals are frightened to get on a bus because of the color of their skin or the way they dress. In virtual worlds, the effects of stereotyping are not quite so worrying, but nevertheless there are a number of areas where people accept the *status quo* without perhaps considering what that means.

Icons

Many virtual worlds draw on iconic or mythical images to sustain their immersive depth. If a player comes across a "little old man" NPC, it's a source of great disappointment if it turns out he really is just a little old man and isn't veiling some immense power or wisdom. If they came across a unicorn, they would feel cheated if it wasn't white (and if they came across a herd of them—say what?!). Although these iconic figures are stereotypical, therein lies their strength; they represent an idealized "knowledge" of a reality that when correctly applied to a virtual world can deliver immersion. So tokenized have these metaphors become that it can forcefully be argued they aren't stereotypes at all, they're shorthand for a parcel of meanings.

The same argument can be used to explain why so many Fantasy virtual worlds have elves and dwarfs (or rebrandings of the same) as character races. Dwarfs are solid, materialist, quick to anger, but dependable; elves are spiritual, aloof, beautiful, yet insular. Players immediately have identifiable stereotypes that they can use to help decide what kind of character they wish to play. Real-life dwarfs might complain about this depiction, but "no, these are *dwarves* not *dwarfs*." Real-life elves rarely comment.

An ethical point that seems to have been missed by most of the designers who employ character races[23] is that it promotes the notion that races are tangibly different. If it's fine to regard all elves as being arrogant, fair-haired aesthetes, that validates the idea of stereotypical races. Why couldn't a dwarf be a dreamer, a poet, a fun-loving bard? Why couldn't an elf be a greedy, bad-tempered, never-satisfied lover of ale? Because they're "not like that"? Or maybe "a few are like that, but most aren't"? So what are "all Japanese" or "all Jewish" or "all Mexican" people like?

Having races as stereotypes in virtual worlds endorses having races as stereotypes in the real world. It's up to designers themselves to decide whether or not this is fine by them, but they should at least make that decision consciously. At the moment, most of them simply follow the flow without thinking about it. They should.

As I mentioned in Chapter 6, most virtual worlds are fine with giving tangible properties to Fantasy races, but they avoid doing this for real races. Players may decide at character-creation time or through their personal descriptive text to reflect a real-life

---

23. Actually—and this is the root of the problem—humanoid sub-species that the designers *call* "races."

race other than the default (there's always a default), but it's purely cosmetic. There is an argument that this homogenizes characters, making them all basically the same; this is indeed the case, but that's unsurprising given that it's the goal. Sure, ethnic groups that have a culture tied to their physical appearance won't thrive in a world where anyone can steal that appearance, but then you have to ask the question as to whether this might not be a good thing. Racial supremacists have lost the war when people can be whatever race they choose to be.

There is a separate issue related to people for whom their race is a fundamental part of their identity. In virtual worlds without their race, or even with their race but with Fantasy ones alongside it, this could prompt a serious crisis. Should designers try to accommodate such individuals? Or is it simply a fact of life that race doesn't transfer to virtual worlds (even though attitudes to race can)?

Other stereotypes exist in virtual worlds, of course, which are less emotive but nevertheless raise similar issues. Character classes, for example, impose conformity. If you're a designer who believes in conformity, have character classes; if you're one who doesn't, don't. If you haven't given the issue the slightest thought, you'd better do some thinking—you may be promoting social values with which you disagree.

Finally, a word on anthropomorphic animal characters.

As I mentioned in Chapter 6, anthropomorphic characters are all to do with symbols. Different animal species have different characteristics that (because animals aren't as free-thinking as humans) they follow strongly. Yes, some can have personalities that are different from those of others, but they're ruled by their instincts far more than are humans. Because of this, people have come to associate certain behaviors with certain animals—the cunning fox, the timid rabbit, the inquisitive mouse—and they use the animals as symbols for the behaviors. In some cases, the link is only metaphorical: A man who prowls around looking for innocent women to prey on might be likened to a wolf that prowls around looking for innocent smaller creatures to prey on, but there's nothing sexual about the wolf's activity. Nevertheless, the image of the wolf as a predator is strong enough that if you referred to a man as acting like a wolf people wouldn't think you meant he attacked sheep.

For some designers, this degree of stereotyping could also be too much. If it's okay to stereotype animals, pretty soon it's okay to stereotype humans, and then where are we? For others, it's merely an example of the general way that languages work using metaphor, and the moment foxes and rabbits complain is the moment their plight deserves to be taken seriously. You can make up your own mind.

Virtual worlds where players take on the role of anthropomorphic characters implicitly accept that this stereotyping is fine; furthermore, they have a well-developed system of codes that associate different animal forms with different kinds of behavior. This leads to a system of self-fulfilling stereotypes: If people think that bears betoken having a macho exterior but a sensitive caring inside, then people who want that image will play as bears. People who want to play as a shy character will not choose to be a bear, even though in a virtual world where all the animals are anthropomorphic anyway there's nothing to stop someone from being a shy bear.

What about non-anthropomorphic animal worlds? What if your character is, say, a dog? If it looks like a dog and can only do things that dogs can do, is that okay? Well if people want to be a dog, then presumably it's up to them, but there are some awkward problems about identity drift here. It could be psychologically damaging for someone who didn't know exactly what they were doing to play for extended periods in virtual worlds in the role of a dog or any other non-sentient creature. Playing a character of a gender, race or age not your own is different because they can all think just as well as each other; playing as a dog, though? You can change, but can the dog?

Although this may seem rather a far-fetched idea, there are already virtual worlds moving toward it[24]. Knowing what you know about immersion, would it be ethical or unethical to go the whole way?

Changing yourself is easier than changing a stereotype. You decide on you; everyone else decides on a stereotype.

---

24. Example: *The Jungle.* `telnet://thejungle.dhs.org:4000`.

Social Engineering

Are virtual worlds a force for good or for evil?

As I have already said, I strongly believe in the former. However, mere faith in my own (clearly biased) judgment is hardly justification. Computer games (along with television, film, and music) are routinely implicated when some disturbed teenager gets hold of a weapon and goes on a killing spree; virtual worlds are also starting to suffer from their perceived negative effects[25]. Do virtual worlds incite, reinforce, or train?

I won't make the case for virtual worlds here, because I hope to have done that already in this book. However, I will examine some of the case against. Without any formal studies to call on, all I can do is provide anecdotal evidence; nevertheless, it's evidence based on years of observation, and therefore not quite as speculative as it may seem.

My argument that virtual worlds are a force for good is based largely on the fact that players can learn to be better people as a result of playing them. That means I intrinsically accept that virtual worlds can bring about change. Given this, why must that change necessarily be for the good?

Well, it isn't always, of course; in a well-designed virtual world it will be most of the time, but some people will indeed replay old issues repeatedly, consolidating points of view that would be better disbanded. The reverse is also true: Some individuals in real life become better people after committing horrific acts that leave others traumatized, but on the whole anyone taking up this kind of activity is on the road to personal destruction.

So, why is it that individuals take "good" things from virtual worlds, rather than "bad" things? I believe that it is due to the similarities between virtual worlds and the real one. The majority of people who learn anything at all from virtual worlds will pick up things such as

➤ Information specific to the virtual world (stats, goals, geography)

➤ Skills specific to the interface (dodging, aiming, feature recognition)

---

25. *EverQuest* has been blamed for at least one suicide, and *Lineage* is habitually held responsible for a wide range of crimes.

➤ Skills specific to the virtual world (tactics, strategy)

➤ More general skills (social, behavioral, educational)

➤ Wider cultural values (as exhibited by the other players)

➤ The difference between the real and the virtual

These are all either innocuous or of benefit to the individual player (the further down the list, the more likely it is to be of use[26]).

People who play virtual worlds will not pick up things such as these:

➤ Desensitization (to evil, to other people's emotions)

➤ The belief that people are just like NPCs, and rules that apply to NPCs apply to people

➤ The idea that everything virtual transfers to the real

If any of these were true, that would indeed be worrying. In general, though, I don't think they are. Let's take a closer look....

The desensitization argument is that people come across something in the virtual world so often that they become used to it, so when the same issue arises in the real world they do no respond appropriately. This is a valid point about virtual worlds (as it is about things like TV news, too); where it becomes invalid, however, is in the suggestion that impressionable players will be unable to distinguish between virtual-world concepts and the real-world concepts that they're based on.

Take "evil," for example. The notion that most players of the big commercial virtual worlds have about evil actually translates as "cool." In practice, the people on the "evil" side exhibit the same kind of behavior that they would were they on the "good" side, except they think they're cooler because they have all the nasty-sounding spells and skills.

---

26. Educational virtual worlds can put in facts they want players to learn, but they'll have to make sure that players know these are true in the real world, otherwise they will not assume it. There are occasional interface skills that are useful too: Many people have learned to type by playing textual worlds, for example.

What evil *really* means is rule by fear. You do what your boss tells you to do because if you didn't you would be tortured, maimed, and (if you were lucky) killed as an example to others who might think of stepping out of line. An evil person is as likely to kill someone on their own side as they are the "enemy." In real life, people fight for evil because

- ➤ They're evil.

- ➤ They think they're evil.

- ➤ They're afraid of what will happen to them or to people they care for if they don't fight.

- ➤ They have no way of escaping.

- ➤ They don't realize they're fighting for evil.

- ➤ They're threatened by what they perceive as an even greater evil.

Now translate this into a Fantasy world. Let's give evil commanding officers the power to take 10% of a player's levels off them for "torture." Who would fight on their side?

Well evil people would, because they get the same powers over their subordinates and they agree with the overall aims of the evil empire. Non-evil people would scream like crazy at customer service the moment such a sanction was imposed on them. Those who felt particularly annoyed would quit and join the good side. If a greater evil was on the way, they'd quit and play another game.

In short, "evil" as a concept doesn't work as a major force in virtual worlds. What we have instead is some kind of sanitized version that gives people a cloak to hide behind if they want to do something they think is a little naughty. It's no more evil than the "good" side is good (when self-sacrifice is cheap, even evil people will do it).

"Evil" in virtual worlds is just an artificial construct that misapplies labels to promote a meaningless conflict. Is it without consequences, though? If players come to see "evil" as just a label, does that indeed desensitize them to the very concept of it? Will they be more likely to side with something labeled as evil in the real world?

At a very superficial level—that of the label—perhaps. If they are told that some dictator is "evil," some individuals may not fully appreciate what this means; this could be true irrespective of whether they have played virtual worlds or not, though. Whatever, contact with the reality of evil will swiftly disabuse them of this naivety.

Nevertheless, the wicked will always prey on the gullible; if desensitizing people to the label means that those to whom it applies can draw innocents closer to them, it can't be a good thing. Whether it's unacceptably bad or merely one poor chord in the great song of popular culture is another matter[27].

Besides, the traffic is not one-way: Real-world ideas can affect virtual world concepts. In the great scheme of things, permanent death for characters is not actually as bad as people make out. However, because death in the real world is bad, this has caused people to redefine what "death" means in virtual worlds. They say their character "died" even when all that happened was it was teleported out of a battle. Are they becoming less sensitized to the notion of death in the real world because of this? Or does their use of "death" in this way arise precisely because they *aren't* insensitive to it?

The remaining two primary concerns about the way that virtual worlds can be a negative influence are related to each other. They say that people who spend long periods in virtual worlds will transfer inappropriate emotional and intellectual understandings to the real world because they cannot subconsciously separate the real from the virtual. If you spend all day beating the guts out of NPCs, and NPCs look just like people, then in the real world you'll start to objectify people too. Similarly, if you find that being lying and deceitful in the virtual world works, you'll change in the real world so that you adopt this strategy too.

The objectification argument is a non-starter. People are acutely aware of whether opponents are computer-controlled or player-controlled. It makes a big difference to them[28]. If anything, they are more likely to subjectify NPCs than to objectify players.

---

27. The word "wicked" has already acquired dual meaning in popular culture, at least temporarily. At the moment, people can refer to a new dance, magazine, candy bar, or whatever as "wicked" and understand it's not the same kind of "wicked" as a "wicked witch." Whether that will always be the case remains to be seen.

28. Advanced AI systems may be able to present as real players and remain undetected. This brings in major philosophical issues concerning sentience, though. Basically, if players can't tell an AI from another player using free-form communication, then the AI *is* another player—it just happens to run on different hardware to human players.

Virtual-to-real transfer does occur. The core of the attack against it is that it happens without critical reflection; in other words, it becomes part of your behavior through rote, rather than because you thought about it. Although I agree that it is possible to learn information and simple skills this way, I do not believe that behavioral changes can also be acquired except under very artificial circumstances. If you find that being lying and deceitful works, you'll notice it consciously; you won't just fall into it with zombie-like mindlessness. This is why, when other players start shunning you because of your behavior change, you may explicitly consider what it is you are doing wrong (that is, lying) and resolve your ways.

The way I see this is like the difference between episodic and semantic memory. Episodic memory is your memory of events ("yesterday I watched a movie"); semantic memory is your memory of procedures and processes ("when you watch a movie, you have to buy a ticket"). People who suffer from amnesia will forget their name, let alone what movies they have seen, but they'll still remember that they have to buy a ticket. Semantic memory is an abstraction of episodic memory[29]; from individual events, you build up a general picture that describes them, such that you can forget the individual events but retain what you have learned. I don't remember how I found out I needed to buy a ticket to see a movie, but then I don't need to; I only need to remember that I do need to buy a ticket.

With virtual worlds, the actions that you undertake lead to individual episodes. Although you remember the episodes immediately when they're over, with time they will fade. Yes, some will be particularly memorable and will remain with you always, but most won't. What does remain are the lessons you *learned* from the episodes, and these are quite different from the mere facts of the episodes themselves.

As a designer, I therefore don't care whether people get a rush from finding a secret passage, from being a leader, from designing their own house, or from laying waste to a nest of vampires. What I care about is whether, in doing so, they develop as people.

---

29. It's wider than I've made out here. You can regard episodic memory as handling facts and semantic memory as handling knowledge. Acquired skills (such as the ability to drive a car) can be considered as compiled actions, and therefore are contenders for being part of semantic memory; it's usually more appropriate to look on them as forming a separate memory of their own, however, which may or may not be part of semantic memory.

So, when someone says that virtual worlds encourage sex or violence, no, they don't. Even if a designer went all out to try to encourage it, they wouldn't. It may be that they encourage play of a sexual or violent nature, but play is play, and it's virtual. The lessons that people learn are the lessons that they can take with them into the real world. They find out about people; they find out about themselves.

I believe that designing virtual worlds is a morally defensible occupation. I believe that designers are on the side of the virtuous.

Mind you, I also believe that one day we'll see more people getting married because of virtual worlds than we'll see getting divorced because of them. Don't let my idealism do your thinking for you. Consider the issues; reflect on them yourself; draw your own conclusions.

Confounding Expectations

There's a gray area to this talk of what people learn from virtual worlds.

Immersion is driven by a virtual world's similarity to Reality. It is founded on players' implicit expectations. Some of those expectations concern virtual worlds themselves. Should these expectations be confirmed or frustrated? Do you, as a designer, give the players what they expect (for example, races) or what they don't (for example, everyone's human)? The issue is not the effect on immersion (it's not all that great); rather, it's the effects that confounding these expectations have on individuals.

If you give someone something that they are not expecting, but which is consistent with the way the virtual world operates, then they will either accept it or reject it. Either way, they'll have to think about it; this is why challenging expectations is good. Obviously, if too many are challenged at the same time it could impact on immersion, but in general this isn't going to happen.

Challenging expectations causes people to think about those expectations. Through such analyses, players can change as people. As I have explained, this is how things should be; the lessons that people learn come from abstractions of events, not from the events themselves. You don't learn that killing is good, you learn how to trust your friends; you don't learn that Zeus is all-powerful, you learn that being all-powerful means being all-responsible. This is how it should be.

Yet immersion subverts this mechanism. You accept the virtual world because of its similarity to the real one. Your implicit view of how the real world works informs your view of how the virtual world should work. Is it not possible that the reverse could at times be true? What you implicitly accept without thinking in the virtual world could transfer to what you implicitly accept in the real world? As I said earlier, obviously anything complicated would require conscious thought—I'm not suggesting that players are likely to be brainwashed like this—but nevertheless there are smaller things that could have real-world consequences.

Example: In a virtual world, acceleration is instantaneous. You go from a standing start to running full speed without an intermediate period of speeding up. If someone who has been playing in a graphical virtual world for 10 hours gets into their car and drives off, could that be dangerous? This kind of low-level skill acquisition is easy to pick up—people who access text-based virtual worlds from a command-line interface will routinely find themselves typing the short forms of "look" or "inventory" at the command prompt.

When designers challenge player expectations at this kind of level (rather than at a more cerebral level), the players have to accept it or reject it. Rejection means stopping playing, so challenges aren't ever going to be major; they do exist, though. For example, in a graphical world if you want to walk between characters who are physically blocking your way, the world may let you do it—even though in the real world you couldn't. The reason this is so is because otherwise players could barricade an area with their own bodies; nevertheless, it challenges players' notions of their own physicality in the virtual world. If they don't like it, they're not going to become immersed and will eventually leave; if they do like it, it becomes part of their implicit knowledge of the way the virtual world works. With deepening immersion, there is the risk that this world view could be taken back to Reality. It may not last there for long, but it could still be enough to cause an accident.

Whose fault is it when such lapses occur? The player, for putting themselves into such a situation in the first place, or the designer for challenging their expectations?

Above the level of immersion, there is still cause for concern. Designers can cause players to re-examine their attitudes, but what happens if the players conclude that they should behave in a way that is bad either for themselves or for society? I argued earlier that players don't learn from the facts of what they do but from abstractions of those facts, but what if what they learn is inappropriate for their real-world culture?

For example, a virtual world may have lax attitudes to sexuality. A player may, after many experimental encounters of virtual sex, decide that they are not attracted to members of the same sex and are therefore heterosexual. This is fair enough, but if as a result of their not enjoying their homosexual encounters they drew all kinds of false conclusions about homosexuals in general, this would not necessarily be regarded as a universally positive view to transfer into the real world. Is the virtual world's designer in any way responsible for this unfortunate result? After all, if they had not promoted lax attitudes to sexuality, the player would not have experimented and would therefore not have drawn any conclusions at all (false or otherwise).

Here's another example. Virtual world designers create an environment in which people can explore their own identity. They can find out who they "really are." It could transpire that they "really are" someone deeply unpleasant, who has previously been subduing their urges behind some façade that they now feel comfortable about dropping. Are virtual worlds best left alone if they regularly produce individuals like this?

Designers can influence the ways in which people change in virtual worlds. When they do so, does this give them a responsibility for the outcome? Or are they merely providing trials that will allow players to find what was already there deep inside them anyway? If I challenge a player's expectations, am I equipping them with the means by which to determine their own solution? Or am I guiding them in a direction that may be inappropriate.

I'd like to believe the former. I can lead a horse to water, but I can't make it drink. Yet I can make it consider drinking. Is it my responsibility if it does drink? Or is it the horse's?

Yourself

When all's said and done, the ethics of a virtual world reflect those of its designer. If *you* don't think about how to behave, about what's right and wrong, about responsibility, about rights, then why should your players? If *you* think ethics are other people's responsibility, so will your players. *Your* beliefs, *your* attitudes, *your* personality—they're all reflected in your virtual world. *You* have to take responsibility, because (at least initially) you *are* the world.

Here's a final ethical problem for you.

Back in Chapter 3, I outlined *A Story About a Tree*. This concerned the death in real life of Karyn, a Norwegian beauty queen who played in *LegendMUD*. I used this anecdote to pose questions concerning what is "real" in a virtual world. At the time, I said I didn't know whether or not Karyn was a real person. Actually, I do know whether or not Karyn was a real person: She wasn't. She was a complete invention.

In February 2002, film producer Tracy Spaight got in touch with me about a documentary he was making, *Real People, Virtual Worlds*. He wanted to know if it would be possible to interview me, and sent along a preview tape of some interviews he'd done already. The centerpiece was a powerful monologue by Raph Koster in which he described and commented on *A Story About a Tree*. Although I had long harbored reservations about Karyn, I'd kept them pretty much to myself. When it came to a movie that was likely to be seen on television by millions of people, though, well, it would have been somewhat embarrassing for Tracy and Raph if Karyn turned out to be fake. I suggested to Tracy that he check out the story, just to be sure. Someone at *LegendMUD* would probably have met or spoken to Karyn in real life when she was alive, so it shouldn't take long; it was just to put my mind at rest. Except, no one at *LegendMUD* had actually met her.

I hadn't reckoned with Tracy's documentary-maker's instincts. He methodically investigated every shred of evidence that remained concerning Karyn's life. It took a great deal of time and patience, but the facts he unearthed were undeniable. Here are some of the highlights:

- ➤ There are only three people in the whole of Norway called Karyn. It's a highly unusual name there.

- ➤ The total number of deaths in road traffic accidents in Norway in 1995 was 352. Road death is relatively uncommon in that country.

- ➤ Only one person died in the crash that supposedly killed Karyn. The report reproduced on Karyn's web site said three people; it had been altered in translation.

- ➤ The University of Oslo, which Karyn said she attended, had no record of a former beauty queen (or anyone else) having died in a road accident in January 1998.

➤ The Frøken Norge (Miss Norway) beauty pageant had no entries named Karyn in 1995 (when Karyn was supposedly a finalist).

➤ Karyn's picture on her web site was of a *bona fide* Frøken Norge contestant. She had never heard of *LegendMUD* until Tracy tracked her down.

There was more—lots more. Police accident reports, depositions from Geocities, newspaper archives, and so on.

So Tracy and I knew that Karyn didn't exist, and could prove so categorically. We sensed that the news would elevate Tracy's documentary to mainstream levels of interest. Real people can have real relationships with imaginary people? That's a great hook! I could imagine reading a syndicated version of the story in UK Sunday newspapers a few years down the line, as happened with Julian Dibbell's *A Rape in Cyberspace*.

But just a moment....

Real relationships? Involving real people, who have suffered real grief? Couldn't it be potentially devastating for them to discover the depths of Karyn's betrayal. It might not be *right* for us to go public with the story. The world might be a better place if we just sat on it.

That wasn't all we had to consider. *A Story About a Tree* is very well known; it's almost iconic. It has been cited many times as a counter to the argument that "it's just a game." Yet for Karyn, it *was* "just a game," at least at some level. Would it be better for the long-term development of virtual worlds for *A Story About a Tree* to keep its integrity? Or could more useful lessons be learned from a reappraisal of it in this new light?

So we had a problem: What should we do?

I won't tell you what we *did* do, although obviously it resulted in our revealing the truth about Karyn (or you wouldn't be reading this[30]). All I'll say is that both Tracy and I felt our actions were right.

---

30. Nor Tracy's account: Tracy Spaight, *Who Killed Miss Norway?*. Salon, 14 April 2003.
   http://www.salon.com/tech/feature/2003/04/14/who_killed_miss_norway/index.html
.

Instead, I'd like to pose the question: What would *you* have done in our position?

Now, ask what your answer says about you. What does that say about your virtual world? What in turn does this say about your players?

It's your design; it's your morality.

From Essex to ethics in one book....

Index

I

Q

R

X-Y-Z

VOICES THAT MATTER

VISIT OUR WEB SITE

WWW.NEWRIDERS.COM

On our web site, you'll find information about our other books, authors, tables of contents, and book errata. You will also find information about book registration and how to purchase our books, both domestically and internationally.

EMAIL US

Contact us at: **nrfeedback@newriders.com**

- If you have comments or questions about this book
- To report errors that you have found in this book
- If you have a book proposal to submit or are interested in writing for New Riders
- If you are an expert in a computer topic or technology and are interested in being a technical editor who reviews manuscripts for technical accuracy

Contact us at: **nreducation@newriders.com**

- If you are an instructor from an educational institution who wants to preview New Riders books for classroom use. Email should include your name, title, school, department, address, phone number, office days/hours, text in use, and enrollment, along with your request for desk/examination copies and/or additional information.

Contact us at: **nrmedia@newriders.com**

- If you are a member of the media who is interested in reviewing copies of New Riders books. Send your name, mailing address, and email address, along with the name of the publication or web site you work for.

BULK PURCHASES/CORPORATE SALES

The publisher offers discounts on this book when ordered in quantity for bulk purchases and special sales. For sales within the U.S., please contact: Corporate and Government Sales (800) 382-3419 or **corpsales@pearsontechgroup.com**. Outside of the U.S., please contact: International Sales (317) 581-3793 or **international@pearsontechgroup.com**.

WRITE TO US

New Riders
1249 Eighth Street.
Berkeley, California 94710

CALL/FAX US

Toll-free (800) 283-9444
If outside U.S. (510) 524-2478
FAX: (510) 524-2221

New Riders

WWW.NEWRIDERS.COM

Publishing the Voices that Matter

You already know that New Riders brings you the **Voices That Matter**.

But what does that mean? It means that New Riders brings you the

Voices that challenge your assumptions, take your talents to the next

level, or simply help you better understand the complex technical world

we're all navigating.

Visit **www.newriders.com** to find:

- ▸ **10% discount** and **free shipping** on all book purchases
- ▸ Never before published chapters
- ▸ Sample chapters and excerpts
- ▸ Author bios and interviews
- ▸ Contests and enter-to-wins
- ▸ Up-to-date industry event information
- ▸ Book reviews
- ▸ Special offers from our friends and partners
- ▸ Info on how to join our User Group program
- ▸ Ways to have your Voice heard

WWW.NEWRIDERS.COM

Peachpit
Essential books for the creative community

Visit Peachpit on the Web at www.peachpit.com

- Read the latest articles and download timesaving tipsheets from best-selling authors such as Scott Kelby, Robin Williams, Lynda Weinman, Ted Landau, and more!

- Join the Peachpit Club and save 25% off all your online purchases at peachpit.com every time you shop—plus enjoy free UPS ground shipping within the United States.

- Search through our entire collection of new and upcoming titles by author, ISBN, title, or topic. There's no easier way to find just the book you need.

- Sign up for newsletters offering special Peachpit savings and new book announcements so you're always the first to know about our newest books and killer deals.

- Did you know that Peachpit also publishes books by Apple, New Riders, Adobe Press, Macromedia Press, palmOne Press, and TechTV press? Swing by the Peachpit family section of the site and learn about all our partners and series.

- Got a great idea for a book? Check out our About section to find out how to submit a proposal. You could write our next best-seller!

You'll find all this and more at www.peachpit.com. Stop by and take a look today!

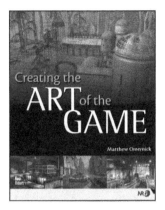